Routledge Handbook of Democratization

This exciting new handbook provides a global overview of the process of democratization, offering chapter-by-chapter discussion at both the country and regional levels and examining the interaction between the domestic and external factors that affect the progression of countries from authoritarian to democratic rule.

Bringing together 29 key experts in the field, the work is designed to contrast the processes and outcomes of democratic reform in a wide range of different societies, evaluating the influence of factors such as religion, economic development, and financial resources.

It is structured thematically into four broad sections:

- **Part I** provides a regional *tour d'horizon* of the current state of democratization and democracy in eight regions around the world.
- **Part II** examines key structures, processes, and outcomes of democratization and democracy.
- **Part III** focuses on the relationship between democratization and international relations through examination of a range of issues and actors including: the third and fourth waves of democracy, political conditionality, the United Nations, the European Union, the African Union, and the Organization of African States.
- **Part IV** examines the interaction between democratization and development with a focus on poverty and inequality, security, human rights, gender, war, and conflict resolution.

A comprehensive survey of democratization across the world, this work will be essential reading for scholars and policy-makers alike.

Jeffrey Haynes is Associate Dean in the Faculty of Law, Governance, and International Relations at London Metropolitan University. He is the editor of the series *Routledge Studies in Religion and Politics* and co-editor of the journal *Democratization*.

Routledge Handbook of Democratization

Edited by Jeffrey Haynes

Routledge
Taylor & Francis Group

LONDON AND NEW YORK

First published 2012
by Routledge
2 Park Square, Milton Park, Abingdon, Oxon, OX14 4RN

Simultaneously published in the USA and Canada
by Routledge
711 Third Avenue, New York, NY 10017

Routledge is an imprint of the Taylor & Francis Group, an informa business

British Library Cataloguing in Publication Data
A catalogue record for this book is available from the British Library

Library of Congress Cataloging-in-Publication Data
Routledge handbook of democratization / edited by Jeffrey Haynes.
p. cm.
Includes bibliographical references and index.
1. Democratization. I. Haynes, Jeffrey.
JC423.R715 2012
321.8–dc23
2011024481

ISBN: 978-0-415-57377-1 (hbk)
ISBN: 978-0-203-14843-3 (ebk)

Typeset in Bembo
by Integra Software Services Pvt. Ltd, Pondicherry, India

Printed and bound in Great Britain by the MPG Books Group

Contents

Contents

Illustrations

Tables

Figures

Abbreviations

ABS	AsiaBarometer Survey
ACP	African, Caribbean, Pacific
ADEMA	Alliance for Democracy in Mali
AKP	Justice and Development Party (Turkey)
AL	Awami League (Bangladesh)
AN	National Assembly
ANC	African National Congress
ANC	National Constitutional Assembly
APRM	African Peer Review Mechanism
ARENA	Nationalist Republican Alliance (El Salvador)
ASEAN	Association of Southeast Asian Nations
AU	Africa Union
BFDA	Burmese Freedom and Democracy Act
BiH	Bosnia and Herzegovina
BJP	Bharatiya Janata Party/Indian People's Party
BNP	Bangladesh Nationalist Party
BSP	Bahujan Samaj Party (India)
CACM	Central American Common Market
CEDAW	United Nations Convention on the Elimination of All Forms of Discrimination Against Women
CEE	Central and Eastern Europe
CEO	chief executive officer
CFSP	Common Foreign and Security Policy
CIS	Commonwealth of Independent States
CNE	National Electoral Council (Venezuela)
CNPC	China National Petroleum Corporation
CONADEP	National Commission on Disappeared Persons (Argentina)
CPI	Consumer Price Index
CSI	first phase of the modern theory of civil society
CSII	second phase of the modern theory of civil society
CSO	civil society organization
CSTO	Collective Security Treaty Organization
DECO	Department for Electoral Cooperation and Observation (OAS)
DFID	Department for International Development (UK)
DPP	Democratic Progressive Party (Taiwan)
ECOSOCC	Economic, Social and Cultural Council (Africa)

ECOWAS	Economic Community of West African States
EIDHR	European Instrument for Democracy and Human Rights
EIU	Economist Intelligence Unit
EMGFA	Estado-Maior General das Forças Armadas (Portugal)
ENPI	European Neighbourhood and Partnership Instrument
EP	European Parliament
EU	European Union
EurasEC	Eurasian Economic Community
FDI	foreign direct investment
FES	Friedrich Ebert Stiftung (Germany)
FMLN	Farabundo Martí National Liberation Front
FRELIMO	Frente de Libertação de Moçambique
FSLN	Sandinista National Liberation Front
GDP	gross domestic product
GLC	government-linked-company
GN	National Guard (Nicaragua)
GNP	gross national product
GRO	grass-roots organization
GSP	Generalized System of Preferences
HIPC	Heavily Indebted Poor Country
HUMINT	human intelligence
IACHPR	Inter-American Court of Human Rights
IACHR	Inter-American Commission on Human Rights
ICC	International Criminal Court
ICCPR	United Nations International Covenant on Civil and Political Rights
ICTY	International Criminal Tribunal for the former Yugoslavia
ID	democracy index
IDEA	International Institute for Democracy and Electoral Assistance
IEM	international monitoring of elections
IfS	Instrument for Stability (EU)
IMF	International Monetary Fund
INGO	international non-governmental organization
IPR	index of power resources
IPU	Inter-Parliamentary Union
IRI	International Republican Institute (US)
KAS	Konrad Adenauer Stiftung (Germany)
KMT	Kuomintang (Taiwan)
MCC	Millennium Challenge Corporation
MCCE	Movement against Electoral Corruption
MDC	Movement for Democratic Change (Zimbabwe)
MDD	mechanisms of direct democracy
MEDA	Mesures d'Accompagnement
MENA	Middle East and North Africa
MFA	Armed Forces Movement (Portugal)
MOD	Ministry of Defence
MPRP	Mongolian People's Revolutionary Party
MVR	Fifth Republic Movement (Venezuela)
NATO	North Atlantic Treaty Organization

NDC	National Democratic Congress (Ghana)
NDI	National Democratic Institute for International Affairs (US)
NDU	National Defence University (Mongolia)
NED	National Endowment for Democracy (US)
NEP	New Economic Policy (Malaysia)
NEPAD	New Partnership for Africa's Development
NGO	non-governmental organization
NIP	National Indicative Programme
NPP	New Patriotic Party (Ghana)
NSC	National Security Council
OAS	Organization of American States
OAU	Organization of African Unity
ODA	official development assistance
OECD	Organisation for Economic Co-operation and Development
OIC	Organization of the Islamic Conference
OPEC	Organization of the Petroleum Exporting Countries
PAN	National Action Party (Mexico)
PAP	People's Action Party (Singapore)
PDP	People's Democratic Party
PKR	Parti Keadilan Rakyat
PLC	Liberal Constitutionalist Party
PLD/PAD	People's Alliance for Democracy (Thailand)
PLH	Liberal Party of Honduras
PLN	National Liberation Party (Costa Rica)
PML-N	Pakistan Muslim League Nawaz
PN	Nationalist Party (Honduras)
PNA	Palestinian National Authority
PP	Panamanianist Party
PPP	Pakistan People's Party
PPP	People's Power Party (Thailand)
PR	proportional representation
PRD	Party of the Democratic Revolution (Mexico)
PRD	Revolutionary Democratic Party (Panama)
PRI	Institutional Revolutionary Party (Mexico)
PSC	Peace and Security Council (Africa)
PSD	Social Democratic Party (Portugal)
PSO	peace support operations
PT	Worker's Party (Brazil)
PTS	Purdue Political Terror Scales
QoD	quality of democracy
RENAMO	Resistência Nacional Moçambicana
RPI	Retail Price Index
SCO	Shangai Cooperation Organization
SIGI	Social Institutions and Gender Index
TRT	Thai Rak Thai
TSJ	Supreme Tribunal of Justice (Venezuela)
UDHR	Universal Declaration of Human Rights
UMNO	United Malays National Organization

UN	United Nations
UNDP	United Nations Development Programme
UNECA	United Nations Economic Commission for Africa
UNEP	United Nations Environmental Programme
UNICEF	United Nations Children's Fund
UNIFEM	United Nations Development Fund for Women
UNIPW	United Nations International Protection Workshop
UNRWA	United Nations Relief Works Agency for Palestinian Refugees in the Near East
UNTAC	United Nations Transitional Authority in Cambodia
UPD	Unit for the Promotion of Democracy (OAS)
URNG	Guatemalan National Revolutionary Union
UTO	United Tajik Opposition
WB	World Bank
WBG	Women's Budget Group
WBI	Women's Budget Initiative
WHO	World Health Organization

Contributors

Abdul–Gafaru Abdulai is a Ph.D. candidate at the University of Manchester, UK. He holds an M.Phil. in Development Studies from the University of Cambridge and worked as a Research Officer at the Institute for Democratic Governance (IDEG), Ghana, from March 2007 to September 2009.

Ludvig Beckman is Associate Professor at the Department of Political Science, Stockholm University, Sweden, where he is currently running research projects on various aspects of the problem of democratic inclusion. His fields of research include democratic and political theory. His publications include *The frontiers of democracy. The right to vote and its limits* (Palgrave Macmillan, 2009) and articles in international journals, including *Democratization*, *Environmental Politics* and *Ratio Juris*.

David Beetham is Professor Emeritus, University of Leeds, UK; Fellow, Human Rights Centre, University of Essex, UK; Associate Director, Democratic Audit. Relevant publications include: *Democracy and Human Rights* (1999); (jointly) *International IDEA Handbook on Democracy Assessment,* Kluwer, 2001; (jointly) *Democracy under Blair* (Politico's, 2002); *Democracy, a Beginner's Guide* (Oneworld Publications, 2005); *Parliament and Democracy in the Twenty-first Century: a Guide to Good Practice* (Inter-Parliamentary Union, 2006); (jointly) *Power to the People? Assessing Democracy in Ireland* (TASC at New Island, 2007); (jointly) *Assessing the Quality of Democracy: A Practical Guide* (International IDEA, 2008). He has undertaken many international consultancies: for UNESCO and the UNDP on democracy; for the UN High Commission on Human Rights on human rights and democracy; for International IDEA on democracy assessment; for the Inter-Parliamentary Union (IPU) on parliament and democracy. Recent journal articles include several on aspects of human rights and their relation to democracy.

John A. Booth is a researcher and consultant on Latin American politics, having retired as Regents Professor of political science from the University of North Texas, USA, in 2011. His published research focuses on attitudes toward democracy and democratic change in Latin America and on political violence and revolution in Central America. He is affiliated with the Latin American Public Opinion Project Americas Barometer 2010 and 2012 public opinion survey rounds, and has consulted and lectured on democratization, revolution, and Central American politics, and a political risk consultant for the Department of State, other government agencies, interest groups, foundations, and corporations and several universities. He is the author or co-author of *Understanding Central America*, (5th ed., 2010), *The Legitimacy Puzzle in Latin America* (2009), *Costa Rica: Quest for Democracy* (1998), and *The End and the Beginning: The Nicaraguan Revolution* (revised 2nd ed. 1985).

Vincent Boudreau is a professor of political science at the City College of New York, USA, and a member of the City University of New York graduate faculty. He also directs CCNY's Colin Powell Center for Policy Studies. A specialist in the politics of social movements, particularly in Southeast Asia, his latest book is *Resisting Dictatorship: Repression and Protest in Southeast Asia*. He also conducts research and writes on repression, government transitions to democracy, and collective violence, and is currently completing a book manuscript that examines Philippine and Indonesian social movements across their transitions from dictatorship. In addition to his academic work, Dr. Boudreau has undertaken projects with ActionAid Asia, Jubilee South Asia, and The Philippine Rural Reconstruction Movement, and has consulted for Oxfam Asia, Action of Economic Reform (Philippines), and Freedom House. He received his Ph.D. from Cornell.

Anita Breuer holds a Master in Area Studies Latin America and received her doctoral degree in Political Science from the University of Cologne, Germany, in 2008. Her research interests involve processes of democratic transition, as well as good governance and citizen participation in post-transition democracies. She is the author of several articles dealing with direct democracy in Latin America which have been published in *Democratization, Latin American Politics and Society, Bulletin of Latin American Research, Representation, and Revista de Ciencia Política*. She acts as a reviewer for several peer-reviewed journals including *Comparative Political Studies, Democratization* and *Swiss Political Science Review*. In 2007, she was awarded the Frank Cass Prize for the best article by a junior scholar in *Democratization*. In 2008 she obtained a postdoctoral research grant from the Fritz Thyssen Foundation. She currently holds a post as researcher at the German Development Institute, an independent policy think tank based in Bonn, Germany, where her research focuses on the impact of social digital media on political participation.

Rasmus Broms is a Ph.D. candidate at the Department of Political Science, University of Gothenburg. His Master's thesis focused on the relationship between social capital and judicial institutions in Western Europe. From 2009 to 2011 he worked as a research assistant at the Quality of Government Institute, where he currently is active writing his dissertation, which revolves around the relationship between taxation, state building and institutional quality.

Thomas C. Bruneau is a Distinguished Professor of National Security Affairs at the Naval Postgraduate School. He joined the NSA Department in 1987 after having taught in the Department of Political Science at McGill University in Montreal, Canada since 1969. Dr. Bruneau became Chairman of the Department in 1989, and continued in that position until 1995. He became Director of the Center for Civil Military Relations in November 2000, a position he held until December 2004. He has researched and written extensively on Latin America, especially Brazil, and Portugal. Dr. Bruneau has published more than a dozen books in English and Portuguese as well as articles in journals including *Latin American Research Review, Comparative Politics, Third World Quarterly, Journal of Interamerican Studies and World Affairs, Journal of Latin American Studies, Encyclopedia of Democracy*, and *South European Society and Politics*.

Matthew Carlson is an Associate Professor of Political Science at the University of Vermont, USA. He specializes in Asian politics, public opinion, electoral systems, and human rights. Recent publications include *Money Politics in Japan: New Rules, Old Practices* (2007) and 'Financing Democracy in Japan: The Allocation and Consequences of Government Subsidies to Political Parties', forthcoming in *Party Politics*.

Francesco Cavatorta is Senior Lecturer in the School of Law and Government, Dublin City University, Ireland. His research focuses on the politics of the Middle East. He is the author of over

30 refereed journal articles. He is currently editing a manuscript on civil society dynamics in Syria and Iran.

Gordon Crawford is Professor of Development Politics at the School of Politics and International Studies, University of Leeds. He is Director of the Centre for Global Development at Leeds. He is co-editor of *Democratization*, and co-convenor of the Governance and Development Working Group of the European Association of Development Research and Training Institutes (EADI).

Renske Doorenspleet is associate professor in comparative politics in the Department of Politics and International Studies, University of Warwick, UK. She is also director of the Centre for Studies in Democratization. Her book *Democratic Transitions: Exploring the Structural Sources of the Fourth Wave* (2005) focuses on theoretical and empirical explanations of recent transitions to democracy around the world. She has also published several book chapters and articles in various journals, including: *World Politics*, *European Journal of Political Research*, *Acta Politica* and *Democratization*.

Charles Manga Fombad is Professor of Law and Head of Department of Public Law at the Faculty of Law, University of Pretoria, South Africa. He is the author/editor of eight books and has published more than two dozen book chapters and over 50 articles in internationally refereed journals. He has received numerous prizes for his research and publications and is a rated scholar of the South African National Research Foundation. Professor Fombad is a member of the editorial board of several international Journals. His main areas of research interests are comparative constitutional law, delict (tort law), media law, legal history, international law and law of international institutions. He has written many papers on the issue of constitutionalism, democracy and the African Union.

Verena Fritz holds a Ph.D. in Political Science from the European University Institute, Italy. Her research and her work in international development have focused on democratization, state-building, and political economy dynamics that enable or hinder development in the former Soviet Union and Mongolia, as well as in other world regions. Verena is currently a Governance Specialist with the World Bank's Public Sector Governance unit. She is the author of *State-building: A Comparative Study of Ukraine, Lithuania, Belarus, and Russia*.

Sonja Grimm is Assistant Professor of International Relations and Comparative Politics in the Department of Politics and Management at the University of Konstanz, Germany. She specializes in studies of transition to democracy, state-building and democracy promotion in post-conflict societies. In 2008, she edited (with Wolfgang Merkel) a special issue of *Democratization*, entitled: 'War and Democratization: Legality, Legitimacy, and Effectiveness' (Vol. 15, No. 3), and in 2012 she co-edited (with Julia Leininger and Tina Freyburg) another special issue of *Democratization*, entitled: 'Do all Good Things Go Together? Conflicting Objectives in Democracy Promotion' (Vol. 19, No. 3). She obtained her Ph.D. ('Imposing Democracy: Political Re-organisation under External Oversight after Military Intervention') from Humboldt University, Berlin, Germany, and has a Masters degree in Political Science, History and History of Art from the Ruprecht-Karls-University Heidelberg. Germany. Sonja Grimm coordinates the research network 'External Democratization Politics (EDP)'.

Jeffrey Haynes is co-editor of *Democratization*. He is also Professor of Politics, Associate Dean (Research & Postgraduate) of the Faculty of Law, Governance, and International Relations, and

Director of the Centre for the Study of Religion, Conflict and Cooperation at London Metropolitan University, UK. His research interests are: religion and international relations; religion and politics; democracy and democratization; development studies; and comparative politics and globalization. He is the author of more than 30 books, 55 refereed journal articles, 75 book chapters and two reports: a 17,000-word discussion paper for the Geneva-based United Nations Research Institute for Social Development, 'Religion, Fundamentalism and Identity: A Global Perspective' (1995) and a 15,000-word study for the Commonwealth Secretariat, 'Political Transformation in the Commonwealth' (2009). His most recent books are: *Religious Actors in the Public Sphere: Means, Objectives, and Effects* (co-edited with Anja Hennig) (2011), and *Religion, Politics and International Relations: Selected Essays* (2011).

David Herbert is Professor of Religious Studies at the University of Agder, Norway, where he teaches on the Religion, Ethics and Society Ph.D. and Masters programmes. He previously taught religious studies and sociology at the University of Groningen, The Netherlands, The Open University, UK, and Trinity College, Dublin, Ireland. His main research interests are in religion and civil society, religion and the politics of multiculturalism, and religion and media. His writings include *Religion and Social Transformations* (ed., 2001), *Religion and Civil Society* (2003), and *Creating Community Cohesion: Religion, Media and the Public Sphere in Multicultural Societies* (forthcoming, 2012).

Monica Herz is an associate professor at the Catholic University of Rio de Janeiro, Brazil. She has a Ph.D. from the London School of Economics and Political Science and has written three books : *Organizações Internacionais: histórias e práticas* (with Andréa Ribeiro Hoffman) (2004), *Ecuador vs. Peru: Peacemaking Amid Rivalry* (with João Pontes Nogueira) (2002), and *Global Governance Away From the Media* (2010), as well as several articles and chapters on Latin American security and Brazilian foreign policy.

Farida Jalalzai has a Ph.D. in Political Science from University at Buffalo, USA, and a B.S. in Political Science and African and African American Studies from SUNY College at Brockport (1996), USA. She is Assistant Professor of Political Science at the University of Missouri-St Louis. Her research analyses the representation and behaviour of women and minorities in politics and the role of gender in the political arena. Her work focuses on women national leaders and she has published in *Women and Politics, Politics & Gender, International Political Science Review, Journal of Women, Politics, & Policy* and *German Politics, Politics & Policy*. She has recently completed a book-length manuscript on women national leaders worldwide called *Women Rule*. She has also published research dealing with Muslim American political behaviour and the impact of discrimination on Muslim Americans since 9/11.

Kanishka Jayasuriya is Professor of International Politics, University of Adelaide, Australia. Prior to this he was Principal Senior Research Fellow at the Asia Research Centre (ARC), Murdoch University, Australia. His most recent book is *Statecraft, Welfare, and Politics of Inclusion* (2006). His current research focuses on political regimes and inequality in emerging market economies.

Paul G. Lewis is Emeritus Professor of Politics at the Open University, UK. He has published extensively on issues of Central and East European politics during the communist and post-communist periods. In terms of the latter he has focused on various dimensions of democratiza-tion, and particularly on the process of party development and integration with the European Union. He has recently published a co-edited volume titled *Europeanising Party Politics? Comparative Perspectives on Central and Eastern Europe* (2011). He is currently preparing a further edition (5th) of Developments in Central and East European Politics for Palgrave Macmillan.

Fabrice Lehoucq is Associate Professor, Department of Political Science, University of North Carolina, Greensboro, USA. He is a specialist in comparative politics, democratic politics, and political economy. Lehoucq is the author of several books, including the first author of *Stuffing the Ballot Box: Fraud, Democratization, and Electoral Reform in Costa Rica* (2002) and of *Civil War, Democratization, and Underdevelopment in Central America* (2012). He has published articles in *Comparative Political Studies*, *Comparative Politics*, and *Electoral Studies*. He has received support for his research from the Inter-American Development Bank, Kellogg Institute (University of Notre Dame), the Alexander von Humboldt Foundation, the National Endowment for the Humanities, the Social Science Research Council, and the World Bank. At present, he is at work on a book manuscript called 'Political Institutions, Instability, and Democratic Performance in Latin America'. He holds a Ph.D. in Political Science from Duke University.

Wolfgang Merkel is Director of the 'Democracy and Democratisation' research program at the Social Science Research Centre Berlin (WZB) and Professor of Political Science at the Humboldt University Berlin, Germany. He is a member of a number of key bodies, including the Berlin-Brandenburg Academy of Sciences and Humanities and the International Council of Advisors to the Spanish Prime Minister José Luis Rodríguez Zapatero. He is also a non-party member of the Basic Values Commission of the Executive Committee of the German Social Democratic Party (SPD) and a member of the social sciences review board of the German Research Foundation (DFG). His most recent publications include the co-edited volume *The Future of Representative Democracy* (2011); *System transformation* (2010); *Social Democracy in Power: The Capacity to Reform* (2008), which has been translated into German, Chinese and Vietnamese; and more than 200 journal articles on such subjects as democracy and democratization, twenty-first-century dictatorships, political parties, comparative public policy, the future of social democracy, welfare states and social justice.

Michelle Pace is Reader in Politics and International Studies at the Department of Political Science and International Studies, University of Birmingham, UK. From April 2007 until March 2009 she was Principal Investigator (PI) on a British Academy large research project on Arab Mediterranean perceptions on democratization and since February 2008 she has been PI on an ESRC First Grant Scheme large research project on Paradoxes and Contradictions in EU Democracy Promotion Efforts in the Middle East. She is the founder and convenor of the BISA working group on International Mediterranean Studies as well as the research group on EU democracy promotion efforts in the Middle East. Her publications include *The Politics of Regional Identity. Meddling with the Mediterranean* (2006); *Conceptualizing Cultural and Social Dialogue in the Euro-Mediterranean Area: A European Perspective* (co-ed., 2007); *The European Union's Democratization Agenda in the Mediterranean: A Critical Inside-Out Approach* (ed., 2009); *Europe, the USA and Political Islam: Strategies for Engagement* (ed., 2010); and numerous journal articles.

Vicky Randall is Emeritus Professor of Government at the University of Essex, UK. She is the co-editor of *Politics in the Developing World* (just published in its third edition) and author of numerous articles and book chapters concerned with political parties in developing democracies.

Garry Rodan is an Australian Professorial Fellow (2010–2014) of the Australian Research Council and Professor of Politics and International Studies at the Asia Research Centre, Murdoch University, Australia. His thematic research interest is in the relationship between capitalist development and political regime directions in Southeast Asia. Attempting to characterize and explain dynamics of authoritarian rule has been a particular focus. He is the author of

Transparency and Authoritarian Rule in Southeast Asia: Singapore and Malaysia (2004) and *The Political Economy of Singapore's Industrialization* (1989). His edited and co-edited books include *Neoliberalism and Conflict in Asia After 9/11* (2005), *The Political Economy of Southeast Asia* (1997, 2001, 2006), *Political Oppositions in Industrializing Asia* (1996), *Singapore Changes Guard* (1993) and *Southeast Asia in the 1990s: Authoritarianism, Capitalism and Democracy* (1993).

Bo Rothstein holds the August Röhss Chair in Political Science at the University of Gothenburg, Sweden, where he is head of the Quality of Government (QoG) Institute. The Institute conducts research about the importance of trustworthy, reliable, competent, non-corrupt government institutions. In 2006, he served as Visiting Professor at Harvard University. In 2003, he was awarded a six-year grant from the Swedish Science Council for long-term support for leading scholars. In 2010, he was awarded a similar five-year grant from the Knut and Alice Wallenberg foundation which is the largest private foundation promoting research in Sweden. Rothstein has also served as adjunct professor at the University of Bergen and University of Aalborg. His latest book, *The Quality of Government: Corruption, Inequality and Social Trust in International Perspective* was published in 2011. His articles have appeared in scholarly journals such as *World Politics, Governance, Comparative Politics, Scandinavian Political Studies, American Behavioral Scientist, European Journal of Political Research* and *Comparative Political Studies*. He is also a regular contributor to the Swedish debate about public policy and has published more than 100 op-ed articles in all major Swedish daily newspapers.

Martin Slann received a doctorate in political science from the University of Georgia, USA. He is a member of the political science faculty and dean of the College of Arts and Sciences at The University of Texas at Tyler. Professor Slann is the co-author of the *Encyclopedia of Terrorism* (Facts on File) and *The Ethnic Dimension in International Relations* (Lynne Rienner) as well as several journal articles. Professor Slann is also the author or co-author of several textbooks on introductory American Government and Introduction to Politics. He is an *ex officio* member of the Board of Directors for the Southern Regional Model United Nations. He has delivered numerous presentations at regional and national meetings of political science associations and the International Studies Association.

Wendy Stokes is Academic Leader for research and graduate studies in the Faculty of Law, Governance and International Relations at London Metropolitan University, UK. Her long-standing research interests include equality, democracy and participation, in particular, the implications of equalities policies, political ideas, and political activism for women and gender. Her recent publications include *Women in Contemporary Politics* (2006), as well as journal articles and book contributions. Currently, her research interests include: women's political parties, feminist theatre, citizenship, and women members of the Greater London Authority. She is interested in the development of strategies for increasing the numbers of women in public life, but conceives of this as part of a larger movement towards greater equality and peace for all.

Jay Ulfelder is an independent consultant and writer. He received his Ph.D. in Political Science from Stanford University, USA, in 1997 and his B.A. in Comparative Area Studies (USSR and Eastern Europe) in 1991. From 2001 until 2011, he worked for Science Applications International Corporation as research director for the Political Instability Task Force, a US Government-funded research programme that seeks to forecast and explain various forms of political change in countries worldwide. He has published work on regime survival and change in the journals *Comparative Political Studies, Democratization,* and *International Political Science Review* and in a book entitled *Dilemmas of Democratic Consolidation: A Game-Theory Approach* (Lynne Rienner, 2010).

Jonathan Wheatley is a senior researcher at the Centre for Research on Direct Democracy (c2d), Switzerland. He is also lecturer at the University of Zurich and the Swiss Federal Institute of Technology at Zurich (ETH). Dr Wheatley's research interests include democratization, state-building, parties and party systems in developing democracies and the impact of new forms of media and information-communication technologies on party systems in established democracies. In addition to publishing a number of scholarly articles, Wheatley has also published *Georgia from National Awakening to Rose Revolution: Delayed Transition in the Former Soviet Union* (2005), an analysis of the political regime in Georgia from 1988 to 2004.

Richard Youngs is director general of FRIDE, Madrid, Spain, and assistant professor at the University of Warwick, UK. Prior to joining FRIDE, he was EU Marie Curie research fellow at the Norwegian Institute for International Relations, Oslo (2001–4), and senior research fellow at the UK Foreign and Commonwealth Office (1995–8). He has a Ph.D. and an MA in International Studies from the University of Warwick and a BA from the University of Cambridge. His research focuses on democracy promotion, European foreign policy, energy security and the Middle East region. He has published six books on different elements of European external policy, edited eleven volumes and published over forty articles and working papers, while writing regularly in the international media. His latest book is *Europe's Decline and Fall: The Struggle against Global Irrelev*ance (2010).

Elke Zuern is an Associate Professor of Politics and Chair of the Social Sciences at Sarah Lawrence College, USA. She has been a visiting scholar at both the University of Witwatersrand and the University of Johannesburg, in South Africa. Her work engages questions of democracy, economic and political inequality, protest, violence, and memory. She has published articles in various journals including *Comparative Politics, Democratization, African Affairs, African Studies Review, Politique Africaine, Transformation* and *Politikon* as well as numerous book chapters. Her book *The Politics of Necessity: Community Organizing and Democracy in South Africa* (2011) demonstrates the shifting challenges faced by poor citizens in South Africa and other new democracies, exposes the impoverishment of discussions of democracy that overlook this pattern, and reveals the consequences of these silences.

Introduction

Thirty-five years of democratization: the third and fourth waves of democracy in perspective

Jeffrey Haynes

Four decades ago, there were few democratically elected governments outside Western Europe and North America. Non-democracies had various kinds of authoritarian, unelected governments, including, military, one-party, no party and personalist dictatorships. From the mid-1970s, there was an unexpected, not regionally specific, shift from unelected to elected governments – a process of democratization. The US political scientist, Samuel Huntington, was quick to identify the phenomenon and decided to give it a name: the 'third wave of democracy'. The democratization process continued in the 1980s and, after a brief hiatus, took further energy in the 1990s and early 2000s with the 'decommunization' of Central and Eastern Europe (CEE) in what some observers call the 'fourth wave of democracy' (McFaul 2002). Taken together, the third and fourth waves of democracy highlight that competitive electoral politics are now being conducted in a record number of countries, in most parts of the world. In 2011, Freedom House characterized 147 countries as 'free' or 'partly free', indicating a significant level of democracy, while 47 other states were identified as 'not free', suggesting a palpable lack of democracy.[1] Overall, then, of the 194 countries identified by Freedom House in 2011, just over three-quarters (75.8 per cent) had extant, recognizably democratic regimes 35 years after the start of the third wave in the mid-1970s.

The third wave of democracy

The third and fourth waves of democracy followed two earlier 'waves' of democracy. The first took place during the nineteenth century and the early years of the twentieth century, when democratization occurred in various European and North American countries. The second wave began directly after the Second World War, when several countries, including Italy, Japan and West Germany, moved from authoritarian to democratic rule.

The third wave of democracy began in 1974 with three Southern European countries – Greece, Portugal and Spain – moving from authoritarian to democratically elected governments. Following this, in the 1980s and 1990s, numerous authoritarian regimes in Latin America, Eastern Europe, Asia and Africa, also democratized. The extent of these changes is shown by the fact that in 1972 only one-quarter of countries had democratically elected governments. Twenty years later, in the early 1990s, the proportion had grown to more than 50 per cent, and by the end of the first decade of the twenty-first century, around 75 per cent of the world's nearly 200 countries had democratically elected governments.

Explaining the shift from authoritarian to democratic rule

Processes of democratization can occur in four identifiable stages, although not all democratizations conform to this model. The four stages are: (1) political liberalization; (2) collapse of authoritarian regime; (3) democratic transition; and (4) democratization consolidation. *Political liberalization* is the process of reforming authoritarian rule. *Collapse of the authoritarian regime* refers to the – often prolonged – stage when a dictatorship falls apart. *Democratic transition* is the material shift to democracy, commonly marked by the democratic election of a new government. *Democratic consolidation* is the typically lengthy, often unfinished, procedure of embedding democratic institutions and perceptions among both elites and citizens that democracy is the best way of 'doing' politics.

The four stages are complementary and can overlap. For example, political liberalization and transition can happen simultaneously, while aspects of democratic consolidation can appear when certain elements of transition are barely in place or remain incomplete. Or they may even be showing signs of retreating. On the other hand, it is nearly always possible to observe a concluded transition to democracy. This is when a pattern of behaviour developed ad hoc during the stage of regime change becomes institutionalized, characterized by admittance of political actors into the system – as well as the process of political decision-making – according to previously established and legitimately coded procedures.

Until then, absence of or uncertainty about these accepted 'rules of the democratic game' make it difficult to be sure about the eventual outcome of political transition. This is because transition dynamics revolve around strategic interactions and tentative arrangements between actors with uncertain power resources. Key issues include: (1) defining who is legitimately entitled to play the political 'game'; (2) the criteria determining who will win and who will lose politically; and (3) the limits to be placed on the issues at stake. What chiefly differentiates the four stages of democratization is the degree of uncertainty prevailing at each moment. For example, during regime transition *all* political calculations and interactions are highly uncertain. This is because political actors find it difficult to know: (1) what their precise interests are; and (2) which groups and individuals would most usefully be allies or opponents.

During transition, powerful, often inherently undemocratic political players, such as the armed forces and/or elite civilian supporters of the exiting authoritarian regime, characteristically divide into 'hard-line' and 'soft-line' factions. 'Softliners' are relatively willing to achieve negotiated solutions to the political problems. 'Hardliners' are less willing to arrive at solutions reflecting compromise between polarized positions. Democratic consolidation is most likely when 'softliners' triumph because, unlike 'hardliners', they are willing to find a compromise solution.

A consolidated democracy is said to be in place when political elites, recognizable political groups such as political parties, and the mass of ordinary people apparently accept the formal rules and informal understandings that determine political outcomes: that is, 'who gets what, where, when and how'. If achieved, it signifies that groups are settling into relatively predictable positions involving politically legitimate behaviour according to generally acceptable rules. More generally, a consolidated democracy is characterized by normative limits and established patterns of power distribution. Political parties emerge as privileged in this context because, despite their divisions over strategies and their uncertainties about partisan identities, the logic of electoral competition focuses public attention on them and compels them to appeal to the widest possible clientele. In addition, 'strong' – or at least relatively unfragmented – civil societies are often said to be crucial for both meaningful democratization and eventual democratic consolidation, not least because they help keep an eye on how the government operates and what it does with its power. In sum, democratic consolidation is said to be present when all significant political actors take for granted the fact that democratic processes dictate governmental renewal.

Yet, despite numerous relatively free and fair elections over the last few decades in many formerly authoritarian countries in most parts of the world, ordinary people often lack clear and consistent ability significantly to influence political outcomes. This is because small groups of elites – whether, civilians, military personnel or a combination – still often control national political processes, despite democratization, while also managing more widely to continue to dictate political outcomes. Under such conditions, because power is still focused in relatively few elite hands, political systems continue in many cases to have rather narrow bases from which most ordinary people are, or feel, excluded. This can be problematic because, by definition, a democracy should not be run by and for the few, but should signify popularly elected government operating in the broad public interest.

In sum, during the third wave of democracy, increased numbers of governments came to power via the ballot box – yet not all of them have strong democratic credentials.

Democratization: the comparative importance of domestic and external factors

The third and fourth waves of democracy occurred during a period of enhanced and deepening globalization, which in general highlighted the impact of external factors on many countries' domestic political and economic structures and processes. However, focusing on external factors alone is insufficient to get a full understanding of democratic outcomes in the post-1970s. We also need to consider countries' internal political characteristics and assess how they interact with external factors in different political contexts.

Regime change and democratization: domestic factors

Most analyses of democratization take into account three main domestic factors: civil society, social capital and political society.

Civil society

Most examples of democratic transition during the third and fourth waves reflected the importance of consistent pressure from 'below' on authoritarian regimes. Such pressure, normally focused through civil society organizations, not only helps push the limits of newly created political space but can also be instrumental in the process of democratization – especially when civil society links up with representative political parties. In such cases, pressure led non-democratic governments to liberalize, articulate political reform agendas and, eventually, allow relatively free and fair multiparty elections.

The term 'civil society' crept quietly and largely unexamined into the literature on political economy in the 1980s. It began to be used in relation to the discourse of opposition leaders and groups in many non-democratic countries, especially the communist countries of CEE. However, civil society is not a new term. Often associated with the German philosopher Hegel (1770–1831), the term began to appear in the literature on Western political philosophy from the time of the emergence of the modern nation state in the eighteenth century. However, in contemporary usage, 'civil society' refers to associations and other organized bodies that are intermediate between the state and the family. These include: labour unions, social movements, professional associations, student groups, religious bodies and the media. Collectively, such entities are said to help maintain a check on the power of the state and its totalizing tendencies; ideally, civil society amounts to an ensemble of arrangements to advance the socio-political interests of society, with the state and civil society forming mutually effective counterweights. 'Sturdy' civil societies nearly always stem from strong societies. 'Strong societies' are characterized by a comparative lack of ideological and class cleavages, by rather 'politicized' civil societies that can be easily mobilized for political causes, and by centralized social organizations such as business, labour and religious organizations. In sum, 'civil society' is not only a key defender of society's interests against state (over)dominance, but is also in most cases highly influential in democratization outcomes.

Civil society organizations are not directly involved in the business of government or in overt political management. But this does not necessarily prevent some from their exercising sometimes profound influence on various political issues, from single issues to the characteristics of national constitutions. In CEE, many observers highlight the role of civil society in helping to undermine apparently strong communist regimes that uniformly toppled like dominoes during 1989–91.

There are three broad categories of civil society. First, there are *weak civil societies*, characteristic of societies fragmented by ethnic and/or religious divisions, and found in many African, Middle Eastern and Central Asian countries. In these countries, civil society is typically ineffective and disjointed, not an effective, united counterweight to state power. This is frequently linked to wider problems of governance, such as inadequate popular participation and lack of governmental transparency and accountability. In such circumstances, governments are typically adept at buying off or crushing expressions of discontent. Overall, these circumstances reflect failure or inability of social groups to organize in such a way as to defend and promote their interests, while seriously reducing societal capacity to counter the hegemonic drives of the state.

Relatively strong civil societies are found in various East and Southeast Asian countries, including South Korea and Taiwan, and some Latin American and CEE nations, including Argentina, Chile and the Czech Republic. *Strong civil societies* are found in most established democracies, for example in India, Germany, Sweden and France. In both categories, civil societies are both vibrant and robust, with numerous civil rights organizations, social movements and local protest groups. One of the differences between 'strong' and 'relatively strong' civil societies is the length of time over which they have developed. Most Western European and North American countries have been nation states for lengthy periods, and their civil societies have also had a long time to develop, in some cases hundreds of years. On the other hand, Latin American and East Asian countries, while also in most cases existing as states for decades or longer, have nevertheless democratized much more recently. Countries with such civil societies are also not normally seriously divided by ethnic and/or religious schisms. They also tend to be relatively industrialized and urbanized, with well-organized trade unions and politically active working classes. In sum, in relation to democratization, civil society's effectiveness is often linked to:

- Societal – especially ethnic and religious – diversity, reflecting the quantity of social capital
- The level of economic development, urbanization and industrialization

Social capital

Civil society is said to be most effective when it builds upon society's store of social connections, that is, its *social capital*. Whereas *human* capital comprises formal education and training, and *economic* capital is material and financial resources, *social* capital is the interpersonal trust that makes it easier for people to do things together, neutralize free riders, and agree on sanctions against non-performing governments. The importance of social capital in helping build and sustain democracy has been noted in the literature on the subject, and the level of trust in a society is said to vary according to the vibrancy of associational life. Increasing stock of social capital – from both extensive and growing membership in voluntary associations – is likely to promote the deepening of democracy. Two main relational characteristics of social capital can be noted: first, 'bonded solidarity', that is, the sense of common nationhood and cultural identity that helps focus group resources. Second, 'enforceable trust' that controls the mutual assistance supplied and demanded, permitting a higher degree of resource-sharing than would be conceivable through more informal channels. This 'bank' of social capital is likely to be undermined by:

- inefficient government performance
- authoritarian regimes that frown on the growth of societal solidarity
- widespread societal hardship
- social disintegration, due in part to development shortfalls.

Under such circumstances, it will be very difficult or impossible to build recognizably democratic political systems.

Political society

To take the next steps from the collapse of authoritarianism through democratic transition, to arrive at consolidated democracy, *political society* needs to be actively and consistently involved. This is because to build a recognizably democratic system requires a great deal of serious thought and action about core institutions – including political parties, elections, electoral rules, political leadership, intra-party alliances and legislatures, and most of the relevant work is carried out by political society actors. While political society is analytically separate from civil society, the two are closely linked. Not least, civil society, expressed through political society, can constitute itself politically to help select governments and monitor their performance in office.

According to Alfred Stepan (1988: 4), political society is the 'arena in which the polity specifically arranges itself for political contestation to gain control over public power and the state apparatus'. Political parties are the main component of political society. Chances of democracy taking root are said to be bolstered when there are relatively few, not ideologically polarized, political parties competing for power. Autonomous, democratically organized political parties can help to keep in check the personal power aspirations of political leaders. Such political parties are said to be a crucial key to democratic consolidation, especially when a pervasive pro-democracy legitimacy does not prevail during democratic transition. The more rapidly the party spectrum forms during transition, then the more likely is eventual democratic consolidation. When party systems become institutionalized in this way, parties typically orient themselves towards the goal of winning elections through focused appeals to voters. But when the party structure is only slowly established, then citizens may respond better to personalistic appeals from populist leaders rather than to those of parties. This scenario tends to favour the former, who may attempt to govern without bothering to establish and develop solid institutions underpinning their rule.

The main point is that institutionalizing party systems matters a great deal as they are much more likely to help sustain democracy and to promote effective governance than the likely alternative: amorphous party systems dominated by populist leaders. An institutionalized party system can help engender confidence in the democratic process in four main ways. First, it can help moderate and channel societal demands into an institutionalized environment of conflict resolution. Second, it can serve to lengthen the time horizons of actors because it provides electoral losers with the means periodically to mobilize resources for later rounds of political competition. Third, an effective party system can help prevent disenchanted groups' grievances from spilling over into mass street protests, likely to antagonize elites and their military allies and help facilitate a return to authoritarian rule ('the need for strong government'). Finally, an effective party system, linked to a capable state, can be important in helping imbue the mass of ordinary people with the idea that the political system is democratically accountable.

In sum, chances of democratization are enhanced when there is: (1) a strong civil society; (2) relative extensive amount of social capital; and (3) a robust political society, with a cohesive party system.

Regime change and democratization: external factors

Much analytical attention is devoted to processes of democratization at the level of the nation state. It is also often noted that the deepening of globalization after the Cold War focused attention on the third and fourth waves of democratization as processes that cannot be fully understood by looking at internal factors alone. As a result, it is widely accepted that democratization outcomes are affected by what various external actors do. For example, at the very least, democratization requires that no foreign power, hostile to this development, interferes in the political life of a country with the intention of subverting the political system. On the other hand, democratization during the third and fourth waves highlighted that the influence of external actors is typically secondary to that of domestic factors. In other words, external actors can hasten or retard but rarely if ever *fundamentally* influence democratization outcomes over time. Both background factors and more overt pressure from both state and non-state actors can be noted.

Background factors

'Background factors' are the generally favourable or unfavourable geostrategic circumstances in relation to regime change and democratization during the third and fourth waves. This is not a new phenomenon, and the significance of background factors can be noted in relation to regime change, including earlier waves of democratization, throughout the twentieth century. For example, after the First World War, President Woodrow Wilson's references to the desirability of 'national self-determination' in relation to the founding of the League of Nations encouraged nationalists in the Middle East and elsewhere to demand self-rule. A decade later, during the 1930s, tentative moves towards democracy in several Latin American countries could not make consistent headway against a background of deepening regional – and global – economic depression. After the Second World War, during the 1960s and 1970s, US fears of the spread of the Cuban revolution led throughout Latin America to a regional crackdown on calls for democracy, and growing US support for non-democratic – mainly military – governments. More recently, in the 1980s and 1990s, global circumstances (including the short-lived chimera of George H. W. Bush's 'new world order') became more advantageous for democracy, following the unforeseen and total collapse of CEE's communist regimes. The overall point is that external background factors were influential in relation to democratization during the twentieth century and in the early years of the present one. However, background factors are never sufficient on their own to lead to fundamental changes of regime unless they interact with what pro-democracy actors in both civil society and political society are seeking to achieve.

External pressures to democratize

During the current era of deepening globalization, the scope for external actors to determine the course of regime change has increased. Partly as a result of the influence of globalization, less powerful states must accept both their external setting, and their vulnerability to it, as a given. The task of their leaders is to manage external influences as best they can. In particular, many post-colonial countries in the developing world are not only weak but also characterized by 'negative sovereignty' implying adverse civil and socio-economic conditions. Consequently, they may well be objects of the policies of other, stronger states.

But not even weak states are necessarily powerless in relation to powerful external states. For example, in the 1990s and early 2000s, the only remaining superpower – the US – was not able decisively, quickly or consistently to influence political outcomes in several apparently 'weak' states, including: Afghanistan, Haiti, Iraq, Liberia, Nigeria, Somalia and Sudan. These countries all had important 'negative' power resources that lay principally in their potential for 'chaos power', that is, capacity to create or make worse regional problems that powerful countries such as the US might be expected – perhaps through the United Nations or regional organizations – to deal with. In short, the ability of external actors to influence democratization is linked to the presence or absence of functioning states in the countries they enter; when functioning states are particularly 'fragile' – as in most of the countries noted in this paragraph – then even powerful external actors such as the government of the US struggle both to implement their preferred policies and to preside over regime change of the kind they wish to see. Where functioning states do exist, external state actors may encourage their political preferences through the media of 'political conditionality'. There are two main forms: (1) 'positive' political conditionality to encourage further democratization; and (2) 'negative' political conditionality to promote desired political reforms in hitherto unreceptive countries.

From the 1980s, the largest aid donors in quantitative terms – Britain, France, Japan and the US, plus the Scandinavian countries – sought to encourage both democratization and economic liberalization among countries receiving their aid. These governments, along with the International Monetary Fund and the World Bank, attached political conditionality to aid, loans and investments to recipient countries. If the latter denied their citizens basic human rights – including democratically elected governments – they would be denied assistance. The reasoning behind political conditionality was partly economic. Western governments and intergovernmental organizations claimed that economic failures were directly linked to an absence of political accountability. Consequently, it was claimed that, without meaningful democratization, economic liberalization would struggle to achieve desirable results.

The United States is a key player in relation to political conditionality, with both the government and various non-state – albeit state-linked – organizations, such as the National Endowment for Democracy (NED), actively supporting both democratization and economic liberalization. This is not a new policy, but has developed from the 1950s. Fifty years ago, then newly democratic governments in Latin America – including Costa Rica, Venezuela and Colombia – received considerable financial and diplomatic support from the US government. Later, in the 1970s, US foreign policy goals were reflected in President Jimmy Carter's pro-human rights foreign policy, while in the 1980s President Ronald Reagan's government promoted democracy primarily as a counter to perceived communist expansionism directed by, but not limited to, the US's regional *bête noire* – Cuba's communist government, then led by Fidel Castro. In the 1990s President William Clinton developed new policies linked to political conditionality, a strategy continued by the administrations of Presidents George W. Bush and Barack Obama, which regarded democratization as a useful way to arrive at more peaceful and cooperative international relations. During the 1990s alone, successive US governments provided more than $700 million to over 100 countries, mainly in the developing world and CEE, to further their democratization efforts.

US state assistance is typically focused in a standard democracy template. This involves offering financial support to help develop electoral processes and democratic structures, including constitutions and political institutions, including, the rule of law, legislatures, local government structures, political parties, improved civil-military relations and civil society. However, it takes more than simply external sources of finance to develop democracy. This is because money alone cannot create and embed concrete manifestations of good governance, without which democracy cannot develop. This outcome is not simply available on order, but requires a particular kind of politics to institute and sustain it.

Superficially, democratization may be encouraged if external actors limit their perusal of the democratic process to elections alone; indeed, international observation of elections seems often the only test used to judge a shift from authoritarian to democratic rule. But when elections are complete, and the attention of the corpus of international observers moves on, 'democracy' is at best partially achieved. Anti-democracy elites may remain powerful, and political systems still have narrow bases, characterized by the survival of authoritarian clientelism and coercion. In sum, external democracy funding will not be effective if target regimes are able to acquire democratic legitimacy internationally without substantially changing their mode of operation.

This book's structure and contents

This book is a collective effort, bringing together 33 experts on the multifarious, endlessly fascinating topic of democratization. Following this introductory chapter, the volume is structured thematically into four sections, encompassing overall 28 separate contributions. Part I provides a regional *tour d'horizon* of the current state of democratization and democracy in eight regions: Central and Eastern Europe, Central America, South America, sub-Saharan Africa, the Middle East and North Africa, Central Asia, South Asia, and East and Southeast Asia. Part II comprises eight chapters grouped together under the rubric of 'democratization and governance', which collectively examine key structures, processes and outcomes of democratization and democracy: democratic transitions; elections; hybrid regimes; deviant democracies; the military; political parties; civil society; and social capital.

Part III comprises six chapters, which overall focus on the relationship between 'democratization and international relations'. The individual chapters do this through an examination of the following issues and actors: the third and fourth waves of democracy; democratic conditionality; the United Nations; the European Union; the African Union; and the organization of American states. The last four chapters of the section examine the roles in recent democratization of the stated international and regional organizations.

The final section of the book, Part IV, comprises six chapters grouped under the heading 'democratization and development'. The aim here is to examine the relationship between the two, through a focus on: poverty and inequality; security; human rights; gender; war and conflict resolution.

Note

1. See http://www.freedomhouse.org/images/File/fiw/FIW_2011_MOF_Final.pdf (accessed 20 September 2011).

References

McFaul, M. (2002) 'The Fourth Wave of Democracy and Dictatorship: Noncooperative Transitions in the Postcommunist World', *World Politics*, 54 (2), pp. 212–244.

Stepan, A. (1988) *Rethinking Military Politics: Brazil and the Southern Cone*. Princeton, NJ: Princeton University Press.

Part I
Democratization – the regional picture

1

Central and Eastern Europe

Paul G. Lewis

The regional pattern of democratization

From the end of the Second World War and the Yalta Agreement of 1945, Central and Eastern Europe fell – or, in the case of the Soviet Union itself, remained – under communist rule and was thus subject to an authoritarian system of government. Various popular uprisings or reform movements were crushed by Soviet military intervention (East Germany 1953, Hungary 1956 and Czechoslovakia 1968), some states removed themselves – partly or wholly – from Soviet influence (Yugoslavia, Albania and Romania), while the Polish leadership put an end to the conflicts of the Solidarity period and preserved one-party rule by declaring a domestic state of war in 1981. Authoritarian rule of somewhat different kinds was nevertheless maintained for some 40 years, and the regional picture only began to undergo significant change with the accession to power in the Soviet Union of Mikhail Gorbachev in 1985.

In the Soviet Union there was soon much talk of glasnost' (openness) and perestroika (reconstruction), and political life gradually began to open up. In 1990 the leading role of the party was expunged from the constitution, and the communist power monopoly thus formally abolished, while diverse reform measures and processes of more radical change were already under way in the countries of Eastern Europe, as it had gradually become clear that the Soviet Union under Gorbachev was no longer committed to maintaining communist rule by force. The basic decision seems to have been taken in late 1986, although there is much uncertainty about the date and when the information was conveyed to the leaders of the satellite countries.

Various measures of liberalization were undertaken after this date, particularly in Poland and Hungary, the nations that led the reform movement. Moves to establish independent political parties were thus taken in Hungary in 1988, and in Poland a referendum was held in late 1987 on economic reform proposals, and steps taken the following year to reinstate the Solidarity trade union and involve it in a new stabilization programme. It soon became clear that a broader process of democratization was under way throughout the region. The key public events that marked the early stages of this process took place in 1989 and included, in May, the dismantling of parts of the barbed-wire fence that formed the Iron Curtain from the Hungarian side, the holding of semi-free elections in Poland during June and the breaching of the Berlin Wall in November. By the end of the year, the authoritarian regime had collapsed in these countries (as well as in Czechoslovakia), and the transition to democracy was clearly under way.

Free, competitive parliamentary elections were held in Czechoslovakia, East Germany and Hungary in 1990 (although not in Poland until 1991), as well as in Bulgaria and Romania – although in the latter case, in particular, there were doubts as to the fairness of the election. The Soviet Union itself began to break up in 1991, and free national elections were held in Estonia and

Lithuania in 1992. Competitive elections in what were soon to become the successor states to Yugoslavia had already been held in 1990, so the transition to democracy in Central and Eastern Europe got under way with amazing speed once the possibility of peaceful change opened up and the leading nations took the first steps. The pace of change was such that democratic opposition forces were sometimes ill-prepared and outmanoeuvred by established power-holders, as in Serbia, thus blocking prospects for further reform and delaying the process of more fundamental regime change for some years.

But it was not just because of the political astuteness of former communist leader Slobodan Milošević that democratic change encountered particular obstacles in Yugoslavia and its successor states. Democratization in Central and Eastern Europe was part of a broader, or multifaceted, process of change. It was pointed out at an early stage that the post-communist region faced a triple transition, one involving not just regime transformation but also marketization and fundamental economic reform as well as processes – in many cases – of state formation or even nation-building (Offe 1991). These were processes that were hardly unproblematic in themselves but their mutual interaction could have highly negative consequences, not least for democratization. Nowhere was this more apparent than in Yugoslavia, where Milošević set out to create a greater Serbia as the communist federation underwent rapid disintegration. The ensuing war involved Croats and Bosnians, lasted for several painful years and delayed the prospects for peaceful political change for a yet longer period. In Serbia, for example, Milošević was only ousted in 2000 and the path to democratic change finally opened. The unification of Germany and the dissolution of the Czechoslovak federation (into the Czech Republic and Slovakia) also changed state borders, although to far less deleterious effect. The demise of the Soviet Union produced yet more independent states, but this was a process that – in the core European area at least – did not involve any major border disputes.

While the process of democratization has been relatively straightforward in some areas, in others it has been considerably more complicated. Twenty years after the beginning of the process, the record of post-communist democratization in Central and Eastern Europe has therefore, not surprisingly, been a mixed one, although in simple terms the pattern is quite clear. According to the ratings of the US-based Freedom House (http://www.freedomhouse.org/template.cfm?page=1), all the former communist countries that are now members of the European Union were 'free' in 2009 (i.e. Bulgaria, Czech Republic, Estonia, Hungary, Latvia, Lithuania, Poland, Romania, Slovakia and Slovenia, as well as parts of the now united Germany), as were Croatia, Montenegro, Serbia and Ukraine. Albania, Bosnia, Kosovo, Macedonia and Moldova are 'partly free', implying substantial but not complete democratization (Puddington 2010).

According to the slightly different ratings of Nations in Transit, eight of the new EU members are also now regarded as consolidated democracies, excluding only Bulgaria and Romania. Russia, however, is no longer transitional and now has a consolidated authoritarian regime, as has Belarus. Most of the partly free countries (the exception is Bosnia) are also seen as semi-consolidated democracies (Nations in Transit 2009). So the bulk of Central Europe has democratized successfully, and things are now moving in a positive direction in much of the West Balkans.

Key features of democratization in Central and Eastern Europe

What accounts for the stronger current of democratization in the countries to the west (and to some extent the north) of the region? A number of explanations are readily apparent. From what has already been stated, two main factors – location and the role of the 'West' (in practice the effect of potential membership of the European Union (EU) and the North Atlantic Treaty

Organization (NATO)), and the impact of border disputes (the established idea that in order to become a democracy a territory has first to become a coherent state) – are obvious candidates. Throughout the post-communist world, it has been argued, 'there is a positive correlation between distance from the West and regime type' (McFaul 2002: 241). Where the initial balance of forces was unfavourable to democratic reformers, the attraction of EU and NATO membership gradually strengthened the hand of reformers by providing incentives to change and deepen democracy. Serbia has already been mentioned in passing in this respect, and Romania, Bulgaria and Croatia may also be placed in this category. Anti-communist mobilization was certainly sufficient to bring down Romanian communism and eliminate President Nicolae Ceauşescu and his wife, but, at least partly in consequence of the relatively totalitarian rule of the communist period, was unable to provide new leaders or any organizational basis for democratic change. It took time for these features to emerge, and many observers agree that the attractions of EU membership played a major part in bringing this about (Morlino and Sadurski 2010).

The observation that a polity (generally a state) needs defined borders for a democratic regime to emerge and put down strong roots is not a recent one, and has long been accepted as a major condition for successful democratization. The wars of the Yugoslav succession in the 1990s provide strong evidence of this, and it was only when they were resolved that the alternative attractions of Western integration began to exert a stronger influence. In contrast to Serbia, democratic challengers did well in the first free elections to be held in the Yugoslav republics of Croatia and Bosnia-Herzegovina but, as independent states, they were soon drawn into the bitterest conflict seen in Europe since the Second World War. Much of the responsibility for this can be attributed to the political ambitions of Milošević, who adopted a strongly nationalist orientation towards the end of the communist period. Only Slovenia was able to escape the post-communist conflicts and make a rapid transition to democracy.

However, it must also be recognized that the Yugoslav state had never had a settled history. Established in 1918 and formalized at the Versailles Conference, there were bitter conflicts between its constituent nationalities before, during and after the Second World War. Equally, while Franjo Tudjman did well in the Croatian free elections of 1990, his political orientation was a strongly nationalist one that did little for democratic change and much to perpetuate the conflict with the Serbs, in which Bosnians were also involved and suffered much destruction at the hands of both other groups. While the war is now over, though, and Tudjman's legacy may well be withering following his death more than a decade ago, the political travails of Bosnia continue and in 2011 it remains subject to the authority of a high representative appointed by the United Nations (UN). Once the Bosnian conflict was over, Macedonia – another constituent republic of the former Yugoslavia – also saw the outbreak of major ethnic violence, in 2001, when an uprising of part of the Albanian minority came near to leading the country into civil war. After a recurrence of violence during the 2008 parliamentary elections, though, the political situation has stabilized as the EU came to exert greater influence. While a far less extreme case, the establishment of a separate Slovak state in 1993 also strengthened the position of Vladimir Mečiar, a nationalist with strong ties to the communist regime, whose behaviour raised doubts about his (and the country's) democratic commitment. This was a development that prompted the EU to adopt a more sceptical attitude to Slovakia than the other seven post-communist candidates (Czech Republic, Estonia, Hungary, Latvia, Lithuania, Poland and Slovenia), which joined the Union in 2004.

While there is general agreement that Slovakia, Bulgaria and (particularly) Romania were slower to take the transition path than Poland, Hungary and the Czech Republic, there are different ways in which the explanatory variables are put together – even if there is wide agreement on the factors that were involved. Vachudová and Snyder (1997), for example, direct attention to the nature of regime change (whether there were opposition forces in 1989 able to take power and initiate fundamental transformation of the state), the state of the economy at the beginning of democratization and the vigour with which an economic reform programme was applied, as well as the ethnic geography of the countries concerned and the appeals that nationalist politicians were able to make. Other writers have placed greater emphasis on the extent of social modernization, levels of economic development, the nature of cultural legacies, and the role of religion (Huntington 1996; Przeworski and Limongi 1997).

From the standpoint of contemporary Central Europe, though, the attractions of the European Union seem to have prevailed over the various impediments to democratization that have been identified. The obstacles were clearly more difficult to overcome in countries situated more to the east and the south. But geographical location is hardly an explanation in itself and does nothing to identify the processes of change that were involved. As one example, Møller (2009: 95) sets out to throw more light on post-communist transformation by identifying and discussing three specific structural factors that seem to be important in explaining the striking success of the Central European countries.

First, there is the EU factor itself and explanations linked with the idea of the countries' vicinity to Western Europe. This can range from a quite general idea – that all (or at least most) countries are now subject to some kind of international liberal discursive hegemony – to Vachudova's (2005) argument that the EU began to exercise an active leverage over potential EU members in the mid-1990s. Second, there is the political legacies approach, associated particularly with Kitschelt (2001), who calls for an integration of the deep and proximate causes. Thus communist, or even pre-communist legacies, including histories of bureaucratic-authoritarian practices or a national accommodative communist regime, provided for a cleaner break and better democratic prospects when the opportunity presented itself. Third, there is the modernization explanation linked with ideas current for several decades and dating back to an early phase of democracy studies (see Lewis 2003).

Møller's correlation analysis suggests that all these structural factors and the key constraints associated with them exert some effect, particularly over a longer time-span. Morlino and Sadurski (2010: 231) also point to the importance of the interaction of EU influence with relevant domestic factors in producing effective democratization outcomes, and a greater EU impact when the influence is consistent with the existing domestic situation and actor willingness to implement European policy. The strength of the structural argument also suggests that such 'deep' variables have exercised a determinant effect on the longer-term fate of the post-communist countries. A corollary of this view is that alternative perspectives that focus on actor salience, an argument particularly associated with di Palma (1990), are not likely to be persuasive in the long run. This also fits with the growing doubts now expressed in many areas about the role of external influences and the effectiveness of the international democracy promotion process. The efforts to develop democratically oriented political parties and restrain tendencies to extremist populism have, for example, been judged to have had limited success in some areas, as have EU attempts to reduce corruption and encourage good governance in the wider European region.

The role of domestic factors

Increasingly, then, it is domestic structural factors that are given particular emphasis in explaining democratization. A number of aspects come into the analysis here. **Civil society** became a major focus of discussion in the 1980s as dissidents and opposition forces (particularly) in Central Europe sought to carve out an area of autonomous activity. They distinguished this sphere from that open to the direction of the communist state which, despite its weakened condition and the tentative steps taken towards liberalization, was still in essence a totalitarian entity and claimed virtually unlimited authority over social organizations and processes. There are different ideas on how a civil society should best be defined, but broadly speaking it concerns the space between individuals (and perhaps their family) and the state. The communist authorities in Hungary (1956) and Czechoslovakia (1968) had clearly shown that they would not tolerate any challenges to the power of the states they controlled, although the experience of Poland during the Solidarity period (August 1980 to December 1981) was considerably more ambiguous. Accordingly, civil society in communist Poland was judged to be more integrative than it was in Hungary or Czechoslovakia, which in turn were more advanced in this area than other communist countries (Nagle and Mahr 1999: 66).

A number of features contributed to this situation. Poland had abandoned its attempt to collectivize agriculture in 1956 and left most land in the private hands of an independent peasantry, while its economy as a whole was more open to reform initiatives. The historically powerful Catholic Church retained its autonomy throughout the communist period, and political leaders hung back from any direct assault on its position. This left Church activists with greater freedom to support Polish opposition initiatives undertaken in defence of workers' and human rights in the 1970s. Hungarian civil society initiatives were considerably more limited, although environmental activists and others concerned to revive national memories were active in the 1980s. Equally, Charter 77 was launched in Czechoslovakia with the support of only about 250 signatories, even if it received far more international publicity than this small number might have suggested. Nevertheless, even these quite modest developments helped place Hungary and Czechoslovakia, together with Poland, in the forefront of changes towards democratization, while the prominent role it gave to intellectuals provided a rapid impetus to the development of a free press and the removal of other media from the hands of communist functionaries. On the other hand, civil society influences have been far weaker in the Balkans and areas outside the Central European core. There is little domestic base for the development of civil society in the Balkans, where the concept itself is not a familiar one and is regarded as a Western import. For example, in Albania, where society suffered some of the worst state repression in the whole region during the communist period, the political culture has been described as being just about the opposite of civil society (Mavrikos-Adamou 2010: 516–517).

But it is not clear as to how far such civil society resources have contributed to the further stages of democratic development or how they satisfy the requirements of an open democratic regime. Civil participation has been quite limited in post-communist Poland, for example, and it has been suggested that the civil society qualities that sustained a large mass protest movement in the 1980s were based on ethical motivations that do not square well with the pragmatic and compromise-seeking orientations needed for the operation of a contemporary liberal-democratic system (Siemienska 2006: 231). While a strong civil society is generally supportive of an effective human rights regime, too, in practice the operation of a democratic system involves a balance being struck between collective and group rights. Minority language rights have been a particularly sensitive area. For the sizable Russian minorities in Latvia and Estonia, fluency in the language of the new dominant nationality was linked with limits being placed on citizenship rights, and this was a major factor in the 1990s that prevented those countries from being recognized as full democracies. The numerically significant Hungarian minorities in Romania and Slovakia have also produced major tensions, which are still far from finding resolution after 20 years of post-communist transformation. A new Slovakian law that required Hungarians to use the majority language in government affairs was regarded as particularly offensive by the new, nationalistically inclined Hungarian government elected in April 2010. The decision of the new Hungarian government to offer Hungarian citizenship to the minority populations of neighbouring countries provoked further problems.

Such aspects of civil society are closely associated with issues of **political culture** and the subjective orientations to politics that helped end communist rule in Central and Eastern Europe, and sustain, to a greater or lesser extent, the advance of democratization. Here, too, there are major differences between different groups of countries. During the 1990s, with respect to the proportion of citizens who held views that identified them as 'strong democrats', there was a significant difference between a reference-group of established democracies, where between 44 and 60 per cent fell into this category – and most Central European countries, where between 28 and 42 per cent of citizens could be thus regarded. Poland, however, stood outside this group with only 20 per cent holding views that marked them as 'strong democrats'. Populations in post-Soviet Eastern Europe were even less likely to hold such views – as few as 7 per cent in Ukraine and Lithuania, and just 4 per cent in Russia. Yet again, there seemed to be 'an East-West axis which is connected with a diminishing support for democracy as an ideal' (Klingemann *et al.* 2006b: 6). Here, then, is another apparent geographical difference, which in fact relates less to the pull of the EU or the West but more to a distribution of values that is likely to render the population of a given society more or less susceptible to EU-promoted democratic values.

Twenty years after the beginnings of democratization in the region, there were still marked differences in how the change was perceived in different countries. In 1991, all countries had a majority of the population approving of the regime change, and most still did in 2009. Yet only two countries – Poland and Slovakia – had *more* citizens who approved of the change in 2009 than 18 years earlier. Most were less enthusiastic about regime change than they had been, with barely more than half of Bulgarians, Russians or Lithuanians now endorsing the change. In Ukraine, though, the percentage approving of the change to democracy fell from 72 to 30 per cent, which suggests that the implantation of democratic norms and values has not made any progress at all since the end of communism but actually regressed (Pew Research Center 2009).

Another related dimension is **social capital**, which directs attention more to individual characteristics and issues of trust. Analysis of the 2002 European Social Survey suggests that social trust is lower in Central Europe (Poland, Hungary and Slovenia) than – particularly – northern Europe (Denmark, Norway, Finland and Sweden), although trust levels in Greece are the lowest of all (Neller 2008: 107). Similar findings emerge concerning the relationship between social capital and political involvement in that new democracies in general (i.e. Southern as well as East-Central European) are significantly less participant than well-established northern states (van Deth 2008: 197). The same conclusions have been reached in other studies. More detailed analysis shows that two factors – the experience of communist rule and how long the democratic system has been in place – by themselves have very little explanatory value. The Poles might indeed be considerably less trusting of political activities – and thus display qualities less conducive to democratization – than the Swiss or Danes but it is not because of their communist past. Individual factors such as satisfaction with the performance of political leaders and the system in general, feelings of responsiveness, and social trust are more relevant in this context (Gabriel and Walter-Rogg 2008: 242).

Establishment of the **rule of law** is a development that many, though not all, analysts regard as a significant component of democratization. It is arguably, though, particularly salient in the post-communist cases (Börzel *et al.* 2010). In this respect it is interesting to consider why two EU-member countries (Bulgaria and Romania) are not considered to be consolidated democracies while all the others are. Conventional wisdom, as well as Nations in Transit scores, suggests that the major impediments are high levels of corruption and lack of judicial independence and effectiveness – meaning that the full rule of law is not yet established. In 2008, Bulgaria lost more than €200 million of EU funds because of their unprecedented misuse, while a former minister was indicted in February 2010 for the 'biggest theft' of the transition period, involving €5.5 million derived from corrupt land transfers. In March 2010 a serving minister was accused of corruption concerning the placing of flu vaccine contracts. The European Commission played a significant part in uncovering at least some of these activities. The relevance of these factors is hardly surprising, and such malfunctions are prevalent throughout the Balkans and other areas less susceptible to robust democratization (Mavrikos-Adamou 2010: 519–520). Fukuyama (2010) has, indeed, recently asked why it is that political scientists have paid far less attention to the transition to the rule of law than to the transition to democracy – although implicitly many would probably link the two developments, as Nations in Transit scores actually do (http:www.free domhouse.org/images/File/nit/2010/NIT-2010-Tables-final.pdf).

Møller (2009: 20–24) also directs attention to this linkage and points out that Dahl's (1989) relegation of the rule of law to a background condition in one of his major works on democratization is not really satisfactory. In the regional context, too, it is surely significant that adherence to the rule of law is one of the Copenhagen criteria (the conditions of EU membership for the post-communist countries spelt out by the European Commission in 1993). We also see an increasing use of managed elections by populist, quasi-authoritarian governments (seen in some Asian countries – such as Thailand – as well as some successor states of the former Soviet Union, with signs of this in Russia itself), which suggests that the core definition of democracy in electoral terms might now be less appropriate than it once was and that 'background conditions' are now more salient to a basic conception of democratization.

Moving further along the democratization path, there is also the contentious question of when the consolidation of democracy actually occurs (a question clearly related to the corruption issue in Bulgaria and Romania) – and whether or not we can ever really know when it does. Consolidation is often associated with the idea of democracy being the only game in town – but O'Donnell (1996) raised serious questions about what this implies. People play political games in different ways, and the games actually played inside democratic institutions may be rather different from those dictated by the formal rules. In the public arena the game can be played by the book, while rather different things – and corrupt practices – might be going on behind the scene.

This is explicitly pointed out by Saari (2009) in a discussion of Russia – which, despite being classified by Nations in Transit as a consolidated authoritarian regime, actually defines itself as a democracy, either managed or sovereign. Such informal practices – or particularism – O'Donnell (1996) also notes, is rife in a number of enduring polyarchies (generally thought of as established or consolidated democracies) such as Japan, India and (closer to home) Italy. The protracted experience of one-party rule in these countries is also significant and likely to be associated with these practices – although it has not prevented electorally induced changes of government. This also suggests some parallels with Eastern Europe and countries where the influence of the communist establishment persisted long after the formal change of regime. The Transparency International report released in November 2009, further, showed Greece to be at the same level as Bulgaria and Romania in terms of perceived corruption – which says, amongst other things, little for the reforming effect of the EU (http://transparency.org/policy_research/surveys_indices/cpi/2009/cpi_2009_table).

A final dimension involves the core institutions and processes of **political society** that define the democratic polity and sustain its operation. Central here are elections, political parties, party systems, parliaments and other formal political institutions. Competitive elections, free and fairly organized, are the core of democratization to the extent that they enable the peaceful transfer of political power in accordance with the popular will. All 'free' countries are understood to hold free elections, and the 'partially free' Moldova is also now defined as an electoral democracy. The partially free states of the West Balkans (Albania, Bosnia, Kosovo and Macedonia) are also progressing in this area, according to the Freedom House judgments made in 2010 (http://www.freedomhouse.org/template.cfm?page=1). Kosovo held well conducted municipal elections in November 2009, the first since independence was declared in 2008, while Macedonia also held fair presidential and local elections in 2009 as well as implementing the reforms recommended after elections in 2008. Properly competitive elections have, however, been absent in Belarus and Russia, where authoritarianism has persisted or been re-established.

Competitive elections require reasonably well organized parties, and all countries that hold valid elections fulfil the basic requirements in this area. The absence of a party that fully straddles the ethnic divides is still prominent in Bosnia-Herzegovina and has been one important reason why the country has made limited progress towards democracy after the war of the 1990s. It was because of this that the establishment of a transnational party (Our Party) was hailed as a major development in April 2010. But even where reasonably effective parties do exist in Central and Eastern Europe they are not particularly strong. Membership levels are low, organization and local implantation quite weak and public trust in them low. In 2008 only 16 per cent of citizens in the new EU member states expressed any trust in parties, against 32 per cent in old member states (Eurobarometer 69, 2008). This, nevertheless, represented a slight increase over previous levels, as trust averaged only 12 per cent between 2001 and 2008.

Partly in consequence of this, party systems are also weak and generally unstable. They have shown high levels of multipartyism, extensive volatility and considerable fragmentation. The post-communist systems have been more fluid and fragmented than those in other areas at equivalent stages of development in other regions (South America and postwar Western Europe). It has remained questionable as to whether or not some countries have anything that can be called a party system at all (Lewis 2006). Another way of describing this state of affairs is to state that party systems in Central and Eastern Europe are weakly institutionalized, which has consequences for democratic stability and the effectiveness of the regime overall. Institutionalized systems are thought to be more firmly rooted in the electorate, offer clearly defined political alternatives, facilitate policy formulation and implementation, and guard against instability and populist outbursts – although it can also be argued that the Central European record of achievement in most of these areas has not been too bad.

Finally, where competitive elections have been held and independent parties have a reasonable public existence, parliaments have been properly organized and conducted their business efficiently. The more problematic developments in this area have been seen in the less consolidated democracies and countries with restricted freedoms. In Albania, for example, contested elections were held in June 2009 but the parliament thus formed was deadlocked and unable to function effectively as both main parties accused each other of fraud and the opposition blocked legislation and organized anti-government protests. In accordance with prevailing regional tendencies, EU mediators were called on to help solve the problem. Moldova's procedures were equally deadlocked for many months in the attempt from April 2009 to elect a new president, as a parliamentary majority of more than 60 per cent could not be obtained. In the Ukrainian parliament, fisticuffs broke out after the pro-Russian government appointed in 2010 proposed to give the Russian fleet extended rights in the port of Sebastopol. In view of these factors, and the various national weaknesses that can be identified, it is reasonable to endorse the view that only the eight Central and East European countries that joined the EU should be regarded as consolidated democracies, with some doubts persisting about Bulgaria and Romania because of the patchy rule of law in those countries. Of the remaining 11 countries, Croatia, Montenegro and Serbia are now those closest to democratic consolidation (see Table 1.1).

Table 1.1 Freedom House combined average ratings and regime types (2010)

	Democracy score	Regime type
Czech Republic	1 (free)	consolidated democracy
Estonia	1 (free)	consolidated democracy
Hungary	1 (free)	consolidated democracy
Lithuania	1 (free)	consolidated democracy
Poland	1 (free)	consolidated democracy
Slovakia	1 (free)	consolidated democracy
Slovenia	1 (free)	consolidated democracy
Latvia	1.5 (free)	consolidated democracy
Croatia	1.5 (free)	semi-consolidated democracy
Bulgaria	2 (free)	semi-consolidated democracy
Romania	2 (free)	semi-consolidated democracy
Serbia	2 (free)	semi-consolidated democracy
Montenegro	2.5 (free)	semi-consolidated democracy
Ukraine	2.5 (free)	hybrid regime
Albania	3 partly free	semi-consolidated democracy
Macedonia	3 partly free	semi-consolidated democracy
Bosnia-Herzegovina	3.5 partly free	hybrid regime
Moldova	3.5 partly free	semi-consolidated authoritarian
Kosovo	4.5 partly free	semi-consolidated authoritarian
Russia	5.5 not free	consolidated authoritarian
Belarus	6.5 not free	consolidated authoritarian

Sources: (column 2) http://www.freedomhouse.org/uploads/fiw10/CombinedAverageRatings(IndependentCountries) FIW2010.pdf, (column 3) http://www.freedomhouse.org/images/File/nit/2010/NIT-2010-Tables-final.pdf.

Democratization and the context of economic transformation

Democratization has been successful in Central and Eastern Europe to the extent that 14 of the region's 21 states are now judged to be free, while another five are partly free and showing signs of moving in a democratic direction. Eight, moreover, are judged to be consolidated democracies. But the quality of democracy, even in the new EU member countries, continues to raise doubts among informed observers, and many express some disappointment about its limited achievements. Participation is limited, publics are mistrustful of their representatives, corruption is thought to be widespread, and parties are quite weak. This has produced a general conception of post-communism as having produced a 'thin' democracy loosely rooted in society and supported by quite weak structures – but one sustained by steady economic development and growing consumer satisfaction.

Many were sceptical from the start about the prospects for democracy after communism, partly because of the poor conditions for its development supposedly inherited from the communist period but also because of the historic record of the interwar years, which saw the emergence of a number of populist movements and extremist parties. Similar doubts emerged following a number of elections in 2005 and 2006 that saw the rise of a number of unorthodox parties, prompting the *Journal of Democracy* to produce an issue in 2007 entitled Is East-Central Europe Backsliding? The answer from most writers was a relatively confident 'no'. Krastev (2007: 58) summed it up by observing that there was something of a political crisis in Central Europe, but that it should not be subject to a 'Weimar interpretation' because the 'economies of the region are not stagnating but booming. Standards of living are rising and unemployment is declining'. Similar comments were made by Krzysztof Jasiewicz (2007) and Jacques Rupnik (2007). This is not intended to score points by confronting experts with their partly mistaken views but rather to show that virtually all seasoned observers were surprised and taken aback by the economic crisis that broke in 2008. The important question is what this means for democratization in the region and how developments two or three years on should be interpreted.

If the process has really been sustained to a significant extent by economic development and continuing growth, the prospects may indeed be more uncertain than previously thought. First, it is, questionable whether or not the economic transformation has been as successful as many have argued, particularly in terms of its impact on people's standard of living. Second, less debatable are the impacts of the post-2007 economic crisis in Central and Eastern Europe. Some declines in gross domestic product (GDP) occurred in 2008 but more serious falls were seen in 2009, ranging from 18 per cent in Latvia to 6 per cent in Hungary, with Lithuania, Estonia and Romania somewhere in between. Continuing (though more modest) falls were projected in Latvia and Lithuania for 2010. Unemployment rose, and reached the highest levels in Latvia and Lithuania at 16 per cent during 2009. Electoral responses, in distinction to demonstrations and street protests, did not initially seem to be marked. Bulgaria was the only country to hold a parliamentary election that year, and the extreme right made modest gains (the emergence of a new party – Order, Law and Justice – with 4 per cent of the vote, and a gain of 1 per cent for Ataka). European Parliament (EP) elections were also held in 2009, giving Greater Romania three new seats and awarding the Slovak National Party their first EP seat. More dramatic was the rise of Jobbik ('Movement for a Better Hungary'), which gained 15 per cent of the vote in that country. This was a nationalist party founded in 2002 and located on the extreme right, expressing anti-roma and anti-semitic sentiments. Its performance in the EP elections was repeated in the Hungarian parliamentary election of April 2010, when Jobbik gained nearly 17 per cent of the vote.

It is, of course, not clear how far the rise of Jobbik should be attributed to economic developments, but in general terms the success of the extreme right in Central and Eastern Europe has been limited, particularly in comparison with developments in West European countries such as Austria, the Netherlands, Italy, Switzerland, Belgium, Denmark, etc. Some post-communist governments have shown particular vigilance in this area. In February 2010 the top court of the Czech Republic took the unusual step of banning the extremist Workers' Party as a threat to democracy. To this extent, the eight post-communist countries that joined the EU in 2004 seem indeed to have become consolidated democracies, in that their institutions and processes are well placed to withstand the pressures of economic recession. Indeed, at the time of writing (July 2010), it is the Greek regime that appears to be most challenged by contemporary economic problems and the failure of the growth process. Neither, in electoral terms, does the electoral success of Jobbik necessarily carry any clear implication about the stability of the Hungarian party system, let alone about democratic con-solidation. Until 2010 Hungary had one of the most stable systems in Central Europe. Another, however, was in the Czech Republic, which held parliamentary elections in May 2010 – and in that country, too, the two established parties both lost seats and two new parties entered parliament. Perhaps it was just time for a change, as established parties had lost their impetus and popularity.

On the face of it, then, the Nations in Transit classification of eight of the post-communist democracies as consolidated appears to be accurate, and a 'Weimar scenario' is not likely to suddenly take centre stage. Some, such as Roberts (2010), endorse this view and produce positive appraisals of Central European democratization. Many, however, take a less positive approach and emphasize its shortcomings, which are indeed not difficult to identify. It is appropriate to bear in mind that no perfect democracy ever exists, though, and even a consolidated democracy will have its weak points.

Transition states and non-free countries

It is indeed not those identified as consolidated democracies that seem to be most under threat in the current situation but countries still in a more transitional state. Ukraine occupies a particular position here – a rare case of a free post-Soviet country in 2009 but classified (still) by Nations in Transit as a transitional case, and described in the accompanying National Report as a fragile democracy. Copsey and Shapovalova (2010), however, are adamant that the country's 'orange revolution' of 2004 had indeed transformed it into a proper democracy. As a 'free' country it had relatively free media, basically secure human rights, and a pluralistic and competitive political order – but an inefficient system of governance and an 'evident deficit of rule of law'. It was the particularly low scores for judicial independence and a weak legal process, combined with a high corruption rating, which contributed to its low democracy rating. Other indicators are not positive either, and its population's declining attachment to democratic principles has already been noted. Its economy also shrank by up to 15 per cent in 2009, which may go some way to account for the negative appraisal of post-communist developments (and seems to have had a greater impact on the popular mood than it did in the more advanced Central European democracies). Nevertheless, Ukraine did hold free elections in 2010, which led to the emergence of a more pro-Russian president, although whether or not this augurs well for long-term democratization remains to be seen.

Ukraine shows other differences from the more consolidated democracies of the region. Unlike Central Europe and the Balkans, the nature of EU influence was also weak from a very early stage. Ukraine fell into the EU category of Newly Independent States (rather than those defined as Central and East European), which were offered fewer resources and weaker inducements for reform. Equally, and probably more important, Ukraine was a bifurcated society (regionally, linguistically, culturally and economically) with divided elites, which made it difficult for the EU to identify and cooperate with an effective domestic partner and help overcome the ambivalent foreign policy orientation that emerged. It now seems pretty clear that for the democratizing influence of the EU to be exerted effectively, through conditionality and socialization, reform-minded domestic actors need to be firmly in place and in control of government processes (Solonenko 2009: 711).

While Ukraine's 'orange revolution' is generally portrayed as the outcome of successful popular mobilization, this was only partly true and elite characteristics were very important – if not actually decisive. Reformist president Viktor Yushchenko was head of the National Bank of Ukraine before becoming prime minister. Yulia Tymoshenko, appointed prime minister in 2005 and again in 2007, was an extremely rich businesswoman with a background in the gas industry and links with the prominent Dnipropetrov'sk economic clan (Cheterian 2009: 144). As with other 'colour revolutions' (which include Kyrgyzstan and Georgia, where outcomes were less than fully democratic), elite divisions provided the main thrust for political change in Ukraine (Lane 2009: 131). While not fully comparable, developments in Ukraine reflect the primary importance of state-building in the democratization of Central and Eastern Europe, although in this case it is less a case of territorial integrity that is at issue but more the development of an integrated national community and a unified political system. This is a characteristic yet to be achieved in Ukraine, and the further economic strains placed on the country by the economic crisis clearly played a part in the loss of support for Yushchenko and the swing to Viktor Yanukovych, whose orientation to Russia promised greater economic stability.

Russia, of course, in common with Belarus, is classified both as an 'unfree' country and a consolidated authoritarian regime, which means that it does not play much of a part in a regional account of democratization. As regional hegemon until 1989 it is in some ways not surprising that it has reverted to a dominant authoritarian tradition – which extends way back beyond the communist period, of course. In common with the other countries in the region, however, there were domestic forces pressing for democratic change and major reform groups that hoped to carry forward the transformation begun by Gorbachev. Until the mid-1990s, for example, it was classified in the freedom ratings on a par with Ukraine, Albania and Romania but, unlike most other countries, moved away from democracy rather than towards it.

But in many ways, Russia is the exception that proves the rule in the region. It clearly lacks many of the features identified in this chapter as those which encourage and sustain democratization. It has never had a strong civil society or political culture conducive to democracy, nor has it seen much development of the rule of law or political society separate from a narrow circle of power-holders. Equally, it was hardly a viable candidate for EU membership or an area over which the EU might exert much influence. In a rather different way, issues of state-building and nationalism have played an important role and provided obstacles to democratization. The attempt of the Chechens in southern Russia to achieve independence unleashed a bitter war and violent confrontations that seem to have little prospect of reaching a peaceful conclusion. The resistance of the authorities to journalists' attempts to accurately report the war led to stronger censorship, repression and more limitations on press freedom (the murder of Anna Politkovskaya being the most well known victim of this political response from the authorities). The continuing struggle also fed nationalist forces, however, and strengthened the position of Vladimir Putin, who as president and prime minister was able to satisfy the aspirations of many Russians for stability. In this process his position was strengthened by the country's extensive oil, gas and other natural resources, which channelled funds into the domestic economy (as well as the pockets of a small number of multimillionaires) and supported the living standards of many Russian citizens. The development of a state and the strengthening of its authority on the basis of revenues from oil and other energy resources have rarely (if ever) been conducive to democratization, however, and this has also been the case with Russia.

The other consolidated authoritarian regime in the region is Belarus, where Alyaksandr Lukashenka has been president since 1994 and has every likelihood of being 're-elected' for another term. Like Russia, Belarus has a weak civil society and undeveloped political society, features not helped by widespread repression (if not greatly violent in most cases), limited media freedom and the absence of free elections. But on Russian lines, too, there is substantial support for the leadership, limited popular opposition to the regime and a restricted range of organized parties capable of offering a political alternative. Unlike Russia, though, Belarus has very limited experience or substantial sentiments of nationhood and virtually no legacy of independent statehood (Marples 2009). Much of the passive support for the regime derived until 2006 from a stable and largely unreformed economy that delivered reasonable standards of living for much of the population. This has now changed. Although a small and relatively weak country, Belarus, has made political overtures both to Russia and the EU but has not developed stable links with either of them. In practice, the future both of the economy and the regime is likely to be dependent on developments in Russia, and recurrent problems over energy supplies and the outbreak of 'gas wars' does not offer much promise in this area.

Conclusion

Major political change in Central and Eastern Europe began with Gorbachev's accession to power in the Soviet Union in 1985 and soon developed into a process of fundamental democratization in many countries. Problems of state formation, as in the former Yugoslavia, emerged as one obstacle to the process, while the attractions of EU membership were an important factor facilitating democratization. Domestic factors were, however, also significant and certain national conditions had to be present for EU influence to be effective. These have included a number of features such as a strong civil society, the existence of a political culture supportive of democratic principles, reserves of social capital that encourage trust and political participation, establishment of the rule of law so as to minimize corruption and strengthen judicial independence, and the development of a political society that institutionalizes the core organizations and processes that sustain a working democracy. In practice, the role of such factors is quite complex, and precisely how a civil society should integrate collective and minority rights, for example, is a problematic issue. Institutional development has also been quite patchy, and the functioning of political parties and parliaments has often been quite poor. The relation of post-communist economic transformation to democratization – and the impact of the economic crisis on political processes – raise further questions. Electoral responses to economic stringency have so far been quite moderate, in fact, and the rise of an extremist right-wing party in Hungary has been the most visible response, providing some evidence for the effectiveness of democratic consolidation in many countries of the region. Belarus and Russia stand out as countries that have resisted democratization and, in the case of Russia, retreated from a certain level of democratic achievement. Ukraine, on the other hand, is characterized as a hybrid regime with a government still in transition; the future of its status as a 'free' country remains uncertain.

References

Börzel, T. A., A. Stahn and Y. Pamuk (2010) 'The European Union and the Fight against Corruption in Its Near Abroad: Can it Make a Difference?', *Global Crime*, 11 (2), pp. 122–144.

Cheterian, V. (2009) 'From Reform and Transition to "Coloured Revolutions"', *Journal of Communist Studies and Transition Politics*, 25 (2–3), pp. 136–160.

Copsey, N. and N. Shapovalova (2010) 'Europe and the Ukrainian Presidential Election of 2010'. European Parties, Elections and Referendums Network (University of Sussex), Election Briefing No. 49.

Dahl, R. (1989) *Democracy and Its Critics*. New Haven, CT: Yale University Press.

van Deth, J. W. (2008) Social Capital and Political Involvement'. In *Social Capital in Europe: Similarity of Countries and Diversity of People?*, ed. H. Meulemann. Leiden: Brill, pp. 191–218.

Eurobarometer 69 (2008) [Online] available at http://ec.europa.eu/public_opinion/archives/eb/eb69/eb69_part1, pp. 66–73 (accessed 1 September 2009).

Fukuyama, F. (2010) 'Transitions to the Rule of Law', *Journal of Democracy*, 21, pp. 33–44.

Gabriel, O. W. and M. Walter-Rogg (2008) 'Social Capital and Political Trust'. In *Social Capital in Europe: Similarity of Countries and Diversity of People?*, ed. H. Meulemann. Leiden: Brill, pp. 219–250.

Huntington, S. P. (1996) *The Clash of Civilizations and the Remaking of World Order*. New York: Simon and Schuster.

Jasiewicz, K. (2007) 'The Political-Party Landscape', *Journal of Democracy*, 18 (4), pp. 26–33.

Kitschelt, H. (2001) 'Accounting for Post-Communist Regime Diversity. What Counts as a Good Cause?' In *Transformative Paths in Central and Eastern Europe*, ed. R. Markowski and E. Wnuk-Lipiński. Warsaw: Institute of Political Studies/Friedrich Ebert Foundation, pp. 11–46.

Klingemann, H-D., D. Fuchs and J. Zielonka, eds (2006a) *Democracy and Political Culture in Eastern Europe*. London: Routledge.

——, —— and —— (2006b) 'Introduction: Support for Democracy and Autocracy in Eastern Europe'. In Klingemann *et al.* (2006a), pp. 1–21.

Krastev, I. (2007) 'The Strange Death of Liberal Consensus', *Journal of Democracy*, 18 (4), pp. 56–63.

Lane, D. (2009) ' "Coloured Revolution" as a Political Phenomenon', *Journal of Communist Studies and Transition Politics*, 25 (2–3), pp. 113–135.

Lewis, P. G. (2003) 'Central and Eastern Europe'. In *Democratization through the Looking-Glass*, ed. P. Burnell. Manchester: Manchester University Press, pp. 153–168.

—— (2006) 'Party Systems in Post-Communist Central Europe: Patterns of Stability and Consolidation', *Democratization*, 13 (4), pp. 562–583.

McFaul, M. (2002) 'The Fourth Wave of Democracy *and* Dictatorship: Noncooperative Transitions in the Post-Communist World', *World Politics*, 54, pp. 212–244.

Marples, D. R. (2009) 'Outpost of Tyranny? The Failure of Democratization in Belarus', *Democratization*, 16 (4), pp. 756–776.

Mavrikos-Adamou, T. (2010) 'Challenges to Democracy Building and the Role of Civil Society', *Democratization*, 17 (3), pp. 514–533.

Møller, J. (2009) *Post-communist Regime Change: A Comparative Study*. London: Routledge.

Morlino, L. and W. Sadurski, eds (2010) *Democratization and the European Union*. London: Routledge.

Nagle, J. D. and A. Mahr (1999) *Democracy and Democratization*. London: Sage.

Nations in Transit (2009) *Tables*. [Online] available at www.freedomhouse.hu/images/nit2009/tables.pdf (accessed 11 June 2010).

Neller, K. (2008) 'What makes People Trust in their Fellow Citizens?' In *Social Capital in Europe: Similarity of Countries and Diversity of People?*, ed. H. Meulemann. Leiden: Brill, pp. 103–133.

O'Donnell, G. (1996) 'Illusions about Consolidation', *Journal of Democracy*, 7 (2), pp. 34–51.

Offe, C. (1991) 'Capitalism by Democratic Design? Democratic Theory Facing the Triple Transition in East Central Europe', *Social Research*, 58, pp. 865–892.

di Palma, G. (1990) *To Craft Democracies: An Essay on Democratic Transition*. Berkeley: University of California Press.

Pew Research Center (2009) 'The Pulse of Europe 2009: 20 Years after the Fall of the Berlin Wall'. [Online] available at http://pewglobal.org/reports/display.php/ReportID=267 (accessed 12 June 2010).

Przeworski, A. and F. Limongi (1997) 'Modernization: Theories and Facts', *World Politics*, 49 (2), pp. 155–183.

Puddington, A. (2010) *Freedom in the World 2010: Erosion of Freedom Intensifies*. [Online] Freedom in the World Press Release, 12 January; available at www.freedomhouse.ord/uploads/fiw10/FIW_2010_Overview_Essay.pdf (accessed 11 June 2010).

Roberts, A. (2010) *The Quality of Democracy in Eastern Europe: Public Preferences and Policy Reforms*. Cambridge: Cambridge University Press.

Rupnik, J. (2007) 'From Democracy Fatigue to Populist Backlash', *Journal of Democracy*, 18 (4), pp. 17–25.

Saari, S. (2009) 'European Democracy Promotion in Russia Before and After the "'Colour'" Revolutions', *Democratization*, 16 (4), pp. 732–755.

Siemienska, R. (2006) 'Poland: Citizens and Democratic Politics'. In Klingemann *et al.*, pp. 203–234.

Solonenko, I. (2009) 'External Democracy Promotion in Ukraine: The Role of the European Union', *Democratization*, 16 (4), pp. 709–731.

Vachudova, M. A. (2005) *Europe Undivided: Democracy, Leverage, and Integration after Communism*. Oxford: Oxford University Press.

—— and T. Snyder (1997) 'Are Transitions Transitory? Two Types of Political Change in Eastern Europe since 1989', *East European Politics and Societies*, 11, pp. 1–35.

2

Central America

John A. Booth

The six countries of the Mesoamerican isthmus share historic and economic experiences that similarly affected their political systems. Despite unique traits, their economies and polities fit within the world economy in similar ways. Common domestic economic and external pressures acted upon them after 1960 to establish five new democracies in a region where before only one had developed that form of government.

After independence from Spain, agrarian elites dominated Central American politics and excluded ordinary citizens. Civil wars between conservative and liberal elite factions brought militaries into politics and nurtured authoritarianism in most countries. The region's geography, especially two narrow land passages between the Atlantic and Pacific that shortened trade between the Atlantic and Pacific, attracted foreign intervention in Nicaragua and Panama. US security promotion efforts during the Second World War and the Cold War reinforced the region's authoritarian regimes.

Central American nations attempted to strengthen their dependent agricultural export economies beginning in the late 1950s. A regional economic cooperation scheme accelerated growth and integrated Central America more deeply into the world economy, while also increasing inequality and poverty. The Organization of the Petroleum Exporting Countries' (OPEC) oil embargo of 1973 nearly collapsed Central America's economies and unleashed mobilization for economic redress and political reform. Governments that violently repressed such demands for change experienced rebellions. Nicaragua's Sandinista rebels seized power in 1979, an event that brought a tsunami of foreign intervention to shape the region's conflicts and had elites scrambling for solutions to unrest. Democratization seemed an unlikely prospect in 1980. Yet by divergent paths of reform, liberalization, revolution, negotiation and foreign imposition, the denouement of the turmoil and intervention was transition to democracy.

This chapter draws upon theory and empirical evidence from extensive scholarship to describe and explain the democratization of Central America. It evaluates available empirical evidence about what happened and provides sketches of the democratization process in each country.

Overview of Central America's democratization

Explanations of transition to democracy take three broad approaches – cultural, structural and process-related theories (see Welzel 2009). *Cultural theories* argue that the attitudes of citizens determine the rules of political systems (Adorno *et al.* 1950; Almond and Verba 1963; Inglehart 1988, 1990; Putnam 1993, 2000; Inglehart and Welzel 2005). *Structural theories* contend that large-scale features of social systems determine the onset of democracy. Most emphasize how shifts in the distribution of material and organizational resources among political actors can lead to democracy (Lipset 1959, 1994; Rueschemeyer *et al.* 1992; Vanhanen 1997; Gasiorowski 2000; Przeworski *et al.* 2000; Boix 2003; Epstein *et al.* 2006). *Process theories* examine not the causes but the mechanics of democratization, including pacts among powerful elites that determine the rules of the new political game, and on the imposition of democracy by external actors.[1] It is helpful to discuss Central America's democratization in terms of these theories, most of which have clear relevance and empirical support, often in combination with each other.

As of 1970, among Central American states only Costa Rica enjoyed democracy. Two types of authoritarianism prevailed elsewhere – military-dominated rule in El Salvador, Guatemala, Honduras and Panama; and the personalistic military rule of the Somozas in Nicaragua. In Honduras and Panama, the armed forces ruled outright without the trappings of constitutionality. El Salvador, Guatemala and Nicaragua held elections regularly but the armed forces (or the Somozas in Nicaragua) dominated the parties and fraudulently manipulated votes. The next section of this chapter considers relevant evidence from the three theoretical approaches to democratization outlined above – cultural, structural and process-related theories. They vary considerably in explanatory power and in the evidence available to test them.

Evidence concerning the democratization of Central America

Political culture

Despite a recent explosion of survey data from Latin America, little of value is available in terms of understanding culture's contribution to Central America's democratization. The region's authoritarian governments provided conditions adverse to conducting survey research on political topics. Thus data on political norms in authoritarian Central America are missing; most 'evidence' consists of scholarly conjecture.

One minor exception is that, near the end of Nicaragua's Sandinista revolution but a scant five years after its adoption of elections, one 1989 survey found that Nicaraguans held high levels of democratic norms – indeed roughly the same as Costa Ricans of the same era who had by then enjoyed almost four decades of democracy (Booth and Seligson 1991, 1994). Nicaraguans were not expected to be democrats, because they had experienced little democracy and because (by the received wisdom) neither the country's economic development nor its general political culture were propitious for democratic attitudes. Lipset (1959), for instance, would have viewed Nicaragua as too underdeveloped to have lost the predominant working-class authoritarianism believed to be typical of poor countries – although recent empirical evidence strongly challenges this theory (Krishna 2008). Others believed the prevalence of Catholicism and centuries of elite-dominated social relations would have made Nicaragua unlikely to develop mass democratic norms (Dealy 1974; Morse 1974; Wiarda 1974; Inglehart 1988). However, these surprising empirical findings left unresolved whether or how Nicaraguans' attitudes may have shaped the country's transition to full electoral democracy in 1990.

Social and economic structures

The evidence concerning structural influences on Central American democratization is stronger because of, for decades, much better tracking/evaluation of political and economic systems. Seligson applied Lipset's theory that modernization and economic growth created conditions for democracy. Lipset analysed many developing nations and found that once a country attained an economic production threshold of approximately $250 per capita in 1950 US dollars, as well as 50 per cent literacy, democracy became more likely to occur and to survive. Seligson's analysis of five Central American countries using this framework found that Costa Rica passed the literacy threshold in the early twentieth century, and that Honduras, El Salvador and Nicaragua did so between the late 1950s and early 1960s. Only Guatemala lagged below that literacy rate after 1970. As to the approximate dates of attaining the US$250 per capita threshold, Costa Rica did so in the mid-1940s, El Salvador and Guatemala in the 1960s, and Nicaragua in the mid-1970s (Seligson 1987). Honduras had not attained the threshold by 1982 (the end of Seligson's data).

I here replicate and extend Seligson's analysis using more recent data. Figures 2.1 and 2.2 present, respectively, gross domestic product (GDP) per capita in constant 1986 US dollars, and literacy rates. The equivalent to Lipset and Seligson's democratization threshold of $250 in 1950 US dollars is US$1,050 expressed in 1986 dollars, indicated in Figure 2.1 by the broken red line. There we see that Costa Rica democratized (c.1950) at approximately the point it achieved the theorized economic threshold for democratization. Figure 2.2 demonstrates that literacy in Costa Rica far exceeded the 50 per cent threshold when it democratized. Panama passed the development threshold around 1975 and the literacy threshold well before that. El Salvador passed the economic threshold in the 1980s and that for literacy in the late 1960s. Guatemala passed the economic threshold in the early 1960s but did not attain the literacy threshold until the 1980s. Honduras approached the economic threshold in 1980 but did not quite reach it; Honduras attained the literacy threshold in the 1970s. Nicaragua attained the economic threshold around 1970 but subsequently declined and has not regained it, while it crossed the literacy threshold around 1980. Panama reached the economic threshold for democracy in the mid-1970s, having attained the literacy threshold decades earlier.

These data suggest that Central American democratization roughly conforms to the structural democratization theory. Actual democratization dates hew closer to the hypothetical economic threshold than they do to the hypothesized 50 per cent literacy threshold. The latter was attained in Panama and Costa Rica decades before democratization. Panama tarried almost two decades in democratizing after attaining the hypothetical economic threshold. One may surmise that the

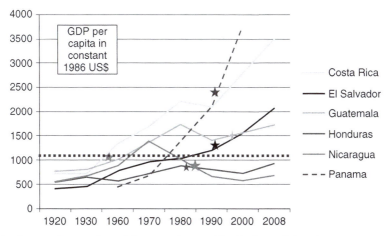

Figure 2.1 Economic growth and democratic transition in Central America
Note: Stars indicate approximate dates of formal adoption of electoral democracy

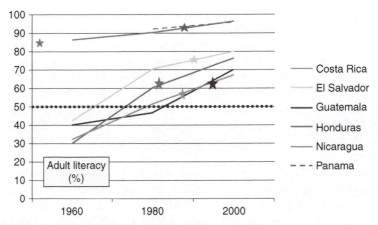

Figure 2.2 Adult literacy and democratic transition
Note: Stars indicate approximate dates of adoption of formal democracy

presence of US forces and the Panama Canal's security risks may have enabled the national economic and political elite and the armed forces to delay democratization there.

Figure 2.1 indicates that Honduras has never quite attained the hypothetical threshold for democratization ($1,050 GDP per capita in constant 1986 US dollars), and that Nicaragua surpassed the threshold but subsequently fell back below it. Obviously the empirical evidence leading to the proposed democratization thresholds are estimates, so one must view these numbers with caution. To the extent of structural theory's validity, these data suggest that Honduras and Nicaragua may suffer from weaker constraints towards democratization and may therefore be more vulnerable to democratic breakdown. Przeworski *et al.* (2000) claim that there is no democratization threshold, but only a democratic survival threshold – failure to attain the threshold leaves democratized but insufficiently developed countries vulnerable to democratic breakdown. Indeed, there is contemporary evidence to support this: Nicaragua's deteriorated electoral quality and increasing concentration of executive authority during the 2000s, and the Honduran coup d'état of 2009 (Seligson and Booth 2009, 2010; Booth and Seligson 2010).

Another empirical approach is that of Vanhanen, who theorizes that the dispersal of power resources in society away from elites conditions the transition to democracy. (The power resources are per cent urban population, per cent non-agricultural population, current university student enrolment as a proportion of the population, adult literacy, the per cent of all agricultural holding in family farms, and the degree of decentralization of non-agricultural resources.) He measures democracy as a combination of the per cent of the losing party vote in the most recent national elections) and the voter turnout rate. Vanhanen (1997) has found in many regions over many decades that when the index of power resources (IPR) reaches a certain empirically determined range, democracy tends to appear. Of America he says:

> The surprising victory of democracy in Latin America in the 1980s was not unexpected from the perspective of resource distribution, for IPR values were high enough to support democracy in nearly all countries … In fact I predicted democratization in Latin American countries in my studies published in 1975 and 1979.

Seligson questions whether some of Vanhanen's power resource items adequately measure relevant conditions in Central America (Seligson 1997). Close inspection of the distribution of

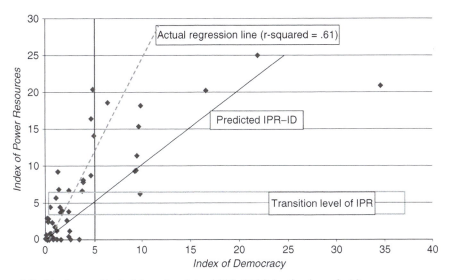

Figure 2.3 Vanhanen Central America data, 1900–2000 (author's analysis)

power resources (IPR) and Vanhanen's democracy index (ID) in Central America from 1900 to 2000 (Figure 2.3) reveals that 61 per cent of the variance in ID is explained by the IPR. However, democratization seems to lead IPR rather than the other way around (as the theory suggests). Analysis of the cases supports this for Costa Rica, Honduras, Guatemala and El Salvador. Panama has the closest ID-IPR fit over time. Only in Nicaragua did IPR lead ID at the time the country reached the democracy threshold of 5.0.

On the other hand, evident both in Figure 2.3 and even more clearly in Figure 2.4, for the region as a whole, mean ID levels tend to somewhat exceed mean resource distribution levels. The general correlation between the two trends over time is evident, with IPR reaching Vanhanen's 3.3 threshold for democratization about the same time as ID reaches his 5.0 democracy threshold. Nevertheless, ID levels tend to lead IPR, an oddity in a region rife with dictatorships. The

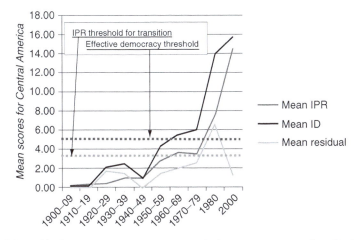

Figure 2.4 Mean Vanhanen power resources and democracy scores for Central America, 1900–2000 (author's analysis)

disparity (residual) between the ID and IPR indices (indicated in Figure 2.4 as the green line) grows sharply during the 1970s and 1980s, then recedes by 2000. One reasonable implication of the disparity and its growth in the crucial 1970s and 1980s is that Vanhanen's IPR measure does not capture critical factors such as international pressure and domestic turmoil that probably drove rising voter turnout and party competitiveness in his democratization index. Moreover, Vanhanen's reliance on voter turnout and party competitiveness probably inflates democracy scores during periods when Central America's military regimes regularly held phony elections.

These analyses provide evidence that modernization/economic development and power resource dispersion relate to Central American democratization, yet do not provide clarity about how the processes unfolded. They suggest but do not establish causality, nor do they account for many factors addressed in process theories – including, civil society, elites and external forces.

Process explanations

Two of three process approaches to democratization in Central America focus on elites. Huntington examines elite roles in regime changes to democracy, classifying them as 'transformation' (controlled liberalization by incumbents), 'replacement' (overthrow of authoritarian elites by challengers), and 'transplacement' (negotiated settlement of a conflict) (Huntington 1991). Huntington discussed Honduras's 1981–2 shift to civilian rule as a transformation. Using his categories, three replacements occurred: Costa Rica's National Liberation movement in 1948 and Nicaragua's Sandinistas in 1979 toppled the incumbent regimes, and in 1989 the US invasion replaced Panama's Noriega regime. By Huntington's scheme there were two transplacements – in El Salvador (1992) and Guatemala (1996) negotiated settlement of their civil wars initiated democracy.

Peeler (1985, 1992, 1995, 1998) has compared the roles of elites in negotiating democratic regimes in Central America. Elites enmeshed in system crises forged inter-elite agreements of varying breadth to establish electoral democracy in Costa Rica (1949–50), Honduras (1981), El Salvador (1992) and Guatemala (1996). Peeler views Nicaraguan elites as having failed to reach a broad inter-elite settlement as transition to electoral democracy transpired in 1987–90 and beyond. Several authors have provided detailed accounts of negotiated transitions in Costa Rica (Peeler 1985; Booth 1998), Guatemala (Azpuru et al. 2007; Williams and Walter 1997; Jonas 2000), and El Salvador (Karl 1992; Williams and Walter 1997; Azpuru et al. 2007). In Nicaragua, elites have failed to reach a broad settlement in favour of democracy because of anti-democratic provisions in a late 1990s pact between the leaders of the Sandinista and Liberal parties (Close and Deonandan 2004; Booth et al. 2010; Walker and Wade 2011).

The other process approach examines external pressures for democratization and the direct outside imposition of democracy. Extensive literature exists about the evolution of US, European, Catholic Church and international organization pressures on Central American governments to democratize during the 1980s. Until then most scholars viewed US Cold War pressures on the region as antagonistic to democratization; this literature is vast (Diskin 1983; LaFeber 1983; Booth 1985; Schoultz 1987, 1998; Moreno 1990; Robinson 1992; Smith 1996; Walker and Wade 2011). However, by the mid-1980s there were human rights abuses by US-supported regimes in El Salvador, Honduras and Guatemala. Growing US congressional resistance to funding Nicaragua's contras, and for military aid to El Salvador and Honduras, became liabilities for the Reagan administration's containment efforts. This led US administrations to adopt a tactic of pressing isthmian governments for human rights improvement, constitutional reform and electoral democracy. Containing Nicaragua's Sandinista revolution and the Salvadoran and Guatemalan insurgencies remained US goals, but there was growing pressure on regional governments to adopt different styles of rule, including system democratization. Other Latin American and European countries, the Organization of American States, and the United Nations, also increasingly promoted peace and democratization in the region after 1980. In 1989 the Cold War ended, lowering America's perceived threat of communist expansion in the region and making negotiated settlements with the Left more palatable around the region (Carothers 1991, 1999; Lowenthal 1991a, 1991b; Martz 1995; Moreno 1996; Robinson 1996; Weeks 2008; Booth *et al.* 2010). These external pressures, backed by conditioned assistance from donors and international lenders, facilitated democratization by making it easier for Central American elites to allow the Left back into the legal political arena.

Finally, the United States directly intervened to help democratize Panama in December 1989. Following an election fraud by the Noriega regime that blocked the opposition from taking power, the US deployed troops to the country, defeated the resistance and facilitated the real 1989 election victors' assumption of power. With the military effectively abolished, Panamanian parties began following democratic rules of the game and peacefully alternated in power (Pérez 1995, 2011; Ropp 1995, 2007).

Multiple factors – an overview

Single-factor explanations of democratization do not account satisfactorily for the sweep of what transpired in Central America. The more holistic analysis of the region's democratization that follows below knits together structural and process theories. It argues that economic transformation beginning in the 1960s, and an ensuing crisis in the late 1970s and 1980s, drove political change and civil society mobilization. It also discusses elite behaviour and how external actors shaped the democratization process (Booth 1991; Booth *et al.* 2010).

Accelerated economic growth in the 1960s and early 1970s had a mobilizing effect across Central America. Differential reactions by political elites to this mobilization shaped how democratization occurred. Accommodation of pressure from below and anticipation of growing popular anger caused Honduran military elites to liberalize. Repressive responses drove dramatic upsurges of political violence that led to rebellions in three countries. A revolution in Nicaragua eventually established the framework for democracy there. Where incumbent elites retained power in Guatemala and El Salvador, a combination of external pressure and pressure from rebels and civil society eventually brought about political reforms that moved each country towards democratization via peace agreements. In Panama, where a left-populist regime accommodated demands from below, pressure for democratization from an increasingly active civil society was forestalled until the United States ousted the military from power in 1989.

The principal motor for change in Central America was five governments' promotion of economic growth through the Central American Common Market (CACM). Founded in 1959, CACM promoted managed regional economic growth based on infrastructure development and attracting foreign and domestic investment. Political stability would come from the benefits of capitalist-mode economic growth trickling down to workers, a strategy designed to undercut the appeal of leftist movements after the Cuban revolution of 1959. CACM was partly successful; it accelerated economic growth, diversified economies, and increased manufacturing and agricultural exports. It also had deleterious effects, masked for a decade by rapid GDP growth: concentration of agricultural holdings, growing unemployment, increased dependency on economic inputs, and greater economic inequality. Economic diversification and these growing problems caused a rapid proliferation of labour and peasant unions, new political parties, political reform efforts, and social justice movements rooted in liberation theology. When the OPEC oil embargo of 1973 drove up energy prices, a severe recession ensued, causing unemployment, inflation and protests to increase.

Governments in the mid-1970s met civil society's narrowly based demands for better wages, more services and political reform with two types of responses. Democratic Costa Rica and military-ruled Honduras responded with reform, concessions, amelioration of poverty and low to modest repression. Both countries weathered their crises without a major insurrection, and Honduras gradually liberalized into an electoral democracy. In contrast, dictatorships in Guatemala, Nicaragua and El Salvador responded to popular demands with violent repression and refusal to ameliorate the parlous conditions of their working classes. This further angered and energized civil society, which refocused narrow demands for specific reform into generalized wrath towards ruling regimes. Civil society increasingly forged alliances with extant or emerging Marxist guerrilla groups. Turmoil and conflict aggravated negative economic trends, reinforcing growing resistance and calls for reform.

A catalytic moment in the regional democratization process was the defeat of the Somoza regime by the Sandinista National Liberation Front (FSLN) in July 1979. Although a Marxist insurgency in Guatemala had begun in 1960 and had subsequently waxed and waned, the Sandinista victory in Nicaragua served to encourage rebels and cooperating opposition from civil society elsewhere. It also prompted elites elsewhere in the region to reconsider and amend their strategies for survival. Abroad, the Sandinista victory prompted greater US intervention to forestall another revolution in the region, and led other Latin American nations to broker the resolution of Central America's conflicts before they spread or deepened US intervention.

Following the Sandinista victory in Nicaragua, massive civil society mobilization for reform, and escalating repression, rocked El Salvador. Seeking to head off a replay of Nicaragua, disgruntled elites in the Salvadoran military, opposition parties and business community staged a coup in October 1979. The United States, anxious to contain leftist unrest, immediately bet on the de facto government by providing it with economic and military assistance. Hardliners quickly took over the junta and escalated repression rather than abating it, which contributed to the unification of five Marxist guerrilla groups into the Farabundo Martí National Liberation Front (FMLN) and to a coordinated rebellion. Violence escalated with the rebels gaining considerable ground, prompting commitment of new US aid and military advisers. US strategy for El Salvador by the mid-1980s shifted towards pushing the junta to adopt political and administrative reforms and redress some grievances of the poor in order to undercut the rebels and legitimize the regime.

Honduras exemplified an alternative strategy. The Honduran military regime in the late 1970s undertook an extensive land redistribution programme to benefit landless peasants. Witnessing the events of 1979–80 in neighbouring Nicaragua and El Salvador with alarm, the Honduran military opted to liberalize. A constituent assembly elected in 1981 drafted a new constitution; a presidential election followed in 1982. In a contradictory process driven by Washington's desire to contain the Sandinista revolution and Salvadoran rebels, the United States provided Honduras military and economic assistance. This secured Honduran tolerance and support for a US-backed counter-revolutionary effort by anti-Sandinista Nicaraguan forces based in Honduras, allowed a major US troop presence in Honduras during the 1980s, and weakened the new civilian governments in Tegucigalpa. Though greatly strengthened by US assistance, the military stuck to the liberalization strategy. National Party and Liberal Party presidents alternated in power, and Honduras muddled through in the constitutional democratic mode for almost three decades before its democracy would again stumble.

In summary, rapid economic development also bred civil society mobilization and economic distress that spurred demands for reform, especially after the OPEC oil embargo badly damaged already wobbling economies. Governments responded either with low to modest repression and some reforms (Costa Rica and Honduras), or with violent repression (Nicaragua, El Salvador and Guatemala). The governments that kept repression low and made even modest amelioration efforts avoided rebellions. In contrast, violent uprisings backed by civil society mobilization ensued where repression constituted the main government response to protest mobilization. When the Sandinistas and their allies ousted the Somozas, ruling elites in other countries modified their strategies – gradually and under US pressure – to include liberalizing reforms. With the end of the Cold War in 1989, US perceptions of an ideological and strategic threat subsided. This idea was reinforced by the opposition electoral defeat of the FSLN in Nicaragua's 1990 election and the end of the Sandinista revolution. Further pressure for democratization as a key to peace came from Central and Latin American neighbours, European countries and international organizations. Altered elite threat perceptions and external efforts to broker peace eventually led to the settlement of the Salvadoran civil war in 1992 and of the Guatemalan conflict in 1996. Each peace agreement provided for demobilized rebel forces and other formerly excluded political parties to enter the legal political arena and compete for power. These relatively broad elite settlements resulted in constitutional, electoral rule that survived several presidential cycles in both Guatemala and El Salvador.

The evidence above omits the Panamanian case. As it is not part of CACM, Panama did not experience quite the same processes. Two differences stand out. First, Panama's economy grew much more rapidly even than those of CACM (Figure 2.1). It did so under a leftist military government that implemented programmes to assist the working classes while allowing the commercial bourgeoisie to prosper. The rapidly expanding economic pie, better distributed than in previous decades, attenuated demands for political reform. Second, repression under Panama's military leader Omar Torrijos never attained the horrific levels of dictatorial Nicaragua, El Salvador and Guatemala. This likely avoided strengthening anti-regime grievances. In the 1980s, Manuel Noriega was less adroit than his predecessor, Torrijos, at placating social forces and staying on the good side of the United States. In the late 1980s civil society exerted pressure for civilians to retake power. The United States supported this demand under its new pro-democracy strategy for the region and diminished strategic concerns for Panama. When Noriega frustrated the expectations for democratization in the 1989 election and undermined US drug interdiction programmes by assisting narcotics smuggling, the US stepped in, removed the dictator and handed the government to civilians.

Case studies

Costa Rica

Throughout the first century of its independent history Costa Rica experienced authoritarian strongman rule, political domination by agrarian elites, indirect elections, quasi-democracy, coups and military intervention in politics. Indirect elections and civilian rule, however, became normal practices as early as the mid-nineteenth century. A trend towards democratization began when citizens protested at a stolen indirect election in 1889. The incumbent Liberals and the army relented and ceded power to the actual winner. Agrarian elites continued to dominate thereafter, but in the early twentieth century direct presidential elections were adopted. Growing literacy caused by Costa Rica's heavy promotion of education expanded suffrage. Popular and elite resistance to military rule (1917–19) again underscored citizen support for elections and civilian rule. For two decades from the 1920s, a corrupt election system gradually improved, as new parties, labour unions and other civil society actors mobilized into the political arena with increased economic and social diversity (Booth 1998, 1989; Molina Jiménez and Lehoucq 1999; Lehoucq and Molina Jiménez 2002; Molina Jiménez 2005).

Costa Rica's democracy arose from social conflict, election fraud and civil war. In the early 1940s President Rafael Angel Calderón Guardia of the agrarian-elite-dominated Republican Party forged an unexpected alliance with the Catholic Church and communist labour unions and passed major social security and labour legislation. Angry upper-class parties and a middle-class social democratic movement, led by José Figueres Ferrer, attempted to steal the 1948 presidential election for Otilio Ulate Blanco in order to prevent Calderón Guardia's re-election. When the legislature nullified the fraudulent presidential results, Figueres and his National Liberation forces revolted and won a brief civil war. A stalemate among the major actors ensued: neither mobilized labour, middle-class or upper-class forces could control the system alone. During an 18-month period of de facto rule by the National Liberation junta, a constituent assembly rewrote the constitution, further reforming the electoral system and abolishing the army. To resolve the stalemate, Ulate received the presidency in 1950, while social reforms were retained to placate the organized working class. Meanwhile Figueres and his social democratic backers formed the National Liberation Party (PLN). An informal elite settlement evolved in which the PLN and a coalition of upper-class parties became an effective two-party system that alternated in power for the next five decades. The elimination of the military (widely anti-democratic in Latin America), truly clean elections, and this informal inter-elite accord on electoral democracy constituted the basis for democratization and democratic consolidation (Bell 1971; Ameringer 1982; Peeler 1985; Booth 1998, 2008).

Nicaragua[2]

US forces occupied Nicaragua for most of the 1912–32 period, seeking to maintain the US monopoly of the Panama Canal and to suppress the anti-American rebel Augusto C. Sandino, while establishing Nicaragua's National Guard (GN) from which arose dictatorial Somoza family rule. Founded in 1934, the Somoza dynasty cultivated US support to enhance their power, practiced kleptocracy to enrich themselves, governed through the Liberal Party, co-opted the Conservative Party, and used the GN to repress critics and opponents. Upon the assassination of founder Anastasio Somoza García in 1956, his older son Luis became president and his younger son Anastasio Somoza Debayle headed the GN.

Nicaragua embraced the CACM and experienced rapid growth, burgeoning inequality, unemployment and mobilization for political reform. Liberation theology-inspired Catholic activists, unions, the private sector, and new political parties mobilized and demanded change. The FSLN and other guerrilla groups formed in 1959–60, hoping to unseat the dictatorship. All failed except the FSLN, although a US-supported counter-insurgency contained the FSLN for more than a decade.

Upon Luis Somoza's death in 1967, Anastasio became president amid growing unrest. The CACM-driven boom was aggravating popular socio-economic conditions and these caused demands for reform, protests and strikes. In December 1972, an earthquake devastated Managua and killed an estimated 10,000 people. National Guard troops disbanded and looted; Somoza embezzled relief aid and imposed predatory recovery policies. Soon afterwards, the OPEC oil embargo began, elevating prices and unemployment. When the FSLN staged a hostage-taking in late 1974, Somoza declared a state of siege and unleashed a three-year reign of terror that convinced many to support or join the FSLN. In January 1978 the editor of the opposition newspaper *La Prensa* was assassinated and spontaneous popular attacks on GN posts erupted nationwide. The government brutally quelled these incidents. The FSLN seized its opportunity amid this rage and spontaneous rebellion: it opened its recruiting and broadened its alliance with civil society.

The Sandinistas militarily defeated the regime in July 1979. The Marxist-Leninist Sandinistas and their diverse allies took power as a coalition government, but the FSLN dominated the revolutionary government. The Sandinistas eschewed radicalization, leaving political space for opposition, nationalizing only part of the economy, and avoiding formal alliances with leftist governments. Not persuaded by these policies, the United States, Liberal Party exiles, and former GN elements who had escaped, forged counter-revolutionary (*contra*) forces that attacked the revolutionary government. The government adopted a military draft and counter-insurgency programmes in response.

Seeking external and internal legitimacy, the revolution held a 1984 national election (boycotted by Liberals). The FSLN's Daniel Ortega won the presidency and the National Assembly wrote a new constitution that took effect in 1987. These changes failed to convince Nicaragua's flight capital to return, and government economic policy accelerated the economic decline. The US-financed contra war intensified in the late 1980s and the United States imposed an economic embargo. The war, the draft, and economic deterioration eroded the government's support.

For Nicaragua's 1990 election, the United States helped unify the opposition behind Violeta de Chamorro. Nicaraguans voted the Sandinistas out of power by 55 per cent, an outcome the FSLN accepted. In 1996 Nicaraguans elected the Constitutionalist Liberal Party (PLC) candidate Arnoldo Alemán president. (Following his term he was convicted of embezzlement and imprisoned.) Ortega and Alemán later forged a pact that has since undermined democracy. FLSN-PLC legislative cooperation altered election laws to allow PLC-FLSN domination of election administration and eliminate small parties, and packed the supreme court. In 2006 the Liberals split, which allowed Ortega's re-election with only 38 per cent. Observers denounced the 2008 municipal elections as fraudulently manipulated to the FSLN's benefit. The supreme court ruled Ortega could run for president again, despite a constitutional provision blocking re-election, and overturned Alemán's embezzlement conviction, allowing him, too, to seek re-election. Consequently, in the November 2011 presidential election Ortega is expected to win re-election for a second consecutive term.

El Salvador[3]

A military regime formed following an abortive 1932 leftist insurrection and massacre of thousands of suspected supporters by the army and landowners. For five decades the military, supported by much of the national bourgeoisie, controlled government through repression and military-dominated parties. Concentrating land ownership and the CACM boom in the 1960s and 1970s stimulated growth but simultaneously concentrated wealth and elevated rural poverty and unemployment. This drove the growth of civil society, unions, liberation theology-inspired popular groups and reformist political parties. In the 1970s an opposition coalition twice won enough votes to force the regime to openly steal presidential elections to retain the presidency. Several leftist insurgent groups formed during the 1970s, each with links to opposition civil society. The government used security forces to repress popular reform demands, with increasingly sanguinary results.

As Nicaragua's insurrection accelerated and overthrew the Somoza regime in 1979, disgruntled Salvadoran military officers temporarily allied with opposition progressives and some business factions to overthrow President Romero in October 1979. The Carter administration gambled that the putatively reformist coalition might stem regime and revolutionary violence, and quickly endorsed the new government. As American military and economic assistance began to flow, the junta's reformist pretensions evaporated. Extreme rightist elements took over and official violence escalated. Within months, five Marxist guerrilla groups united into the FMLN and escalated military operations. US assistance swelled under the Carter and Reagan administrations. This increased the regime's capacity to fight the insurgency and eventually produced, at very high levels of violence, a protracted stalemate in the conflict.

In the early 1980s, increasingly embarrassed by the Salvadoran government's behaviour and fearful of growing congressional resistance to fund the war, the Reagan administration opted to press for human rights and political reforms. El Salvador adopted a new constitution in 1983 and held a 1984 presidential election (won by Christian Democrat José Napoleón Duarte) and a 1985 legislative election. Critics denounced irregularities in both elections, which excluded the Left. Duarte's weak government helped legitimize US support for El Salvador in the United States, but he could neither control the military, implement reform nor undertake peace negotiations. The Central American Peace Accord of 1987 encouraged negotiated settlements to Central America's civil wars. By 1989 the Cold War's end had reduced US fears of a negotiated settlement and the Bush administration endorsed peace negotiations. Talks remained stalled through El Salvador's elections of 1988 and 1989 in which the rightist Nationalist Republican Alliance (ARENA) party's Alfredo Cristiani won the presidency. The FMLN, by then committed to negotiating peace, remained frustrated by the government dragging its feet. In late 1989 the FMLN attacked the capital San Salvador in order to jar the regime to move forward with negotiations. The tactic revealed the FMLN's high capacity for disruption and sparked government interest in negotiations.

The logjam broken, the Chapultepec peace agreement was struck in 1992. It provided for civilian democratic rule, allowed the centre-left and insurgent-left to form parties and enter legal politics, reduced and reformed the military, reformed the police, gave amnesty for crimes committed during the war, and set up a truth commission to investigate the war. The United Nations provided implementation monitoring. The armed forces reduced its size and returned to the barracks. The FMLN demobilized and participated in the 1994 elections. Although it lost three successive presidential elections to ARENA, the FMLN won major mayoral elections and increased its legislative representation. In 2009 FMLN nominee Mauricio Funes won the presidency and the FMLN obtained the greatest number of seats in the legislature. While violence and crime remained very high, democratic governance was less problematic than many observers expected, given the country's legacy of conflict.

Guatemala[4]

Guatemala first experienced democracy in 1944 when middle-class and labour unrest prompted the resignation of the dictator Jorge Ubico. The election of President Juan José Arévalo initiated ten years of democracy, modernization and energized civil society. In 1950 Jacobo Arbenz Guzmán became president. He pushed more economic and social reforms (legalization of the Communist Party and agrarian reform) and hundreds of peasant unions formed. This antagonized major landowners, the United Fruit Company, and the United States. In 1954, US-backed forces led by Carlos Castillo Armas invaded Guatemala with CIA air support. Castillo Armas seized power when the army refused to defend the government and forced Arbenz to resign.

Repression ensued against worker and peasant organizations, political parties and other suspected opponents. The government jailed and killed thousands and rolled back the agrarian reform. Foreign policy aligned closely with that of the United States as the Cold War deepened. When Castillo Armas was assassinated in 1957, the army took power, imposing General Miguel Ydígoras Fuentes as president and continuing heavy repression. In 1960 Guatemala's first rebel group appeared, adopted a Marxist-Leninist line, and sought to emulate the successful guerrilla strategy of Castro in Cuba. US counter-insurgency aid to the Guatemalan military escalated in the

1960s, as did repression by military-based death squads. From 1970 to 1982 civilians effectively ceded political control to the military. Most parties nominated generals, and election fraud imposed the military's preferred winners, although repression failed to contain opposition growth as liberation theology-inspired activist groups and new reformist political parties arose. Escalating inequality, inflation and unemployment driven by the CACM boom reactivated unions and strikes. The OPEC embargo of 1973 and Guatemala's severe 1976 earthquake prompted further mobilization among the poor. New leftist guerrilla groups also formed in highland indigenous areas, while dormant older rebel groups reactivated. Insurgent activity rekindled in the late 1970s, and five guerrilla groups united into the Guatemalan National Revolutionary Union (URNG) in 1982.

A 1982 coup replaced the president General Romeo Lucas García with General Efraín Ríos Montt. He escalated counter-insurgency and created involuntary rural militias to control indigenous communities, dissolved congress, suppressed parties, and imposed a state of siege. This led to international opprobrium, including withholding US military aid and, eventually, to a controlled liberalization process. A constituent assembly elected in 1984 drafted a new constitution. In 1985, with only centrist and conservative parties participating, Christian Democrat Vinicio Cerezo Arévalo won the presidency. Although counter-insurgency continued, this political opening gradually drew parts of the business community, civil society and moderate parties towards the legal political arena and undercut the formation of guerrilla–civil society links.

With electoral democracy nominally established, peace negotiations began under Cerezo but stagnated for several years despite the end of the Cold War, international encouragement and the demise of Nicaragua's Sandinsta revolution. Cerezo's successor, Jorge Serrano Elías, attempted an 'executive coup' in 1993, but Guatemala's Court of Constitutionality removed him from office. His successor, Ramiro de León Carpio, initiated more political reform and reactivated peace talks, facilitated and monitored by the United Nations. A peace agreement, leading to more civilian authority and a curtailed role for the armed forces, was signed in December 1996, which ended 36 years of civil war that cost 200,000 lives. The government undertook police reform, but a crime wave ensued. Violence escalated rather than declined – much of it criminal but some by police 'cleansing' of 'undesirables'. Guatemalans failed to ratify several constitutional reforms specified in the settlement, leaving many issues pending. Electoral democracy survived, at times seemingly threatened by poor elite commitment. Elections nevertheless took place and power changed hands peacefully several times.

Honduras[5]

Geographically isolated and with few natural resources, Honduras remained mainly a subsistence economy throughout the nineteenth century. Its people were among the hemisphere's poorest, yet Honduras remained relatively stable compared with its neighbours. Political and economic elites were regionally rather than nationally integrated. Commercial banana production by foreign firms began around 1900 but displaced few peasants or indigenous peoples. Land shortages and concentrated land ownership only developed in the mid-twentieth century (Durham 1979). With little rural protest or need to manage an agrarian proletariat, the Honduran military (like Costa Rica's) remained weak, while banana-worker unions developed relatively freely.

The Liberal Party of Honduras (PLH) became ascendant in politics after the 1870s, until a schism in 1932 allowed the conservative National Party (PN) to take power. PN efforts to deny a Liberal return to power through elections prompted a military coup in 1956. After that the armed forces assumed an active political role, either ruling directly or powerfully influencing civilian leaders from behind the scenes. US military assistance enhanced the military's strength and political power. At first neutral between the PN and PLH, the military by the 1960s tilted towards the National Party and became increasingly repressive of organized labour. Honduras joined CACM in 1960, but benefitted the least from its policies.

Colonel Oswaldo López Arellano seized power in 1963, following which Honduras experienced popular unrest and a trade disadvantage with Central America. In 1969 Honduras fought briefly with El Salvador over Salvadoran peasants' squatting on Honduran land, border security and trade tensions. López Arellano stepped down in 1969, but the government that followed him failed to calm unrest. López Arellano again seized power and this time implemented populist programmes, including an agrarian reform. Embarrassed by a corruption scandal in 1975, López Arellano transferred power to two subsequent military rulers whose governments made little economic progress. Under pressure from the Carter administration, adversely affected by the wobbly CACM, and uneasy about the Nicaraguan revolution and Salvadoran civil war, the Honduran military opted to liberalize. In 1980 it held constituent assembly elections. In 1981, a presidential election saw the PLH's Robert Suazo Córdova accede to the presidency.

US military aid rapidly reinforced the Honduran military's political role in the early 1980s, and Honduras lent its territory to the Reagan administration's harassment of Nicaragua's Sandinista government. In 1984 President Suazo provoked a constitutional crisis by seeking to alter the constitution to allow his re-election, but senior officers convinced him to relent. National Party candidates won the next two presidential elections, and the military retained its enormous influence. In 1994 Liberal human rights lawyer Carlos Roberto Reina became president and began curtailing human rights abuses and military power. Reina's successors alternated between the PN and PLH.

By the early 2000s, Honduras appeared to have consolidated formal democratic rule. In June 2009, however, a dispute between President Manuel Zelaya, congress and the courts over a proposed referendum on constitutional revision turned into a coup d'état. Ruling against Zelaya in a dispute over the proposed referendum, the supreme court charged him with constitutional violations and ordered his arrest. The military then unconstitutionally exiled Zelaya, and congress replaced him with the President of Congress Roberto Micheletti. Heavy international pressure failed to persuade the de facto government to relent. A new government was elected on the normal constitutional schedule in November 2009. Thus Honduras provided the region with its first full-on failure of one of its fledgling constitutional democracies.

Panama[6]

Panama's special position uniting North and South America, and the Atlantic and Pacific, has always shaped its economic and political destiny. Its canal has fuelled relative prosperity, but transit-related geopolitics and external interference have deeply shaped Panamanian politics.

Canal construction under the US's aegis brought new racial and ethnic groups to Panama and swelled the working class. The canal's completion in 1914 stimulated new trade and growth, but lost construction jobs and the foreign canal-monopoly skewed the distribution of wealth. The 1930s depression deepened workers' poverty and mobilized them politically. Arnulfo Arias, promoting anti-American nationalism and racial exclusion, led the populist Panameñista Party (PP) to electoral victories in 1940, 1949 and 1968. His programme offended the United States and canal operators, the bourgeoisie and the military, who overthrew Arias each time he was elected. US security interests during the Second World War and the Cold War prompted repeated direct intervention in Panamanian affairs by US troops based in the Canal Zone. With the advent of nuclear warfare and intercontinental ballistic missiles, the canal's geostrategic importance declined. US administrations from the 1950s onwards negotiated to amend the canal treaty, seeking to defuse US-Panamanian tensions and local unrest.

In 1968 General Omar Torrijos overthrew Arias, suppressed political parties, and implemented a left-populist programme beneficial to the poor. Torrijos promoted his own Revolutionary Democratic Party (PRD) to mobilize the working classes behind his regime, and, in 1977, successfully completed negotiations to redraw the canal treaty. During the 1970s, political parties were allowed to resurface and elections (often fraudulent) resumed. After Torrijos's death in 1981, General Manuel Noriega seized power as head of the armed forces. Noriega quickly escalated repression and corruption but stayed in power by juggling conflicting demands from the United States for cooperation and domestic constituencies. Opposition parties, the commercial elite and civil society grew increasingly unhappy with Noriega's rule.

Ceding to domestic and foreign criticisms, Noriega held elections in 1989 – but then fraudulently manipulated the results. Washington's newly elected Bush administration invoked the US policy of promoting democracy – and mounting evidence of Noriega's drug connections and human rights abuses – to justify direct intervention. Using its remaining US bases in Panama, the United States invaded in December 1989. The Panamanian military, quickly defeated, was disbanded and the putative victors of the 1989 election, a coalition of bourgeois reform parties led by Guillermo Endara, assumed power.

Elections since 1989 have been clean. The military has not been reconstituted. No single segment or party dominates Panama's politics, the presidency has peacefully passed between parties on multiple occasions, and human rights performance has been good. Panama has largely remained calm, in part because of strong economic growth and capable government.

Notes

1 On elites and pacts see Rustow (1970); O'Donnell *et al.* (1986); Stepan (1986); Huntington (1991); Higley and Gunther (1992); on imposed democracy see Whitehead (1991); Enterline and Greig (2005, 2008). Other chapters of this volume discuss these theories in more detail.
2 This section draws primarily from these sources: Booth (1985); Walker and Wade (2011); Robinson (1992); Booth, Wade and Walker (2010); Booth and Seligson (2010); Close (1999); Close and Deonandan (2004); Prevost and Vanden (1997).
3 This section draws heavily on the following sources: Chapter 6 of Booth, Wade and Walker (2010); and from works by Montgomery (1982, 1994); Azpuru *et al.* (2007); Williams and Walter (Herman and Brodhead 1984; Williams and Walter 1997); Chapter 4 of Herman and Brodhead (1984); and Baloyra (1982).
4 This section is drawn heavily from the following sources: Booth, Wade and Walker (2010) (chapter 7); Jonas (1991, 2000); Azpuru *et al.* (2007); Immerman (1982); Berger (1992); and the Historical Clarification Commission (1999).
5 This section drawn especially upon these sources: Morris (1984); Euraque (1996); Mahoney (2001); Ruhl (2007).
6 Material on Panama is drawn mainly from Ropp (1984, 1992, 2007); Zimbalist and Weeks (1991); Booth and Seligson (2009), Peeler (2004); and Schneider (2007).

References

Adorno, T. W., D. J. Levinson, E. Frenkely-Brunswik and R. N. Sanford (1950) *The Authoritarian Personality*. New York: Harper and Row.
Almond, Gabriel A. and Sidney Verba (1963) *The Civic Culture: Political Attitudes and Democracy in Five Nations*. Princeton, NJ: Princeton University Press.
Ameringer, Charles (1982) *Democracy in Costa Rica*. New York: Praeger.
Azpuru, Dinorah, Ligia Blanco, Ricardo Córdova Macías, Nayelly Loya Marín and Adrián Zapata, eds (2007) *Construyendo La Democracia En Sociedades Posconflicto: Guatemala Y El Salvador, Un Enfoque Comparado*. Guatemala City Guatemala and Ottawa, Canada: Asociacion de Investigación y Estudios Sociales (ASIES) – Centro Internacional de Investigaciones para el Desarrollo (IDRC) – F&G Editores.
Baloyra, Enrique (1982) *El Salvador in Transition*. Chapel Hill: University of North Carolina Press.
Bell, John Patrick (1971) *Crisis in Costa Rica: The Revolution of 1948*. Austin: University of Texas Press.

Berger, Susan A. (1992) *Political and Agrarian Development in Guatemala*. Boulder, CO: Westview Press.

Black, George (1981) *Triumph of the People: The Sandinista Revolution in Nicaragua*. London: Zed Press.

Boix, Carles (2003) *Democracy and Redistribution*. Cambridge: Cambridge University Press.

Booth, John A. (1985) *The End and the Beginning: The Nicaraguan Revolution*. Boulder, CO: Westview Press.

—— (1989) 'Costa Rica: The Roots of Democratic Stability'. In *Democracy in Developing Countries: Latin America*, eds Larry Diamond, Juan Linz and Seymour Martin Lipset. Boulder, CO: Lynne Rienner.

—— (1991) 'Socioeconomic and Political Roots of National Revolts in Central America', *Latin American Research Review*, 26 (1), pp. 33–73.

—— (1998) *Costa Rica: Quest for Democracy*. Boulder, CO: Westview Press.

—— (2008) 'Democratic Development in Costa Rica', *Democratization*, 15(4), pp. 714–732.

—— and Mitchell A. Seligson (1991) 'Cultura Política y Democratización: Vías Alternas En Nicaragua y Costa Rica'. In *Transiciones a La Democracia En Europa y América Latina*, eds Carlos E. Barba Solano, José Luis Barros Horcasitas and Javier Hurtado. México: FLACSO–Universidad de Guadalajara, pp. 628–681.

—— and —— (1994) 'Political Culture and Democratization: Evidence from Mexico, Nicaragua and Costa Rica'. In *Political Culture and Democracy in Developing Countries*, ed. Larry Diamond. Boulder, CO: Lynne Reinner, pp. 107–138.

—— and —— (2009) *The Legitimacy Puzzle in Latin America: Democracy and Political Support in Eight Nations*. Cambridge: Cambridge University Press.

—— and —— (2010) *Cultura Política De La Democracia En Nicaragua, 2010:Consolidación Democrática En Las Américas En Tiempos Difíciles*. Nashville, TN: Vanderbilt University.

——, Christine J.Wade and Thomas W. Walker (2010) *Understanding Central America: Global Forces, Rebellion and Change*. Boulder, CO: Westview Press.

Brockett, Charles D. (1988) *Land, Power, and Poverty: Agrarian Transformation and Political Conflict in Central America*. Boston, MA: Unwin Hyman.

—— (2005) *Political Movements and Violence in Central America*. New York: Cambridge University Press.

Carothers, Thomas (1991) *In the Name of Democracy: U.S. Policy toward Latin America in the Reagan Years*. Berkeley: University of California Press.

—— (1999) *Aiding Democracy Abroad: The Learning Curve*. Washington, DC: Carnegie Endowment for International Peace.

Close, David, ed. (1999) *Nicaragua: The Chamorro Years*. Boulder, CO: Lynne Rienner Publishers.

—— and Kilowatie Deonandan, eds (2004) *Undoing Democracy: The Politics of Electoral Caudillismo*. Lahham, MD: Lexington Books.

Dealy, Glen (1974) 'The Tradition of Monistic Democracy in Latin America'. In *Politics and Social Change in Latin America: The Distinct Tradition*, ed. Howard J. Wiarda. Amherst: University of Massachusetts Press.

Diskin, Martin, ed. (1983) *Trouble in Our Backyard: Central America and the United States in the Eighties*. New York: Pantheon Books.

Dunkerley, James. (1988) *Power in the Isthmus: A Political History of Modern Central America*. London; New York: Verso.

Durham, William H. (1979) *Scarcity and Survival in Central America: Ecological Origins of the Soccer War*. Stanford, CA: Stanford University Press.

Enterline, Andrew J. and J. Michael Greig (2005) 'Beacons of Hope? The Impact of Imposed Democracy on Regional Peace, Democracy, and Prosperity', *Journal of Politics*, 67 (4), pp. 1075–1098.

—— and J. Michael Greig (2008) 'The History of Imposed Democracy and the Future of Iraq and Afghanistan', *Foreign Policy Analysis* 4 (4), pp. 321–374.

Epstein, David L., Robert Bates, Jack Goldstone, Ida Kristensen and Sharyn O'Halloran (2006) 'Democratic Transitions', *American Journal of Political Science*, 50 (3), pp. 551–569.

Euraque, Dario A. (1996) *Reinterpreting the Banana Republic: Region and State in Honduras, 1870–1972*. Chapel Hill: University of North Carolina Press.

Gasiorowski, Mark J. (2000) 'Democracy and Macroeconomic Performance in Underdeveloped Countries: An Empirical Analysis', *Comparative Political Studies*, 33 (3), pp. 319–349.

Herman, Edward S. and Frank Brodhead (1984) *Demonstration Elections: U.S.-Staged Elections in the Dominican Republic, Vietnam, and El Salvador*. Boston, MA: South End Press.

Higley, John and Richard Gunther (1992) *Elites and Democratic Consolidation in Latin America and Southern Europe*. Cambridge; New York: Cambridge University Press.

Historical Clarification Commission (1999) *Guatemala: Memory of Silence* (Guatemala City: Historical Clarification Commission).

Huntington, Samuel (1991) *The Third Wave: Democratization in the Late Twentieth Century*. Norman: University of Oklahoma Press.

Immerman, Richard H. (1982) *The Cia in Guatemala: The Foriegn Policy of Intervention*. Austin: University of Texas Press.

Inglehart, Ronald (1988) 'The Renaissance of Political Culture', *American Political Science Review*, 82 (4), pp. 1203–1230.

—— (1990) *Culture Shift in Advanced Industrial Society*. Princeton, NJ: Princeton University Press.

—— and Christian Welzel (2005) *Modernization, Cultural Change, and Democracy*. New York: Cambridge University Press.

Jonas, Susanne (1991) *The Battle for Guatemala: Rebels, Death Squads, and U.S. Power*. Boulder, CO: Westview Press.

—— (2000) *Of Centaurs and Doves: Guatemala's Peace Process*. Boulder, CO: Westview Press.

Karl, Terry Lynn (1992) 'El Salvador's Negotiated Revolution', *Foreign Affairs*, 71 (2), pp. 147–164.

Krishna, Anirudh (2008) *Poverty, Participation, and Democracy: A Global Perspective*. New York: Cambridge University Press.

LaFeber, Walter (1983) *Inevitable Revolutions: The United States in Central America*. New York: W.W. Norton.

Lehoucq, Fabrice Edouard and Iván Molina Jiménez (2002) *Stuffing the Ballot Box: Fraud, Electoral Reform, and Democratization in Costa Rica, Cambridge Studies in Comparative Politics*. New York: Cambridge University Press.

Lipset, Seymour Martin (1994) 'The Social Requisites of Democracy Revisited', *American Sociological Review*, 59, pp. 1–22.

—— (1959) 'Some Social Requisites of Democracy: Economic Development and Political Legitimacy', *American Political Science Review*, 53, pp. 65–105.

Lowenthal, Abraham F. (1991a) *Exporting Democracy: The United States and Latin America: Themes and Issues*. Baltimore, MD: Johns Hopkins University Press.

—— (1991b) *Exporting Democracy: The United States and Latin America: Case Studies*. Baltimore, MD: Johns Hopkins University Press.

Mahoney, James (2001) *The Legacies of Liberalism: Path Dependence and Political Regimes in Central America*. Baltimore, MD: Johns Hopkins University Press.

Martz, John D. ed. (1995) *United States Policy in Latin America: A Decade of Crisis and Challenge*. Lincoln: Univeristy of Nebraska Press.

Molina Jiménez, Iván (2005) *Demoperfectocracia: La Democracia Pre-Reformada En Costa Rica (1985–1948)*. Heredia, Costa Rica: Editorial Universidad Nacional.

—— and Fabrice Lehoucq (1999) *Urnas De Lo Inesperado: Fraude Electoral Y Lucha Política En Costa Rica*. San José: Editorial de la Universidad de Costa Rica.

Montgomery, Tommie Sue (1982) *Revolution in El Salvador: Origins and Evolution*. Boulder, CO: Westview.

—— (1994) *Revolution in El Salvador: From Civil Strife to Civil Peace*. Boulder, CO: Westview Press.

Moreno, Dario (1990) *U.S. Policy in Central America: The Endless Debate*. Miami: Florida International University Press.

—— (1996) *The Struggle for Peace in Central America*. Gainesville: University Presses of Florida.

Morris, James D. (1984) *Honduras: Caudillo Politics and Military Rulers*. Boulder, CO: Westview Press.

Morse, Richard M. (1974) 'The Heritage of Latin America'. In *Politics and Social Change in Latin America: The Distinct Tradition*, ed. Howard J. Wiarda. Amherst: University of Massachusetts Press.

O'Donnell, Guillermo, Philippe C. Schmitter and Laurence Whitehead, eds (1986) *Transitions from Authoritarian Rule*. Baltimore, MD: Johns Hopkins University Press.

Peeler, John (1985) *Latin American Democracies: Colombia, Costa Rica, and Venezuela*. Chapel Hill: University of North Carolina Press.

—— (1992) 'Elite Settlements and Democratic Consolidation in Latin America: Colombia, Costa Rica, and Venezuela'. In *Elites and Democratic Consolidation in Latin America and Southern Europe*, ed. John Higley and Richard Gunter. New York: Cambridge University Press, pp. 81–112.

—— (1998) *Building Democracy in Latin America*. Boulder, CO: Lynne Reinner Publishers.

Peeler, John A. (1995) 'Elites and Democracy in Central America'. In *Elections and Democracy in Central America, Revisited*, ed. Mitchell A. Seligson and John A. Booth. Chapel Hill: University of North Carolina Press.

—— (2004) *Building Democracy in Latin America*. 2nd ed. Boulder, CO: Lynne Rienner,.

Pérez, Orlando J. (1995) 'Elections under Crisis: Background to Panama in the 1980s'. In *Elections and Democracy in Central America, Revisited*, ed. Mitchell A Seligson and John A. Booth. Chapel Hill: University of North Carolina Press.

—— (2011) *Political Culture in Panama: Democracy after Invasion.* Houndmills Basingstoke, Hampshire: Palgrave Macmillan.

Prevost, Gary and Harry E. Vanden, eds (1997) *The Undermining of the Sandinista Revolution.* New York: St Martin's Press.

Przeworski, Adam, Michael E. Alvarez, Jose Antonio Cheibub and Fernando Limongi (2000) *Democracy and Development: Political Institutions and Well-Being in the World, 1950–1990.* Cambridge: Cambridge University Press.

Putnam, Robert D. (1993) *Making Democracy Work: Civic Traditions in Modern Italy.* Princeton, NJ: Princeton University Press.

—— (2000) *Bowling Alone: The Collapse and Revival of American Community.* New York: Simon & Schuster.

Robinson, William I. *A Faustian Bargain: U.S. Intervention in the Nicaraguan Elections and America Foreign Policy in the Post-Cold War Era.* Boulder, CO: Westview Press, 1992.

—— (1996) *Promoting Polyarchy: Globalization, U.S. Intervention, and Hegemony.* Cambridge: Cambridge University Press.

Ropp, Steve C. (1984) 'Leadership and Political Transformation in Panama: Two Levels of Regime Crisis'. In *Central America: Crisis and Adaptation*, ed. Steve C. Ropp and James A. Morris. Albuquerque: University of New Mexico Press.

—— (1992) 'Explaining the Long-Term Maintenance of a Military Regime: Panama before the U.S. Invasion', *World Politics*, 44 (2), pp. 210–234.

—— (1995) 'The Bush Administration and the Invasion of Panama: Explaining the Chjoice and Timing of the Military Option'. In *United States Policy in Latin America: A Decade of Crisis and Challenge*, ed. John D. Martz. Lincoln: Univeristy of Nebraska Press, pp. 80–109.

—— (2007) 'Panama: New Politics for a New Millennium'. In *Latin American Politics and Development*, ed. Howard Wiarda and Harvey F. Kline. Boulder, CO: Westview Press.

Rueschemeyer, Dietrich, Evelyne Huber Stephens and John D. Stephens (1992) *Capitalist Development and Democracy.* Cambridge: Cambridge University Press.

Ruhl, J. Mark (2007) 'Honduras: Problems of Democratic Consolidation'. In *Latin American Politics and Development*, ed. Howard J. Wiarda and Harvey F. Kline. Boulder, CO: Westview Press.

Rustow, Dankwart (1970) 'Transitions to Democracy: Toward a Dynamic Model', *Comparative Politics*, 2, pp. 337–363.

Schneider, Ronald M. (2007) *Latin American Political History: Patterns and Personality.* Boulder, CO: Westview Press.

Schoultz, Lars (1987) *National Security and United States Policy toward Latin America.* Princeton, NJ: Princeton University Press.

—— (1998) *Beneath the United States: A History of U.S. Policy toward Latin America.* Cambridge, MA: Harvard University Press.

Seligson, Mitchell A. (1987) 'Development, Democratization and Decay: Central America at the Crossroads'. In *Authoritarians and Democrats: The Politics of Regime Transition in Latin America*, ed. James M. Malloy and Mitchell A. Seligson. Pittsburgh: University of Pittsburgh Press.

—— (1997) 'The Vanhanen Thesis and the Prospects for Democracy in Latin America'. In *Prospects for Democracy: A Study of 172 Countries*, ed. Tatu Vanhanen. London: Routledge, pp. 277–283.

——and John A. Booth (2009) *Special Report on Honduras: Predicting Coups? Democratic Vulnerabilities, the Americasbarometer and the 2009 Honduran Crisis*, available online at http://sitemason.vanderbilt.edu/lapop/AmericasBarometerInsightsSeries/2009/8/1/i0821-special-report-on-honduras-predicting-coups-democratic-vulnerabilities-the-americasbarometer-and-the-2009-honduran-crisis-by-mitchell-a-seligson-and-john-a-booth-.

—— and John A. Booth (2010) 'Crime, Hard Times and Discontent', *Journal of Democracy*, 21 (2), pp. 123–135.

Smith, Peter H. (1996) *Talons of the Eagle: Dynamics of U.S.-Latin American Relations.* New York: Oxford University Press.

Stepan, Alfred. (1986) 'Paths toward Redemocratization: Theoretical and Comparative Considerations'. In *Transitions from Authoritarian Rule*, ed. Guillermo O'Donnell, Philippe C. Schmitter and Laurence Whitehead. Baltimore, MD: Johns Hopkins University Press.

Vanhanen, Tatu (1997) *Prospects of Democracy: A Study of 172 Countries.* London: Routledge.

Walker, Thomas W. and Christine C. Wade (2011) *Nicaragua: Living in the Shadow of the Eagle.* 5th ed. Boulder, CO: Westview Press.

Weeks, Gregory (2008) *U.S. And Latin American Relations.* New York: Pearson Longman.

Welzel, Christian (2009) 'Theories of Democratization'. In *Democratization*, ed. Christian W. Haerpfer, Patrick Bernhagen, Ronald F. Inglehart and Christian Welzel. Oxford: Oxford University Press.

Whitehead, Lawrence (1991) 'The Imposition of Democracy'. In *Exporting Democracy: The United States and Latin America*, ed. Abraham Lowenthal. Baltimore, MD: Johns Hopkins University Press.

Wiarda, Howard J. (1974) 'Social Change and Political Development in Latin America: Summary, Implications, Frontiers'. In *Politics and Social Change in Latin America: The Distinct Tradition*, ed. Howard J. Wiarda. Amherst: University of Massachusetts Press.

Williams, Philip J. and Knut Walter (1997) *Militarization and Demilitarization in El Salvador's Transition to Democracy*. Pittsburgh, PA: University of Pittsburgh Press.

Zimbalist, Andrew and John Weeks (1991) *Panama at the Crossroads: Economic Development and Political Change in the Twentieth Century*. Berkeley: University of California Press.

3

South America

Anita Breuer

This chapter analyses the relationship between democratization, citizen participation and democratic consolidation in South America. The third wave of democratic transitions that spread across the region started in 1978. It triggered a subsequent wave of constitutional reform and constitution-writing exercises. A significant aspect of these reforms was the introduction of alternative mechanisms of citizen participation. These reforms raised hopes that the development of a new participatory style of democracy would help to overcome the elitist and socially exclusionary character of the outgoing military regimes. Focusing on a particular institutional feature, the adoption of mechanisms of direct democracy (MDD), this chapter sets out to assess the impact of participatory institutions on democratic consolidation and the quality of democracy in the region. To do so, it proceeds in three steps. The first section renders a comparative account of the political settings that brought about the adoption of national level MDD in South America. The second section provides an overview of the institutional frameworks regulating these mechanisms. The third section introduces some of the most critical and significant practical applications of MDD, in order to illustrate their interaction with existing institutional settings and the impact on democratization and democratic consolidation.

The starting point is to note the wave of authoritarianism that engulfed South America between the 1960s and 1970s, ending seven of the region's existing democracies. At the height of this wave, in the mid-1970s, only two countries – Colombia and Venezuela – remained with civilian governments constituted through contested elections. Starting with Ecuador in 1978, electoral democracy made a comeback in South America and by 1990 virtually every country in the region had restored democratically elected governments. This comeback of democracy was remarkable since it took place amidst a severe economic crisis that forced many of the region's countries to undergo conflictive processes of neoliberal restructuring, which met with considerable degrees of popular resistance. By the end of this turbulent decade, however, major inroads had been made in pursuit of democracy.

A significant aspect of this re-democratization was the ensuing wave of constitutional reforms that swept South America in the 1990s. In what Grindle (2000) has pointedly termed 'audacious reforms', over the course of that decade many South American countries adopted institutional innovations designed to open up their political systems. Significant electoral reforms included the elimination of electoral colleges for the election of presidents (Argentina 1994, Brazil 1985) and the switch from simple majority to run off elections in order to strengthen the legitimacy of presidential mandates (Peru 1981, Argentina 1994, Colombia 1991, Uruguay 1997), as well as the reinforcement of the independence and functional autonomy of National Electoral Institutes throughout the region (Zovatto and Orozco 2008). At the same time, a wave of political decentralization led to the introduction of elected state and municipal governments in some countries (Venezuela 1989, Bolivia 1993), or re-introduced them where such elections had been suspended during the authoritarian period (Argentina 1983, Brazil 1986 and 1988) (Tuchlin and Selee 2004). However, democratizing reforms did not remain limited to the sphere of representative democracy. They also introduced a variety of alternative institutions allowing for citizen participation beyond representative elections.

In the context of South American politics, this opening up of additional participation channels represented a remarkable shift in direction. During the 1980s, the region saw a wave of democratic enthusiasm, with South Americans mainly approving the reinstallation of democratic institutions. At the beginning of the 1990s, there was much optimism about the future perspectives of regional democracy. During the 1990s, this optimism gave way to more sober assessments. The poor record of the re-established democracies in effectively combating poverty, more equitably distributing wealth and providing social security, as well as the survival of informal, non-democratic practices – such as clientelism and systematic corruption – led to increasing levels of electoral volatility and voter abstention. As citizens increasingly 'checked out' of involvement in public life (Grindle 2000), governments became less accountable. Lack of citizen participation is therefore judged to be one of the major obstacles for democratic progress in the region (Mainwaring and Hagopian 2005).

A core problem was the survival of closed and elitist decision-making, which remained dominant in many spheres of public life. For one thing, most of the region's transitions to democracy, except those of Argentina and Bolivia, which resulted from the collapse of the authoritarian regimes, were the result of inter-elite pacts, with little participation of ordinary citizens. The usual transitional pattern, which consisted in negotiations between authoritarian regime incumbents, regime defectors, and democratic opponents, allowed the outgoing elites to exert control over transition with serious costs in terms of socio-economic equity of the re-established democratic systems (O'Donnell *et al.* 1986). The region also showed considerable variation concerning the degree of attachment of citizens to political parties. In Venezuela, Chile and Uruguay, parties maintained strong connections to organized social interests and managed to structure citizens' political interests during the 1990s. By contrast, the post-authoritarian party systems of Brazil, Bolivia and Ecuador were mainly dominated by elite interests, thus losing touch with social groups they claimed to represent (Mainwaring and Scully 1995).

Against the background sketched out above, I pose several questions pertaining to democratic progress in the region. First, what motivated South American policymakers to redistribute power downwards? Second, which institutions were adopted and what were their effects in practice? Third, what impact did the adoption of participatory institutions have on overall democratic quality in the region?

To answer these questions, this chapter focuses on the introduction of mechanisms of direct democracy (MDD). This particular institutional feature poses an interesting and suitable object for the study of the impact of participatory reforms in South America for two reasons. First, theoretically, there has been a controversial scholarly debate concerning the relation between direct democracy and democratic consolidation and quality. Advocates of direct democracy emphasize the potential of MDD to foster participation and enhance the political awareness of citizens as well as their ability to exercise vertical control over their representatives (Barber 1984; Smith and Tolbert 2004). At the same time, critics warn about their eroding impact on representative democracy and the risk of their populist misuse (Shifter 1996; Ellner 2003). Second, technically, each of South America's ten presidential democracies – except Uruguay and Chile, where direct democracy dates back to the early twentieth century – introduced one or more forms of MDD on the national level following the third wave of democratization. This enables us to evaluate the impact of MDD by means of cross-national comparison.

This chapter proceeds in three sections, in order to illustrate the regional impact of MDD on democratization, democratic quality and consolidation. First, it offers a comparative account of the political settings and motivational contexts that brought about the adoption of national level MDD in South America. Second, it provides an overview of institutional frameworks regulating these mechanisms. Third, it examines some of the more critical and significant practical applications of MDD.

Background of post-third-wave reforms introducing MDD in South America

It would seem naive to assume that the institutional innovations dealt with in this study were promoted by political elites on the high moral grounds of a genuine participatory understanding of democracy. Rather than that, we have to bear in mind that constitutional designers are often incumbent politicians facing the possibility of re-election. It is thus more reasonable to assume that, rather than by a pronounced desire to maximize social utility, their institutional choices are – at least partially – targeted at maximizing their own benefits as career politicians.

Table 3.1 shows that, between 1978 and 2010, 13 new constitutions were adopted in South America. Each of the region's countries, except Uruguay, ratified at least one new constitution during this period and almost all of these new constitutions implied the introduction or expansion of direct democratic participation rights. The adoption of these new constitutions came about under three conditions. First, new constitutions were adopted in the course of transition to democracy. In these cases, the previous democratic constitution had either been replaced or seriously discredited by the outgoing authoritarian regimes, or the country lacked a pre-authoritarian democratic charter

Table 3.1 New constitutions and mechanisms of direct democracy in South America, 1978–2010

Country	New constitution	Change of political regime (transition to democracy)	Institutional crisis	Change of preference or re-distribution of power among main political actors	Direct democracy introduced or expanded
Argentina	1994			YES	YES (Introduced)
Bolivia	2009			YES	YES (Expanded)
Brazil	1988	YES			YES (Introduced)
Chile	1980	YES			NO
Colombia	1991		YES		YES (Introduced)
Ecuador	1978	YES			YES (Introduced)
Ecuador	1996			YES	YES (Expanded)
Ecuador	1998		YES		YES (Expanded)
Ecuador	2008			YES	YES (Expanded)
Paraguay	1992	YES			YES (Introduced)
Peru	1979	YES			NO
Peru	1993			YES	YES (Introduced)
Venezuela	1999			YES	YES (Expanded)

The "Operant event" header spans the three middle columns: Change of political regime (transition to democracy), Institutional crisis, and Change of preference or re-distribution of power among main political actors.

altogether (Negretto 2009). This was the case in Ecuador (1978), Peru (1979), Brazil (1988) and Paraguay (1992). Chile represents a special case in this category. Its Constitution of 1980 was ratified in a tightly controlled plebiscite and established the itinerary to the restoration of democracy. It provided for an eight-year presidential term (March 1981–March 1989) for General Pinochet, and required the military junta to submit a presidential nominee to a plebiscite in 1988 for another eight-year term. Chosen as that candidate, Pinochet lost the plebiscite in 1988, thus allowing for elections in 1989. The outgoing military government unilaterally proposed a set of constitutional changes, which were approved in yet another plebiscite in 1989. Despite the prominent role of citizen participation in this process, neither the Constitution of 1980 nor its reform in 1989 introduced new MDD on the national level.

Second, serious crises of the representative institutions led to a redistribution of power among the country's main political actors, allowing traditionally excluded political interests or neo-populist politicians to control the process of constitutional reform. The constitutions adopted in Peru (1993), Argentina (1994), Ecuador (1996, 2008), Venezuela (1999) and Bolivia (2009) came about under this condition.

Third, the process of constitutional reform was not fully controlled by outside interests. However, situations of extreme institutional stress and civil disturbance forced the political elites to consent to the introduction of MDD in order to restore civil order and prevent regime breakdown (Barczak 2001). The constitutions of Colombia (1991) and Ecuador (1998) were adopted under these conditions. Bolivia represents a special case in this category. In 2003 the government's decision to allow foreign investors to exploit natural gas led to violent anti-government protests. The 'gas war' crisis, which involved the deaths of several protestors and the destitution of President Sánchez de Lozada, sparked a considerable legitimacy crisis. While this crisis did not result in the adoption of a new constitution, it led to a constitutional reform in 2004 that introduced several MDD at the national level (Breuer 2007, 2008).

However, the introduction (or expansion) of direct democratic rights did not unleash the wave of new participatory style politics in South America that some had hoped for. Again, the answer to why this failed to occur partly has to be sought in the strategic reasoning of institutional designers. Participatory institutions are advocated as a way of loosening the political establishment's grip on political power. Their practical application will therefore generally imply a criticism of the performance of the governing elites. As Beramendi et al. (2008) point out, the wish of lawmakers to shield themselves from citizen attempts to do away with their legislative monopoly may be reflected in a restrictive institutional design that renders MDD's practical application difficult. In the section below, I present three cases that exemplify the dynamics of constitutional reform and logic of subsequent institutional design described above.

Ecuador

The Ecuadorian case illustrates constitutional reforms that came about as part of the process of democratic transition. In 1972, President Velasco Ibarra was deposed in a military coup headed by General Rodríguez Lara. Initially, the Lara regime had perceived itself not as an interim government, but as a progressive long-term venture to introduce structural changes aimed at kick-starting the country's deadlocked development process. However, the entrepreneurial sector's discontent with the military regime's poor economic performance, popular disillusionment with the slow pace of reform, and a failed coup attempt in 1975, all combined to persuade the armed forces to initiate a re-transition to civilian rule in early 1976 (Isaacs 1991). Consequently, the military junta appointed three commissions of civilian politicians and political scholars to design democratic institutions. The first commission was charged with revising the pre-authoritarian constitution of

1949, the second with drafting a new constitution, and the third with development of a new electoral law. In a referendum pitting the two constitutions against each other, voters gave preference to the new charter, which included innovations such as the enfranchisement of illiterates, the abolition of the Senate, and the introduction of MDD. However, as Pachano (2008) points out, the concept guiding the establishment of MDD in Ecuador did not genuinely respond to the idea of empowering citizens vis-à-vis the state. Quite the contrary: the Constitution of 1978 endowed the president with unconstrained authority to submit to plebiscite any subject he deems of national importance. Effectively, in the past, Ecuadorian presidents faced with opposition by highly fragmented congresses, repeatedly made use of this instrument to circumvent congress and submit reform projects directly to the electorate (Breuer 2009). Meanwhile, citizen-initiated mechanisms of direct democracy were tightly regulated, including the proportion of votes required to recall the mandate of an elected representative, which was higher than the proportion of votes to elect him or her to office. Other bottom-up mechanisms, such as the popular initiative, remained moribund due to the fact that no legislation was developed to regulate their practical application (Pachano 2008).

Peru

The Peruvian case falls into the category of constitutional reform process controlled by a neo-populist leader. In 1990, Alberto Fujimori won a personalistic presidential campaign that epitomized the disintegration of the traditional Peruvian party system. Once in charge of government, he continued a strategy of confrontation with the political parties and congress and increasingly relied on a team of technocrats and the military to carry out a drastic neoliberal restructuring programme. As tensions between the executive and the legislature grew acute in April 1992, Fujimori dissolved congress and instructed the army to take over the congressional palace. Having to legitimize his regime in the light of mounting national and international pressure, Fujimori called elections for a new congress in 1992 and endowed a handpicked group of notables with the task of drafting a new constitution (Cotler 1995). The new charter, ratified by plebiscite in 1993, implied a considerable concentration of power in the executive. At the same time, it introduced several direct democratic procedures that theoretically added to Peruvians' participatory rights. A close look at the design of these newly created institutions, however, raises the question whether or not Peruvian constitutional drafters and legislators indeed intended to create operative participatory mechanisms. The right to revoke the mandate of elected officials, for instance, is listed among the 'fundamental rights of the person' in the first chapter of the Peruvian constitution. The same constitution, however, indirectly denies the application of this right to national level deputies and the president. It indicates that there are no alternative means to revoke a parliamentary mandate other than the procedures for the dissolution of congress,[1] and fails to include the revocation of mandate into the list of possible reasons for the vacancy of the presidential office (Maraví 1998).[2] The exercise of the right to derogate existing laws via referendum, in turn, was hampered by the fact that a respective citizen petition not only had to be endorsed by signatures of 10 per cent of the national electorate but also required approval by a vote of 40 per cent of congress's constituent members. Interestingly, this restriction was only introduced in 1996, in reaction to a signature campaign that sought to derogate a newly passed law intended to pave the way for Fujimori's second re-election.

Colombia

Colombia fulfils the condition under which outsider interests do not fully control the constitutional reform process yet exercise sufficient pressure to achieve the adoption of participatory institutions in exchange for appeasement. Throughout the 1980s, Colombia saw a wave of violence motivated by 'narco-politics'. A series of 'magnicides' affected politicians and high-level civil servants, revealing a failing state that lost its monopoly of physical coercion. The state's legitimacy crisis culminated with the murder of the charismatic liberal presidential candidate, Luis Carlos Galán, at the hands of the Medellín drug cartel in 1989. The murder led to the founding of the student movement, 'Seventh Ballot', which urged Colombians to cast an extra-legal ballot demanding to convoke a National Constituent Assembly (ANC) in the 1990 local and congressional elections. Two million voters responded to the students' call, in the light of which the supreme court decided to validate the Seventh Ballot.

The election process, which transcended the traditional bipartisan election dynamics, produced a heterogeneous constituent body whereby outsider interests – including the ADM-19 (representing the former guerrilla group M-19) and various civic groups – gained representation. Participatory democracy loomed large on the ANC's agenda. Many contend that the Colombian Constitution of 1991 is one of the most ambitious projects of modern constitutionalism, providing an exceptionally wide range of participatory devices. However, the participatory euphoria and inclusive spirit dampened when the ANC concluded that the mandate of congress's sitting legislators would have to be revoked to prevent counter-reform. It was feared that incumbent legislators would try to neutralize most of the newly adopted institutions when developing the legislation to regulate them. Unsurprisingly, most people in congress opposed the claim for early elections, especially the liberal faction that controlled a majority of seats in congress but only 36 per cent of seats in the ANC. After negotiations between liberal leaders and the ANC's chairpersons, it was agreed that the celebration of early elections would be subject to a ban on ANC members to run for office. This agreement, which disqualified the opposition's most prestigious candidates, facilitated the triumph of the traditional parties in the subsequent elections, securing them a resounding majority in congress, while the ADM-19 obtained less then 10 per cent of the seats. The legal development of the new constitution thus fell into the hands of the traditional political elites, while the renovating forces that had taken part in its design again saw themselves relegated to the margins of the political process. In 1994, congress passed Law 134 that regulates constitutional provisions concerning participation. Said law imposed a number of burdensome requirements for the practical application of the new participatory mechanisms, which according to the legislators were adopted in order to 'prevent their irresponsible and irrational use'.[3] Restrictive features introduced by Law 134 include excessively high signature and turnout requirements in recall procedures and the necessary intervention of congress in the process of citizen law-making by means of popular initiatives.

The above cases demonstrate that the adoption of MDD may constitute a mere declaration of goodwill rather than progressing genuine participatory democracy. On several occasions, in situations of institutional stress or imminent regime collapse, South American politicians have used the promise of increased participation as 'pressure relief valve' in order to de-escalate conflict and prevent regime collapse. Yet when it came the to institutional design of the newly adopted mechanisms, the same elites that professed support for participatory democracy often sought to minimize the risk that these mechanisms could practically implement by issuing restrictive legislation on the regulation of these mechanisms.

Institutional frameworks regulating MDD in South America

Direct democracy constitutes a broad category that incorporates different types of mechanisms, implying different levels of control that political actors may exercise over political decision-making.

The degree of control hinges on assignment of two abilities: Ability to (a) set a referendum's agenda by formulating the ballot proposal; and (b) trigger the referendum, i.e. the authority to actually submit the proposal to popular vote (Hug and Tsebelis 2002).

Depending on how these competences are distributed between the citizenry and formal political actors, a referendum can be allocated to one of three basic referendum types:

(1) **citizen-initiated** – in which an organized group of citizens formulates a ballot proposal to introduce a new piece of legislation, derogate an existing law, or revoke a representative's mandate, and the referendum vote is triggered by collection of a stipulated number of signatures;

(2) **government–initiated** – in which the competence to formulate the referendum question and to trigger the vote belongs to the formal political actors, i.e. either the executive, or a stipulated number of legislators, or the executive and legislative branch in cooperation;

(3) **mandatory** – which must be held in situations or on issues explicitly stipulated by the constitution. Here, the ballot question is determined by the formal political actors who wish to alter the legislative status quo, while the convocation of the vote is constitutionally mandatory, i.e. the referendum is triggered automatically.

The first type shifts control over political decision-making from formal political actors to the citizenry. Given that these referendums are triggered by the citizens, i.e. 'from below', they are commonly referred to as 'bottom-up MDD'. Mechanisms belonging to this category are considered appropriate to foster different aspects of democratic quality such as participation (Beetham 2004), accountability (Setälä 2006; Breuer 2007) and consensus (Linder 1998). Subtypes in this category are the popular initiative, the derogative referendum and the recall.

A participatory institution that is frequently miscategorized as a bottom-up MDD is the instrument referred to in several Latin American constitutions as *iniciativa popular legislativa*. It constitutes citizens' rights to propose law projects to congress, which is obliged to proceed on these proposals, provided that they are endorsed by a specified number of citizen signatures. However, the decision to accept, reject or convoke a referendum on the project rests with the legislature. Rather than a tool of citizen political decision-making, this instrument is considered as an instrument of agenda control and has therefore been judged as less effective for the exercise of vertical political control (Altman 2010).

By contrast, the convocation of government-initiated referendums and mandatory referendums is controlled 'from above' by political elites, which is why they are referred to as 'top-down' MDD. These mechanisms largely retain control over political decision-making in the hands of the political establishment. Critics of these instruments emphasize that they leave ample room for manipulation by governments who wish to obtain additional legitimacy for their policies, often bypassing parliamentary deliberation, existing laws and constitutional rules (e.g. Gross and Kaufmann 2002). This aspect has led to concern that in the context of presidential systems, top-down MDD can contribute to 'delegative democracy' (O'Donnell 1996), i.e. a variant type of democratic regime in which the executive is only insufficiently subjected to horizontal checks and balances.

As if to confirm this concern, top-down MDD are dominant in South American legislation on direct democracy. All South American constitutions currently in force provide for this type, with the Uruguayan constitution being the only one that forecloses the government from triggering a referendum vote. Bottom-up MDD, by contrast, are absent in four of the ten South American constitutions (Argentina, Brazil, Chile and Paraguay) under study here. It should be noted that this contrast was even more pronounced prior to what has already been referred to as the 'new wave' of constitutional reform in the Andes (Cameron 2010).[4]

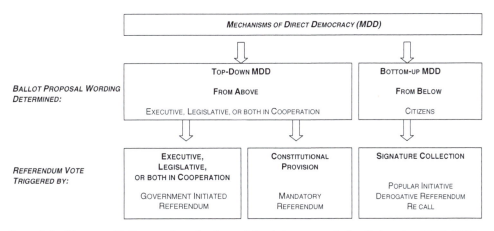

Figure 3.1 New constitutions and mechanisms of direct democracy in South America, 1978–2010

Table 3.2 Provisions for MDD in South American constitutions

	Constitutional provisions for MDD initiated from below			Constitutional provisions for MDD initiated from above	
	Popular initiative	Derogative referendum	Recall	Government-initiated referendum	Mandatory referendum
Argentina 1994				Art. 40	
Bolivia 2009	Arts. 11, 162 411,		Arts. 11, 157, 170, 240	Art. 298	Arts. 257, 411
Brazil 1988				Art. 49	
Chile 1980					Art. 117
Colombia 1991	Arts. 40, 103, 378	Arts. 40, 103, 170	Arts. 40, 13	Arts 103, 378	
Ecuador 2008	Arts. 61, 441		Arts. 61, 105	Art. 441	Arts. 420, 442
Paraguay 1992				Arts. 121, 122	Art. 290
Peru 1993	Arts. 31, 206		Art. 31	Art. 206	
Uruguay 1967	Art. 331	Art. 79			Art. 331
Venezuela 1999	Art. 71	Arts. 73, 74	Art. 72	Arts. 71, 73	Arts. 344, 345

Practical applications of MDD in South America

Looking at South America's empirical experience with direct democracy, the dominance of top-down MDD becomes even more evident. Out of 38 national level direct democratic events that took place between 1978 and 2009, 12 were mandatory referendums and 16 were government-initiated procedures, which in the majority of cases were triggered by the executive branch of government. Only ten events resulted from citizen initiatives, eight of which took place in Uruguay, thus making it the sole Latin American country that consistently uses bottom-up MDD.

Direct democracy in South America – Citizen participation or plebiscitary authoritarianism in participatory disguise?

Rather than contributing to citizen empowerment, adoption of MDD in South America served primarily the purposes of political elites. Notwithstanding this conclusion, however, regionally, direct appeals to the citizenry appear to be increasingly popular. On various occasions, South American governments have tried to use the majoritarian tool of the referendum as a shortcut to the often cumbersome decision-making processes of liberal deliberative democracy. However, they have not always been successful in these endeavours. Next, I present two country cases to illustrate this contention.

Venezuela

Achieving power in 1999, Venezuelan President Hugo Chávez repeatedly resorted to the referendum to consolidate his political regime termed 'participative and protagonist democracy'. This concept prizes popular sovereignty over liberal norms (Coppedge 2003), and combines a democratic mandate with populist socialism and efforts to concentrate power in the executive. The presidential election of 1998 that brought Chávez into office was the culmination of a prolonged process of party system decay. During the 1960s and 1970s, the country enjoyed a reputation as one of the most stable democracies in the developing world. During the 1980s and 1990s, however, economic decline induced grave social changes that, combined with government corruption, led to increasing disaffection of voters with the traditional social democratic AD and the Christian democratic COPEI and finally provoked the collapse of the traditional bipolar party system in 1998 (McCoy and Myers 2004). Chávez's anti-establishment platform reflected the popular sentiment of the moment and secured him a landslide victory with 56 per cent of the vote in the presidential elections of 1998. However, anti-Chávez forces still controlled two-thirds of seats in the National Assembly, which enabled them to obstruct the most radical reforms of the presidential agenda. Responding to this obstacle, Chávez scheduled two nationwide referendums for July 1999 to establish and select the members of a National Constitutional Assembly (ANC). The ANC was created when the referendum on its convocation passed with a 92.37 per cent 'yes' vote, with the pro-Chávez Polo Patriotico winning 95 per cent of the seats (Coppedge 2003). The Constitution of 1999, drafted by the ANC, considerably expanded citizen participation rights, introducing mandatory and facultative referendums, citizen initiatives and national level recall. At the same time, however, it also concentrated power in the executive branch by introducing features such as the creation of a unicameral National Assembly (AN) with limited oversight over presidential decision-making, increase of the presidential term from five to six years with the possibility of immediate re-election, and presidential power to dissolve the National Assembly.

In 2004, Venezuela saw the region's first and so far only vote to recall a presidential mandate. In October 2003, the Coordinadora Democrática, an organization comprising opposition parties and non-governmental organizations, organized a petition-drive requesting the vote on the revocation of Chávez's mandate. Following an intense campaign of which the highly polarized dynamics mobilized large parts of the electorate, on 15 August Chávez's mandate was reaffirmed with 59 per cent of votes. The process and outcome of the vote were evaluated to be controversial. While the Organization of American States (OAS), which observed the vote, endorsed the result, the political opposition and other international observers denounced the vote as fraudulent. Claims of manipulation were levelled mainly against the government-friendly National Electoral Council (CNE), which was accused of having created unequal opportunities for the contending sides and whose restrictive conditions did not allow for an objective monitoring of the electoral process by independent observers.[5] Another

Table 3.3 Direct democratic events in South America by type, 1980–2009

Type of MDD	Subtype	Event	Total
From Above	Mandatory Referendum	Bolivia Jan. 2009 Brazil April 1993 Chile Oct. 1988 Chile June 1989 Uruguay Aug. 1994 Uruguay Dec. 1996 Uruguay Oct. 1999 Uruguay Oct. 1999 Venezuela April 1999 Venezuela Dec. 1999 Venezuela Dec. 2007 Venezuela Feb. 2009	12
	Government Initiated Referendum	Argentina Nov. 1984 Bolivia July 2004 Bolivia Aug 2008* Brazil Oct. 2005 Chile Sept. 1980 Colombia Dec. 1990 Colombia Oct. 2003 Ecuador June 1986 Ecuador Aug. 1994 Ecuador Nov. 1995 Ecuador May 1997 Ecuador Nov. 2006 Ecuador Apr. 2007 Ecuador Sept. 2008 Peru Oct. 1993 Venezuela Dec. 2000	16
From Below	Popular Initiative	Colombia Mar. 1990 Uruguay Nov. 1989 Uruguay Nov. 1994 Uruguay Nov. 1994 Uruguay Oct. 2004 Uruguay Oct. 2009	6
	Derogative Referendum	Uruguay Apr. 1989 Uruguay Dec. 1992 Uruguay Dec. 2003	3
	Recall	Venezuela Aug. 2004	1
			38

* In August 2008, Bolivia saw a national confidence vote on President Morales, the vice-president, and the departmental governors. Although this event has frequently been referred to as a recall, it was in fact a government-initiated procedure, given that its convocation was not triggered by signature collection but by a congressional majority vote.

highly critical issue in the context of the recall referendum was the release of the so-called Tascón List. Prepared by a deputy to the National Assembly, Luis Tascón, the list gave the names of citizens who had signed the recall petition. There is ample evidence that these data were subsequently used to deny jobs and government services to opposition supporters (Jatar 2006).

In view of this, in November 2005, six opposition parties announced their boycott of the upcoming legislative elections. The opposition's pull-out was prompted by an audit of electronic voting machines, watched by international observers, which produced evidence that a specific combination of voting machines and fingerprinting devices at polling stations threatened the secrecy of the vote. In what has been interpreted as a lack of motivation to participate in uncompetitive elections, on 4 December, only 25 per cent of Venezuelans turned out to vote. The polls produced an Assembly in which Chávez's Fifth Republic Movement (MVR) controlled 114 seats out of 167 with the remaining seats split among government-allied parties. With the Supreme Tribunal of Justice (TSJ) and the CNE already controlled by Chávez supporters, this clean sweep in the AN removed the last remaining institutional check on the executive. However, in stark contrast to the 2005 legislative elections, in the presidential elections of 2006, 75 per cent of voters turned out to provide an unequivocal electoral endorsement for Chávez, with 61 per cent over 31 per cent for his opponent – the single, unified opposition candidate Manuel Rosales. Motivated by this electoral success, in August 2007 Chávez announced the holding of a referendum to reform the 1999 Constitution, which according to him was imperative to accelerate the transformation from the state model of 'participative and protagonist democracy' to the proclaimed new model of 'socialism of the 21st Century'. The reform package, elaborated by a confidential president-appointed committee and hastily rubber-stamped by the National Assembly, was released to the public only one month prior to the referendum (López Maya 2010). It consisted of 69 amendments to the constitution's 350 articles, implying a further radical concentration of power in the executive. Most importantly, the reform package sought to increase the presidential term from six to seven years and eliminate term limits entirely. With the CNE in the hands of the government, and state-run media giving almost no coverage to the no-campaign, the referendum was largely expected to be a foregone conclusion. However, in the referendum held on 2 December, 51 per cent of participating voters rejected the reform. While the government quickly admitted defeat, Chávez also made it clear that he would not take no for an answer. Speaking at a televised news conference alongside armed forces chiefs on 5 December, he warned the opposition not to provoke the military, and announced plans to resubmit the constitutional reform to referendum in 'the same or a transformed, simplified form'.[6] In fact, following the referendum defeat, most of the rejected measures were implemented via presidential decree, which was facilitated by the AN's approval of an 'enabling-law' bill granting the president the power to rule by decree in important issue areas for the duration of 18 months (López Maya 2010).

As for the question of term limits and re-election, in 2009 the executive instructed the AN to repropose the respective constitutional amendment. The ballot proposal's cumbersome wording carefully avoided mention of the issue of indefinite re-election. Instead voters were asked, in barely intelligible terms, whether or not they approved of 'expanding people's rights', by reforming five articles of the constitution. Following a massive campaign that involved the mobilization of the entire government apparatus and a brazen use of public resources (López Maya 2010), in February 2009 the reform was approved by 55 per cent of voters.

Colombia

In 2002, Alvaro Uribe obtained the first one-round victory in presidential elections since the introduction of the two-round run-off system in Colombia in 1991. Uribe had campaigned on an anti-corruption ticket, which gained him enormous popularity. One of his campaign promises was to submit a referendum proposal on constitutional reform to congress. Although the Colombian constitution does not prescribe ratification of constitutional amendments by a mandatory referendum, the president can try to abbreviate the lengthy ratification procedure by submitting a referendum proposal on constitutional reform to congress, which needs to approve it with an absolute majority in both chambers. To understand why Uribe chose to promote the reform via referendum despite having a broad support base in congress, one needs to take a closer look at his reform proposal. Many of the proposal's measures were directed at the abolition of privileges of Colombian legislators and the suppression of traditional 'pork barrel' and vote-buying practices. The issue that met with strongest resistance in the legislature was the merger of the bicameral congress into a unicameral body, involving the reduction of legislative seats by 40 per cent and the convocation of early elections. This proposal was criticized as an attempt to eliminate party mediation through a bicameral congress and a blueprint for a highly authoritarian presidency. Upon his inauguration in August 2002, Uribe submitted the referendum bill to congress. Initially, Uribe showed an intransigent posture towards the legislature, stating that the bill was non-negotiable; and his interior minister, Fernando Londoño, the referendum's main architect, even threatened congress with dissolution should it obstruct the bill's passage.[7] In view of the notoriously opportunistic allegiances of Colombian legislator's, however, Uribe was anxious to have legislative proceedings on his bill concluded before congress's winter recess in December and, as time grew short, he gradually adopted a more conciliatory attitude. The negotiated bill, finally approved by congress, contained significant concessions on behalf of the executive, such as the preservation of bicameralism, the agreement to reduce the number of legislators by 20 per cent instead of 40 per cent, and renunciation from the demand of early legislative elections. To promote participation, Uribe opted to capitalize on his popularity and turn the referendum into a vote of confidence in his government, arguing that a failure of the referendum would severely affect his ability to govern. However, despite the government's massive investment of resources in the referendum campaign, in the referendum vote only one of the 15 proposed reform measures achieved the minimum turnout of 6.3 million votes. In reaction, Uribe filed a claim with the CNE asking to purge the electoral roll after the publication of the results, contending that approximately 10 per cent of voting cards had been issued to persons who were either dead or ineligible to vote.[8] However, the president's hopes to reverse the referendum result through a recalculation of the electoral denominator were disappointed when the CNE declined his claim and officially confirmed the failure of the remaining 14 questions, leaving Uribe no choice but to negotiate a significantly trimmed-down version of his original proposal with the legislature.

Despite the referendum's failure, Uribe continued to enjoy high popular approval and obtained a sweeping re-election victory in 2006 after the legislature had earlier agreed to lift a constitutional ban on a second consecutive term. Towards the middle of his second term, Uribe began to push for yet another constitutional reform, which should allow him to run for a third term in 2010. In April 2008, a citizen committee headed by the President's former campaign manager, Giraldo Hurtado, registered a petition drive for holding a referendum on the constitutional article, which prohibits a second consecutive presidential re-election. According to the complicated wording of the question, which citizens were asked to sign, Uribe could only have sought re-election after a four-year gap in 2014. Having complied with the signature threshold of 1.4 million signatures, the petition was presented to congress, which needs to pass the bill that convokes the referendum. While the lower chamber approved the bill in its original wording, the senate chose to reword the ballot question so as to facilitate Uribe's candidacy in the 2010 presidential elections. In this context, several opposition legislators denounced that government officials had offered political favours to congress members in exchange for their votes on the altered referendum bill. However, before a referendum can be held, the Colombian Constitutional Court must review both its text and the procedures by which it was passed. In one of the most awaited rulings of Colombia's recent history, in February 2010 the constitutional court concluded that a referendum allowing Uribe to run for a third term violated the spirit of the constitution. The court furthermore judged that legislative proceedings on the referendum bill had been fraught with irregularities and 'substantial violations to demoratic principles'.

As the cases of Venezuela and Colombia show, while MDD's potential to contribute to delegative democracy in the context of presidential systems cannot be summarily dismissed, it needs both revision and contextualization. In both cases, first, presidents whose government style – albeit different ideological persuasions – is considered personalistic and neo-populist (Dugas 2003; Ellner 2003) and whose concept of 'direct democracy' relies almost exclusively on state patronized citizen participation, attempted to push their agenda by making a debatable use of MDD. Second, presidential agendas intended a considerable concentration of power in the executive, implying the weakening of democratic checks and balances. While Venezuela's Chávez was largely successful in this endeavour, given that horizontal control of the executive by independent state institutions had previously been eroded, his Colombian counterpart, Uribe, saw his ambitions subjected to and, ultimately, frustrated by legislative opposition and judicial oversight.

Having discussed the downside aspects of MDD in South America brought forward by critics, the next section of this chapter will explore some of the upside aspects of participation by MDD, as sustained by their supporters.

MDD in South America – Effective tools of citizen control over politics?

It is often contended that direct democracy, especially bottom-up MDD, is positively associated with various democracy-enhancing features, including vertical control and government accountability, and increased citizens' political participation and knowledge. My contention is that this argument needs to be fine-tuned and contextualized. For example, bottom-up MDD are not immune to instrumentalization and manipulation by governing authorities, as illustrated in the cases of Venezuela and Colombia. In addition, when bottom-up MDD implementation results from authentic citizen effort and leads to organized citizen groups' success in achieving political goals, we cannot assume that this is exclusively due to the virtuous properties of bottom-up MDD, as other – external – factors may be as important. Next, I present two country studies to illustrate this contention.

Uruguay

In terms of citizen participation, Uruguay represents an outlier in the region insofar as it is the only South American country that regularly applies bottom-up MDD. Different to other South American countries, direct democracy did not emerge as a result of the third wave of democracy. Rather, it is linked to the Uruguayan process of state-building and institutionalization of democratic norms. Early in the twentieth century, Uruguay imported some elements of the Swiss political milieu, including the collegiate executive and use of top-down MDD. It is important to note, here, that direct democracy was not adopted to meet the demands for increased participation of concrete societal groups, but as the result of partisan interests in the context of constitutional evolution (Altman 2008). More precisely, in cases where the legislature opposed executive projects of constitutional reform, direct democracy offered an opportunity for the executive to transfer the political stalemate to the arena of the citizenry (Lissidini 1998). In fact, and very similar to the post-third-wave experiences of the region's other countries, early expansions of direct democratic rights in Uruguay occurred simultaneously with executive concentration of power.

Bottom-up MDD were first incorporated into the constitution in 1967 and only began to be used on a regular basis after democratic restoration in 1985. Citizen organizations repeatedly succeeded in using these tools to prevent the state's withdrawal from the provision of public goods in the process of neoliberal restructuring. Examples are the 1992 derogative referendum, which overturned a law to privatize the national airline, telecommunication and energy companies, and a 2004 constitutional initiative enshrining free access to drinking water. A distinctive feature of bottom-up MDD use in Uruguay is that the passage of ballot measures largely depends on the mobilization efforts of political parties and that voters' choices are heavily conditioned by the suggestions of their party leaders. That is, rather than civil society organizing to bypass distrusted political leaders, in Uruguay the use of citizen initiatives is linked to a degree of party loyalty that is unparalleled in the region (Altman 2002).

Brazil

Besides the top-down forms of MDD, the Brazilian Constitution of 1988 provides for bottom-up participation on the national level only in the semi-direct form of the legislative popular initiative. As mentioned earlier, this tool is generally associated with minor potential for citizen control over the political process, since legislators are not obliged to accept and legislate on citizen-proposed measures. Furthermore, in the Brazilian case, the practical application of this mechanism is restrained by the requirement that a citizen law project needs to be endorsed by signatures of 1 per cent of the national electorate, distributed throughout at least five states, with minimum 0.3 per cent of the voters in each of them. Despite this exigent institutional setting, in 2010 the country saw a successful citizen campaign, unprecedented in scope and impact.

In May 2008, the Brazilian Movement against Electoral Corruption (MCCE) launched a campaign to improve the profile of candidates running for legislative office. The Brazilian Congress has a general reputation of being particularly unruly and corrupt (Geddes and Ribeiro 1992).[9] Part of the reason is that the Brazilian Constitution grants an extraordinary degree of immunity to congress members which, unlike elsewhere, extends to capital crimes committed outside a parliamentarian's official duties. Numerous reform efforts in this field were nullified by a strong legislative *esprit de corps*.

Under the tag line 'A vote has no price, it has consequences', the MCCE's *Ficha Limpa* (clean slate) bill proposed to tighten the criteria for legislative eligibility. Specifically, the bill sought to bar from election persons previously convicted or with pending court proceedings for specific crimes such as murder, drug trafficking, misuse of public funds and vote buying. Initially, even supporters of the campaign were pessimistic about its chances of success. On one hand, in absence of government support for initiative campaign financing and logistics in Brazil, it seemed unlikely that promoters would be able to attract the necessary 1.3 million signatures (equivalent to 1 per cent of the national electorate). Then again, considering that an estimated 25 per cent of sitting legislators were facing ineligibility under the new law,[10] obtaining the legislative approval necessary for the bill's passage appeared to be a scenario akin to turkeys voting for Christmas. Initially, the signature collection campaign made slow progress. However, the project's fate changed once its promoters decided to take the campaign to the Internet. As an increasing number of sympathizers began to follow the campaign on social network sites such as Facebook, Twitter and Orkut, the process of signature collection gained pace,[11] and in December 2009 the promoters submitted 1.5 million signatures to the Chamber of Deputies. In the run-up to the bill's voting in congress in April 2010, the promoters continued to push online-mobilization. In the first ten days of April, more than 2,000,000 citizens signed an online petition calling for the *Ficha Limpa* law to be passed, and 40,000 followed the campaigners' call to flood legislators' inboxes and voicemails with messages to remind them of their democratic duties. Most importantly, however, online-organized campaign events (e.g. a symbolic clean-up with brooms and buckets performed by activists outside the national congress) attracted coverage by major television channels and newspapers.[12] As the Internet campaign spilled over into traditional media, the bill's momentum became irreversible and in June 2010 the law was promulgated by President Lula da Silva after having been unanimously approved by congress.

In both of the above cases, South American citizens effectively used participatory institutions to exercise vertical control over their representatives and reverse unwanted policies. However, their success was crucially conditioned by non-institutional, external factors. In Uruguay, the tranquil and routine use of bottom-up MDD is clearly related to the country's long-institutionalized direct democratic practice and extraordinarily high levels of party loyalty. The sustained record of political elites in successfully employing MDD to promote their agenda, and the assuredness of party leaders that voters will follow their parties' recommendations when faced with a ballot choice, has contributed to the adoption of bottom-up MDD as a routine tool in the country's political decision-making process. Meanwhile, in Brazil, the success of the *Ficha Limpa* campaign can be attributed to the Internet's increasing role in mobilizing and vocalizing public interest, rather than to the institutional properties of the legislative popular initiative, which is regarded a bland weapon of citizen control. In the light of these findings, the argument on the democracy-enhancing virtues of bottom-up MDD clearly needs to be qualified.

Conclusions

Focusing on the adoption and empirical implementation of MDD, this chapter set out to discuss the background of participatory reforms carried out throughout South America following the third wave of democracy, and to provide an assessment of their impact on democratic consolidation and quality in the region.

The mixed record of positive and negative aspects that emerged from this analysis is interesting as it challenges some of the conventional wisdoms on citizen participation by direct democracy. The incorporation of participatory institutions in South American constitutions, following the region's redemocratization, raised hopes that increased citizen participation in the political process would help to overcome the elitist and socially exclusionary character of the outgoing military regimes. However, as this chapter has shown, the implementation of participatory reforms need not necessarily be motivated by the wish to empower citizens *vis-à-vis* the state. The South American experience demonstrates that the adoption of participatory institutions may constitute a mere declaration of will rather than reflecting a genuine participatory under-standing of democracy on behalf of political elites. On several occasions, South American politicians used the promise of increased participation as a preventive de-escalation strategy in situations of extreme institutional stress or imminent regime collapse. Such hidden agendas become evident when studying the legislative frameworks that regulate MDD in South America and the record of their empirical applications. The majority of direct democratic institutions found in South American belong to the category of top-down MDD, which reserve the facility to control the agenda of a referendum and trigger the popular vote to governing authorities. At the same time, bottom-up MDD, which allow citizens to shape the political agenda, reverse unwanted policies and remove irresponsive officials from office, are not only less often found in South American constitutions – they are also often regulated by restrictive legislation that renders their practical application difficult. As a consequence, direct democratic practice in South America has so far almost exclusively been dominated by the use of government-sponsored plebiscites.

This tendency has spurred scholarly concern, that the combination of presidential systems with participatory institutions may contribute to a delegative style of leadership that exploits the weakness of representative institutions, such as parties and legislatures, in order to enhance executive power. This concern intensified as, starting from the late 1990s, several countries of the Andean region shifted towards what has been labelled 'leftist neopopulism'. Growing citizen disaffection with the conventional vehicles of representative democracy led to the emergence of Hugo Chávez in Venezuela, Evo Morales in Bolivia, and Rafael Correa in Ecuador. They share the common idea of a participatory, direct form of democracy, which they portray as superior to representative democracy and its institutions. Indeed, the constitutional reforms promoted by these leaders combined the expansion of citizens' participatory rights with a considerable concentration of power in the executive. This aroused suspicions that what some welcome as a new wave of 'participatory democracy' in South America may in fact be a dangerous development towards plebiscitary authoritarianism. However, as the comparative analysis of the Venezuelan and the Colombian case shows, the problem does not rest with the adoption of participatory institutions per se, but rather with how they interact with the institutional set-up surrounding them.

Where independent state agencies retain the ability to subject the practical implementation of these institutions to robust scrutiny, as in the case of Colombia, this risk will be considerably lower than in situations where this ability has been eroded by executive control over other key constitutional bodies, as has been the case in Venezuela. As both cases show, even government-controlled MDD enable citizens to remain veto players in the political game and assert positions that oppose the agenda of governing authorities – independent electoral oversight provided (Altman 2010). Citizens may exercise this veto right actively by rejecting a government proposal at the ballot box, as in the Venezuelan constitutional referendum in 2007, or passively by abstaining to vote in a referendum, as in the Colombian constitutional referendum in 2003. This challenges Lijphart's supposition that 'when governments control the referendum, they will tend to use it only when they expect to win' (Lijphart 1984: 203).

South America has also seen several instances, although scarce, of citizens successfully using institutions of bottom-up participation to exercise control over their representatives. However, this success could only come about through the favourable interaction of these institutions with external factors. In Brazil, the success of a popularly driven bill on electoral corruption was facilitated by the expansion of the space for public debate through Internet technology, which increased civil society's ability to fulfil its watchdog function. Meanwhile, in Uruguay, a long history of direct democracy and high levels of party loyalty have contributed to the willingness of political elites to develop a positive attitude towards bottom-up MDD and adopt them as routine tools of political decision-making. That said, it would be a futile effort to formulate a simple categorical claim concerning the relation between the adoption of participatory institutions and democracy's prospective development in South America. Undisputedly, the promise of participation and enhanced democratic quality related to post-third-wave reforms has remained partially unfulfilled. Notwithstanding, the participatory institutions these reforms enshrined in South American constitutions are there to stay and will, by all signs, continue to play a significant role in future political decision-making in the region. Whether this will act to the benefit or detriment of democratic consolidation depends on the development of the institutional and non-institutional factors that interact with them. On the institutional side, the separation of powers and the stability and integration capacity of party systems appear to be the most critical aspects. As for non-institutional factors, the continued freedom of the press and increasing accessibility of alternative media are crucial for civil society's ability to mobilize citizens for the use of bottom-up institutions of participation and to monitor governments' use of top-down institutions of participation.

Notes

1 Constitution of 1993, Art 134.
2 Ibid., Art. 113.
3 Proyecto de Ley # 92 de 1992 – Senado de la República –, *Gaceta del Congreso* (23), Bogotá, año 1, ago.11, 1992, p. 10.
4 The Venezuelan Constitution of 1961 prescribed mandatory referendums for constitutional reforms (art. 246) but only knew a semi-direct form of the popular initiative allowing 20 citizens to present a legislative initiative to congress, which had to approve the project. The Bolivian Constitution of 1967 knew a similar form of the popular initiative; here, an unspecified number of citizens was entitled to present law projects to the legislative power (art. 71). In Ecuador, both the government-initiated referendum (art. 78) and the popular initiative were introduced by the Constitution of 1978. however, the latter mechanism remained inoperative since it was never regulated by law. The recall was only adopted by the Constitution of 1998.
5 European Union: 'Declaration by the Presidency on behalf of the European Union on the Presidential Revocatory Referendum in Venezuela', Brussels, August 2004.
6 BBC News: Chavez belittles opposition win. 6 December 2007. http://news.bbc.co.uk/2/hi/americas/ 7130347.stm (accessed 21 June 2010).
7 *Latin American Weekly Report*. Minister Says the State is Bankrupt. 15 October 2002.
8 *Latinnews Daily*. Uribe Tries to Reverse Referendum Result. 19 December 2003.
9 In 2007, the majority of respondents in a poll assessed their legislators as self-serving, and dishonest. Two in five assessed that democracy would be better off without congress (*The Economist*, 'Parliament or pigsty?', 8 February 2007).
10 *Le Monde*, 'Opération "fiches propres" au Brésil', 26 May 2010.
11 The campaign attracted 24,000 followers on Facebook and 10,000 on Twitter. More than 50,000 users downloaded the campaign video from YouTube, and between April and June 2010 on several occasions *Ficha Limpa* became the most cited issue of the week on Twitter Brazil.
12 AVAAZ Media: 'Avaaz activists clean up Congress with brooms buckets and soap.' http://www.avaaz. org/act/media.php?press_id=181 (accessed 16 June 2010).

References

Altman, David (2002) 'Popular Initiatives in Uruguay: Confidence Votes on Government or Political Loyalties?', *Electoral Studies*, 21, pp. 617–630.
—— (2008) 'Collegiate Executives and Direct Democracy in Switzerland and Uruguay: Similar Institutions, Opposite Political Goals, Distinct Result', *Swiss Political Science Review*, 14 (3), pp. 438–520.
—— (2010) 'Plebiscitos, referendos e iniciativas populares en América Latina', *Perfiles Latinoamericanos*, 18 (35), pp. 9–34.
Barczak, Monica (2001) 'Representation by Consultation? The Rise of Direct Democracy in Latin America', *Latin American Politics and Society*, 43 (3), pp. 37–60.
Beetham, David (2004) *Defining and Measuring Democracy*. London: Sage.
Beramendi, Virginia *et al.* eds (2008) *Direct Democracy: The International IDEA Handbook*. Stockholm: International IDEA.
Breuer, Anita (2007) 'Institutions of Direct Democracy and Accountability in Latin America's Presidential Democracies', *Democratization*, 14 (4), pp. 554–579.
—— (2008) 'The Problematic Relation Between Direct Democracy and Accountability in Latin America: Evidence from the Bolivian Case', *Bulletin of Latin American Research*, 27 (1), pp. 1–23.
—— (2009) 'The Use of Government Initiated Referendums in Latin America: Towards a Theory of Referendum Causes', *Revista de Ciencia Política*, 29 (1), pp. 23–55.
Coppedge, Michael (2003) 'Venezuela: Popular Sovereignty versus Liberal Democracy'. In *Constructing Democratic Governance in Latin America*, ed. J. Jorge Dominguez and M. Shifter. Baltimore, MD: John Hopkins University Press, pp. 165–192.
Cotler, Julio (1995) 'Political Parties and the Problems of Democratization in Peru'. In *Building Democratic Institutions. Party Systems in Latin America*, ed. S. Mainwaring and T. Scully. Stanford, CA: Stanford University Press, pp. 323–353.
Dugas, John C. (2003) 'The Emergence of Neopopulism in Colombia? The Case of Alvaro Uribe', *Third World Quarterly*, 24 (6), pp. 1117–1136.

Ellner, Steve (2003) 'The Contrasting Variants of the Populism of Hugo Chávez and Alberto Fujimori', *Journal of Latin American Studies*, 35 (1), pp. 139–162.

Geddes, Barbara and Artur Ribeiro Neto (1992) 'Institutional Sources of Corruption in Brazil', *Third World Quarterly*, 13 (4), pp. 641–661.

Grindle, Merilee S. (2000) *Audacious Reforms: Institutional Invention and Democracy in Latin America*. Baltimore, MD: Johns Hopkins University Press.

Gross, Andreas and Bruno Kaufmann (2002) 'IRI Europe Country Index on Citizen Lawmaking 2002'. In *Report on Design and Rating of the I&R Requirements and Practices of 32 European States*, ed. A. Gross and B. Kaufmann. Amsterdam: Initiative and Referendum Institute (IRI) Europe.

Hug, Simon and Georg Tsebelis (2002) 'Veto Players and Referendums around the World', *Journal of Theoretical Politics*, 16 (3), pp. 321–356.

Isaacs, Anita (1991) 'Problems of Democratic Consolidation in Ecuador', *Bulletin of Latin American Research*, 10 (2), pp. 221–238.

Jatar, Ana J. (2006) *Apartheid del siglo XXI: La informática al servicico de la discriminación política en Venezuela*. Carácas: SÙMATE.

Lijphart, Arend (1984) *Democracies: Patterns of Majoritarian and Consensus Government in Twenty-One Countries*. New Haven, CT: Yale University Press.

Linder, Wolf (1998) *Swiss Democracy*. Basingstoke: Macmillan.

Lissidini, Alicia (1998) 'La historia de los plebiscitos uruguayos durante el siglo XX: ni tan democráticos ni tan autoritarios', *Revista Uruguaya de Ciencias Sociales*, 23 (1–2), pp.195–217.

López Maya, Margarita (2010) *¿Qué nos dicen los resultados 'contradictorios' de los referendos de 2007 y 2009 sobre el uso de MDD en Venezuela?*. Paper presented at the 2nd Latin American and Carribbean Congress of Social Sciences. Latin American School of Social Scienes (FLACSO), Mexico City, 26–29 May.

Mainwaring, Scott and Frances Hagopian eds (2005) *The Third Wave of Democratization in Latin America*. Cambridge: Cambridge University Press.

McCoy, Jennifer and David Myers eds (2004) *The Unravelling of Representative Democracy in Venezuela*. Baltimore, MD: Johns Hopkins University Press.

Mainwaring, Scott and Timothy Scully eds (1995) *Building Democratic Institutions: Party Systems in Latin America*. Stanford, CA: Stanford University Press.

Maraví, Milagros (1998) 'El funcionamiento de las instituciones de la democracia directa en el Perú a partir de la constitución política de 1993', *Ius et Praxis*, pp. 135–147.

Negretto, Gabriel (2009) 'Paradojas de la Reforma Constitucional en América Latina', *Journal of Democracy* (Spanish Edition), 1 (1), pp. 38–54.

O'Donnell, Guillermo (1996) 'Delegative Democracy'. In *The Global Resurgence of Democracy*, ed. L. Diamond and M. Plattner. Baltimore, MD: Johns Hopkins University Press, pp. 55–69.

O'Donnell, G., P. Schmitter and L. Whitehead eds (1986) *Transitions from Authoritarian Rule: Latin America*. Baltimore, MD: Johns Hopkins University Press.

Pachano, Simon (2008) 'Democracia directa en Ecuador'. In *Democracia directa en América Latina*, ed. A. Lissidini and Y. Welp. Buenos Aires: Prometeo Libros, pp. 145–158.

Setälä, Maija (2006) 'On the Problems of Responsibility and Accountability in Referendums', *European Journal of Political Research*, 45 (5), pp. 701–723.

Shifter, Michael (1996) 'Tempering Expectations of Democracy'. In *Constructing Democratic Governance in Latin America*, ed. J.I. Domínguez and M. Shifter. Baltimore, MD, and London: Johns Hopkins University Press, pp. 3–10.

Smith, D. and C. Tolbert (2004) *Educated by Initiative. The Effects of Direct Democracy on Citizens and Political Organizations*. Ann Arbor: The University of Michigan Press.

Tuchlin Joseph S. and A. Selee (eds) (2004) *Decentralization and Democratic Governance in Latin America*. Woodrow Wilson Center Report on the Americas No. 12, Washington, DC , http://www.wilsoncenter.org/topics/pubs/ACF18E5.pdf.

Zovatto, Daniel and Jesús Orozco (eds) (2008) *Reforma política y electoral en América Latina 1978–2007*. Mexico, DF: IDEA Internacional.

4

Sub-Saharan Africa

Elke Zuern

Sub-Saharan Africa is a vast and incredibly diverse region with a population of roughly 800 million people living in 48 states. From 1990 to 2010, despite the great differences among regimes in the region, all but three (Eritrea, Somalia and Swaziland) held at least one election contested by more than one party (africanelections.tripod.com). This marks a significant shift, as prior decades saw only a small number of countries offering multiparty elections.[1] Coups, once a widespread mechanism for changing power, have decreased dramatically since 1990. But the mere holding of elections is not an indicator of the triumph of democracy. Of the 45 states that have held multiparty elections, just more than one-third have held two consecutive, reasonably free and fair legislative and presidential elections in the last decade.[2] These elections provide an easy indicator of a very basic requirement for democracy, but they neither signal democratic governance nor do they unilaterally create it. As states increasingly hold elections, incumbents are becoming more adept at employing subtle forms of manipulation that can be difficult to trace. Many ordinary citizens continue to perceive their governments as inaccessible and unresponsive to their enquiries, needs and demands.

Democracy is notoriously difficult to measure. There are two key reasons for this: disagreement over the very definition of democracy, and the related question of what indicators should be employed to measure it across countries and over time. A number of key questions follow: how thick or thin should the definition be? Is it possible to offer a single definition to apply to regimes across the globe? Minimalist (or thin) definitions of democracy are most amenable to measurement because they include the fewest requirements for a regime to be considered a democracy. It is easy to count, for example, the number of sub-Saharan African states that have held at least one multiparty election since 1990. As soon as we add the criteria of free and fair elections, a significant judgment is necessary to draw the line between elections that allowed opposition forces to campaign and opposition voters to vote with relative ease – and those where incumbents engaged in subtle and not-so-subtle tricks to reduce the prospects for opposition candidates. Generally, the more minimalist the definition of democracy, the easier it is to measure, but the less it actually tells us about citizens' experiences and governments' responsiveness and accountability.

For this reason, most measures of democracy include additional criteria beyond the simple holding of elections in which multiple parties participate. As additional criteria are added, analysts are forced to prioritize the most important aspects of democracy while casting aside factors presumed to be of lesser immediate relevance. This requires a highly subjective assessment of what democracy should be, which is dependent upon the model of success used as a template. Since states in Western Europe and the United States were the first to take significant steps to develop national representative systems of rule, in which leaders were elected by some subset of the citizenry, these states have most often formed the basis for templates of modern democracy. Ironically, as the two largest colonial powers on the African continent (Great Britain and France) made their own transitions to democracy in the late 1800s, they also colonized African territories. For those areas under colonial rule, democracy – understood as an expression of self-rule – was clearly impossible. Most sub-Saharan African countries did not receive independence until the 1960s, some only decades later, significantly delaying their opportunities to experiment with their own ideals of democracy.

Models of democracy and democratization have followed the historical development of multiparty systems and the rise of powerful states. Western European states and the United States have long served as templates for democracy. The academic literature investigating contemporary democratization developed in response to a growing trend towards more democratic rule, beginning in the 1970s in Southern Europe and Latin America. As a result, while the ideal of democracy tends to be based on the European and American experience, the model for late twentieth century transitions was largely drawn from Latin American, and later from Eastern European, experiences. It is unsurprising that African states have not neatly followed either the models of Western democracy or of post-authoritarian democratization. Historically, the differences are obvious. In comparison to other world regions, sub-Saharan African states were subject to late colonialism. The continent was carved up by the European powers towards the end of the nineteenth century, a time at which European methods of colonial rule had been developed and tested elsewhere and technical advances gave Europeans seemingly unstoppable military power. Colonial rule on the African continent was more comprehensive than that seen in most of Asia and the Middle East. It was also much shorter than that in most Latin American states, so it did not go so far as to create new societies in the image of European states (Young 1994). When most Africans achieved independence after less than a century of colonial rule, they inherited the extractive, repressive, divisive state apparatus that had been developed as the antithesis of the democratic state by the colonial powers.

In order to create new democracies in sub-Saharan Africa, both the state and imported ideals of democracy required decolonization. In order to create models of democracy that address local challenges and capture citizens' aspirations, African theorists have moved beyond notions of liberal democracy developed in the West to argue for a broader concept of liberation. Those actively seeking to create democratic systems on the ground have worked to build new – and redesign existing – formal and informal institutions. These processes understandably play out quite differently across the wide diversity of states on the continent. In order to demonstrate both the range and the similarities of the obstacles facing African states, three quite different regimes are briefly investigated in this chapter: Mali, South Africa and Ghana. Together, the lessons drawn both from the *ideal* and the *practice* of democracy offer an important corrective to common measures and understandings of democracy in the West.

Decolonizing democracy

To decolonize democracy (Lucero 2010), both the process of change and the end goal need to be re-evaluated. Much of the comparative literature on democratization has implicitly relied upon a presumed sequence of processes necessary for democratic development (Collier and Levitsky 1997). The assumption that different states undergoing regime change would follow similar steps echoes the notion of a singular form of 'progress' central to modernization theory. By breaking discussions of democracy into key components – such as reasonably free and fair multiparty elections; basic civil liberties including speech, assembly and association; and the power of elected governments to govern (Strom 2008) – and accepting that different states will not pursue each in the same order, theorists have moved away from the presumption of 'democracy by numbers'. Procedural elements of democracy such as multiparty elections, a free press and an independent judiciary offer an important measure of the potential for responsive governance. But, any analysis that focuses solely on formal procedures, excludes the crucial, but difficult to measure, experiences of ordinary people in their attempts to access government services and hold their leaders to account. Investigations that include substantive elements, which consider the responsiveness of government institutions and the empowerment of citizens across ethnic, racial, gender, class and other lines, offer the potential to better reflect the lived experiences of ordinary people.

This is a tall order and one that most popular measures do not follow. The most frequently cited index of democracy is actually a measure of freedom constructed by US-based Freedom House (www.freedomhouse.org), which closely reflects the aspirations of US foreign policy (Giannone 2010). The indicators measure civil and political rights in order to construct a liberal democratic framework that includes economic freedoms within civil rights but excludes socio-economic rights. Equality, an ideal underlined by famed analysts of American democracy from Alexis de Tocqueville (1853, 2003) to Robert Dahl (1961), has completely disappeared from the ranking system, and *freedoms* – largely from state intervention – predominate. On this model, the European states as well as Australia, New Zealand, Canada and the US consistently receive the highest scores. Though a large number of the world's regimes do deserve low scores on any measure of democracy, the overall picture of rankings presented by Freedom House clearly rewards those regimes that most closely follow the American ideal of liberal democracy.

Other measures of democracy offer some additional criteria for measurement. The UK-based Economist Democracy Index (www.eiu.com) strives to offer a broader assessment of democracy by moving away from a simple equation between freedoms and democracy. Aside from basic civil and political rights, it includes: the functioning of government, political culture and participation (Kekic 2007). Scores for participation, interestingly, pull down a number of otherwise highly ranked democracies, both globally and on the African continent. The index is still, however, modelled on an ideal of liberal democracy and economic freedoms rather than focusing on measures of equality. For the African continent, the Ibrahim Index offers an interesting counter-point by measuring good governance via four indicators that include: safety and the rule of law, participation and human rights, sustainable economic opportunity and human development. The addition of human development raises the score for countries not as highly ranked on other indicators of democracy such as the Seychelles and the north African states, and drags down others such as Benin, Senegal and Mali (www.moibrahimfoundation.org). The unavoidable shortcoming of each of these indicators is that they work with their own particular biases and demonstrate the degree to which regimes approximate the ideals set by those who design the measures.

No global or regional index of democracy can be designed to measure the degree to which individual democracies meet the ideals of governance set by their own population. But, if democracy is understood as 'rule by the people', both the practice and the design of governance must address each society's particular needs. Koelble and Lipuma (2008: 7) argue: 'The analytical choice is this: if the peoples across the postcolony must necessarily produce inflected forms of democracy that depart from the EuroAmerican model, then political science can either judge their democratic efforts as inherently deficient or measure their democracy in respect to their attainment of their versions of these critical values.' For many post-colonial states, this begins by distinguishing their trajectory from that of their former colonizers. European states formed largely through warfare and competition among European rivals. In Africa, on the other hand, the boundaries of almost all present-day states were drawn by former colonial powers with little regard for existing political units. African colonial states were defined by territory and presumed resources for extraction, rather than any concern for the indigenous construction of nations. The challenge of building post-colonial nations has presented a significant obstacle to the development of united state apparatuses able to effectively govern and offer services to all parts of their territory. State weaknesses provide an additional challenge to the development of democracy.

The quest for democracy in sub-Saharan Africa therefore requires societies to address the negative legacies of both colonial and many post-colonial regimes. On the continent, many have referred to the quest for democracy not merely as a process of democratization but as a process of liberation (Ekeh 1997; Osaghae 2005). The first struggle for liberation was against colonial rule, but while independence brought an end to direct European political control, in most countries it did not lead to the creation of democratic societies. Both political and economic oppression continued under African leaders, often maintained in power through the support of foreign allies and donors. The movement for a 'second liberation', beginning in the late 1980s and spreading across much of the continent, has been understood by most Western analysts as a wave of democratization, but this is only part of the struggle. This second quest for liberation parallels earlier demands for independence in important respects: popular agitation was in both cases focused on the expansion of political rights and the improvement of socio-economic conditions and included demands that Africans be free to define their own future without external interference or control (Zuern 2009). Measures of democratization that exclusively look to multiparty elections and formal guarantees of political and civil rights as measures of success fail to comprehend the depth of the ideal of liberation.

Proponents of a second liberation see democracy and basic socio-economic rights as mutually dependent, each unobtainable without the other. They also take an additional step to address broader concerns of independence. As Osaghae (2005: 4) argues 'liberation was used to describe the [re]assertion of [African] initiative and authenticity to rid the state, society and economy of foreign domination and psychological fixation or colonial mentality.' This notion of liberation therefore includes a psychological process of decolonization and a struggle to bring local knowledge to the fore to empower formerly colonized societies (Fanon 1961; Biko 1978; Okere et al. 2005). The term democratization fails to capture the full essence of this hoped for transformation as it offers liberal democracy as its goal. In contrast, liberation seeks a more substantive form of democracy that not only grants freedoms to individuals but also works to mitigate stark inequalities in economic and political power. Afrobarometer surveys in 2005 and 2006 asked people in 18 African countries[3]: 'What if anything does democracy mean to you?' (afrobarometer.org). Their responses demonstrate the importance that ordinary people ascribe to both civil liberties and norms of equality and justice in their definitions of democracy. While the most cited understanding of democracy includes civil liberties, the second most common were measures of equality and justice. In Benin, the second most popular meaning of democracy was national independence. In three other countries (Botswana, Mozambique and Uganda) peace and unity were the second most popular response. In five countries (Lesotho, Namibia, Senegal, South Africa and Zimbabwe) at least one-fifth of respondents chose equality and social/economic development as key to democracy. In each case, people's understandings of what democracy should entail went beyond liberal ideals. The meanings that people attach to democracy are clearly tied to the political, social and economic history of their respective countries.

In the early 1990s, Claude Ake (1993: 244) presciently argued:

> The process towards democracy must be shaped by the singular reality that those whose democratic participation is at issue are the ordinary people of Africa … So long as this fact is kept steadily in focus, democracy will evolve in ways that will enhance its meaning … But it will be quite different from the contemporary version of liberal democracy, indeed, different

enough to elicit suspicion and even hostility from the international community that currently support African democratization. If, however, African democracy follows the line of least resistance to Western liberalism, it will achieve only the democracy of alienation.

Ake's warning regarding the alienating potential of systems based on Western liberalism is crucial to understanding democracy's overall success. If the pursuit of democracy is viewed by many as a process of liberation, external pressure to adopt a particular set of institutions and policies will dramatically undermine, and delegitimize, the entire process. While the emphasis in African quests for liberation and democratization is, as in liberal democracy, on basic freedoms, it also includes socio-economic rights and the autonomy to create locally defined systems of rule.

The pursuit of democracy and liberation

African experiences in the quest for a second liberation differed fundamentally from the Latin American transitions that preceded them. Unlike in much of Latin America (O'Donnell and Schmitter 1986), the shift to inclusive multiparty elections in Africa did not occur through elite pacts (although South Africa is a partial exception). The majority of African transitions occurred only after sustained popular protest (Bratton and van de Walle 1997). This protest was most often driven by economic hardship, but as governments failed to effectively respond to the causes of that hardship, protesters increasingly demanded political reform and democratic govern-ance. Analysts such as Bratton and van de Walle, and many others after them, have pointed to the economic origins of protest action, but have not fully considered its significance for the kind of democracy that ordinary Africans were demanding. After the end of the Cold War, expectations around the world were high for the triumph of democracy, but the enthusiasm with which many embraced the end of communist rule seemed to leave little room for considering if liberal democracy would be the best model for a wide diversity of post-colonial states and societies (see, for example, Bratton et al. 2005).

At the same time, external donors led by the International Monetary Fund (IMF) and the World Bank (WB) required economic liberalization in order to receive the loans that most sub-Saharan African countries needed to stay afloat. The WB's good governance agenda prescribed a minimal state that balanced its budgets, reduced subsidies and liberalized trade. As Abrahamsen (2000: 51) has persuasively argued: 'In the good governance discourse, [liberal] democracy emerges as the necessary political framework for successful economic development, and within the discourse democracy and economic liberalism are conceptually linked: bad governance equals state intervention, good governance equals democracy and economic liberalism.' On the African continent, policies of economic redistribution simply became unfeasible (Lewis 2008: 104). But, without some mechanism to empower ordinary people, the political equality promised by democracy is dramatically undermined by the disproportionate power of political and economic elites, often one and the same, who not only determine policy decisions and their implementation but also set the very agenda for discussion.

Most presidents across the continent, regardless of the type of regime they lead, have very strong executive powers (Van Cranenburgh 2008), and legislatures that might check their powers tend to be institutionally weak (Rakner and van de Walle 2009). This centralization of power leaves little room for ordinary citizens to hold their leaders to account. The fact that incumbents still win 85 per cent of the elections in which they compete demonstrates the challenges activists face in reigning-in sitting leaders. Posner and Young (2007: 131) argue: 'The institutionalization of political power thus depends less on whether sitting presidents are willing to permit challengers to run against them than on whether incumbents will stand down (thereby forgoing likely reelection) when they have completed as many terms as their respective countries' constitutional laws allow.'

The numbers are not that encouraging. The authors demonstrate that from 1990 to 2005, of the 18 presidents who were legally barred from running for another term, six immediately announced they would not seek an additional term. Three (Daniel arap Moi of Kenya, Joaquim Chissano of Mozambique, and Benjamin Mkapa of Tanzania) initially pursued extending or removing term limits, but backed down in the face of significant domestic opposition. The remaining nine attempted to change their respective constitutions. Three failed (Frederick Chiluba of Zambia, Bakili Muluzi of Malawi, and Olusegun Obasanjo of Nigeria), while six others succeeded (Idriss Déby of Chad, Omar Bongo of Gabon, Lansana Conté of Guinea, Samuel Nujoma of Namibia, Gnassingbé Eyadéma of Togo, and Yoweri Museveni of Uganda) (Posner and Young 2007: 131–134). Five years later, in 2010, three of the six remain in office, two died while in office, and only one, Samuel Nujoma of Namibia, stepped down after his third term. An optimistic spin on these results would be that 12 presidents stepped down after serving their constitutional maximum number of terms, and an additional one stepped down after a constitution-changing third term.[4] In each of these cases, domestic and international pressure for the presidents to step aside played a significant role in determining their actions.

A comparison between the classification of sub-Saharan African regimes in 1989 and their success in holding reasonably free and fair elections in the twenty-first century demonstrates the highly contingent nature of moves towards democracy. The five categories defined by Bratton and van de Walle (1997) include, from most to least competitive: multiparty democracies, settler oligarchies (apartheid), competitive one-party systems, military oligarchies and plebiscitary one-party systems. While those regimes characterized as more competitive in 1989 are slightly more likely to hold multiparty elections today, each category of 1989 regimes includes countries commonly considered democracies today. Of the five multiparty systems in 1989 (Botswana, Gambia, Mauritius, Senegal and Zimbabwe), three have seen reasonably free and fair consecutive elections in the last decade; one, Zimbabwe, became one of the most repressive regimes on the continent; and another, Gambia, is best labelled a hybrid system. The states ruled under apartheid systems, Namibia and South Africa, have held repeated multiparty elections leading to a change in leadership but not in ruling party.

The previous competitive one-party systems include Mali, Malawi and Sierra Leone, which have held repeated elections and seen a change in the party dominating the legislature, but also the authoritarian regimes of Cameroon, Central African Republic, Côte d'Ivoire and Togo. The previous military oligarchies include the often-praised democracy in Ghana, Nigeria's highly manipulated electoral system, and repressive regimes such as Chad and Sudan. Finally, the plebiscitary systems include the more successful electoral systems of Benin, Cape Verde and Comoros, as well as the repressive states of Angola, Equatorial Guinea, Niger and Swaziland. States that have experienced sustained violence through civil and interstate wars also have experienced widely differing trajectories. While Sierra Leone has now held two reasonably free and fair elections since the end of its civil war, Angola has struggled to establish even minimally free elections. Somalia lacks a functioning state and Rwanda has a tightly controlled system in which there is almost no room for opposition. Similarly, resources, despite the much-repeated argument of a 'resource curse', do not help to predict success in achieving basic democratic attributes. Diamond-rich Botswana has consistently held multiparty elections since its independence in 1966, while oil-rich Nigeria struggles to hold just one reasonably free and fair election at state and national level.

Broad indicators from prior regime type to history of warfare, to resources or gross domestic product (GDP) do not offer accurate predictors of whether or not present-day regimes hold consistent and reasonably free and fair multiparty elections. They also tell us nothing about the content of democracy and how those states that consistently hold free and fair elections have developed and defined their democratic regimes. In order to understand this, we need to look at individual country experiences.

Experiences of democracy

Mali, South Africa and Ghana offer three examples of African states frequently praised for their success in establishing functioning democracies. They also vary widely on measures of income and human development, with Mali classified as one of the lowest income states on the continent and across the globe (databank.worldbank.org) and a correspondingly low human development score (UNDP 2010). At the other extreme, South Africa stands among the wealthiest states on the continent and is classified as an upper-middle-income economy with medium human development. Ghana falls between the two. All three are ethnically and linguistically diverse. Mali's population is overwhelmingly Muslim; the other two are majority Christian with significant religious diversity. South Africa is the one state with a sizeable population of European descent (roughly 9 per cent). Ghana and South Africa were both British colonial territories, while Mali was colonized by the French. Prior to their transition to multiparty elections, Ghana and Mali experienced several coups. Their previous regimes also pursued a heterodox leftism while South Africa was consistently capitalist (though also protectionist). In 1989 Bratton and van de Walle (1997: 79) classified the three as distinct regime types: Ghana as a military oligarchy, Mali a competitive one-party system and South Africa a settler oligarchy (apartheid). Five years later, Mali and South Africa had completed multiparty elections with a change in national government, while Ghana had held flawed elections with no change in leadership. By 2010, all three were labelled democratic by international indicators and the majority of their citizens. The cases are discussed below in order of their first multiparty elections that led to the ousting of the incumbent president.

Communitarian democracy in Mali

In early 1992, Mali held a series of multiparty elections in which a new coalition of opposition parties, the Alliance for Democracy in Mali (ADEMA), won the majority of seats in parliament and the presidency. These elections followed a period of significant turbulence and negotiation. In March 1991, protests led by students, labour unions, human rights organizations and many others demanded reforms including the end of repression, torture and corruption (Smith 2001: 73–74). When protesters marched to government buildings demanding the resignation of the president, Moussa Traoré, the armed forces responded with violence, killing hundreds. The president, who had come to power in a military coup 23 years earlier but introduced single-party elections in 1979, declared a state of emergency. Within days, he was removed by another military coup. A coalition of opposition forces refused to accept the new military government and announced plans for a national conference to schedule elections and organize the writing of a new constitution. Mali thereby became one of ten Francophone countries in which citizens demanded a national conference in the early 1990s. This uniquely African method of transition succeeded in ousting incumbents in three cases: Benin, Congo-Brazzaville and Mali (Clark 1995). In Mali, the conference included representatives from opposition groups, trade unions, other local organizations and the transitional government. Such inclusiveness and participation in the process of constitutionalism proved to be crucial in determining the legitimacy and durability of the democratic transition (Wing 2008).

Drawing on a political culture of interdependence, power-sharing, tolerance and trust, citizens of Mali have defined their ideal of democracy. Bratton *et al.* (2002: 208) sum up the findings of the 2001 Afrobarometer poll in Mali: 'the Malian conception of democracy is largely communitarian. It centers on a set of political values such as "equality and justice," "mutual respect", "unity" and "working together", which describe an idealized version of political community derived from the country's past.' The results of the next Afrobarometer survey, held in 2005, reinforce these findings.[5] Of the respondents, 28 per cent defined democracy with: equality/justice, peace/unity/power sharing or working together, while 25 per cent answered with civil liberties and personal freedoms (afrobarometer.org). For Malians, social justice is a key component of democracy, and many citizens actively participate in community-level organizations.

Mali has experienced per capita economic growth (measured in 2000 US$) averaging almost 4 per cent per year since 1995 (databank.worldbank.org). The country's compliance with structural adjustment reforms has helped to keep loans and aid flowing (Soares 2005), but debt remains high despite some debt-relief. Mali ranks 160 out of 169 countries on the United Nations Development Programme (UNDP) (2010) index for human development. The country continues to lag behind the already low averages for sub-Saharan Africa and performs poorly even for a country with its level of GDP. Its adult literacy rate in 2006 was a mere 26.2 per cent, compared with 65.8 per cent for Ghana (2008) and 89.0 per cent for South Africa (2008) (databank.worldbank.org). Poverty and the distance of many small communities from the capital present significant challenges for the empowerment of all citizens. Decentralization reforms - meant to bring government closer to the people, and move Mali 'closer to the World Bank ideal of good governance' (Seely 2001: 517) – have led to little devolution of authority (Hetland 2008). While a majority (67 per cent) of citizens state that they have attended a community meeting in the past year (another 25 per cent say they would if they had the chance), only one-third say they have actually contacted a local government councillor. Citizens remain more likely to go to traditional rulers to raise their concerns.

In a low-income country such as Mali, in which an estimated 80 per cent of the population lives in rural areas and which has been ranked by the UNDP as among the lowest in the world for human development and women's empowerment, including a diversity of voices in participatory institutions poses a great challenge. While Mali faces clear hurdles in making government more accessible, it defies several common assumptions concerning the challenges of democracy in multi-ethnic and Muslim countries. First, with the exception of the Tuareg rebellion, which ended with successful negotiations in 2009, Mali's ethnic diversity has not generally divided the country's citizens. Dickovick (2008: 1132) comments: 'as in Benin and Ghana, ethnicity took a back seat to parties and movements constructed on a national basis, although, with democratization, some local and regional parties inevitably did emerge'. Afrobarometer data support this conclusion. In 2008, almost 80 per cent stated that they identified as Malian more than or equal to their ethnic identity, and a clear majority believed that leaders should not favour their own family or group. Similarly, citizen's religious identity has not led to preferences for the exclusion of others. While greater freedom of association has led to an increase in religious associations since the early 1990s, Villalón (2010: 389) argues that 'accommodation and bargaining are the central features of the evolving political dynamics'.

The pursuit of social justice in South Africa

Like Mali, South Africa's path to democracy was led by popular protest, but in South Africa this protest spanned decades. Since the banning of the country's largest opposition movement, the African National Congress (ANC) in 1960, South African history was marked by extensive anti-apartheid organizing, periods of intense mobilization, protest, uprisings and stark repression and violence. By the late 1980s, the economic and political costs of the domestic insurgency had pressed the government to embark upon a series of steps towards political liberalization and negotiation. In early 1990, the ANC and several other organizations were unbanned and Nelson Mandela was released after 27 years in prison. This opening paved the way for a series of difficult multiparty negotiations, dominated by the ruling National Party and the opposition ANC. During the four years between the unbanning of the ANC and South Africa's first non-racial democratic elections, more than 15,000 people died as a state of civil war raged in a number of areas across the country (Klopp and Zuern 2007). This violence was encouraged and, in some cases, a direct product of the actions of state security agents who sought to derail negotiations and fan rivalries among opposition parties. As media and human rights organizations published increasing evidence of the state's complicity in the violence, government leaders were forced to take steps to attempt to create peace. Though fears remained that the April 1994 elections would be marked by significant violence, three days of voting ran remarkably smoothly and the ANC won nearly two-thirds of the national vote.

Since the end of apartheid, South Africans have consistently equated democracy with social justice and the need to address inequality. These demands are a clear legacy of decades of anti-apartheid activism seeking not just political equality but also a greater equality of basic conditions and opportunities (Zuern 2011). Looking at survey results from 1995, Bratton and Mattes (2001: 454–455) noted: '91.3 per cent of respondents equated democracy with "equal access to houses, jobs and a decent income" (with 48.3 per cent seeing these goods as "essential" to democracy). ... To be sure, a majority of South Africans did associate democracy with procedures to guarantee political competition and political participation, but their endorsement of these political goods was far less ringing than the almost unanimous association of democracy with improved material welfare.' The 2006 survey reinforced these findings. Asked to define democracy, only 29 per cent of respondents offered 'civil liberties' and 'personal freedoms' while 39 per cent equated democracy with 'equality', 'social/economic development', 'peace/unity' and 'working together' (afrobarometer.org).

It is difficult to overstate the challenges faced by South Africans in the aftermath of apartheid. The UNDP (2003: 12) carefully stressed the severity of the economic and social crisis: 'The first democratically elected government in South Africa inherited apartheid policies and institutions that had resulted in a stagnant economy, an exceptional level of poverty, inequalities in income and wealth and extremely skewed access to basic services, natural resources and employment.' South Africa has seen relatively slow average per capita economic growth since 1994, and its distribution of income remains one of the most unequal in the world. Unemployment has risen in the post-apartheid period, and, including frustrated job seekers, remained well above 30 per cent in 2010 (statssa.gov.za). Although South African incomes have grown since 1995, they have grown at a faster rate for whites than for Africans. From 1995 to 2008, white mean per capita income grew more than 80 per cent while African income grew by less than 40 per cent (RSA 2009). Poverty, therefore, remains overwhelmingly among black South Africans. The poorest are almost exclusively black, but a small black elite has joined the wealthiest, formerly all white, quintile (Martins 2007: 217). Inequality is therefore significant both across former population groups and within them.

Despite South Africa's status as an upper-middle-income country, it struggles not only to address poverty and economic inequality but also to assure citizens access to a responsive government. While the 1996 Constitution stresses the importance of participation, local government – the tier of government closest to the people – has overwhelmingly failed to engage communities. Concern over the state of local government has been expressed repeatedly by various government-sponsored studies, the national ministry responsible for local government, politicians across the political spectrum, local activists, the media and many ordinary people, who describe it as inefficient, ineffective and often corrupt (Zuern 2011). Despite the significant shortcomings of the government's efforts to address inequality, unemployment and crime, the governing party – the ANC – has repeatedly won elections due to its continuing popularity as the party of liberation. The danger in any system marked by a dominant party is that it will lead to reduced checks upon power and fewer opportunities for the development of an effective opposition. Protest, which reached new highs in 2009, has therefore remained one of the key avenues citizens employ to express their discontent (Alexander 2010).

Freedom and inequality in Ghana

In contrast to Mali and South Africa, Ghana did not see a change in the presidency via multiparty elections until 2001, when President Rawlings, who came to power in a coup in 1981, stepped down and opposition leader John Kufuor defeated Rawlings' chosen successor. This significant step followed years of dramatic economic reform as part of a WB/IMF structural adjustment programme as well as a gradual, managed process of political reforms referred to as 'political structural adjustment' by Rawlings (Lyons 1997: 69). By 1990, Rawlings faced donor pressure from the WB/IMF and key bilateral donors, along with a newly united domestic opposition front, the Movement for Freedom and Justice, for the expansion of civil and political rights (Whitfield 2003: 387). Though a new multiparty constitution was adopted in 1992, the national elections that year were marred by charges of fraud, leading to an overwhelming win for the president and his party, the National Democratic Congress (NDC). In the following elections in 1996, electoral reforms allowed opposition parties to win one-third of the seats in the National Assembly, but Rawlings maintained the presidency. By 2000, when term limits prevented Rawlings from running for re-election, further electoral reforms, increased monitoring by local organizations, a freer media, and a well-organized opposition led to a victory for the New Patriotic Party (NPP). This was celebrated by many Ghanaians as their country's 'second independence' (Gyimah-Boadi 2001: 112).

Ghanaians, much more than Malians and South Africans, tend to define democracy with civil liberties and personal freedoms; 36 per cent described democracy this way in 1999 and an even greater 48 per cent did so in 2005. Of the three countries, Ghanaians are also most likely to believe people are treated equally before the law. But, in 2005, almost one in four Ghanaians, far more than in either Mali or South Africa, replied that they did not know what democracy was (afrobarometer.org). While the majority of Ghanaians do not include principles of equality and social justice in their definition of democracy, they do believe that reducing poverty and economic inequality should be a top government priority. Whitfield (2003: 389) reports that 'advocacy of social and economic rights and the discourse of "civil society" have replaced movements for multiparty, constitutional rule and the discourse of "democracy"'.

Ghana has experienced consistent economic growth over a longer period of time than either Mali or South Africa, with an average of just over 2 per cent growth per capita since 1984. The country's life expectancy (57 years) is also higher than that in either Mali (47) or South Africa (52, largely due to AIDS). While poverty levels have declined significantly, almost 30 per cent of the population still live below the national poverty line of just under US$1.25 a day (UNDP). '[G]ross inequalities persist, with poverty largely concentrated in the three northern regions, and among food crop farmers and women' (Abdulai and Crawford 2010: 45). Despite these considerable economic challenges, Ghana has developed a strong electoral system. In stark contrast to Kenya in 2007, where a close vote and manipulation of the outcome by the incumbent led to significant violence, deaths and displacement, a similarly close vote in Ghana the following year produced a peaceful handover of power from the NPP to the NDC, even after a bitterly fought campaign (Whitfield 2009). Ghana's two central political party groups have remained remarkably stable throughout half a century of dramatic political and economic change. The NPP and NDC win roughly equal percentages of the national vote, totalling approximately 90 per cent together. The presence of two strong, alternating parties has provided a significant check on power and abuse. It has also led each party to move towards the political centre (Morrison 2004: 438). Ethnicity plays a role in voting, but it does so alongside other factors, including economic conditions and perceptions of government corruption, that mitigate its impact (Arthur 2009).

Like Mali and South Africa, Ghana's democracy still faces considerable challenges. Donors have encouraged Ghana to decentralize power to increase the accountability and responsiveness of local government, but Crawford (2009: 68) demonstrates that 'overall, the opportunities that exist in theory for local voters to monitor and sanction the actions of their elected representatives are very restricted in practice'. Power remains concentrated in the executive branch. Afrobarometer polls also demonstrate that, despite decentralization reforms meant to make local government more accessible, citizens who want to address a concern remain more likely to go to religious leaders rather than their local assembly representative. Like Mali, Ghana also has a high debt-to-income ratio (databank.worldbank.org), even after qualifying for and receiving debt relief through the Heavily Indebted Poor Country (HIPC) initiative. This reliance on external support requires the government to respond to the demands of lending institutions, and thus undermines democratic accountability to the electorate.

The significance of elections and inequality for the future of democracy

In a region as large and diverse as sub-Saharan Africa, it is impossible to draw broad conclusions concerning the nature of democracy in all 48 states. The three regimes investigated here count among the relatively small but growing number of African countries labelled as democratic both by their citizens and by outside analysts. They demonstrate that there is no singular model for the development of a democratic system and that citizens of each country have distinct ideals for their democracy. In each case, both elites and ordinary people played a crucial role in the transition to, and establishment of, a new democratic regime. Despite their divergent historical trajectories, and widely different economic bases, the three exhibit a number of important similarities. Each country experienced some degree of political and economic liberalization at the end of the Cold War, but the ordering of economic and political reform varied. In Ghana, economic reform came more than a decade before political reform allowed a change in the ruling party and the office of the president. In South Africa, political reform and the legal end of apartheid opened the door to greater economic opportunities as well as significant pressure for the new governing party to adopt liberal policies. These pressures were brought to bear even without the formal requirements of structural adjustment. In all three cases, popular protest played an important role in pressuring the incumbent government to allow multiparty elections. Protests were triggered in good part by widespread hardship and significant economic inequality between those with political power and the overwhelming majority of citizens. In Mali, protest and the state's violent response led to a coup, which was followed by a transitional government that was willing to negotiate with opposition parties demanding a national conference and a new constitution. In Ghana, protest raised the political cost of economic reforms that caused widespread hardship, and external funders pressed for greater political liberalization. Local opposition forces then maintained pressure on the government to make multiparty reforms a reality. In South Africa, protest reached the level of popular insurgency threatening both political and economic power-holders, and pressing business leaders to join the popular chorus demanding some form of change. In each of these three cases, the willingness of incumbents to step down was crucial to the creation of a more democratic regime.

Elections have become relatively standard across the region, but the quality of these elections, and incumbents' responses to their outcomes, continue to vary widely. In contrast to Mali, South Africa and Ghana, incumbents in recent elections in Kenya, Zimbabwe and Côte d'Ivoire refused to step down. In the 2007 Kenyan elections, incumbent Mwai Kibaki was defeated at the polls but manipulated the results to declare himself the winner. The violence that followed displaced hundreds of thousands and more than 1,000 people were killed (Rutten and Owuor 2009; Wolf 2009). In Zimbabwe's 2008 elections, incumbent Robert Mugabe lost the first round of voting to his challenger Morgan Tsvangirai. Tsvangirai withdrew from the second round as opposition supporters were threatened, beaten and killed by forces allied with the ruling party (Howard-Hassmann 2010). This allowed Mugabe to claim a pyrrhic victory at the polls. Most recently, Côte d'Ivoire's 2010 elections led, according to domestic and international election monitors, to the defeat of incumbent Laurent Gbagbo. As Gbagbo was nonetheless initially sworn in as president for another term, hundreds of opposition supporters were reported killed. In all three cases, international actors intervened to attempt to prevent further violence and provide a basis for future democratic elections, but the case of Côte d'Ivoire, a country divided after years of civil war, stood out for the unity shown by African and non-African states in condemning the actions of the incumbent (Hill 2011). The Economic Community of West African States, the African Union, the United Nations, and the European Union all pronounced Gbago's opponent Alassane Ouattara to be the winner of the election. It remains to be seen whether or not this transnational solidarity will help to usher in increased prospects for democracy in Côte d'Ivoire and across the region.

Democracy faces many challenges in sub-Saharan Africa and across the globe. Intransigent elites are the most visible hurdle for democratic forces to overcome. Economic inequality, which threatens to undermine democracy's promise of political equality, has long received less attention. Based on a comprehensive empirical test of the relationship between inequality and democracy, Christian Houle (2009: 613) concludes 'income distribution is a leading candidate in explaining why some poor democracies, such as India, have been remarkably stable, while others, like Peru and Nigeria, have not'. The key difference between these states, he argues, is not their ability to create democratic regimes via multiparty elections but to maintain them. In each of the three cases of largely successful African democracies discussed here, political reform, greater political and civil rights, and even the change in government, did not address the longstanding inequalities that remain a significant barrier to the practice of democracy. The new democracies all adopted liberal economic policies and worked to keep state intervention in the market to a minimum for fear of deterring potential investors and loans. While few states, except South Africa, collect adequate data to demonstrate growing inequality, Afrobarometer's 2008 survey responses show increased perceptions of inequality across the continent (afrobarometer.org). Economic inequality provides the basis for starkly different life chances based on proximity to medical care, adequate housing, educational opportunities and social connections. These factors, in turn, reinforce an already uneven political playing field. In their different definitions of democracy, people across 18 states in sub-Saharan Africa importantly underline not only the centrality of freedoms, so prominent in discussions of liberal democracy, but also that of equality, which has largely fallen by the wayside in Western academic discussions of democracy in the early decades after the end of the Cold War. The enforcement of free and fair elections, greater attention to the challenges posed by inequality, and the autonomy to define and develop local models of democracy will be crucial to the future of democracy in sub-Saharan Africa.

Notes

1 Only Botswana, Gambia, Mauritius, Sénégal and Zimbabwe had multiparty systems in 1989 (Bratton and van de Walle 1997: 79).
2 As of the end of 2010 these include: Bénin, Botswana, Cape Verde, Ghana, Lesotho, Malawi, Mali, Mauritius, Namibia, São Tomé and Príncipe, Sénégal, Seychelles, Sierra Leone, South Africa, Tanzania and Zambia (Botswana, Lesotho and Mauritius only hold legislative elections). Liberia seems to be on the way to joining the group but has not yet completed two presidential and legislative elections.
3 The 18 include Benin, Botswana, Cape Verde, Ghana, Kenya, Lesotho, Madagascar, Malawi, Mali, Mozambique, Namibia, Nigeria, Senegal, South Africa, Tanzania, Uganda, Zambia and Zimbabwe.
4 This chapter was written in New York City, the site of another example of a sitting leader's legal manoeuvres against existing laws to extend term limits. In 2008, Mayor Michael Bloomberg convinced just over half of the city council members to vote to overturn the outcome of two voter referenda that imposed a two-term limit on the mayor. In 2009, he ran for a third term and won re-election.
5 The survey question probing the meaning of democracy was not asked in the most recent (2008) survey.

References

Abdulai, Abdul-Gafaru and Gordon Crawford (2010) 'Consolidating Democracy in Ghana: Progress and Prospects', *Democratization*, 17 (1), pp. 26–67.

Abrahamsen, Rita (2000) *Disciplining Democracy: Development Discourse and Good Governance in Africa*. London: Zed Books.

Afrobarometer (2009) 'Neither Consolidating Nor Fully Democratic: The Evolution of African Political Regimes, 1999–2008'. Briefing Paper No. 67. http://www.afrobarometer.org (accessed 20 September 2011).

Ake, Claude (1993) 'The Unique Case of African Democracy', *International Affairs*, 69 (2), pp. 239–244.

Alexander, Peter (2010) 'Rebellion of the Poor: South Africa's Service Delivery Protests–A Preliminary Analysis', *Review of African Political Economy*, 37 (123), pp. 25–40.

Arthur, Peter (2009) 'Ethnicity and Electoral Politics in Ghana's Fourth Republic', *Africa Today*, 56 (2), pp. 45–73.

Biko, Steve (1978) *I Write What I Like. Steve Biko: A Selection of His Writings Edited with a Personal Memoir by Aelred Stubbs*. London: Bowerdean Press.

Bratton, Michael and Nicolas van de Walle (1997) *Democratic Experiments in Africa: Regime Transitions in Comparative Perspective*. Cambridge: Cambridge University Press.

—— and Robert Mattes (2001) 'Support for Democracy in Africa: Intrinsic or Instrumental?', *British Journal of Political Science*, 31 (4), pp. 447–474.

——, Massa Coulibaly and Fabian Machado (2002) 'Popular Views of the Legitimacy of the State in Mali', *Canadian Journal of African Studies*, 36 (2), pp. 197–238.

——, Robert Mattes and E. Gyimah-Boadi (2005) *Public Opinion, Democracy and Market Reform in Africa*. Cambridge: Cambridge University Press.

Clark, Andrew (1995) 'From Military Dictatorship to Democracy: The Democratization Process in Mali', *Journal of Third World Studies*, 12, pp. 201–222.

Collier, David and Steven Levitsky (1997) 'Democracy with Adjectives: Conceptual Innovation in Comparative Research', *World Politics*, 49 (3), pp. 430–451.

Crawford, Gordon (2009) ' "Making Democracy a Reality"? The Politics of Decentralization and the Limits to Local Democracy in Ghana', *Journal of Contemporary African Studies*, 27 (1), pp. 57–83.

Dahl, Robert (1961) *Who Governs? Democracy and Power in an American City*. New Haven, CT, and London: Yale University Press.

Dickovick, J. Tyler (2008) 'Legacies of Leftism: Ideology, Ethnicity and Democracy in Benin, Ghana and Mali', *Third World Quarterly*, 29 (6), pp. 1119–1137.

Ekeh, Peter (1997) 'The Concept of Second Liberation and the Prospects of Democracy in Africa: A Nigerian Context'. In *Dilemmas of Democracy in Nigeria*, ed. Paul Beckett and Crawford Young. Rochester: University of Rochester Press, pp. 83–110.

Fanon, Franz (1961) *The Wretched of the Earth*. New York: Grove Press.

Giannone, Diego (2010) 'Political and Ideological Aspects in the Measurement of Democracy: the Freedom House Case', *Democratization*, 17 (1), pp. 68–97.

Gyimah-Boadi, Emmanuel (2001) 'A Peaceful Turnover in Ghana', *Journal of Democracy*, 12 (2), pp. 103–117.

Hetland, Øivind (2008) 'Decentralization and Territorial Reorganization in Mali: Power and Institutionalization of Local Politics', *Norwegian Journal of Geography*, 62, pp. 23–35.

Hill, Evan (2011) 'Africa's Old Guard on the Run?', Aljazeera (5 January). English.aljazeera.net.

Houle, Christian (2009). 'Inequality and Democracy: Why Inequality Harms Consolidation but Does Not Affect Democratization' *World Politics* 61 (4), pp. 589–622.

Howard-Hassmann, Rhoda (2010) 'Mugabe's Zimbabwe, 2000–2009: Massive Human Rights Violations and the Failure to Protect', *Human Rights Quarterly*, 32 (4), pp. 898–922.

Kekic, Laza (2007) 'The Economist Intelligence Unit's Index of Democracy', *Economist The World in 2007*.

Klopp, Jacqueline and Elke Zuern (2007) 'The Politics of Violence in Democratization', *Comparative Politics*, 39 (2), pp. 127–146.

Koelble, Thomas and Edward Lipuma (2008) 'Democratizing Democracy: A Postcolonial Critique of Conventional Approaches to the "Measurement of Democracy" ', *Democratization*, 15 (1), pp. 1–28.

Lewis, Peter (2008) 'Growth Without Prosperity in Africa', *Journal of Democracy*, 19 (4), pp. 95–109.

Lucero, José Antonio (2010) 'Decolonizing Democracy? Lessons from Bolivia and Peru'. Manuscript.

Lyons, Terrence (1997) 'A Major Step Forward', *Journal of Democracy*, 8 (2), pp. 65–77.

Martins, Johan H. (2007) 'Household Budgets as a Social Indicator of Poverty and Inequality in South Africa', *Social Indicators Research*, 81, pp. 203–221.

Morrison, Minion (2004) 'Political Parties in Ghana through Four Republics: A Path to Democratic Consolidation', *Comparative Politics*, 36 (4), pp. 421–442.

O'Donnell, Guillermo and Phillipe Schmitter (1986) *Transitions from Authoritarian Rule: Tentative Conclusions about Uncertain Democracies*. Baltimore, MD: Johns Hopkins University Press.

Okere, Theophilus, Chukwudi Anthony Njoku and René Devisch (2005) 'All Knowledge is First of All Local Knowledge: An Introduction', *Africa Development*, 30 (3), pp. 1–19.

Osaghae, Eghosa (2005) 'The State of Africa's Second Liberation', *Interventions: The International Journal of Postcolonial Studies*, 7 (1), pp. 1–20.

Posner, Daniel and Daniel Young (2007) 'The Institutionalization of Political Power in Africa', *Journal of Democracy*, 18 (3), pp. 126–140.

Rakner, Lise and Nicolas van de Walle (2009) 'Opposition Weakness in Africa', *Journal of Democracy*, 20 (3), pp. 108–121.

Republic of South Africa (RSA), Presidency (2009) 'Development Indicators 2009'. http://www.thepresidency.gov.za/learning/me/indicators/2009/indicators.pdf (accessed 20 September 2011).

Rutten, Marcel and Sam Owuor (2009) 'Weapons of Mass Destruction: Land, Ethnicity and the 2007 Elections in Kenya', *Journal of Contemporary African Studies*, 27 (3), pp. 305–324.

Seely, Jennifer (2001) 'A Political Analysis of Decentralization: Coopting the Tuareg Threat to Mali', *The Journal of Modern African Studies*, 39 (3), pp. 499–524.

Smith, Zeric (2001) 'Mali's Decade of Democracy', *Journal of Democracy*, 12 (3), pp. 73–79.

Soares, Benjamin (2005) 'Islam in Mali in the Neoliberal Era', *African Affairs*, 105 (418), pp. 77–95.

Strom, Lisa (2008) 'An Elemental Definition of Democracy and its Advantages for Comparing Political Regime Types', *Democratization*, 15 (2), pp. 215–229.

de Tocqueville, Alexis (1853/2003) *Democracy in America and Two Essays on America*. London and New York: Penguin Books.

United Nations Development Programme (UNDP) (2003) 'South Africa Human Development Report– the Challenge of Sustainable Development: Unlocking People's Creativity'. http://hdr.undp.org/en/reports/nationalreports/africa/southafrica/name,3190, en.html

United Nations Development Programme (UNDP) (2010) *Human Development Report 2010–The Real Wealth of Nations: Pathways to Human Development*. New York: United Nations Development Programme.

Van Cranenburgh, Oda (2008) ' "Big Men" Rule: Presidential Power, Regime Type and Democracy in 30 African Countries', *Democratization*, 15 (5), pp. 952–973.

Villalón, Leonardo (2010) 'From Argument to Negotiation: Constructing Democracy in African Muslim Contexts', *Comparative Politics*, 42 (4), pp. 375–393.

Whitfield, Lindsay (2003) 'Civil Society as Idea and Civil Society as Process: The Case of Ghana', *Oxford Development Studies*, 31 (3), pp. 379–400.

—— (2009) ' "Change for a Better Ghana": Party Competition, Institutionalization and Alternation in Ghana's 2008 Elections', *African Affairs*, 108 (433), pp. 621–641.

Wing, Susanna (2008) *Constitutionalism and Deliberation in Mali*. New York: Palgrave Macmillan.

Wolf, Thomas (2009) ' "Poll Poison"?: Politicians and Polling in the 2007 Kenya Election', *Journal of Contemporary African Studies*, 27 (3), pp. 279–304.

Young, Crawford (1994) *The African Colonial State in Comparative Perspective*. New Haven, CT: Yale University Press.

Zuern, Elke (2009) 'Democratization as Liberation: Competing African Perspectives on Democracy', *Democratization*, 16 (3), pp. 585–603.

—— (2011) *The Politics of Necessity: Community Organizing and Democracy in South Africa*. Madison: University of Wisconsin Press.

5

The Middle East and North Africa

Francesco Cavatorta

The Middle East and North Africa (MENA) is often referred to as an exception to the democratizing trends that characterized global politics since the late 1980s.[1] This is because the majority of the countries in the region have remained solidly authoritarian, often with the same families or ruling elites in power since the achievement of independence. This has begun to change with the Arab Spring of 2011, although the outcome of the uprisings in Tunisia, Libya, Egypt and Yemen is still uncertain. The persistence of authoritarian rule has occurred despite, or precisely because of, the introduction of both economic and political reforms aimed at transforming the nature of political rule in a democratic direction. Interestingly, even countries that are considered regional exceptions because of their institutional democratic arrangements, such as Israel, Turkey and Lebanon, are controversial democracies at best and struggle to be unanimously accepted as full-fledged democracies. However, it is the Arab countries in the MENA region that truly have bucked the trend of democratization. The absence of successful democratizations so far should not, however, be equated with socio-economic and political stagnation, as the MENA countries have undergone profound transformations since the late 1980s.

This chapter will first describe the different types of political systems that are present in the region and outline how the 'third wave of democratization' positively influenced domestic political events in the late 1980s and early 1990s. At the time, all countries in the region, with the exception of Iraq, undertook a number of liberal reforms that seemed to anticipate full democratization. Electoral processes were put in place, political institutions modernized, individual freedoms expanded and economies transformed. During those 'demo-crazy' years (Valbjørn and Bank, 2010), scholars, eager to dismiss the perceived exceptionalism of the Arab world when it comes to democratic rule, focused their attention on such reforms as if political change at the top of MENA states were imminent. The main argument and hope was that democratization would soon characterize the region. The academic debate in and about the region was firmly placed within the democratization literature. This chapter will next analyse some of the main explanations that have been given for the failure of the early liberal reforms to consolidate and lead to the democratic transformation that many expected. These explanations range from structure-led to agency-led. The chapter will then move away from 'democracy-spotting' and will focus on the ways in which authoritarian rulers in MENA countries have been able to survive. Rather than attempting to explain the reasons why there is little or no democracy in the Middle East and North Africa, more recently scholars have begun to focus on accounting for the survival of authoritarianism in the context of the significant social and economic changes that occurred in the region due to the effects of globalization. This leads to an examination of MENA regimes with new theoretical tools that differ from the ones of the democratization literature. In fact, scholars are progressively abandoning the assumption that MENA countries are inevitably moving, either slowly or quickly, towards a liberal form of democratic governance and prefer now to study them as new and enduring political systems that should be analysed in their own right. This means looking at the survival of authoritarian rule and at the governance mechanisms that have permitted such survival. While the 2011 uprisings have partially undermined the validity of the authoritarian survival paradigm, a return to the democratization paradigm as a guide for explaining the events of the Arab Spring is unlikely given that the transformations brought about do not conform to the traditional assumptions of transitology. In addition, many countries in the region have yet to experience the same degree of political contestation as Tunisia, Egypt, and Libya.

The Middle East and North Africa – the absence of democracy

There is very little doubt that in world politics the region is considered to be uniquely authoritarian, and that the third wave of democratization that Huntington (1991) identified as sweeping across the globe, starting in the mid-1970s, does not seem to have had any influence in MENA. At first glance, it appears that MENA countries did not change much since they first achieved independence, when small democratic advances were quickly overturned in favour of authoritarian rule. This is particularly evident in the Arab countries where the same ruling elites and, in some instances, the same families have been in power for decades.

Until the Arab Spring, a brief overview of the power-holders in Arab countries painted a picture of immutability at the top of the political system. The wave of popular uprisings that has shaken the region in 2011 has partially modified this picture of secure authoritarianism. Long-serving dictators and ruling families are being successfully challenged and although the transformations taking place might not lead to the establishment of democracy, the removal of Ben Ali in Tunisia, of Gaddafi in Libya and Mubarak in Egypt are a powerful testimony to the successful contestation of authoritarian political power. Other countries in the region however have remained rather stable and are still characterized by the politics of authoritarian survival. It follows that the enthusiasm with which the momentous Arab Spring has been received should be tempered in the knowledge that many Arab dictators are still in place and that in the case of Tunisia, Yemen and, crucially, Egypt 'the presidents have left, but the regimes have remained in place' (Ottaway 2011). A cursory look at rulers in the region confirms that old power structures and arrangements are still prevalent. Since independence in 1956, Morocco has had three kings who have passed on power to each other, ruling as absolute executive monarchs over the Moroccan population. Tunisia, which also achieved independence in 1956, has been governed for more than 50 years by only two presidents: Habib Bourguiba until 1987 and Ben Ali until 2011. His departure following mass protests has been followed by a carefully managed transition with politicians and military officers linked to the old regime in charge. In Algeria, despite a façade of civilian rule, high-ranking officers in the military and intelligence services still hold enormous powers, a legacy of the prominent role soldiers had in achieving independence in 1962 from France. Even the current civilian President Bouteflika is a throwback to the Algerian political past, as he had occupied a number of high offices, including the post of foreign minister, following independence. In neighbouring Libya, Colonel Gaddafi has been removed from power and this constitutes a veritable shift in the politics of the country and Libya, with a small population and significant oil wealth, could be on its way to democracy if the obstacles of regional and ideological divisions among the opposition groups can be overcome. In Egypt the removal of Mubarak has confirmed rather than challenged the powerful role that the military plays in the politics of the country, just as in Yemen where large sections of the military and society are loyal to President Saleh despite increasing opposition to his rule. The picture in the Mashreq is not very different where Jordan, much like Morocco, has remained an absolute monarchy, with the king enjoying considerable executive powers. To the north of Jordan, the Arab Republic of Syria has been turned into the personal fiefdom of the Assad family despite increasing open popular opposition since March 2011. In 2000, upon the death of Hafez al-Assad, president since 1970 after taking over in a military coup, his son Bashar was proclaimed president and rules the country to this day, having been re-elected president in an uncontested election in 2007. To the south of Jordan, the Arab states of the Arabian Peninsula are still ruled by the same monarchical families that were central, post-independence, to state-formation, with power being passed within the family itself (Herb 1999).

Potential exceptions to the persistence of authoritarian rule or political uncertainty following the Arab Spring among Arab countries are Lebanon and Iraq. Lebanon has a tradition of democratic politics and is not a classic authoritarian state, but the weakness of the central state due to the overbearing role that sectarian allegiances play in the political system makes it difficult to categorize it as a democracy. The consociational arrangements that characterize Lebanese politics, institutions and electoral rules can hardly be considered democratic in so far as they respond to pre-arranged sectarian divisions. For example, the appointment to the top government posts responds to clear sectarian lines with the presidency always occupied by a Christian, the prime minister office by a Sunni and the speaker of the house always a Shi'a. This occurs irrespective of demographic changes or electoral results. If one adds to this the Syrian interference in Lebanese politics and the presence of the Hizballah armed militia, independent from the country's military, the country can hardly be categorized as fully democratic. As for Iraq, while the post-Saddam period might have the potential to lead to democracy, it is still too early, following the US-led invasion of March 2003, to make confident claims about the degree of democracy that is present in the country. Recent developments, such as the 2010 legislative elections (Visser 2010), seem to indicate that the steadily increasing sectarianism of politics is more likely to deliver Lebanese-style political arrangements, with all the negative and undemocratic consequences that this has, rather than the full-fledged liberal democracy that invading countries had hoped for. Finally, the Islamic Republic of Iran, while not an Arab state, can also be considered an authoritarian state. Despite the presence of democratic elements in its constitution, the supreme role of unelected officials and the restriction of individual liberties prevent Iran from being classified as a fully democratic state. A cursory look at Table 5.1, drawn from Freedom House scores ranging from 1 (free) to 7 (not free), indicates that democratic governance and associated freedoms are indeed largely absent in the region.

Some scholars argue that the regional picture is different and by implication more positive and less exceptional when one looks outside the Arab world and Iran. The contention is that there are non-Arab democratic countries in MENA, notably Turkey and Israel. There is no doubt that in comparative regional perspective, these two countries have working democratic institutions and seem to have embraced liberalism and can therefore legitimately claim to be much more democratic than their neighbours. Turkey, in particular, has undergone a vibrant democratic transformation since the dark days of regular military coups in the 1970s and 1980s. The strengthening of democratic institutions, due to both domestic factors and the continuous engagement with the European Union, has led to the breaking of the ultimate Turkish taboo: the election to power of a party with its roots in political Islam despite the staunchly secular constitution and the opposition of a powerful army. In some quarters, however, Turkey is not considered fully democratic because of the absence of full civilian control over the military, and the treatment of the Kurdish minority despite the legislative improvements of recent years. In

Table 5.1 Freedom House scores 2010

Algeria	Not Free (5.5)
Bahrain	Not Free (5.5)
Egypt	Not Free (5.5)
Kuwait	Partly Free (4.0)
Jordan	Not Free (5.5)
Iran	Not Free (6.0)
Iraq	Not Free (5.5)
Israel	Free (1.5)
Lebanon	Partly Free (4.0)
Lybia	Not Free (7.0)
Morocco	Partly Free (4.5)
Oman	Not free (5.5)
Qatar	Not free (5.5)
Saudi Arabia	Not free (6.5)
Syria	Not free (6.5)
Tunisia	Not Free (6.0)
Turkey	Partly Free (3.0)
United Arab Emirates	Not free (5.5)
Yemen	Not free (5.5)

Source: Freedom House Index 2010. Available at http://www.freedomhouse.org/uploads/fiw10/CombinedAverage Ratings(IndependentCountries)FIW2010.pdf.

contrast to Turkey, Israel has been considered part of the liberal-democratic family since its inception. The country seems indeed unique in the region for the democratic responsiveness of its elected institutions and the degree of liberalism that characterizes its society, with traditional liberal rights featuring prominently in legislation. A number of commentators argue, however, that Israel does not fit the category of liberal democracies because of the highly discriminatory policies in place against its Arab citizens (Davis 2003), the growing militarization of the political system with an increasing of career military men entering politics (Goldberg 2006), and the treatment of Palestinians in the occupied territories (Cypel 2007). However, the militarization argument is not entirely convincing because the Israeli civilian governments are fully in control of the military, and army men elected to government posts no longer have active positions in the military. Equally, the Israelis' treatment of Palestinians in the occupied lands is not considered overly problematic for democracy because Palestinians in the territories are not citizens and Israel does not enjoy sovereignty rights there. This does not, therefore, undermine Israel's democratic credentials. The fundamental problem for such democratic credentials is mostly due the contradiction that exists between liberal democracy, with its emphasis on both individual rights and democratic procedures, and Zionism with its emphasis on the Jewish character of the state, which leads to the exclusion of non-Jews from fully enjoying their individual rights, and therefore prevents them from being part of the democratic institutions of the state (Davis 2003). It is for this reason that Israel is sometimes labelled an 'ethnic democracy' (Smooha 1997).

Failure to consolidate – how did it all go so wrong for democracy in the Arab world?

From the survey above we can see what appears to be an authoritarian continuity as the principal trait of regional political regimes. This would, however, be a mistake. With the exception of Iraq, all the other Arab countries in the region have experimented with liberal reforms and even democratization during the late 1980s and 1990s. If anything, regional trends anticipated the sweeping changes that occurred in Eastern Europe and the Soviet Union. Countries such as Tunisia and Algeria began undertaking liberal political reforms in 1987 and 1988 respectively, with Algeria experiencing genuine democratization between 1989 and 1992. Other Arab countries followed suit and the 1990s was the decade of regional 'democratization', with authoritarian leaders seemingly intent on sharing power with other political and social groups. Elections occurred more frequently, individual liberties expanded and democratic rhetoric informed public debate. Tangible signs of democratization affected institutions as well, with a number of legislative chambers acquiring more powers (Denoeux and Desfosses 2007) and with the creation of seemingly independent authorities. According to Valbjorn and Bank (2010), these were the 'demo-crazy' years, when the principal sport of area specialists was 'democracy-spotting' – an attempt to identify democratization in any political reforms. Certainly, there was a certain normative eagerness on the part of area specialists to place the Arab world firmly within the democratization framework and to examine changes in the region within that context, so as to avoid the extant label of 'exceptional'. The main problem of democracy-spotting, however, became quite evident early on: meaningful processes of transition to democracy did not materialize and liberal-democratic reforms very quickly floundered. This might change following the Arab Spring, although the actors and factors that are the protagonists of the Spring are not the ones that the literature on transitology expected and identified as central.

There are numerous examples of the failure of democratic reforms launched in the 1980s and 1990s. The Algerian democratic experiment ended in a brutal internal conflict, and the dangers of the Algerian scenario affected how other authoritarian leaders conceived of the political changes they were introducing and the possible unintended consequences. The Tunisian experiment, while not ending as violently as the Algerian one, was also terminated with the reassertion of the power of the presidency and the security services, which closed down all the pockets of democracy that had opened up in the country (Beau and Tuquoi 1999). The rest of the region followed suit and by 1999–2000, when a new generation of leaders came to power in Jordan, Morocco and Syria, it was clear that they did not intend to introduce fundamental political changes and that, apparently liberal reforms – including elections – were actually a façade seeking to hide continued authoritarian political rule. As a result, the Arab world's failure to democratize became both a scholarly and policymaking puzzle that needed to be solved.

Broadly speaking, two sets of explanations were offered: structure-led and agency-led. Within these two categories, scholars identify subsets of more specific explanatory variables. This section analyses the validity of such explanations, keeping in mind that the region and the countries within it are very diverse and, therefore, different explanations should have different weight according to context. Among the structure-led accounts for the failure of processes of transition we find international factors, the role of hydrocarbons and political culture. We will deal with each in turn.

It is impossible to exclude international factors from an analysis of MENA, given the region's global geostrategic and economic centrality (Hinnebusch 2003). The standard argument is that meaningful democracy and democratization in the region would destabilize the international system, risking major world powers' key interests. From this, it follows that the West-dominated international community provides support for democracy only rhetorically, while materially supporting authoritarian rulers if they are deemed to be defenders of crucial Western interests, including: Egypt (Durac 2009), Morocco (Cavatorta 2005), Tunisia (Durac and Cavatorta 2009) and Jordan (Yom and al-Momami 2008). This argument tends to place the Arab world outside the 'normal' arena of international politics, where the expansion of the democratic area of peace has long been a declared objective of Western policymakers. Following from the theory of democratic peace, democracy and democratization are believed to be the best form of insurance against international instability, as democracies are said not to go to war with each other, rather seeking cooperation to solve common problems. In this context, authoritarian regimes present a threat to stability and development, as they are said to be both aggressive and untrustworthy internationally. When it comes to the Arab world, however, such logic and assumptions do not apply and scholars such as Burhan Ghalioun (2004) and Mohammed Ayoob (2005) have highlighted how the most powerful states in the global system support authoritarian rule in the region in the name of regional and international stability. The reason for this lies with the potential beneficiaries of meaningful political change in the region, notably Islamist parties and movements, which *inter alia* have an anti-imperialist discourse that concerns Western powers. This is in stark contrast to Western policies in Eastern Europe and Latin America in the late 1980s and 1990s, which were highly supportive of democratization. Thus, it makes much more strategic sense for the US and its allies to distribute material and legitimacy resources to allied authoritarian leaders in order to strengthen their position and prevent the success of the Islamist opposition. The upshot is that the international community, despite its rhetorical commitment to democratization, provides such ruling regimes with both legitimacy (i.e. participation to international forums and the shunning of genuine opposition parties and figures) and material resources (i.e. military and economic aid), which allow them to postpone genuine democratic reforms indefinitely. The post-9/11 War on Terror simply reinforced this existing trend. The provision of external resources to help maintain political power made attempts at reforming Arab political regimes impossible, as there were no incentives for authoritarian ruling elites to change. In return for support for authoritarianism, the ruling elites maintain regional stability and avoid pursuing policies that might be perceived as anti-Western, such as taking a hard stance on the Arab-Israeli conflict. Thus, for some analysts, the role of international actors in augmenting the resources available to the ruling elites and their supportive domestic constituencies is crucial in accounting for the failure of transition processes.

While there is a degree of truth in this view, the international community is not entirely responsible for the failure of transitions. Theoretically, it is disputable whether or not international factors can be so important as to dominate domestic variables. In addition, there are also countries, such as Syria and Iran, that are certainly not pro-Western, which have also failed meaningfully to democratize. Some commentators argue that Israel's regional role – a state of almost permanent conflict with many neighbouring countries – allows various Arab governments, and the Iranian regime, to keep a very tight control on domestic politics, ostensibly not to weaken resistance to the Zionist enemy. This, however, is only a very partial explanation. While there is no doubt that the presence of Israel affects both the international and domestic politics of countries in the region, it would be a mistake to argue that it single-handedly prevents democratization, as this would ignore complex internal dynamics between social groups and the weight that the distribution of resources, notably oil rents, has on where the political power lies. The way in which Western powers reacted to the Arab Spring confirms their ambivalence towards democratization. Early on during the mass protests, there was the tendency to support the incumbents, but when it became clear that ordinary Arab citizens were genuinely intent on getting rid of their leaders Western powers backed the protesters and, in the case of Libya, helped the anti-Gaddafi insurgency.

Another popular structural explanation for the failure of transitions in the Arab world is related to Arab political culture, in particular the controversial relationship between Islam and democracy, often said to be incompatible sets of values. Further evidence of the importance of political culture in determining authoritarian outcomes in the Arab world is seen in the fact that non-Arab countries, such as Turkey and Israel, are democracies. The religion of the vast majority of Arabs is perceived to be an obstacle to democracy because Islam is considered an inherently undemocratic religion (Lewis 2002). As a set of values and beliefs that have gone unchallenged by any form of Enlightenment, it produces a political culture that is imbued with political quietism. If Islam is about submission, and this belief goes unquestioned, it is said to be inevitable that a submissive political culture will continue. As a result, incumbent political leadership is never openly challenged as this would create conditions for internal divisions that, in turn, would undermine the unity of believers in a country. Political pluralism is therefore extremely problematic, and unlikely to be the outcome of any political reform project. Authoritarian political systems are said therefore to be inevitable.

The problem with this interpretation is that political quietism is not really a characteristic of Arab societies, as the rise of numerous opposition movements, including Islamist ones, demonstrates. In fact, the degree of political contestation is much higher in the Arab world than elsewhere precisely because authoritarian political arrangements do not reflect the wishes of the majority of the population (Fattah 2008). This clearly indicates that Muslim societies, as much as other societies, are divided on issues related to how to govern. A corollary to the explanation focusing on Islam is the one related specifically to Arab political culture. A number of studies (Stepan and Robertson 2003) demonstrate empirically that Islam is not necessarily an obstacle to democracy, as there are a number of democratic states where the vast majority of the population is Muslim, including Turkey, Bangladesh and Indonesia. In addition, Muslims participate in the democratic process in Europe, North America and India, where they constitute significant religious minorities. The focus therefore shifts to what are believed to be fundamental traits of Arab culture that prevent successful democratization in MENA.

The most cited of these is the tribalism affecting Arab societies, whereby the leader of a country becomes like a tribal chieftain surrounding himself with trusted members of his tribe and distributing the 'booty' to them (in this case state resources) in order to secure regime survival. Such a conceptualization of how the state should serve the interest of a clan or tribe goes to the detriment of the concept of citizenship, which, in turn, renders competition for political power a zero-sum game between different tribes or clans. Superficially, this type of explanation carries a degree of explanatory power. When one examines the tribal links that rulers such as Saddam Hussein in Iraq, or Hafez al-Assad in Syria, put in place – upon getting and keeping power in order to secure the regime – one could legitimately argue that both 'tribalism' and 'familism' serve to prevent democracy. The problem with this account is that it might confuse causes with consequences. As Gambill (2003) convincingly argues, tribalism is more a consequence of the inability of the Arab state to provide security and material goods for its citizens. It is worth mentioning that tribalism was not a strong trait of Arab societies immediately after independence, when popular, nationally focused development projects were pursued. Tribalism seems therefore a reaction of the regime and society to the failures of the state to deliver on its developmental promises.

A third structural explanation for the failure of democratization has to do with 'rentierism'. In their seminal study of oil revenues, Beblawi and Luciani (1987) argue that the externally generated rents that ruling elites are able to secure has significant consequences for their political systems. Brynen (1992) demonstrates that 'rents' can also be derived from workers' remittances and foreign aid because such revenues also permit a degree of insulation of the ruling elites from popular pressure. Broadly speaking, rents allow authoritarian ruling elites to buy off political dissent through the provision of essential services for the population and by strengthening the repressive apparatus. Democratization becomes impossible in such rentier states because the rulers have the resources available to control the transition and reverse it if they deem it necessary. In terms of rentier states' ability to provide for the population in order to quell political dissent, this is possible because, ideally, rentierism does not require productive mobilization of vast sectors of society. For Sadiki (1997) this is a 'democracy of the bread' that does not conceive of political opposition or pluralism and can only be shaken, as it was in the late 1980s, when rents decrease and the authoritarian state can no longer maintain its side of the bargain with its citizens. This is what happened in Algeria in the late 1980s when a drop in the price of oil significantly reduced the regime's resources. Algeria's rulers were thus forced to undertake a number of cost–cutting measures that had a negative impact on the standard of living of the vast majority of the population and, in turn, the population took to the streets demanding political changes (Cavatorta 2009). Furthermore, the control of political dissent in rentier states is facilitated because the state is not only the main employer, but because the resources available through rents can be invested in constructing a security apparatus, the main goal of which is to suppress domestic dissent (Bellin 2004). Overall, absence of significant personal taxation and provision of essential services, in exchange for political acquiescence, form the basis of an unwritten social contract, which isolates ruling elites from the necessity of political pluralism.

The idea that financial autonomy insulates the regime from social pressures is not without critics. Gwenn Okruhlik (1999), for instance, argues that rentier states, through the political choices they make when spending rent money, inevitably create an internal opposition at the same time as they buy off dissent. Thus, the manner in which the rents are distributed and allocated matters, because this process sees the emergence of both winners and losers, with the consequence of generating opposition to the distributional choices as a constant feature of rent distribution.

In terms of agency-led explanations, the focus is on ruling elites and Islamist movements and how their intentions and interactions undermine chances of democratic transition. When it comes to the ruling elites, it is often argued that they never had the genuine intention to truly move the country away from authoritarianism. With this in mind, it becomes obvious that the liberal political reforms that most Arab ruling elites implemented in the late 1980s and throughout the 1990s are nothing but a façade to assuage the democratic rhetoric emanating from the West after the end of the Cold War – and find renewed domestic legitimacy. The problem was that, as soon as it became clear that moving the reform process forward would lead to significant political changes – maybe the regime's demise, and the accession to power of new social groups' political representatives – then rulers made sure that reforms were not meaningful. Cosmetic changes to the political system were implemented and presented as steps towards political pluralism, but in fact they were simply a sham. There is no doubt that the reform process was not a genuine one, but the problem with an exclusive focus on the 'devious' intentions of the ruling elites is that it fails to take into account how very rarely authoritarian rulers begin processes of liberalization with the objective of creating a genuinely plural political system. Most transitions begin when ruling elites have no other option but to liberalize in the presence of a serious crisis of legitimacy, and they therefore hope that liberalization can be controlled and eventually reversed in order to reassert their own exclusive power in a superficially renewed political system. It is usually the snowballing effect of the initial opening up that prevents ruling elites, in successful democratizations, from controlling the process as other actors emerge and change the dynamics of the game (Huntington 1991). Liberalizing, whatever the reason for doing it, might have unforeseen consequences and the Arab Spring might be precisely one of them in so far as liberal reforms intended to stop further democratization generated unintended dynamics that new actors and political groups were able to exploit to undermine the regime.

A second agency-led explanation concentrates on political Islam. Islamist movements have been the most popular opposition since the early 1980s in the Arab world and, thanks to a powerful combination of ideological zeal, charity work and militant opposition to the regimes in power, they marginalized all other opposition political actors and set themselves up as the main beneficiary of any democratic opening. At the beginning of their political activism, Islamist movements did not have a positive image of democracy, which in many circles was equated with Western ideological imperialism and was therefore 'anti-Islamic'. The goal of Islamist movements was the creation of an Islamic state, largely without conventional democratic characteristics in the conceptualization of leading Islamist thinkers and leaders. In addition, the Islamist agenda also seemed to be profoundly anti-liberal, particularly on women's and minority rights. Islamist movements began to change their discourse in the 1980s, with some parties openly embracing democracy as the best option to win political power and create an Islamic state through the ballot box. This meant that they were poised to benefit from the tentative liberal reforms being carried out in the late 1980s and 1990s across the region. The problem, however, for Islamist parties was, and still is, that they are not perceived to be genuine democrats by the ruling elites, the non-Islamist domestic opposition and the international community. The outcome of carrying liberal reforms to their logical conclusion, namely free and fair elections for meaningful competition for political office, is that Islamist parties would instrumentally use democratic openings often to take power through elections, would then abolish democratic procedures, and install an authoritarian-theocratic regime (Khalil 2006). For some, the Islamist political project of creating an Islamic state is inherently authoritarian and can only be achieved through violence and authoritarian behaviour (Ben Mansour 2002). This means that processes of transition in the Arab world have failed because ruling elites and other opposition movements cannot or will not trust the democratic credentials of Islamist parties. The problem with this approach, Brumberg (2002a) argues, is the impossibility of determining the true essence or nature of any political movement, including the Islamists, if one does not examine the environment and the constraints within which they have to operate. There is considerable evidence to demonstrate that Islamist movements, aside from their ideological stances, are very much shaped in their behaviour and type of activism by environmental constraints (El-Ghobashy 2005; Cavatorta 2007). Ultimately, the presence of and support for Islamist movements should not be seen as the confirmation that Islam and authoritarian rule are inextricably linked, as Islam per se can support and legitimize any type of political action and system of government (Esposito 2002).

The scholarly and policymaking debate over the explanations for the failure of democratization produced a significant number of studies, but their point was not clear, as they tended to discuss a political phenomenon that was just not occurring: democratization itself. In the early years of the new millennium it became increasingly clear that scholars and policymakers were debating about theoretical assumptions only. In a sobering 2002 article, Thomas Carothers debunked many of the notions surrounding the validity of the democratization paradigm and illustrated the problems that emerge with studying political change in authoritarian contexts only through the prism of transitology. The problems and issues that Carothers raised were of a theoretical nature and applied to cases across the globe, but were of particular relevance in the Arab world, where no transition has yet occurred, although the Arab Spring might change that in some countries. The questioning of the fundamental assumptions of democratization led a number of regional specialists to end their 'democracy-spotting' exercises and to focus instead on the daily reality of governance in the region and how it is practised. These studies can be grouped under the label of 'post-democratization' and examine not only how authoritarianism survives, but also what kind of changes have taken place within the continuity of authoritarianism (Schlumberger and Albrecht 2004; Anderson 2006). More generally, this paradigm shift has led to a renewed interest in forms of governance that are on a continuum from authoritarianism to democracy rather than believing that democratic outcomes are inevitable. Concerning the Arab world, the questions being asked focus on ways in which and under what circumstances economic and political reforms have been introduced and to what extent they have strengthened new forms of authoritarianism. The question of the renewal of authoritarian rule in the Arab world is important because it connects not to 'transiting' political systems but to authoritarian continuity. The next section analyses the most important mechanisms through which current Arab rulers have managed to maintain power. It is in this context of renewal that some of the factors examined above become relevant rather than their link to democratization per se. This approach remains valid even in the context of the Arab Spring in so far as future arrangements in countries that have undergone some sort of regime change will be path-dependent on the arrangements and governance mechanisms that preceded them.

The transformation of authoritarianism in the Arab world

At the end of the Cold War in the late 1980s, defeat of socialism, victory of the liberal-democratic and capitalist camp, and Arab regimes' failures, triggered both liberal economic and political reforms across the Arab world. With the exception of Iraq, all Arab countries undertook a number of reforms that, in the eyes of many scholars and policymakers, would likely lead to regime change and democratic transformation. This did not occur, but it would be a mistake to believe that this is symptomatic of immobility. Instead, as the next section illustrates, liberal economic and political reforms have transformed how authoritarianism operates in the Arab world and, in light of the Arab Spring, might have sowed the seeds of its own undermining.

The conflation of elections with democracy and pluralism has been exploited by Arab ruling elites, and one of the first major reforms that were introduced in many Arab countries in order to shore up both domestic and international legitimacy was the holding of multiparty and multi-candidate elections. Before the late 1980s, elections were indeed held across the region but they were either obviously rigged – when more than one party competed as in the case of Morocco – or were 'Soviet-style' elections with only one party or one candidate allowed to run. The impossibility of maintaining that system in the face of increasing external and internal criticism forced Arab rulers to permit the formation and re-emergence of political parties with the intent of providing the regime with increased legitimacy. As a result, the vast majority of Arab countries can now claim to have functioning multiparty systems. Opposing political parties are allowed openly to operate, hold party conferences and stand for election. However, ruling elites have managed this process in order to avoid genuine electoral contestation and, therefore, the emergence of multiple political parties is not the same thing as genuine political pluralism. While numerous parties have indeed been created and elections tend to be fairer, they are usually held for institutions that are emasculated of any real policymaking power, which firmly remains in the hands of unaccountable and often unelected groups of people isolated from the pressures that opposition political parties 'should' exercise.

In traditional monarchies such as Morocco and Jordan, the king is the chief executive and decision-maker. Elected parliaments simply function as debating chambers. In the Arab republics, the president is the main decision-maker and therefore a similar arrangement is in operation. Michael Willis (2002: 4) concludes that 'rather than controlling the state, [political parties] are controlled by the state'. The formal existence of multiparty politics prevents the international community from being too critical of Arab allies because, after all, the rulers do indeed allow for a degree of pluralism and, for their part, most opposition parties prefer to take advantage of these very limited openings. This is because the current forms of 'repression' are 'softer' than they used to be, often involving complex legislation that places tight operational controls. Their participation in the political system, however, diminishes their status in the eyes of ordinary citizens. Political parties are frequently discredited in public opinion both because they are perceived as instruments of the regime and because they are ineffective. It is evident that this 'façade' political pluralism does very little in the long term for the legitimacy of the system and for the parties themselves, but popular disenchantment with the parties is actually quite useful for the ruling elites because it contributes to the depoliticization and apathy of society – in which they thrive (Maghraoui 2002). A possible exception to this trend is Islamist parties and movements, which often enjoy considerable popularity. The problem for them is that when they constitute a genuine oppositional force and demand participation, they are often prevented from doing so (as is the case of the Islamic Salvation Front in Algeria and was the case in Tunisia). In addition to repression, which is supported by sectors of domestic society and the international community, ruling elites have also been able to co-opt some Islamists by giving in to some of their demands in exchange for the renunciation to advocate systemic change. This is clearly seen in the Algerian and Moroccan cases, where some Islamist parties sit in parliament and are included in the political system, while other more radical ones are excluded (Boubekeur 2007). The Arab Spring has confirmed the very low status of political parties and traditional opposition movements, including the Islamists, as they were not central to the uprisings and were surprised by them as much as the ruling elites. New political actors loosely organized along horizontal structures were the initiators of the revolts with opposition political parties lagging behind.

Accompanying the introduction of elections and other institutional reforms, there has been a significant expansion of liberal freedoms. Thus, there is today across the region more freedom of speech and a wider social space within which social forces can organize, helping in some cases to create a more active civil society. Since the late 1990s, as Marvine Howe (2005) describes, there has been a patchy yet significant increase in the number of civil society organizations across the region, leading to an overall growth in civil society activism. The issues that new civil society actors tackled ranged from apolitical to deeply political and problematic ones such as human rights, women's rights and democratic reforms. The growth of civil society was perceived as a positive development in many policymaking and scholarly circles and it also encouraged local activists because it seemed to promise the possibility of reducing the overbearing power of the state on society and increasing autonomous civil space, in turn accelerating the process of political change.

Civil society activism has not, however, brought about democratization and once again the events of the Arab Spring indicate how traditional, official and vertically-organised civil society movements were unprepared for the uprisings and did not commit to them until they were well on the way. Studies by Wiktorowicz (2000) and Jamal (2007) suggest that traditional civil activism has strengthened authoritarian rule. According to this scholarship, rather than functioning as an independent and autonomous sphere, civil society has often become an aspect of the state. The ruling elites have almost artificially created a civil society that functions as a means enabling them to exercise social control. This approach is too stark, however, as it does not mean that truly independent civil society groups and organizations do not exist. The main problem for them, however, is that the authoritarian constraints force them to use authoritarian practices and networks if they want to carry out some of their activities. For instance, in order to operate they have to avail themselves of the authoritarian and corrupt networks of patronage they might wish to eliminate in the name of democracy and transparency. This is true in most respects of their work, whether it is obtaining an official permit to operate, to leasing a building or securing permission for demonstrations or other activities. This, as Clark (2004) shows, also applies to Islamist organizations, which rhetorically thrive from presenting themselves as real opposition actors. Much like with political parties and elections, the state therefore can project a pluralist image because there is an active civil society – while securing its own survival through careful management of civil society activism. It should be noted that the ruling elites, as in the case of political parties, do not simply use repression to control society, but increasingly rely on tried and trusted strategies of co-optation. In the Arab world such strategies are viable because of the almost irreconcilable ideological differences between opposition movements and figures, such as between secularists and Islamists. In particular, the divide between Islamists and secularists seems to play into the hands of the ruling elites, which can put in place 'divide and conquer' tactics, preventing coalition-building. Generally speaking, when a regime decides to liberalize, coalition-building strategy between opposition parties and/or civil society movements for both electoral purposes and for everyday contestation of the political system is a crucial aspect of intra-opposition politics. Most political actors acknowledge that through the creation of a 'united front' the regime can be pressurized more strongly to democratize. Unfortunately, in the Arab world, coalition-building is very rarely successful, whether in the short- or long-term. Very deep ideological and strategic differences characterize relationships between Islamist political actors and secular/liberal ones. While opposition to the regime should function as a catalyst for united opposition, wide-spread ideological differences that underpin, respectively, Islamist and secular-liberal projects, fundamentally impede chances of coalition-building. For Islamists, the creation of a liberal democracy may be at odds with their Islamist ethos, opposed to 'importing' foreign political systems and, more importantly, changed personal behaviour. For secularists, the very idea of an Islamic state is anti-democratic and illiberal and therefore they would not want to participate in its creation. Thus, fear and mutual suspicions characterize the relationships between the two sets of regime opponents (Cavatorta and Elananza 2008). While there has been a degree of cross-ideological cooperation between the two sectors, this has failed to be sustained and potent. In countries where the uprisings have been successful such as Egypt and Tunisia, the dividing line between Islamists and seculars is once again deepening after their temporary unitary stand against Ben Ali and Mubarak respectively. In addition to ideological differences about the outcome of regime change, there are also significant strategic divergences. Secular opposition actors, both in the party system and in civil society, are very aware of the popularity of Islamists. Secularists believe that regime change would benefit almost exclusively the Islamists, who, in turn, would set about creating institutional rules and legislation detrimental to secular beliefs and ideas. Given this expectation, the secular/liberal parties prefer to be co-opted by governing regimes, while attempting to win concessions from them. Ultimately, it is the incumbent authoritarian regime that benefits most from these divisions. The Arab Spring has weakened this explanation, although the cross-ideological rivalry has resurfaced powerfully in Tunisia after the departure of Ben Ali that both seculars and Islamists greeted with enthusiasm.

A third set of reforms that had a significant impact in transforming authoritarianism in the Arab world has to do with the radical economic changes. Until the late 1980s, Arab states were almost exclusively reliant on state-led development, with the bureaucracy and state-owned enterprises employing most people. The private sector had a small role in countries such as Jordan, Egypt and Morocco, but the state was the largest economic actor by far. This was even more the case in hydrocarbon-exporting countries. The economic failures of most regimes, however, called for a radical overhaul of the economy, ideologically underpinned by the 'Washington Consensus'. The collapse of the socialist model of development confirmed the necessity for the state to withdraw from the economic sphere if it wanted to generate economic growth. Developing countries, including oil-rich ones in the Arab world, needed to adapt to the requirements of the neoliberal age and to integrate the global economy. This was done through the introduction of market reforms that progressively moved Arab states away from the state-led developmental model. While the retreat of the state from economic planning is today by no means complete, and Arab states still retain a significant economic role, most have a form of market economy. Over the last two decades trade has been liberalized, foreign investment encouraged, privatization has occurred, currency values permitted to fluctuate, subsidies ended, and states' budgets slashed. The picture is not exactly the same for all countries, but there has been a discernible trend towards embracing a market economy. Overall, Arab economies have performed well during this time and, while still lagging behind many other world regions, economic development is now relatively healthy compared with the years of stagnation (1970s and 1980s). The introduction of market-oriented reforms has had a substantial influence on state-society relations and on the way in which authoritarianism has been renewed, particularly in Arab republics, but also in monarchies such as Morocco and Jordan. Generally speaking, the introduction of market reforms has resulted in the creation of a 'facade market economy' with business elites drawn from the ranks of the ruling elites and dependent on political links to secure business-related rents (Dillmann 2001, 2002). Privatization has profited people close to the rulers, as has the granting of licences for trading abroad. This has led to the creation of networks of privilege (Heydemann 2004) that have strengthened the hold of the regime because resulting business elites profit from their close relationships with those in power. This Arab regime pro-business attitude means that traditional support constituencies such as workers and peasants have been replaced by emergent middle-class, big-business and technocratic groups. This is a significant shift in terms of support bases under-pinning Arab regimes, particularly former socialist ones such as Syria, Algeria and, to an extent, Tunisia. In addition to the problematic nature of the beneficiaries of market reforms, it should be highlighted that economic inequalities have increased in most states, a trend that might eventually encourage even further political extremists. Interestingly, the Arab Spring has a very strong economic component in so far as neoliberal market reforms were perceived to be as much of an obstacle to a better and more just life as political authoritarianism. Thus, market reforms rather than creating a pro-democracy bourgeoisie have created a strong mass movement that demands democracy in order to install regimes that would do away with neoliberalism.

Overall, what clearly emerges is that the Arab world has experienced a phase of what Heydemann (2007) refers to as 'authoritarian upgrading' – and has not gone through a failed process of democratization. Extant explanations for the failure of the transition process would be better advised to determine *how* they have been instrumental in helping achieve this 'authoritarian upgrade' and under what circumstances one explanation is more valid than others. In turn this upgrading has had unintended consequences that the Arab Spring has rendered visible.

Conclusion

The most salient feature of the MENA region is the persistence of authoritarian rule, although this is challenged in the context of the Arab Spring. Turkey and Israel are problematic democracies, and the future of both Lebanon and Iraq is still very uncertain due to the weight of sectarianism. The Arab world and Iran are as authoritarian today as they have ever been, but they have radically changed since the 1980s. The consequences of neoliberal market reforms, the impact of new technologies and significant international events have combined to alter these polities, both socially and economically. These changes have not led to effective democratization yet and might not do so in the future, but they have re-awakened Arab societies where authoritarian forms of governance and unfair economic circumstances are increasingly under contestation. The theore-tical tools of transitology are ill suited to explain events in the region, particularly because ruling elites have been able to avoid the central issue of transfer of power and popular involvement in politics and because the actors and factors that are central to its theoretical assumptions do not play a role in the Arab Spring. While adopting some of the trappings of democracy, most regional regimes retain unaccountable and unrepresentative decision-makers. It is therefore no surprise that much of the current scholarship focuses on attempting to account for the ways in which this has been possible, and tries to explain what mechanisms are in use to secure such regimes. Some factors provide better answers than others. There is no doubt, for instance, that external rents are helpful in solidifying security apparatuses and buying a degree of political acquiescence, giving rulers the ability to structure both politics and society, although the case of Libya indicates that even hydrocarbon revenues cannot save a regime under immense popular pressure. International support is also crucial in a number of MENA countries because it provides a degree of legitimacy that the international community does not grant to other authoritarian rulers elsewhere. However, it should be noted that authoritarian leaders across the Arab world display strongly adaptive abilities, including the ability to oversee radical transformations without losing power. In this respect, it seems that their greatest achievement is to contain Islamist parties and movements. Islamists are said to be inherently inimical to both democracy and liberalism, leading the international community, liberal sectors of domestic society, and 'crony capitalists' reluctantly to support incumbent authoritarian rulers. Consequently, those in power can introduce changes that acquire international and domestic supporters without actually putting in place political pluralism. When all else fails, the rulers retain the support of the security apparatus, which has its own vested interest in the survival of the regime; it is the 'weapon' of last resort when other softer strategies fail. Bahrain and Syria in the spring of 2011 used it to great effect to put down popular uprisings.

The 1990s were spent on 'democracy-spotting' when the reality was that the signs of democratization that were being spotted were simply signs of authoritarian upgrading. It seems that the 'liberalized autocracies' (Brumberg 2002b) emerging from that process of should be studied as political systems in their own right because even when they change they do not do so according to the assumptions of transitology.

Note

1 Please note that this chapter was completed before the final political outcomes of the 'Arab Spring' 2011 were clear.

References

Anderson, L. (2006) 'Searching Where the Light Shines: Studying Democratization in the Middle East', *Annual Review of Political Science*, 9, pp. 189–214.

Ayoob, M. (2005) 'The Future of Political Islam: The Importance of External Variables', *International Affairs*, 81 (5), pp. 951–961.

Beau, N. and J.P. Tuquoi (1999) *Notre Ami Ben Ali*. Paris: La Decouverte.

Beblawi, H. and G. Luciani (eds) (1987) *The Rentier State*. London: Croom Helm.

Bellin, E. (2004) 'The Robustness of Authoritarianism in the Middle East', *Comparative Politics*, 36 (2), pp. 139–158.

Ben Mansour, L. (2002) *Frères musulmans, frères féroces. Voyage dans l'enfer du discourse Islamiste*. Paris: Editions Ramsay.

Boubekeur, A. (2007) 'Political Islam in Algeria', *CEPS Working Documents*, 268, pp. 1–12.

Brumberg, D. (2002a) 'Islamists and the Politics of Consensus', *Journal of Democracy*, 13 (3), pp. 109–115.

—— (2002b) 'The Trap of Liberalized Autocracy', *Journal of Democracy*, 13 (4), pp. 56–68.

Brynen, R. (1992) 'Economic Crisis and Post-Rentier Democratization in the Arab World: the Case of Jordan', *Canadian Journal of Political Science*, 25 (1), pp. 69–97.

Carothers, T. (2002) 'The End of the Transition Paradigm', *Journal of Democracy*, 13 (1), pp. 5–21.

Cavatorta, F. (2005) 'The International Context of Morocco's Stalled Democratisation', *Democratization*, 12 (4), pp. 549–567.

—— (2007) 'Neither Participation nor Revolution: The Strategy of the Moroccan', *Jamiat al-Adl wal-Ihsan*. *Mediterranean Politics*, 12 (3), pp. 381–397.

—— (2009) *The International Dimension of the Failed Algerian Transition*. Manchester: Manchester University Press.

—— and A. Elananza (2008) 'Political Opposition in Civil Society. An Analysis of the Interactions of Secular and Religious Associations in Algeria and Jordan', *Government and Opposition*, 43 (4), pp. 561–578.

Clark, J. (2004) *Islam, Charity and Activism*. Bloomington: Indiana University Press.

Cypel, S. (2007) *Walled: Israeli Society at an Impasse*. New York: Other Press.

Davis, U. (2003) *Apartheid Israel*. London: Pluto Press.

Denoeux, G.P. and H. Desfosses (2007) 'Rethinking the Moroccan Parliament: The Kingdom's Legislative Development Imperative', *Journal of North African Studies*, 12 (1), pp. 79–108.

Dillman, B. (2001) 'Facing the Market in North Africa', *Middle East Journal*, 55 (2), pp. 198–215.

—— (2002) 'International markets and Partial Economic Reforms in North Africa: What Impact on Democratization?', *Democratization*, 9 (1), pp. 63–86.

Durac, V. (2009) 'The Impact of External Actors on the Distribution of Power in the Middle East: the Case of Egypt', *The Journal of North African Studies*, 14 (1), pp. 75–90.

—— and F. Cavatorta (2009) 'Strengthening authoritarian rule through democracy promotion? Examining the Paradox of the US and EU Security Strategies: The Case of Tunisia', *British Journal of Middle Eastern Studies*, 36 (1), pp. 3–19.

El-Ghobashy, M. (2005) 'The Metamorphosis of the Egyptian Muslim Brothers', *International Journal of Middle East Studies*, 37 (3), pp. 373–395.

Esposito, J. (2002) *Unholy War: Terror in the Name of Islam*. Oxford: Oxford University Press.

Fattah, M. (2008) *Democratic Values in the Muslim World*. Boulder, CO: Lynne Rienner.

Gambill, G. (2003) 'Explaining the Arab Democratic Deficit: Part I', *Middle East Intelligence Report*, 5 (2).

Ghalioun, B. (2004) 'The Persistence of Arab Authoritarianism', *Journal of Democracy*, 15 (4), pp. 126–132.

Goldberg, G. (2006) 'The Growing Militarization of the Israeli Political System', *Israel Affairs*, 12 (3), pp. 377–394.

Herb, M. (1999) *All in the Family. Absolutism, Revolution and Democracy in the Middle Eastern Monarchies*. Albany: State University of New York Press.

Heydemann, S. (ed.) (2004) *Networks of Privilege in the Middle East: The Politics of Economic Reform Revisited*. London: Palgrave Macmillan.

—— (2007) 'Upgrading Authoritarianism in the Arab World. The Brookings Institution', *Analysis Paper*, 13, pp. 1–37; available at http://www.brookings.edu/~/media/Files/rc/papers/2007/10arabworld/10arab world.pdf (accessed 20 September 2011).

Hinnebusch, R. (2003) *The International Politics of the Middle East*. Manchester: Manchester University Press.

Howe, M. (2005) *The Islamist Awakening and Other Challenges*. Oxford: Oxford University Press.

Huntington, S. (1991) *The Third Wave of Democratization*. Norman: Oklahoma State University.

Jamal, A. (2007) *Barriers to Democracy. The Other Side of Social Capital in Palestine and the Arab World*. Princeton, NJ: Princeton University Press.

Khalil, M. (2006) 'Egypt's Muslim Brotherhood and Political Power: Would Democracy Survive?', *Middle East Review of International Affairs*, 10 (1), pp. 44–52.

Lewis, B. (2002) *What Went Wrong? Western Impact and Middle Eastern Responses*. London: Phoenix Press.

Maghraoui, A. (2002) 'Depoliticization in Morocco', *Journal of Democracy*, 13 (4), pp. 24–32.

Okruhlik, G. (1999) 'Rentier Wealth, Unruly Law, and the Rise of the Opposition', *Comparative Politics*, 31 (3), pp. 295–315.

Ottaway, M. (2011) 'The Presidents Left, the Regimes are Still Tthere', Carnegie Endowment (February 14, 2011). Available at http://carnegieendowment.org/publications/?fa=42627 (accessed 14 February 2011).

Sadiki, L. (1997) 'Towards Arab Liberal Governance: From the Democracy of Bread to the Democracy of the Vote', *Third World Quarterly*, 18 (1), pp. 127–148.

Schlumberger, O., and H. Albrecht (2004) 'Waiting for Godot: Regime Change Without Democratization in the Middle East', *International Political Science Review*, 35 (4), pp. 371–392.

Smooha, S. (1997) 'Ethnic Democracy: Israel as an Archetype', *Israel Studies*, 2 (2), pp. 198–241.

Stepan, A. and G. Robertson (2003) 'An Arab More than a Muslim Electoral Gap', *Journal of Democracy*, 14 (3), pp. 30–44.

Valbjorn, M. and A. Bank (2010) 'Examining the "post" in Post-Democratization. The Future of Middle Eastern Political Rule through Lenses of the Past', *Middle East Critique*, 19 (3), pp. 183–200.

Visser, R. (2010) 'Iraq Moves Backward', *Middle East Report*, 40 (2), pp. 2–7.

Wiktorowicz, Q. (2000) 'Civil Society as Social Control: State Power in Jordan', *Comparative Politics*, 33 (1), pp. 43–61.

Willis, M. (2002) 'Political Parties in the Maghrib: The Illusion of Significance?', *The Journal of North African Studies*, 7 (2), pp. 1–22.

Yom, S. and M. al-Momami (2008) 'The International Dimension of Authoritarian Regime Stability: Jordan in the Post Cold-War Era', *Arab Studies Quarterly*, 30 (3); available at http://findarticles.com/p/articles/mi_m2501/is_1_30/ai_n27947386/?tag=content;col1 (accessed 20 September 2011).

6

Central Asia

Verena Fritz and Jonathan Wheatley

In Central Asia expectations of democratization have remained largely unfulfilled. The only year in which all five countries – Kazakhstan, Kyrgyzstan, Uzbekistan, Tajikistan, and Turkmenistan[1] – were rated as 'partly free' by Freedom House was in 1991–2. Over the subsequent years, all countries except Kyrgyzstan reverted rather quickly to a 'not free' status (Figure 6.1 below shows the combined Freedom House index of political rights and civil liberties between 1986 and 2009). In Kazakhstan and Uzbekistan, presidents have held power since before the collapse of the Soviet Union in 1991. In Turkmenistan, autocrat Saparmurat Niyazov held power from 1985 until his death in 2006, when he was replaced by one of his own protégés. In Tajikistan, President Emomali Rahmon, a collective farm boss during the Soviet era, has been head of state since 1992. Only in Kyrgyzstan is autocratic control less secure with President Askar Akayev and his successor Kurmanbek Bakiyev both overthrown in popular uprisings led by rival elites in 2005 and 2010 respectively. Of the five Central Asian states, four can be described as 'consolidated authoritarian', while the fifth (Kyrgyzstan) can best be described as a 'non-consolidated, non-democratic' regime. In all five Central Asian states, power has never changed hands by means of the ballot box.[2] Among all post-communist transition countries and subregions (such as the Balkans or the South Caucasus), Central Asian countries form the most solid block of authoritarian countries and currently Central Asia is one of the most authoritarian 'subregions' in the world.

At the same time, there is a sharp contrast between the five Central Asian republics and neighbouring Mongolia, which, against the odds, has developed a democratic regime. The first competitive elections in Mongolia were held in 1990 and produced an overwhelming victory for the ruling communist party, known as the Mongolian People's Revolutionary Party (MPRP). The MPRP ceded power to the opposition Democratic Party in elections held in 1996, but won the subsequent elections in 2000 with an overwhelming majority. In 2004 an inconclusive election led to a coalition government between the two main parties, before the MPRP won again in 2008 in elections that the Democratic Party claimed were rigged. Nevertheless, in 2009 Mongolia held a fair and competitive presidential election in which the Democratic Party won. Despite the hiccup in 2008, Freedom House has rated Mongolia as 'free' in every year since 1992 and, by 2010, the country scored 2 for both political rights and civil liberties, the same as Bulgaria and Romania, both EU members.

From a democratization perspective, this raises two important questions: one is why the Central Asian countries have 'underperformed' in terms of their democratic trajectory since 1990, both in comparison with their former Soviet neighbours and in comparison with Mongolia (and even in comparison with many African 'democratizers' with similar or even lower

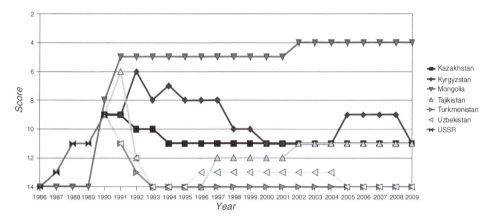

Figure 6.1 Freedom House scores, 1986–2009

Note: Freedom House scores for civil liberties and for political rights range from 1 to 7. Adding these yields a range of possible ratings from 2 (fully democratic political rights and civil liberties) to 14 (fully autocratic regime with no civil liberties).

levels of economic development). The second question is what this evolution to date means in terms of prospects for future democratization in these countries.

This chapter considers several aspects that various strands of democratization theory suggest could have an impact on the political regime. These include socio-economic development, the role of political elites, nation-building and state-building, the role of natural resources and the effect of the external (international) environment. A key marker of regime trajectories in Central Asia has been the consolidation of power by individual leaders, which was achieved in Kazakhstan, Turkmenistan and Uzbekistan, and, after bloody civil war and postwar manoeuvring, in Tajikistan. Leaders in Kyrgyzstan were initially less bent on power consolidation, and successive leaders failed when they tried to monopolize power; in contrast in Mongolia, power was continuously more broadly shared among shifting groups. These varying regime trajectories were facilitated by structural factors, in particular legacies, dynamics of natural resource exploitation and the external environment. Importantly, the type of power and regime evolution observed in Central Asia over the past 20 years is not unique to that region but has parallels with developments in countries elsewhere, which earlier underwent both decolonization and state-building, e.g. countries in Africa. Several of these countries experienced periods of political crises and/or conflict, while many eventually embarked on democratization during the 'Third Wave' (Huntington 1991).

Explaining Central Asian non-transitions and the Mongolian exception: modernization theory

According to 'classic' modernization theory, the modernization of society through socio-economic development is the key factor that determines whether or not democratization occurs, and, if so, whether or not democracy takes root. Lipset (1959) argues that economic development is conducive to democracy first because it leads to higher levels of education, which in turn promote a tolerant, rational or 'civic' culture, and second because it ameliorates class conflict.

More recent formulations of 'modernization' theory acknowledge that democratization can occur also in much less developed settings, but they continue to maintain that economic development is important insofar as it can trigger other development conditions (such as literacy)

Table 6.1 Per capita incomes in 1992: Central Asia, Mongolia, Ghana and Kenya

	KAZ	KYR	TAJ	TUR(*)	UZB	MNG	GHA	KEN
GNI per capita PPP current int'l $ 1992	4510	1480	1480	2200	1290	1260	700	980

(*) Data for 1993.
Source: World Development Indicators database (World Bank).

that are favourable to successful and sustained democratization. For Diamond, 'economic development produces or facilitates democracy only insofar as it alters favourably four crucial intervening variables: political culture, class structure, state society relations, and civil society' (Diamond 1992: 487).

At the outset of independence, Central Asia presented a mix of developmental factors. Certainly, the emerging new republics were backward in comparison with Central Eastern Europe (CEE) and the western parts of the former Soviet Union in terms of socio-economic development (e.g. see Kitschelt 2001). However, compared with other regions in the developing world that embarked on democratization in the 1990s, levels of education and of industrialization were relatively high and initial conditions were therefore not unfavourable (see also Huntington 1991).

In terms of per capita incomes, five of the six countries that are the focus of this chapter were within a relatively close range between PPP$1,200 and PPP$2,200 per capita in purchasing-power terms. Kazakhstan was an outlier within the region with a starting per capita income of around PPP$4,500. This compares to per capita incomes in the early 1990s of PPP$700–1,000 in African countries transitioning to democracy during this period (see Table 6.1).

Furthermore, literacy was more or less universal throughout Central Asia and Mongolia in the early 1990s, while literacy rates in democratizing African countries such as Ghana were only around 50 per cent of the adult population. According to modernization theory, high literacy rates are especially conducive to the endurance of democratic regimes over time (Lipset 1959, 1994).

Consequently, in terms of modernization, democratization certainly appeared as a possibility in Central Asia. While modernization theory would suggest that a successful transition to democracy would be less likely here than in Central Eastern Europe, where per capita income levels were higher (Vanhanen 2003), democracy would still be more likely to take root in Central Asia than in many less developed regions, e.g. countries in Africa, where democratization emerged during this period. Moreover, while little or no democratization occurred in the five Central Asian countries, substantial democratization took place in neighbouring Mongolia even though its starting level of per capita income was at the lower end by comparison (see Table 6.1).

Dynamics of political leadership and contestation

Given that modernization theory does not explain either the absence of democratization in the five Central Asian republics or the divergence in regime trajectories between these five countries and Mongolia, it is worth considering other factors that may encourage (or impede) democratization. An alternative conceptual approach emphasizes the importance of contingent choices and strategic calculations of actors during the transition process (O'Donnell and Schmitter 1986; Karl 1990; Karl and Schmitter 1991; Przeworski 1992). In terms of internal regime dynamics, what stands out in Central Asia is the consolidation of power in the hands of individual leaders. Most of these leaders had already assumed power by the time the Soviet Union collapsed, and subsequently consolidated their positions. At the same time, and in contrast to several post-Soviet republics that experienced greater democratization, there was little mobilization of an opposition. Political leadership dynamics were also very different between the five Central Asian countries and Mongolia.

In the Central Asian countries, the power struggles that emerged when the Soviet Union collapsed were largely dominated (and except in Kyrgyzstan won) by individual leaders who had been appointed to top positions at the end of the Soviet era. This contestation over power involved rival elite networks, especially regional ones (Jones Luong 2002); but there was little contestation by genuine counter-elites and as the result of popular mobilization. While the newly independent countries initially adopted constitutions with somewhat limited presidential powers, presidents subsequently used referendums and other initiatives for constitutional amendments to formalize their extensive personal powers and to create 'hyper-presidential' systems.

Most of the Central Asian countries have been ruled by the same men who had been the last heads of the republican government (and so-called first secretaries of their republican communist parties) during the Soviet era: Nursultan Nazarbaev in Kazakhstan (since 1989), Islam Karimov in Uzbekistan (since 1989) and Saparmurat Niyazov in Turkmenistan (since 1985). The head of the Kyrgyz Republic, Askar Akayev, had been appointed in 1990 during the dying days of the Soviet Union. In Tajikistan, Emomali Rahmon, who had been elected as a people's deputy to the Supreme Council of the Tajik SSR in 1990, became head of state in November 1992 after two other leaders resigned during and due to the emerging civil war that had started in May.

Central Asian presidents used the collapse of Soviet hegemony and the ensuing sequence of events to reconfigure power relations. To cite Uzbekistan as an example, Communist Party First Secretary Islam Karimov was elected as president in March 1990, i.e. nearly two years prior to independence. Karimov was a representative of a regional, Samarkand-centred network.[3] His power was initially balanced by Shukrullo Mirsaidov, a representative of the rival Tashkent-based network, who was appointed vice-president in November 1990. However, in the autumn of 1991, Karimov managed to dissolve the Communist Party (in the wake of the anti-Gorbachev putsch in Moscow), re-creating it as the People's Democratic Party (PDP). The reconfigured PDP was dominated by networks and individuals loyal to Karimov, who also assumed the role of the party's chairman. Thus, when Uzbekistan became independent at the end of 1991, the personal power of the president was already rather well entrenched. In January 1992, Karimov felt emboldened enough to abolish the post of vice-president and remove Mirsaidov from power (Collins 2006).

The development and adoption of new constitutions and subsequent constitutional referenda were then used to further consolidate a 'hyper-presidential', authoritarian regime. In Turkmenistan, an almost identical scenario was played out as former First Secretary Saparmurat Niyazov renamed the Communist Party the Democratic Party of Turkmenistan, under his own leadership, and then set about establishing a personality cult around his own person. In Kazakhstan, Nursultan Nazarbayev relied more on compromise and co-optation to strengthen his power base, but by 1995 was able to amend the constitution in his favour and secure full control.

In Tajikistan and Kyrgyzstan, presidents Emomali Rahmon and Askar Akayev also strove to consolidate power, but there the process was more fraught. In both countries, the main challenges to a consolidation of power by individual leaders came from rival elite networks. In Kyrgyzstan, Akayev struggled with southern elites based around the network of former Communist Party First Secretary Absamat Masaliev.[4] Although Akayev managed to consolidate his authority partially, successfully increasing powers of the presidency by referendum in 1996, he was never able to fully outmanoeuvre his southern opponents. One factor that appears to have hindered the process of monopolizing power in Kyrgyzstan was the relatively rapid privatization process, which provided a number of local leaders in the south with private capital, some of which was used to buy the loyalty of citizens and build opposition networks (Radnitz 2006, 2010). Akayev was driven from power in March 2005 after disputed elections led to an uprising in the southern cities of Jalalabad and Osh. Akayev's successor as president, Kurmanbek Bakiyev, met a similar fate in 2010, when economic mismanagement and cronyism led to a popular uprising led by northern elites.

In 1992 in Tajikistan, regional rivalries between elites from Leninobod and Kulob, on the one hand, and those from Gharm and Badakhshan on the other, escalated into civil war. While inter-regional grievances and rivalries were a key cause of the conflict, the United Tajik Opposition (UTO) also included Islamist groups as well as more liberal-reformist groups. After the initial outbreak of the war, the country's first post-independence president, Rahmon Nabiyev, and then also the acting president Akbarsho Iskandarov were forced to resign. This opened the way for Emomali Rahmon, a member of the former Soviet *nomenklatura* and of the Kulobi regional network, to become the acting head of state in late 1992. He was confirmed as president in an election organized in November 1994, while the war was still ongoing. Russia and Uzbekistan supported the government led by Rahmon and helped the regional networks that Rahmon represented to prevail in the bloody conflict. Eventually, a United Nations, US and Russian-backed peace deal was reached in 1997, which formally instituted a power-sharing arrangement with the UTO. However, the president was able to use the resulting post-conflict situation to successively disempower the opposition. While the country has been at peace since 1997, the regime became increasingly authoritarian and power became increasingly concentrated.

One noticeable feature of the authoritarian trajectories in Central Asia is that the emerging presidents (who in three out of five cases were the former Communist Party boss) rather quickly sidelined the communist parties. None of the newly independent states established a party-led authoritarian regime as in Vietnam or China.[5] This was accomplished by co-opting local Communist Party bosses or playing off different party networks against each other. Referring to Kazakhstan, Jones Luong (2002: 140) argues that: 'Nazarbayev made a concerted effort to reassure regional leaders that they would continue to play a significant role in the selection and supervision of local level cadre'. New presidential administrations took over the old Communist Party function in terms of supervising and controlling all other branches of power. At the same time, these dominating presidential administrations reflect the fact that power was now more narrowly held by a single individual and a rather small entourage.

In Mongolia, by contrast, no individual leader sought total control. Like the five post-Soviet republics, Mongolia had no significant internal opposition in the 1980s. It did experience a leadership change in 1984, when Mongolia's long-term, Brezhnev-era leader Yu Tsedenbal was replaced as head of state by Ja Batmunkh. However, subsequent events in Mongolia were sharply different from those in the five Central Asian countries. In 1989-90, several opposition parties emerged to challenge the MPRP-led regime.[6] Remarkably, no single dominant leader emerged from within the MPRP. In March 1990, Batmunkh dissolved the MPRP government and stepped down as head of state in response to protests by the newly formed opposition – opening the way for the country's first elections. The absence of an assertive leader also enabled the MPRP to remain strong as a party. By early 1992, Mongolia adopted a constitution that enshrined a mixed parliamentary-presidential system (see Fritz 2008a).

The pattern of presidential power and authoritarian regime consolidation across Central Asia suggests that these were not 'accidental' outcomes, attributable to the particularities of the individual leaders involved. Rather, the pattern across the region suggests that there were shared and hence more systemic factors involved. The following sections turn to four key issues: the weakness of focal points for opposition movements in Central Asia, the absence of established statehood, the role of natural resources, and the role played by external influences. The following sections explore these wider factors in turn, considering how they were uniform or varied across the region, and also whether or not they can account for why Mongolia took such a different trajectory.

The weakness of focal points for opposition movements and the exigencies of state-building

The rise of strong leaders in Central Asia was facilitated by weak national identities and by the challenge of state-building. In Central Asia, there was neither a strong sense of national identity nor a strong tradition of independent statehood 'available' at the outset of independence. This absence of strong national identity had roots in the 'artificial' creation of political entities in the region during the early years of the Soviet regime. The Central Asian republics were the last to declare independence from the USSR and only did so when the Soviet collapse became inevitable. With regard to state-building, emerging leaders portrayed themselves as guarantors of state-building progress.

In many other (post-)Soviet republics, non-communist, nationalist counter-elites emerged in the late 1980s. They began to undermine the dominance of the incumbent communist elites, a potentially important component of political liberalization.[7] This took different forms in the Baltic countries, in Moldova and Ukraine, in the South Caucasus, as well as in Russia itself; initial outcomes included early wins for the nationalist opposition, uneasy coexistence between old and new elites, crackdowns by old elites, all-out civil conflict, and co-optation among old and new elites.

In these other republics, opposition movements emerged and rallied around the theme of nationalism, language and historical memories of being separate from the Soviet Union. Certainly, nationalism is not a general precondition for (successful) democratization, and may even be inimical to it through its tendency to generate conflict and to marginalize or even persecute those who do not support the 'national project'. However, in the post-communist region, nationalism was a potent unifying theme for opposition forces, an important focal point for the formation of successful counter-elites (Wheatley 2005; Beissinger 2007; Wheatley and Zuercher 2008). The example of other former Soviet republics that made significant progress towards democracy – most importantly the Baltic republics, Moldova, Georgia and Ukraine – underlines the presence or absence of a strong national identity as a rallying point for the opposition (see also Bunce 2003).

The existence of a functioning state as a prerequisite of democracy has been proposed by a number of authors. Linz and Stepan (1996) argue that without a state with 'statelike attributes' and with capacities normally associated with a modern state (e.g. monopoly over the legitimate use of force, capacity to collect taxes and provide public services and the implementation of a judicial system), democratic governance is impossible. Focusing on Africa, Bratton and Chang (2006) argue that new democracies can emerge only in the context of effective statehood based on the establishment of the rule of law.

In the five Central Asian countries, a sense of statehood was rather weak. None of the Central Asian republics that were delineated territorially during the Soviet period previously existed as independent states within those borders. There had been several khanates – the Kazakh khanate in the north, and to the south the khanates of Bukhara and Khorazm, and later on of Quqon – but these were rather limited as organized polities.[8] In the nineteenth century, Central Asian lands became absorbed by the Russian Empire progressively from north to south. During the Soviet period, borders were created in ways that did not reflect earlier borders, cutting across population groups. This contrasts sharply with the experience of the three Baltic republics, where the existence of independent statehood during the period 1921–40, and the establishment of genuine state institutions, would later serve as a template for the new states when independence was regained in 1991.

In a sense, of course, there was a rather well-developed degree of state capacity in Central Asia during the Soviet period in terms of the existence of state structures that organized the public sphere throughout the territories, imposing order, collecting taxes and delivering services (Nettl 1968; Fritz 2008b; Tansey 2009). However, the state in question was the Soviet state and the republics themselves had few attributes of independent statehood. Most of the ministries that ran the economy were all-union ministries (i.e. they had no counterparts at republican level); the only important union-republic ministry (with its own structure at the level of the republic) was the Ministry of Internal Affairs. Fiscal resources were subsidized by the union, especially in Kyrgyzstan and Tajikistan. Corruption and associated forms of bad governance were particularly entrenched at the republican level as the case of the so-called 'Uzbek Cotton Scandal' in Uzbekistan demonstrates.[9] Such scandals showed that republican elites tended to see the state as a source of revenue for personal enrichment, rather than as a mechanism to order society and to provide public goods to all. It is not surprising, therefore, that the collapse of the USSR led to a reduction in state capacities and an increase in dysfunctional governance. The new governments in Central Asia struggled to continue to raise revenues to fund their own existence, while the supply of public services that the Soviet state had provided sharply declined.

The contrast with Mongolia is illustrative. Even though Mongolia had not been an independent state from around 1700 to 1911, it had a prehistory of earlier independent statehood and even empire. Genghis Khan was available as a Mongolian identification figure and national symbol. During the communist period, although Mongolia was a Soviet satellite, it had its own state institutions, unlike its Central Asian neighbours. Consequently, at the potential 'transition moment' in the early 1990s, Mongolia had a more established sense of statehood, as well as a clearer sense of national identity.

Other former Soviet republics also faced 'stateness' challenges. Moldova, Georgia and Azerbaijan all experienced violent conflict over how the state was to be (re-)configured. While none of these republics could today be described as fully democratic, only perhaps Azerbaijan can be considered as a consolidated authoritarian regime like those of the Central Asian republics. One other factor that may affect the way a new state is constituted is the presence of natural resources, which appears to have had a major impact on how the new state functions. This factor appears to have been relevant in many parts of Central Asia and it is to this factor that we now turn our attention.

The role of natural resources as an influencing factor in democratization

Having an economy that is strongly reliant on resource-extractive industries has been argued to have potential negative effects on political stability as well as on the likelihood of democratization – as various forms of a potential 'resource curse'. With regards to the political regime, state elites can seek to control cash flows from primary commodities such as oil or mineral ores and use the funds to maintain or entrench authoritarian control (Friedman 2006; Collier 2007). Hydrocarbons are seen as particularly problematic in this regard, since extraction is usually geographically concentrated and the rents – i.e. profits that exceed the cost of production plus a 'standard' rate of return – can be very significant. For Jensen and Wantchekon, 'discretion in the distribution of oil or mineral revenues causes democratic governments to break down or authoritarian governments to endure' (Jensen and Wantchekon 2004: 817). Political leaders in resource-rich states may find it sufficient to rely on a small 'winning coalition' (Bueno de Mesquita *et al.* 2003) that benefits from control over these resources and pay little heed to interests of the citizens at large. In short, it is argued that an economy that is based on primary resources makes it easier for autocrats to consolidate power.

As Haber and Menaldo (2010) emphasize, across a longer historical perspective, resource wealth is not *inevitably* associated with authoritarian government. For example, in the Middle East, many countries were authoritarian prior to the discovery or exploitation of significant resources, while neighbouring countries that were resource poor(er) have also remained authoritarian (e.g. Yemen or Jordan). At the same time, in the nineteenth century, natural resources played a significant role in the US's economy – without causing democratic breakdown. This suggests that while resources are likely to matter given the potential rents involved, they do not determine regime outcomes – but interact with other factors.

Central Asia and Mongolia are rich in natural resources, but with significant variation in types, distribution and development of these resources relative to the potential democratization period in the early 1990s. Turkmenistan had already become a major gas producer by the early 1990s, with production running at 80 billion cubic meters annually. By 2008 gas accounted for 57 per cent of total exports, while oil and oil products made up a further 37 per cent. Oil and gas between them accounted for more than 70 per cent of Turkmenistan's gross domestic product (GDP) in 2008.[10]

Similarly, Uzbekistan was already producing around 37 billion cubic meters of natural gas in 1990, and the country was also a significant exporter of cotton fibre (a different type of primary commodity), as well as gold. In the mid-1990s, cotton fibre made up 40 per cent of total exports (subsequently declining to around 20 per cent by 2006), gold 16 per cent and natural gas 15 per cent (IMF 2008). In addition, Uzbekistan exports significant amounts of copper.

Kazakhstan produced substantial volumes of oil in the early 1990s, but this mostly served to satisfy internal demand, with little exports. A significant increase in oil production occurred subsequently, especially from the late 1990s onwards. Oil now accounts for nearly one-quarter of GDP, 60 per cent of total exports, and 40 per cent of all budget revenues. Moreover, in 2009, around three-quarters of foreign direct investment (FDI) in Kazakhstan was targeted at the oil and gas sectors (IMF 2010b).

Like Uzbekistan, Tajikistan was also a major cotton producer during the Soviet period and, according to World Bank figures, cotton fibre still accounted for 18 per cent of the country's exports in 2007. The other key export is aluminium, accounting for nearly 50 per cent of exports in the early 1990s, and still 39 per cent by 2007.[11] Kyrgyzstan is somewhat less reliant on primary commodities than its post-Soviet neighbours: gold exports are estimated to make up around 40 per cent of total exports.[12] Finally, Mongolia today exports significant volumes of copper concentrate and gold; in 2008, the former made up 33 per cent of total exports, the latter 24 per cent (IMF 2010a).

In Central Asia, the presence of major natural resources, including a range of minerals and natural gas, was well known to political elites on the eve of independence (i.e. when the potential 'window of opportunity' for liberalization and democratization was open). The post-independence leaders and their entourage have sought to use control over these commodities in order to solidify their political control.

The companies that exploit these natural resources largely remained under the control of the state elites. In Kazakhstan, oil and gas production is dominated by the state-owned KazMunayGas. Foreign competitors with an interest in Kazakhstan's oil have faced strong pressure from Kazakhstan's government. Kazakhstan recently passed a law declaring its right to pre-empt the sale of any oil property in the country.[13] In Turkmenistan, the emerging authoritarian government established firm control over gas production through the state monopoly Turkmengaz.

In Uzbekistan, most cotton has to be sold to state ginneries, which then sell it to approved import–export companies. This system establishes a situation in which significant rents can be reaped by the state and associated business elites, while leaving many cotton farmers and their families poor and exploited.[14] In Tajikistan, the cotton 'value chain' remains similarly controlled via ginneries owned by the state and associated business elites, while the country's most significant economic asset, the Talco aluminium plant, is tightly controlled by the country's leadership.

In Kyrgyzstan, natural resources and primary commodities have been less dominant. Cotton is less significant than in Tajikistan and Uzbekistan. While Kyrgyzstan produced gold already during the Soviet period, most of the country's mineral deposits were too costly to develop due to the nature of the deposits as well as their remote locations. Since independence, gold mining has intensified, but the state did not secure a monopoly over gold production. The state-owned gold company Kyrgzaltyn owns one-third of shares in the country's largest gold mine, Kumtor.[15]

Mongolia is rich in mineral deposits, but similar to Kyrgyzstan, most of these had been too remote and costly to develop during the Soviet period. In 1990, the country had one major copper-producing mine (Erdenet), which remained 51 per cent owned by the Mongolian government, with the other half owned by Russia. Soviet-era prospecting had suggested the presence of major other mineral deposits in the country (including copper, gold, uranium and others, as well as large coal deposits); but none of these had been proven in detail or started to be developed during the initial period of democratization. The larger potential was known amongst elites, but the potential rents from these deposits initially remained uncertain. Mongolia's resource potential only became financially viable and highly attractive as China's economy expanded and as the latter became a voracious importer of raw materials in the course of the 1990s and 2000s.

The trajectories of different countries in Central Asia appear to support the regime-focused hypotheses related to the 'resource curse'.[16] Those countries with the most significant natural resources relative to GDP (Turkmenistan, Kazakhstan and Uzbekistan) are also the most authoritarian. In Tajikistan, there was neither gas nor minerals; cotton and aluminium were the key commodities. The fact that significant resource rents were less readily available meant that rival factions could not as easily be 'bought off'. After the end of Tajikistan's civil war, and as part of its efforts at consolidating power, the Rahmon government then pursued consolidation of its economic control over cotton and aluminium. Kyrgyzstan was relatively resource poor – and experienced the relatively greatest degree of liberalization in Central Asia. In Mongolia, there is substantial natural resource wealth, but only one main mine was developed during the Soviet period. The main existing mine remained under state control, while small new mines started to develop in various locations for many years prior to some major deals and resource developments in the late 2000s. This constellation proved compatible with democratization.

What appears to be most relevant for regime trajectories in Central Asia is the fact that resource wealth provided incentives and opportunities for authoritarian consolidation. This was facilitated both by the internal elite dynamics discussed above, and by international factors, discussed in the following sections. The key incentive for emerging leaders was to bring potentially vast wealth under their personal control, and that of a relatively narrow group of supporters. In Turkmenistan, Uzbekistan, Kazakhstan and, later, Tajikistan, resource wealth and the 'easy' rents that it generated allowed elites to co-opt, bribe, cajole or repress opponents and to achieve monopoly control of the country's media and other potential sources of challenge. As will be discussed below, the region's resource wealth furthermore contributed to a relationship with the outside world that was focused on resources (and security) rather than democratization or human rights, and made these countries less aid-dependent than they would otherwise have been.

External environment: confluence of negatives

Way and Levitsky (2007) identify two international factors that may influence the spread of democratization. The first is proximity to well-established democratic polities that influence regimes in democratizing states through networks of exchange and interaction, which they refer to as *linkage*, while the second they term *leverage*, which occurs where democratic change is in the clear interest of influential foreign powers and where external actors actively pressurize a state to democratize. In a similar way, Whitehead (1996) and Schmitter (1996) refer to such external influences as *contagion* (i.e. the spread – or retreat – of democracy between neighbouring or closely associated countries), and *conditionality*, whereby outside actors impose conditions or incentives in return for democratic change.

The most important external actors in the 1990s for Central Asia and Mongolia were the US, Europe and Russia, as well as actors from Arab and other Muslim countries that sought to promote Islam (Adamson 2003). Over time, China has become much more important, especially in economic terms, but other than as a general 'model' of development, it was not an active political player during the initial window of opportunity around independence. Generally, the West (i.e. Europe and the US) would be expected to be an external actor supportive of democratization, and seeking to build linkages as well as using leverage.

However, in Central Asia the US and Europe have played an ambiguous role with regards to democratization. On the one hand, they have sought to promote democracy, as they did in Central and Eastern Europe. On the other hand, they have also been quite willing to cooperate directly or indirectly with the emerging authoritarian regimes, as long as these regimes were useful from an energy or security perspective. This tendency became especially noticeable in the early 2000s, when the US developed close relations with the authoritarian regime in Uzbekistan as part of planning the attacks on Afghanistan and Iraq (Daly *et al.* 2006).[17] Europe collectively and European countries individually have been rather subdued in their engagement in Central Asia in terms of democratization and have limited their criticism of human rights violations. Geographic distance to Europe and the US reduced the potential for linkage.

The extent and impact of Islamic influence is hard to assess accurately as the flow of funds – much of which is private – does not appear in public records. The influence is also difficult to assess because Central Asian governments themselves have generally been rather opposed to Islamic influences, while having some incentives to exaggerate the degree and danger of Islamist influence in order to legitimize the persecution of potential opposition groups (Mihalka 2006; Naumkin 2006).

As Adamson (2003) notes, three distinct types of Islamic groups have been active in Central Asia: Wahhabism, from the Arab Gulf region, especially Saudi Arabia; Hizb ut-Tahrir, an Islamist network with roots in Jordan and Palestine; and groups from Turkey promoting 'moderate' Islam. Hizb ut-Tahrir is assumed to be the group with the greatest number of supporters across Central Asia (see Weitz 2004). The strongest influence of these groups appears to be in Uzbekistan, Tajikistan and Kyrgyzstan, while they have been less relevant in Kazakhstan (ICG 2009: 3). To the extent that an influence exists (and existed in the early 1990s) it appears to have been opposed to democratization.

A third key source of influence has been Russia. During the initial period of regime formation and state-building in Central Asia in the 1990s, Russia was significantly weakened (and preoccupied with transition at home), while more recently, it sought to reassert its influence. However, even while weakened, Russia was supportive of incumbent 'Soviet-successor' presidents. Russia's engagement has been driven in part by the association of democratization with a pro-Western foreign policy orientation, which is seen as opposed to Russia's interests. Jointly with Uzbekistan, Russia actively supported the dominant Leninobod and Kulob groups in their struggle against their rivals from Gharm and Badakhshan during the civil war in Tajikistan. Russia began sending its own election observers, nominally under the auspices of the Commonwealth of Independent States (CIS), which endorse the result of elections – even if these are clearly not free and fair. Also, Russia started promoting various multilateral associations in the region to promote regional economic, foreign policy and security cooperation, such as the Eurasian Economic Community (EurasEC), the Collective Security Treaty Organization (CSTO) and the Shangai Cooperation Organization (SCO) (see Schmitz 2008). After 2000, Russia began to reassert its influence in its so-called 'near abroad'. This support was aimed at bolstering incumbent regimes against potential challenges and at promoting Russia-friendly politics. Russia lent support to Uzbekistan's President Karimov after Uzbek special forces opened fire on demonstrators in the eastern Uzbek town of Andijan in May 2005. In late 2010, Russia was rather closely engaged with the political parties preparing to form a coalition government in Kyrgyzstan.

Over the last decade, China has begun to play a far greater role in Central Asia, especially in terms of commercial interests. Over the last few years the state-owned China National Petroleum Corporation (CNPC) has built a 2,200 km long gas pipeline from northern Turkmenistan, across Uzbekistan and Kazakhstan, and into Western China. As well as Turkmen gas, it will also be fed by gas from fields in western Kazakhstan. At present, only small amounts of gas flow along the pipeline, but it is estimated that by 2014 it will be carrying around 40 billion cubic metres per year.[18] In 2009 an oil pipeline was completed that conveys oil from Kazakhstan's Caspian Basin to Xinjiang in China. Chinese and Kazakh companies are also creating joint ventures for the extraction of copper and uranium.

A fifth external influence – particularly relevant for Tajikistan, Turkmenistan and Uzbekistan – has been the drugs trade and general instability emanating from Afghanistan. These three Central Asian countries are the first stop on major drug-trading routes from Afghanistan to Europe, and especially Tajikistan's mountainous borders have been difficult to control. According to Cornell (2006: 38): 'Greater Central Asia has been one of the regions whose security has been most negatively affected by [drugs-related] organized crime.' Drugs smuggling and the crime networks associated with it have had corrosive effects on societies (through the spread of addiction) as well as on states (through corruption and state-capture). The trade in drugs appears to have become increasingly important in recent years also in Kyrgyzstan (ICG 2010).

Considering again the strikingly diverging trajectory of Mongolia, external factors here have differed in very significant ways. A Buddhist country, its religious influences have come from Tibet, most notably the Dalai Lama's network in exile. Given its location, Mongolia has been removed from the conflicts around Afghanistan and Iraq, and has not been of interest as a transit route for drugs. Furthermore, it has not been a source of energy (although a mining boom based on copper, gold and coal has emerged since 2006).

Situated between Russia and China, Mongolia has been the subject of considerable geopolitical interest, especially from the US and Japan. However, in contrast to the Central Asian countries, this geopolitical interest translated into support for democratization, rather than collusion with incumbent elites. The US and Japan provided ample development assistance, and the US (as well as Germany) actively engaged in democratization (Fritz 2008a). Russia by and large 'let go' of Mongolia in the 1990s, but has sought to rebuild its influence in the 2000s in the economic as well as the political spheres. Mongolia itself has pursued good relations with the US as a way to balance the influence of its two powerful neighbours. At the same time, it has sought to be on 'good enough' terms with Russia and China, and has been able to pursue this three-way balance with greater ease than, for example, Uzbekistan (Telford 2004).

Moreover, being an independent country to start with was a boon to democratization in rather subtle ways. Mongolia soon established both diplomatic and aid relations with key Western partners, and as a result benefited from implicit or explicit democratization assistance earlier. Mongolia also had significantly closer relationships with Central and Eastern Europe (especially Poland and what was then Czechoslovakia) than the five Central Asian states, due to its long-standing role as an aid-dependent country within the Council for Mutual Economic Assistance (COMECON) block. Thus, despite being geographically even more remote from established democracies than the five post-Soviet countries, during a critical period Mongolia had denser links with successfully democratizing countries and established democracies (Levitsky and Way 2005).

The combination of 'negative' external influences that have blighted democratization in Central Asia is striking and contrasts starkly with the benign external influences that the new European Union member states in Central Europe have been able to benefit from. Overall, external influences have favoured the emergence and consolidation of authoritarian rather than democratic regimes and have compounded rather than counterbalanced other factors that have made democratization challenging.

What are the prospects for eventual democratization?

Many countries – and regions such as Latin America or parts of Asia and Africa – that experienced authoritarian regimes for long periods of time eventually developed hybrid or even fully demo-cratic regimes. It is therefore worth asking whether or not there are any medium-term prospects of change in Central Asia.

Importantly, while the authoritarian regimes are consolidated in four out of the five Central Asian countries, these regimes have a very mixed record with regards to socio-economic devel-opment on the one hand, and state-building on the other. Uzbekistan, Tajikistan, Kyrgyzstan and, to a lesser degree, Turkmenistan are considered as potentially unstable states (see Table 6.2).

Poverty levels are still high across the region even after some decline in the 2000s, with the exception of Kazakhstan (see Table 6.3).[19] Elite groups have absorbed much of the countries' wealth and economic opportunities. The 2005 armed protests in Andijan (Uzbekistan) by citizens discontented with poverty, official corruption and elite rent-seeking – and the government's heavy-handed reaction (killing several hundred or possibly a few thousand protesters) – reflect these underlying tensions (ICG 2006).

Table 6.2 Indices on state and political stability

	FfP/Failed States Index 2007	FfP/Failed States Index 2010	WGI Pol Stab 2000	WGI Pol Stab 2009
Kazakhstan	72.3	72.7	50.0	69.8
Kyrgyzstan	88.2	88.4	30.8	26.4
Mongolia	58.4	60.1	73.1	55.2
Tajikistan	88.7	89.2	4.8	16.0
Turkmenistan	87.5	82.5	44.7	50.9
Uzbekistan	93.5	90.5	12.0	18.4

Note: The Fund for Peace's Failed Index (www.fundforpeace.org) is a combined score across 12 categories and can range from 12 (highly stable) to 120 (extremely fragile). The World Governance Indicators score on Political Stability and Absence of Violence ranges from 0 to 100 with lower ratings indicating a higher risk of instability. Both indices draw on a range of existing indicators.

Table 6.3 Percentage of population living below poverty PPP$2/day and national lines

	poverty headcount ratio at <$2 a day (PPP) c.2003	poverty headcount ratio at national poverty line	poverty headcount ratio at <$2 a day (PPP) c.2007
Kazakhstan	17.2	n/a	2.0
Kyrgyzstan	51.9	43.1 (2005)	27.5
Mongolia	49.1	n/a	13.6
Tajikistan	50.8	53.5 (2007)	n/a
Turkmenistan	n/a	n/a	n/a

Source: World Bank.

Again, there is a notable contrast with Mongolia, which is considered a relatively stable state by various ratings, and which appears to have rather successfully reduced extreme poverty in recent years (despite a much lower per capita GDP than Kazakhstan). While the emerging wealth of the country's resource boom is also being absorbed by small groups of elites, the parliamentary system allows for greater competition over these rents. It has also given rise to populist social welfare policies (the introduction of universal, unconditional payments for children; and promises of giving annual lump-sum payments to all citizens from natural resource revenue flows) that seem to have contributed to poverty reduction.

In several ways, Central Asian countries exhibit similarities with post-colonial personal regimes that emerged in parts of Asia and Africa in the 1970s (see Gammer 2000). In particular, similarities include personalized autocratic regimes that proclaim to be engaged in state-building while de facto contributing to state weakness because power is very much personalized rather than becoming embedded in institutions. There are still important differences – for example, full adult literacy has largely been preserved across Central Asia, while in many African countries initial attempts after decolonization to expand access to education quickly stalled. In addition, the volatile international environment is different from that during the Cold War. However, the emergence of highly personalized rule after independence, economic dependence on commodities and related rent-seeking by well-connected elites, as well as an external environment that is not favourable to democratization, are traits that Central Asian countries share with a number of post-colonial countries during the 1970s.

In terms of what the future holds, Mongolia has been rated as 'free' by Freedom House for 19 consecutive years. The country has experienced changes in power as the result of elections, and in this sense, democracy can be considered as consolidated – although threats to the quality as well as the durability of democracy remain. In contrast, Turkmenistan, Uzbekistan, Kazakhstan and Tajikistan have all been categorized as 'not free' for at least 16 years and have become consolidated authoritarian regimes. The presidents of all four countries are deeply entrenched in their positions and have kept any potential challengers closely in check. So far, a leadership change has happened only in one of these four countries, Turkmenistan, where the autocratic president Saparmurat Niyazov died in December 2006 and was replaced by his Health Minister Gurbanguly Berdymuhamedov. Despite dismantling some of the more extreme elements of Niyazov's personality cult, Turkmenistan remains fully authoritarian. Leadership successions will eventually also have to occur in Kazakhstan, Uzbekistan and Tajikistan. While they may reduce elite cohesion, there is a real risk that any change will involve prolonged periods of instability, rather than a real democratic opening and rapid transition to a democratic regime.

Recent events in Kyrgyzstan are an example. While presidents Akayev and Bakiyev in Kyrgyzstan sought to exercise authoritarian leadership, they never achieved a *consolidated* authoritarian regime. In April 2010, the Bakiyev government was toppled by opposition protests in the north. In June 2010, the power vacuum that existed in southern Kyrgyzstan provided the backdrop for bitter intercommunal fighting in Osh between Kyrgyz and Uzbeks that left hundreds killed and many thousands (mainly Uzbeks) displaced. In the immediate aftermath of these events, a constitutional referendum took place in which the country adopted a mixed parliamentary-presidential system. The constitution also limits the number of parliamentary seats that can be won by any one party to 65 out of a total of 120, in order to prevent the authoritarian consolidation of power. In October 2010, Kyrgyzstan held parliamentary elections that in the words of the Organization for Security and Cooperation in Europe (OSCE) monitoring mission 'constituted a further consolidation of the democratic process' and were widely held to be the first elections in Central Asia in which the outcome was uncertain. Thus, the situation in Kyrgyzstan corresponds well to what Lucan Way describes as 'pluralism by default' in which 'institutionalized political competition survives not because leaders are especially democratic or because societal actors are particularly strong, but because the government is too fragmented and the state too weak to impose authoritarian rule' (Way 2002: 127). Such democratization by default would be a benign outcome; while the risk remains that the same elite pluralism that opens up a window of opportunity for democratization could just as likely tear the country apart.

Kazakhstan is relatively more stable as well as more developed than the southern countries. While the political regime is a consolidated authoritarian one, since independence it has delivered a degree of economic growth, as well as of state modernization and institution-building. The most likely medium-term scenario for Kazakhstan is to remain a consolidated authoritarian regime – especially if the leadership transition from President Nazerbaev (who turned 70 in 2010) to a successor is managed without an internal weakening of the regime.

Conclusion

Against a backdrop of an unexpected need for state-building and economic crisis at the beginning of the 1990s, late Soviet or early post-Soviet leaders embarked on creating systems of personal rule. With little experience of democracy and surrounded by an institutional setting that – both formally and informally – rewarded arbitrary and authoritarian acts, such consolidation, if success-ful, was bound to lead to authoritarianism. The weakness of any effective counter-elites enabled this regime development.

In Central Asia, the ruling elites of Turkmenistan, Uzbekistan and Kazakhstan (all led by the former Communist Party boss) were able to consolidate authoritarian control relatively rapidly, and Tajikistan's Emomali Rahmon was able to do so somewhat later (i.e. after the 1997 peace agreement). Despite the best efforts of Kyrgyzstan's President Askar Akayev, however, his net-works were never able to fully consolidate their authority. Consolidation of power in Central Asia allowed the leadership to establish a hyper-presidential system in which parliaments were largely reduced to a rubber-stamping role.

In Mongolia, on the other hand, no single leader was able to emerge as *primus inter pares*. The MPRP was able to retain its collective power as an organization and was not usurped by any one leader. Given the apparent absence of a 'father of the nation', the constitution that was approved by the Mongolian parliament (the *Ikh Khural*) in January 1992 was a mixed parliamentary-presidential system in which the parliament retained significant powers.

The ready availability of primary commodities provided the Central Asian elites with the opportunity to entrench the authoritarian systems further. In Turkmenistan, Kazakhstan, Uzbekistan and Tajikistan, state elites consolidated control over rents from oil, gas, minerals and cotton and used these to reward loyalists and punish dissenting voices.

There remain two further factors that were conducive to democratization in Mongolia, but not in Central Asia. The first was Mongolia's history of independent statehood. The fact that Mongolia was already an independent state meant that it had readily available a set of state institutions that could not easily be usurped for the benefit of any one leader. In Central Asia, however, state institutions had to be rebuilt from an array left by the Soviet Union. The second factor that was relatively beneficial for democratization in Mongolia was that, despite its remote geographical location, links between Mongolia and the West were rather strong and such linkages made a positive contribution to the democratization process. In Central Asia, on the other hand, the West was more interested in commercial and security issues than democratization and provided little incentives and engagement.

Overall, the prospects for successful democratization and for eventual consolidation of democracy in Central Asia remain highly uncertain, and are currently limited to Mongolia and potentially Kyrgyzstan. In terms of domestic actors, a major challenge is the fact that any organized opposition has been systematically prosecuted, especially in Tajikistan, Turkmenistan and Uzbekistan, reducing the likelihood that a transition triggered by opposition-organized events would result in successful democratization. Natural resource dependence is likely to continue and may even increase as new deposits are being developed in reaction to growing demand. The external environment will continue to play an important role, and in particular regime developments in Russia and China on the one hand, and, on the other hand, wider foreign, security and energy policy interests in the region.

Notes

1 There are a variety of definitions of 'Central Asia'. The most restrictive definitions define Central Asia as Kyrgyzstan, Uzbekistan, Tajikistan and Turkmenistan only. In a wider geographic sense, Mongolia, as well as territories within China, Iran, Afghanistan, India, Pakistan and Russia are considered part of Central Asia. For the purposes of this chapter, the term 'Central Asian countries' will be used to refer to the five former Soviet republics: Kazakhstan, Kyrgyzstan, Uzbekistan, Tajikistan and Turkmenistan.

2 In October 2010, relatively free and fair parliamentary elections were held in Kyrgyzstan. However, the initial 'change in power' resulted from protests against the government of President Bakiyev in April (who resigned and fled the country), and was furthermore preceded by a burst of ethnic violence in June 2010 in the south of Kyrgyzstan.

3 Late communist and early post-communist networks were primarily regional patronage networks. These networks were usually linked to crucial economic assets (such as major enterprises or collective farms and agro-industries) as well as to positions in the Soviet *nomenklatura* hierarchy.

4 Masaliev was Akayev's principal opponent in presidential elections held in December 1995. Although he won just 24.4% of the vote in the presidential elections, he was elected to parliament in his Osh constituency in February of the same year with 84% of the vote.

5 While communist parties still exist throughout the region, they are not centres of power. Moreover, although new ruling parties were created out of the old Communist Party in Uzbekistan and Turkmenistan (the People's Democratic Party and the Democratic Party of Turkmenistan respectively), they were no longer the main source of power – the president was.

6 The Mongolian People's Revolutionary Party or MPRP was the country's Communist Party that had held a monopoly of power for close to 70 years.

7 The major exception to nationalist mobilization in the western part of the Former Soviet Union remained Belarus, where national sentiment was weak.

8 'Khanate' is a Turco-Mongolian term used to describe chiefdoms or principalities (which could be of varying size and durability).

9 This refers to the massive falsification of cotton-production figures during the 1960s and 1970s, which was masterminded by Uzbek Communist Party First Secretary Sharof Rashidov and his followers for the purpose of private profit.

10 World Bank, 'Turkmenistan at a glance' (2009), available at http://devdata.worldbank.org/AAG/tkm_aag.pdf (accessed 14 August 2010).

11 World Bank, 'Tajikistan at a glance' (2009), available at http://devdata.worldbank.org/AAG/tjk_aag.pdf (accessed 14 August 2010). Tajikistan does not produce any bauxite, and the raw material for producing aluminium is imported. The key ingredient for aluminium production is cheap energy. Tajikistan produces hydropower, and has significant undeveloped potential. However, Talco consumes about 40% of the existing energy supply, while the rest of the economy suffers frequent electricity shortages.

12 Joomart Otorbaev, Rafkat Hasanov, Gulzhan Ermekbaeva, Dinara Rakhmanova, Sergey Slepchenko and Murat Suyunbaev, 'The Kyrgyz Republic' (2008) at www.silkroadstudies.org/new/docs/publica tions/GCA/GCAPUB-08.pdf (accessed 14 August 2010).

13 *New York Times*, 'China Ups the Ante in Its Bid for Oil' (23 August 2005), available at http://www. nytimes.com/2005/08/23/business/worldbusiness/23oil.html?_r=1 (accessed 14 August 2010).

14 International Crisis Group, 'The Curse of Cotton: Central Asia's Destructive Monoculture'. Crisis Group Asia Report N°93, 28 February 2005.

15 The rest of the shares are owned by the Canadian company Centerra Gold. The agreement to divide shares in Kumtor in that proportion was made in 2009 after a rather conflictual relationship between the Canadian and Kyrgyz sides saw Kyrgzaltyn stake in the mine oscillate between16% and around 60% in the period since 1992. Fergana.ru: Central Asia news, 'Kyrgyzstan: New Agreement on Kumtor Divides Kyrgyz Elites' (30 April 2009) at http://enews.ferghana.ru/article.php?id=2529 (accessed 14 August 2010).

16 At the same time, the region does not support extreme forms of 'resource curse' hypotheses, which assume that natural resources can be a trigger for civil wars.

17 Relations between Uzbekistan and the US eventually soured by 2005, when the US became more critical of Uzbekistan's human rights record, and the country rebuilt closer ties with Russia.

18 BBC News, 'Struggle for Central Asian energy riches' (1 June 2010) at http://www.bbc.co.uk/news/ 10185429 (accessed 15 August 2010).

19 Data is patchy. For example, there is no recent data for Turkmenistan.

References

Adamson, F. (2003) 'The Diffusion of Competing Norms in Central Asia: Transnational Democracy Assistance Networks vs. Transnational Islamism'. Paper prepared for delivery at the 2003 Annual Meeting of the American Political Science Association.

Beissinger, Mark R. (2007) 'Ethnic Identity and Democratization: Lessons from the Post-Soviet Region', *Taiwan Journal of Democracy*, 3 (2), pp. 73–99.

Bratton, Michael and Eric Chang (2006) 'State Building and Democratization in Sub-Saharan Africa: Forwards, Backwards, or Together?', *Comparative Political Studies*, 39 (9), pp. 1059–1083.

Bueno de Mesquita, Bruce, Alastair Smith, Randolph M. Siverson and James D. Morrow (2003) *The Logic of Political Survival*. Cambridge, MA: MIT Press.

Bunce, Valerie (2003) 'Rethinking Recent Democratization Lessons from the Postcommunist Experience', *World Politics*, 55 (2), pp. 167–192.

Collier, Paul (2007) 'Managing Commodity Booms: Lessons of International Experience', a paper prepared for the African Economic Research Consortium, available at www.cabri-sbo.org/uploads/files/ Managing%20Commodity%20Booms%20by%20Paul%20Collier.pdf (accessed 25 August 2010).

Collins, Kathleen (2006) *Clan Politics and Regime Transition in Central Asia*. Cambridge: Cambridge University Press.

Cornell, Svante E. (2006) 'The Narcotics Threat in Greater Central Asia: From Crime-Terror Nexus to State Infiltration?', *China and Eurasia Forum Quarterly*, 4 (1), pp. 37–67.

Daly, John C.K., Kurt H. Meppen, Vladimir Socor, and S. Frederick Starr (2006) 'Anatomy of a Crisis: US-Uzbek Relations 2001–2005', Silk Road Paper, Washington, DC: Central Asia-Caucasus Institute, available at http://www.isdp.eu/images/stories/isdp-main-pdf/2006_daly-et-al_anatomy-of-a-crisis. pdf (accessed 29 August 2011).

Diamond, Larry (1992) 'Economic Development and Democracy Reconsidered', *American Behavioural Scientist*, 35 (4/5), pp. 450–499.

Friedman, Thomas (2006) 'The First Law of Petropolitics', *Foreign Policy*, 154, pp. 28–39.

Fritz, Verena (2008a) 'Mongolia: The Rise and Travails of a Deviant Democracy', *Democratization*, 15 (4), pp. 766–788.

—— (2008b) 'Transition and State-Building in the Southern CIS', Paper prepared for the Central Eurasian Studies Society's 9th Annual Meeting, 18–21 September 2008, Georgetown University, Washington DC.

Gammer, Moshe (2000) 'Post-Soviet Central Asia and Post-Colonial Francophone Africa: Some Associations', *Middle Eastern Studies*, 36 (2), pp. 124–149.

Haber, S. and V. Menaldo (2010) *Do Natural Resources Fuel Authoritarianism? A Reappraisal of the Resource Curse*. Paper available at https://iriss.stanford.edu/sites/all/files/sshp/docs/Haber%20and%20Menaldo%20March%2019%202010.pdf (accessed 20 September 2011).

Huntington, Samuel (1991) *The Third Wave*. Norman: University of Oklahoma Press.

ICG (International Crisis Group) (2006) 'Uzbekistan: In for the Long Haul', Asia Briefing N° 45.

ICG (International Crisis Group) (2009) 'Central Asia: Islamists in Prison', Asia Briefing N° 97.

ICG (International Crisis Group) (2010) 'The Pogroms in Kyrgyzstan', Asia Report N° 193.

IMF (International Monetary Fund) (2008) 'Republic of Uzbekistan: 2008 Article IV Consultation—Staff Report; Public Information Notice on the Executive Board Discussion; and Statement by the Executive Director for the Republic of Uzbekistan'. IMF Country Report No. 08/235.

IMF (International Monetary Fund) (2010a) 'Mongolia: Fourth Review under the Stand-By Arrangement and Request for Modification of Performance Criteria'. IMF Country Report No. 10/84.

IMF (International Monetary Fund) (2010b) 'Republic of Kazakhstan: 2010 Article IV Consultation—Staff Report; Public Information Notice on the Executive Board Discussion; and Statement by the Executive Director for Kazakhstan'. IMF Country Report No. 10/241.

Jensen, Nathan and Leonard Wantchekon (2004) 'Resource Wealth and Political Regimes in Africa', *Comparative Political Studies*, 37 (7), pp. 816–841.

Jones Luong, Pauline (2002) *Institutional Change and Political Continuity in Post-Soviet Central Asia: Power, Perceptions, and Pacts*. Cambridge and New York: Cambridge University Press.

Karl, Terry (1990) 'Dilemmas of Democratization in Latin America', *Comparative Politics*, 23 (1), pp. 1–21.

—— and Philippe Schmitter (1991) 'Modes of Transition in Latin America, Southern and Eastern Europe', *International Social Science Journal*, 128, pp. 269–284.

Kitschelt, Herbert (2001) 'Post-Communist Economic Reforms: Causal Mechanisms and Concomitant Properties', presented at the 2001 annual meeting of the American Political Science Association.

Levitsky, Steven and Lucan Way (2005) 'International Linkage and Democratization', *Journal of Democracy*, 16 (3), pp. 20–34.

Linz, Juan and Alfred Stepan (1996) *Problems of Democratic Transition and Consolidation: Southern Europe, South America, and Post-Communist Europe*. Baltimore, MD: Johns Hopkins University Press.

Lipset, Seymour Martin (1959) 'Some Social Requisites of Democracy: Economic Development and Political Legitimacy', *The American Political Science Review*, 53 (1), pp. 69–105.

—— (1994) 'Social Prerequisites of Democracy Revisited', *American Sociological Review*, 59, pp. 1–22.

Mihalka, Michael (2006) 'Counterinsurgency, Counterrerrorism, State-building and Security Cooperation in Central Asia', *China and Eurasia Forum Quarterly*, 4 (2), pp. 131–151.

Naumkin, Vitalii (2006) 'Uzbekistan's State-building Fatigue', *The Washington Quarterly*, 29 (3), pp. 127–140.

Nettl, J.P. (1968) 'The State as a Conceptual Variable', *World Politics*, 20, pp. 559–592.

O'Donnell, Guillermo and Philippe C. Schmitter (1986) *Transitions from Authoritarian Rule*. Baltimore, MD: Johns Hopkins University Press.

Przeworski, Adam (1992) 'The Games of Transition'. In *The New Transitions in Latin America: Problems of Transition and Consolidation*, ed. Scott Mainwaring, Guillermo O'Donnell and Samuel Valenzuela. Notre Dame: Notre Dame University Press.

Radnitz, Scott (2006) 'What Really Happened in Kyrgyzstan?', *Journal of Democracy*, 17 (2), pp. 132–146.

—— (2010) 'The Color of Money: Privatization, Economic Dispersion, and the Post-Soviet "Revolutions" ', *Comparative Politics*, 42 (2), pp. 127–146.

Schmitter, Philippe (1996) 'The Influence of the International Context upon the Choice of National Institutions and Policies in Neo-Democracies'. In *The International Dimensions of Democratization: Europe and the Americas*, ed. Laurence Whitehead. New York: Oxford University Press, pp. 26–54.

Schmitz, Andrea (2008) 'Partner aus Kalkuel: Russische Politik in Zentralasien' [Calculating partner: Russian policy in Central Asia] *SWP-Study 5*. Berlin: Stiftung Wissenschaft und Politik.

Tansey, Oisín (2009) *Regime-building: Democratization and International Administration*. Oxford and New York: Oxford University Press.

Telford, Sarah (2004) 'To What Extent Does Post-1990 Mongolia Pursue an Independent Foreign Policy?', *UNISCI Discussion Paper*. Madrid: Universidad Complutense Madrid.

Vanhanen, Tatu (2003) *Democratization: A Comparative Analysis of 170 Countries*. London: Routledge.

Way, Lucan A. (2002) 'Pluralism by Default in Moldova', *Journal of Democracy*, 13 (4), pp. 127–141.

—— and Steven Levitsky (2007) 'Linkage, Leverage, and the Post-Communist Divide', *East European Politics and Societies*, 21 (1), pp. 48–66.

Weitz, Richard (2004) 'Storm Clouds over Central Asia? Revival of the Islamic Movement of Uzbekistan (IMU)?', *Studies in Conflict and Terrorism*, 27, pp. 505–530.

Wheatley, Jonathan (2005) *Georgia from National Awakening to Rose Revolution: Delayed Transition in the former Soviet Union*. Aldershot: Ashgate.

Wheatley, Jonathan and Christoph Zürcher (2008) 'On the Origin and Consolidation of Hybrid Regimes: The State of Democracy in the Caucasus', *Taiwan Journal of Democracy*, 4 (1), pp. 1–31.

Whitehead, Laurence (1996) 'Three International Dimensions of Democratization'. In *The International Dimensions of Democratization: Europe and the Americas*, ed. Laurence Whitehead. New York: Oxford University Press, pp. 3–25.

7

Democracy in South Asia

India and Pakistan: parallel pasts, divergent futures

Farida Jalalzai

This chapter examines several questions related to two key countries in South Asia – India and Pakistan – and their differing experiences with democratic transition and consolidation. The key question that the chapter addresses is: how and why do India and Pakistan differ in terms of democracy both historically and at the present time? What are their future democratic prospects? Although once part of the same country, Pakistan and India have had divergent democratic trajectories. On the one hand, India is a consolidated but illiberal democracy. Many among Indian elites and ordinary citizens have a philosophical commitment to democracy, and politics is generally governed by democratic procedures. However, while citizens' civil liberties are continually encroached upon by the state, India's democratic prospects are quite promising. Pakistan, on the other hand, has been under authoritarian rule for most of its history; several governments have been military dictatorships (McGrath 1996). Although the country's democratic position has recently improved, a toxic combination – including, pervasive and persistent military influence on politics, weak and fragmented civil society, and strong linkages between religious extremism and the state – combine to make full democratic transition and consolidation unlikely.

Measuring democracy

The approach this chapter takes in analysing and explicating democratic outcomes in India and Pakistan requires outlining the scholarly debate regarding whether democracy is a matter of degree or kind. Sartori (1970) argues that a dichotomy differentiating democracies from non-democracies is valid conceptually. Similarly, Collier and Levitsky argue that with democratic gradations comes the risk of conceptual stretching (1997). As such, a country is either a democracy or it *is not* (Huntington 1996). However, democracy is complex and nuanced (Collier and Adcock 1999). Larry Diamond (1999) combines approaches, first differentiating generally between a democracy and a non-democracy, and then further distinguishing between different kinds of democracy as follows:

(1) **Pseudo-democracies** may have multiple parties and other features of electoral democracy, 'but lack at least one key requirement: an arena of contestation sufficiently fair that the ruling party can be turned out of power' (Diamond 1999: 15).

(2) **Delegative democracies** have formal constitutional structures of democracy and may meet some empirical standards of liberal democracy but are very hollow and weak. Power is delegated to the presidency with no checks and horizontal measures of accountability between branches.

(3) **Illiberal democracies** are also weak and institutionally shallow, but meet some of the qualifications of electoral democracy.

(4) **Electoral democracies** are civilian and constitutional systems where offices are filled through regular, competitive, multiparty elections with universal suffrage (Diamond 1999: 10).

(5) **Liberal democracies** encompass all aspects of electoral democracy but provide power only to those who are accountable to the electorate, ensure vertical accountability between branches and are characterized by freedom and pluralism. Human rights are a very important aspect of this conception.

In this chapter, I will utilize Diamond's categories of democracy, in relation to India and Pakistan.

Variables and data sources

Utilizing Diamond's categorization, the main dependent variable is the *degree* of democracy in a polity. In this chapter, the sources used are the Freedom House surveys available since the early 1970's. Linking these surveys to a wide variety of scholarship engaged with throughout this chapter, I analyse the following independent variables in relation to India and Pakistan: democratic history; political autonomy; political equality; rule of law; civil liberties; ability to change government; religion in government; population heterogeneity; civil society/cultural norms; and international factors. Data for the independent variables come from numerous sources. Along with several scholarly studies, I refer to the Purdue Political Terror Scales (PTS), annual reports from Human Rights Watch, Amnesty International, the US State Department, as well as data from the International Monetary Fund (IMF), government documents and court rulings. I begin by looking at levels of democracy in the two countries under discussion.

India and Pakistan: political rights, 1972–2010

Freedom House ratings range from 1 to 7, with 1 indicating the most freedom and 7 the least. One score assesses civil liberties and the other political rights. Scores are averaged resulting in the following ratings – 'free' (1–2.5); 'partly free' (3.0–5.0); and 'not free' (5.5–7).[1] As far as political rights are concerned, Pakistan has never been free. It has been considered partly free for a total of 23 years, generally during civilian rule (see Figure 7.1). India, in contrast, apart from five years when it was partly free, has been firmly in the free camp.

India and Pakistan civil liberties, 1972–2010

Pakistan's civil liberties ratings are consistently partly free or not free (see Figure 7.2). Over the last five decades, the country has received a '5' from Freedom House, only just in the partly free range. In India's case, protection of civil liberties is weaker than its political guarantees towards democracy. Freedom House has rated India free for only five years; during the remaining period is has been partly free, including at the current time (2011).

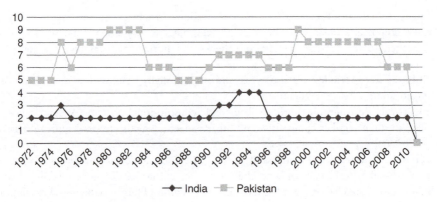

Figure 7.1   Political rights, 1972–2010

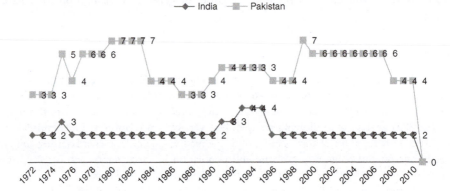

Figure 7.2   Civil liberties, 1972–2010

India and Pakistan overall freedom, 1972–2010

In combining political rights and civil liberties, Pakistan was rated partly free between 1972–9, 1985–6 and 1998–2007 (see Figure 7.3). For all other years it has been considered by Freedom House as not free, as coinciding with the ul Haq (1978–88) and Musharraf (2001–8) military dictatorships. Pakistan has never been rated free overall. India, however,

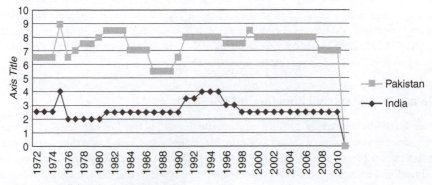

Figure 7.3   Overall freedom, 1972–2010

has been rated free a majority of the time. In spite of a partly free classification for four years (two in the 1970s and two in the 1990s) India has been considered free, though only barely, because of its relatively poor civil liberties regime. Therefore, India is both currently and historically a democracy while Pakistan is neither. However, India is an illiberal democracy, with weak and hollow democratic institutions, albeit in the context of regular, competitive, multiparty elections with universal suffrage (Diamond 1999: 10). Although Freedom House data indicate the extent of democracy in both countries, specific factors contributing to these classifications require further elaboration. Next, I outline key findings related to the main independent variables.

Democratic history

Linz and Stepan (1996) argue for a path-dependent approach to democracy; democracy is more likely when a country has past democratic experiences. According to Ziring (2000), Pakistan's earliest democratic exposure is best characterized as pseudo-democratic under the leadership of Mohammad Ali Jinnah (1947–8) and Liaquat Ali Khan (1947–51). Even during more recent democratic periods – including the governments of Zulfiqar Ali Bhutto (1971–1977), Benazir Bhutto (1988–90; 1993–6) and Nawaz Sharif (1990–3; 1993; 1997–9), full democratic transition was not achieved. Civilian rule has been repeatedly interrupted by the military, notably under Generals Ayub Khan (1958–69), Zia ul Haq (1977–88) and Pervez Musharraf (1998–2008). Following the assassination of Benazir Bhutto in 2007, and President Musharraf's resignation in 2008, Asif Zardari (Benazir Bhutto's widower) attained the presidency. Since then, Pakistan's democratic status has improved, though still leaving much to be desired as it navigates various security concerns in the post-9/11 environment (Ziring 2004).

In contrast, India is a long-standing, consolidated democracy. India's first prime minister, Jawaharlal Nehru, significantly influenced its future political direction. According to Ganguly (2002: 39): 'Nehru encouraged parliamentary debate, maintained internal democracy within the Congress party, continued the British tradition of a politically neutral civil service, fostered judicial independence, encouraged press freedom, boosted secularism, and firmly entrenched civilian control of the military.' For most of India's history, the Congress Party (later splitting into the Congress-I and the New Congress parties), has been the dominant political force. However, politics is sometimes unstable in India. For example, parliament has been dissolved several times, often following charges of corruption against its members. Some regimes were more repressive than others. Yet, although India's degree of democracy has left much to be desired, it has had an uninterrupted tradition of democratically settled conflict. Nevertheless, food shortages, inflation and regional political grievances combined to stimulate growing civil unrest in the early 1970s. Prime Minister Indira Gandhi's response was one of suppression as she centralized control of the government and the New Congress Party. There were charges of corruption, a mass opposition movement in Bihar, and resistance to her within the New Congress Party. In addition, Mrs Gandhi was convicted of election fraud during her 1971 campaign and was ordered to resign. However, she declared a state of emergency, imprisoning numerous opposition leaders and journalists. During emergency rule, she initiated economic development programmes and managed to oversee a reduction in price inflation. However, many of her policies were seen as repressive. After free elections, Gandhi lost her seat in parliament, though she returned to power in the 1980s until her assassination by Sikh extremists in 1984. In short, although blemished, India clearly has a longer lasting and more robust democracy than Pakistan.

Political autonomy

Political autonomy is determined by the degree to which the executive, legislative and judicial branches are able to perform necessary duties. Although these branches need autonomy, they also require constraints and accountability deriving from a variety of constitutional checks and balances. Pakistan has not been able to disperse power among these branches very evenly. The president has historically been more powerful than the prime minister and could require him to obtain a vote of confidence in the National Assembly and even dissolve the entire National Assembly (Syed 1997: 48). The 1973 Constitution increased prime ministerial powers, but still permitted presidential dismissal. The supreme court ruled this procedure unconstitutional in 1993 when President Khan dismissed Prime Minister Sharif. Re-elected later with a two-thirds parliamentary majority, Sharif passed Amendments 13 and 14 strengthening his position by removing presidential powers to dissolve the government and ban defection of parties. However, President Musharraf's Legal Framework Order – passed in 2002 – amended the previously suspended constitution to allow him to dismiss the prime minister and dissolve parliament (State Department 2003).[2] After Musharraf left power, parliament passed the 18th Amendment, again limiting presidential power and giving parliament, the prime minister, the judiciary and provincial governments greater autonomy. Overall, civilian presidents are vulnerable to being overthrown by the military. In fact, if the current president – Zardari – is able to stay in power for the next two years, that is, until mid-2012, then he will be the first to complete a full term.

India also has a dual executive. However, in contrast to Pakistan, the balance of power rests with the prime minister while the office of the president is largely ceremonial. Powers are constitutionally fixed with a division of responsibilities between national and state governments. The national government has exclusive powers over some areas such as foreign affairs while states have responsibility over other policies (for example, health care), and share some responsibility over others (for example, education). In practice, this division has worked, although we should note that the national government has, numerous times over the last 50 years, suspended the powers of states to administer policies under emergency powers (Kohli 1990). Leaders in India generally are subject to checks, and those proven corrupt are ousted or not re-elected. However, executive power has been concentrated in the hands of a small number of elite families. Furthermore, leadership has increasingly been based on populism (Kohli 1990: 17). Under Indira Gandhi, power struggles in the Congress Party erupted and conflict was hard to resolve within the existing party framework. Gandhi sought to ensure her control, not through democratic solutions but by appointing loyal followers to positions of power (Kohli 1990: 16). In sum, although democratically their power needs to be curtailed, unlike in Pakistan, political executives in India are not challenged by non-elected figures from key national institutions, especially the armed forces.

In Pakistan, the legislative branch is comprised of the directly elected National Assembly and the indirectly selected Senate. However, the legislature has little autonomy. The National Assembly has lost favour with the public over time – largely because successive presidents have not taken it seriously; as a result, it does not operate diligently, creating a vicious circle of underperformance that some analysts contend gets worse over time (Syed 1997: 57). Public esteem was further eroded when National Assembly members unanimously passed a bill that doubled their salaries and allowances, and permitted them to import (duty free) cars of their choosing: 'The bill was passed at a time when the federal budget was expected to show a huge deficit' (Syed 1997: 59). The National Assembly has been abolished several times – in 1958, 1969, 1977 and 1999 – and dismissed in 1953, 1988, 1990 and 1993. However, passage of the 18th Amendment in 2010 has recently helped to provide greater parliamentary autonomy.

India has a bicameral parliament comprising the appointed Council of States and the directly elected People's Assembly. In India, parliament occupies a more prestigious position than that in Pakistan, largely because 'popularly elected governments, after losing their mandate, peacefully remit power to successful opponents' (Ganguly 2002: 1). Years of Congress Party dominance also fostered parliamentarianism.

The Pakistan Constitution (Article 175) provides for a judiciary, although it was not autonomous until 1987. Structurally complex, the judiciary consists of several courts with overlapping and competing jurisdictions. Special courts have been established for banking, drugs, terrorism and sharia (Islamic) law. However, the judiciary is still subject to great executive influence. For example, the supreme court validated the 1999 coup granting the then General Musharraf both executive and legislative authority for three years (World Fact Book 2003: 13). After the coup, Musharraf suspended the constitution, and no court could issue orders against Musharraf or anyone exercising power under his authority (State Department 2000: 16). In July 2001, Musharraf reconstituted the National Security Council, dominated by 12 senior military officers, becoming 'in effect the highest deliberative body in Pakistan' (Shah 2002: 70). In 2007, Musharraf removed Supreme Court Chief Justice Iftikhar Muhammad Chaudhry after the latter ruled that executive encroachments were unconstitutional. This was the first time that the courts engaged in direct confrontation with the executive (Bajoria 2011). This touched off a wave of anti-government protests among lawyers. Chaudhry was eventually reinstated. The current president, Zardari, has largely respected the independence of the supreme court (Rumi 2011c). However, the judiciary has now taken aim at some key democratic reforms in parliament (Rumi 2011c).

India has an independent judiciary with strong constitutional safeguards but limited legislative review. Courts exist at the sub-district, district and federal levels. Unlike Pakistan, India established a fully autonomous judiciary following independence. In theory, citizens are assured a fair trial and this happens in practice more often than in Pakistan. The Criminal Procedure Code provides for open trial, except in cases involving official secrets, which hinders democracy in India. Still, 'India's activist judiciary is trying to restore some probity and efficacy to a variety of institutions. For example, it is primarily due to the supreme court's willingness to entertain public interest litigation that former Prime Minister Rao is still under investigation on corruption charges' (Ganguly 2002: 2). The supreme court greatly aided India's democratic transition and consolidation: 'With executive power slipping and wobbly coalition government the order of the day, the Court's activism emphasizes lawfulness and predictability, often in the face of state abuses' (Rudolph and Rudolph 2002: 61). Since the late 1970s, the supreme court has been noted for its judicial activism against abuses of the poor and for seeking to try corrupt ministers: 'To this end, the Court introduced a system of public-interest litigation that enabled bonded laborers, disenfranchised tribal people, indigent women, the homeless … to approach the bench in search of justice' (Ganguly 2002: 43).

The military

In both India and Pakistan, the military interacts with political elites and the mass public, playing integral and complex roles in both democratic transition and consolidation (Wintrobe 2008). Pakistan's most institutionalized and autonomous political actor is the military. The conflict over Kashmir, which involves India, has led to an expansion of the size of the army, with 60 per cent of Pakistan's budget spent on defence during the first ten years following independence (1947–57), placing the military in a powerful position (McGrath 1996: 24). According to Syed (1997: 61): 'The army has no constitutional or legal authority … but its self-perception encourages it to think that it is entitled to do what it does … The army has overthrown governments when politicians stood in low esteem (1958 and 1977) or when the political system appears to be breaking down (1969).' The strength of the military has kept elected institutions weak and hence unable to govern efficiently. Consequently, civilian leaders have often become unpopular, giving the military (the country's strongest and most stable institution) 'moral authority' to intervene in politics. Nevertheless, since 11 September 2001, the military has faced heightened criticism from both domestic and international sources. More recently, the US use of drones to seek out and kill Taliban and al-Qaida militants necessitates cooperation of the Pakistan military. While the United States complains that the government of Pakistan is not doing enough to curb domestic extremism, many significant domestic voices believe that the military acts too rashly and strongly – as it has killed hundreds of civilians as a result of its anti-extremist operations in recent years (Perlez and Kahn 2011).

India's military influence differs by state, with the military playing a key political and security role in conflict prone areas such as Jammu–Kashmir while, on the other hand, many citizens take up arms against one another in private armies, often formed between different castes (Kohli 1990). Overall, India devotes large amounts of resources to the military but not at the expense of other institutions. Like Pakistan, early political decisions regarding the role of the military led to the military's current influence. Shortly before independence in 1947, members of the Indian National Army defected from the British Indian Army to join the Japanese during the Second World War. British forces sought to kill or imprison defectors. Although Prime Minister Nehru defended the renegades, he nevertheless 'categorically refused to reinstate them into the Indian Army since they had broken the oath of office and had become politicized' (Ganguly 2002: 8). Nehru thus established the supremacy of civilian authority over the military, with lasting effects.

Political parties

Political parties are critical both to democratic elections and for the representation of citizens between elections (Diamond 1999). The Pakistan Muslim League dominated Pakistan from 1947–50, although forming cohesive parties soon proved problematic. Free and fair elections were not held until the 1970s. Emerging parties soon became involved in the war leading to Bangladesh's independence in 1971. The Pakistan People's Party (PPP), while under Ali Bhutto (1971–77), dominated the party system. Bhutto, however, did not advance the role of parties in the 1973 Constitution. After Bhutto's removal, General Zia ul Haq proved unsuccessful in abolishing parties and was especially plagued by the PPP, headed by Benazir Bhutto (Ali's daughter). Nawaz Sharif also formed the Pakistan Muslim League Nawaz (PML-N). Prior to President Musharraf's coup in 1999, Pakistan had about 15 parties, although the PPP and PML-N were the most significant. Many smaller parties were ethnically and religiously based.

Political alliances in Pakistan have shifted frequently. The PPP suffered from factionalism mainly due to its inability to accommodate interests and provide jobs to party supporters, while the state bureaucracy became threatened by its increasing influence. According to Shafqat (1997: 244):

> The PPP needed to evolve a policy choice to co-opt the bureaucracy, appease its institutional needs, and restore the confidence in party government … In addition, the regime, without mustering sufficient organizational strength and support made futile attempts to weaken the military's hegemony. It presumed that the power had been transferred to a civilian leadership while the military had conceded only the sharing of power.

This aggravated the situation and the president dissolved the government. Another election was held in 1990 (the results of which many observers considered rigged) when Sharif came into power. When parties *are* permitted in Pakistan, they are largely non-inclusive and elite-dominated. Most are non-democratic in their structure (forms), as well as their norms (Shafqat 1997: 248). Over time, the strong powers of the institutions of the military and bureaucracy 'inhibited further the development of the Muslim League into a well-organized political party and the development of political parties in general' (Shafqat 1997: 250).

Co-opting a splintered branch of the PML, Musharraf formed his own political party – the PML-Q. During his spell in power, the autonomy of all political parties was severely undercut, not least because Musharraf exiled the two major party leaders – Sharif and Benazir Bhutto. He also placed many restrictions on party activity. Benazir Bhutto returned to Pakistan from exile in 2007 with hopes of achieving a power-sharing arrangement with Musharraf. However, she was assassinated following a campaign rally in December. Many observers have speculated that her party would have won a majority of seats in the upcoming parliamentary elections, positioning her for a third prime ministerial term. Following her assassination, Bhutto's husband, Asif Zardari, assumed command of the PPP and won presidential elections when Musharraf left power in 2008. At the time of writing (mid-2011), the PPP dominates parliament, followed by the PML-N, while the PML-Q is the third largest. In December 2010, Musharraf (then exiled in London) announced the launching of a new party: the All Pakistan Muslim League.[3] In addition, there are several minor parties. In sum, parties have generally proved more resilient than would be expected.

Largely due to the leadership of the Congress Party, which operated under democratic rules and procedures, Indian parties learned to accept parliamentary democracy (Kohli 1990: 8). Generally, one-party domination is conducive to an undermining of democracy. However, under Nehru (1947–64) power-sharing and consensus-building characterized Congress Party rule. In addition, under Indira Gandhi, the Congress Party was: 'transformed from an internally democratic, federal, and consensual organization to a centralized and hierarchical party' (Lijphart 1996: 264). But, as previously noted, divisions eventually led to the split of the Congress Party. More recently, however, elections in India have become more competitive. In 1998, the Bharatiya Janata Party (BJP), a Hindu nationalist party, won the most parliamentary seats (Heller 2000).

Although the Congress Party re-emerged as the largest party in India following the elections of 2004, it is true to say that India now has a new era of party politics, characterized by multiparty, coalition rule. According to Wilkinson (2005: 155):

> The importance of electoral alliances has become increasingly clear over the past 15 years, a period in which no Indian party has been able to win an outright majority in parliament. The relative electoral success of Congress and the BJP is now determined by how well they work out their alliances and seat-adjustment deals with: 1) the many state-level parties, which now provide almost 30 percent of the MPs, up from 5 percent in the late 1980s; 2) the CPI-M, which has won 7–10 percent of seats in parliament in recent elections; and 3) regional parties that are too small to be officially considered state parties but which nonetheless win 8–10 percent of the seats. Collectively, these three groups of parties now occupy almost half of the seats in the Lok Sabha.

Note, however, that the Congress Party benefits more from this situation because it has more coalition partners than the BJP (Wilkinson 2005). Finally, Congress Party member Manmohan Singh has been India's prime minister since 2004.

Rule of law

Rule of law is critical to democracy and is measured by the existence of a constitution that protects citizens from unjustified detention, exile, terror, torture and 'undue interference in their personal lives not only by the state, but also by non-state and anti-state forces' (Diamond 1999: 12). Pakistan has promulgated four constitutions (1956, 1962, 1973 and 1985): an indication of instability. Musharraf suspended the constitution in October 1999, restoring it in December 2002 with the amendments mentioned earlier. He temporarily suspended it again in 2007. Major constitutional revisions discussed throughout this chapter were made beginning in April 2010 (Bajoria 2011).

Chapter 1 of the Constitution of the Islamic Republic of Pakistan – on fundamental rights – explicitly excludes members of the armed forces or the police, who are charged with the maintenance of public order, from adherence to the constitution.[4] Those arrested under preventative detention are not given the same rights as other detainees; rights of assembly are subject to 'reasonable restrictions'; and the right to property is protected save in accordance with Islamic law based on the Qur'an and the Sunnah. Rule of law can be determined by the prevalence of political violence tolerated by the state. Pakistani police often deliver 'street justice' when the courts fail to find suspected criminals guilty (State Department Report 2003). The general population is also targeted and, although forbidden by the constitution and the penal code, torture and degrading treatment by police is common. Often, police make arrests so that families will pay bribes to have detainees released. Women are frequently raped in police custody. Very few police officers are investigated or punished for abuse. Overall, Pakistanis are not adequately protected under the rule of law. Further, there is no guarantee that the constitution will not be suspended by a future coup (Bajoria 2011).

India has operated under the same constitution since 1950 although several amendments have been added over time. India has a secular constitution. All citizens are guaranteed freedom of speech and expression, peaceful assembly, association, movement and residence.[5] However, the state has broad discretion over rights, based on its own interests. On paper, rights in India appear to be more democratically orientated and liberal than in Pakistan, although their realization is often problematic.

Mores systematic evidence regarding the efficacy of the rule of law can be gleaned from the Purdue Political Terror Scales (PTS), which analyse the extent to which states violate human rights. Countries are rated from 1 to 5, with 1 being the least violent and 5 the most.[6]

Purdue Political Terror Scales 1976–2009

Here, we see a lot more similarities between India and Pakistan. Both countries have alarmingly high scores, averaging 3.7 and 3.5 respectively (see Figure 7.4). State terror has become more common and severe over time in both countries. Currently, violence against citizens in both India and Pakistan is very problematic. This inhibits democracy since these states are unable to protect citizens from arbitrary arrest and imprisonment, political torture, murder and rape.

Political equality

Political equality in Pakistan is limited and complicated. The Hudood Ordinances, based on sharia law, were passed under Zia ul Haq's rule (from 1978 to 1988). Applying both to Muslims and non-Muslims, it contradicted the constitution clause stating non-Muslims are not subject to Muslim codes. In 1991, the Enforcement of Shari'ah Act further embedded Islamic doctrine in Pakistani

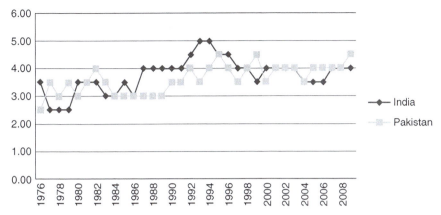

Figure 7.4   Purdue Political Terror Scales, 1976–2009

law requiring all Muslims, who are then not equally protected, to follow such injunctions and submit themselves to sharia law. Although the constitution restricts gender discrimination (Article 25), women are not equal before the law. A woman's testimony was worth half of a man's in court, and inheritance only half of what she would get if she were a man. Above all, if a rape victim failed to provide four male witnesses, she was imprisoned for adultery or premarital sex and denied bail (Zakaria 2006). While President Musharraf initially pledged to entirely repeal the Hudood Ordinances, he only partially nullified it with the 2006 Women's Protection Act. All rape cases were moved to civil courts, removing the necessity of four male witnesses (Weaver 2007). However, in December 2010, the Federal Sharia Court ruled important aspects of the Women's Protection Act to be unconstitutional (Rumi 2011b).

Minority religious groups are discriminated against in Pakistan. In 1984, the Ahmadis (a minority Muslim group) were prohibited from calling themselves Muslims and using Islamic words or greetings (violating their freedom of speech). This was upheld by the supreme court in 1996 (State Department Report 2000). In 2010, violent attacks in Lahore resulted in the deaths of nearly 100 Ahmadis (Rumi 2011b). The constitution prohibits non-Muslims from running for the offices of president and prime minister. Elected officials must take an oath (including non-Muslims) to preserve Pakistan's Islamic state ideology. A Christian from the state of Punjab was recently the first woman to be sentenced to death for violating the blasphemy law. Vocal critics of the law have been intimidated and even assassinated (Rumi 2011a).

In India, various religious groups follow different laws – thus violating equal protection before the law. Muslim personal laws govern aspects of family law, inheritance and divorce, including those discriminating against women. The Hindu Succession Act (1956) provides equal inheritance rights for Hindu women, but, in practice, married daughters are rarely given a share in parental property and, under many tribal land systems (especially in Bihar), women do not have the right to own land. Although India is generally characterized as a secular state, religious equality has been problematic. According to Summit Ganguly (2008: 171): 'The Indian State, especially in the last two decades, has failed to serve as a neutral arbiter of Hindu-Muslim discord. On one occasion in 2002, it became a blatantly partisan actor, allowing Hindu zealots to slaughter innocent Muslims in the western state of Gujarat.' This coincided with the dominance of the BJP, the Hindu nationalist party. Finally, though the caste system has long been officially abolished, lower-status castes continue to face discrimination in a wide variety of institutions and have difficulty achieving full equality. At the same time, constitutional provisions have led to an increase in their political influence, through the promotion of reserved seats (Guha 2007).

Ability of citizens to change their government

Are citizens guaranteed universal suffrage in regular elections providing for real opposition with the absence of fraud? Since independence, Pakistan has permitted universal suffrage for citizens aged 21 years and older. However, the first free and fair elections were not held until December 1970. In practice, suffrage is limited. Many women are disenfranchised due to family persuasion and religious and social custom, especially in rural areas. Several military takeovers dismissed votes cast in national, local and provincial elections, although some of these elections were fraudulent anyway. In April 2002, Musharraf won a referendum by 98 per cent, extending his presidency for five years. The referendum process was anything but democratic. Musharraf banned public rallies by political parties, preventing them from campaigning against the referendum. Evidence from independent observers indicated extensive fraud and coercion:

> Electoral rolls and national identification cards were dispensed with, ballots were routinely stamped in the presence of, or even by, polling officials, and observers reported cases of repeat voting. Police and local government officials ... transported busloads of voters to polling stations. Both public and private employees reportedly said that they had cast 'yes' votes on the orders of supervisors.

(State Department 2003)

Musharraf announced amendments in August 2002 that increased the formal political role of the military and further restricted party activities, while limiting the ability of individuals to run for office. He was re-elected in 2007, under similarly democratically problematic conditions (Bajoria 2011). Following Musharraf's fall from power, multiparty elections have been held for parliament and the presidency, bringing the PPP back to lead the government. The next federal elections are scheduled for 2013.

India has a longer history of regular elections, with presidential elections last held in 2007. As suggested in the party section of this chapter, political opposition exists in India and most elections are considered free and fair. The last parliamentary elections of 2009 resulted, again, in a coalition government led by the Congress Party.

Civil liberties

The protection of civil liberties and other human rights are important ingredients of liberal democracy (Diamond 1999). This includes press freedom from state incursion. Media freedom in Pakistan is limited and investigative journalism is virtually non-existent. The constitution prohibits criticism of Islam, the military and the courts. Islam is used to deny fundamental rights, such as speech and the press, by deeming them un-Islamic if they are critical of Islam. Under Musharraf, freedom of the press was further restricted. Books needed to pass government censors before publication; and the government had a virtual monopoly of the broadcast media. While human rights reports now find generally greater press freedom than during previous times, Pakistani courts have punished journalists critical of court decisions, resulting in their hesitancy to document abuses (Rumi 2011b). Freedom of assembly and association among the general public is also very limited. Security fears routinely result in detentions of terrorist suspects without charge (Rumi 2011a).

India has a more vigorous and freer press than Pakistan, publishing more critical accounts of those in power. However, there are limits: under the Official Secrets Act, the government may restrict the publication of sensitive stories. The 1971 Newspaper (Incitements to Offences) Act – prohibiting publications that may instigate violence – remains in effect in Jammu and Kashmir.

Obviously, this might be used to censor stories critical of the government. Since 1998, the state government of Manipur has limited publication of insurgency-related news. Although some of these laws aim to have a positive impact, they are rather undemocratically formulated and executed and, in addition, do not address the root causes of violence. The government continues to ban 'controversial books'. Although the police must obtain warrants for searches and seizures, authorities in Jammu and Kashmir, Punjab and Assam have special powers to search and arrest without a warrant (State Department Report 2003). The Indian Telegraph Act allows for monitoring telephone conversations and personal mail when it is deemed in the state's interest. The constitution provides for the rights of assembly and is generally respected in practice, although this differs state to state. In Jammu and Kashmir, separatist parties are denied permits for gatherings and it is not uncommon for rights of assembly to be infringed under the Criminal Procedure Code. According to the latest Human Rights Watch (2011) report on India, security-forces abuses against civilians are rampant.

Religion in government

Religion is critical to address in relation to democracy in two respects. First, are particular religious traditions dominant in countries less supportive of democracy? Second, does the country operate as a religious state, a theocracy, resulting in the suppression of religious minorities? Addressing the former, Huntington (1996) asserts that it is especially difficult for Muslim countries and those based on 'Eastern' religious traditions to establish liberal democracy. Both India and Pakistan, therefore would be unlikely to have democratic success, according to Huntington. Regarding Pakistan, the constitution states that it is an Islamic country and that government representatives will be chosen by the people, and will adhere to the principles of democracy, freedom, equality, tolerance and social justices (albeit freedoms are to confirm to Islam and subject to public morality). The constitution established the Islamic Council, which interprets holy readings in numerous cases, including those involving blasphemy. As the Hudood Ordinances demonstrated, there is a clear infiltration of religion (Islam) in politics. This is problematic for democracy, since crucial liberal freedoms (it is frequently observed) are denied under many interpretations of Islamic law. India, on the other hand, is primarily a secular state. Still, it is problematic to have both laws providing religious equality while religious groups are subject to different legal codes. Religion, however, is also playing a more prominent role since the rise of the BJP, with several examples discussed in this chapter.

Population heterogeneity

It is widely believed that the greater the heterogeneity of people in a country, then the less successful democracy will be. The argument is that extreme pluralism can produce fragmentation and conflict, ultimately hampering democracy (Linz and Stepan 1996: 33). Lijphart (1999: 158) contends that heterogeneity does not necessarily lead to democratic breakdown as long as a consociational system is in place, characterized by: (1) grand coalition governments that included representatives from all major language and ethnic groups; (2) cultural autonomy; (3) political representation in proportion to their population; and (4) a minority veto with regard to issues specific to them.

India and Pakistan are divided religiously and ethnically, and India is further divided by caste and language. Different ethnic groups in Pakistan include Punjabi, Sindhi, Pashtun, Muhajir and Baluchi (World Factbook 2011). Pakistan is more religiously homogenous than India with 95 per cent of the population Muslim, while Christians and Hindus mainly account for the remainder (World Factbook 2011). Muslim are further divided between Sunni and Shi'a: 77 per cent and 20 per cent respectively, a situation that is sometimes linked to outbreaks of sectarian violence. Some religious minorities are subject to violence and harassment, especially Ahmadis and Christians. While Pakistan does not have a strong power-sharing system, minorities are reserved some seats in parliament, although tribal people are greatly under-represented in government. According to Malik (1997: 164), lack of minority representation perpetuates ethnic conflict and, on occasion, military intervention is used to maintain law and order.

India's vast population is also ethnically heterogeneous, divided mainly between Indo-Aryan (77 per cent) and Dravidian (25 per cent) (World Factbook 2011). India has 300 officially designated tribes. Heterogeneity is further illustrated by language. Hindi, the national language, is the first language for only 30 per cent of the population. There are 14 other official languages, and many other languages spoken that do not have official status. India is more diverse in terms of religion than Pakistan, comprising 81 per cent Hindus, 12 per cent Muslims, 2.4 per cent Christians, 2 per cent Sikhs, 1.9 per cent Buddhists and 2.5 per cent others (World Factbook 2011).

Competing elites have tried to mobilize ethnic groups, seeking to use religion, language or race for political leverage, which sometimes leads to conflict. India has a further dimension of diversity: the caste system that divides the Hindu majority. However, Lijphart (1996) contends that India has all necessary power-sharing characteristics. These include: (1) grand coalitions in the cabinet produced inclusively of the population (under the Congress Party), balancing religious, linguistic and regional interests of society; (2) cultural autonomy in federal arrangements – in that state and linguistic boundaries largely coincide and the constitutional rights of states for minorities to establish educational institutions supported by public funds (Article 30), and personal laws concerning marriage, divorce, custody and inheritance; (3) proportionality in power-sharing with groups in the population: the constitution reserves seats in parliament and state legislatures for 'tribes' and castes in proportion to their population; and (4) a de facto minority veto. Indeed, it may be due to India's commitment to such structures that democracy has taken root. On the other hand, there are many indications that power-sharing has declined over the last half century (Lijphart 1996).

Civil society/democratic norms

According to Diamond (1999), democracy is most likely to thrive when there is a flourishing civil society and widespread acceptance of basic democratic norms. Both civil society and democratic norms in Pakistan are weak, while India has, more than Pakistan, ensured individual rights. As Di Palma suggests (1990), democratic norms can take hold prior to their acceptance by the masses, via elite influence. Shafqat (1997: 248) asserts that:

> Since military rule has been persistent, and democratic government has remained an illusion, the political elites have little experience with democratic rule. In the 1970's, although Bhutto assumed power through the electoral process and framed a constitution, he found it difficult to rule through democratic means. Even Benazir Bhutto and Nawaz Sharif reveal unfamiliarity with democratic norms.

Democratic cultural norms are more prevalent in India than in Pakistan; in the former, political conflicts are normally resolved via the working of democratic institutions. On the other hand, many Pakistanis lack a sufficient level of education, which many observers contend is a basic necessity for becoming politically active. Although literacy rates have substantially risen since

2000, only half of the population can read and women's literacy rates substantially lag behind those of men (World Factbook 2011). The premise is that without basic education, people are unable to fully exercise citizenship: 'A free and lively civil society makes the state and its agents more accountable by guaranteeing that consultation takes place not just through electoral representation but also through feedback and negotiation' (Heller 2000: 488). In Pakistan, civil society has not developed during the frequent periods of military government. During other times, government has been weak, unable to develop strong democratic institutions, largely because of the baleful influence of the military. Instead of providing for citizens equally, government leaders have typically opted to give more resources and autonomy to those who can stir up the most conflict (for instance, religious elites) resulting in a patron–client relationship between the state and parts of society. Still, there are indications that a middle class is beginning to articulate demands, evident in the 2007 'lawyers' uprising' noted above. Such activity within the masses is promising for civil society, but could be also be negative if increased demands by the public are not addressed by government.

India does not provide universal free, compulsory primary education, even though it is guaranteed in the constitution (Article 45). During the late 1990s, the BJP government pledged that it would finally implement Article 45, but it did not take place. The literacy rate in India, at 61 per cent, is higher than in Pakistan, although there are similar gender gaps between males and females (World Factbook 2011). The case of the southern state of Kerala is illustrative of the effects of education on informed citizenship. According to Heller (2000: 497):

> Literacy in Kerala has reached 91 percent ... Successive governments maintained the highest rates of educational expenditures in India ... Associational life has been further strengthened by the provision of public goods. The provision of basic health care and subsidized food staples and the regulation of the labor market have reduced material dependencies and eroded traditionalist clientalist networks.

Economics

The literature on the relationship of economic prosperity to successful democratization is quite vast and conflicting. Przeworski *et al.* (1996, 2000) find that democratic transition is not a consequence of economic growth, as argued in the classic work by Lipset (1959). However, it is pivotal in democratic consolidation. In contrast, Epstein *et al.* (2006: 566) provide convincing evidence that economic growth promotes *both* democratic transition and consolidation. In short, economic development may be a necessary though not sufficient condition for democratization (Linz and Stepan 1999). Pakistan's PPP per capita rate in 2009 was $2,683,[7] while gross domestic product (GDP) real growth rate is 2.7 per cent and the most recent inflation rate is 13 per cent.[8] India's PPP per capita was $3,039 in 2008,[9] though it is projected to nearly double in the next few years. Growth in GDP is much higher than in Pakistan, currently nearly 9 per cent, while its current inflation rate is 8.8 per cent.[10] Thus, India's economic circumstances appear very promising for democratic survival, even amidst the global economic crisis (Panagariya 2008), though this is not the case for Pakistan.

International factors

Beyond the domestic environment, the international context has helped shape democratic prospects in both countries. The United States was the largest developmental donor to Pakistan until the late 1990s, when Pakistan conducted nuclear weapons testing in response to those carried out by India. Since 11 September 2001, the US has provided more financial assistance, including a US$1 billion package (Shah 2002). On one hand, the international attention given to Pakistan as an important ally in the 'War on Terror' may result in stricter public scrutiny of the democratic process in Pakistan. However, well-organized militants continue to threaten both government and stability. Further, increased financial packages to Pakistan from the United States come with a cost, resulting in numerous civilian casualties from drone strikes (as outlined earlier). This has fuelled domestic tension.

India has also been dependent on international donors such as the International Monetary Fund and the World Bank. These organizations pressurized India to liberalize economically, a development supported by both the business elite and middle classes (Kohli 1990: 334). However, such pressure can actually make democracy less stable in the short run. Unlike Pakistan, India's recent international payments position is strong, with good foreign exchange reserves, reasonably stable exchange rates and growing exports of computer software.

The long-running conflict between India and Pakistan impacts on democracy in both countries. After partition in 1947, Pakistan spent a great deal of money on establishing its military at the expense of other institutions because of violent conflicts with India, one of the factors leading to the repeated breakdown of democracy in Pakistan. India aiding East Pakistan's (Bangladesh) liberation and the long-standing Kashmir conflict have contributed to conflict and influenced the foreign policies of both countries. Civil liberties in war-torn states such as Jammu and Kashmir have been suspended because of the military threats by both countries, and there is no end to this in sight, due to the escalation of conflict and increase in terrorist activity against both sides. Since 11 September 2001, Pakistan's alliance with the United States has led to greater conflict with India and increased violence in the disputed territory, and many of the groups that have been prominent in the war in Kashmir have had their funds frozen and have been put on the US State Department's list of foreign terrorist organizations (Shah 2002: 68). The roots of this run deep and are still palpable.

Conclusions

Although once part of the same country, over time Pakistan and India have taken diverging democratic trajectories. Pakistan has yet to achieve a full – or even clear cut and consistent – democratic transition. We have seen that this is the result of several factors – including the continuing influence of Islamic law and conventions, which may conflict with liberal democratic norms; political interference by the military; a weak and fragmented civil society; and lack of democratic cultural norms. While its democratic ratings have recently improved, periods of civilian rule are notably sporadic. If President Zardari is able to complete a full term, something no civilian leader has been able to do, this may bode well for Pakistan's democratic future.

India has been an electoral democracy for more than 50 years, with only a four-year lapse. However, since it lacks a positive record of protecting civil liberties and human rights, it is a consolidated but illiberal democracy. Much of India's current democratic success can be traced back to the commitment to democratic norms among its founders such as Nehru and the historical dominance of the democratically aware Congress Party. On the other hand, India has recently faced many notable challenges, including the development of numerous political factions, some of which are guided by particular – not necessarily pro-democracy – religious agendas. However, India has managed to remain committed to electoral democracy, though less so to the promotion of civil rights and liberties.

Notes

1 Freedom House website, available at http://www.freedomhouse.org/template.cfm?page=594 (accessed 1 April 2011).
2 Both Sharif's and Bhutto's prime-ministerships resulted in their removal by the president.
3 'Sorry Musharraf launches new political party' 2010, *BBC News* (online), 1 October, available at http://www.bbc.co.uk/news/world-south-asia-11450507 (accessed 15 April 2011).
4 'The Constitution of the Islamic Republic of Pakistan'. Available at Constitution Finder. http://www.pakistani.org/pakistan/constitution/ (accessed 22 April 2011).
5 'The Constitution of India'. Available at Constitution Finder. http://lawmin.nic.in/coi/coiason29july08.pdf (accessed 22 April 2011).
6 The ratings are comprised of two scores – one by the US State Department and the other from Amnesty International reports. I average the two scores annually. Available at http://www.politicalterrorscale.org/download.php (accessed 30 March 2011).
7 Value is from 2009. http://www.tradingeconomics.com/pakistan/gdp-based-on-purchasing-power-parity-ppp-per-capita-gdp-imf-data.html (accessed 22 April 2011).
8 Value is from April 2011. http://www.tradingeconomics.com/pakistan/indicators.
9 Value is from 2008. http://www.tradingeconomics.com/india/gdp-per-capita-ppp (accessed 22 April 2011).
10 Value is from March 2011. http://www.tradingeconomics.com/india/inflation-cpi (accessed 22 April 2011).

References

Bajoria, J. (2011) 'Pakistan's Constitution'. Council on Foreign Relations Website. 21 April; available at http://www.cfr.org/pakistan/pakistans-constitution/p15657 (accessed 22 April 2011).
Collier, D. and R. Adcock (1999) 'Democracy and Dichotomies: A Pragmatic Approach to Choices about Concepts', *American Political Science Review*, 93(2), pp. 537–565.
—— and S. Levitsky (1997) 'Democracy with Adjectives: Conceptual Innovation in Comparative Research', *World Politics*, 49 (3), pp. 430–451.
Diamond, Larry (1999). *Developing Democracy: Towards Consolidation*. Baltimore, MD: Johns Hopkins University Press.
Di Palma, G. (1990) *To Craft Democracies*. Berkeley: University of California Press.
Epstein, D. L., R. Bates, J. Goldstone, I. Kristensen and S. O'Halloran (2006) 'Democratic Transitions', *American Journal of Political Science*, 50 (3), pp. 551–569.
Ganguly, S. (2002) 'India's Multiple Revolutions', *Journal of Democracy* 13 (1), pp. 39–51.
—— (2008) 'India's Improbable Success', *Journal of Democracy*, 19 (2), pp. 170–174.
Guha, R. (2007) *India after Gandhi: The History of the World's Largest Democracy*. London: Macmillan.
Heller, P. (2000) 'Degrees of Democracy', *World Politics* 52 (4), pp. 484–519.
Huntington, S. P. (1996) *The Clash of Civilizations*. New York: Simon and Schuster.
Kohli, A. (1990) *Democracy and Discontent*. Cambridge: Cambridge University Press.
Lijphart, A. (1996) 'The Puzzle of Indian Democracy: A Consociational Interpretation', *American Political Science Review*, 90 (2), pp. 258–268.
—— (1999) *Patterns of Democracy*. New Haven, CT: Yale University Press.
Linz, J. and A. Stepan (1996) *Problems of Democratic Consolidation: Southern Europe, South America, and post-communist Europe*. Baltimore, MD: Johns Hopkins University Press.
Lipset, S. M. (1959) 'Some Social Requisites of Democracy', *American Political Science Review*, 53 (1), pp. 69–105.
McGrath, A. (1996) *The Destruction of Pakistan's Democracy*. Oxford: Oxford University Press.
Malik, I. (1997) 'Ethnic Politics in Sindh Establishment'. In *State, Society, and Democratic Change in Pakistan*, ed. R. Rais. Oxford: Oxford University Press, Chapter 7.
Panagariya, A. (2008) *India: The Emerging Giant*. Oxford: Oxford University Press.
Perlez, J. and I. Kahn (2011) 'Drone Strikes Militants in Northwest Pakistan'. *New York Times* (online). 21 April; available at http://www.nytimes.com/2011/04/23/world/asia/23pakistan.html?_r=1&hp (accessed 22 April 2011).
Przeworksi, A., M. E. Alvarez, J. Cheibub and F. Limongi (1996) 'What makes Democracies Endure?', *Journal of Democracy*, pp. 39–55.

——, M. E. Alvarez, J. Cheibub and F. Limongi (2000) *Democracy and Development*. New York: Cambridge University Press.

Pye, L. W. (1967) *Southeast Asia's Political Systems*. Englewood Cliffs, NJ: Prentice-Hall.

Rais, R. B. (1997) 'Elections, Regime Change and Democracy'. In *State, Society, and Democratic Change in Pakistan*, ed. R. Rais. Oxford: Oxford University Press, Introduction.

Rudolph, Lloyd and Susan Rudolph. 2002. 'South Asia Faces the Future: New Dimensions of Indian Democracy', *Journal of Democracy* 13 (1), 52–66.

Rumi, Raza (2011a) 'Pakistan: Disastrous Year for Rights', *Friday Times* (online), 24 January; available at http://www.hrw.org/en/news/2011/01/24/pakistan-disastrous-year-rights (accessed 21 April 2011).

—— (2011b) 'Pakistan: A Year of Abuses', *Friday Times* (online), 28 January; available at http://www.hrw.org/en/news/2011/01/28/pakistan-year-abuses (accessed 21 April 2011).

—— (2011c) 'Pakistan: Democracy Three Years Later', *Friday Times* (online), 5 April; available at http://www.hrw.org/en/news/2011/04/05/pakistan-democracy-three-years-later (accessed 21 April 2011).

Sartori, G. (1970) 'Concept Misformation in Comparative Politics', *The American Political Science Review* (64), pp. 1033–1053.

Sayeed, Khalid Bin (1997) 'Some Reflections on the Democratization Process'. In *State, Society, and Democratic Change in Pakistan* , ed. R. Rais. Oxford: Oxford University Press, Chapter 1.

Shafqat, Saeed (1997) 'Transition to Democracy, an Uncertain Path'. In *State, Society, and Democratic Change in Pakistan*, ed. R. Rais. Oxford: Oxford University Press, Chapter 11.

Shah, A. (2002) 'Democracy on Hold in Pakistan', *Journal of Democracy* (1), pp. 67–75.

Syed, Anwar H. (1997) 'The Ouster of Nawaz Sharif in 1993: Power Plays within the Ruling Establishment'. In *State, Society, and Democratic Change in Pakistan*, ed. R. Rais. Oxford: Oxford University Press, Chapter 3.

Weaver, K. (2007) 'Women's Rights and Shari'a Law: A Workable Reality?', *Duke Journal of Comparative and International Law* (17), pp. 483–509.

Wilkinson, S. (2005) 'Elections in India: Behind the Congress Comeback', *Journal of Democracy*, 16 (1), pp. 153–167.

Wintrobe, R. (2008) *The Political Economy of Dictatorship*. New York: Cambridge University Press.

Zakaria, Rafia (2006) 'Veils and Jails', *Frontline Magazine (online)*, 1 September; available at http://www.altmuslim.com/a/a/a/2374 (accessed 21 April 2011).

Ziring, L. (2000) *Pakistan in the 20th Century*. New York: Oxford University Press.

—— (2004) *Pakistan: At the Crosscurrent of History*. Chino Valley, CA: Oneworld Press.

Web reports

CIA World Factbook. Pakistan(2011) Available at https://www.cia.gov/library/publications/the-world-factbook/geos/pk.html (accessed 22 April 2011).

CIA World Factbook. Pakistan(2003) Available at http://www.theodora.com/wfb2003/pakistan/pakistan_government.html (accessed 2 March 2011).

CIA World Factbook. India(2011) Available at https://www.cia.gov/library/publications/the-world-factbook/geos/in.html (accessed 22 April 2011).

State Department Report on Human Rights in Pakistan(2000) Available at http://www.state.gov/g/drl/rls/hrrpt/2000/sa/710.htm (accessed 15 April 2011).

State Department Report on Human Rights in Pakistan(2003) Available at http://www.state.gov/g/drl/rls/irf/2003/24473.htm (accessed 15 April 2011).

Human Rights Watch (2011) India-World Report-2010. Available at http://www.hrw.org/en/world-report-2011/india (accessed 22 April 2011).

8

East and Southeast Asia

Matthew Carlson

Although the number of democratically elected governments in Asia has increased, the consolidation of democracy has proven to be a difficult business. An important ingredient in the democratization process is the role of public opinion and the extent that the public embraces democratic principles and practices. This chapter uses public opinion data from the 2005 to 2007 AsiaBarometer Survey (hereafter ABS) conducted in 12 East and Southeast Asian societies (Japan, Taiwan, South Korea, China, Hong Kong, Mongolia, the Philippines, Indonesia, Thailand, Malaysia, Singapore and Cambodia) to analyse popular perceptions of democracy, and principles and practices associated with liberal democratic governments.[1] Specifically, it focuses on several of the following inter-related questions: do democratic institutions work well in the short and long term? To what extent are citizens in these societies satisfied with various political and civil rights? Does the current political system and government perform well? The results revealed that while there are strong majorities that support many of the ideals of democracy and commitment to elections, respondents are much less satisfied in areas related to government accountability, responsiveness and the efforts of the central government. With the exception of only a few countries, there is a considerable gap between how citizens evaluate the ideals of democracy versus how they perceive its specific practices.

The starting point is to note that transitions to and consolidation of democracy in East and Southeast Asia has proved to be both fragile and tenuous since the third wave of democratization began some 30 years ago (Huntington 1991). The wave has washed over the shores of the Philippines (1986), South Korea (1987), Mongolia (1990), Thailand (1992), Cambodia (1993), Taiwan (1996) and Indonesia (1998). It had little effect on resolutely authoritarian regimes in China, North Korea, Vietnam, Laos and Myanmar. However, even the 'democratic' regimes retained some characteristics of an authoritarian nature and have been classified under such labels as 'hybrid' (Diamond 2002), 'semi-authoritarian' (Ottaway 2003), 'pseudo-democracy' (Case 2001) or 'semi-democratic' (Samudavanija 1995). For democracy to survive and prosper, many argue that there must be wide mass support for the new democratic 'rules of the game' (Linz and Stephan 1996; Diamond 1999; Carothers 2002; Shin and Wells 2005; Park 2007). This includes mass support for the electoral process but also for democratic ideals, processes and values. How citizens view the ideals and practices of democracy is thus a critical ingredient in the process of democratization itself.

The purpose of this chapter is to evaluate public support for democracy and democratic governance among two Asian subregions: East Asia (Japan, South Korea, China, Hong Kong, Taiwan and Mongolia) and Southeast Asia (Cambodia, Indonesia, Malaysia, the Philippines,

Thailand and Singapore).[2] Several empirical questions are considered using survey data: to what extent are citizens in these societies satisfied with various political and civil rights? How do they evaluate the performance of their country in terms of values associated with a liberal democratic system? By scrutinizing how citizens in this part of the world perceive democracy and democratic governance, we can better evaluate East and Southeast Asian governments and contribute to debates over their prospects for democratic consolidation. The multinational survey responses were collected through face-to-face interviews with approximately 11,882 randomly selected citizens.

This chapter is organized into six parts. The first section reviews previous studies that have focused on assessing democracy. Based on this review, the second section develops a framework for evaluating public support for democracy and democratic governance using survey data in East and Southeast Asia and discusses key measurement issues. The third section examines general citizen orientations towards specific regime types. The fourth section examines public support for specific qualities associated with liberal democracy: rule of law, satisfaction with political and civil freedoms (e.g. right to vote, freedom of expression and associational rights), accountability and responsiveness. The fifth section explores variations in demographic differences in the support for properties at the heart of liberal democracy. The final, sixth section summarizes key findings and discusses their implications for further democratization in East and Southeast Asia.

Prior research on democratization

Democracy is a contested concept and thus has been the focus of considerable debate. Minimalist or procedural definitions are captured in Joseph Schumpeter's (1976: 279) definition of democracy as a system 'for arriving at political decisions in which individuals acquire the power to decide by means of a competitive struggle for the people's vote'. In this view, elections are heavily emphasized as a necessary condition for democracy. Maximalist or substantive definitions, in contrast, include free and fair elections, but add other freedoms such as freedom of speech, freedom of the press and freedom of association.

The debate over procedural and substantive democracy is reflected in a popular regime classification scheme used in comparative politics: electoral democracies, liberal democracies and pseudo-democracies (Diamond 1999). Electoral democracies are a minimalist conception that privileges elections over fuller dimensions of democracy. Liberal democracies, in contrast, can be identified by a long list of characteristics, including a system where citizens have considerable freedoms of belief, speech, assembly and demonstration; are politically equal under the law; and are protected from detention and torture. Finally, pseudo-democracies – or 'non-democracies' – are a broad range of regimes that have some formally democratic institutions that typically obscure the presence of authoritarian domination.

In addition to the efforts of individual scholars, many national and international organizations have attempted to critically assess the level of democracy around the world. The Freedom House organization, based in Washington, publishes a yearly report that assesses democracy using a questionnaire that contains a detailed checklist of questions about political rights and civil liberties.[3] The democracy scores derived from experts' responses to this checklist are widely used in comparative politics by researchers interested in specific countries and time frames. The International Institute of Democracy and Electoral Assistance (IDEA) in Sweden has created a handbook on democratic assessment that has also proven useful in comparative research (Beetham et al. 2001). Specifically, it offers a list of guiding principles that can be used to conceptualize what is considered democratic. These include participation, inclusion, representation, transparency, accountability, responsiveness and competition.

Another mode of democratic assessment has derived from scholarship on the 'quality' of democracy (Montero 1998; Munck 2001; Altman and Pérez-Liñán 2002). In one of the most recent efforts, Larry Diamond and Leonardo Morlino (2005) offer a framework for evaluating democratic quality that purports to distinguish 'high-quality' democracies from 'low-quality' ones. They argue that a 'good' democracy satisfies citizen expectations regarding governance, allows citizens' associations to enjoy liberty and political equality, and provides a means for citizens to hold government accountable through elections. In short, 'high-quality' democracies should reflect quality of results, quality of content and procedural quality.

The existing body of literature has generated much valuable information for assessing the level and quality of democracy for different political systems. However, it suffers from a few major weaknesses. First, the emphasis on procedural definitions of democracy has meant that few studies have been able to offer a full and comprehensive assessment of the quality of liberal democracy. Existing studies agree on many of the underlying principles of liberal democracy but there is little actual empirical research that links these qualities to specific countries or public opinion. Second, most of the survey-based studies have been undertaken in Africa, Latin America and Europe.[4] Consequently, many of the survey findings from these regions have yet to be examined in the context of East and Southeast Asia. In an attempt to remedy these deficiencies in the literature, this chapter analyses popular perceptions of democracy and democratic governance in 12 Asian societies. It also considers what qualities of liberal democracy are most lacking in the surveyed countries.

Conceptualization and measurement of democratization and democracy

This section examines the 'quality' of democracy by first measuring general levels of support for a democratic political system in comparison to authoritarian regime alternatives. Democratic political systems are structured to maximize opportunities to be responsive to the preferences of their citizens and to offer those citizens the opportunities for public contestation and active participation in political life (Dahl 1971). Democracies are also considered to represent a unique process of making collective and binding decisions that are better at delivering desired common goods than alternative systems (Dahl 1989). This is expressed in Winston Churchill's (1947) claim that democracy is the worst form of government except all the others that have been tried. Thus, when citizens evaluate their general preference for a democratic system, it is important to distinguish not only what they think of the ideal of democracy itself as compared with alternative forms of government, but also how they evaluate the effectiveness of the democratic system to deliver common goods.

The examination of general levels of citizen support for democracy does not reveal how well citizens are satisfied with specific qualities of liberal democracy. Consequently, the fourth section of this study builds upon some of the dimensions mentioned in Diamond and Morlino's (2005) framework for gauging democratic quality as well as the quality of liberal democracy: rule of law, satisfaction with political and civil freedoms (e.g. right to vote, freedom of expression and associational rights), accountability, and responsiveness. The rule of law, right to vote and accountability are mainly concerned with procedural aspects of a democracy, whereas freedom of expression and associational rights are substantive. Responsiveness is a dimension that bridges both procedure and substance.

In terms of measurement, this section will first examine support for democracy and its alternatives by comparing citizen preferences for a democratic system with three authoritarian types: rule by powerful leader, military government and rule by experts. Second, it will examine the qualities of liberal democracy by focusing on six specific properties. The first two capture the minimalist definition of democracy: rule of law and the right to vote. The measures for rule of law are based on two questions that tap the extent of trust in the legal system and police. The right to vote is based on a sole question that asks respondents the extent to which they are satisfied with this right.

The dimensions employed to go beyond the minimalist definitions include freedom of expression, associational rights, accountability and responsiveness. Freedom of expression is measured by examining the levels of citizen satisfaction with freedom of speech and the right to criticize the government. Associational rights are examined by looking at satisfaction with the right to participate in any kind of organization and the right to gather and demonstrate. Accountability is based on two items: whether respondents feel there is widespread corruption among those who govern and whether elected officials stop thinking about the public once they are elected. Finally, responsiveness is based on two questions: whether respondents believe government officials pay little attention to people and whether people believe they do not have the power to influence government policy.

Prior to the analysis of these measures, it is useful to comment briefly on the 12 East and Southeast Asian societies represented in the ABS. Table 8.1 shows the last ten years' of Freedom House's ratings of political rights and civil liberties. While it could be argued that most of the countries qualify as democracies under the most minimalist definition of having a record of national elections, there are obvious differences in the degree of democracy. Among the East Asian societies, Freedom House has assigned the 'free rating' to Japan, Taiwan, South Korea and Mongolia. Japan's democracy is East Asia's oldest, having democratized in the Taisho Era (1912–26), reversed to authoritarian rule, and democratized once again in the aftermath of the Second World War, with considerable assistance from the US government. In contrast, Taiwan, South Korea and Mongolia are considered much newer democracies, having begun the path in the late 1980s.

Among the Southeast Asian countries, Freedom House rates Indonesia as the region's newest democracy, as the only 'free' country, and places the Philippines, Thailand, Malaysia and Singapore in the intermediate category of 'partly free'. Cambodia is currently classified as 'not free'. Thailand enjoyed a 'free' rating for several years until a military coup in 2006 relegated it to the 'not free'

Table 8.1 Ten years' of Freedom House ratings

Countries	1999	2000	2001	2002	2003	2004	2005	2006	2007	2008
Japan	1/2/F	1/2/F	1/2/F	1/2/F	1/2/F	1/2/F	1/2/F	1/2/F	1/2/F	1/2/F
Taiwan	2/2/F	1/2/F	1/2/F	2/2/F	2/2/F	2/1/F	1/1/F	2/1/F	2/1/F	2/1/F
South Korea	2/2/F	2/2/F	2/2/F	2/2/F	2/2/F	1/2/F	1/2/F	1/2/F	1/2/F	1/2/F
China	7/6/NF	7/6/NF	7/6/NF	7/6/NF	7/6/NF	7/6/NF	7/6/NF	7/6/NF	7/6/NF	7/6/NF
Hong Kong	5/3/PF	5/3/PF	5/3/PF	5/3/PF	5/3/PF	5/2/PF	5/2/PF	5/2/PF	5/2/PF	5/2/PF
Mongolia	2/3/F	2/3/F	2/3/F	2/2/F	2/2/F	2/2/F	2/2/F	2/2/F	2/2/F	2/2/F
Philippines	2/3/F	2/3/F	2/3/F	2/3/F	2/3/F	2/3/F	3/3/PF	3/3/PF	4/3/PF	4/3/PF
Indonesia	4/4/PF	3/4/PF	3/4/PF	3/4/PF	3/4/PF	3/4/PF	2/3/F	2/3/F	2/3/F	2/3/F
Thailand	2/3/F	2/3/F	2/3/F	2/3/F	2/3/F	2/3/F	3/3/PF	7/4/NF	6/4/PF	5/4/PF
Malaysia	5/5/PF	5/5/PF	5/5/PF	5/5/PF	5/4/PF	4/4/PF	4/4/PF	4/4/PF	4/4/PF	4/4/PF
Singapore	5/5/PF	5/5/PF	5/5/PF	5/4/PF	5/4/PF	5/4/PF	5/4/PF	5/4/PF	5/4/PF	5/4/PF
Cambodia	6/6/NF	6/6/NF	6/5/NF	6/5/NF	6/5/NF	6/5/NF	6/5/NF	6/5/NF	6/5/NF	6/5/NF

Notes: The first score is political liberties followed by civil liberties and status; both are coded on a 1–7 scale where 1 is the most free and 7 is the least free (F = Free; PF = Partly Free; and NF = Not Free).
Source: http://www.freedomhouse.org/.

category in the same year. However, the citizens' experience with democracy up until this point may mean that respondents will express opinions developed under more democratic conditions.[5] In contrast, Cambodia has experienced regular elections and continues to do so, but the hegemony of the Cambodian People's Party, the weakness of opposition parties, widespread corruption and major concerns about the rule of law have led to Freedom House's 'not free' classification. Beyond basic differences in the degree of democracy are such things as the level of socio-economic development, population size, contrasting colonial histories and variation in social structure.

General orientations towards a democratic political system

This section examines the proportions of respondents who support a democratic political system as well as authoritarian regimes such as a military government. In particular, respondents are asked at a fairly abstract level to evaluate what sort of political systems are perceived to be good or bad for their country.

Support for specific regime types

How much support is there among the populace for a democratic political system in the sample of East and Southeast Asian countries? To what extent do citizens orient and commit themselves to a democratic system in comparison to authoritarian alternatives of rule? These are selected as the main questions to be analysed when examining the proportions of respondents who support specific regime types.

Several questions were used from ABS to evaluate whether citizens prefer a democratic political system or the alternative regimes. Specifically, the questions ask respondents whether a democratic political system, rule by a powerful leader, by military government or by experts would be very good, fairly good or bad for the country. This set of questions reflects attitudes towards democratic values as well as attitudes towards institutions.

Table 8.2 reports the percentages affirming the support for democracy and its alternatives in each country separately and together. In all 12 countries, large majorities expressed support for a democratic political system. Only in the Philippines and Hong Kong did the figure dip below 90 per cent. Of the possible regime choices, a democratic system was the most preferred in all of the countries, irrespective of the country's Freedom House ratings. This result confirms findings derived from global opinion surveys that the majority of respondents in almost all countries share the opinion that having a democratic system is good (Dalton 2004: 41).

Preference for a democratic system does not mean that 'non-democratic' or authoritarian alternatives are unpopular or unfamiliar. In terms of recent political history, respondents from many of the surveyed countries have experienced rule by a powerful leader (e.g. Chiang Kai-shek in Taiwan, Park Chung-hee in South Korea, Ferdinand Marcos in the Philippines, Mahathir Mohamad in Malaysia, Hun Sen in Cambodia) or military rule (e.g. in Indonesia and Thailand). There is also a history of rule by experts and bureaucratic authoritarianism in places such as Thailand, Indonesia, the Philippines and China. Thailand's political system, for example, has been described as a 'bureaucratic' polity dominated by the military and civilian bureaucracy (Funston 2001: 359), while technocrats held key state positions during Suharto's New Order in Indonesia (c.1965–98; see Hill 2000). Certainly, familiarity with authoritarian forms of rule, even if unpopular, is still likely to exert considerable influence in citizen reactions to democracy.

In all the countries in East and Southeast Asia, the most popular regime after a democratic system is 'rule by experts, where governance is presumably decided by technocrats and other

Table 8.2 Support for democratic system and competing regimes

	Democratic system	Powerful leader	Military government	Rule by experts
Japan	94.1	51.3	14.4	67.5
Taiwan	94.2	19.7	25.9	85.4
South Korea	91.6	57.6	28.0	81.0
China	94.2	16.4	53.2	88.1
Hong Kong	88.9	23.5	25.6	71.4
Mongolia	92.4	69.4	31.3	60.8
Philippines	66.6	51.0	39.5	57.8
Indonesia	90.6	38.0	57.7	70.4
Thailand	96.4	26.2	53.1	60.5
Malaysia	94.7	30.5	32.0	69.5
Singapore	90.9	20.3	27.1	59.2
Cambodia	97.5	12.0	41.1	93.0
All countries	91.0	34.7	35.7	72.1

Notes: Support for democratic system combines those who answered very good or fairly good. The number in parentheses is the rank of the survey item from highest to lowest for each country. The percentages of don't know (DK) and no answer (NA) responses are not reported.
Source: 2005–7 ABS.

technical elites as opposed to democratic rule with elected politicians. Majorities in all of the surveyed countries affirmed support for this option, which ranges from a high of slightly above 9 out of 10 respondents in Cambodia, to a low of less than 6 out of 10 for the Philippines. Military rule ranks third out of the four possibilities across all of the countries. Bare majorities in China, Thailand and Indonesia supported this option, whereas the lowest percentages of support herald from the East Asian societies of Japan and Taiwan. The least preferred type of government across most of the countries was rule by powerful leader. Majorities supported this option in Japan, South Korea, Mongolia and the Philippines, but in the remaining countries, a minority endorsed this regime type, plummeting to lows of 12 per cent in Cambodia and 16.4 per cent in China.

These responses tell us something about what sorts of political systems respondents desire for their country, but they can only take us so far. Most of the available literature describes the level of democracy in many of the surveyed Asian countries using adjectives such as 'pseudo-democracy', 'semi-democracy', 'unconsolidated democracy' and 'low quality democracy' (Case 2002). Consequently, there is likely to be much conceptual fuzziness in exactly how citizens in many of these countries react to the process of democratization. For example, citizens may express support for a democratic system but also support for military rule or rule by experts. Citizen orientations in many of the surveyed countries are not expected to be fully crystallized.

To examine this further, let us consider how many non-democratic regime types were selected by respondents in each country. Table 8.3 shows that between 5 per cent and about 35 per cent of respondents in all countries did not select any of the non-democratic alternatives. In other words, majorities in all countries selected one to three of the non-democratic regimes: rule by powerful leader, military rule or rule by experts. In democratic Japan, for example, approximately 36 per cent selected two non-democratic regimes. Although democracy as an ideal is embraced by many respondents, these patterns suggest that democracy is not seen as the 'only game in town'. Many respondents support democracy in principle but also rule by experts, rule by strong leaders or rule by military.

Table 8.3 Number of non-democratic regimes accepted

	None	*One*	*Two*	*Three*
Japan	23.6	30.0	36.0	10.4
Taiwan	9.8	59.1	20.4	10.7
South Korea	11.7	31.3	37.5	19.5
China	7.4	39.2	41.9	11.5
Hong Kong	21.6	47.2	21.6	9.6
Mongolia	14.5	34.7	29.3	21.5
Philippines	25.5	24.5	26.1	23.9
Indonesia	15.9	24.8	35.2	24.0
Thailand	22.3	34.6	24.0	19.2
Malaysia	23.0	39.9	19.4	17.8
Singapore	34.5	38.0	16.3	11.2
Cambodia	4.9	49.9	39.4	5.8
All countries	17.9	37.8	28.9	15.4

Source: 2005–7 ABS.

Assessing the quality of democratic principles and practices

How to interpret general citizen orientations towards democracy and democratic systems may be challenging, as there are multiple factors involved when citizens make such determinations (Dalton 2004). Consequently, it is necessary to disaggregate democratic quality by focusing on how respondents evaluate specific democratic principles and practices as well as their attitudes towards the existing political system and regime.

Trust in institutions

The first area of investigation is to what extent respondents in East and Southeast Asia trust specific institutions to operate in the best interests of their society. Specifically, we examine trust in four institutions: central government, parliament, the legal system and the army. By examining the responses from ABS, we are able to consider the degree of popular trust in central government and parliament as well as the legal system and police. Trust in institutions represents long-term support for the political system and regime, and can be contrasted with popular perceptions of the current political system or government.

Respondents in the ABS were asked to indicate to what extent they trust institutions to operate in the best interests of society, selecting one of four main response categories: (1) trust a lot; (2) trust to a degree; (3) don't really trust; and (4) don't trust at all. Respondents who answered 'trust a lot' and 'trust to a degree' are combined for each of the four institutions.[6] An overall trust average is then taken that captures the percentages of respondents that place trust in all of the institutions. The results are reported in Table 8.4.

When asked about the degree of trust in central government, there was a high level of trust in all of the surveyed countries, with the exception of the three East Asian cases of Japan, Taiwan and South Korea. Overall, about 65 per cent of citizens answered that they trust the government. Those that indicated the most trust herald from Singapore (90.7 per cent) and China (85.5 per cent), while those with the least are from South Korea (20.1 per cent) and Taiwan (35 per cent).

Table 8.4 Trust in government institutions

	Central government	Parliament	Legal system	Army	Trust average
Japan	42.4	31.3	59.8	63.6	49.3
Taiwan	35.0	21.4	32.4	53.7	35.6
South Korea	20.1	8.0	34.7	52.8	28.9
China	85.5	72.0	65.1	81.9	76.1
Hong Kong	58.8	45.7	56.0	42.6	50.8
Mongolia	62.5	51.0	47.7	71.5	58.2
Philippines	73.2	71.2	66.2	70.7	70.3
Indonesia	77.7	64.8	74.6	79.0	74.0
Thailand	63.4	64.1	74.6	83.8	71.5
Malaysia	85.4	80.0	80.7	84.5	82.7
Singapore	90.7	84.0	90.7	90.9	89.1
Cambodia	77.8	71.1	60.1	68.9	69.5
All countries	64.4	55.4	61.9	70.3	63.0

Note: The percentages represent the sum of the two positive responses, 'trust a lot' and 'trust to a degree'. Don't know responses have been omitted.
Source: 2005–7 ABS.

Majorities in most of the surveyed countries also believe that their National Assembly can be trusted, with the exception of several East Asian societies. The strongest support comes from Singapore (84 per cent) and Malaysia (80 per cent). The lowest percentages are found in South Korea (8 per cent) and Taiwan (21.4 per cent). The moderate trust figures registered by Thai respondents are somewhat peculiar as there was no elected National Assembly when the survey was conducted. It is plausible that respondents were evaluating the elected assembly that preceded this survey and the incumbent military government.

The responses for trust in the legal system are included because they reflect citizen support for one of the important underlying notions of the rule of law. Under the rule of law, citizens are equal before the law, which is fairly applied by an independent judiciary (O'Donnell 2005). As Diamond and Morlino (2005) argue, the rule of law is the base on which every other aspect of democratic quality rests. Many of the legal systems among the surveyed countries have been criticized for incompetence and corruption (see e.g. Quah 2003; Harding 2001). However, when it comes to citizen evaluations, majorities in 9 of the 12 surveyed societies believe that the legal system operates in the best interests of society. The levels of trust are highest in Singapore (90.7 per cent) and Malaysia (80.7 per cent) and lowest in Taiwan (32.4 per cent) and South Korea (34.7 per cent).

Across the 12 surveyed countries, the average trust score for the army (70.3 per cent) fared higher than trust in central government, parliament and the legal system. The trust indicators range from Hong Kong (42.6 per cent) and South Korea (52.8 per cent) to Malaysia (84.5 per cent) and Singapore (90.9 per cent). In Hong Kong, the responsibility of national defence is maintained by the People's Liberation Army Hong Kong Garrison of the People's Republic of China, which maintains a largely invisible and symbolic presence. With the exception of Hong Kong, the moderate to high levels of trust appear to support the prominent role that the military has played in politics. What is surprising about the positive endorsement in most of the countries surveyed in Table 8.4 is that the military's role has not always been viewed in positive terms. In Thailand, for example, there is a long history of coups and military-bureaucratic rule, including the government at the time of the survey; in Cambodia, the military has been strongly associated with the establishment of an authoritarian government.

The final column in Table 8.4 captures the overall trust averages for each of the surveyed countries. The highest trust ratings belong to Singapore (89.1 per cent) and Malaysia (82.7 per cent), whereas the lowest ratings herald from South Korea (28.9 per cent) and Taiwan (35.6 per cent). In sum, trust in the four institutions is moderately high with clear majorities in half or more of the societies expressing positive evaluations.

Trust in institutions may capture more long-term evaluations towards the current political system and government. The next section examines citizen satisfaction with current political and civil liberties. Political and civil rights consist of both procedural and substantive practices central to liberal democracy. In contrast to trust in institutions, citizen satisfaction with rights measures short-term evaluations, in that citizens were asked to judge the current scope of political and civil rights in their country.

Satisfaction with current political and civil freedoms

Minimalist definitions of democracy focus on procedural aspects, especially the presence of free and fair elections. The ABS has one question – satisfaction with the right to vote – that is relevant to the minimalist procedural aspects of the political systems in Southeast Asia. The survey asked respondents how satisfied they are with the right to vote by selecting one of four response categories: (1) very satisfied; (2) somewhat satisfied; (3) somewhat dissatisfied; and (4) very dissatisfied.

According to the survey, there is considerable satisfaction that reaches proportions above 70 per cent in all societies except for China. Satisfaction is highest in Cambodia (96.4 per cent), Malaysia (96.2 per cent) and Singapore (95.1 per cent). In China, citizens are able to vote for deputies to local-people congresses and for leadership elections to work units or villages, although the Chinese Communist Party controls the process. Nonetheless, more than half of the Chinese respondents (56.2 per cent) expressed satisfaction with their right to vote. The high levels of satisfaction suggest that most of these countries meet minimalist definitions of democracy as far as the voting and election process is concerned. However, the high levels of satisfaction with voting rights do not mean that citizens are satisfied with other aspects of the political system. It is thus necessary to examine levels of citizen satisfaction with other principles that underlie democratic governance: specifically, how satisfied Asian publics are with the current scope of civil liberties in their country.

The ABS asked respondents about a range of civil freedoms using the same four response categories. Two of the items are concerned with freedom of expression: freedom of speech and the right to criticize the government. The other two items deal with associational freedoms: the right to participate in any kind of organization and the right to gather and demonstrate.[7] These freedoms can be distinguished as 'negative' rights because they require forbearance on the part of others, in contrast to 'positive' rights that require others to provide goods or opportunities (Donnelly 2003: 31).

Citizen satisfaction with the specific civil freedoms is illustrated in Figure 8.1. Across the pooled averages for the surveyed countries, around 6 out of 10 respondents were satisfied with all four of the specific rights. The overall proportion of respondents satisfied with the right to participate in any kind of organization and the right to gather and demonstrate is roughly equal to the proportion satisfied with freedom of speech and the right to criticize the government. Satisfaction with freedom of expression is highest in Japan (69.2 per cent) and Cambodia (61.8 per cent), and lowest in China (29.3 per cent) and Singapore (29.5 per cent). Satisfaction with associational rights is highest in Japan (79.2 per cent) and Indonesia (70.9), and lowest in China (30.4 per cent) and Cambodia (42.3 per cent). Considerable variation exists within each of the

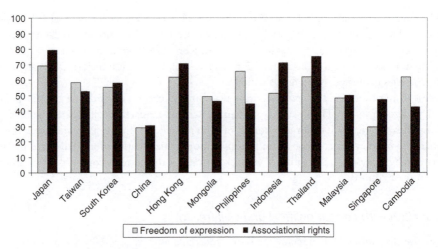

Figure 8.1   Satisfaction with civil liberties

Note: Freedom of expression represents the combined average for two items: citizen satisfaction with freedom of speech and the right to criticize the government. Associational rights represent the average for citizen satisfaction with the freedom to participate in any kind of organization and the ability to gather and demonstrate.
Source: 2005–7 ABS.

surveyed countries in terms of the degree of satisfaction expressed for specific civil rights. When compared with satisfaction with electoral rights, it is also evident that citizens are generally less satisfied with freedom of expression and associational rights.

Accountability and responsiveness of government

Two additional principles associated with liberal democratic rule are considered in this section: accountability and responsiveness. Accountability is the responsibility of elected leaders to represent and carry out the popular will – with the obligation to report, justify and be judged on their actions; accountability also requires that state institutions are transparent and open (Beetham *et al.* 2001). The idea of responsiveness in a democracy is that state institutions should be able to respond to demands of citizens in terms of the formulation and delivery of policies (Beetham *et al.* 2001). Responsiveness thus combines procedural and substantive aspects by considering the extent that public policies correspond to citizen demands and preferences (Diamond and Morlino 2005).

Four questions from ABS are used to examine the principles of accountability and responsiveness of government. Each question asked respondents to agree or disagree with the following statements: (1) there is widespread corruption among those who govern the country; (2) generally speaking, the people who are elected to the [national parliament] stop thinking about the public once they're elected; (3) government officials pay little attention to what citizens like me think; and (4) generally speaking, people like me don't have the power to influence government policy or actions. Whereas the first two items tap accountability, the third and fourth items are closer to the notion of responsiveness. Respondents were given five possible response categories: (1) strongly agree; (2) agree; (3) neither agree nor disagree; (4) disagree; and (5) strongly disagree.

The percentages of respondents who answered affirmatively to the accountability and responsiveness items are specified in Figure 8.2. Higher percentages are considered to indicate more critical assessments of these principles. Across the surveyed countries, nearly half of the respondents

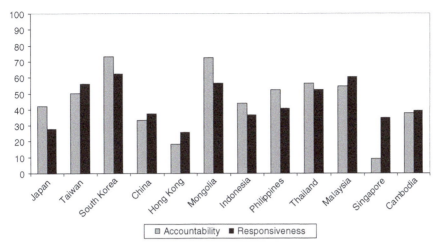

Figure 8.2 Accountability and responsiveness
Note: Accountability is the percentage of respondents who strongly agree or agree to the following statements: (1) corruption is everywhere; and (2) people elected don't think about the public. Responsiveness is the percentage of respondents who strongly agree or agree with the following items: (1) government officials pay little attention; and (2) people like me don't have the power to influence government policy.
Source: 2005–7 ABS.

offered a critical evaluation for the accountability items, agreeing that there is widespread corruption among those who govern and that people who are elected stop thinking about the public once they are elected. Respondents in South Korea and Mongolia reported the highest scores for both these items; Hong Kong residents and Singaporeans were the least critical. For the next items pertaining to responsiveness, the overall pattern across the surveyed countries was almost evenly divided between those critical and supportive. The proportion taking the most critical view of accountability issues heralds from South Korea and Malaysia, whereas the smallest percentages come from Hong Kong and Japan. In sum, majorities in almost half of the surveyed countries rated the measures for accountability and responsiveness in critical terms.

Evaluation of the central government

An important dimension of democratic governance is how the public evaluates the central government. Respondents from East and Southeast Asia may trust government institutions or be satisfied with specific civil liberties, but how they evaluate the central government itself may be quite different. Specifically, this section considers how well respondents in ABS evaluate the central government's efforts when it comes to dealing with four specific issues: the economy, corruption, human rights and public services. The focus on the central government and how well it is doing with these specific issues moves us from the more abstract questions such as trust and satisfaction with civil rights to the more specific focus on the existing regime. The results of the survey are reported in Table 8.5.

Compared with many of the survey questions scrutinized thus far, respondents are fairly critical when it comes to how well the central government is managing specific issues. Across the surveyed countries, only half of the respondents believe it is doing well when the average is taken for all four items. In terms of the specific areas that warranted praise and criticism, the average rating was the highest for public services (56.6 per cent) and human rights (52.8 per cent) followed by the

Table 8.5 How well central government is managing specific issues

	Economy	*Corruption*	*Human Rights*	*Public Services*	*Average*
Japan	36.3	15.8	41.9	36.4	32.6
Taiwan	12.7	9.3	54.3	52.8	32.3
South Korea	7.2	7.4	27.2	52.3	23.5
China	48.0	14.7	44.3	54.5	40.4
Hong Kong	58.9	56.3	63.8	66.3	61.3
Mongolia	49.5	14.8	32.6	34.0	32.7
Philippines	44.6	23.5	43.5	45.6	39.3
Indonesia	28.5	16.8	57.5	70.9	43.4
Thailand	27.7	21.7	47.4	50.7	36.9
Malaysia	75.8	35.3	71.5	63.7	61.6
Singapore	91.9	94.1	84.1	85.4	88.9
Cambodia	59.1	14.3	65.3	66.1	51.2
All countries	45.0	27.0	52.8	56.6	53.6

Note: The figures represent the sum of the two positive responses, 'doing well' and 'fairly well'. Don't know responses have been omitted. The number in parentheses represents the relative ranking of each country.
Source: 2005–7 ABS.

economy (45 per cent) in third place. The least highly rated item was corruption, where only 27 per cent of respondents praised how their central government handles this issue.

In terms of specific countries, the central government was rated the highest in Singapore (88.9 per cent) followed by Malaysia (61.6 per cent) and Hong Kong (61.3 per cent). In Cambodia, a bare majority endorsed the central governments' efforts across the four issues. In the remaining countries, majorities did not endorse the efforts of their central government. The particular issue of corruption is viewed as one of the most problematic areas in both consolidated as well as consolidating democracies and across the varieties of authoritarian systems.

Patterns in citizen support for democratic principles and practices

The previous section examined how respondents evaluated specific democratic principles and practices as well as their attitudes towards the existing political system and regime. One means of summarizing the various patterns is to consider which aspects of democratic governance were most and least highly rated in each society. Table 8.6 reports the highest and lowest rated aspects for each country using four dimensions: (1) trust in institutions (four items); (2) satisfaction with civil liberties (four items); (3) accountability and responsiveness (four items); and (4) evaluation of central government efforts (four items).[8]

There are several common patterns across the surveyed countries as captured in Table 8.6. The most highly rated aspect is trust in institutions in 8 out of 12 countries. For the three East Asian democracies of Japan, Taiwan and South Korea, civil liberties is rated the highest. For the least highly rated aspects, public perceptions of central government efforts fare the lowest in 8 out of 12 societies. These patterns roughly suggest that citizen perceptions become more critical as we move from the abstract to the specific and from long to short-term considerations. Of the four aspects, it was argued earlier that trust in institutions taps long-term performance considerations, whereas satisfaction with civil liberties is more immediate as respondents are asked to evaluate the current scope of rights. Accountability and responsiveness, and central government efforts, deal more

Table 8.6 Most and least highly rated aspects of democratic governance

	Most highly rated	*Least highly rated*
Japan	Civil liberties	Central government efforts
Taiwan	Civil liberties	Central government efforts
South Korea	Civil liberties	Central government efforts
China	Trust in institutions	Civil liberties
Hong Kong	Accountability & responsiveness	Trust in institutions
Mongolia	Trust in institutions	Central government efforts
Philippines	Trust in institutions	Central government efforts
Indonesia	Trust in institutions	Central government efforts
Thailand	Trust in institutions	Central government efforts
Malaysia	Trust in institutions	Accountability & responsiveness
Singapore	Trust in institutions	Civil liberties
Cambodia	Trust in institutions	Central government efforts

Note: The four aspects of democratic governance are: trust in institutions, satisfaction with civil liberties, accountability and responsiveness, and evaluation of central government efforts.
Source: 2005–7 ABS.

specifically with the political system and government. Thus, respondents in East and Southeast Asia appear more content in the abstract but become more critical when evaluating specific practices of the political system and regime.

How the Asian publics rate democratic principles and practices can also be compared with their preferences for a democratic system. This is one avenue for comparing how much of a gap exists between the ideals and institutional support for a democratic system versus its principles and practices. In Figure 8.3, the gap is calculated by subtracting the average scores taken from the four aspects of democratic governance (examined earlier) from the support for a democratic system measure reported in Table 8.2. To be consistent across the four aspects, the measures for

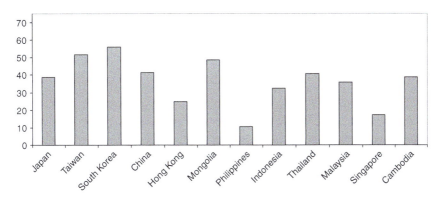

Figure 8.3 Gap between support for democratic system and democratic practices
Note: The gap is calculated by subtracting democratic practices from support for a democratic system. Support for democratic system combines those who answered 'very good' or 'fairly good' and is based on the figures reported in Table 8.3. Democratic practices represent the average score taken from four dimensions of governance: trust in institutions, satisfaction with civil liberties, accountability and responsiveness, and evaluation of central government efforts.
Source: 2005–7 ABS.

accountability and responsiveness have been recoded so that higher values indicate more positive evaluations.

Figure 8.3 shows that in all countries except for the Philippines and Singapore, support for a democratic system is rated much higher than how democracy performs in practice. In South Korea, Taiwan and Mongolia the gap is the greatest and ranges from 49 to 56 points. In China and Thailand, the gap falls in the low 40s. In the Philippines and Singapore, the gap is the least pronounced, which suggests that citizen support for a democratic system is somewhat close to how citizens evaluate its practices. In most of the surveyed countries, however, a considerable gap exists between the desirability of a democratic system and how citizens rate its practices.

Conclusion

The purpose of this chapter has been to evaluate the quality of democratic governance in East and Southeast Asia on the basis of public opinion polls recorded in ABS. The analysis examines general citizen support for a democratic system as well as alternative regime types. It also analyses citizen evaluations of a variety of democratic principles and practices important in the literature on democratic governance, including trust in institutions, satisfaction with political and civil liberties, accountability and responsiveness, and how well the central government is dealing with specific issues.

In terms of general public support for a democratic system, strong majorities in all countries responded positively. However, when examining citizen orientations towards the democratic system in combination with the alternative regimes, it became clear that many respondents may have embraced democracy but did not reject military rule, rule by strong leaders or rule by experts. In some countries, there were sizeable percentages of respondents who accepted two or three non-democratic regimes. Clearly, democratic consolidation in East and Southeast Asia will require a greater proportion of respondents to embrace democracy as the 'only game in town' if it is to succeed.

In terms of how citizens rated democratic principles and practices, a strong majority of citizens were satisfied with the right to vote. However, when the quality of democracy extends to fuller liberal democratic principles and practices, it is clear that the same high levels of enthusiasm do not hold. Across the surveyed countries, about 6 out of 10 respondents reported they trust government institutions and a little more than 5 out of 10 were satisfied with specific civil liberties as well as the measures for accountability and responsiveness. When it comes to how well the central government is doing on specific issues, less than 5 out of 10 responded positively.

Differences were also uncovered in how the Asian publics evaluated abstract and specific principles and practices of democratic rule. Across most of the surveyed countries, there were relatively high levels of trust in government institutions and high levels of satisfaction with civil liberties, with lower levels when the measures dealt with accountability and responsiveness or the central government. Consequently, there appears to be many sizeable gaps when it comes to citizen perceptions of democratic ideals on one hand, and the actual practices of democratic rule on the other. One of the key challenges for many of the countries in East and Southeast Asia in this regard will be to better balance the two, to make performance match the citizens' ideals.

In the meantime, additional research is required to better refine how democratic quality is understood and measured in Asia and other regions of the world. If we take the view that democratic consolidation requires at least more than half of a country's population to embrace democracy as the 'only game in town', when and how this level is reached will be unclear until we know more about the dynamics that shape citizen orientations.

Notes

1 For more information, see http://www.asiabarometer.org.
2 This chapter is an expanded and revised version of Carlson (2008); and Carlson and Turner (2008).
3 See http://www.freedomhouse.org/template.cfm?page=1 (accessed 20 September 2011).
4 Among the best-known survey projects are the New Democracies Barometer, the New Europe Barometer, the Latinobarometer, Afrobarometer, World Values Survey and Eurobarometer (for a review of these studies, see Heath *et al.* 2005).
5 Mikami and Inoguchi (2008) analyse Thai responses both before and after the coup using ABS, and find some decline in perceptions related to the quality of governance, but also note that people's commitment to a democratic system was fragile before the coup.
6 Respondents who answered 'don't know' or 'haven't thought about it' (categories not read out to respondents) were coded as missing data. In both cases, the numbers of respondents in these categories were extremely small and not predominantly from any particular country.
7 'Don't know' responses averaged between 2% and 6% for each item and were treated as missing data.
8 The values for the accountability and responsiveness items have been recoded in the same direction as the three other dimensions with higher values indicating more positive evaluations.

References

Altman, D. and A. Pérez-Liñán (2002) 'Assessing the Quality of Democracy: Freedom, Competitiveness, and Participation in 18 Latin American Countries', *Democratization*, 9 (2), pp. 85–100.

Beetham, D., S. Bracking, I. Kearton and S. Weir (2001) *The International IDEA Handbook on Democracy Assessment*. The Hague: Kluwer Law International.

Carlson, M. (2008) 'Assessing the Quality of Democracy in Southeast Asia', paper presented at the AsiaBarometer conference, Chuo University, Japan.

Carlson, M. and M. Turner (2008) 'Public Support for Democratic Governance in Southeast Asia', *Asian Journal of Political Science*, 16 (3), pp. 219–239.

Carothers, T. (2002) 'The End of the Transition Paradigm', *Journal of Democracy*, 13 (3), pp. 5–21.

Case, W. (2001) 'Malaysia's Resilient Pseudodemocracy', *Journal of Democracy*, 12 (1), pp. 43–57.

—— (2002) *Politics in Southeast Asia: Democracy or Less*. Richmond: Curzon Press.

Churchill, W. (1947) *The Official Report, House of Commons* (5th Series), 11 November 1947, vol. 444, cc. 206–207.

Dahl, R. (1971) *Polyarchy: Participation and Opposition*. New Haven, CT: Yale University Press.

—— (1989) *Democracy and Its Critics*. New Haven, CT: Yale University Press.

Dalton, R. J. (2004) *Democratic Challenges, Democratic Choices*. Oxford: Oxford University Press.

Diamond, L. (1999) *Developing Democracy: Toward Consolidation*. Baltimore, MD: Johns Hopkins University Press.

—— (2002) 'Thinking about Hybrid Regimes', *Journal of Democracy* 13 (2), pp. 21–35.

—— and L. Morlino, eds (2005) *Assessing the Quality of Democracy*. Baltimore, MD: Johns Hopkins University Press.

Donnelly, J. (2003) *Universal Human Rights: In Theory and Practice*. New York: Cornell University Press.

Freedom House. n.d. *Freedom in the World: Country Ratings*; available at http://www.freedomhouse (accessed 20 September 2011).

Funston, J. (2001) 'Thailand: Reform Politics'. In *Government and Politics in Southeast Asia*, ed. J. Funston. Singapore: Institute of Southeast Asian Studies, pp. 328–371.

Harding, A. (2001) 'The Economic Crisis and Law Reform in South East Asia', *Asia Pacific Business Review*, 8 (2), pp. 49–58.

Heath, A., S. Fisher and S. Smith (2005) 'The Globalization of Public Opinion Research', *Annual Review of Political Science*, 8, pp. 297–331.

Hill, H. (2000) *The Indonesian Economy*, 2nd ed. Cambridge: Cambridge University Press.

Huntington, S. (1991) *The Third Wave: Democratization in the Late Twentieth Century*. Norman: University of Oklahoma Press.

Linz, J. and A. Stephan (1996) *Problems of Democratic Consolidation: Southern Europe, Southern America, and Post-Communist Countries*. Baltimore, MD: Johns Hopkins University Press.

Mikami, S. and T. Inoguchi (2008) 'Legitimacy and Effectiveness in Thailand, 2003–2007: Perceived Quality of Governance and its Consequences on Political Beliefs', *International Relations of the Asia Pacific*, 8 (3), pp. 279–302.

Montero, A. P. (1998) 'Review Essay: Assessing the Third Wave Democracies', *Journal of Interamerican Studies and World Affairs*, 40 (2), pp. 117–134.

Munck, G. L. (2001) 'The Regime Question: Theory Building in Democracy Studies', *World Politics*, 54 (1), pp. 119–144.

O'Donnell, G. (2005) 'Why the Rule of Law Matters'. In *Assessing the Quality of Democracy*, ed. L. Diamond and L. Morlino. Baltimore, MD: Johns Hopkins University Press, pp. 3–17.

Ottaway, M. (2003) *Democracy Challenged: The Rise of Semi-Authoritarianism*. Washington, DC: Carnegie Endowment for International Peace.

Park, C. (2007) 'Democratic Consolidation in East Asia', *Japanese Journal of Political Science*, 8 (3), pp. 305–326.

Quah, J. (2003) 'Causes and Consequences of Corruption in Southeast Asia: A Comparative Analysis of Indonesia, the Philippines and Thailand', *Asian Journal of Public Administration*, 25 (2), pp. 235–266.

Samudavanija, C-A. (1995) 'Thailand: A Stable Semidemocracy'. In *Politics in Developing Countries: Comparing Experiences with Democracy*, ed. L. Diamond, J. Linz and S. Lipset. Boulder, CO: Lynne Rienner, pp. 323–368.

Schumpeter, J. (1943, 1976) *Capitalism, Socialism and Democracy*. London: George Allen and Unwin.

Shin, D. and J. Wells (2005) 'Is Democracy the Only Game in Town?', *Journal of Democracy*, 16 (2), pp. 88–101.

Part II
Democratization and governance

9

Democratic transitions

Jay Ulfelder

The replacement of rulers who hold power through tradition or violence with officials chosen by citizens in free, fair and inclusive elections marks a singular, and usually celebratory, moment in any country's political history. This chapter selectively reviews social-science theories on the forces leading societies to that moment, which we will call a 'democratic transition'. Here, the relevant officials are understood to be the ones charged with establishing and executing national laws and policy – that is, both legislators and the chief executive, who may be a prime minister or president – and any regime in which those rulers have not been chosen by free, fair and competitive elections is regarded as authoritarian.

This meaning of the term 'democratic transition' rests on a categorical idea of democracy – a national political regime either is or is not democratic – and privileges elections as the essential procedural criterion for attaining that status. Although this conceptualization of democracy is sometimes referred to as a 'minimal' one, the threshold it establishes is not easy to cross. For elections to be considered largely free, fair and inclusive, an array of supporting conditions must be met throughout the period of political campaigning and then sustained through and beyond the elected government's installation, essentially in perpetuity. As Dahl (2000) shows, that is not a weak standard. This definition also differs from common usage in the post-Cold War period, when countries experiencing almost any kind of positive change in political institutions have often been described as 'in transition' to democracy, sometimes for a decade or more.[1] Here, the term 'democratic transition' is reserved for the (culminating) event, not the larger process in which that event is embedded.

Metaphorically speaking, democratic transitions mark a kind of birth. These occasions can be viewed as discrete events, but the relationships that produce them – and the life courses they initiate – exhibit remarkable variety that is not contained in the event itself. Arrival at the transitional moment depends on processes that began far in advance of the new government's installation and the elections that produced it. What is more, the institutional forms present on either side of that singularity vary tremendously, and there do not seem to be any enduring patterns in the trajectories countries follow into and away from it.

So, why do these 'births' happen where and when they do? Despite a marked increase in the incidence of democratic transitions in the latter half of the twentieth century – and despite intensive analysis of those events by social scientists, and the acute interest of policymakers and activists seeking to promote them and autocrats seeking to prevent them – the causes of demo-cratic transitions are still poorly understood. There is no shortage of analysis on how and why democratic regimes have been established in specific countries at specific times. Nevertheless, the large body of thoughtful work in this field has yet to produce more than a handful of generalizations that seem to apply to many or most relevant cases, and the most ambitious theories on the subject have all proven to be of limited use.

Scholars attempting to review and summarize literatures on democratic transitions have often contrasted structural theories – emphasizing the causal role of deeply rooted and slow-changing conditions – with voluntarist theories centred on choices made by people involved in the process of democratization. This distinction, however, has become something of a false dichotomy. In much of the recent work on the subject, theorists focused on structural conditions have responded to earlier criticisms ('structure is destiny') by attempting to specify mechanisms that probabilistically link those conditions to processes of change; and most voluntarist theories now acknowledge that structure both motivates and constrains the behaviour of the people involved.

For reasons that should eventually become clear, this chapter takes a different tack, juxtaposing theories that have attained paradigmatic status in the field with mid-range theories, which aim more modestly to explore the effects of individual variables or to explain transitions (or the lack thereof) in clearly defined subsets of cases. The trouble with the handful of paradigms that have come to dominate scholarly and policy discourse on democratic transitions is that each one poorly explains and inaccurately predicts the occurrence and timing of many of the real-world events to which it is meant to apply. Lacking a reliable grand theory, a collection of mid-range theories about the probabilistic effects under specific conditions of one or a few variables – such as the presence of natural-resource wealth, the occurrence of an economic crisis, the emergence of social movements, and the thickness and form of international linkages – seems to provide more reliable insights into the causal origins of these events.

Paradigms

A few theories on the causes of democratic transitions make such broad claims and have produced such extensive literatures that we may reasonably describe them as paradigms in the study of comparative democratization. While many authors who have contributed to, or drawn upon, these approaches would not assert or even aspire to paradigmatic status, the ideas on which these literatures are based have become lenses through which specific democratic transitions are most often viewed and 'explained'. As it happens, though, none of these paradigms hold up especially well in the face of empirical evidence.

Modernization theory

For the latter half of the twentieth century, modernization theory dominated American and, arguably, Western thinking about the origins of democratic regimes.[2] The kernel of modernization theory is the claim that the phase of economic 'development' that carries societies from agricultural to pronounced industrial activity produces a variety of social changes conducive to liberal democratic government. In Lipset's (1959) foundational formulation of this theory, the affinity among these streams of change meant that societies grew more likely to establish and then sustain democratic government as they became wealthier, more industrialized, more urban and better educated. In particular, the middle class that was thought to emerge and grow from these intertwined streams of social change was expected to push for the establishment of democratic government, and then to help defend it once in place. Inglehart and Weltzel (2005) have recently restated the theory by identifying a specific pattern of changes in popular values as the causal link between 'modernization' and democratization, but the basic logic is the same. Although this theory is not inherently deterministic, its proponents in the latter decades of the twentieth century often presented it as such. 'All good things go together,' went the glib encapsulation.

Modernization theory provides an intellectual framework in which we can place and interpret several profound, common and apparently interrelated forms of economic, social and political change that have occurred in many countries in the twentieth and twenty-first centuries. As it happens, though, modernization theory does a poor job of explaining the occurrence or absence of democratic transitions at specific times in specific cases. In spite of the strong associations documented by Lipset, Inglehart and Weltzel, and others, authoritarian regimes sometimes survive for decades in wealthy and apparently 'modern' countries (e.g. Singapore at the extreme), and numerous democratic transitions have occurred in poor countries with large rural populations, little heavy industry and low literacy rates (e.g. much of sub-Saharan Africa after the end of the Cold War).[3] The gap between theory and reality was evident from the start, and as early as the 1960s and 1970s, scholars such as Huntington (1968) and O'Donnell (1973) were developing theories that were motivated, at least in part, by the need to explain the numerous exceptions to modernization theory. As political science, at least in the United States, has turned increasingly towards statistical methods, cross-national studies using techniques tailored to the analysis of change over time within cases have often failed to find strong links between increases in wealth, urbanization and education on the one hand, and the location and timing of democratic transitions on the other (e.g. Przeworski *et al.* 2000; Epstein *et al.* 2007; Ulfelder and Lustik 2007).[4]

Defenders of modernization theory sometimes respond to these challenges by pointing out that the theory is meant to be probabilistic, not deterministic, and that the expected association between socio-economic 'modernity' and democracy will prove true in the long run. It is certainly reasonable to offer different theories for different time scales, and long-term secular trends are still broadly consistent with modernization theory; over the past several decades, the world has become much more urban, industrialized and better educated, and many more political regimes are democratic than was true at the start of that period. In the face of the many exceptional cases, however, modernization theory seems to offer an awfully blunt instrument for explaining specific democratic transitions, or even democratic transitions in general, when they are understood as discrete events or even phases instead of an almost glacial process of evolutionary change. Even if the broad correlations ultimately hold over the course of several decades or a century, some other forces must be powerfully shaping variations in the prospects that countries will or will not newly attempt elected government – and those short-term and medium-term variations are of primary concern for most scholars and practitioners in this field.

Transitology

Among advocates for democracy and scholars of democratization, the pessimism that arose in the 1960s and 1970s as many newly democratic countries reverted to authoritarian rule flipped into unabashed optimism in the late 1980s and early 1990s, when a flurry of democratic transitions occurred around the world, often in countries that had never attempted democracy before. A crucial feature of this 'wave' of post–Cold War transitions was that it was not restricted to the more industrial, urban and literate societies escaping communist rule in Europe; instead, its reach also extended to societies in sub-Saharan Africa and Asia that were mainly deeply impoverished, still mostly rural and often lacking in formal education. By the mid-1990s, for the first time in human history, there were more democratic governments in the world than authoritarian ones.[5]

In this ebullient period, many observers proclaimed that the structural conditions previously seen as prerequisites for democratic transitions were no longer relevant, if they ever had been at all. Picking up on Rustow's (1970) observation that democracy in some sense always results from elite 'choice', a body of work had already emerged in the 1980s that shifted the focus of research on democratic transitions from structural preconditions to the wilful actions of political figures during the period spanning the relaxation of authoritarian control to the establishment of democratic government (O'Donnell and Schmitter 1986). Inspired by the sense of possibility implicit in this voluntarist perspective, many scholars and practitioners began to assert that democracy could be installed almost anywhere at any time, as long as political leaders were sufficiently committed to it and possessing of the right political skills. The 'transitional' period running from political liberalization in authoritarian regimes to the installation of an elected government became the focal point for much of the work on this topic, and efforts to describe and explain the dynamics and outcome of that period – a practice sometimes referred to as 'transitology' – became intermingled with attempts by governments and advocates to effect political change in the real world.

For scholars and practitioners alike, transitology marked a gestalt shift away from the structural determinism of modernization theory into a world driven by human agency in which anything was possible, even if some pathways might be more difficult to achieve than others. That same sense of open-ended possibility, however, is precisely what marks transitology's failure as a social-scientific theory. If anything is possible, then every real-world outcome is potentially consistent with the original theory. Whenever things fail to turn out as well as hoped, we can blame the leaders involved for lacking the will and skill to get the job done. So, the theory can never be contradicted, and without the prospect of contradiction, we have an outlook or ideology instead of a theory. In a sense, we are left with the banality that the proximate cause of all political outcomes is human action, so we need only ascribe the right motivations to the people involved to understand why they did what they did.

While transitology does not lend itself to generalization (or falsification) beyond its basic emphasis on the causal pre-eminence of elite intentions and interaction, one sharper conjecture that did arise from this body of work is the notion that the mode of transition shapes the prospects that democracy will arise and survive. In Di Palma's (1990: 8) words: 'Democracies can be made (or unmade) in the act of making them.' More specifically, many scholars working in this vein have argued that pacts – explicit agreements among rival elites on rules governing the exercise of power under the new regime – greatly favour the establishment and survival of democratic government. According to O'Donnell and Schmitter (1986), pacts are important because they reduce the threat that democratization poses to wary leaders by providing guarantees for the future protection of their 'vital' interests. For other scholars, the content of pacts matters less than the process by which they arise, and it is the experience of successful negotiation and compromise that provides the foundation for durable democracy (Levine 1978).

The claim that pacting greatly improves the prospects for a democratic transition is probably the single most-testable conjecture to emerge from this literature, but it has not fared especially well in the face of empirical evidence. Without a shared sense of what kinds of negotiations and agreements constitute 'pacting', the concept has sometimes been stretched to cover almost any kind of elite interaction, which occurs to some extent in every instance of national, political transformation. Some scholars have argued that pacting is often epiphenomenal to the transition process, and that transitology's myopic focus on elite behaviour has obscured the important causal role of popular mobilization and radical challengers (e.g. Adler and Webster 1995; Bermeo 1997). Meanwhile, democratic regimes have fallen in some iconic cases of pacting, such as Venezuela, while they have survived in many others where explicitly negotiated agreements were absent, suggesting that pacts are neither necessary nor sufficient to explain why some authoritarian openings produce democratic transitions while others do not. Ultimately, transitology's turn towards elite will and skill seems to have taught us less about the causes of democratic transitions than it has about our own predilection to imagine opportunities for manufacturing change we hope to see, even under apparently difficult circumstances.

In contradistinction to the extreme voluntarism that has pervaded much of the work in transition studies, some scholars developed game-theoretic models that were intended to capture essential features of the transition process and thereby help to identify regularities in their outcomes. In a pioneering work in this vein, Przeworski (1991) portrayed the transition process as a series of strategic interactions among 'hardliners' and 'reformers' within the authoritarian regime, and 'moderates' and 'radicals' in civil society. In his analysis, this process always began with some kind of political liberalization initiated by the regime, and it could only produce democracy when reformers within the regime allied themselves with moderates or radicals in the opposition. What's more, the ensuing democracy was said to be more likely to consolidate – i.e. to survive much beyond the transition period – when that alliance involved moderates instead of radicals in civil society. Focusing on transitions from Communist Party rule, Colomer (2000) further subdivided the actors identified by Przeworski and thereby identified additional alliances and sequences, including ones in which change occurred by revolution rather than negotiation.

These attempts to formalize the strategic interplay of the transition period succeed in imposing some intellectual constraints on the voluntarism that pervades much of transitology. At the same time, the formal models developed by these and other authors have not yet produced durable insights that would help us predict the trajectory of transition processes in other places. Divisions always exist within authoritarian regimes and among opposition forces over the appropriate depth, pace and form of political change, and those divisions do not always provide the initial impetus to political reform. The crucial questions are how and why certain of those forces gain the upper hand at specific moments, what tactics they use, and how those patterns affect the prospects that a functioning democratic regime will ensue. So far, attempts to capture these interactions in formal models have helped to spotlight those questions, but they have not succeeded in connecting broader conditions to specific patterns or outcomes in ways that would allow us to use them not just to describe but also to anticipate events.

Economic inequality

The most recent addition to the small collection of paradigmatic theories of democratic transitions shares modernization theory's basis in structural political economy, but responds to the evidence that wealth and democracy do not move hand in hand and finds more revolutionary forces at play. Centred on endeavours by Boix (2003) and Acemoglu and Robinson (2006), this body of work uses the methods of game theory and draws inspiration from Marxist political sociology to cast politics as, at its roots, a struggle between rich and poor over the distribution of wealth. These authors argue that democratic transitions are likely to occur when the threat of rebellion against a dictatorship is both credible and formidable. These events are rare because: successful revolutions are difficult to organize; the credibility of the threat posed by citizens to dictators depends on a variety of forces that are often fleeting; and the constellation of actors with a vested interest in the status quo usually succeeds in deterring or repelling popular challenges. When that threat becomes sufficiently potent, however, wealthy elites will sometimes offer democratic government as a strategic compromise, allowing them to concede some redistribution of wealth without having their assets seized or suffering the costs of sustained repression.

While Boix (2003) and Acemoglu and Robinson (2006) identify several factors that contribute to the relevant actors' strategic calculus, the one around which a paradigm has emerged is economic inequality.[6] According to Boix (2003: 19), democratic transitions are most likely when inequality is low: 'A democratic outcome becomes possible,' he writes, 'when the inequality of conditions among individuals, and therefore the intensity of redistributive demands, falls to the point that an authoritarian strategy to block redistribution ceases to be attractive to the well-off'. Acemoglu and Robinson also identify inequality as a crucial piece in everyone's incentive structures, but their model leads them to hypothesize that democratic transitions are most likely to occur when inequality is either very high or very low. Whichever model we use, though, the basic implication is that democratic transitions occur through elite concession in response to concerns about the distribution and redistribution of wealth in unequal societies.

These authors' theoretical models are explicitly intended to cover hundreds of years' worth of institutional stability and change around the world, and the paradigm that has emerged from these grand theories has inspired many new and interesting research projects in comparative politics. As it happens, though, these theories do not accord well with much of the empirical evidence. In a careful and very thorough statistical appraisal of global data from the period 1960–2000, Houle (2009) finds 'no support' for either Boix's or Acemoglu and Robinson's hypotheses linking inequality to democratic transitions. Summarizing the qualitative evidence, Geddes (2007: 323) suggests that these authors' models are 'plausible simplifications of early democratizations in Western Europe and of many transitions in Latin America', but she concludes that models emphasizing other dimensions of political conflict are more germane to recent struggles over democratization in other, usually poorer, parts of the world. These negative findings are no reason to ignore the insight that the distribution and bases of wealth might shape prospects for democratic transitions, but they should suffice to narrow our sense of the theories' validity and scope.

Mid-range theories

Where paradigmatic theories try to describe the entire proverbial elephant, mid-range theories seek more modestly to capture something essential about just a single portion of the beast. The preceding section argued that paradigmatic ideas about the causes of democratic transitions have failed to live up to the grand ambitions assigned to them, whether by the leading authors in each body of work or by their readers. This section turns to several narrower lines of research that have produced helpful insights about single variables, specific subsets of cases, or both.

Natural-resource wealth

A host of recent comparative studies and cross-national statistical analyses have supported the claim that natural-resource wealth – and oil wealth in particular – shape the likelihood that countries under authoritarian rule will experience a democratic transition (Karl 1997; Ross 2001; Jensen and Wantchekon 2004; Smith 2004; Ulfelder 2007; Dunning 2008). These studies are often motivated, in part, by a desire to explain a cluster of egregious exceptions to modernization theory: countries that couple relatively high levels of per capita income with stable authoritarian regimes. In his seminal paper on the topic, Ross (2001: 332–337) describes a few possible pathways linking resource wealth to the absence of democratic transitions: a 'rentier' effect, whereby rulers use income from natural-resource exploitation to buy loyalty and docility; a 'repression' effect, whereby rulers use that income to buy more effective coercion; and a counter-modernization effect, whereby natural resources allow countries to get rich without experiencing the social changes that are thought to link rising wealth to demands for democratic government. Ross's own analysis offers tentative support for all three claims, and the aforementioned studies, which often use a variety of measures for resource wealth and democratic transitions, also support the broader hypothesis.

The success of theories linking natural-resource wealth to prospects for democratic transitions stems, in part, from their deliberately limited scope. Implicitly or explicitly, scholars working in this vein offer arguments that are only meant to apply to countries that combine a limited tradition of democratic government with an abundance of specific natural resources in an era when the global economy is hungry for those resources. Karl's (1997) comparative study is among the most explicit in linking the 'resource curse' she observes to a historically specific conjuncture regarding some countries' political and economic development, on the one hand, and global appetites for oil, on the other. Yet the contextual nature of the core argument pervades work on the subject. Where initial statistical analyses on the subject failed to use data and models that allowed for this kind of contingency (e.g. Ross 2001; Fish 2002), many of the later large-N studies have allowed for it, and have produced sharper findings as a result.

While the aforementioned studies have shown a statistically significant link between resource wealth and democratic transitions, it is important to acknowledge that the substantive effects associated with this variable are often modest. One reason for that modesty may be that cross-national data on one or even a few common sources of natural-resource wealth do a poor job capturing the dizzying array of resources and other commodities and transactions from which governments can extract rents. A body of scholarship that initially focused on oil wealth has spurred new lines of thinking about the political implications of revenue flows from other licit and illicit sources, such as foreign aid (Wright 2009), drug trafficking (Coppedge et al. 2007), and gems and other minerals (Al-Ubaydli 2009). Process-tracing studies of specific countries may continue to reveal linkages between revenues from these kinds of resources and the survival and demise of authoritarian regimes, but the cross-national time-series data required to test these findings in large-sample statistical studies simply do not (yet) exist.

Types of autocracy

Another important body of work that emerged in the 2000s – not coincidentally a time when it became clear that the post–Cold War wave of democratic transitions would not extend to every country on earth – takes a step back in the causal chain. As Huntington (1991) observed, in order for a democratic transition to occur, an authoritarian regime must fall, and at least some of the causes of the latter might differ from the causes of the former. In a widely cited conference paper, Geddes (1997) took up that proposition and used game theory to deduce a set of hypotheses about how three different (ideal) types of authoritarian regimes – military, personalist and single-party – could be expected to 'crack' under different circumstances. Her analysis identified military regimes as the most fragile form of autocracy; suggested that personalist regimes were most likely to break down violently, often after the 'great leader' dies; and explained why single-party regimes were typically the most resilient of the three types.

Geddes's thoughtful work on the subject has inspired a spate of new research on the relationship between forms of autocratic rule and prospects for regime change. Hadenius and Teorell (2007) have expanded on Geddes's typology of authoritarian regimes and looked explicitly at differences across authoritarian types in the likelihood that a democratic transition would follow a regime breakdown, using statistical analysis to identify 'limited multiparty systems' (that is, 'competitive authoritarian regimes') as especially likely to beget democratic transitions. Brownlee (2007) compares four cases of autocratic rule – Egypt, Iran, Malaysia and the Philippines – and concludes that the outcome of elite and social conflicts at the start of authoritarian regimes often produce institutional legacies that can later either sharply limit or invite opportunities for democratic transitions. Consistent with Geddes's analysis, Brownlee sees broad ruling parties that bind elites together as the basis for durable authoritarian rule and thus, implicitly, as a serious obstacle to democratic transitions. Using Geddes's typology as a starting point, Ulfelder (2005) finds that the effects of contentious collective action on the risk of regime breakdown vary across types of autocracy, implying that their effects on prospects for a democratic transition vary as well, indirectly if not directly.

The findings from this expanding literature on the resilience of different forms of authoritarian rule offer some important insights into the origins of democratic transitions that are overlooked when we treat non-democracies as an undifferentiated mass. That said, this line of reasoning also confronts some challenges that make it difficult to imagine how these insights would ever form the basis for a fuller theory of regime change culminating in democratic transitions. For one thing, while scholars have been creative and insightful in identifying authoritarian 'ideal types', it turns out to be very hard to distinguish these forms in practice – and change within them over time. Geddes's deductive reasoning led her to three types, but her efforts to put real-world autocracies into those categories forced her to acknowledge the existence of many 'hybrid' cases, including 'triple-threat' cases that combine elements of all three. By the time Hadenius and Teorell (2007) had finished grappling with the problem, they had expanded the roster to five main types and a host of other satellite forms (e.g. rebel regimes and theocracies). As the categories get more and more specific, the prospects for developing theories that go beyond description to explain and predict outcomes in other cases inevitably diminishes.

More important for this chapter, this body of work has still not produced much theorizing that connects the causes and forms of authoritarian breakdown to the occurrence or absence of democratic transitions. One reason for that omission may be the artificially sharp distinction this literature sometimes draws between those two events. For deductive theorizing, it makes sense to draw a clear line between the two and see them as sequenced, but this break does not exist in the real world. Instead, the two processes often overlap and are intertwined, making it more difficult to distinguish the causes of the one from the other. Still, the basic insight has encouraged scholars working in this field to think carefully about how the causes of a democratic transition might be conditional on the nature of the extant authoritarian regime, and that is undoubtedly a good thing.

Contentious politics

Theories of democratic transitions make competing claims about the role played by popular protest and rebellion in the occurrence and outcome of a transition process. In the transitology tradition, the pre-eminent view is that transitions occur because of a split between hardliners and reformers within the ruling elite, and popular protest that occurs in response to that split is largely epiphenomenal to the ensuing transition (O'Donnell and Schmitter 1986). The effects of popular unrest are thought for the most part to be indirect; mobilized civil society can serve as a valuable resource for elites who favour 'reform', but the threat of violence can also frighten elites away from agreeing to a democratic transition.

This elite-centred view has been undercut, if not completely contradicted, by numerous recent studies, some of which touch on the same cases that informed the classic works in the transitology tradition. As a result, a growing body of work sees citizen action as an important, if not essential, ingredient in many democratic transitions. Reassessing some transition theorists' claim that popular mobilization can spoil chances for democratization by radicalizing reformers' demands, Bermeo (1997) concludes that popular upsurges will only drive liberalizing elites away from democratization if those elites believe those radical forces will dominate electoral politics after the transition.[7] Wood (2001) draws on evidence from South Africa and El Salvador to argue that liberalization and, later, democratic transition only occurred in those countries because mobilization by marginalized citizens imposed substantial costs on ruling elites, a trajectory she calls the 'insurgent' path to democracy. Schock (2005) compares the fate of non-violent social movements across several authoritarian regimes and concludes that the ability of such movements to provoke democratic transitions depends, in part, on the organizational forms they adopt and tactics they use.

The findings from these and other studies on links between what some sociologists call 'contentious collective action' and the occurrence and outcome of democratic transitions do not accumulate into a cogent theory. They do, however, serve as an important corrective to theories and practices that focus almost exclusively on elite bargaining and choice as the engine of democratic change. Consistent with the more modest ambitions of mid-range theories, they also show how and why the effects of popular mobilization are likely to depend on other factors, making it difficult if not impossible to produce broad generalizations about the role of popular forces in the transition process.

Economic growth

While modernization theory and neo-Marxist theories both cast socio-economic structure as the driving force behind democratization, other scholars have considered the short-term effects of economic growth (and decline) on the chances that a democratic transition will occur. Focusing on 'authoritarian withdrawals' in middle-income countries in the 1970s and 1980s, Haggard and Kaufman (1995: 26) argue that the probability of a democratic transition increases 'during periods of economic distress', in part because of the popular unrest economic crises often begets. At the same time, they also posit that the effect of economic distress is contingent on regime type; they see military regimes as more vulnerable to these shocks than single-party regimes, in which the party can mediate the government's response to elite and popular frustrations. Although their theoretical framework portrays enduring tensions over the distribution of wealth as the fuel for change in political institutions, Acemoglu and Robinson (2006) also identify economic distress as a vital catalyst for democratic transitions. Economic crises are so important because they help citizens overcome collective action problems and reduce the opportunity costs associated with rebellion. Those changes, in turn, raise the expected costs of repression for defenders of the status quo, making the democratic alternative look more appealing.

While the view that economic crisis begets democratic transitions seems to be widely held, statistical studies examining this question have produced different results. Przeworski et al. (2000) find a significant relationship in their models between short-term fluctuations in economic growth rates and the probability of a democratic transition, but Gasiorowski (1995) and Ulfelder and Lustik (2007) do not. Importantly, though, Geddes's (1997) statistical analysis supports Haggard and Kaufman's conjecture that the strength of the association between economic growth and the likelihood of an authoritarian breakdown is contingent on the nature of the authoritarian regime, with military regimes proving the most vulnerable, and personalist regimes the least. These results are certainly plausible in light of their consistency with earlier comparative research, and they could help explain why studies considering transitions in all kinds of authoritarian regimes worldwide across several decades would produce muddier findings. While hardly a definitive test of these arguments, Geddes's results suggest once again that patterns in the forces driving democratic transitions will sometimes come into clearer focus when we narrow the scope of our inquiries to similar cases in similar historical contexts.

International forces

Research aimed at understanding the origins of democratic transitions has traditionally focused on domestic forces as the causes of these events. As economic globalization and international political integration have continued to deepen, however, scholars have increasingly recognized that politics are not neatly contained by national borders, so theories of regime change must grapple with the effects of regional and global forces as well.[8]

While the notion that international forces shape prospects for democratic transitions within countries is now widely accepted, recent analyses of specific international forces have not produced unambiguous results. Several recent statistical studies conclude that democracy is contagious, with transitions in regional neighbours (Brinks and Coppedge 2006; Gleditsch and Ward 2006) and stronger ties to the United States (Brinks and Coppedge 2006) increasing the likelihood of a democratic transition in countries under authoritarian rule, but at least one similar study has considered similar measures and found no significant effect (Ulfelder and Lustik 2007).[9] Focusing more narrowly on the consequences of participation in intergovernmental organizations, Pevehouse (2005) finds that membership in regional bodies can increase the likelihood of democratic transitions, but the strength of this effect varies with the degree of democracy among the organization's member states. Ulfelder (2008) considers similar evidence but reaches a different conclusion, finding that aspects of economic integration, including participation in the global free-trade regime now embodied in the World Trade Organization, have had stronger effects on the likelihood of democratic transitions in recent decades than membership in regional organizations or participation in regional and global human-rights treaty regimes.[10]

The divergence of these results could reflect differences in the data and models used by the various authors. Still, if the effects were strong and unambiguous, we would expect them to be robust to some variation in measures and methods. It seems more likely that the results are inconsistent because these effects are contingent in ways that these global statistical analyses are not always capturing. If that is the case, then efforts to understand the effects of international forces on democratic transitions will have to descend a rung or two on the ladder of generalization and be more explicit about the (narrower) conditions under which specific relationships ought to hold.

A conceptual framework developed by Levitsky and Way (2006) offers an instructive example in how this kind of conditional analysis might proceed. These co-authors focus their analysis on two kinds of ties to the West in the immediate post-Cold War period: linkage, defined as 'the density of ties (economic, political, diplomatic, social, and organizational) and cross-border flows (of trade and investment, people, and communication) between particular countries and the United States, the European Union (EU), and Western-led multilateral institutions'; and leverage, defined as 'the degree to which governments are vulnerable to external democratizing pressure' as a result of economic and political circumstances. Drawing lessons from the pathways followed by many countries in different parts of the post-Cold War world, they conclude that the effectiveness of external pressure to democratize is contingent on the density of the target country's linkages to the West. In their view, leverage is only conditionally effective because linkage is required to carry those external pressures into the domestic political arena, where democratic transitions actually happen. This contingency means that Western attempts to prod the democratization process will usually be ineffective, because Western leverage is often weak.[11]

Implications

The difficulty that paradigmatic theories of democratic transitions have had in trying to explain many of the events to which they are ostensibly meant to apply suggests that our understanding of the origins and dynamics of those events is still limited. Of course, limited is not the same as non-existent. While the paradigms have been questioned, a number of mid-range theories have succeeded in producing sharp insights into subsets of cases that share important background conditions. The success of these less ambitious attempts to explain democratic transitions suggests that some generalization is still possible, as long as the conditions under which the relationships in question are expected to hold are clearly stated.

Our collective inability to produce a general theory of democratic transitions after decades of scrutinizing those important events might seem like a failure, but there is valuable information in those negative findings. Apparently, democratic transitions can take many different forms and follow many different paths, so it is not surprising to discover that the causes of those diverse events vary considerably across contexts and probably over time as well. Thus, while there is clearly a long-term secular trend favouring the establishment of democratic governments in countries around the world, the ways in which authoritarian rulers resist this trend, citizens try to drive it forward, and other interested parties get involved in that process, continue to evolve.

Meanwhile, the fact that grand theories of democratic transitions have not yet succeeded does not mean that they are not worth trying to develop. Acemoglu and Robinson's (2006) work is illustrative in this regard. Those authors offer their theory as a covering law that can explain persistence and change in certain kinds of political institutions – elections and suffrage – in all parts of the world throughout recent history. That the theory fails to do so does not negate the value of the insights it offers us into the politics of economic inequality, and the valence between those politics and certain institutional forms. The same may be said of modernization theory, the emphasis of which on the political implications of social changes associated with the transformation from predominantly rural and agricultural societies to urban, industrial ones continues to ring true, even as the world continues to produce exceptions to it. As long as we reinterpret these grand theories as partial ones and recognize that their predictions are probabilistic rather than deterministic, we can draw useful insights from them without doing too much violence to the messier reality we observe.

As a closing thought, it is worth revisiting an important but often overlooked point made by Tilly (1995) about the importance of timescale to theories of democratization to help understand why it is so hard to formulate grand theories that can explain and predict not just broad patterns, but also specific events. As Tilly points out, the process of democratization could occur on the political equivalent of a geological timescale, like the process by which organic matter is transformed into an oil field; or it could occur on a much shorter (and more familiar) timescale, like the planting and cultivation of a garden; or it could fall somewhere in between. The challenge for scholars of comparative democratization is that we still do not know which timescale applies, but the answer has profound implications for our attempts to understand and affect that process. Both long-term and short-term processes can lead to predictable regularities, but where to look for those regularities, and what kinds of interventions are likely to be effective at changing the trajectory a particular case is following, will differ radically.

What is more, without knowing which time-scale is most applicable, we do know that the way we frame our research problem often carries implicit assumptions about the answer to that question. By slicing democratization into a series of discrete phases, we sharply narrow our historical focus, thereby privileging explanations that rely on proximate conditions and human choices made during the period of observation. As Pierson (2004) compellingly argues, though, the fact that institutional changes cannot occur without human action does not mean that we can fully understand those changes by considering the immediate environment in which the choices were made. Sometimes, we need to situate those choices in a much longer sequence of events and processes in order to understand why they arise, which decisions are taken, and where they lead. The difficulty we have had so far in formulating broad theories of democratic transitions could result from limitations of our understanding and imagination, but they could also stem, at least in part, from how we are framing the question.

Notes

1 For example, Freedom House publishes an annual report on Soviet successor states that it calls 'Countries in Transition', even though those countries gained their independence more than two decades ago and have followed a variety of political trajectories since then. On the conceptual flaws attached to these semantics, see Carothers (2002).

2 For an insightful intellectual history on this topic, see Nils Gilman, *Mandarins of the Future: Modernization Theory in Cold War America* (Baltimore, MD: Johns Hopkins University Press, 2007).

3 Modernization theorists would also have a hard time explaining a case such as contemporary Thailand, where much of the urban middle class apparently supported a return to authoritarian rule, while citizens from rural areas swarm the capital to defend democracy (but that is a topic for a separate discussion).

4 But see Inglehart and Weltzel (2005), and Boix and Stokes (2003), for statistical analyses that confirm the link between development and democracy posited by modernization theory.

5 Using Freedom House's list of electoral democracies as one measure of this trend, the proportion of regimes worldwide that were democratic rose above 50% for the first time in 1993 and then peaked at 59% in 2005. At the end of 2009, the figure stood at 53%. For these data, see 'Freedom in the World 2010' at www.freedomhouse.org.

6 Where Boix emphasizes the mobility of capital as an important co-determinant of the relative costs of repression and rebellion, Acemoglu and Robinson emphasize the capital intensity of the economy and the form and extent of globalization, among other things.

7 For an exemplary statement of the argument that mass action hurts prospects for a democratic transitions, see Karl (1990).

8 Here, international political integration refers not only to explicit unification through the expanded European Union, but also to the strengthening of other regional organizations such as the African Union and Organization of American States, and to the strengthening of international law through treaty regimes and bodies such as the International Criminal Court.

9 Surprisingly, the widely cited statistical analysis by Przeworski *et al.* (2000) did not consider international variables.

10 The European Union (EU) is widely considered a special case with regards to its impact on democratization, because of the strength of its preconditions for membership and the high degree of formal political integration it entails. The prospect of joining the EU is thought to have helped produce some democratic transitions in Eastern Europe following the collapse of Communist Party rule, but its chief effects have probably been on the prospects that democracy would survive in those countries once established.

11 In an earlier but also important work on the subject, Whitehead (1996) identifies three categories of international forces affecting prospects for democratization: contagion, control and consent.

References

Acemoglu, Daron and James A. Robinson (2006) *The Economic Origins of Dictatorship and Democracy*. New York: Cambridge University Press.

Adler, Glenn and Eddie Webster (1995) 'Challenging Transition Theory: The Labor Movement, Radical Reofrm, and Transition to Democracy in South Africa', *Politics & Society*, 23 (1), pp. 75–106.

Bermeo, Nancy (1997) 'Myths of Moderation: Confrontation and Conflict during Democratic Transitions', *Comparative Politics*, 29 (3), pp. 305–322.

Boix, Carles (2003) *Democracy and Redistribution*. New York: Cambridge University Press.

—— and Susan Carol Stokes (2003) 'Endogenous Democratization', *World Politics*, 55 (4), pp. 517–549.

Brinks, Daniel and Michael Coppedge (2006) 'Diffusion Is No Illusion: Neighbor Emulation in the Third Wave of Democracy', *Comparative Political Studies*, 39 (4), pp. 463–489.

Brownlee, Jason (2007) *Authoritarianism in an Age of Democratization*. New York: Cambridge University Press.

Carothers, Thomas (2002) 'The End of the Transitions Paradigm', *Journal of Democracy*, 13 (1), pp. 5–21.

Colomer, Josep M. (2000) *Strategic Transitions: Game Theory and Democratization*. Baltimore, MD: Johns Hopkins University Press.

Coppedge, Michael, Angel Alvarez and Lucas González (2007) 'Drugs, Civil War, and the Conditional Impact of the Economy on Democracy'. Working Paper #341 (October), Kellogg Institute for International Studies, Notre Dame University.

Dahl, Robert (2000) *On Democracy*. New Haven, CT: Yale University Press.

Di Palma, Giuseppe (1990) *To Craft Democracies: An Essay on Democratic Transitions*. Berkeley: University of California Press.

Dunning, Thad (2008) *Crude Democracy: Natural-Resource Wealth and Political Regimes*. New York: Cambridge University Press.

Epstein, David L., Robert Bates, Jack Goldstone, Ida Christensen and Sharyn O'Halloran (2007) 'Democratic Transitions', *American Journal of Political Science*, 50 (3), pp. 551–569.

Fish, M. Stephen (2002) 'Islam and Authoritarianism', *World Politics* 55, 1, pp. 4–37.

Gasiorowski, Mark (1995) 'Economic Crisis and Political Regime Change: An Event History Analysis', *American Political Science Review*, 89 (4), pp. 882–897.

Geddes, Barbara (1997) 'Authoritarian Breakdown: An Empirical Test of a Game Theoretic Argument'. Paper presented at the Annual Meeting of the American Political Science Association, Atlanta, Georgia.

—— (2007) 'What Causes Democratization?' In *The Oxford Handbook of Comparative Politics*, ed. Carles Boix and Susan C. Stokes. Oxford: Oxford University Press.

Gleditsch, Christian and Michael D. Ward (2006) 'Diffusion and the International Context of Democratization', *International Organization*, 60 (4), pp. 911–933.

Karl, Terry Lynn (1990) 'Dilemmas of Democratization in Latin America', *Comparative Politics*, 23 (1), pp. 1–21.

Hadenius, Axel and Jan Teorell (2007) 'Pathways from Authoritarianism', *Journal of Democracy*, 18 (1), pp. 143–157.

Haggard, Stephan and Robert R. Kaufman (1995) *The Political Economy of Democratic Transitions*. Princeton, NJ: Princeton University Press.

Houle, Christian (2009) 'Inequality and Democracy: Why Inequality Harms Consolidation But Does Not Affect Democratization', *World Politics*, 61 (4), pp. 589–622.

Huntington, Samuel P. (1968) *Political Order in Changing Societies*. New Haven, CT: Yale University Press.

—— (1991) *The Third Wave: Democratization in the Late Twentieth Century*. Norman: University of Oklahoma Press.

Inglehart, Ronald and Christian Weltzel (2005) *Modernization, Cultural Change, and Democracy: The Human Development Sequence*. New York: Cambridge University Press.

Jensen, Nathan and Leonard Wantchekon (2004) 'Resource Wealth and Political Regimes in Africa', *Comparative Political Studies* 37, 7, pp. 816–841.

Karl, Terry Lynn (1997) *The Paradox of Plenty: Oil Booms and Petro-States*. Berkeley: California: University of California Press.

Levine, Daniel H. (1978) 'Venezuela Since 1958: The Consolidation of Democratic Politics'. In *The Breakdown of Democratic Regimes*, ed. Juan Linz and Alfred Stepan. Baltimore, MD: Johns Hopkins University Press.

Levitsky, Steven and Lucan A. Way (2006) 'Linkage versus Leverage: Rethinking the International Dimension of Regime Change', *Comparative Politics*, 3 (4), pp. 379–400.

Lipset, Seymour Martin (1959) *Political Man: The Social Bases of Politics*. Garden City, New York: Anchor Books.

O'Donnell, Guillermo A. (1973) *Modernization and Bureaucratic-Authoritarianism: Studies in South American Politics*. Berkeley: Institute of International Studies, University of California.

—— and Philippe C. Schmitter (1986) *Transitions from Authoritarian Rule: Tentative Conclusions*. Baltimore, MD: Johns Hopkins University Press.

Pevehouse, Jon C. (2005) *Democracy From Above? Regional Organizations and Democratization*. New York: Cambridge University Press.

Pierson, Paul (2004) *Politics in Time: History, Institutions, and Social Analysis*. Princeton, NJ: Princeton University Press.

Przeworski, Adam (1991) *Democracy and the Market: Political and Economic Reforms in Eastern Europe and Latin America*. New York: Cambridge University Press.

——, Michael E. Alvarez, Jose Antonio Cheibub and Fernando Limongi (2000) *Democracy and Development: Political Institutions and Well-Being in the World, 1950–1990*. New York: Cambridge University Press.

Ross, Michael L. (2001) 'Does Oil Hinder Democracy?', *World Politics*, 53, 3, pp. 325–361.

Rustow, Dankwart A. (1970) 'Transitions to Democracy: Toward a Dynamic Model', *Comparative Politics* 2, 3, pp. 337–363.

Schock, Kurt (2005) *Unarmed Insurrections: People Power Movements in Nondemocracies*. Minneapolis: University of Minnesota Press.

Smith, Benjamin A. (2004) 'Oil Wealth and Regime Survival in the Developing World, 1960–1999', *American Journal of Political Science*, 48 (2), pp. 232–246.

Tilly, Charles (1995) 'Democracy Is a Lake'. In *The Social Construction of Democracy: 1870–1990*, ed. George Reid Andrews and Herrick Chapman. New York: New York University Press.

Al-Ubaydli, Omar (2009) 'Diamonds Are a Dictator's Best Friend: Natural Resources and the Tradeoff between Authoritarianism and Development'. GMU Working Paper in Economics No. 10–03 (April). Available at SSRN: http://ssrn.com/abstract=1542179 (accessed 20 September 2011).

Ulfelder, Jay (2005) 'Contentious Collective Action and the Breakdown of Authoritarian Regimes', *International Political Science Review*, 26 (3), pp. 311–334.

—— (2007) 'Natural-Resource Wealth and the Survival of Authoritarian Regimes', *Comparative Political Studies*, 40 (8), pp. 995–1018.

—— (2008) 'International Integration and Democratization: An Event History Analysis', *Democratization*, 15 (2), pp. 272–296.

—— and Michael Lustik (2007) 'Modelling Transitions To and From Democracy', *Democratization*, 14 (3), pp. 351–387.

Whitehead, Laurence, ed. (1996) *The International Dimensions of Democratization: Europe and the Americas*. Oxford: Oxford University Press.

Wood, Elisabeth Jean (2001) 'An Insurgent Path to Democracy: Popular Mobilization, Economic Interests, and Regime Transition in South Africa and El Salvador', *Comparative Political Studies*, 34 (2), pp. 862–888.

Wright, Joseph (2009) 'How Foreign Aid Can Foster Democratization in Authoritarian Regimes', *American Journal of Political Science* 53 (3), pp. 552–571.

10

Democratization and inclusion

Ludvig Beckman

The claim that political rights should not be conditional on class, gender or race is not just a symbolic recognition of equality but is also supportive of an equal distribution of a basic political instrument for change. A century ago, this claim was at the heart of the struggle for democratization and the call for a more inclusive suffrage. A century later, we know that the call was largely successful, in at least the formal sense, as today no one would accept as democratic a political system where the vote excludes people on such grounds. In fact, it has been observed that suffrage expansions represent manifest evidence for democracy's progress in the twentieth century (Arat 1991: 52). Universal suffrage is the norm and is recognized as such by international law and in most national constitutions (Fox 1992; Wilson 2009). As concluded by Andreas Schedler (2002: 44) 'legal apartheid' in the realm of electoral politics is 'not a viable model anymore'.

Past victories have made students of more recent 'waves' of democratization somewhat oblivious to the problems related to inclusion. The booming literature on transitions from authoritarian to democratic regimes is rarely concerned with suffrage restrictions and the reason is perhaps the belief that they no longer represent much of a problem. In understanding the causes and effects of democratic institutions, suffrage is said to be of much less significance than it used to be (Bobbio 1987: 56; Alvarez *et al.* 1996: 5). The impression that the problem of inclusion belongs to the past derives some support from the observation that 'universal suffrage' is no longer a unique property of democracy. The right to vote is frequently 'universal' also in hybrid regimes and even in countries where purely authoritarian regimes remain in place, as is indicated by the rise of 'electoral authoritarianism' (Schedler 2009; see also Zakaria 2004; Diamond 2002). As a consequence, the extent of suffrage in national elections scarcely constitutes a credible basis for a distinction between democratic and authoritarian regimes. More crucial to this end is the effectiveness of competition for political power and the protection of political liberties and rights. Given this picture, it may appear that inclusion should no longer be of major concern for students of democracy.

However, in this chapter I argue that inclusion is still a relevant dimension. Whereas the inclusiveness of the vote may not be what separates democratic government from its rivals today, it is a useful reminder that it once did. To ignore inclusion in the study of democracy because it is less important *now* is to build historical specificity into our conceptual tools, which may distort perceptions of the past development of democracy. For example, without sensitivity to the importance of inclusion, it is easy to overlook the fact that restrictions on the basis of gender remained in force in Belgium, France and Switzerland several decades after they had been recognized as 'stable democracies' (Ramirez *et al.* 1997; Paxton 2000; Caraway 2004). Also, ethnic or indigenous groups continued to face substantial barriers to electoral participation in parts of the US and in Australia until the 1960s (Grofman *et al.* 1992: 21).

A further and ultimately more important reason for devoting more attention to inclusion is the questionable assumption that it no longer represents much of a problem. The received view is invariably that all democracies are 'fully inclusive' (Coppedge and Reinecke 1991: 48; Munck and Verkuilen 2002). It is a frequent contention that legal barriers to electoral participation are 'more a matter of a degree than of a legal phenomenon' (IDEA 2002: 26). Yet, the claim that contemporary democracies are 'fully inclusive' is correct only if existing regulations of the vote are defined as the end point of inclusion, in which case the claim is no more than a tautology. In fact, the vote is a strictly regulated activity and access to the ballot is always more or less exclusionary in all countries that are recognized as either electoral democracies, polyarchies or simply as representative democracies. Thus, a broad variety of exceptions and limitations on the right to vote remain even after the transition from authoritarian rule has been completed (Paxton *et al.* 2003). People afflicted by cognitive disabilities, prisoners, and residents who are not citizens, are denied the right to vote in most if not all democracies (Massicotte *et al.* 2004). Also, restrictions on the basis of age remain contested and have been gradually reduced along the way. These observations are important since they raise questions about the 'internal' democratization of political systems.

Thus, the aim of this chapter is to examine how the dimension of inclusion may challenge and enrich established perspectives on democratization. A basic assumption for this endeavour is that democratization is 'also the story of the extension of the suffrage' (Caraway 2004: 457). It should be noted, though, that this claim allows for at least two different readings, depending on which of two distinct conceptions of democratization are accepted (Storm 2008; Geddes 2009). First, democratization can be understood as the process that takes place in the transition from an authoritarian type of regime to a more democratic form of government. For inclusion to be relevant here, we should be able to show that variation in the extension of the suffrage is either affecting or affected by the character of this process. Second, the notion of democratization may refer to the gradual development towards the perhaps never fully achievable ideal of democracy. This process does not end with the transition to democratic government, and therefore applies even to countries regularly recognized as democracies. To the extent that full inclusion is a constitutive element of the ideal of democracy, it should by implication be pertinent to the study of democratization. Though inclusion may be relevant to democratization in either sense, it is also true that this remains controversial. As noted above, the significance of inclusion to democracy is frequently challenged. One reason for this, as we shall see, is to be found in the way democracy is conceptualized.

Inclusion and the meaning of democracy

The study of the development of political institutions through the conceptual lens of 'democracy' invariably raises issues about the appropriate angle to look from. The episodes selected and the properties that are analysed are determined by the way democracy is conceptualized (Collier 1999: 24). The question whether or not the right to vote should be pertinent to the study of democratization is, in fact, decided by the extent to which 'inclusion' is among the properties packed into the 'basic level' or 'root' concept of democracy (Goertz 2006: 6; Collier and Levitsky 2009: 271). In order to identify current positions on this topic, a brief survey of the literature is necessary, paying particular attention to the treatment of inclusion in conceptualizing democracy.

As is frequently the case with regard to quibbles about concepts, the problem is the multiplicity of desiderata for a good definition. Since little agreement seems to exist, the attempt to define democracy is sometimes regarded as a highly unproductive activity. The sole result expected from definitional exercises is nothing but 'endless debates' and 'perennial disputes' (Rosanvallon 1995: 153; Collier and Levitsky 1997: 450). Nevertheless, there are two major perspectives on definitions that should be distinguished. On the one hand, the selection of conceptual properties can be conceived of as a methodological question that should be decided by the analytic utility of the proposed terminology. On the other hand, the task of concept formation is never taking place in a vacuum of either historical established usage or semantic conventions. Given these background conditions, the art of definition inevitably involves a decision between potentially conflicting criteria (Gerring 2001). In fact, different priorities between analytic usefulness and semantic faithfulness are represented in the literature on democratization and may at times have dramatic implications for the study of democratic inclusion.

In one view, democracy is characterized by the presence of effective rules of political competition among rival elites. The distinction between democratic and authoritarian regimes is essentially that only in the former are rulers accountable to citizens and their elected representatives by regularly applied and formally specified procedures (Schmitter and Karl 1991). The noteworthy feature of this approach is that the presence of a single property – competition – is doing all the work identifying and characterizing institutions we call 'democratic' (Alvarez *et al.* 1996: 4). The inclusiveness of the suffrage simply is of no import because, as pointed out by advocates of this approach, effective competition is clearly possible even where suffrage is limited (Przeworski *et al.* 2000: 34).

A second approach introduces inclusion among the defining properties of democracy. The most well known proponent of this view is Robert Dahl (1971: 4), who long ago identified contestation and inclusion as two separate and equally necessary criteria of democracy. According to Dahl, democracy is the name of a procedure for the making of binding collective decisions that allows for the effective and enlightened political participation among all adult members of the association (Dahl 1989: 129). Democracy is hence conceptualized not simply as competition for public power under roughly equal conditions, but also as the inclusion of all members in this process. Rightly understood, a democracy is the type of political system where all members of an association are offered equal opportunities to participate in the race for political power. Inclusion is undoubtedly an essential requirement for democracy in this sense.

These approaches represent distinct definitional strategies. Dahl's construct is an ideal-type definition that provides a multidimensional account of 'democracy'. It is an ideal-type since the conceptual content is a derivation of a general political idea rather than of observable phenomena in the political world. It is multidimensional due to the recognition that democracy is a composite notion and hence not reducible to any singular property. By contrast, the competitive view, endorsed by Adam Przeworski and perhaps first identified by Joseph Schumpeter, represents neither an ideal-type nor a multidimensional conception. Rather, it must be characterized as a real-type by incorporating empirical observable phenomena in its conceptual core. 'Democracy' is hence fully attributable to existing political systems. Furthermore, the notion of competitive democracy is unidimensional by virtue of the fact that democracy is identified with a single property.

The competitive conception of democracy is sometimes rejected out of hand for the reason that it fails to encapsulate the full meaning of rule by the people and thereby unsettles the semantic field. The exclusive focus on political competition is said to be contrary to the way the term 'democracy' is generally understood (Wedeen 2004: 279). Also, the competitive view is said to be 'profoundly misleading' exactly because it does not pay any attention to the participatory dimension of politics (Moon *et al.* 2006). In response, it must be realized that moving away from semantic conventions may be justified for methodological reasons. In fact, minimizing the intension of a concept and maximizing its extension is providing greater leverage for empirical testing. The less that is decided by 'definitional fiat', the more empirical phenomena remain open for causal analysis (Przeworski *et al.* 2000: 14; Adcock and Collier 2001: 553). In that respect, Dahl's ideal-type conception is obviously less successful by virtue of the fact that it throws together a larger number of properties into the bowl of democracy.

However, the basis for choosing between real-type and ideal-type conceptions of democracy is not evident. Should democracy be conceptualized in terms of what it *should* be or in terms of what it *could* be? Arguably, the choice is decisive to the question whether inclusion has a place in the study of democratization or not. A useful reminder in connection to this predicament is that the *causal* properties of a phenomenon depend on how it is conceptualized (Goertz 2006: 148). That is to say, that the decision whether inclusion should be among the defining properties of democracy is likely to have repercussions for the causal analysis of processes of democratization. If the definition of democracy is silent on inclusion, then studies of democracy are also likely to remain silent on inclusion. That this is indeed the case is illustrated by the remark that explanations of competitive political systems are not matched by any comparable effort to explain variations in inclusion. Accordingly, there 'is practically no research on the causes of inclusiveness' (Coppedge *et al.* 2008: 645). The costs of ignoring inclusion in the study of democratization are, in other words, substantial and not restricted to the semantic field.

Conceptions of inclusion

The decision as to whether or not inclusion should be accepted as a dimension of the concept of democracy is only the first step. The second step is to specify the meaning of inclusion once it is acknowledged as a distinctive dimension of democracy. The fact is, the notion of inclusion is potentially ambiguous and vague, allowing for many distinct conceptions with more or less fuzzy borders. And yet, inclusion is a very popular term in political analysis. At times, inclusion is associated with responsiveness to the interests of individuals or groups (Dryzek 1996: 475; Holden 2006). Thus, studies of exclusion/inclusion engage a variety of phenomena such as the representation in parliament by members of indigenous groups (Lawoti 2008: 368). This perspective is also applied in studies of the responsiveness of public discourse and public policy to the interests of minorities and disempowered groups (Young 2000: 53ff.; Hero and Wolbrecht 2005: 4).

Another way to conceptualize inclusion is by looking at acts of political participation. Since to vote is undoubtedly to participate in politics, it is sometimes concluded that turnout in national elections provides an appropriate yardstick for measuring the inclusiveness of a political system as a whole. Tatu Vanhanen's index of inclusion represents the perhaps most consistent and ambitious endeavour in that direction (Vanhanen 2000, 2003). In a similar vein, it has been argued that a defining feature of 'exclusionary democracies' is the prevalence of extremely low rates of electoral turnout (Remmer 1985: 72).

However, in order to be faithful to Dahl's procedural account of democracy, an even narrower understanding of inclusion is called for. Inclusion refers to the existence of formally recognized opportunities for participation in the process of making collectively binding decisions. An individual is included if he or she enjoys a recognized capacity for the expression of a preference among political alternatives. Though voting is not strictly necessary in associations ruled by direct participation, large-scale associations rely on voting in order to aggregate individual preferences to a collective decision. The right to vote is therefore at the heart of democratic inclusion and should be the primary focus in deciding whether or not a political system is inclusive. The conception of inclusion as opportunities for electoral participation is consequently distinct from conceptions that identify inclusion with acts of political participation or even with responsiveness to such acts (Verba 2003: 665).

Criteria for inclusion

The proposition that inclusion is a necessary condition for a democratic process conveys no information about the extent of inclusion required. The next question, therefore, is how a democratic distribution of the right to vote should be specified. The customary answer is that a democratic suffrage is recognized by being 'universal'. A political system with less than universal suffrage is, by implication, defective in terms of democratic inclusion. 'Universal' is nonetheless a notoriously vague notion and it is far from clear what is entailed by characterizing a distribution of anything as such. For instance, it is a frequent contention that universal suffrage is 'not negated' either by the disenfranchisement of prisoners or of people with intellectual disabilities (Nohlen 1995: 1356). Yet, the basis for accepting certain exclusions as consistent with universal suffrage, while rejecting others, is rarely explained. In fact, it has been suggested that universal suffrage is compatible with the exclusion even of women. According to one study 'universal suffrage is considered to exist when virtually all adult males have the vote' (Hewitt 1977: 456). Though this view is no longer widely accepted, it raises severe doubts about the analytic value of the adjective 'universal'. This suspicion is further supported by the somewhat trivial observation that universal suffrage is never meant to include 'everyone': few would accept the view that *any* member of humanity (let alone, of other species) should be able to vote in an election in order for it to be democratic. Moreover, the exclusion of children and young people is deemed by most people to be consistent with a 'universal' distribution of voting rights.

In current literature, the ascription of universality to a distribution is to imply that anyone within the designated class of people is included. A distribution may, in other words, be 'universal' by reference to any conceivable classification of people, such as a nation's population, the citizenry, all adult citizens, all male adult citizens, and so forth. In each case, the resulting distribution is 'universal' as long as every member of the designated class of people is granted the vote. The decisive issue is consequently not the meaning of 'universal' but the meaning of 'the people' in a democracy. The literature conveys at least four distinct approaches to this issue.

The first identifies the democratic people by reference to the rules characteristic of the countries regularly recognized as liberal democracies. A virtue of this 'institutionalist' approach is said to be that it avoids the complexities of deciding who should be included as a matter of conceptual necessity (Collier 1999: 24, n. 14). A democratic suffrage is simply defined as any distribution congruent with the restrictions that are observable among political systems recognized as democracies. 'Usual exclusions' (Still 1981: 378) or 'generally accepted exclusions' (Kekic 2007: 9) are therefore perfectly acceptable. Obviously, it follows from this view that any restrictions of the vote adopted by Western democracies must be considered to be fully consistent with the idea of democratic inclusion. The reason why is simply that they are de facto recognized by democratic nations. The result is that the meaning of democratic suffrage is considered purely 'a matter of convention' (Alvarez *et al.* 1996: 36, n. 3).

A second alternative is to conceptualize democratic suffrage as the equivalent to a distribution of the vote that satisfies some heuristic criteria. For example, students tracing the origins of democratization in the West have been much inspired by the hypothesis that democratic institutions are the outcome of struggles between workers and the privileged classes. An appropriate understanding of universal suffrage is, from this perspective, that voting transcends the division of classes. The point in time where workers are, in significant numbers, granted the vote is considered as the decisive moment in the transition towards democracy (Rueschemeyer *et al.* 1992: 44; cf. Caraway 2004: 457). In fact, Hewitt justified the decision to ignore exclusions by sex or age by explicit reference to the aim of locating the effects of suffrage extensions on the 'class system' (Hewitt 1977: 457).

A third alternative is to emphasize the lexical meaning of the people that are members of an association. According to this view, the vote is more inclusive the more extensive it is among its members. Lipset seemingly adopts this formula in characterizing democracy as 'the social mechanism which permits the largest possible part of the population to influence major decisions' (Lipset 1959: 71). Every restriction on the right to vote represents a limitation of democratic inclusion. A similar understanding is extractible from the notion that democracy is essentially about conditions of 'symmetry' between rulers and ruled (Held 1995). Democratic inclusion is achieved when everyone subject to a political authority is recognized as an equal participant in the making of the decisions of that authority.

A fourth perspective originates in normative theories of justice. An influential starting point for discussions of democracy and the right to vote is that any public action must consider the interests of anyone affected in order to be justified. On the assumption that voting is a mechanism for considering the interests of affected people, it is argued that the opportunity to vote should extend to anyone affected by government policy (e.g. Young 2000: 237; Morriss 2001: 692). A notable feature of this view is that exclusion is not limited to national borders. In contemplating the global reach of economic and environmental problems, it is potentially true that literally everyone ought to be enfranchised on at least some decisions (Goodin 2007). Moreover, since the effects of government action are not confined to the living generation, the 'all affected principle' raises challenging questions about that applicability of democracy to intergenerational relations (Beckman 2008).

Given the frequency by which 'universal suffrage' is invoked in public discourse, the persistent disagreement about its content appears quite remarkable. However, divergent conclusions on this topic are to a certain extent traceable to more fundamental controversies about the nature of the concept of democracy. Some would hold that the meaning of democracy is contested, that the concept is indeed 'essentially contested' (Collier et al. 2006). Any account of democratic inclusion is accordingly contestable as well. Others would insist that a descriptive concept of democracy is available (Sartori 1987). To accept a descriptive conception is to recognize that normative aspects of democracy, such as the justifiability of suffrage restrictions, represent a distinct set of problems that cannot be resolved by the definition. A descriptive concept of democracy would permit us to say that certain exclusions are inconsistent with the meaning of democracy, while at the same time potentially justified in normative terms (Beckman 2009). As illustrated by these remarks, the study of inclusion and democratization represents important theoretical and conceptual challenges, in addition to the many empirical questions that remain unsolved.

Explaining inclusion

The dominant framework for explaining past suffrage extensions is highly shaped by the historic conditions that characterized the first wave of democratization in the early twentieth century. It is developed in order to identify the forces and reasons that account for the pivotal decision to introduce suffrage for workers and women. A basic question is whether these decisions are to be understood either in terms of the calculated political benefit of the ruling elite or by recourse to the ability of the excluded groups to mount a credible threat of violent action (Collier 1999: 2). In Adam Przeworski's (2008: 294) fitting phrase, the question is whether suffrage was 'conquered' by the disenfranchised members of society or 'granted' them by those already enfranchised. Hence, Przeworski (2008: 308) maintains that historical data supports the conclusion that workers 'conquered' the vote by mobilizing and eventually enforcing concessions from the ruling elites (see also Acemoglu and Robinson 2006: 29).[1]

The framework has been employed for the purpose of explaining the first extensions of the suffrage, but not yet applied to the remaining cases of exclusion. As mentioned above, the relevant categories by which the right to vote is commonly restricted is: age, citizenship, residence, mental sanity and criminal record. It is, of course, less likely though perhaps not impossible that the members of any of these groups are able to mobilize and to conquer the vote. In any case, the capacity of either non-citizens, felons or young people to mobilize for inclusion are infinitely smaller than for the groups excluded 100 years ago. In order to explain cases where suffrage has been partially or fully extended to any of these groups, it is necessary to appeal to the interests of ruling coalitions themselves. The question, though, is what the interests in extending suffrage may possibly be.

As previously noted, the 'historical timing' of transitions to democracy must be taken into account in the study of inclusion (Ramirez *et al.* 1997; Caraway 2004). The struggle for inclusion in the past is characterized by radically different circumstances than more recent cases of democratization. Nations building democratic institutions in more recent times are being influenced and inspired by the institutions already in place before them in other nations. For instance, female suffrage had only been adopted by three nations at the time when the Swedish parliament first decided to widen the suffrage in 1907. When the opportunity for democratic suffrage was given to India in 1949, more than 50 nations had already introduced female suffrage. It is hardly surprising, then, that male and female suffrage was introduced simultaneously in India, whereas in Sweden women had to wait another decade after men had won the vote. But the difference between India and Sweden is clouded by the mere claim that, in both cases, women were 'granted' the vote. Plausibly, new and ultimately more inclusive conceptions of the people in the world did something to convince the members of the Constituent Assembly of India that withholding the vote for women was not an option.

In addition to the hypothesis that suffrage extension is the product of strategic decisions by the political elite, we should consider the force of conventions and norms emerging in society and the international community. In order to understand why some democracies have opted for greater inclusion, and why others have not, we should consequently pay attention to a wider set of possibilities than those present in the first wave of democratization.

Exclusions of the young

Age is recognized by most people as a necessary condition for electoral participation. Hence, no political democracy has ever existed that does not impose a voting-rights age. Today, most democracies (with few exceptions, e.g. Japan) typically adopt 18 as the requisite age for voting in national elections. This norm is of rather recent origin, however. Only in the 1970s did a substantial number of democracies reduce the voting-rights age to 18. In 1970, the electorate in United Kingdom, Germany and France included 18-year-olds for the first time. In the US, all citizens 18 years or older were granted the vote following Amendment 26 to the constitution, adopted in 1971 (Cheng 2008).

The changes introduced in the 1970s started a trend towards lowering of the voting-rights age that continues until this day. The age of 18 was introduced in India in 1989, in Switzerland in 1991 and in Turkey in 2001, to name a few. Also, a few countries lowered the voting-rights age still further. The first Western democracy to do so was Austria, which in 2007 granted all citizens age 16 or older the right to vote in national elections. The 16-years rule was also introduced in the Isle of Man (2006) and Guernsey (2007) and by some local or regional constituencies in Germany (e.g. Bremen in 2009) and in Switzerland (Glarus in 2007).

A somewhat different pattern is found in Latin America. Though democratic institutions in Latin America have for a long time been 'fragile', this part of the world has generally been more inclined to include young people in the electoral process. By 1870, voting at the age of 18 was effective in Paraguay, and introduced by Argentina and Uruguay in 1918, followed by both Peru and Brazil in 1932. Moreover, in Latin America we find more examples of the 16-years rule than in any other part of the world. Nicaragua (1984), Brazil (1988) and Ecuador (2008) all provide for voting in national elections at that age. This is an interesting observation, given the view that suffrage extensions should be less likely in more unequal societies (e.g. Engerman and Sokoloff 2005). The basis for this view is that the costs of an inclusive suffrage for the ruling elite are expected to be higher the more badly off the disenfranchised groups.

Although increasing opportunities for the young to participate in elections may be expected to follow naturally from the process of democratization, the relationship between democratic transitions and the voting-rights age has not always been positive. Indeed, the age of voting has sometimes been raised rather than lowered as a result of the transition process. This was the case in Sweden, where the age of voting was raised from 21 to 24 years at the same time as universal male suffrage was introduced. A similar pattern is found in Italy. The age of voting was raised from 21 to 30 years in 1911, when the parliament finally approved universal male suffrage. At the time, the political elite appeared keener to accommodate the adult members of the working class than the young generation.

Fifty years later, the situation looked very different. By the 1960s the young generation had indeed turned politically self-conscious and were raising demands that governments could no longer afford to ignore. Thus, it is difficult not to relate the veritable flood of amendments to the voting-rights movement that began at the end of the 1960s. Yet, other concurrent events may have contributed. The urgency of extending the vote to young people in the US may have been associated with the experience of the Vietnam War and the draft of millions of young Americans. Recalling a theme from the times of the Second World War, a popular slogan used to be 'old enough to fight, old enough to vote' (Neale 1983). The idea that suffrage extensions are related to the need by governments to mobilize the masses for war is familiar from the literature (e.g. Ticchi and Vindigni 2008). The plausibility of this theory in explaining a lowering of the voting age is rather limited, however. Apparently, countries have reduced the voting age, on most occasions, during peaceful times. Another potential explanation for growing incentives to reduce the voting age today is the demographic transformation of the electorate. Increasing life expectancy means older median voters and, some would say, electoral results increasingly skewed towards the interests of old people (Hinrichs 2002: 38). These considerations apparently influenced leading Austrian politicians in the decision to allow 16-year-olds to vote (Council of Europe 2009).

Exclusions of non-citizens and non-residents

Next to the voting-rights age, the exclusion of non-citizens is clearly the most significant in terms of the number of people affected. Non-citizens are denied access to suffrage for the simple reason that citizenship is a formal requirement for participation in national elections in most democratic nations. Only New Zealand is offering reasonable access to participation in national elections for non-citizens. A few other countries do not explicitly require citizenship to vote but an extended period of residence only (Paraguay, Uruguay, Ecuador, Chile and Malawi). The practice of reserving voting rights to citizens may seem natural, but is in fact an invention of the 'golden era' of the nation state, tracing back to the French Revolution and the invention of the modern conception of citizenship (Brubaker 1992). For instance, in the US citizenship was not necessary in order to vote during the nation's first decades of existence. Though most states soon introduced restrictions, these were generally abolished in the mid-nineteenth century when it became fashionable to let all 'inhabitants' vote. In the end, however, by the end of the nineteenth century these rules were in turn removed (Keyssar 2000: 32). The era of alien suffrage ended in 1926 when the last state (Arkansas) abolished the opportunity for non-citizens to vote (Rosberg 1976: 1100).

Citizenship requirements undoubtedly serve to exclude great numbers of asylum seekers, guest workers, refugees and other foreigners from access to democratic rights. By connecting the vote to the legal status of citizenship, the severity of the exclusion is essentially decided by the character of naturalization policies and citizenship laws. Nations that tolerate dual citizenship typically encourage people to become citizens and to gain access to the vote. However, conditions for naturalization are frequently austere and require at least years of continued residence (Kondo 2001; Weil 2001). The importance of the citizenship regime in accounting for the attitude towards non-citizens voting rights is most visibly revealed by David Earnest's comprehensive study of the subject. According to Earnest, regimes that admit for citizenship on the basis of place of birth, rather than ethnic or cultural affinity, are twice as likely to recognize non-citizens as voters in local elections (Earnest 2008: 102).

It is nevertheless hard to explain the reluctance to allow non-citizen voting rights solely by reference to the electoral self-interest of governing parties. This is especially true given the fact that many Western governments have generally been willing to extend social and economic rights to non-citizens, resulting in what some have termed a 'post-national citizenship' (Soysal 1994). On the other hand, as demonstrated by Earnest (2008: 102), there is a strong positive relation between welfare spending and hospitality towards non-citizen voting. By hypothesis, the norms of equality that serve to justify extensive welfare programmes are also affecting the conception of political equality in a more expansive direction. Dominant perceptions of the vote as a unique privilege for citizens may, therefore, be increasingly in tension with a more fundamental conception of equal consideration of all inhabitants' interests.[2]

Exclusions of prisoners

The question whether people sentenced to imprisonment should be able to participate in national elections is answered quite differently by contemporary democracies. Though the practice of 'felon disenfranchisement' is found in a majority of democratic systems, a substantial number of countries have reached the contrary conclusion as is indicated by the fact that, according to one source, 16 countries impose no restrictions at all on prisoners voting (Massicotte et al. 2004: 32).

Felon disenfranchisement is politically sensitive. Clearly, political opposition in democratically transitional countries may suffer as a result of practices of felon disenfranchisement. Arbitrary arrests of important figures not only prevent them from voting but also prevent others from voting for them. Restrictions on prisoners' rights to vote usually goes hand in hand with restrictions on prisoners' rights to candidacy. Indeed, the number of people disenfranchised by criminal sentence is considerable in some places and is potentially affecting electoral outcomes (Manza and Uggen 2006). It is also clear that the practice of felon disenfranchisement has uneven consequences for major groups in society. Since the distribution of prison sentences among major groups is uneven, the proportion of citizens disenfranchised as a result of imprisonment is certain to be unevenly distributed as well. Looking at the US, it has been pointed out that felon disenfranchisement constitutes a disproportionate penalty on the democratic rights of the black population (Fellner and Mauer 1998). In fact, a frequent contention is that the practice of felon disenfranchisement in the US is fundamentally at odds with developments in Europe (Demleitner 2009).

The exclusion of prisoners from the vote is equally common among recently democratized nations and old democracies. Yet, there are signs that the slow coming of a 'new legal world order' is making it more difficult to sustain the practice of felon disenfranchisement. Recent years have witnessed a number of rulings by constitutional and international courts, effectively invalidating statutes imposing restrictions on prisoners' rights to vote. Most important is undoubtedly the ruling by the European Court of Human Rights in 2005 (*Hirst v. United Kingdom*), where the court found that a blanket ban is inconsistent with the provisions of the European Convention on Human Rights. In Canada, South Africa and Australia, the ruling of constitutional courts have invalidated felon disenfranchisement on the basis of a similar interpretation of the legitimate aims of democratic society. The most significant aspect of these developments is that the courts are increasingly referring to a common understanding of democratic values. Hence, a potential conclusion is that the right to vote is for the first time becoming a 'basic right by international consensus' (Wilson 2009: 111).

It is, of course, a possibility that felon disenfranchisement may be abolished for mere strategic reasons. After all, prisoners are potential voters. But low expected turnout rates among prisoners, and the sentiment that it is more rewarding to remain 'tough on crime', may significantly hamper these incentives. A more probable explanation for any future expansions of suffrage in this direction is therefore that international norms emphasizing a more literal understanding of universal suffrage will eventually take hold of legislators and judges in democratic nations.

Exclusions of the intellectually disabled

A majority of the democratic countries in the world enforce restrictions on the right to vote for people with pronounced intellectual disabilities or who suffer from mental illness.[3] Most common are restrictions on the electoral participation of any person placed under guardianship or declared mentally incompetent by a court of law. Yet some countries explicitly deny voting to 'insane' persons or anyone judged to be of 'unsound mind'. In the United States, where important aspects of the vote remain the prerogative of the state, only six states permit people with intellectual disabilities the right to vote. Other states have typically endorsed the legal provision that 'no idiot, or insane person, shall be entitled to the privileges of an elector' (Schriner *et al.* 1997: 76). Countries where suffrage has been extended to people with intellectual disabilities are not just few in numbers, but also made the decisions rather recently. In the UK, the Electoral Administration Act abolished the last restrictions in 2006. In Ecuador, the new constitution and electoral law introduced in 2009 effectively removed restrictions on the vote for 'mentally disabled'. In Canada and Sweden, legal barriers to the vote for intellectually disabled persons were brought to an end in the 1980s. As a result, there is scant evidence for a relationship between suffrage extensions of this kind and transitions to democracy.

Only in Ireland and Italy have people with intellectual disabilities been included in the *demos* for a sustained period of time. Since both are obviously Roman Catholic nations it may be surmised that Catholicism has something do with it. Speaking against this view is the observation that a majority of Catholic countries have not enfranchised people with intellectual disabilities. Moreover, the history of suffrage expansions in general does not speak in favour of Catholic countries being more inclusive. Female suffrage was introduced later in Catholic countries than elsewhere. The last observation may not be fatal to the hypothesis, however. As noted by Przeworski (2008: 315), the Pope had already expressed support for female suffrage in 1919. The lagged acceptance of female suffrage by Catholic democracies is explained by Przeworski by reference to the limited electoral benefit of enfranchising Catholic women, as perceived by the dominant political parties at the time. At present, it remains an open question as to whether or not the early decision by Italy and Ireland to recognize the vote for intellectually disabled is, in fact, related to Catholicism.

The recognition of the vote for people with intellectual disabilities in Canada and Sweden is of rather recent origin. Sweden removed legal barriers to their electoral participation in 1988. In Canada, the vote for all disabled people was implemented a few years earlier, following the introduction of the Canadian Charter of Rights and Freedoms in 1981. The Federal Court of Appeal subsequently ruled that limitations on the right to vote for people with intellectual disabilities were not 'reasonable' given the Charter's provision that the vote should be guaranteed to 'all citizens'. The changes introduced by Sweden at about the same time must be explained differently, however. The vote by people with intellectual disabilities is essentially a by-product of new legislation removing the institute of 'legal incompetence'. The primary aims of the reforms enacted in Sweden were to enhance the status of disabled people in society and not to expand suffrage. Whereas in Canada suffrage was extended as a result of efforts to provide a more stringent protection for the constitutional rights of all citizens, the extension of the vote in Sweden is more appropriately characterized as the outcome of efforts to improve the welfare of disabled citizens in particular. The potential electoral benefit of extending the franchise in this direction was by implication never contemplated. This is true for Canada because the change was not initiated by legislators, and true for Sweden because the purpose of the change was different.

Conclusions

Inclusion in the precise meaning of access to the vote in national elections is pertinent to the study of democratization in more than one sense. First, the notion of inclusion raises fundamental questions about the conceptualization of democracy. Second, inclusion is a relevant dimension in describing and measuring democracy, in the past as well as in the present. Third, it elicits important and so far poorly understood questions about how best to explain variation in the extent of inclusion among democratic nations. Contrary to popular perceptions, the relation between democratization and suffrage should attract our attention not just for historical reasons.

Notes

1 The rationalist perspective does not necessarily imply that a broadened suffrage was the intended outcome of institutional reform. As emphasized by Johnson (2005: 293), it may more often have been the unintended result of 'ongoing, unstructured conflict among political and economic actors in pursuit of narrow advantage'.
2 While jealously guarding the vote against non-citizens, many governments in both the developed and the developing world have in recent years been more hospitable towards voting by their own citizens living abroad (IDEA 2007).
3 Terminology is controversial in this context for historical reasons. Following the recommendations of a number of scholars in the field, I will mostly refer to 'intellectual disability' (Editorial 2005).

References

Acemoglu, D. and J. A. Robinson (2006) *Economic Origins of Dictatorship and Democracy*. Cambridge: Cambridge University Press.

Adcock, R. and D. Collier (2001) 'Measurement Validity: A Shared Standard for Qualitative and Quantitative Research', *American Political Science Review*, 95 (3), pp. 529–546.

Alvarez, M., J. A. Cheibub, F. Limongi and A. Przeworski (1996) 'Classifying Political Regimes', *Studies in Comparative International Development*, 31 (2), pp. 3–36.

Arat, Z. (1991) *Democracy and Human Rights in Developing Countries*. Boulder and London: Lynne Rienner Publishers.

Beckman, L. (2008) 'Do Global Climate Change and the Interest of Future Generations have Implications for Democracy?', *Environmental Politics*, 17 (4), pp. 610–624.

—— (2009) *The Frontiers of Democracy. The Right to Vote and Its Limits*. London: Palgrave Macmillan.

Bobbio, N. (1987) *The Future of Democracy: A Defence of the Rules of the Game*. Translated from Italian by R. Griffin. Minneapolis: University of Minnesota Press.

Brubaker, R. (1992) *Citizenship and Nationhood in France and Germany*. Cambridge, MA: Harvard University Press.

Caraway, T. (2004) 'Inclusion and Democratization: Class, Gender, Race and the Extension of Suffrage', *Comparative Politics*, 36 (4), pp. 443–460.

Cheng, J. D. (2008) *Uncovering the Twenty-sixth Amendment*, Ph.D. The University of Michigan.

Collier, D. and S. Levitsky (1997) 'Democracy with Adjectives: Conceptual Innovation in Comparative Research', *World Politics*, 49 (3), pp. 430–451.

—— and —— (2009) 'Conceptual Hierarchies in Comparative Research'. In *Concepts and Method in Social Science. The Tradition of Giovanni Sartori*, ed. D. Collier and J. Gerring. London: Routledge.

——, F. Hildago and A. O. Maciuceanu (2006) 'Essentially Contested Concepts: Debates and Applications', *Journal of Political Ideologies*, 11 (3), pp. 211–246.

Collier, R. (1998) *Paths toward Democracy: The Working Class and Elites in Western Europe and South America*. Berkeley: University of California.

Coppedge, M. and W. Reinicke (1991) 'Measuring Polyarchy'. In *On Measuring Democracy. Its Consequences and Concomitants*, ed. A. Inkeles. New Brunswick: Transaction.

——, A. Alvarez and C. Maldonado (2008) 'Two Persistent Dimension of Democracy: Contestation and Inclusiveness', *The Journal of Politics*, 70 (3), pp. 632–647.

Council of Europe (2009) *Parliamentary Assembly*, Doc. 11895.

Dahl, R. (1971) *Polyarchy: Participation and Opposition*. New Haven, CT: Yale University Press.

—— (1989) *Democracy and Its Critics*. New Haven, CT: Yale University Press.

Demleitner, N. V. (1999) 'Continuing Payment on One's Debt to Society: The German Model of Felon Disenfranchisement as an Alternative', *Minnesota Law Review*, 84, pp. 753–804.

Diamond, L. (2002) 'Thinking about Hybrid Regimes', *Journal of Democracy*, 13 (2), pp. 21–35.

Dryzek, J. S. (1996) 'Political Inclusion and the Dynamics of Democratization', *The American Political Science Review*, 90 (3), pp. 475–487.

Earnest, D. (2008) *Old Nations, New Voters*. New York: State University of New York Press.

Editorial (2005) 'Emerging Trends in Accepting the Term Intellectual Disability in the World Disability Literature', *Journal of Intellectual Disabilities*, 9 (3), pp. 187–192.

Engerman, S. L. and K. L. Sokoloff (2005) 'The Evolution of Suffrage Institutions in the New World', *Journal of Economic History*, 65 (4), pp. 891–921.

Fellner, M. and J. Mauer (1998) *Losing the Vote: The Impact of Felony Disenfranchisement Laws in the United States*. Washington/New York: Human Rights Watch and the Sentencing Project.

Fox, G. (1992) 'The Right to Political Participation in International Law', *Yale Journal of International Law*, 17, pp. 539–607.

Geddes, B. (2009) 'Changes in the Causes of Democratization through Time'. In *Sage Handbook of Comparative Politics*, ed. T. Landman and N. Robinson. London: Sage, pp. 278–298.

Gerring, J. (2001) *Social Science Methodology: A Criterial Framework*. Cambridge: Cambridge University Press.

Goertz, G. (2006) *Social Science Concepts*. Princeton, NJ: Princeton University Press.

Goodin, R. (2007) 'Enfranchising All Affected Interests, and Its Alternatives', *Philosophy and Public Affairs*, 35 (1), pp. 40–68.

Grofman, B., L. Handley and R. G. Niemi (1992) *Minority Representation and the Quest for Voting Equality*. New York: Cambridge University Press.

Held, D. (1995) *Democracy and the Global Order*. Cambridge: Polity Press.

Hero, R. E. and C. Wolbrecht, eds (2005) *The Politics of Democratic Inclusion*. Philadelphia, PA: Temple University Press.

Hewitt, C. (1977) 'The Effect of Political Democracy and Social Democracy on Equality in Industrial Societies: A Cross-National Comparison', *American Sociological Review*, 42 (3), pp. 450–464.

Hinrichs, K. (2002) 'Do the Old Exploit the Young? Is Enfranchising Children a Good Idea', *Archives Européennes de Sociologie*, 63 (1), pp. 35–58.

Holden, M. (2006) 'Exclusion, Inclusion, and Political Institutions'. In *The Oxford Handbook of Political Institutions*, ed. R. A. W. Rhodes, S. Binder and B. A. Rockman. New York: Oxford University Press.

IDEA (International Institute for Democracy and Electoral Assistance) (2002) *Voter Turnout since 1945. A Global Report*. Stockholm: IDEA.

IDEA (International Institute for Democracy and Electoral Assistance) (2007) *Voting from Abroad: The International IDEA Handbook*. Stockholm: IDEA.

Johnson, J. (2005) 'What the Politics of Enfranchisement can Tell Us about how Rational Choice Theorists Study Institutions'. In *Preferences and Situations. Points of Intersection Between Historical and Rational Choice Institutionalism*, ed. I. Katznelson and B. Weingast. New York: Russell Sage Foundation.

Kekic, L. (2007) 'The Economist Intelligence Unit's Index of *Democracy* in The World in 2007', *The Economist Intelligence Unit*.

Keyssar, A. (2000) *The Right to Vote: The contested History of Democracy in the United States*. New York: Basic Books.

Kondo, A., ed. (2001) *Citizenship in a Global World*. London: Palgrave Macmillan.

Lawoti, M. (2008) 'Exclusionary Democratization in Nepal, 1990–2002', *Democratization*, 15 (2), pp. 363–385.

Lipset, S. M. (1959) 'Social Requisites of Democracy: Economic Development and Political Legitimacy', *American Political Science Review*, 53 (1), pp. 69–105.

Manza, J. and C. Uggen (2006) *Locked Out. Felon Disenfranchisement and American Democracy*. New York: Oxford University Press.

Massicotte, L., A. Blais and A. Yoshinaka (2004) *Establishing the Rules of the Game: Elections Laws in Democracies*. Toronto: University of Toronto Press.

Moon, B. E. J. H. Birdsall, S. Ceisluk, L. M. Garlett, J. J. Hermias, E. Mendenhall, P. D. Schmid and W. H. Wong (2006) 'Voting Counts: Participation in the Measurement of Democracy', *Studies in Comparative International Development*, 41 (2), pp. 3–32.

Morriss, P. (2001) 'Suffrage'. In *Encyclopedia of Democratic Thought*, ed. P. B. Clarke and J. Foweraker. London: Routledge.

Munck, G. and J. Verkuilen (2002) 'Conceptualizing and Measuring Democracy', *Comparative Political Studies*, 35 (1), pp. 5–34.

Neale, T. H. (1983) *The Eighteen Year Old Vote: The Twenty-sixth Amendment and Subsequent Voting Rights of Newly Enfranchised Age Groups*. Report No 83-103 Gov., Congressional Research Archives: The Library of Congress.

Nohlen, D. (1995) 'Voting Rights'. In *Encyclopedia of Democracy*, ed. S. M. Lipset. Washington, DC: Congressional Quarterly Books.

Paxton, P. (2000) 'Women's Suffrage in the Measurement of Democracy: Problems of Operationalization', *Studies in Comparative International Development*, 35 (3), pp. 92–111.

——, K. A. Bollen, D. M. Lee and H. Kim (2003) 'A Half-century of Suffrage: New Data and a Comparative Analysis', *Studies in Comparative International Development*, 38 (1), pp. 93–122.

Przeworski, A. (2008) 'Conquered or Granted? A History of Suffrage Extensions', *British Journal of Political Science*, 39 (2), pp. 291–321.

——, M. Alvarez, J. A. Cheibub and F. Limongi (2000) *Democracy and Development. Political Institutions and Well-Being in the World, 1950–1990*. Cambridge: Cambridge University Press.

Ramirez, F. U., Y. Soysal and S. Shanahn (1997) 'The Changing Logic of Political Citizenship: Cross-national Acquisition of Women's Suffrage', *American Sociology Review*, 62 (5), pp. 735–745.

Remmer, K. L. (1985) 'Exclusionary Democracy', *Studies in Comparative International Development*, 20 (4), pp. 64–85.

Rosanvallon, P. (1995) 'The History of the Word 'Democracy' in France', *Journal of Democracy*, 6 (4), pp. 140–154.

Rosberg, G. (1976) 'Aliens and Equal Protection: Why not the Right to Vote', *Michigan Law Review*, 74, pp. 1092–1136.

Sartori, G. (1987) *The Theory of Democracy Revisited. Part One and Two*. New Jersey: Chatham House.

Schedler, A. (2002) 'The Menu of Manipulation', *Journal of Democracy*, 13 (2), pp. 5–21.

—— (2009) 'Electoral Authoritarianism'. In *The SAGE Handbook of Comparative Politics*, ed. T. Landman and N. Robinson. London: Sage, pp. 381–393.

Schmitter, P. C. and T. L. Karl (1991) 'What *Democracy* Is ... and Is Not', *Journal of Democracy*, 2 (3), pp. 75–88.

Schriner, K., L. A. Ochs and T. G. Shields (1997) 'The Last Suffrage Movement: Voting Rights for Persons with Cognitive and Emotional Disabilities', *Publius: The Journal of Federalism*, 27 (3), pp. 75–96.

Soysal, Y. N. (1994) *Limits of Citizenship: Migrants and Postnational Membership in Europe*. Chicago: University of Chicago Press.

Still, J. (1981) 'Political Equality and Election Systems', *Ethics*, 91 (3), pp. 375–394.

Storm, L. (2008) 'An Elemental Definition of Democracy and its Advantages for Comparing Political Regime Types', *Democratization*, 15 (2), pp. 215–229.

Ticchi, D. and A. Vindigni (2008) 'War and Endogenous Democracy'. IZA Discussion Paper No. 3397.

Vanhanen, T. (2000) 'A New Dataset for Measuring Democracy', *Journal of Peace Research*, 37 (2), pp. 251–265.

—— (2003) *Democratization. A Comparative Analysis of 170 Countries*. London: Routledge.

Verba, S. (2003) 'Would the Dream of Political Equality Turn Out to be a Nightmare?', *Perspectives on Politics*, 1 (4), pp. 663–679.

Wedeen, L. (2004) 'Concepts and Commitments in the Study of Democracy'. In *Problems and Methods in the Study of Politics*, ed. I. Shapiro, R. M. Smith and T. Masoud. Cambridge: Cambridge University Press, pp. 251–273.

Weil, P. (2001) 'Access to Citizenship: A Comparison of Twenty-Five Nationality Laws'. In *Citizenship Today. Global Perspectives and Practices*, ed. A. Aleinikoff and D. Klusmeyer. Washington, DC: Brookings Institution Press.

Wilson, R. J. (2009) 'The Right to Universal, Equal and Non-discriminatory Suffrage as a norm of Customary International Law: Protecting the Prisoner's Right to Vote'. In *Criminal Disenfranchisement in an International Perspective*, ed. A. C. Ewald and B. Rottinghaus. Cambridge: Cambridge University Press, pp. 109–135.

Young, I. M. (2000) *Inclusion and Democracy*. Oxford: Oxford University Press.

Zakaria, F. (2004) *The Future of Freedom: Illiberal Democracy at Home and Abroad*. New York: W. W. Norton.

11

Hybrid regimes

A social foundations approach

Garry Rodan and Kanishka Jayasuriya[1]

By the turn of the twenty-first century a new concept was gaining traction in accounting for disappointed expectations of the so-called 'third wave' of democratization: the *hybrid regime*. The now pervasive influence of the concept reflects diverse attempts to describe and explain the absence or partial nature of democratization in many countries around the world. It emphasizes not just the combining of elements of both democracy and authoritarianism, but also the possibility of qualitatively distinct regimes transcending existing categories.

For some, hybrid regimes are necessarily transitory ones, even if their collapse is not imminent. Other theorists countenance the possibility that we may be witnessing the development of sustainable regime alternatives to democracy. Crucially, the very notion of a hybrid regime is a manifestation of transition theory's underlying assumption that capitalism and liberal democracy are natural partners. This has constrained regime analysis, systematically discouraging more open-ended enquiries into the nature and causes of political change outside the West.

Thus, despite greater recognition of the complexity and uncertainty of democratic consolidation and transition, much hybrid regime literature is consumed with developing detailed descriptions and typologies of different hybrid regime variants. Moreover, as per the earlier transition paradigm, analysis remains largely focused on the institutional and strategic incentives of political actors to engage with and support 'competitive authoritarian' or other forms of hybrid regimes, with evaluation of the functional quality of political institutions against democratic criteria a central focus.

There are several problems with this quality of democracy (QoD) approach, which appears to take inspiration from democracy audits on established democracies (Beetham 2004; Morlino 2004; Roberts 2005). First, benchmarking regimes against ideal typical liberal democracies reinforces the questionable assumption that democracy is the natural outcome or measure of political change. Second, definitions of democracy have become expansive and misleading (Morlino 2009; Mazzuca 2010). Third, the crucial question of why particular regimes emerge at all often gets lost or marginalized. At the heart of our problems with this literature is the continuing focus on the 'transition problematic', that is, the question of 'why no effective democratic institutions?' rather than the question 'what explains the particular dynamics of hybrid regimes?

To move beyond the transition problematic we need to incorporate the analysis of political institutions within a wider analysis of power relations and historical context. To be sure, existing literature contains attempts to analyse social and economic bases of hybrid regimes and associated political institutions. This includes the importance of civil society and informal institutions for the trajectories of formal political institutions (Ottaway 2003; Slater 2003; Hawthorne 2004; Merkel 2004; Carothers 2006). This literature provides insights about the social foundations of hybrid regimes, such as how the nature and extent of differing organizational cohesiveness of party and state institutions – including 'massive *informal* advantages' to dominant political elites – mediate regime directions (Levitsky and Way 2010: 321; see also Brownlee 2008). However, this literature remains limited in comprehending the nature of the interests and ideologies combining or competing to create or undermine organizational cohesiveness.

In contrast, our social foundations approach starts with examination of the historical conditions of capitalist development and its implications for alliances and conflicts affecting political regime possibilities. We argue that capitalist development in many recently democratized or post-authoritarian societies has failed to produce comparable alliances of social forces to those that led in Western Europe to the consolidation of representative liberal democracy. These relationships influence the nature and trajectory of political institutions. Crucially, our focus is not on the effectiveness and/or cohesiveness of political and state institutions but on understanding the social and political relationship that underpins them. This allows for the countenancing and evaluating of a range of regime trajectories – not just the prospects or otherwise for the flourishing of democratic institutions.

The discussion is structured as follows. First, we examine the emergence of the hybrid regime as a concept, the varying meanings and significances attributed to it and how it has been used to highlight concerns about the democratic quality and effectiveness of institutions. Second, attempts to link political institutions of hybrid regimes to civil society, informal institutions and the cohesiveness of party and state institutions are examined. Third, in distinguishing and demonstrating our social foundations approach, we analyse regime dynamics in three Southeast Asian countries: Thailand, Malaysia and Singapore. The failure to consolidate democratic transition in Thailand has been linked, by QoD authors, to the dysfunctional nature of democratic institutions, which we challenge. In our analysis of Malaysia, we distinguish our particular structural approach in going beyond highlighting the social embeddedness and organizational cohesiveness of state and party institutions to identify the political economy bases of this cohesiveness, allowing us to explain variations among a wide range of regimes – not just hybrid ones – in this cohesiveness. We illustrate this by comparing Malaysia with Singapore.

Hybrid regimes and the quality of democracy

The origins of the hybrid regime as a concept can be traced at least as far back as Diamond's (1989) notion of 'semi-democratic countries' (see also Huntington 1991: 12) and O'Donnell's (1994) 'delegative democracies'. Subsequently, though, there is a proliferation of terms intended to characterize regimes thought to be simultaneously composed of democratic and authoritarian elements or appearances. This includes reference to 'halfway house' regimes (Case 1996), 'partial democracies' (Robinson 2003; Epstein *et al.* 2006; Zinecker 2009), 'pseudo-democracies' (Volpi 2004), 'semi-democracies' (Rich 2002), 'defective democracies' (Croissant and Merkel 2004; Merkel 2004; Boggards 2009), 'illiberal democracies' (Zakaria 2003), 'limited democracies' (Haynes 2001), 'competitive authoritarianism' (Levitsky and Way 2002, 2010), 'electoral authoritarianism' (Diamond 2002) and 'semi-authoritarianism' (Ottaway 2003). These concepts vary in their level of specificity, some being generic terms that may or may not have associated subtypes, others intended to capture only a specific form of hybrid regime. Amidst variations in how hybrid regimes are distinguished, and the conceptual rigour with which the concept is applied, scrutiny of political institutions' democratic integrity looms large in most attempts at specifying hybrid regimes.

When Diamond (1989) first referred to 'semi-democracies' and 'pseudo-democracies', it was by way of trying to identify the emergence of new variants of authoritarian rule. He argued that 'the existence of formally democratic political institutions, such as multiparty electoral competition, masks (often, in part, to legitimate) the reality of authoritarian domination' (Diamond 1989: xvii–xviii). By contrast, O'Donnell (1994) maintained that newly installed regimes in Argentina, Brazil, Peru, Ecuador, Bolivia, South Korea and the Philippines met Dahl's (1956) definition of polyarchy without necessarily being destined for representative democracy. His concept of delegative democracy was meant to capture this 'new species' of democracy that involved 'high stakes' competitive elections, after which 'voters are expected to become a passive but cheering audience of what the president does' (O'Donnell 1994: 99). O'Donnell's key observation was that, in delegative democracies, vertical and horizontal accountability institutions are ineffective or non-existent.

Subsequently, authors increasingly opted for conceptualizing such regimes not so much as variants of either authoritarianism or democracy but as a new and separate hybrid category. For example, in Volpi's analysis of political regimes in Muslim countries, he argues: ' "pseudo-democracy" does not simply correspond to a deviation from a "democratic" normative framework and teleological order – a case of liberal democracy minus "x" or authoritarianism plus "y" – but that it forms a distinct analytical category and political phenomenon' (Volpi 2004: 1061). However, the precise mix of authoritarian and democratic elements could vary significantly from case to case. Indeed, specifying and comparing institutional variations of the democratic-authoritarian mix has been the primary preoccupation within much of the hybrid regime literature.

In one of the early explicit elucidations of the hybrid regime concept, Karl (1995) emphasized how some regimes in Central America combined authoritarian clientelism and coercion at the local level with greater pluralism at the national level. These were not merely 'façade' democracies, according to Karl (1995: 80), since elections were 'often free and fair', but nor were they genuine democracies. Militaries may support civilian presidents, he noted, but they also 'resist efforts by civilians to control internal military affairs, dictate security policy, make officers subject to the judgment of civil courts, or weaken their role as the ultimate arbiters of politics. Impunity is condemned, yet judiciaries remain weak, rights are violated, and contracts are broken.'

Subsequently, Levitsky and Way (2002: 52) identified 'competitive authoritarianism' as a distinctive form of hybrid regime. Here, 'democratic institutions are widely viewed as the principal means of obtaining and exercising political authority', yet formal rules of electoral competition are so systematically violated that the regime 'fails to meet conventional minimal standards for democracy' (Levitsky and Way 2002: 52) – something O'Donnell's delegative democracy is considered to have met (Levitsky and Way 2002: 53). Crucially, though, political competition is not completely absent: 'Although incumbents in competitive authoritarian regimes may routinely manipulate formal democratic rules, they are unable to eliminate them or reduce them to a mere façade' (Levitsky and Way 2002: 53).

Meanwhile, Ottaway's (2003: 15) more general concept of 'semi-authoritarian' regime acknowledges the widespread adoption of elections alongside 'the existence and persistence of mechanisms that effectively prevent the transfer of power through elections from the hands of the incumbent leaders or party to a new political elite or organization'. The precise mechanisms responsible for this may vary from one semi-authoritarian regime to another, but Ottaway (2003: 16) cites the absence of fully institutionalized formal frameworks reinforced by informal patronage networks as critical factors shaping how power is actually allocated.

Another attempt to encapsulate the idea of a distinctive regime embodying features of both democracy and authoritarianism, but with the emphasis tilted more towards the former than in the cases above, is Zakaria's (1997, 2003) characterization of 'illiberal democracy'. Zakaria (2003: 99), too, observed a post-Cold War expansion of regimes combining elections and authoritarianism, involving varying degrees of limits on political competition – ranging from 'modest offenders' such as Argentina to 'near-tyrannies' such as Kazakhstan, with countries such as Romania and Bangladesh somewhere between. However, many of these regimes permit levels of political participation uncharacteristic of authoritarianism: 'Along much of the spectrum, elections are rarely as free and fair as in the West today, but they do reflect the reality of popular participation in politics and support for those elected' (Zakaria 2003: 23).

Carothers's (2002) important essay, 'The End of the Transition Paradigm', went further in challenging core transition theory assumptions, particularly the notion that most countries are in transition to democracy via a process of opening, breakthrough and consolidation. Yet while Carothers helped disabuse many transition theorists of the view that hybrid regimes may be a mere historical pit stop en route to democracy, the transitions paradigm is far from dead. On the contrary, categorizations and analyses of non-democratic regimes continue to take liberal demo-cratic institutions as the point of reference. Terms such as 'defective', 'semi' and 'pseudo' democracy only make sense in relation to a democratic ideal type.

The persistent adoption of liberal democracy as the reference point for categorizing and evaluating hybrid regimes is well illustrated in the work of Wigell (2008), which comprises in our view one of the most sophisticated and detailed typologies of hybrid regimes. His schema is grounded in the understanding of liberal democracy as comprising two constitutive dimensions: electoral and constitutional. On this basis, regimes can be distinguished around four essential regime types – democratic, constitutional-oligarchic, electoral-autocratic and authoritarian – and numerous other subtypes. Of the eight conditions Wigell (2008: 237) identifies that must be present for democracy, four relate to electoral institutions – free, fair, competitive and inclusive elections – while another four relate to constitutional institutions – freedom of organization, freedom of expression, freedom from discrimination and the right to alternative information.

However, towards further differentiating between assorted hybrid regimes, Wigell (2008: 238–241) submits another four electoral conditions – electoral empowerment, integrity, sover-eignty and irreversibility – and four constitutional conditions – executive accountability, legal accountability, bureaucratic integrity and local government accountability. Wigell (2008: 247) does not disguise that his typology is infused with normative overtones and a methodological privileging of liberal democracy: 'Based on a two-dimensional conceptualization of liberal democracy it proceeds to create *diminished* [our emphasis] subtypes that are logically related to each other on the basis of a clear set of defining attributes.'

Often, then, hybrid regime analysis has centred narrowly on trying to establish the existence of effective democratic institutions, presupposing a somewhat technical notion of institutions leading to emphasis on institutional design and elite choices (see, for example, Robinson 2003; Henderson 2004). Inadequate attention is paid to the relationship between institutional effectiveness, on the one hand, and structural and historical factors, on the other. There are, however, theorists who have attempted just this sort of analysis – whose work we now examine.

Structural approaches to hybrid regimes

As analyses rooted in the transitions paradigm gathered momentum, the relative influence of structural analyses from a range of theoretical perspectives declined. However, renewed recogni-tion that structural factors may be essential to explaining the durability of hybrid regimes is evident – particularly through emphasizing the relationship between formal and informal political institutions. Such analyses are especially valuable in bypassing the circular logic inherent in the QoD explanation for the so-called 'defective' character of political institutions.

Mazzuca (2010) explains that the QoD approach to the categorization and analysis of hybrid regimes conflates access to power – defining the character of a political regime – with the exercise of power – concerned more with administrative processes. He argues that aspects of institutional quality – highlighting corruption, clientelism, abuses of executive decree authority, and the absence of effective checks and balances on power – are 'best characterized not as indicators of authoritarianism and deficiencies in democratization but as reflecting – in Weberian terms – patrimonialism and failures in bureaucratization' (Mazzuca 2010: 334). Within Wigell's (2008) framework, legal accountability and bureaucratic integrity would, for example, constitute administrative rather than political regime considerations. Consequently, the low institutional quality identified often pertains to bureaucratic or administrative institutions rather than political ones, and may be quite compatible with a democratic regime. Indeed, Mazzuca (2010: 341) points out that, in Latin America, the champions of democracy 'have strong vested interests in the preservation of patronage networks, and the continuation of other symptoms of low institutional quality'. Mazzuca argues that the timing of Weberian bureaucratic revolutions matters greatly to the complexion of contemporary democratic regimes. This has two implications. First, the causes of 'poor quality' political institutions may reside in factors beyond the purview of prevailing approaches. Second, so-called institutional failure may be nothing of the sort from the perspective of interests embedded in the regime.

Morlino (2009: 281) also charges that the QoD literature adopts far too expansive a notion of political regime, emphasizing the importance of historical legacies. He contends that: 'a hybrid regime is always a set of ambiguous institutions that maintains aspects of the past', be these remnants of traditional, authoritarian or democratic rule. Like Mazzuca, Morlino injects more conceptual precision in attempting to understand the effectiveness of political institutions within an historical perspective.

Among the more explicit attempts to link the performance of political institutions to patterns in social and economic relationships is Merkel's (2004) incorporation of the concept of 'social embeddedness' into his account of divergent paths of 'defective' regimes. He identifies a range of structural factors favourable to fully democratic institutions, including a developed economy, the prevention of extreme poverty, social pluralism, and the fair distribution of the material and cognitive resources of society. These are seen to 'create a shield for democracy and, in most cases, enhances the quality of democracy with regards to the rule of law and participation' (Merkel 2004: 45).

The concept of social embeddedness also features in policy-oriented work intended to inform better democracy promotion strategies in hybrid regimes. In this vein, analysing different variants of semi-authoritarianism in Egypt, Azerbaijan, Venezuela, Senegal and Croatia, Ottaway (2003, 2004) highlights such structural factors as the weak link between political and economic reform and the nature of civil society. Ottaway's key contribution is in exposing the complex, dynamic and variable components of civil society that affect the character of formal political institutions. The mere existence of extensive civil societies is not in itself a plus for democracy. Rather: 'In some countries, organizations of civil society reflect the social pluralism of religion and ethnicity … Thus, civil society simply ends up reflecting old social division' (Ottaway 2003: 18–19).

In her analysis of the Middle East, Ottaway (2004) thus emphasizes the importance of broad-based political organizations, including social movements and unions, for democratic institutions to take root. The prospect of democracy in the Arab world depends on the growth of constituencies committed to furthering the democratic goal, ideally because they are truly committed to democracy, but at a minimum because they see democracy as a means to gain power and further their interests (Ottaway 2004: 3–6). Ottaway's analysis is complemented by the work of Hawthorne (2004) about the conditions needed for civil society organizations to play a democratizing role in the Middle East: autonomy from the regime, a pro-democracy agenda, and an ability to form coalitions with other organizations. The autonomy condition speaks of the interests and relationships that can exist between civil society and the state, and the ways these organizations can be co-opted.

Historical and institutional background is paramount for Brownlee (2008) in his exploration of why some regimes endured the 'third wave' while others didn't. Assessing the impact of electoral practices and other institutional variables, he concludes that regime longevity is not causally related to established multiparty elections and legislatures. He specifically parts company with Geddes's (1999) emphasis on elite preferences and behaviour on the basis that her analysis 'does not account for how institutions affect elite preferences years before the regime appears under strain or why such institutional effects may drive elites to enlist with otherwise beleaguered opposition movements' (Brownlee 2008: 90). Comparing the Philippines and Malaysia, he argues that the fall of Ferdinand Marcos's regime was the 'culmination of an extended process of institutional decline and elite defection, catalysed years earlier by the president's pursuit of personal control over organizational continuity' (Brownlee 2008: 91). By contrast, Mohamad Mahathir's capacity to withstand five electoral cycles in Malaysia was a function of 'the redoubtable premier's ultimate deference to United Malays National Organisation (UMNO) and its capacity for resolving elite conflict' (Brownlee 2008: 91). Brownlee (2008: 112) concludes that 'the maintenance or demise of hybrid regimes may depend less on the elections they hold than on the coalitions they hold together'.

The most extensive and sophisticated comparative study yet of hybrid regimes, by Levitsky and Way (2010), specifically asks why some competitive authoritarian regimes have democratized between 1990 and 2008, while others have not. In their study of 35 countries, three paths are observed: democratization, unstable authoritarianism and stable authoritarianism. They argue that two main factors explain these variations. The first is the extent and nature of linkages with the West that mediate the political impact of structural economic crises, domestic opposition forces and other stresses on incumbent rulers. Here, differences in the depth of economic, political, diplomatic, social and organizational ties and cross-border flows of capital, goods and services, people and information are important. The second mediating factor is the incumbents' organizational power, namely the 'scope and cohesion of state and governing party structures' (Levitsky and Way 2010: 23). Whereas some incumbents enjoyed well-developed structures and, thus, had at their disposal the 'coercive tools to prevent elite defections, steal elections, or crack down on protest', others didn't and were thus 'vulnerable to relatively weak opposition challenges' (Levitsky and Way 2010: 23). Clearly this builds on Brownlee's earlier insights about party organizational factors.

This emphasis on ruling party or incumbents' organizational power contrasts sharply with the analytical preoccupation of some of the QoD focus on institutional design. Constitutional design, Levitsky and Way (2010: 346) conclude, 'had no notable impact on regime outcomes', and parliamentary systems were 'no more likely to democratize (and, in fact, were *less* likely to democratize) than those with presidential or semi-presidential systems' (Levitsky and Way 2010: 346).

Compared with the QoD literature, these studies represent a refreshing return to some earlier scholarship of regime analysis sensitive to historical specificity and the wider social, political and economic context of formal institutions. Consequently, they shift analysis from voluntarist conceptions of leadership choices in shaping regime trajectories. Thus, to the extent that we can debate the idea of institutional effectiveness, these authors ensure this is not conducted in isolation from some form of theorization of state power.

The social foundations approach and Southeast Asia

These valuable studies are nevertheless constrained by two limitations. First, analytical interest in structural and historical relationships is locked into the transition problematic of primarily seeking to explain the absence of democratic institutions. In effect, analysis of informal institutions, civil society and the social distribution of economic resources is harnessed to the same question preoccupying QoD analysts: what is blocking democratic transition? The difference is that these authors view this problem through consideration of whether or not democratic institutions are, or can be, socially embedded. Meanwhile, exploration of what these structural factors mean for the character and direction of hybrid regimes is far from exhaustive.

Second, notwithstanding important insights by Brownlee (2008), and Levitsky and Way (2010), about the importance of the organizational cohesion of party and state institutions for understanding hybrid regime directions, the social foundations of this cohesion are underexplained. Conspicuously absent from these frameworks is consideration of relationships between the organizational power of political parties or state organizations and the dynamic and complex interests associated with capitalist development. Yet these relationships not only help explain the discrepancy between the persistence of authoritarian rule in Singapore and the extremely strong international linkages of Singapore with established democracies – which Levitsky and Way (2010: 343) admit is starkly at odds with their theory – they also strengthen explanations of regime directions in other Southeast Asian countries, including Thailand and Malaysia.

Our theoretical starting point is that capitalist development fundamentally influences the nature of societal forces and the conflicts between them. Friction associated with capitalist development obviously includes patterns of ownership and control in the economy, around which a host of political conflicts and alliances ensue. But it also encompasses the way that power and authority is exercised to constrain and/or enable certain forms of political organization to function. Thus, through the advent of economic globalization, complex divisions of labour have altered the relative power of capital and labour – especially labour's reduced capacity for collective organization in late industrializing countries.

Geopolitical factors also need to be taken into account in the analysis of political regimes since they are inseparable from the organization of economic power. The Cold War, for instance, not only produced close trade and aid relations between Western countries and various authoritarian governments, but a more general suppression in the region of civil society organizations – especially independent trade unions – with tacit or even active support from Western governments (Deyo 2006). As Luebbert (1991: 314) points out, in Western Europe: 'the institutions of the modern state, of the economy, and of the party system were the projects of mass movements; they were institutions that reflected the balance of interests those movements contained'. Political institutions have thus developed in a very specific structural context in many late industrializing countries.

Bellin's (2000) concept of 'contingent democrats' is, therefore, especially useful. She maintains that: 'the peculiar conditions of late development often make capital and labour much more ambivalent about democratization than was the case for their counterparts among early industrializers' (Bellin 2000: 178). In late industrializing countries, middle-class support for democratic consolidation is as contingent as it was in interwar Europe. But this contingency is now in the context of weak working-class movements and generally fragmented, if not underdeveloped, civil societies (Rodan and Jayasuriya 2009).

By way of demonstrating the analytical reach of our social foundations approach for regime analysis, the following discussion draws on the respective Southeast Asian countries of Thailand, Malaysia and Singapore. Thailand is a fascinating case where social and political forces have embraced reform agendas entirely consistent with, and often in the language of, the QoD literature to legitimize the overthrow of democratically elected governments. This puzzle cannot be explained without seeing political institutions as part of complex and wider power struggles of capitalist development. Analytically privileging conflicts and alliances associated with the dynamics of late industrializing capitalism – in the comparison of Malaysia and Singapore – also affords more precision explaining variations in the nature and impact of organizational power of party and state political institutions within and beyond hybrid regimes.

Thailand: institutions as sites of social conflict

Often referred to as the 'People's Constitution', the 1997 Thai Constitution was widely thought to have marked a democratic highpoint in the country's political development (Dressel 2009). It explicitly recognized the importance of political participation and expression, Section 76 proclaiming that: 'The State shall promote and encourage public participation in laying down policies, making decisions on political issues, preparing economic, social and political development plans, and inspecting the exercise of State power at all levels' (Kingdom of Thailand 1997). The 1997 Constitution also incorporated a range of vertical and horizontal accountability institutions, including the Constitutional Court, the Election Commission and the National Counter Corruption Commission, as well as procedures and regulations that governed the appointment of members to regulatory bodies in sectors such as telecommunications. Furthermore, the Constitution was designed to create a strong and stable executive government between elections. To this end, it limited the capacity of parliament to move motions of no confidence in the government, and constrained MPs' rights to resign from parties. All of this solidified executive power.

Yet rather than lay the basis for stable, democratic politics, what transpired was a dramatic escalation of tensions between so-called 'Red Shirts' and 'Yellow Shirts,' to be followed by the abandonment of political pluralism and a return to authoritarianism (Nostitz 2009). Ironically, authoritarianism's comeback involved extensive checks and balances on the powers of elected officials, presented as a protection of democratic institutions by curbing corruption and money politics. Resonances with various QoD institutional reform prescriptions were striking.

Unlike the QoD theorists who focus on evaluating the 'effectiveness' of the 1997 Constitution, we argue that it was an outcome of a political compromise between conservative elites and more liberal middle-class social forces represented by the non-governmental organizations (NGOs) and technocrats who were keen to broaden political participation (Connors 2003; Hewison 2007). Under that compromise, greater political participation was accommodated but the possibilities of political contestation and representative democracy were narrowed. Hostility to democratic representation by some liberal NGOs and technocrats, linked to what McCargo (2005) refers to as the 'network monarchy', was exemplified by the provision in the 1997 Constitution barring parliamentary candidates without university degrees. As Hewison (2007: 933) points out, royalist technocrats and liberal elite proponents of constitutional change argued that while participation must be permitted, it needs to be 'carefully managed to prevent its radicalization'.

It was in this political context that Thaksin Shinawatra and his Thai Rak Thai (TRT) Party captured government, campaigning on a populist platform against the austerity programme of the previous Chuan Leekpai government that dampened economic growth. The policies of the TRT were closely aligned to the interests of newly emerging elements of the domestic bourgeoisie, including those in the telecommunications and construction sectors. Indeed, the TRT arose as a kind of insurance for those elements of domestic capital hit hard by the Asian financial crisis of 1997–8 and the various IMF reform programmes (Jayasuriya and Hewison 2004).

New political institutions under the 1997 Constitution, designed to create strong executive government and parties, enabled the TRT to cement a more centralized system of money politics, which to some extent bypassed or subordinated local systems of political patronage (Pasuk and Baker 2004). The local system of patronage was part of the network monarchy entrenched within the state apparatus, working through such institutions as the Privy Council and elements of the military (McCargo 2005; Handley 2006; Hewison 2007). Yet, what was interesting about Thaksin was his and the TRT's appeal to a broad cross-class coalition that included urban and rural poor groups (Jayasuriya and Hewison 2004; Hewison 2005), which translated into a resounding re-election in February 2005.

Meanwhile, this new populist politics allowed Thaksin to challenge some of the social forces whose interests were protected in the compromise of the 1997 Constitution. Consequently, after the TRT's 2005 re-election, tensions mounted between the pro-royal middle-class liberals and business interests of the network monarchy, or Yellow Shirts, on the one hand, and Red Shirts comprising business interests linked to TRT and the urban and rural poor beneficiaries of the TRT's policies on the other hand.

Soon after Thaksin's re-election, corruption allegations surfaced, leading to anti-government demonstrations by a complex of urban social forces that were tacitly backed by the network monarchy. Thaksin responded by calling yet another election for April 2006, which was boy-cotted by major opposition parties. The TRT landslide election result was subsequently annulled by the constitutional court, which ordered new polls. However, before this government could form, a military coup in September 2006 abandoned the 1997 Constitution and removed Thaksin and the TRT (Ungkaporn 2007). Coup leaders created a commission that drafted a new constitution, approved in a tightly controlled referendum in August 2007. What was to transpire under the 2006 Constitution was a sharp reversal of the previous attempt to strengthen political parties and executive powers, with a substantial bolstering of institutions of horizontal accountability – notably through greatly enhanced judicial powers over politics (Dressel 2009, 2010). Meanwhile, the Constitutional Court disbanded the TRT. Nevertheless, when elections were called under the new constitution, the pro-Thaksin People's Power Party (PPP) won most seats of any party and formed government.

However, the underlying social conflicts that institutional reforms were meant to contain were yet to fully play out. Instead, the constitutional court, which claimed to be acting as the guardian of democratic institutions, subsequently dissolved the PPP in December 2008. After parliamentary manoeuvring, the pro-royalist technocrat Abhisit Vejjajiva of the Democrat Party – the hitherto champions of institutions for greater political participation – was installed as prime minister without a general election. In escalating and increasingly violent clashes, Red Shirts mobilized against the government leading to the occupation of commercial and civic areas of central Bangkok, resulting in a brutal military crackdown authorized by the Abhisit government. Intensified repression of political opposition followed (International Crisis Group 2010).

Case (2007: 639) has argued that the 2006 coup can be explained in terms of poor quality democratic institutions. According to him:

> executive abuses and corrupt practices failed to share out patronage in ways that encouraged forbearance among elites. Rather, a skewed distribution of favours so excluded some elites that they re-energized their constituents in ways that further eroded democracy's

quality. Spiraling downwards, quality was finally so seriously depleted that this in itself formed a pretext for authoritarian reversal.

However, this does not tell us what caused the 'poor democratic performance' in the first place. Moreover, apparent institutional dysfunction may be perfectly functional for certain social interests. From a social foundations perspective, the hybrid nature of the regime under Thaksin, and ensuing political instability, resides more in the unravelling of the institutional compromise embodied in the 1997 Constitution.

Similarly, the 2006 military coup – and what subsequently transpired – needs to be understood in terms of the broader power relationships that found institutional expression within the political regime and the state. This was in part an ideological conflict, pitting a conservative and communitarian notion of political order against the TRT's populist politics. The 2006 coup reflected competing notions of representation held by the conservative forces of the network monarchy and by those embracing the populist politics of the TRT. It was a contest that had a foundation in the structure of the broader political economy because, as Hewison (2005) points out, the special economic benefits for Thaksin and his allies threatened the vast business interests of the Crown Property Bureau – the entity that controlled the economic assets of the monarchy. The coup reflected the fundamental absence of a cohesive civil society capable of exerting pressure on the state through intermediary organizations and the powerful role of entrenched social and political interests tied to the monarchical institutions (Kengkij and Hewison 2009).

Intriguingly, notions of representation were mediated through an ideological configuration articulated by organized middle-class-led civic groups in Bangkok. As Nelson (2007) points out, the protests against Thaksin that eventually led to his ousting were strongly supported by NGOs with a predominantly middle-class leadership that came together under the banner of the People's Alliance for Democracy (PAD). The PAD was the vehicle of Sondhi Limthongkul, a media tycoon who had fallen out with Thaksin. Some of the middle-class-led NGOs shared with the conservatives a common distrust of broad-based political participation, arguing that it led to money politics requiring the protection of democratic institutions.

Trying to make sense of paradoxical claims by Thai civil society activists to be protecting democratic institutions through support for authoritarian measures, Connors (2008: 161) argues that middle-class liberals: 'have entrusted the mission of establishing liberal democracy in the ideologies and institutions simultaneously derived from and legitimated by a mythic social contract embodied in the monarchy'. The social foundation of this middle-class preference for a 'regulated democracy' is to be found in historical legacies of the Cold War. Not least of these is the absence of strong intermediary organizations, especially independent labour, linking civil society and the state. Harriss's (2006: 461) general argument that, 'middle class people have responded to their impotence in the political sphere by devoting their energies to activism in civil society, and in doing so de-valorize party political activity', is applicable here.

Malaysia and Singapore: state capitalism and contrasting organizational power

Some theorists, attempting to explain the reproduction of hybrid regimes by emphasizing structural relationships, have argued that the existence of an organizationally cohesive set of party and/or state institutions is pivotal. However, here organizational cohesiveness tends to be equated with the institutional management of intra-elite conflict and the coercive capacity of the state, without incorporating into the analysis the dynamic social bases for the conflicts being managed or suppressed. Using the example of Malaysia, we argue that tensions within state capitalism have led to a relative decline in UMNO's capacity to manage intra-elite conflict, opening up political space for internal and external critics of UMNO. Com-paring Malaysia and Singapore, we highlight how different structures and dynamics of state capitalism have produced differing degrees and forms of party and state organizational power, resulting in contrasting degrees of oppositional political space.

For Brownlee (2008), the durability of UMNO and the regime in Malaysia over which it presides emanates from the capacity of that organization to contain and resolve elite conflicts. Similarly, for Levitsky and Way (2010) state and party organizational cohesiveness, which extends to the capacity for effective coercion, is pivotal to UMNO's success. This cohesiveness is reflected in extensive patronage networks that include control over access to vast economic resources. However, for these insights to realize their full analytical potential they need to be linked with the underlying political economy dynamics of Malaysian development integral to organizational cohesiveness, or lack thereof.

Arguably, organizational cohesiveness – in the way defined by Levitsky and Way (2010) – has been declining in Malaysia, even if it remains sufficient to reproduce the regime for the foreseeable future, as they reasonably maintain. Despite UMNO's continued political supremacy, increased formal and informal oppositional political space has been achieved, reflected partly in the emergence of the multiethnic Parti Keadilan Rakyat (PKR), under Anwar Ibrahim, and massive opposition gains at the 2008 elections. For the first time since 1969, the ruling coalition was denied a two-thirds majority (required to legislate constitutional change), winning just 51.2 per cent of the popular vote compared with 64 per cent in 2004. The coalition also went from controlling government in all but one of the thirteen states to controlling only eight.

However, our point is not to contest the degree of UMNO cohesiveness but to contend that Levitsky's and Way's framework is ill equipped to detect emerging sources of threat to UMNO's organizational capacity. Their analytical emphasis is on how conflicts within the elite are managed. Our emphasis is on the underlying dynamics to conflicts requiring UMNO's management. If the durability in the existing hybrid regime in Malaysia is to continue, this will be in part a function of whether or not tensions inherent to state capitalism can be accommodated through UMNO's organizational capacity.

Capitalism in Malaysia has involved the active cultivation of an ethnic Malay domestic bourgeoisie through the New Economic Policy (NEP) launched in 1971. However, state patron-age has been selectively dispensed to promote a coterie of politically trusted entrepreneurs. Factionalism within UMNO pre-dated the NEP, but the NEP gave it a new structural base and dynamic. As Khoo (2003: 22) notes, though, in periods of high economic growth, tensions between contending factions over patronage spoils are politically manageable, but in periods of economic downturn levels of intra-elite friction have tended to intensify.

The expulsion from UMNO and subsequent imprisonment of the then Deputy Prime Minister Anwar Ibrahim in the wake of the 1997–8 Asian financial crisis was a dramatic demonstration of this point and how UMNO has retained an importance as a site for struggles over state patronage in its own right. Historically, UMNO was involved in direct investments, but subsequently proxy investors on the party's behalf have assumed a central role. This has meant that a degree of autonomy has been open to de facto state capitalists in Malaysia. However, whereas Levitsky and Way emphasize how such elite tensions have not fundamentally undermined UMNO's grip on the regime, the question is what produces such tensions and the implications of this for reproducing organizational power over time.

Tensions inherent in Malaysian capitalism translate not just into periodic UMNO factional clashes reflecting personality differences, but structured conflicts that also involve their own dynamic political opportunities for contending political elites and related business interests

(Gomez 2002; Tan 2007). The 1997–8 Asian financial crisis presented opportunities for a reallocation of power within UMNO and the state at the expense of particular business tycoons and patrons, rather than a dismantling of patronage per se. Certainly the economic and political costs to UMNO of supporting indebted connected companies were being compounded in a context of financial globalization, a point seized on by Anwar and others within UMNO in advocating selective market-oriented reforms. The financial crisis enhanced the argument that patronage itself should be more selective – a point that ultimately Mahathir made some concessions to by promoting entrepreneurs and state managers seen to be more adept at the challenges of a competitive, globalized market. Transparency and accountability rhetoric has thus not been without utility in intra-elite struggles, not to mention those elements within the state genuinely seeking reform towards a less politicized regulatory system. Such a climate is more conducive for democratic-minded civil society activists and opposition political parties seeking to mobilize against UMNO.

Thus, the opportunity for *reformasi* and the way its prospects were determined cannot be explained without reference to emerging contradictions between global capitalism and Malaysian state capitalism, and resulting intra-elite ruptures. This facilitated increased political space to challenge established political institutions and the social foundations on which they rested.

In a similar fashion to Malaysia, organizational cohesiveness in Singapore is intimately related to state capitalism. Yet, here, less volatility is evident in conflicts linked to state capitalism and the need and capacity of the ruling party to contain them. The explanation lies in the different social foundations of state capitalism.

The leadership of the ruling People's Action Party (PAP) realized soon after the PAP internal split in 1961, resulting in the formation of the *Barisan Sosialis* and the loss of links with mass organizations, that repressing opponents would not be a sufficient basis for contesting elections in the long term: the PAP also needed to develop its own power base. Towards this end, a merger of state and party reshaping the political economy of Singapore was affected. This entailed not just a powerful new class of politico-bureaucrats predisposed towards more bureaucratic and administrative techniques of political control and mobilization, but also a form of state capitalism that rendered many Singaporeans directly or indirectly dependent on the state for economic and social resources, including housing, employment, business contracts and access to personal savings. Such a structural relationship has fostered vulnerability to political co-option and intimidation, and further undermined the possibility of independent social and economic bases from which challenges to the PAP could be effectively mounted.

Instead of this state capitalism diluting as Singapore's economy progressed, it flourished as vast sums of capital generated by government-linked-companies (GLCs) bolstered the economic and political power of the PAP state (Low 1998; Worthington 2003; Rodan 2004). Consequently, the domestic bourgeoisie's economic opportunities have been heavily conditioned by, and dependent on, state capitalism – most recently through offshore investment strategies by GLCs (Rodan 2006). The political inclinations and capacities of the middle class have been no less influenced by the structural relationships embodied in Singapore's state capitalism. Much of that class is either employed within the state in one or another of the government departments, statutory bodies or GLCs, or indirectly derives its livelihood from servicing state capitalism through the provision of professional, legal, commercial or other services. Moreover, this structural relationship to the state brings with it systematic exposure to an institutionalized ideology that champions the role of technocratic political elites at the expense of ideas of representation and citizenship rights. For those exercising power or enjoying some status as a result of state capitalism, this ideology can be seductive.

Understanding the organizational power of the political incumbents in Singapore in terms of these social foundations allows more than an explanation of why democracy has not transpired; it also lays the basis for comprehending the changing institutional and ideological characteristics of authoritarianism largely missed by analysts preoccupied with explaining the absence of democracy rather than the character of the regime (see Rodan and Jayasuriya 2007; Rodan 2009). The increasing sophistication and range of 'consensus politics' and the expansion of the political space of the state through which these have been institutionalized, including through initiatives such as the Nominated Members of Parliament scheme and assorted mechanisms for public policy feedback and suggestions, reflects not just 'organizational power', but also a particular coalition of interests integral to the PAP brand of state capitalism.

Conclusion

An important benefit of the hybrid regime concept and literature has been a greater acknowledgement that democratic transitions may not only be much more complex and protracted processes than was previously thought, but also that transitions are by no means inevitable. Nevertheless, this literature remains locked within a transition theory problematic in one way or another: either to benchmark institutional progress or lack thereof towards democratic transition; or to locate the socially based impediments to effective democratic institutions. Consequently, the full range of political regime possibilities is not explored. This is precisely the advantage of the social foundations approach illustrated above. It is designed to locate the interests and conflicts driving pressures for and against institutional reform, leaving open for enquiry where regimes might be headed and why.

Moreover, this approach exposes how the popular depiction of struggles for democratic transition and consolidation – as struggles of establishing good quality institutions – empties analysis of politics. Good quality democratic institutions such as judicial review processes are themselves products of particular social coalitions and interests. In the Thai case, the deepening of the judicialization of politics through the 2007 Constitution, far from ushering in so-called good democratic institutions, has 'heightened the influence of palace networks' (Dressel 2009: 312). These networks remain hostile to popular democratic expression. Therefore it is paramount to understand who is actually supporting particular institutional reform projects, why, and what conflicts and interests might be marginalized or privileged as a result. What really matters to politics is not whether a regime is a hybrid form, however that might be conceptualized, but whose interests are being advanced or suppressed through institutional reform agendas.

Note

1 Research for this chapter was supported by Australian Research Council funding for a Discovery Project (1093214), 'Representation and Political Regimes in Southeast Asia', for which the author is grateful.

References

Beetham, David (2004) 'Towards a Universal Framework for Democracy Assessment', *Democratization*, 11 (2), pp. 1–17.
Bellin, Eva (2000) 'Contingent Democrats: Industrialists, Labor, and Democratization in Late-Developing Countries', *World Politics*, 52 (1), pp. 175–205.
Boggards, Matthijs (2009) 'How to Classify Hybrid Regimes? Defective Democracy and Electoral Authoritarianism', *Democratization*, 16 (2), pp. 399–423.
Brownlee, Jason (2008) 'Bound to Rule: Party Institutions and Regime Trajectories in Malaysia and the Philippines', *Journal of East Asian Studies*, 8, pp. 89–118.
Carothers, Thomas (2002) 'The End of the Transition Paradigm', *Journal of Democracy*, 13 (1), pp. 17–33.

—— (2006) *Confronting the Weakest Link: Aiding Political Parties in New Democracies*. Washington, DC: Carnegie Endowment for International Peace.

Case, William F. (1996) 'Can the "Halfway House" Stand? Semidemocracy and Elite Theory in Three Southeast Asian Countries', *Comparative Politics*, 28 (4), pp. 437–464.

—— (2007) 'Democracy's Quality and Breakdown: New Lessons from Thailand', *Democratization*, 14 (4), pp. 622–642.

Connors, Michael K. (2003) *Democracy and National Identity in Thailand*. London: RoutledgeCurzon.

—— (2008) 'Article of Faith: The Failure of Royal Liberalism', *Journal of Contemporary Asia*, 38 (1), pp. 143–165.

Croissant, Aurel and Wolfgang Merkel (2004) 'Introduction: Democratization in the Early Twenty-First Century', *Democratization*, 11 (5), pp. 1–9.

Dahl, Robert (1956) *A Preface to Democratic Theory*. Chicago: University of Chicago Press.

Deyo, Frederic C. (2006) 'South-East Asian Industrial Labour: Structural Demobilisation and Political Transformation'. In *The Political Economy of South-East Asia: Markets, Power and Contestation*, ed. Garry Rodan, Kevin Hewison and Richard Robison. Melbourne: Oxford University Press, pp. 283–304.

Diamond, Larry (1989) 'Preface'. In *Democracy in Developing Countries: Asia*, ed. Larry Diamond, Juan J. Linz and Seymour Martin Lipset. Boulder, CO: Lynne Rienner, pp. ix–xxvii.

—— (2002) 'Thinking About Hybrid Regimes', *Journal of Democracy*, 13 (2), pp. 21–35.

Dressel, Björn (2009) 'Thailand's Elusive Quest for a Workable Constitution, 1997–2007', *Contemporary Southeast Asia*, 31 (2), pp. 296–325.

—— (2010) 'Judicialization of Politics or Politicization of the Judiciary? Considerations from Recent Events in Thailand', *Pacific Review*, 23 (5), pp. 671–691.

Epstein, David, Robert Bates, Jack Goldstone, Ida Kristensen and Sharyn O'Halloran (2006) 'Democratic Transitions', *American Journal of Political Science*, 50 (3), pp. 551–569.

Geddes, Barbara (1999) 'Authoritarian Breakdown: Empirical Test of a Game Theoretical Argument', paper presented at the annual meeting of the American Political Science Association, Atlanta.

Gomez, Edmund Terence (2002) 'Political Business in Malaysia: Party Factionalism, Corporate Development, and Economic Crisis'. In *Political Business in East Asia*, ed. Edmund Terence Gomez. London: Routledge, pp. 82–114.

Handley, Paul (2006) *The King Never Smiles*. New Haven: Yale University Press.

Harriss, John (2006) 'Middle-Class Activism and the Politics of the Informal Working Class: A Perspective on Class Relations and Civil Society in Indian Cities,' *Critical Asian Studies*, 38 (4), pp. 445–465.

Hawthorne, Amy (2004) 'Middle Eastern Democracy: Is Civil Society the Answer?,' Washington, DC: Carnegie Endowment for International Peace, Carnegie Papers Number 44, Middle East Series.

Haynes, Jeff (2001) ' "Limited" Democracy in Ghana and Uganda. What Is Most Important to International Actors: Stability or Political Freedom?,' *Journal of Contemporary African Studies*, 19 (2), pp. 183–204.

Henderson, Karen (2004) 'The Slovak Republic: Explaining Defects in Democracy,' *Democratization*, 11 (5), pp. 133–155.

Hewison, Kevin (2005) 'Neo-liberalism and Domestic Capital: The Political Outcomes of the Economic Crisis in Thailand,' *Journal of Development Studies*, 41 (2), pp. 310–330.

—— (2007) 'Constitutions, Regimes and Power,' *Democratization*, 14 (5), pp. 928–945.

Huntington, Samuel P. (1991) *The Third Wave: Democratization in the Late Twentieth Century*. Norman: University of Oklahoma Press.

International Crisis Group (2010) *Bridging Thailand's Deep Divide*. Asia Report No. 192, 5 July.

Jayasuriya, Kanishka and Kevin Hewison (2004) 'The Antipolitics of Good Governance: From Global Social Policy to a Global Populism?', *Critical Asian Studies*, 36 (4), pp. 571–590.

Karl, Terry Lynn (1995) 'The Hybrid Regimes of Central America', *Journal of Democracy*, 6 (3), pp. 72–86.

Khoo, Boo Teik (2003) *Beyond Mahathir: Malaysian Politics and its Discontents*. London: Zed Books.

Kingdom of Thailand (1997) 'Constitution of the Kingdom of Thailand'; available at http://www.asianlii.org/th/legis/const/1997/1.html#S002 (accessed 10 November 2010).

Kitirianglarp, Kengkij and Kevin Hewison (2009) 'Social Movements and Political Opposition in Contemporary Thailand', *Pacific Review*, 22 (4), pp. 451–477.

Levitsky, Steven and Lucan A. Way (2002) 'The Rise of Competitive Authoritarianism', *Journal of Democracy*, 13 (1), pp. 51–65.

Levitsky, Steven and Lucan A. Way (2010) *Competitive Authoritarianism: Hybrid Regimes After the Cold War*. Cambridge: Cambridge University Press.

Low, Linda (1998) *The Political Economy of a City-State: Government-Made Singapore*. Singapore: Oxford University Press.

Luebbert, Gregory M. (1991) *Liberalism, Fascism, or Social Democracy: Social Classes and the Political Origins of Regimes in Interwar Europe*. New York: Oxford University Press.

McCargo, Duncan (2005) 'Network Monarchy and Legitimacy Crises in Thailand', *The Pacific Review*, 18 (4), pp. 499–519.

Mazzuca, Sebastian L. (2010) 'Access to Power Versus Exercises of Power Reconceptualizing the Quality of Democracy in Latin America', *Studies in Comparative International Development*, 45, pp. 334–357.

Merkel, Wolfgang (2004) 'Embedded and Defective Democracies', *Democratization*, 11 (5), pp. 33–58.

Morlino, Leonardo (2004) 'What is a "Good Democracy"?', *Democratization*, 11 (5), pp. 10–32.

—— (2009) 'Are There Hybrid Regimes? Or are They Just an Optical Illusion?', *European Political Science Review*, 1 (2), pp. 273–296.

Nelson, Michael H. (2007) 'People's Sector Politics (Kanmueang Phak Prachachon),' in 'Thailand: Problems of Democracy in Ousting Prime Minister Thaksin Shinawatra', *SEARC Working Paper Series* No. 87.

Nostitz, Nick (2009) *Red vs. Yellow, Volume 1: Thailand's Crisis of Identity*. Bangkok: White Lotus Press.

O'Donnell, Guillermo (1994) 'Delegative Democracy', *Journal of Democracy*, 5 (1), pp. 55–69.

Ottaway, Marina (2003) *Democracy Challenged: The Rise of Semi-Authoritarianism*. Washington, DC: Carnegie Endowment for International Peace.

—— (2004) 'Democracy and Constituencies in the Arab World,' in *Carnegie Papers No. 48, Middle East Series*. Washington, DC: Carnegie Endowment for International Peace.

Phongpaichit, Pasuk and Chris Baker (2004) *Thaksin: The Business of Politics in Thailand*. Chang Mai: Silkworm Books.

Rich, Gary (2002) 'Categorizing Political Regimes: New Data for Old Problems', *Democratization*, 9 (4), pp. 1–24.

Roberts, Andrew (2005) 'Review Article: The Quality of Democracy', *Comparative Politics*, 37 (3), pp. 357–376.

Robinson, Neil (2003) 'The Politics of Russia's Partial Democracy', *Political Studies Review*, 1 (2), pp. 149–166.

Rodan, Garry (2004) *Transparency and Authoritarian Rule in Southeast Asia: Singapore and Malaysia*. London: Routledge.

—— (2006) 'Singapore: Globalisation, the State, and Politics'. In *The Political Economy of South-East Asia: Markets, Power and Contestation*, ed. Garry Rodan, Kevin Hewison and Richard Robison. Melbourne: Oxford University Press, pp. 137–169.

—— (2009) 'New Modes of Political Participation and Singapore's Nominated Members of Parliament', *Government and Opposition*, 44 (4), pp. 438–462.

—— and Kanishka Jayasuriya (2007) 'The Technocratic Politics of Administrative Participation: Case Studies of Singapore and Vietnam', *Democratization*, 14 (5), pp. 795–815.

—— and —— (2009) 'Capitalist Development, Regime Transitions and New Forms of Authoritarianism in Asia', *Pacific Review*, 22 (1), pp. 23–47.

Slater, Dan (2003) 'Iron Cage in an Iron Fist: Authoritarian Institutions and the Personalization of Power in Malaysia', *Comparative Politics*, 36 (1), pp. 81–101.

Tan, Nathaniel, ed. (2007) *Mahathir vs Abdullah: Covert Wars and Challenged Legacies*. Kuala Lumpur: Kinibooks.

Ungkaporn, Giles Ji (2007) *A Coup for the Rich: Thailand's Political Crisis*. Bangkok: Workers Democracy Publishing.

Volpi, Frederic (2004) 'Pseudo-Democracy in the Muslim World', *Third World Quarterly*, 25 (6), pp. 1061–1078.

Wigell, Mikael (2008) 'Mapping "Hybrid Regimes": Types and Concepts in Comparative Politics', *Democratization*, 15 (2), pp. 230–250.

Worthington, Ross (2003) *Governance in Singapore*. London: RoutledgeCurzon.

Zakaria, Fareed (1997) 'The Rise of Illiberal Democracy', *Foreign Affairs*, 76 (6), pp. 22–43.

—— (2003) *The Future of Freedom: Illiberal Democracy at Home and Abroad*. New York: W. W. Norton & Company, Inc.

Zinecker, Heidrun (2009) 'Regime-Hybridity in Developing Countries: Achievements and Limitations of New Research on Transitions', *International Studies Review*, 11, pp. 302–331.

12

Deviant democracies

Renske Doorenspleet[1]

There is a strong consensus in the literature on democratization that economic development[2] and the presence of democratic neighbours increases the probability of a regime becoming democratic. Under such circumstances, no matter what political leaders, civil society activists or ordinary citizens do, they act within a social and economic context that is more or less favourable for democracy. However, scholarly research also shows that there are important exceptions to this general pattern. These are what I would like to call 'deviant democracies': countries that have seemingly beaten the odds and successfully democratized within an unfavourable structural setting.

Within the so-called 'fourth wave' of democratization, from 1989 onwards (see Huntington 1991; Doorenspleet 2000), Benin and Mongolia represent prime examples of deviant cases of democratization. Prior to this time, historical examples are Costa Rica and India since the late 1940s.[3] These political systems meet the minimal criteria for democracy, in that they have competitive elections and inclusive suffrage (Dahl 1971; Doorenspleet 2005: ch. 2), but they are 'deviant democracies' because they lack the standard requisites for democracy of the modernization and diffusion theories. In other words, they are deviant not because they are democracies of lower or different quality, but because they cannot be explained by the major theories and previous statistical studies on this topic. These poor countries, surrounded by non-democratic neighbours, have followed an exceptional, unusual and unexpected path towards democracy. In this, they are out of the ordinary and deserve attention.

This chapter aims to provide a better understanding of the exceptional and anomalous nature of democratization in these countries. It will first look at the strongest and most robust findings from dozens of previous statistical studies, which have come to the same conclusion: both economic development and diffusion have a positive effect on democracy. Those factors have not only a crucial effect on transitions towards democracy, but also during the consolidation phase. This chapter briefly reviews these convincing theories of democratization and their empirical findings. In doing so, the chapter will lay the ground for specifying more precisely the level of 'deviancy' of the cases under consideration, and offer potential explanations for their unusually successful process of democratization.

Economic development and democracy: findings from large-N studies

The starting point for the quantitative studies on explaining democratization was the article 'Some Social Requisites of Democracy: Economic Development and Political Legitimacy' in the

American Political Science Review of 1959, written by Seymour Martin Lipset (1959; see also Lipset 1994). Lipset's 1959 article generated new insights and was a powerful force in the development of the so-called 'modernization theory'. Lipset asserted that theoretical and empirical explorations show that democracy relates to a state's socio-economic development, meaning that 'the more well-to-do a nation, the greater the chances that it will sustain democracy. From Aristotle down to the present, men have argued that only in a wealthy society in which relatively few citizens lived in real poverty could a situation exist in which the mass of the population could intelligently participate in politics and could develop the self-restraint necessary to avoid succumbing to the appeals of irresponsible demagogues. A society divided between a large impoverished mass and a small favoured elite would result either in oligarchy ... or in tyranny' (Lipset 1959: 75).

Although Lipset's study has often been criticized,[4] there have been a large number of quantitative cross-national studies that followed Lipset's ideas, particularly until the 1990s. Such studies sought to test the relationship between economic development and democracy and all found a positive relationship.[5]

The various studies differed in many ways, so it was particularly noteworthy that the positive relationship between economic development and democracy was universally highlighted. Overall, there were six differences between the studies: measurements of democracy; measurements of development; sample of states analysed; period of investigation; the use of quantitative methods; and other explanatory variables included in the sample.

First, although the studies used the same definition of democracy, the actual measurements differed (cf. Doorenspleet 2000). Conceptualizations of democracy were remarkably similar, relying on the ideas of Joseph Schumpeter (1943) and Robert Dahl (1971) who used very minimalistic criteria; as a consequence, these types of democracy are often called 'minimal' or 'electoral' democracy, while they can develop into more 'liberal' types of democracy, see e.g. Doorenspleet 2005. However, actual measurements of democracy differed. Many studies only considered Dahl's dimension of competition (is there a competitive struggle among political parties to get votes?) and ignored the dimension of the inclusive right to vote (cf. Bollen 1980, 1993; Gastil 1991; Jaggers and Gurr 1995; Alvarez *et al.* 1996). As far as can be determined, only Dahl (1971), Arat (1991), Coppedge and Reinicke (1991) and Vanhanen (1997) collected data on inclusiveness. In addition, some measurements treated democracy and non-democracy as a continuous variable (e.g. Cutright 1963; Jackman 1973; Bollen 1979, 1980, 1983, 1991; Vanhanen 1997), whereas others did not (e.g. Gasiorowski 1996; Przeworski and Limongi 1997a).

The second difference between these quantitative studies is that they used different indicators and measures of (economic) development. While some applied a narrow measurement using gross national income per capita (Bollen and Jackman 1985; Lipset *et al.* 1993; Przeworski and Limongi 1997a, 1997b), others applied a more extensive measurement, including such indicators as education, urbanization and life expectancy (Cutright 1963; Olsen 1968; Diamond 1992).

Third, studies that analysed the relationship between development and democracy differed with respect to the sample of states. Some studies surveyed all independent states (Olsen 1968; Vanhanen 1997). Others focused on, for example, non-African states (e.g. Cutright 1963), non-communist regimes (Jackman 1973), or all developing states (Arat 1991; Gasiorowksi 1996).

Fourth, the studies examined different periods. Most of the studies focused on only one or two specific years (Bollen 1980, 1993; Bollen and Jackman 1985; Coppedge and Reinicke 1991). Others looked at a longer period, e.g. from 1948 to 1984 (Arat 1991), since 1950 onwards (Alvarez *et al.* 1996; Gasiorowksi 1996; Przeworski and Limongi 1997a; Przeworski *et al.* 2000), or from 1850 until the 1990s (Vanhanen 1997).

Fifth, studies that tested Lipset's thesis used different quantitative methods. A number of scholars did cross-tabulations of economic development and democracy (e.g. Coleman 1965;

Huntington 1991). Cutright's (1963) study was the first to use correlational analysis to investigate the relationship. Many others followed him and conducted correlation analyses (e.g. Olsen 1968; Neubauer 1967), multiple regression (Jackman 1973; Bollen and Jackman 1985; Lipset *et al.* 1993), or more sophisticated techniques such as logit, probit or event-history models (Gasiorowski 1996; Przeworski and Limongi 1997a).

Finally, and most importantly, some researchers explored propositions derived from alternative theoretical views. For example, Bollen (1983) and Lipset *et al.* (1991) included variables derived from the insights of dependency and world-system theories. Other researchers included variables such as cultural pluralism (Bollen and Jackman 1985), percentage of Protestants in a state (Bollen 1979, 1983), or levels of military expenditure (Lipset *et al.* 1993). In short, variables included in analyses varied widely.

There are thus many differences among the studies investigating the relationship between development and democratic regimes, and yet each has found a positive association. This long tradition of replication should be sufficient to convince everyone that the correlation between development and the presence of democracy has been a persistent finding in empirical studies. Even researchers belonging to the qualitative research tradition assume a relationship arguing that:

> the main finding of cross-national statistical work – a positive, though not perfect, correlation between capitalist development and democracy – must stand as an accepted result. There is no way of explaining this robust finding, replicated in many studies of different designs, as spurious effect of flawed methods. Any theory of democracy must come to terms with it.
>
> *(Rueschemeyer et al. 1992: 4)*

To be sure, quantitative studies of the past 20 years have accepted and taken for granted the positive influence of economic development on democracy. As a consequence, more recent large-N studies on democratization began to focus on other important explanatory variables such as types of political institutions, mass values, attitudes and beliefs (see e.g. Bratton *et al.* 2005; Inglehart and Welzel 2005), while the independent variable of economic development served as an essential and undisputed control variable.

Transition and consolidation

Until the 1990s, quantitative research did not make the distinction between transitions to democracy, on the one hand, and consolidation of democracy, on the other. For example, for Inglehart (1997) economic development precedes transitions, while Diamond (1992) positively linked economic development to both transition and consolidation. It is arguable, however, that many factors, including the level of economic development, which might help in maintaining democracy (i.e. consolidation), are not necessarily the same as the factors that bring about democracy in the first place (i.e. transition).

Huntington was one of the first scholars working in the quantitative research tradition to deal with the impact of economic development specifically on democratic transitions. He argued that transitions to democracy are unlikely in poor countries; they typically occur in rich countries. The empirical results showed that during the so-called third wave of democratization (1974–90), middle-income countries were most likely to make a transition to democracy: '[A]s countries develop economically and move into this zone, they become prospects for democratization' (Huntington 1991: 60). Gasiorowski (1995) concurs. Both support Lipset's argument that economic development increased the likelihood of democratic transitions from 1950 to 1990.

These findings have not gone unchallenged, however. For example, studies by Przeworski and others (1997, 2000) have suggested that there is no significant relationship between economic development and transition to democracy; democracies may emerge at *any* level of economic development. Moreover, conventional wisdom about a straightforward relationship between economic development and political change was also questioned by the experiences of Eastern European countries, which began their transition from communist regimes to democracy amidst economic crisis and generally declining levels of economic development (Lewis 1997; Kennedy 1999).

Boix and Stokes (2003), in turn, have reassessed Przeworski and Limongi's findings that economic development does not play a significant role in transitions away from autocracy. Their study convincingly challenged and criticized Przeworski and Limongi's results, arguing that economic development does substantially increase the probability that a country will make a transition to democracy. Boix and Stokes also argue that development has a much bigger positive effect on the likelihood of maintaining a democratic regime. All in all, therefore, on the basis of the above-mentioned quantitative studies, it is fair to accept that economic development has a positive impact both on transitions to democracy and on democratic consolidation.

Democratic diffusion and democracy: findings from large-N studies

According to many quantitative scholars, both economic development and democratic diffusion are strong explanations for both democratic transition and consolidation. The dramatic changes in Eastern Europe since 1989 seemed to show that countries are both dependent on each other and influence one another during the process of democratization. Once the non-communists came to power in Poland in August 1989, the breakdown of non-democratic communist regimes swept through Eastern Europe, reaching first Hungary in September 1989, then East Germany in October, Czechoslovakia and Bulgaria in November, and Romania in December. The 'disease' of democracy seemed to spread contagiously. As one citizen of former East Germany remarked: 'We saw what Poland and Hungary were doing. We heard Gorbachev. Everyone felt, why are we being left behind?' (Huntington 1991: 104).

Why not us? Everyone knew from his or her neighbour's experience that transition to democracy was a possibility. Not only in Eastern Europe, but also in parts of Africa and Asia, a diffusion or demonstration effect seemed operative. These processes of diffusion and demonstration encouraged elites and civil society groups to press for change towards democracy. Hence, democratization occurred not only in temporal, but also in spatial clusters. Countries seem to affect each other: living in a democratic region makes it more likely that a regime will democratize.

Indeed, since the third-wave transitions took place, many theorists sought to include the influence of democratic clustering in their research (Huntington 1991; Lipset 1994; Pridham and Vanhanen 1994). Linz and Stepan, for example, emphasized this influence during democratization processes, positing that 'the more tightly coupled a group of countries are, the more a successful transition in any country in the group will tend to transform the range of perceived political alternatives for the rest of the group'. Indeed, they continued, 'international diffusion effects can change political expectations, crowd behaviour, and relations of power within the regime almost overnight' (Linz and Stepan 1996: 76). Lipset (1994: 16) concluded that a 'diffusion, a contagion, or demonstration effect seems operative, as many have noted, one that encourages democracies to press for change and authoritarian rulers to give in'.

Based on these theoretical ideas, cross-national empirical studies show indeed that there is a clear clustering of democratization around the world. In his quantitative large-N study on the impact of economic crises on democracy, Gasiorowski (1995) also paid attention to the possible 'demonstration effects' of democratic neighbours (see also Starr 1991). He was one of the first political scientists who incorporated this variable into a multivariate model, and discovered that it was significant and strong, both during democratic transition and consolidation. However, while the finding that democratic neighbours can facilitate both democratic transition and consolidation was quite novel, few studies sought to follow Gasiorowski's lead by examining this issue.

The few that did made the same conclusion. O'Loughlin *et al.*'s (1998) study provided clear evidence of a spatial clustering of regime types. Democracies are likely to be found in regions with other democracies, while non-democratic regimes also form a strong spatial constellation. In addition, Kopstein and Reilly (2000) showed that democratic diffusion matters, especially in the case of former Eastern European communist countries close geographically to Western Europe. For them, 'location matters more than domestic politics itself' (Kopstein and Reilly 2000: 24) in determining democratic outcomes. Finally, large-N quantitative studies have shown that democratic neighbours do indeed have a strong and positive influence on the likelihood that a country undertakes a democratic transition, especially during the post-1989 fourth wave (see e.g. Chapter 8 in Doorenspleet 2005).

However, while the evidence of this correlation is convincing, the mechanisms are not so clear. Not much has been written yet about why clustering of types of political regimes might occur. Elkins and Simmons (2005) suggest three explanations. First, countries respond similarly, though independently, to similar domestic conditions. This explanation, which is dominant in comparative politics and international political economy, states that countries democratize because of domestic, political and economic pressures and that these pressures simultaneously exist for other countries' leaders. A second explanation is that democratic transition and consolidation are coordinated either by a group of nations, a hegemonic power, or an international organization. Examples might include voluntary international cooperation, or coercion by donor countries or international financial organizations. A third explanation of clustering is uncoordinated interdependence between the countries, what Elkins and Simmons explicitly call 'diffusion'. One country's actions and choices affect others, but not through direct cooperation or imposition. Instead, the kind of interdependence is uncoordinated. Examples of this type not only adapt to altered conditions but also to diffusion via exchange of information or learning.

More research needs to be done in order to find out whether these three explanations of clustering can be supported by empirical evidence and what the specific mechanisms might be. It is now widely accepted, however, that a non-democratic regime surrounded by democratic neighbours will be more likely to make a transition to democracy and vice versa. Whether the presence or absence of democratic neighbours also encourages or hinders the process of democratic consolidation remains underinvestigated, although preliminary research also indicates a strong impact on democratic consolidation (Gasiorowski 1995). In other words, empirical evidence from statistical studies shows that there is a clear spatial clustering of democratization around the world. Non-democratic countries surrounded by democracies are much more likely to make a democratic transition than non-democratic countries in a non-democratic region.

Deviant democracies: democratization against the odds

There are, however, important exceptions to this general pattern: 'deviant democracies'. They are countries that have seemingly beaten the odds and democratized within an unfavourable structural setting. Within the so-called fourth wave of democratization, from 1989 onwards, Benin and Mongolia represent primary examples of deviant cases of democratization. Earlier, there were other examples: Costa Rica and India from the late 1940s.[6] These political systems meet the minimal criteria for democracy in that they have competitive elections and inclusive suffrage (see Doorenspleet 2000). They are 'deviant democracies', however, because they lack the standard 'requisites' for democracy mentioned by the modernization perspective and, at the same time, they have become democratic while neighbouring countries remained undemocratic.

Deviant democracies have democratized against the odds. We need a better understanding of the exceptional and anomalous nature of such countries' democratization. Next, this chapter will describe some of them, show to what extent they can be classified as 'deviant democracies', and try to detect general patterns.

India

India is the largest democracy in the world, with over one billion inhabitants. Following a nationalist campaign, India became independent from British rule on 15 August 1947, with Muslim-majority areas forming a separate state: Pakistan. On 26 January 1950, India became a republic with a new constitution, describing India as a sovereign, socialist, secular, democratic republic.

India adopted a Westminster-style parliamentary system. It has met the minimal requirements of democracy since the late 1940s, holding free and fair elections with a competitive struggle among political parties (see McMillan 2008). At the same time, more than 300 million Indians live in utter poverty, meaning that India is also the country with the world's largest concentration of poor people. India has 30 per cent of the world's births, 20 per cent of the world's maternal deaths, and 20 per cent of the world's child deaths. More than half of the country's children are malnourished. Forty-two of every 1,000 female children die before reaching the age of five. Despite constitutional guarantees, violence against women is widespread and the practice deprives women of education, health care and good nutrition. The majority of Indian women are illiterate (see McMillan 2008, but also Kohli 2001; Nachane 2009).

India is probably the most famous 'deviant democracy' in the world and 'has long been a puzzle for students of comparative democratic politics' (Lijphart 1996: 258). The low level of economic development made it unlikely both that India would democratize and then consolidate democracy. In this sense, Indian democracy clearly is a deviant case. Adam Przeworski and his co-authors noted that '(t)he odds against democracy in India were extremely high' (Przeworski *et al.* 2000: 87) and their models (wrongly) predicted India as a dictatorship for the whole postwar period.

India's transition to democracy was also very unlikely because it was – and still is – surrounded by non-democratic neighbours. During most of its period of democratic transition and consolidation, India was surrounded by authoritarian regimes: various military juntas in Bangladesh, Burma and Pakistan, an absolute monarchy in Nepal, and a communist regime in China. While the transition took place in a period of national independence struggles worldwide, only a few post-colonial states democratized. Today, India is the only major stable democracy in South Asia (see Kohli 2001; McMillan 2008).

Hence, more than 60 years after the struggle for independence, Indian democracy appears to be strong and robust,[7] 'the most surprising and important case of democratic endurance in the developing world' (Diamond 1989: 1). Despite poverty, illiteracy, a largely agrarian society, and with authoritarian neighbours, India has been a long-term democracy: a deviant democracy (McMillan 2008; see also Randall 1997).

Costa Rica

Costa Rica democratized in the late 1940s. It is Latin America's oldest continuous democracy. Following a short civil war, the military was abolished and a new constitution drafted by a democratically elected assembly. After the implementation of democratic reforms, a new democratic government came to power on 8 November 1949. After a coup d'état, President Figueres became a national hero, in 1953 winning the country's first democratic election under the new constitution. Since then, Costa Rica has held 13 presidential elections, the latest being in 2010. All elections were widely regarded by the international community as competitive, free, fair and peaceful.

The democratization process was remarkable in Costa Rica as economic development was not particularly high (see also Seligson 1987). Particularly in comparison to other Latin American countries such as Argentina, Chile or even Panama, let alone various European countries, Costa Rica belonged to the poor(er) countries in terms of gross national product (GNP) per capita, gross domestic product (GDP) or Vanhanen's Index of Power Resources.[8] In terms of per capita income, Costa Rica was well below the Latin American average when its transition started, US\$347 compared with US\$396.[9]

Not only modernization theories, but also diffusion theories cannot convincingly explain Costa Rica's transition to and consolidation of democracy. The democratic regime survived in Costa Rica when other democracies failed all around it. In other words, Costa Rica was clearly a deviant case. Although there were some regional brief surges of democratization after the Second World War, most of these new Latin American democracies became authoritarian again, due to oligarchic resistance or US intervention (see Booth 2008).

The survival of Costa Rican democracy was unusual because it occurred when the United States increasingly intervened to help suppress popular cries for democratization and to support authoritarian regimes in its 'back yard', that is in both Latin and Central America (see Booth 2008; see also Booth *et al.* 2006). As the Americans feared Soviet influence nearby in this period of the Cold War, they preferred friendly dictators above non-compliant democrats. However, in the 1950s, Costa Rica's young democracy escaped the regional rollback of democracy (LaFeber 1983; Smith 2005; Schneider 2007). According to Booth (2008: 716), Costa Rica's 'survival was the more remarkable because Costa Rican democracy was often led by a social democratic party at a time when democratic regimes with leftist and centre-left governments (or nations where the centre-left even contended for power) fell to rightist autocratic or military regimes (e.g. Venezuela, Panama, Guatemala, the Dominican Republic), often with the assistance, encouragement or intervention of the United States'.

In short, only a few Latin American countries democratized when Costa Rica did, and most quickly reverted to authoritarianism. In addition, Costa Rica's new democratic regime was led by social-democrats, yet survived during the 1950s and 1960s when similar regional governments and movements in Latin America were being undermined by US intervention (Booth 2008).[10]

Mongolia

A very unlikely place for democracy – the home of Genghis Khan – Mongolia is the most sparsely populated country in the world. Half the population still lives in round felt tents called *gers*, and livestock outnumber humans eight to one. Mongolian democracy, in light of most social-science theories and commonsense expectations, should never have been (Fish 1998). Still, the country held a constitutional referendum in 1990 and a vote in 1992 that led to its first democratic change of parliament. Since then, it had held peaceful elections every four years, and can be classified as a consolidated minimal democracy.

Mongolia is, however, a deviant democracy in many respects (see Fritz 2008). Most importantly, the country is extremely poor. Before and after its transition to democracy, Mongolia was one of the poorest communist countries, having an annual per capita income of approximately US

$500 in 1990. It is true that there was some degree of modernization despite low overall economic development. Mongolia had, for example, a literacy rate of more than 95 per cent, and it had an elite and middle class educated in the Soviet Union and in other communist countries. However, this high level of literacy was not fundamentally different from other post-communist countries, which subsequently became authoritarian (e.g. Uzbekistan or Kazakhstan). Moreover, modernization in terms of alphabetization of language and industrialization occurred relatively late. Hence, Mongolia contradicts several theoretical expectations, as its level of economic development is low and the democratization process has gone hand in hand with deep economic crisis.

Moreover, Mongolia is geographically far from any consolidated democracy. To the south, Mongolia has borders with China, which had just put an end to its own internal protests for more democracy that took place at Tiananmen Square in 1989 – less than a year before the Mongolian move towards more democracy. To the north, Mongolia bordered the Soviet Union, which, in 1990, was disintegrating. To be sure, a number of Mongolia's initial pro-democracy advocates had studied in democratizing countries such as Poland, Czech Republic and Hungary. In this sense, diffusion may have played a role during the democratization process in Mongolia. The distance to the nearest capital in Western Europe, however, is enormous: Berlin is more than 6,000 km from Ulaanbaatar, Mongolia's capital. Mongolia is geographically a very isolated and deviant democracy.

Overall, factors of modernization and diffusion favoured continuation of authoritarian government. The severe economic crisis that coincided with the initial period of democratization, moreover, might have made democracy as a system of government rather unpopular. Instead, however, Mongolia embarked on substantial democratization, and support for democracy as a regime type has been high since the 1990s (see Fritz 2008).

Benin

Following Benin's independence from France in August 1960, it went through decades of political upheavals, which often resulted in military coups. However, almost 30 years later, the political landscape in Benin started to change radically when a national conference was held in the midst of an economic crisis and growing domestic political unrest. On 19 February 1990, Benin began a national conference with government and civil society actors, in order to discuss a peaceful transition to multiparty rule (Heilbrunn 1993). This led to an interim civilian-led government committed to a change towards a multiparty system of democracy. It all went quite quickly and smoothly. By March 1991, Benin had held free, fair and transparent legislative and presidential elections (see Decalo (1997); Gisselquist 2008).

Under the Beninese constitution, presidential elections have been held every five years since 1991, and legislative elections every four years. Although observers note some irregularities in these elections, they have been considered free and fair enough for their results to be endorsed by the international community. In addition, Benin has experienced successful alternations of executive power. Benin can be classified as a minimal democracy since 1991 (see Seely 2005; Gisselquist 2008).

However, Benin made this transition and consolidated its minimal democracy despite the predictions of modernization and diffusion theories, and empirical quantitative findings. In 1990, which was the year of the National Conference, Benin's level of economic development was low (see Gisselquist 2008: Figure 1): the country's GDP per capita was $273 (in constant 2000 US$). A decade later, it was $313, and it was still just $327 in 2006. Although the level of economic development was comparable to that of its neighbour Togo, Benin's GDP per capita during its democratic transition was well below the sub-Saharan African average of $528.

Moreover, Benin made the transition to democracy before its direct neighbours, and before most other countries in sub-Saharan Africa. Benin was among the first sub-Saharan African states to democratize in terms of holding multiparty presidential elections after a period of authoritarianism (Bratton and van de Walle 1997). Before Benin's transition, the only African countries that had held competitive multiparty elections since independence were Botswana, the Gambia, Mauritius, Senegal and Zimbabwe (Bratton and van de Walle 1997: 197–198). Benin's way of making transition towards democracy was also new: it included the first National Conference in francophone Africa, which was soon imitated by other countries and seen as a desirable model for democratic transition. Hence, the process of democratic diffusion partly originated from Benin.

Deviant democracies: explaining the outliers

Benin, Costa Rica, India and Mongolia can be seen as examples of deviant democracies, in terms of modernization and diffusion theories. They were not only surrounded by non-democracies during transition but were also relatively poor countries during both transition and consolidation. How can these deviant democracies be explained?

Transition

Regarding domestic factors, three key actors can be identified (political elites, the military and civil society) and one structural factor (ethnic fragmentation), which can be seen as the most important explanations of the discussed deviant democracies (see also Doorenspleet and Mudde 2008). The role of internal actors is the most prominent domestic factor mentioned in these deviant democracies, particularly political elites.[11] In line with the actor-oriented literature on democratization (Rustow 1970), domestic elites appear to play an important role as well in the transitions of deviant democracies. This is not a surprising result, as the dominant approach within the quantitative literature on democratic transitions has generally neglected the role of actors in explaining regime change. The actor-oriented approach, which is more influential in qualitative research (see e.g. O'Donnell and Schmitter 1986; Di Palma 1991) states that regime transitions are not determined by structural factors but shaped by the actions of principal political actors (see chapter 4 in Doorenspleet 2005).

Of particular importance is the role of the old elites, which are considered the biggest potential threat to democratic transition. In the deviant democracies the former regime either disappeared, through the process of decolonization (India), or its main actors prepared the transition (Costa Rica, Mongolia). Thus, in none of the cases did remnants of the old regime constitute important blocks of opposition to democratic transition. Therefore, the deviant cases show that democratic transition was more possible when old political elites could not prevent it. Incidentally, this could have happened in India, in the first years of independence, where British colonial elite resided. However, unlike for example Rhodesia, India was simply too big to be controlled by them (see McMillan 2008).

This still leaves many things unexplained, however. For example, the question often remains why the political actors did what they did. Was it indeed political actors that were key decision-makers, or were they so constrained by structures that they did not have an alternative? Whatever the reason, particularly in Costa Rica, politicians seem to have used the state to protect their own economic interests, requiring stability and (therefore) some level of legitimacy, whereas many leaders in failed democracies did not have any wealth except for the rents they accrued from state access.

While most attention in the actor-oriented literature is reserved for political elites, deviant democracies highlight the important role of the army.[12] In fact, the political insignificance of the army has been mentioned as one of the crucial factors in explanations of the overwhelming success of democratization in Central and Eastern Europe in comparison to, for example, Latin America (Barany 1997). Still, whereas the army is considered a major factor in studies of failed democratization, it plays little role in studies of successful democratization (Aka 1999).

In the analyzed deviant democracies, the army was either a weak or a pro-democratization actor. Costa Rica abolished its standing army just before the transition, partly because of its prior anti-democratic behaviour (Booth 2008). Mongolia's army had always been weak, given that the Soviet Union was its main protector (Fritz 2008). Finally, in Benin and India the army chose the side of the democratizers (Gisselquist 2008; McMillan 2008). In fact, the role of the army is the most striking factor in the comparative studies of Benin and other democratizing African countries (Gisselquist 2008; i.e. Table 1). Hence, the deviant cases show that democratic transition was made possible because the military was either relatively weak or pro-democracy.

Another domestic actor that is often discussed in the democratization literature is the role of 'civil society'. Particularly in the literature on the recent democratization in Eastern Europe, the importance of a heroic civil society is often highlighted, referring to the roles of organizations such as the Polish Solidarity and the Czech Charter 77 (see e.g. Geremek 1992). In several of the cases of deviant democracy, such as Benin (Gisselquist 2008), Costa Rica (Booth 2008) and India (McMillan 2008), there was a strong civil society, in terms of activity and independence, before the process of democratization started. However, Mongolia had only a very short period of strong pro-democracy civil society activity at the end of the 1980s (see Fritz 2008), in fact not much different from communist Czechoslovakia.

In short, a strong civil society is not a necessary condition for democratic transition, but it can play an important role. For example, civil society can limit the political space for other actors that may oppose democratization, such as political elites and the army. However, the relationship between civil society and democratization is complex. This is, in part, because of the broadness of the concept of civil society, which delineates roughly a sphere between the state and the family, and encompasses many diverse and opposing values (see e.g. Kopecký and Mudde 2003; Mudde 2007). Hence, it is the nature of the dominant civil society actors that determines the relationship towards democratization, not simply the absence or presence of these actors. That said, transition could also benefit from a lack of civil society activity, as this provides pro-democracy political elites with more space and time to develop their policies.[13]

A further internal factor, a structural one, which is often considered problematic to democracy and democratization, is a society's high ethnic fragmentation.[14] However, the role of ethnic fragmentation in deviant democracies shows that structural factors only influence politicians' actions, but do not determine them. In ethnically fragmented democracies, such as Benin and India, national political elites decided not to play the ethnic card (see Gisselquist 2008; Good and Taylor 2008; McMillan 2008). In India, the success of congress's strategy was undoubtedly 'helped' by the partition of colonial India and the creation of independent India and Pakistan, which significantly weakened the remaining Muslim opposition. Incidentally, the recent successes of the Indian People's Party (BJP) seem to indicate that consolidated democracies can deal better with ethnic politics (see McMillan 2008). In other words, the absence of ethnic politics seems particularly relevant for the transition phase.

While internal factors are the most important, at least in most cases, during the transition phase, external factors also contribute. This is self-evident in the process of decolonization, although this in no way guarantees successful democratization. Three external factors should be noted: the former colonizer, the regional hegemon and external shock.

The position of the former colonizer towards the former colony seems very important. In the case of India in the late 1940s, the United Kingdom actively pushed for democracy (McMillan

2008). In Benin, France did the same from the late 1980s. In fact, France's pro-democracy stand towards Benin differed markedly from its position towards other former African colonies, such as Togo, which failed to democratize (see Gisselquist 2008).

There is another external actor that can play a crucial role during the transition phase: the regional hegemon. In Costa Rica and Mongolia the regional hegemon tolerated the democratization process (Booth 2008; Fritz 2008). In these cases, the external actor in question took an exceptional position, as it had often negatively interfered in democratization in the region: apartheid South Africa in neighbouring states, the US in much of Central and Latin America, and Russia in Central Asia. One could also add France's role in much of francophone Africa (see Gisselquist 2008), where it is both a former colonizer and, to some extent, a regional hegemon.

Explanations for the regional hegemon's exceptional behaviour are primarily linked to internal conditions, notably the limited economic or strategic value (structural) and the non-threatening foreign policy position (actor) of the democratizing country. If one compares the deviant democracies to similar countries in the region that did not successfully democratize, their lack of natural resources stands out. Similarly, the countries do not have a strong geopolitical position. The possible exception is Mongolia, although it seems that all hegemons concerned preferred the country to take a 'neutral' position (see Fritz 2008). In fact, it appears that relatively 'unimportant' countries can prevent significant political interference from their regional hegemon by implementing a neutral or moderately pro-hegemon foreign policy, whereas more geopolitically relevant countries are expected to be more decidedly pro-hegemon. Therefore, deviant cases are more likely where there is a lack of opposition from significant external actors such as former colonizers or regional hegemons.

The final factor, external shock, is more difficult to situate within the dichotomies of structure-agency and internal-external. This notwithstanding, it seems to have played an important role in triggering democratic transition. The transition process in the deviant democracies was preceded by an economic or political shock – leaving aside the shock of decolonization itself. Benin was hit by an economic crisis (Gisselquist 2008), while in Mongolia this was at the very least looming (and the elites were aware of it; see Fritz 2008). Costa Rica and India experienced a civil war and violent conflict (see Booth 2008; McMillan 2008). Despite this partial exception, however, deviant cases are more likely to occur where the existing regime is confronted with an economic or political shock or crisis.

Consolidation

Not surprisingly, many factors that are conducive to democratization in the transition phase also play a role during consolidation. Logically, this is even more the case for internal or external structural factors. However, it also makes sense that the effect of particular factors decreases during the process of democratic consolidation. Overall, domestic actors play a less important role during the phase of democratic consolidation, when institutionalization and routinization increasingly limit the space of political elites and socialize both the elites and the masses. The same applies to the army, although its military power provides it with more possibilities to disrupt the democratization process. With regard to civil society, much depends on the nature of the dominant coalition of active organizations. Democratic consolidation is probably only threatened by civil society when the active dominant coalition is anti-democratic. While a democracy might not be able to 'deepen' without a strong (pro-democratic) civil society, it can definitely consolidate without one.[15]

This is not to say that internal factors do not play a crucial role during consolidation, but rather that these are predominantly structural. Somewhat in line with the modernization theory of democratization, the development of the economy seems highly relevant. Still, it is striking that the deviant democracies experienced economic growth or stability *after* their transition to democracy. While stability might already be enough to appease potential counter-elites, who often have vested economic interests in the country, economic growth will provide the demo-cratic regime with at least passive support from the masses. While elites will probably need to see actual results, the masses will initially be appeased by having hope at positive results in the future.

A second internal structural factor is the state structure, more specifically the centralization of the state. In all cases, the new democratizing state was very centralized, sometimes despite regional legacies (notably India; see McMillan 2008). By centralizing finances and powers, the national political elites have the means to implement their policies and win support for their regime, among others, through economic growth or stability. Moreover, centralization undermines the potential anti-democratic opposition, which is forced to challenge the strong centre to undermine the regime. The latter is probably particularly relevant in ethnically fragmented countries, in which there are too many 'nations' to challenge the centre. In other words, the absence of ethnic groups that are big enough to challenge the democratic centre by themselves, increases the chances at successful democratic consolidation (see also India; McMillan 2008).

Finally, international actors continue to play an important role, although there are some important differences with the transition phase. Rather than former colonizers and regional hegemons, international organizations (such as the International Monetary Fund or World Bank) and foreign states that provide substantial financial aid to democratizing countries weigh significantly on their policies. This was the case, for example, in Benin and Mongolia (Fritz 2008; Gisselquist 2008); and one could argue that Costa Rica (Booth 2008) required foreign expertise to develop natural resources. Where funders explicitly require or support democracy as a condition for the continuation of aid, and democratizing countries are heavily dependent upon this aid, the positive role of external actors is greatest.

This seems to have been the most notable factor in the consolidation phase of Mongolian democracy (see Fritz 2008), particularly during the period of parliamentary dominance of the Mongolian People's Revolutionary Party (MPRP). Cynically, one could say that the MPRP simply copied the political regime of its major funders; it was totalitarian during USSR patronage, and became democratic during Western sponsorship. While the situation might have been less opportunistic in other countries, significant foreign aid can make democratic policies an economic necessity for local elites. Moreover, it can legitimate both the political leaders and the democratic regime – again, through economic growth or stability.

In conclusion, the domestic and international factors as described above can explain the transition and consolidation of deviant democracies, and have often been omitted or underdeveloped in previous quantitative studies comparing most countries in the world.

Conclusion

Numerous studies have convincingly shown that structural factors matter for democratization. Above all, the level of economic development and the presence or absence of democratic neighbours have most impact on a country's prospects for democratization. However, there are some countries that have experienced, in various historical periods, a successful transition to democracy in an unfavourable structural context. Their level of economic development was low *and* they were surrounded by non-democratic neighbours when their non-democratic regimes collapsed.

Yet, after transitions of different lengths, they successfully began to build at last a minimal democracy. Moreover, most also succeeded in consolidating the new democratic order. They have sustained their minimal democracies well beyond the initial period of transition and the first free democratic elections. They are 'deviant democracies': not necessarily perfect democracies by Western liberal-democratic standards, but they do represent unusual success stories, given the context in which their transitions took place.

This chapter showed that deviant cases of democratization include Costa Rica and India, which made their transition to democracy during the second wave of democratization following the end of the Second World War; and Benin and Mongolia that managed to make the transition to democracy in the early 1990s during the more recent fourth wave of democratization. All these countries can be considered as 'democracies against the odds'. In other words, they do not fit the expectations of modernization and diffusion theories. In the light of the exceptional and anomalous nature of democratization in these countries, we need to bring a better understanding of political change in those deviant cases.

This chapter detected the factors that can be seen as the most important explanations of the discussed deviant democracies (see also Doorenspleet and Mudde 2008). It showed that during the transition phase of the deviant democracies, three agency explanations (political elites, the military and civil society), one structural domestic factor (ethnic fragmentation) and international factors (former colonizers and regional hegemons) played a crucial role. During the consolidation phase, two internal structural factors (economic growth/stability and the state centralization) are crucial in the deviant democracies, while international actors continue to play an important role (albeit different actors than during the transition phase; namely, international organizations such as the International Monetary Fund or the World Bank, and foreign states supporting democracy through financial aid).

A comparative study of 'deviant autocracies' seems the most logical next step, as most notably the economic development theory has been criticized most forcefully for underexplaining autocracies (Bromley 1997; Randall 1997). In other words, the limitations of the economic development theory are most visible in the many economically developed countries that remain autocratic or have returned to that state (e.g. China, the Gulf states, Malaysia). A study of the reasons why these countries remain autocratic may provide important additional insights into the process of democratization. Paradoxically, 'deviant autocracies' might reveal more on the success of democratization than deviant democracies did.

Notes

1 While this chapter is revised and updated, it is based on the articles of the special issue on 'deviant democracies' published in *Democratization* (vol. 15, no. 4, 2008), edited by Renske Doorenspleet, Petr Kopecky and Cas Mudde. Renske, Petr and Cas were shocked and saddened to hear of the sudden death of Peter Mair in August 2011. As our Ph.D. supervisor at the University of Leiden in the period between 1992 and 2001, he was a source of encouragement and inspiration, and simply an outstanding scholar who will be greatly missed. This chapter is dedicated to the memory of Prof. Peter Mair.

2 See the next section of this chapter, which focuses on the lively debate in the academic literature on this issue.

3 Another example of a deviant democracy is Botswana since the 1960s (see Good and Taylor 2008) but this case will not be discussed in this chapter.

4 Lipset's followers have pointed out that his study has many conceptual, methodological and technical problems (cf. Cutright 1963; McCrone and Cnudde 1967, Olsen 1968; Jackman 1973; Bollen 1980; Bollen 1991; Diamond 1992). First, Lipset's operationalization of democracy contained indicators of stability. Second, his measurement of economic development was ad hoc. Third, Lipset's sample was limited to European, English-speaking and Latin American states. Fourth, the analysis of data was static from a single time point, although it classified regimes based on their experience over a long period of time (25 to 40 years). Fifth, Lipset made no use of measures of statistical association or statistical controls. Sixth, the means between the two groups differed, yet the spread in the values on almost every indicator was so extreme that it would be very difficult to place a single state in either the democratic

or non-democratic category, knowing, for example, only its score on the number of telephones. Finally, like other classical modernization theorists, Lipset assumed linearity, ignoring the possible negative impact that development at a certain middle level might have on the probability of democracy.

5 See, for example, the following studies: Cutright (1963); Coleman (1965); McCrone and Cnudde (1967); Neubauer (1967); Olsen (1968); Jackman (1973); Coulter (1975); Bollen (1979, 1980, 1983, 1991); Bollen and Jackman (1985, 1989, 1995); Muller (1988, 1995a, 1995b); Inglehart (1988, 1997); Diamond (1992); Muller and Seligson (1994); Burkhart and Lewis-Beck (1994); Alvarez *et al.* (1996); Vanhanen (1997); Przeworksi and Limongi (1997a, 1997b).

6 See also Botswana (cf. Note 3 above).

7 India can be considered an established democracy, but its functioning certainly has important flaws in practice. Political and bureaucratic corruption, for example, has been a major concern in India. See the findings of Transparency International's Corruption Perceptions Index, and notice the growing anti-corruption protests in India.

8 See, for example, Bulmer-Thomas *et al.* (2006); Astorga *et al.* (2005); and Vanhanen (1997), especially Appendix 5.

9 In constant 1970 US dollars. See *Statistical Abstract of Latin America*, 22 (1983), pp. 282–283. However, Booth (2008) argued that economic development was relatively high, so there is still debate about this issue.

10 See however Booth's critique on the notion that Costa Rica is a deviant democracy, given the relatively high level of economic development of this country during crucial phases of the democratization process (Booth 2008).

11 See the special issue in *Democratization*, August 2008. vol. 15, no. 4, edited by Renske Doorenspleet, Petr Kopecky and Cas Mudde.

12 Ibid.

13 See particularly the deviant case of Botswana (Good and Taylor 2008).

14 The idea that ethnic fragmentation is problematic for democracy can be found in classic works in comparative politics in the 1950s, such as Almond (1956), and see for one of the first rational choice argumentations work by Rabushka and Shepsle (1972).

15 This is most clearly exemplified in the case of Botswana (see Good and Taylor 2008). For a detailed description of the difference between consolidation and deepening of democracy, see Schedler (1998); Doorenspleet and Kopecký (2008).

References

Aka, Philip C. (1999) 'The Military and Democratization in Africa', *Journal of Third World Studies*, 16 (1), pp. 71–86.

Almond, Gabriel (1956) 'Comparative Political Systems', *Journal of Politics*, 18 (3), pp. 391–409.

Alvarez, M., J. A. Cheibub, F. Limongi and A. Przeworski (1996) 'Classifying Political Regimes', *Studies in International Comparative Development*, 31 (2), pp. 3–36.

Arat, Z. F. (1991) *Democracy and Human Rights in Developing Countries*. Boulder and London: Lynne Rienner Publishers.

Astorga, Pablo Ame R. Berges and Valpy Fitzgerald (2005) 'The Standard of Living in Latin America during the Twentieth Century', *The Economic History Review*, 58 (4), pp. 765–796.

Barany, Zoltan (1997) 'Democratic Consolidation and the Military: The East European Experience', *Comparative Politics*, 30 (1), pp. 21–43.

Boix, Carles and Susan C. Stokes (2003) 'Endogenous Democratization', *World Politics*, 55 (4), pp. 517–549.

Bollen, K. A. (1979) 'Political Democracy and the Timing of Development', *American Sociological Review*, 44 (3), pp. 572–587.

—— (1980) 'Issues in the Comparative Measurement of Political Democracy', *American Sociological Review*, 45 (3), pp. 370–390.

—— (1983) 'World System Position, Dependency, and Democracy: The Cross-National Evidence', *American Sociological Review*, 48 (1), pp. 468–479.

—— (1991) 'Political Democracy: Conceptual and Measurement Traps'. In *On Measuring Democracy*, ed. A. Inkeles. New Brunswick and London: Transaction Publishers, pp. 3–20.

—— and R. W. Jackman (1985) 'Political Democracy and the Size Distribution of Income', *American Sociological Review*, 50 (1), pp. 438–458.

—— and —— (1989) 'Democracy, Stability, and Dichotomies', *American Sociological Review*, 54 (1), pp. 612–621.

—— and —— (1995) 'Income Inequality and Democratization Revisited: Comment on Muller', *American Sociological Review*, 60 (6), pp. 983–989.

Booth, John A. (2008) 'Democratic Development in Costa Rica', *Democratization*, 15 (4), pp. 714–733.

Bratton, Michael and Nicolas Van de Walle (1997) *Democratic Experiments in Africa: Regime Transitions in Comparative Perspective*. Cambridge: Cambridge University Press.

——, Robert Mattes and E. Gyimah-Boadi (2005) *Public Opinion, Democracy, and Market Reform in Africa*. New York: Cambridge University Press.

Bromley, Simon (1997) 'Middle East Exceptionalism – Myth or Reality?'. In *Democratization*, ed. David Potter, David Goldblatt, Margaret Kiloh and Paul Lewis. Cambridge: Polity Press, pp. 321–344.

Bulmer-Thomas, Victor, John H Coatsworth and Roberto Cortés Conde, eds (2006) *The Cambridge Economic History of Latin America*. Cambridge: Cambridge University Press.

Burkhart, R. E. and M. S. Lewis-Beck (1994) 'Comparative Democracy: The Economic Development Thesis', *American Political Science Review*, 88 (4), pp. 903–910.

Coleman, J. S. (1965) *Education and Political Development*. Princeton, NJ: Princeton University Press.

Coppedge, M. and W. H. Reinicke (1991) 'Measuring Polyarchy'. In *On Measuring Democracy*, ed. A. Inkeles. New Brunswick and London: Transaction Publishers, pp. 47–68.

Coulter, P. (1975) *Social Mobilization and Liberal Democracy: A Macroquantitative Analysis of Global and Regional Models*. London: D.C. Heath.

Cutright, P. (1963) 'National Political Development: Measurement and Analysis', *American Sociological Review*, 28 (1), pp. 253–264.

Dahl, R. A. (1971) *Polyarchy: Participation and Opposition*. New Haven, CT: Yale University Press.

Decalo, Samuel (1997) 'Benin: First of the New Democracies.' In *Political Reform in Francophone Africa*, ed. John F. Clark and David E. Gardinier. Boulder, CO: Westview.

Diamond, Larry (1989) 'Introduction: Persistence, Erosion, Breakdown'. In *Democracy in Democratic Countries: Asia*, ed. Larry Diamond, Juan J. Linz and Seymour Martin Lipset. Boulder, CO: Lynne Rienner.

—— (1992) 'Economic Development and Democracy Reconsidered'. In *Reexamining Democracy: Essays in Honor of Seymour Martin Lipset*, ed. G. Marks and L. Diamond. London: Sage Publications, pp. 93–140.

Di Palma, Giuseppe (1990) *To Craft Democracies: An Essay on Democratic Transitions*. Berkeley: University of California Press.

Doorenspleet, Renske (2000) 'Reassessing the Three Waves of Democratization', *World Politics*, 52 (3), pp. 384–406.

—— (2005) *Democratic Transitions: Exploring the Structural Sources during the Fourth Wave*. Boulder, CO: Lynne Rienner Publishers.

—— and Petr Kopecký (2008) 'Against the Odds: Deviant Cases of Democratization', *Democratization*, 15 (4), pp. 697–714.

—— and Cas Mudde (2008) 'Upping the Odds: Deviant Democracies and Theories of Democratization', *Democratization*, 15 (4), pp. 815–832.

Elkins, Zachary and Beth Simmons (2005) 'On Waves, Clusters, and Diffusion: A Conceptual Framework', *The ANNALS of the American Academy of Political and Social Science*, 598 (1), pp. 33–51.

Fish, Steven (1998) 'Mongolia: Democracy without Prerequisites', *Journal of Democracy*, 9 (3), pp. 127–141.

Fritz, Verena (2008) 'Mongolia: the Rise and Travails of a Deviant Democracy', *Democratization*, 15 (4), pp. 766–789.

Gasiorowski, Mark J. (1995) 'Economic Crisis and Political Regime Change: An Event History Analysis', *American Political Science Review*, 89 (4), pp. 882–897.

Gastil, R. D. (1991) 'The Comparative Survey of Freedom: Experiences and Suggestions'. In *On Measuring Democracy*, ed. A. Inkeles. New Brunswick and London: Transaction Publishers, pp. 21–46.

Geremek, Bronislav (1992) ' Civil Society Then and Now', *Journal of Democracy*, 3 (2), pp. 3–12

Gisselquist, Rachel M. (2008) 'Democratic Transition and Democratic Survival in Benin', *Democratization*, 15 (4), pp. 789–815.

Good, Kenneth and Ian Taylor (2008) 'Botswana: a Minimalist Democracy', *Democratization*, 15 (4), pp. 750–766.

Heilbrunn, John R. (1993) 'Social Origins of National Conferences in Benin and Togo', *The Journal of Modern African Studies*, 31 (2), pp. 277–299.

Huntington, Samuel P. (1991) *The Third Wave: Democratization in the Late Twentieth Century*. Norman: University of Oklahoma Press.

Inglehart, R. (1988) 'The Renaissance of Political Culture', *American Political Science Review*, 82 (4), pp. 1203–1230.

Inglehart, R. (1997) *Modernization and Postmodernization: Culture, Economic, and Political Change in 43 Societies*. Princeton, NJ: Princeton University Press.

—— and C. Welzel (2005). *Modernization, Cultural Change and Democracy: The Human Development Sequence*. New York: Cambridge University Press.

Jackman, R. W. (1973) 'On the Relation of Economic Development to Democratic Performance', *American Journal of Political Science*, 17 (3), pp. 611–621.

Jaggers, K. and T. R. Gurr (1995) 'Tracking Democracy's Third Wave with the Polity III Data', *Journal of Peace Research*, 32 (4), pp. 469–482.

Kennedy, Michael D. (1999) 'Contingencies and the Alternatives of 1989: Toward a Theory and Practice of Negotiating Revolution', *East European Politics and Societies*, 13 (2), pp. 293–302.

Kolhi, Atul (2001) 'Introduction.' In *The Success of India's Democracy*, ed. Atul Kohli. Cambridge: Cambridge University Press, pp. 1–21.

Kopecký, Petr and Cas Mudde, eds (2003) *Uncivil Society? Contentious Politics in Post-Communist Europe*. London: Routledge.

Kopstein, Jeffrey S. and David A. Reilly (2000) 'Geographic Diffusion and the Transformation of the Postcommunist World', *World Politics*, 53 (1), pp. 1–37.

LaFeber, Walter (1983) *Inevitable Revolutions: The United States in Central America*. New York: W.W. Norton.

Lewis, Paul G. (1997) 'Theories of Democratization and Patterns of Regime Change in Eastern Europe', *Journal of Communist Studies and Transition Politics*, 13, pp. 4–26.

Lijphart, Arend (1996) 'The Puzzle of Indian Democracy: A Consociational Interpretation', *American Political Science Review*, 90 (2), pp. 258–268.

Linz, Juan J. and Alfred Stepan (1996) *Problems of Democratic Transition and Consolidation: Southern Europe, South America, and Post-Communist Europe*. Baltimore, MD: Johns Hopkins University Press.

Lipset, Seymour M. (1959) 'Some Social Requisites of Democracy: Economic Development and Political Legitimacy', *American Political Science Review*, 53 (1), pp. 69–105.

—— (1994) 'The Social Requisites of Democracy Revisited, *American Sociological Review*, 59 (1), pp. 1–22.

——, K-R. Seong and J. C. Torres (1993) 'A Comparative Analysis of the Social Requisites of Democracy', *International Social Science Journal*, 45 (2), pp. 155–175.

McCrone, D. J. and C. F. Cnudde (1967) 'Toward a Communications Theory of Democratic Political Development: A Causal Model', *American Political Science Review*, 61 (1), pp. 72–79.

McMillan, Alistair (2008) 'Deviant Democratization in India', *Democratization*, 15 (4), pp. 733–750.

Mudde, Cas (2007) 'Civil Society'. In *Developments in Central and Eastern European Politics*, ed. Stephen White, Judy Batt and Paul G. Lewis. Basingstoke: Palgrave, pp. 223–225.

Muller, E. N. (1988) 'Democracy, Economic Development, and Income Inequality', *American Sociological Review*, 53 (1), pp. 50–69.

Muller, E. N. (1995a) 'Economic Determinants of Democracy', *American Sociological Review*, 60 (6), pp. 966–982.

—— (1995b) 'Income Inequality and Democratization: Reply to Bollen and Jackman', *American Sociological Review*, 60 (6), pp. 990–996.

—— and M. A. Seligson (1994) 'Civic Culture and Democracy: the Question of Causal Relationships', *American Political Science Review*, 88 (3), pp. 635–652.

Nachane, Dilip M. (2009) 'Marketization of the Economy and Democracy.' In *Challenges to Democracy in India*, ed. Rajesh M. Basrur. Oxford: Oxford University Press, pp. 215–248.

Neubauer, D. E. (1967) 'Some Conditions of Democracy', *American Political Science Review*, 61 (4), pp. 1002–1009.

O'Donnell, Guillermo A. and Phillippe C. Schmitter (1986) 'Tentative Conclusions about Uncertain Democracies'. In *Transitions from Authoritarian Rule: Prospects for Democracy*, ed. Guillermo A. O'Donnell and Phillippe C. Schmitter. Baltimore, MD, and London: Johns Hopkins University Press.

O'Loughlin, John, Michael D. Ward, Corey L. Lofdahl, Jordin S. Cohen, David S. Brown, David Reilly, Kristian S. Gleditsch and Michael Shin (1998) 'The Diffusion of Democracy, 1946–1994', *Annals of the Association of American Geographers*, 88 (4), pp. 545–574.

Olsen, M. E. (1968) 'Multivariate Analysis of National Political Development', *American Sociological Review*, 33, pp. 699–712.

Pridham, Geoffrey and Tatu Vanhanen, eds (1994) *Democratization in Eastern Europe: Domestic and International Perspective*. London: Routledge.

Przeworski, A. and F. Limongi (1997a) 'Modernization: Theories and Facts', *World Politics*, 49 (2), pp. 155–183.

—— and F. Limongi (1997b) 'Democracy and Development'. In *Democracy's Victory and Crisis*, ed. A. Hadenius. Cambridge: Cambridge University Press, pp. 163–194.

——, Michael E. Alvarez, José Antonio Cheibub and Fernando Limongi (2000) *Democracy and Development: Political Institutions and Well-being in the World, 1950–1990*. Cambridge: Cambridge University Press.

Rabushka, Alvin and Kenneth A. Shepsle (1972) *Politics in Plural Societies: A Theory of Democratic Instability*. Columbus, OH: Merrill.

Randall, Vicky (1997) 'Why Have the Political Trajectories of India and China Been Different'. In *Democratization*, ed. David Potter, David Goldblatt, Margaret Kiloh and Paul Lewis. Cambridge: Polity Press, pp. 195–218.

Rueschemeyer, Dietrich, Evelyne H. Stephens and John D. Stephens (1992) *Capitalist Development and Democracy*. Cambridge: Polity Press.

Rustow, Dankwart A. (1970) 'Transitions to Democracy; Toward a Dynamic Model', *Comparative Politics*, 2 (3), pp. 337–363.

Schedler, Andreas (1998) 'What is Democratic Consolidation?', *Journal of Democracy*, 9 (2), pp. 91–107.

Schneider, Ronald M. (2007) *Latin American Political History: Patterns and Personalities*. Boulder, CO: Westview.

Schumpeter, Joseph A. (1943) *Capitalism, Socialism and Democracy*. London: Unwin.

Seely, J. C. (2005) 'The Legacies of Transition Governments: Post-transition Dynamics in Benin and Togo,' *Democratization*, 12 (3), pp. 357–377.

Seligson, Mitchell A. (1987). 'Democratization in Latin America: The Current Cycle.' In *Authoritarians and Democrats: The Politics of Regime Transition in Latin America*, eds. James M. Malloy and Mitchell A. Seligson. Pittsburgh: University of Pittsburgh Press, pp. 3–12.

Smith, Peter H. (2005) *Democracy in Latin America: Political Change in Comparative Perspective*. New York: Oxford University Press.

Starr, H. (1991) 'Democratic Dominoes; Diffusion Approaches to the Spread of Democracy in the International System', *Journal of Conflict Resolution*, 35 (2), pp. 356–381.

Vanhanen, T. (1997) *Prospects of Democracy, a Study of 172 Countries*. London: Routledge.

13

The military

Thomas C. Bruneau

This chapter focuses on the military as an actor in the processes of democratic consolidation, and on how newer democracies seek to assert and develop civilian control and achieve effectiveness in the security forces' roles and missions.[1] It elaborates on a framework for analysis that I have developed in the study of newer as well as more mature democracies, and illustrates with examples from countries where I and my research team have done field research for more than a decade. There is some useful conceptual literature on the military in democratic consolidation, but little empirical work on how democratic civilian control is in fact implemented. There is even less on what militaries require in order to implement the roles and missions civilian leaders assign them. Consequently, while the early part of this chapter, which focuses on the conceptualization of the military and democratic consolidation, is documented with academic literature, the four specific case studies in the latter part will rely heavily on empirical research carried out by the author and his colleagues.[2]

The military in democratic consolidation

The most prominent scholars of democratic consolidation, including Juan J. Linz and Alfred Stepan (1996), Adam Przeworski (1991), and Philippe Schmitter (1995), have focused on the role of the military in the process. This is not surprising when we recall Samuel E. Finer's central point in his classic, *The Man on Horseback: The Role of the Military in Politics*, in which he queries: 'Instead of asking why the military engage in politics, we ought surely ask why they ever do otherwise. For at first sight the political advantages of the military *vis-à-vis* other and civilian groupings are overwhelming. The military possess vastly superior organization. And, they possess *arms*' (Finer 2003: 5). Even in those countries, mainly in Eastern and Central Europe, where the military did not constitute the government (although they did in juntas throughout Latin America, sub-Saharan Africa, and East and Southeast Asia), the military, with their organization and arms, has to be taken seriously in the transition to and later consolidation of democracy. Consequently, alongside scholars such as Linz and Stepan, Przeworski and Schmitter, two classic studies on democratic consolidation, edited by Richard Gunther *et al.* (1995), and Larry Diamond *et al.* (1997) have chapters on the military. Finally, from the same perspective of the military's role in democratic consolidation is Larry Diamond and Marc F. Plattner's edited *Civil-Military Relations and Democracy* (1996). In addition, there are a few studies on particular cases of the military in new democracies, including those by Felipe Aguero on Spain (1995), David Pion-Berlin on Argentina (1997), and Marybeth Peterson Ulrich on the Czech Republic and Russia (1999).

Philippe Schmitter (1995) and Alfred Stepan (1988) engage with virtually all of the main issues concerning the military and democratic consolidation. Schmitter explicitly includes the military variable, which he illustrates in two separate figures. In one illustration, 'A Visual Representation of Regime Change from Authoritarian Rule to Democracy', the author assigns the military two roles in the process of democratic consolidation: (1) to negotiate a pact that codifies the relationship between the civilian leadership and the military; and (2) to embed civilian control over military decision-making (Schmitter 1995: 541). Schmitter pursues this idea further in another illustration, 'A Heuristic Model of the Factors Influencing the Type/Extent of Democratic Consolidation' (1995: 564). Unfortunately, neither Schmitter nor Przeworski go into any detail on how civilian control is instituted, by whom, or what the results would be. Przeworski (1991: 29) does not go further than to state the following: '[O]bviously, the institutional framework of civilian control over the military constitutes the neuralgic point of democratic consolidation.' These details, at very early stages of consolidation, are the focus of works by Aguero (1995), Pion-Berlin (1997) and Ulrich (1999), in their specific country studies.

Alfred Stepan (1988: 94–97) provides a framework of 11 'Selected Prerogatives of Military as Institution in a Democratic Regime', which can be rated to evaluate how deeply embedded a country's military is in its governing institutions Stepan's prerogatives all concern civilian control, and if they receive high ratings, the country cannot qualify as a democracy. There is value in Stepan's framework for two reasons: First, it provides a factual basis on which to compare the progress of different countries in asserting what Schmitter and Przeworski posit in terms of civilian control over the military; and second, it sensitizes the researcher to explore the military's involvement in domains of state, society and the economy that would not be acceptable in a mature democracy. In 2004, the Federal Research Division of the US Library of Congress sponsored a global assessment of civil-military relations utilizing Stepan's framework. I had responsibility for Iberia, and while I found the framework useful to assess a state in the early phase of democratic consolidation, in which civilians were extending control over the military, it was not useful in later stages because the ratings were too low to offer much information. And, most importantly, the definitions of the prerogatives tend to be formalistic, while structures and processes are central, and details are critical, for understanding the military's role in a functional democracy.

In response to the perceived gaps in the literature, our work focuses on the institutions that are − or are not − created to assert democratic civilian control over the military (Bruneau and Goetze 2006; Bruneau and Matei 2008). This research shows that states often throw out a great deal of 'smoke and mirrors', whereby they rhetorically assert democratic civilian control but do not actually wield it, because either the institutions have not been created or there are not enough civilians with the expertise to make the institutions operative. Thus, one purpose in this chapter is to examine how civilian control is, in fact, implemented. Once control has been achieved, however, there remains the issue of effectiveness. That is, what the military and other security forces should be, and are, used for. The exploration of this question is another purpose of this chapter. In most new democracies, asserting democratic civilian control is the stage, at least initially, at which the process of dealing with the military ends. This is also where the academic literature stops. Recently, however, emerging threats from international terrorism and organized crime, and global demands for countries' participation in the international community through international peace support operations (PSO), are forcing virtually all governments to re-examine what their militaries and other security forces can do. Today, 117 states provide peacekeepers for United Nations missions, and most provide logistical support to police and other civilian authorities to fight crime and provide humanitarian assistance in natural disasters. The scholarly literature, however, has unfortunately mostly ignored the issue of effectiveness, which is crucial in our framework. Beyond my team's own work, the only exceptions we are aware of are Aguero (2009) and Edmunds (2006).

The institutional requirements for democratic civilian control and effectiveness

Today, in view of the rising trends in global threats, and in both domestic and international requests for military support in areas such as PSO, the variables of control and effectiveness must be analysed in tandem. This is the case for at least three reasons: First, we find from our research that the effectiveness of the military, and other security actors, is increasingly recognized by civilian leaders and the general public as important to national security; second, these two variables, as we will see in some of the case studies, may be in competition with one another; and third, they overlap to some degree, in terms of their institutional requirements. I will discuss these requirements in the case studies later in this chapter. The data for the case studies are drawn from a decade of extensive research, rounded out with in-country interviews conducted by myself and my team in Argentina, Mongolia, Portugal and Romania, where one or more of us spent at least a week between early and mid-2010.

Based on our research, I define what is necessary, if not sufficient, to achieve both control and effectiveness. *Control* over armed forces comprises three elements: civilian authority over institutional control mechanisms, normalized oversight, and the inculcation of professional norms through professional military education. Control must be grounded in and exercised through institutions that range from organic laws that empower the civilian leadership, to civilian-led organizations with professional staffs, such as a ministry of defence – and include one or more committees in the legislature that deal with policies and budgets, and a well-defined chain of authority for civilians to determine roles and missions. Oversight requires the executive, and probably the legislature, to have institutionalized mechanisms to ensure that the security and defence organizations perform in a manner consistent with the direction they have been given. Finally, the inculcation of professional norms supports the first two elements through transparent policies for recruitment, education, training, promotion and retirement.

The second dimension is the *effectiveness* with which the military and other security forces fulfil the assigned roles and missions. It is important to highlight several concerns on the importance of limits on definitions and measurement. First, as mentioned above, armed forces fulfil a very wide spectrum of potential roles and missions, including: disaster relief, support to the police in domestic situations, intelligence collection, peace support operations, counter-terrorism, counter-insurgency and, of course, warfare. Second, no imaginable role or mission in the modern world can be achieved by only one service in the military or one agency outside of the military, without the involvement of other services and agencies. Thus 'jointness' and inter-agency coordination are indispensable. Third, and making things much more complicated, there are the paradoxes of evaluating effectiveness in the contexts of deterrence or secrecy. When wars are avoided precisely because a country is perceived not to be vulnerable, or an intelligence organization supplies secret information that either prevents or induces a specific desired response without the knowledge of anyone but those directly involved, then evaluating the services' effectiveness means, essentially, trying to quantify a negative. Finally, most imaginable roles and missions for today's security services are carried out within a web of coalitions or alliances, thus further complicating attempts to determine a single military's effectiveness. In short, there are challenging methodological and logical issues involved in evaluating effectiveness, yet analysts must grapple with them to begin to understand what support the military and other security forces require if they are to do what is now expected of them. It may be that few scholars attempt to deal with effectiveness, at least in part because of these conceptual and methodological challenges.

Based on the above observations and our empirical research, I posit here that there are three minimum requirements for effectiveness. First, *there must be a plan, a strategy or doctrine*. Examples include defence white papers, national security concepts or strategies, national military strategies, doctrine on intelligence, and counterterrorism doctrine. Prominent strategy analyst Hew Strachan (2005: 52) captures the concept well:

> In the ideal model of civil-military relations, the democratic head of state sets out his or her policy, and armed forces coordinate the means to enable its achievement. The reality is that this process – a process called strategy – is iterative, a dialogue where ends also reflect means and where the result – also called strategy – is a compromise between the end of policy and the military means available to implement it.

Second, there must be structures and processes both to formulate and implement the plans. These would include ministries of defence, national security councils, or other means of inter-agency coordination. Third, a country must commit resources, in the form of political capital, money and personnel, to ensure the military has sufficient equipment, trained forces and other assets needed to fulfil the assigned roles and missions. Lacking any of these three components, it is difficult to imagine how any military could act effectively.

It should be obvious that the data to support the latter two dimensions of this civil-military relations framework are not readily available in the secondary literature, given that scholars have not been investigating effectiveness. Even when material on democratic civilian control is included, the data are generally formalistic. It was thus necessary for my team and I to collect the data first hand in the four countries discussed below – Argentina, Mongolia, Portugal and Romania. While making no claim that these four are a representative sample of the military in democratic consolidation, I believe they represent sufficient variety to provide information and insights that may be useful to other countries, should they find the political will to implement change. To some extent, these four case studies illustrate 'lessons-learned/best-practices', which contrasts them with most newer democracies, where very little is happening in terms of institution-building.

Argentina is a dramatic case, where a military junta constituted the government for most of the post-World War Two era, and acted with particular brutality between 1976-83, when the leadership perpetrated extensive human rights abuses. Consequently, it is not surprising that Argentina's civilian governments since 1983 have focused, although for the most part haphazardly, on controlling the military. More recently, the civilian governments have by definition negated the possibility for military effectiveness by legally restricting the military to external defence against state actors. We will see in the case of Argentina that civilian control is formally robust but problematic, and that military effectiveness is severely restricted.

Mongolia has been independent from China since 1921, but was closely linked to the Soviet Union; the main function of its military, integrated with the Soviet military from the mid-1960s, was to provide a bulwark against the People's Republic of China. The Soviet 39th Army, stationed in Mongolia, had very many tanks and armoured vehicles (1,866 and 2,531 respectively) and air support in the form of helicopters and fighters (315) (*The Military Balance* 1988: 171). Mongolia itself had 650 tanks, 870 armoured vehicles, and 40 fighter jets and helicopters (Worden and Savada 1991: 272). Following the Cold War and the advent of democracy, Mongolia's military was reconfigured. While formally the majority of its forces are now oriented to territorial defence, the main focus of the Mongolian military is now on peace support operations, under both

United Nations and coalition auspices. We will see that the initial institutional arrangements for democratic control, following the long and intense system of Communist Party control, impedes the military's effectiveness in implementing the new and preferred role of PSO.

Portugal initiated the "third wave" of democratization with the military coup on 25 April 1974 that became a revolution and ultimately evolved into democracy. Initially, the military assumed a central role in government, and it took almost 20 years before democratic civilian control was institutionalized in a civilian-led ministry of defence. Portugal was a founding member of the North Atlantic Treaty Organization (NATO), which emphasizes military effectiveness. Partly as a result, both military control and effectiveness developed during Portugal's transition. In addition, since 2006 the civilian government has emphasized increasing military effectiveness as part of a strategy to maximize Portugal's independence in the context of European integration.

Romania was one of the most repressive communist dictatorships during the Cold War. Despite initial setbacks, with stimulus and support from NATO and then the European Union (EU), Romania has consolidated its new democracy, including democratic civilian control of the armed forces. Furthermore, within the framework of NATO, and with troops in the Balkans, Afghanistan and Iraq, Romania has also had to ensure that its military is effective (or at the minimum, compatible at a high operational level, with counterparts from older, established democracies).

The remainder of this chapter will briefly describe and analyse how well these four countries have managed the two dimensions of control and effectiveness. Space limits prevent me from fully illustrating the requirements outlined above. I will instead highlight certain features of the two general dimensions for control and effectiveness for each of the countries under consideration.

Argentina

Argentina is relevant to this chapter for several reasons. First, its military dictatorship, especially during the period 1976-83, was arguably the most repressive in the region. Five thousand deaths have been attributed to the regime, as well as 30,000 unsolved disappearances. The junta proved itself incompetent in both economic policy and military strategy by initiating a disastrous war with Great Britain in 1982 over the Malvinas/Falklands Islands, the final straw that brought down the regime. Much political effort between 1983 and 1990 was spent dealing with the military, mainly to avoid military coups. Second, serious efforts to assert civilian control through institutions began in 2003, when Néstor Kirchner became president, although this is still an unfinished process. Third, similarly to other countries, once defence reform began, it strengthened the civilian-led ministry of defence, established a legal basis for civil-military relations, and allowed the civilian leadership to gradually assume control over key areas of national security and defence policy. Fourth, despite these advances, the institutions remain weak and civilian expertise is still limited, mostly because civilians in the Ministry of Defence (MOD) are not hired on a permanent basis and, consequently, are unable to acquire and consolidate defence and security knowledge. Fifth, while democratic civilian control over the armed forces has been implemented and consolidated, military effectiveness remains a very low priority. Indeed, by limiting the armed forces exclusively to external defence, and only against state actors, potential roles and missions are severely circumscribed. Only in the areas of PSO and possibly military support to civilian authorities in natural disasters can the military act.

Argentina's transition to democracy: the role of the military

Argentina has a long history of military involvement in politics. The twentieth century alone saw five coups that resulted in military governments: in 1930, 1943, 1955, 1966 and, finally, between

1976 and 1983. All aspects of civil-military relations in Argentina must be understood in this historical context, just as all political initiatives after the transition to democracy in 1983 can only be understood as efforts to counter this long history of military predominance in politics and the economy. The Argentines, at least the politicians, have yet to overcome this legacy.

The long, drawn-out process of consolidating democratic civilian control is marked at one level by three fundamental laws – on defence (1988), domestic security (1992) and national intelligence (2001) – all of which seek in some way to counter the legacy of military predominance. They are associated with the presidential administrations of Raul Alfonsin (1983–1989), Carlos Menem (1989–1999) and Fernando de la Rua (1999–2001). What stands out, however, over the long period between the transition to democracy in 1983 and the presidency of Néstor Kirchner (2003–2007), is the lack of real change for most of those two decades. This was due primarily to the political dynamics of the era, characterized by an historically high level of military involvement. The first phase, between late 1983 and 1990, was punctuated by four military uprisings (1987, January 1988, December 1988 and December 1990) by the so-called *Carapintadas*, a group of dissident officers, which, while not classic coup attempts in that they did not seek to take power, nevertheless kept the entire political-military relationship turbulent.

Most analysts view the following decade, between 1990 and 2003, as one of lost opportunities. The Defence Law of 1988, which would have strengthened the Joint General Staff (*Estado Mayor Conjunto*) under a civilian-led MOD was not implemented, with the result that the MOD was not strengthened nor was the power of the chiefs of the three military services reduced. Observers attribute the lack of progress to a lack of political will to take on the military, which was overwhelmingly resistant to the change. But what did emerge from these three laws was a widening sense that the armed forces should not be allowed to engage in domestic activities, and never again be allowed to enter a person's house in Argentina. It was only when Néstor Kirchner won election in May 2003, with 22 per cent of the vote in a field of 19 candidates, following the severe economic problems of late 2001, that he took the opportunity to forcefully implement these laws, and thereby begin to establish civilian control over the armed forces.

From the start of his mandate, Kirchner confronted the armed forces, particularly the army. He immediately forced into retirement a dozen generals and put officers loyal to him into key positions. He removed photos of former President (General) Jorge Rafael Videla (1976–81) from military institutions; and he forced into retirement junior officers who disagreed with his policies.

Kirchner also saw to the implementation of the 1988 Defence Law with Law 727/2006, in June of 2006. This law established the powers of the joint staff, strengthened the civilian-led Ministry of Defence, and took power away from the chiefs of the services. The strengthened MOD itself experienced major accretions in civilian responsibilities in several critical areas of the organization (Bruneau and Goetze 2006; Llenderrozas and Chiappini 2008). They include the following: defining military roles and strategies, with a White Paper that was intended to be published sometime in 2010, but has yet to be completed; control over budgets; management of personnel, including control over military promotions; logistics; overseeing military justice; and limiting military intelligence exclusively to external roles. Several new MOD responsibilities specifically limit the role of the armed forces. For example, the air force has lost authority over the military police, meteorology and air traffic control.

Following interviews with former MOD officials and those currently working in the MOD, and from participant-observation, it is obvious that the Argentine MOD is poorly equipped to adequately fulfil all of its responsibilities bestowed by President Néstor Kirchner and the current incumbent, President Cristina Kirchner. Three chief problems limit its capability. First, the Argentine state itself is weak relative to the country's political parties, unions and civil society.

The state lacks the autonomy and means to implement many new policies. Second, the MOD, with some 700 employees, is the smallest of the ministries, yet is responsible for some 75,000 personnel in the armed forces. Third, despite efforts by past and present civilian leaders in the MOD, there is no area specialization whereby civilians can develop their expertise and make a career in national security and defence.

In short, while it became politically expedient for the two Kirchner presidencies to focus on the military, and to pass a robust set of laws to strengthen the civilian-led MOD, this does not mean that the MOD could in fact fulfil the responsibilities accruing to it. Some interviewees voiced their concern that the then Defence Minister Nilda Garré cast the institutional net too wide, and that the MOD and the personnel working there should have focused on fewer issues.

In law, specifically Law 727/2006, the military's mission is limited to external defence, specifically against state actors. The distinction is made between defence, which is the responsibility of the military, and security, which is the responsibility of the Secretariat for Domestic Security under the Ministry of Interior. Consequently, the military cannot deal with the so-called 'new threats', including terrorism, drug trafficking and organized crime, which militaries in other developing democracies have undertaken lately. What Argentina's armed forces can do are external peace-keeping missions, a bright area in the overall fairly bleak picture presented by Argentine's armed forces. It is also not surprising that the budget for the armed forces is very limited. In 2009 it was just 2.5 per cent of the national budget, and in 2010 is planned to be 2.6 per cent. The military's percentage of gross domestic product (GDP) in 2006 (the most recent data we have) was 0.92 per cent.[3]

Mongolia

Sandwiched between China and Russia, Mongolia is an important case study of civil-military relations because it is unique in the Northeast Asia region, for two reasons: first, the country has successfully consolidated democracy and, second, its decision to embrace peacekeeping as the main role for its armed forces. This very positive evolution took place even though, unlike Portugal and Romania, Mongolia is not a member of Partnership for Peace, NATO or the EU. That is, the initiative for democratic change came from indigenous factors, which, if understood, could possibly be duplicated elsewhere, including the very troubled states of Central and Southwest Asia.

Mongolia began to establish a Soviet-modelled set of defence institutions after independence from China in 1921, henceforward providing a bulwark for the USSR against China. The entire Mongolian political-military complex duplicated the Soviet system: a hierarchy of Communist Party officials exercised parallel – and ultimate – authority over military and political officers at all levels, and over military decision-making. By the end of the 1960s, the Soviet 39th Army had 82,000 men stationed in-country; their accompanying families brought the total to more than 100,000 Soviets citizens in Mongolia. The Soviets trained the Mongolian military primarily in-country, but 35 per cent of the Mongolian officer corps was trained in the USSR, while 80 per cent of the commanding officers graduated from Soviet professional military schools. By 1980, the Mongolian armed forces, designated the 5th Army, were interoperable with the Soviet armed forces, and were prepared to operate jointly with the 39th Soviet Army in Mongolia and the Far Eastern Military District of the USSR.

Mongolia's transition to democracy: the role of the military

The relatively peaceful transition to democracy in Mongolia has been studied by a number of competent foreign observers, and I will not repeat their analyses here except to emphasize that it was achieved without major disruption under the guidance of the socialist Mongolian People's Revolutionary Party (MPRP), which had been the sole political power almost since independence. The MPRP was later joined by other, more democratic political parties in the post-Soviet period (Fish 1998, 2001).

What interests us here is the dismantling of the highly politicized Soviet system of civil–military relations and its replacement by a democratic system. These separate processes encompassed the elimination of the political department of the MOD, the abolition of political training for military personnel, agreements between the MOD and the political parties to keep the military out of politics, and, finally, but just as important, establishment of a firm foundation for democratic civil–military relations. These laws covered virtually all aspects of civil–military relations, including a Law on the National Security Council (1992), the Law on Defence (1993), a National Security Concept (1994) and the Law on the Armed Forces (2002). By my count, between the 1992 Constitution and today, 18 laws have been passed that regulate some aspect of national security and defence. I believe that, despite some problems, including riots and allegations of fraud in the elections in July 2008, democracy has become consolidated in Mongolia and the country is well on its way to embracing a democratic model of civil–military relations. And, while a majority of the country's military forces remain committed to territorial in-country defence, peacekeeping is by far the most important role for the military.

As Jargalsaikhan Mendee and David Last (2008: 6) propose, there are at least four motivations for Mongolia to become involved in peace support operations. First, with its 'third neighbour policy', the country seeks to attract like-minded allies through multilateral action to balance the influence of its large and powerful immediate neighbours. Second, due to limited budgets for the armed forces, reimbursement by the United Nations for equipment and training offers a strong motivation for Mongolia to participate in PSO. Third, external standards for readiness have forced Mongolia's leadership to prioritize training and equipment for the armed forces. And, fourth, 'rebranding' the army for international service helps Mongolia move beyond the Cold War paradigms that no longer serve national purposes. As Mendee and Last (2008: 6) observe: '[T]he four motivations were most acutely perceived within the Ministry of Defence but formed an all-party consensus that survived successive changes of government.' Between approximately 2002, when the first troops were dispatched for UN missions, and today, Mongolia has contributed troops to PSO missions in Kosovo, Iraq and Afghanistan, as well as ten UN-sponsored missions. This, then, is the context in which to examine the key issues of democratic civilian control and effectiveness.

It should not be surprising that these ongoing changes are leading to tensions, analyses and further plans for change. During a research trip to Mongolia in mid-June 2010, I learned that a new National Security Concept is being developed, and many of the laws dealing with national security and defence from the early 1990s are being reviewed and revised. Also, at both the presidential and prime ministerial levels, programmes have been developed to engage broader sectors of the population in issues involving national security and defence. The main tensions regarding democratic civilian control and effectiveness have logically arisen from the nature of Mongolia's democratic consolidation, whereby various institutions, including the National Security Council (NSC), the MOD, and the General Staff, would share authority.

No single institution, including the president, the prime minister or the speaker of parliament (the State Great *Hural*), can monopolize power and, unsurprisingly, there are continuing tensions in national security and defence policy decision-making, including with regard to peacekeeping. While training exercises at the Five Hills PSO training centre are supervised by the General Staff, the National Defence University (NDU), which has a monopoly on professional military education and is supposed to have a department dedicated to studying and teaching PSO, is under the auspices of the MOD. Cooperation between them is minimal because they are in competition for control and resources. Consequently, the main role of the armed forces is not being fully supported by the NDU. Furthermore, because the Mongolian NSC was created to divide powers among the president, prime minister and speaker of parliament, an inter-agency process, which in some countries is sponsored and promoted by an NSC-type body, is not one of its goals (Bruneau and Matei 2009). In short, strategically developed means to consolidate democracy, including removing political officers from the armed forces and the armed forces from politics, have affected military effectiveness, at least from the perspective of PSO. There are current efforts to attempt to reform in order to increase effectiveness while maintaining a balance to ensure democracy.

Peace support operations have helped strengthen the effectiveness of Mongolia's civilian control; diffused new norms of professionalism (especially a corps of non-commissioned officers, which did not exist before); and increased inter-agency collaboration among the loosely connected security institutions – border troops, internal troops, the intelligence community and the police. The current budget commitment of 1.4 per cent of GDP, which the Minister of Defence Luvsanvandan Bold, said he hoped would reach 4 per cent, shows that Mongolia is in fact supporting its military.

Considering its history and location, Mongolia has made impressive progress in democratic consolidation, establishing civilian control over the armed forces, and ensuring effectiveness, especially in PSO. There are adjustments taking place, and a fairly wide awareness of the need to continue updating and adjusting policy and practice.

Portugal

Portugal is a relatively new democracy; the country's military-led coup on 25 April 1974 initiated the third wave of democratization (Huntington 1991). The authoritarian regime that led the country from 1928 to 1974 was not a military dictatorship (although the military supported it), but fighting three separate counter-insurgency wars in its African colonies between 1961 and 1974 caused the Portuguese armed forces to balloon to 200,000 men and absorb half of the national budget. The 1974 coup, and ensuing two years of military rule, under a divided but generally leftist leadership, gave the armed forces extensive legal and de facto prerogatives that were gradually pared down over the next 20 years of civilian-led governments. A civilian-led MOD was empowered in the early 1990s, and civilian control ultimately pervaded all aspects of national defence and security policy. Since 2008 the armed forces are being modernized by law and, increasingly, in fact: the MOD has been further strengthened, the armed forces have set up a joint operational command, and personnel are taking part in joint professional military education. The Portuguese case, in short, embodies both democratic civilian control and effectiveness. The causal factors that allow us to best understand these major reforms are found in both domestic politics and external inputs from NATO and the European Union.

Portugal's transition to democracy: the role of the military

The third wave of democratization began on 25 April 1974 when the Armed Forces Movement (MFA), composed of some 200 junior- and mid-level officers, overthrew the civilian-led authoritarian regime that had been founded almost 50 years before. Following a struggle for political power between different political and military factions over the next two years, the country gradually made a transition to democracy, albeit one with the armed forces playing an important role. The 1976 Constitution grew out of a political pact between the MFA and the four main political parties, and enshrined a continuing role for the armed forces in a non-elected, exclusively military Revolutionary Council, which both monopolized powers regarding the armed forces and defence policy, and served as a constitutional court. In short, while the Portuguese government was not a military regime during the long period of authoritarian rule, the transition to democracy paradoxically inserted the armed forces as a central element of political power. The fact that the cabinet of the civilian government included military officers also guaranteed the military broad powers and privileges. Cementing this trend, when General Ramalho Eanes was elected president in 1976 and again in 1981, he combined the role of head of state with that of chief of the general staff of the armed forces. In short, democratic Portugal began with a very large military component but, contrary to expectations, this fact may actually have been what allowed Portugal to make the transition gradually and peacefully. From the first election in 1976, until 1987, no political party received a majority of seats in parliament; the country saw ten governments and five general elections over that decade. While democratic politics was unstable, the military, with its extensive prerogatives, was relatively stable.

Portugal undertook some tentative reforms to sort out civil–military relations once it opened negotiations for accession to the European Community (EC) in 1978, including the creation in 1982 of an MOD headed by a strong civilian politician. The 1976 Constitution was revised in 1982 and the all-military Revolutionary Council abolished, while other aspects of the constitution were modified to facilitate Portuguese entry into the EC. In that same year the *Lei de Defesa Nacional e das Forças Armadas* ('Law on National Defence and the Armed Forces'), elaborated by Defence Minister Diogo Freitas do Amaral, reformed the structure of the armed forces and began to redefine its relationship to the elected civilian government. It thus took six years of incremental change before the armed forces were tentatively brought under formal democratic civilian control (Bruneau and Macleod 1986).

It would take another decade, beginning in approximately 1992, and a stable government under one political party (the Social Democratic Party (PSD)) before civilian control was consolidated. Beginning in 1990, Defence Minister Fernando Nogueira, the second most powerful figure in the PSD government, developed a public campaign involving a series of public meetings and publications to promote the ascendancy of democratically elected civilians over the armed forces. It was only in February 1993 that the basic laws defining the powers of the MOD in relationship to the three services and the chiefs of the general staff were passed. These laws transferred decision-making powers from the armed forces to the civilian-led MOD, and greatly enhanced the ability of the MOD to control the armed forces. By 1994, 20 years after the coup, Portuguese civil–military relations resembled those of other NATO and EC countries, not in small part because these organizations and several of their prominent members actively influenced the evolution of civil–military relations in Portugal.

It took another 12 years, culminating in 2006, before reforms to the operational structure of the armed forces and joint professional military education would be implemented. Under the leadership of Nuno Severiano Teixeira, defence minister for three years from July 2006, the MOD modernized its operations and further strengthened control and oversight, and set up a joint operational command structure, Estado-Maior General das Forças Armadas (EMGFA). At the time of writing, the joint operational structure is being implemented: on 6 April 2010, Rear Admiral Pereira da Cunha was nominated to be the first chief of the EMGFA. The MOD also redefined professional military education, reducing from three to one the schools that each armed service maintained, and sharing a senior joint school. In my interview with Minister Nuno Severiano Teixeira in March 2010, he specifically emphasized that the major reforms in the MOD, and the creation of the joint operational command, were necessary to increase the effectiveness of Portugal's armed forces for contemporary global, European and NATO, and domestic security.

Romania

Like Portugal, Romania is also a relatively new democracy. The country went through a violent revolutionary transition from being one of the most oppressive authoritarian regimes in Central and Eastern Europe to a functioning democracy, beginning after the fall of the Soviet Union in December 1989. It is now, two decades later, a full NATO and EU member, as well as a security partner to many other countries and organizations. Romania has built the basic institutions to consolidate democracy, and its commitment to democratic norms has included a comprehensive reform of its security and military forces to make them smaller, more flexible, and interoperable with Western counterparts. Institutionalizing democratic civil-military relations was a key component of the overall reform process. Like many other post-Soviet Central and Eastern European countries, NATO and the EU were highly influential in these reforms.

Romania's transition to democracy: the role of the military

Since 1989, the Romanian military has been brought under democratic control and made more effective through a five-phase process that involved NATO, the Partnership for Peace, the United States and the EU in domestic and global levels of cooperation. The first phase (December 1989–February 1990) was dominated primarily by ad hoc attempts to depoliticize the military, hasty promotions to higher ranks for those personnel who had been frozen in rank during the communist regime (to eliminate injustices, and not necessarily based on merit or as a corrective to existing systemic dysfunctions), as well as reactivation and appointments to strategic positions for several generals fired by the deposed dictator Nicolae Ceauşescu. The second phase (February 1990–3), saw the establishment of institutions such as the National Defence Supreme Council (1991), which serves as the main national security and defence coordinator, and the National Defence College (1992), to provide military and defence education for military personnel, civilians within the military system, and others. This phase brought in a legal foundation for civil-military relations, such as the drafting and adoption of several laws and government resolutions on defence matters (including the 1991 Constitution, the National Security Law (1991) and the first draft of the Military Doctrine and National Defence Strategy), and attempts to reform the military, including the preliminary stages of modernization and acquisition programmes.

In the third phase (1993–7), the implementation of democratic military reforms accelerated, especially to meet full NATO membership requirements. This phase started with a breakthrough in democratic civil-military relations – the appointment, in 1993, by then Minister of Defence General Nicolae Spiroiu, the first of two civilians to command positions within the military system: a deputy director of the National Defence College, and a deputy minister of defence (Muresan and Zulean 2008: 155–176). On the same note, it is worth mentioning Romania's adoption in 1994 of the Organization for Security and Cooperation in Europe Code of Conduct, which included a chapter dealing with civilian control of the military. During that same year, Romania became the first East European country to join NATO's Partnership for Peace, membership in which involved a host of reform plans and interoperability programmes (e.g. the Planning and Review Process), which helped NATO identify and evaluate membership candidates' forces and capabilities for training, exercises and operations conducted in cooperation with the Atlantic Alliance.

Despite all these changes, however, Romania's pace of reform was sluggish and, together with other interoperability and civil-military issues, prevented accession in the first wave of enlargement of the Atlantic Alliance, in 1997.[4] The fourth phase of reform (1997–2004) involved more sustained and comprehensive reforms, to ensure integration in the second wave of NATO enlargement.[5] During this period, an important catalyst was the NATO Membership Action Plan, adopted in 1999. In 1998 Romania issued the Government Ordinance on Romania's

National Defence Planning, which set up the legal framework for defence planning. Subsequently, the terrorist attacks of 11 September 2001 acted as a trigger for accelerated and effective defence and security reform in Romania, also encouraged by Romania's involvement in the war in Afghanistan, leading to an invitation to join NATO in 2002. That year, a ministerial guidance stipulated new tasks for the armed forces, which included: collective defence, crisis management, counterterrorism and defence diplomacy (Matei 2002: 1–13). In 2002, at the Prague Summit, NATO formally invited Romania to join the Alliance. This phase culminated in 2004, when Romania became a full NATO member. The fifth phase (2004–present), has seen Romania's military undergo transformation as a full NATO and EU (in 2007) member. An important step in these most recent changes was the shift from conscription to fully professional armed forces in 2007.

It is clear that institutionalizing democratic civilian control of the Romanian armed forces clearly has been a key component of the country's defence reforms. The National Defence Supreme Council, which includes the president as chair and also commander-in-chief of the armed forces, the prime minister as vice-chair, and the chief of the general staff, exerts executive control by providing direction and guidance, and overseeing inter-agency coordination. Legislative control and oversight – besides the passage of laws regarding the scope, use and responsibilities of the armed forces – encompasses roles and missions, budgeting and promotions, and is exercised by Romania's bicameral parliament, through permanent and ad hoc committees.

Legislative control and oversight were actually more rigorous and effective before 2004, when the requirements for accession to NATO and the EU were the Romanians' standard for comparison, and political differences were put aside for the sake of NATO/EU integration. During that time, legislators attached greater importance to both transparency and the effectiveness of the Romanian military. After accession, however, legislators developed a laissez-faire attitude towards defence and security reform, while recent political infighting and instability, the suspension in 2007 of President Traian Basescu for constitutional violations, and especially the recent global economic crisis, pushed security and defence far down legislators' agendas. A relevant example is the delay, for more than five years, of the adoption of a draft national security law package, required by Romania's NATO and EU member status. The constitutional court exercises judicial control and oversight of the armed forces through its responsibility to verify the constitutionality of the basic documents related to defence (Muresan and Zulean 2008: 155–176). Romanian civil society and media play an important oversight role as well, by monitoring governmental actions and inactions related to military reform, and forcing the hand of the executive and legislative bodies to deal with problems (Matei 2007: 219–241).

Over time, the Romanian military has become a small, flexible and effective force. Regional and global cooperation played a key role in improving force effectiveness, by requiring that the Romanians become interoperable with Western and NATO counterparts. Since 1991, Romania's armed forces have contributed troops and intelligence personnel to various stability and reconstruction operations under the umbrella of the United Nations, NATO/EU, and with other partners and allies.[6] In 2009, NATO, acknowledging the Romanian military's excellent intelligence capabilities, established a HUMINT (human intelligence) Centre of Excellence in Oradea, Romania, which was effective during operations in Afghanistan, Kosovo and Iraq.

Overall, despite severe challenges, Romania's military made a successful transition from a big military force prepared for total war against traditional state adversaries to a small, NATO-interoperable expeditionary force. The Romanian government instituted a more comprehensive legal framework, new missions and roles, modern education and training programmes for both military and civilian personnel, and perhaps most importantly, new defence policy and strategy. Romanians' unanimous desire and willingness to join NATO and the EU, as well as the two organizations' membership demands, encouraged these changes. Decision-makers tried to set aside differences; the MOD not only opened its ranks for civilians, but created a system to educate and promote them; members of parliament undertook more effective control and oversight; and the armed forces strove to fulfil the interoperability and capability goals set by NATO.

Conclusions

This chapter argues that contemporary civil-military relations must be understood to include both democratic civilian control *and* military effectiveness. Civilian politicians may be reluctant to spend time on the issue of effectiveness, or provide the necessary resources to the armed forces to ensure they can fulfil their roles, because matters of national security and defence do not bring in votes. Military leaders are reticent because the question of why a country should fund forces that are unlikely to fight wars may come up, an issue that also periodically arises in many older and newer democracies. In the cases of Mongolia, Portugal and Romania, their governments use the military as an instrument for other, non-military purposes. In Mongolia, the military is an important part of the 'third neighbour' strategy, to stay independent from China and Russia. Military democratization and stability have also been a selling point for development donors such as the Millennium Challenge Corporation, and its peacekeeping role a means to solidify relations with Germany, Belgium and France over Kosovo and Afghanistan (for more on this, see Dumbaugh and Morrison 2009). In Portugal, military cooperation, such as allowing the US access to a military base in the Azores, helps keep the United States engaged in regional concerns, while helping balance against Spain and the EU. Similarly, in Romania the military is a means to support national autonomy *vis-à-vis* its Slav neighbours, by cooperating with the US on access to airbases and, recently, a site for an anti-ballistic missile base. Thus, effectiveness cannot be viewed only in domestic security terms – any cost-benefit analysis must consider the global and strategic implications. The leaders of these three nations realize this.

Another lesson that emerges from this chapter, one that pertains to all four countries considered, is that a successful transition from an egregiously non-democratic regime is possible. There is no doubt today that the four countries presented here are consolidated democracies with militaries that are under civilian control. Not surprisingly, it took new, elected leaderships time to assert democratic civilian control in Argentina and Portugal, but the timing seems to have been mainly a matter of political will. Romania clearly was assisted by anticipated membership in NATO and the EU, but even in Mongolia, where there were no alliances to join, democratic consolidation, including civilian control of the armed forces, was rapid.

All four countries also demonstrate that the process of consolidating democratic civilian control and increasing the effectiveness of the armed forces are unfinished tasks. Their governments are continually updating legal bases for control, establishing new policies and processes, and improving training and education of personnel, both civilian and military. Argentina has yet to discover how to have both control and effectiveness, but even that country's experiences can serve as a useful model to other new democracies that emerge from military dictatorships and need to bring their military under democratic control.

Notes

1 The views expressed here are the author's alone and do not necessarily represent those of the Department of the Navy or the Department of Defence.

2 The research team includes Cristiana Matei, who is a lecturer at the Center for Civil-Military Relations (CCMR) in California, and has researched and published extensively on Romania, and Colonel Jargalsaikhan Mendee, who was also my graduate student at the Naval Postgraduate School and has done extensive research on Mongolia.

3 By way of comparison, the world on average spends 2% of GDP on militaries. Brazil spends 1.7%, while Colombia, with its decades-long insurgency, spends 3.4%. Country Comparison – Military Expenditures, CIA World Factbook: https://www.cia.gov/library/publications/the-world-factbook/ (accessed 20 September 2011).

4 Czech Republic, Hungary and Poland.

5 These included, among other measures: reducing the size of the armed forces; increasing the number of civilians in the armed forces and ministry of defence; institutionalizing defence planning, policy and strategy; improving human resource management; strengthening education and training for both military and civilian personnel; speeding up professionalization; improving the budgeting and acquisition processes and modernizing equipment; fostering inter-agency coordination and cooperation; consolidating democratic civilian control; and ensuring regional and international cooperation.

6 These include Iraq-Kuwait, Somalia, Angola, Congo, East Timor, Ethiopia-Eritrea, Bosnia-Herzegovina, Kosovo, Afghanistan and Iraq.

References

Aguero, F. (1995) *Soldiers, Civilians, and Democracy: Post-Franco Spain in Comparative Perspective*. Baltimore, MD, and London: Johns Hopkins University Press.

—— (2009) 'The New "Double Challenge": Democratic Control and Efficacy of Military, Police, and Intelligence.' In *Democracies in Danger*, ed. Alfred Stepan. Baltimore, MD: Johns Hopkins University Press.

Bruneau, T. C. (2011) *Patriots for Profit: The Growth of Private Security Contractors*. Stanford: Stanford University Press.

—— and A. Macleod (1986) *Politics in Contemporary Portugal: Parties and the Consolidation of Democracy*. Boulder, CO: Lynne Rienner Publishers.

—— and F. C. Matei (2008) 'Towards a New Conceptualization of Democratization and Civil-Military Relations', *Democratization*, 15 (5), pp. 909–929.

—— and —— (2009) 'National Security Councils: Their Potential Functions in Democratic Civil-Military Relations', *Defense & Security Analysis*, 25 (3), pp. 255–269.

—— and R. B. Goetze (2006) 'Ministries of Defense and Democratic Control'. In *Who Guards the Guardians and How: Democratic Civil-Military Relations*, ed. T. C. Bruneau and S. D. Tollefson. Austin: University of Texas Press.

Diamond, L. and F. Plattner Marc, eds (1996) *Civil-Military Relations and Democracy*. Baltimore, MD, and London: Johns Hopkins University Press.

—— *et al.* eds (1997) *Consolidating the Third Wave Democracies*. Baltimore, MD and London: Johns Hopkins University Press.

Dumbaugh, K. and W. M. Morrison (2009) *Mongolia and U.S. Policy: Political and Economic Relations*. CRS Report for Congress (7-5700) 18 June 2009.

Edmunds, T. (2006) 'What are Armed Forces For? The Changing Nature of Military Roles in Europe', *International Affairs*, 82 (6), pp. 1059–1075.

Finer, S. E. (2003) *The Man on Horseback: The Role of the Military in Politics*. Second Printing. New Brunswick (USA) and London: Transaction Publishers (Originally published 1962).

Fish, M. S. (1998) 'Mongolia: Democracy Without Prerequisites', *Journal of Democracy*, 9 (3), pp. 127–141.

—— (2001) 'The Inner Asian Anomaly: Mongolia's Democratization in Comparative Perspective', *Communist and Post-Communist Studies*, 34, pp. 323–338.

Gunther, R., P. N. Diamandouros and H-J. Puhle, eds (1995) *The Politics of Democratic Consolidation: Southern Europe in Comparative Perspective*. Baltimore, MD, and London: Johns Hopkins University Press.

Huntington, Samuel P. (1991) *The Third Wave: Democratization in the Late Twentieth Century*. Norman: University of Oklahoma Press.

Linz, J. J. and A. Stepan (1996) *Problems of Democratic Transition and Consolidation: Southern Europe, South America, and Post-Communist Europe*. Baltimore, MD, and London: Johns Hopkins University Press.

Llenderrozas, E. and A. Chiappini (2008) *Metodologia Para El Analisis de Los Ministerios de Defensa: El caso Argentina*. Buenos Aires: Red de Seguridad y Defensa de America Latina (RESDAL).

Matei, M. (2002) 'Transformation of the Romanian Armed Forces in the Post-September 11 Environment: New Principles, New Missions, and New Capabilities for a New NATO'. Geneva: Geneva Centre for the Democratic control of Armed Forces (DCAF).

Matei, C. (2007) 'Romania's Transition to Democracy and the Role of the Press in Intelligence Reform'. In *Reforming Intelligence: Obstacles to Democratic Control and Effectiveness*, ed. T. C. Bruneau and S. Boraz. Austin: University of Texas Press.

Mendee, J. and D. Last (2008) 'Whole of Government Responses in Mongolia: From Domestic Response to International Implications', *The Pearson Papers*, 11 (2), pp. 1–22.

The Military Balance, 1988–1989, London, 1988.

Mongol, T. T. T. (1996) *A Concise History of Mongolian Military, Volume 2 (1911–1990)*. Ulaanbaatar: Institute for Defense Studies, Ulaanbaatar.

Muresan, L. and M. Zulean (2008) 'From National, Through Regional, to Universal … : Security and Defense Reform in Romania'. In *Global Politics of Defense Reform*, ed. T. C. Bruneau and H. Trinkunas. New York: Palgrave-Macmillan.

Palamdorj, Sh. and P. Fluri (2003) *Democratic Oversight and Reform of Civil Military Relations in Mongolia (A Self Assessment)*. Ulaanbaatar-Geneva-Moscow: DCAF and the Mongolian Institute for Defence Studies.

Pion-Berlin, D. (1997) *Through Corridors of Power: Institutions and Civil-Military Relations in Argentina*. University Park, Pennsylvania: Pennsylvania State University Press.

Przeworski, A. (1991) *Democracy and the Market: Political and Economic Reforms in Eastern Europe and Latin America*. Cambridge: Cambridge University Press.

Schmitter, P. C. (1995) 'The Consolidation of Political Democracies: Processes, Rhythms, Sequences and Types'. In *Transitions to Democracy*, ed. G. Pridham. Darthouth: Aldershot, pp. 536–569.

Stepan, A. (1988) *Rethinking Military Politics: Brazil and the Southern Cone*. Princeton, NJ: Princeton University Press.

Strachan, H. (2005) 'The Lost Meaning of Strategy', *Survival*, 47 (3).

Teixeira, N. S. (2009) *Contributos Para Uma Politica de Defesa: Julho de 2006 a Julho de 2009*. Lisbon: Ministerio da Defesa Nacional.

Ulrich, M. P. (1999) *Democratizing Communist Militaries: The Cases of the Czech and Russian Armed Forces*. Ann Arbor: University of Michigan Press.

Worden, R. L. and A. M. Savada (1991) *Mongolia: A Country Study*. Washington, DC: Library of Congress.

Zulean, M. (2002) 'Transformation of the Romanian Civil-Military Relations After 1989'. *Working Paper Series-No. 25*. Geneva: DCAF.

14

Political parties

Vicky Randall

As earlier chapters in this volume have shown, although there is continuing intense academic interest in the question of democratization, the assumptions surrounding this topic are perceptibly changing. While the emphasis has shifted from democratic transition ('transitology') to 'consolidology', there is also growing recognition not only of the limits of democratic achievement in many countries but also of backsliding into authoritarianism. One feature of this analysis that has been remarkably constant, however, is the belief that political parties have a crucial part to play in political outcomes where democracy is concerned.

A succession of authors (for instance Burnell (2004), Scarrow (2005) and Janda (2005)) have echoed Lipset's view (2001) of the 'indispensability of parties' in the process and achievement of democratization. There is, moreover, increasing interest in the specific ways in which parties can play a constructive role in democratization. There is also beginning to be some recognition that their contribution may well vary depending on the stage or aspect of the democratization process one is assessing. Further, there is growing realization that in many cases parties may not only fail to play such a constructive role, but may themselves be a major obstacle to democratization – that is, 'part of the problem'.

These are the issues to be explored further in this chapter. Discussion will focus on the so-called 'developing' world, loosely coterminous with Asia, Africa and South America, regions that have undergone variable processes of democratization over the last three decades. We shall consider the role of parties, and party systems, in not only building but also obstructing and deforming democracy. But before doing so, it is necessary to look more directly at parties themselves, their characteristics, variations, interactions and settings.

Political parties

Political parties take such different forms that there is no entirely satisfactory and encompassing definition. Coleman and Rosberg (1964: 2) offer a useful starting point, which does not, for instance, presuppose a context of multiparty competition. They describe parties as ' associations formally organized with the explicit and declared purpose of acquiring and/or maintaining legal control, either singly or in coalition or electoral competition with other similar associations over the personnel and the policy of the government of an actual or prospective sovereign state'. But there are some parties that are not centrally interested in gaining power and many that lack clear organizational boundaries between themselves and, say, a social or guerrilla movement or the military. To cite Lawson (1994: 296): 'One of the main differences between parties and other organizations is that it is sometimes much harder to know where a party starts and stops'.

There have been many attempts to devise typologies of parties, but these are largely confined to Western party contexts and have tended to focus on organizational features. They have generated such categories as 'cadre parties', 'mass parties', 'catch-all parties' and, more recently, 'cartel' and 'electoral-professional parties'. Yet, whilst these categories are not entirely irrelevant to the developing world, nor are they particularly representative. One widely cited typology that aspires to more universal coverage is provided by Gunther and Diamond (2003). Their classification goes beyond organization to take account of ideology and strategic orientation, which enables them to introduce such conceptual innovations as the 'proto-hegemonic fundamentalist party' as represented by the former Welfare Party, now the Justice and Development Party (AKP), in Turkey, as a subtype of the mass party, and the ethnicity-based party, whether based on ethnic group or multi-ethnic in composition. While this is a distinct improvement, it still fails somehow to capture the central variations among parties in developing countries.

In the absence, then, of any very satisfactory typology applicable to parties in the developing world, I suggest that one important and perhaps underestimated distinction between parties concerns the nature of their origins. On this basis, and very roughly, I further suggest that one can distinguish three main types of parties in developing countries. First, the numerically small but politically important category of parties that have developed out of a pre-existing social or political movement. In the past, this often developed out of an anti-colonial or nationalist movement; more recently it has typically emerged from a religiously based movement or a movement for democracy such as the Movement for Democratic Change (MDC) in Zimbabwe. Brazil's Workers Party (PT), founded in 1980, arguably also belongs to this group. Its original members included new left intellectuals and church activists, but the leading role was played by the politically independent Metalworkers Union. Such parties tend to be relatively 'institutionalized' in the sense of having a considerable mass base, ideological appeal and elaborated organization.

Second is the more commonly found category of parties that have been sponsored in some sense by government, or the state, itself. Recent examples include the National Democratic Congress (NDC) created to represent the Rawlings government in Ghana, following the onset of multiparty politics in 1990, and the Pakistan Muslim League sponsored by General (retd.) Pervez Musharraf, when president of Pakistan between 2001 and 2008. Parties sponsored by government in this way will generally have easy access to resources, including patronage, but are likely to have little organizational autonomy.

The third and numerically most common kind of party is largely built around the ambitions of a single leader and often referred to as 'personalistic'. Such parties, established as vehicles for individual, generally wealthy, politicians, have been numerous in recent competitive elections in tropical Africa but also abound in Latin America and Asia. A particularly striking example has been Thailand's *Thai Rak Thai* Party, formed by media business tycoon Thaksin Shinawatra, which gained an absolute majority in the parliament elected in November 2000, even though it had only been formed a few months before. Such parties tend to be overly dependent on their leader as the basis of popular support, and to enjoy little organizational autonomy from them. Accordingly, they are frequently extremely short-lived.

But individual parties cannot be understood on their own; they need to be seen within the wider party system generally, understood as the system of interaction between component parties. Again, different typologies of party systems have been offered. Sartori's influential (1976) classification takes into account the number of 'relevant' parties, including those with most votes and seats but also others with blackmail or coalition potential, the degree of ideological polarization, and whether or not the overall system is authoritarian or competitive. Out of this scheme, a series of party "system types" emerges. Within the authoritarian party system, various types can be found, including both one-party systems and systems in which one party is hegemonic, while other parties are permitted to exist within narrow constraints, as in Mexico until 1997 under the rule of the Institutional Revolutionary Party (PRI), and in Singapore under the People's Action Party (PAP). Within competitive frameworks, Sartori distinguished two-party systems, and more fragmented systems of limited or extreme pluralism. But, perhaps of special relevance for our topic, he identified the 'predominant party system' where, despite genuine party competition, one party remains dominant over several elections. This has particular purchase in sub-Saharan Africa, where van de Walle (2003: 298) suggested it was indeed the 'emerging modal' type.

Looking more specifically at the process of democratization, with particular reference to Latin America, Mainwaring and Scully (1995) have built on this approach, while adding a new dimension of (competitive or democratic) party system 'institutionalization'. The criteria for institutionalization include that there should be stability in the rules and nature of inter-party competition, and that political actors should accord legitimacy to parties and the party system, as well as requiring that component parties should be organized and well rooted in society.

To spell out the implications of what has been said so far, I have noted that political parties can vary significantly both organizationally and in other respects and, other things being equal, this indicates variation in the relationship between parties and democratic processes, and specifically variation in parties' contribution to democratization and democracy. Within developing democracies, the numerically preponderant personalistic parties are perhaps least likely to make a positive contribution, although government-sponsored and even movement-based parties are by no means assured of doing so. But parties also combine in-party systems that similarly vary on a number of dimensions. While by definition competitive party systems are more likely to be positively associated with democracy than non-competitive systems, within the former category, predominant party systems in particular can pose problems for democratic consolidation.

Before moving on from this discussion of party and party system characteristics, another important, if obvious, point must be stressed: neither party nor party system operate in a vacuum, as they interact dynamically within a wider social and political context. That is to say, there is a limit to the extent that they can be addressed simply as independent variables. Especially relevant will be the extent and character of social or cultural cleavages in a country. In sub-Saharan Africa, for example, this is a reference to the specific degree of ethnic 'fractionalization', which can have an important bearing on political processes and democratic outcomes. In addition, the historical context of elections can have major consequences and, as discussed further below, the very manner in which the process of democratization emerges can itself impact significantly on parties. Finally, much scholarly attention has focused on the constitutional context, especially the nature of the electoral system and of executive power, including the prevalence of strong presidential systems (this is not, of course, a one-way street, since parties may themselves have helped to shape constitutional arrangements).

Parties building democracy

As we have seen, it has become almost axiomatic that political parties have a vital role to play in successful democratization. Next we consider how parties and party systems might be expected to contribute positively to democratization, and the extent to which and in what circumstances these expectations have been realized in recent democratization outcomes in the developing world.

Parties in the early transition phase

While one should be ever conscious of the dangers of teleological thinking, it is reasonable to distinguish between the earliest phases of the democratization process and what follows. In the relevant literature, perhaps surprisingly, the tendency has been for less attention to be paid and for expectation to be lower concerning parties' contribution in the earliest stages of democratization. In fact, curiously, this may be one area where the role of parties has actually been underestimated. Processes of transition are notoriously complex and varied: it is not easy to isolate the contribution of particular sets of actors. Still, there are at least three ways in which particular parties appear to have furthered the process at this stage.

In the first scenario, opposition or pro-democracy parties have formed whilst still risking authoritarian reprisals. Admittedly, more commonly it is social movements or civil society groups that have articulated democratic demands in the initial stages of transition, but the distinction between movement and party can often be difficult to draw and in some cases the movements have formed (into) parties prior to the winning of substantial political concessions. An example is the Democratic Progressive Party (DPP) in Taiwan, formed as a party in 1986, and bringing together different factions of the '*dangwai*' or outside- party movement (including defence lawyers of political prisoners), five years before the founding of new parties was made legal in 1991. It is possible that both the Movement for Democratic Change in Zimbabwe, and the National League for Democracy led by Aung San Suu Kyi in Myanmar, will retrospectively be seen as falling into this category, although sadly neither has yet witnessed the democratic transition it seeks.

A second scenario is when parties have been principal participants in a pact-making process leading to some new kind of proto-democratic settlement. This could be seen in regard to the African National Congress's role in South African transition in the early 1990s, for instance, or the parties involved in the pacted transition in Chile in the late 1980s. A variation on this theme is in the wake of civil wars, where the army-parties, admittedly often under considerable external pressure, have come together to agree the basis of a new, eventually democratic order. Such a role was played by the *Frente de Libertação de Moçambique* (FRELIMO) and *Resistência Nacional Moçambicana* (RENAMO) in Mozambique, for instance, and the Farabundo Marti National Liberation Front (FMLN), which helped to draw up the 1992 peace accords in El Salvador.

Third, formerly ruling parties have, on occasion, themselves taken some of the initiative in introducing reforms to open up the political process. This is relatively uncommon, since ruling parties have generally been more inclined to engineer an electoral transition that ensures their continuing de facto dominance, or, as du Toit (1999) phrases it, to act more as a 'bridgehead' to further dominance and less as a 'bridge' to a more democratic system of rule. Perhaps the least disputed case is that of the KMT (*Kuomintang*) in Taiwan, which as ruling party throughout the 1980s steadily widened the scope for political participation. This observation, of course, has to be squared with the reference above to the role of the DPP as a pro-democracy party. It could also be argued that the KMT was responding to external pressure and that it expected to be able to retain its dominant position. Nonetheless, it triggered a genuine democratization process. Hood (1997) attributes this in part to a quasi-democratic component in the KMT's ideology, ultimately inherited from the party's founder, Sun Yat-sen, while Tan (2002) shows how conflict amongst the party's internal factions provided a vital mechanism of adaptation and change.

Parties' potential contribution to democratic consolidation

If parties' contribution to initial democratizing developments has been downplayed, much more attention has been devoted to their role in democratic consolidation. As is elaborated elsewhere in this volume, democratic consolidation, like democracy, is a thoroughly contested concept. Understandings of consolidation range from the most limited, emphasizing electoral procedures and outcomes, to the most demanding, requiring substantial expansion of participation and the necessary reduction in social and economic inequality to ensure this. This might lead us to expect that perceptions of how parties could contribute would be similarly varied, although in practice the more striking observation is that the ways in which parties could contribute has received little systematic attention. Moreover, there is a tendency to think more in terms of party and party systems functioning to maintain democracy than to consider how they assist in the process of building democracy.

At any rate, drawing on the available literature (King 1969; Dalton and Wattenberg 2000; Randall and Svåsand 2002a) one could suggest that parties and party systems could potentially contribute to democratic consolidation in the following main ways (summarized in box below). First, and perhaps most importantly of all, they could provide a means of *political representation*. This has long been recognized as a key democratic function of parties, captured in Sartori's dictum (1976: 27) that parties are or should be 'an instrument ... for representing the people by expressing their demands'.

Within the general literature on political representation, there is by now a well-established distinction between descriptive and substantive forms of representation and debate about how far the latter requires the former, as encapsulated in the notion of the 'politics of presence' (Phillips 1995). Beyond this, the relationship between political parties and representation is neither theoretically straightforward nor satisfactorily addressed in the literature. But we can draw on Birch (1972) to suggest that, ideally, parties' representative role involves first being attentive to the concerns of their grass-roots supporters. However, rather than simply relaying these concerns or even 'aggregating' them, the party constitutes an arena in which such concerns are put in dialogue with the party's longer-term political orientation or ideology. This process helps to produce the distinctive party platform that is presented to voters. At the same time, the party, or its leadership, especially when it is the party of government, must be attentive to the wider concerns and interests of the public as a whole.

In practice, this model's applicability even to Western democratic parties varies widely. Party ideology (even when 'ideology' is understood broadly) may, for instance, be minimal. Nevertheless, the model helps to indicate aspects of party life that should enhance parties' overall representative capacity, including mechanisms for registering and relaying local people's concerns, procedures allowing for internal party debate, procedures ensuring some degree of party leadership accountability to members, and distinctive party programmes.

Second, parties could help to *instil democratic values and habits* into party supporters, members and leaders. They could do this, for instance, through their public declarations, through the way in which they conduct their internal affairs and through the manner in which they interact with other parties.

Parties' potential contribution to democratic consolidation

- political representation
- instilling democratic values
- making government vertically accountable
- organizing opposition

Thereby contributing to

- institutionalization of democracy
- regime legitimacy

Third, parties should help to *make government vertically accountable*. That is, accountable to the people. Parties should help to channel popular demands but should also, through their participation in competitive elections, enable the electorate to judge and sanction government performance. To quote Dalton and Wattenberg (2000: 9), 'with parties controlling the government (alone or in coalition), it is clear who is responsible for the government's actions'.

Fourth, parties should *facilitate horizontal accountability and organize opposition*. Horizontal accountability refers to the scrutiny of government actions or the executive provided by other governing institutions. In the case of parties, this is primarily in relation to the legislature. Parties should help to make government more accountable to the legislature. In particular, given that members of the ruling party or coalition have little incentive to criticize government, the question is how far non-governing parties are able to provide effective parliamentary opposition.

Having said that effective opposition is important, we should nonetheless note a strand of the current democratization literature that warns against the dangers of too strong an opposition, too soon. To cite Burnell (2005: 9): 'in fragile democratic transitions and especially in post-conflict situations ... sharp political confrontation between parties could be very unhelpful'. Even in somewhat more stabilized contexts, opposition needs to be responsible and respectful of parliamentary procedure.

To the extent that parties and party systems contribute to these democracy-building processes, they help to ensure consolidation of the democratic regime, in at least two further and broader respects. First, by instilling appropriate attitudes and expectations in the public, and by contriving through their own actions to 'give substance to constitutional rules and thus confirm and enlarge on the formal outcome of transition' (Pridham 1990: 22), they contribute to the *institutionalization* of democracy. Second, they help to bolster *regime legitimacy*, building reserves of goodwill to help tide fragile new democracies over bad times (Mainwaring and Scully 1995).

Assessing parties' contribution in practice

So how have political parties contributed to the process of democratic consolidation in practice? Obviously there is no simple or single answer to this question, as parties' contributions have varied enormously. Still, an overall comment could be that their positive contribution has been less significant than might be supposed. Of course, we should recognize that, even in developed democracies, parties' contribution may be overestimated. More than four decades ago, when King (1969) set out the main functions for parties in established democracies, he was sceptical concerning the extent to which they actually performed these functions.

We can organize the discussion in terms of the democracy-building functions listed above, beginning with political representation. Those favouring minimalist, procedural notions of democracy might argue that so long as parties help to organize competitive elections and provide the electorate – almost by the mere fact of their simultaneous existence – with an element of choice, they perform a representative function. Beyond this, however, assessment is more complicated.

Taking up first the distinction between descriptive and substantive representation, it could be argued that descriptive representation has indeed become an increasing concern. There are a number of parties, such as ethnically based parties in various sub-Saharan African countries, or parties such as the Bahujan Samaj Party (BSP) standing for a particular social community, the Dalits, in India, in which it is almost essential though not necessarily explicit that party leaders should be of the same group that they claim to represent. The principle of descriptive gender representation has received a special boost from the growing international support, catalyzed by events such as the Fourth World Conference on Women, held in Beijing in 1995, and transmitted by donor agencies and international non-governmental organizations, for measures to increase the political representation of women. Most of all in Latin America but also in a number of African countries, and either on the initiative of individual parties themselves or as a result of new national requirements, women's descriptive representation within parliaments has increased to such an extent that the highest rate of representation in the world – 56 per cent, following elections in 2008 – is in Rwanda. In addition, in South Africa, Costa Rica, Cuba, Mozambique, Angola, Ecuador, Argentina, Guyana and Burundi, the rate is more than 30 per cent (see the Inter-Parliamentary Union website at www.ipu.org). The value of these developments in relation to descriptive gender representation in and through political parties should not be underestimated.

But when it comes to more substantive forms of representation, most parties' contribution is arguably very limited. Contextual factors including the limited scope for programme differentiation, together with authoritarian tendencies within parties help to ensure this. The negative consequences of clientelism are especially relevant. Although some parties offer scope for more corporatist forms of group representation, the predominant idiom of representation remains clientelistic. Thus van de Walle and Butler (1999: 26) observe that: 'In Africa today, parties serve a representation function in a context of clientelistic politics.' Clientelism may offer short-term gains to party supporters, but militates against collective political consciousness and the formulation and pursuit of more long-term political interests. Within the party, it undermines the possibility of internal party democracy – discussed shortly – and forecloses the possibility of meaningful debate.

Returning to the attributes of parties identified above – that is, helping them to play a representative role – party manifestos and programmes are typically limited in content and there is frequently little attempt to differentiate them. For example, according to Wanjohi (2003: 251), 'nearly all party manifestos in Kenya look alike, often using the same phraseology, and even identical paragraphs', while in Indonesia: 'Party leaders feel no embarrassment in stating openly that all parties' platforms are "the same" or "almost the same" ' (Sherlock 2004). In this sense, voters are provided with restricted choice, although it is true that parties may embed other more symbolic cues or coded messages invoking particular community interests or identities.

We can also look more directly at evidence of the extent of inner-party democracy. Internal party democracy is not a universally accepted ideal; some see it as an encumbrance on party leadership that needs to be responsive both to the wider electorate and to political contingencies as they arise (Scarrow 2005). In practice, too, there is an innate tendency (iron law is probably an overstatement), first diagnosed by Michels (2001, originally 1915) even in avowedly democratic parties, towards oligarchic patterns of internal rule. It is clear that even in established democracies, the extent of internal democracy in many if not most parties is quite modest, although typically substantially greater in developed than in developing countries. Even so, some degree of internal democracy is needed if a party is to perform its representative function (this argument is developed further in Randall 2007).

There is a growing trend in the developing world for national laws or constitutions to require parties to include in their own rules provisions for internal democracy. Thus, in anticipation of European Union membership requirements, Article 69 of the Turkish Constitution was amended in 2001 to require that: 'The activities, internal regulations and operation of political parties shall be in line with democratic principles.' In South Asia, India, and, since 2002, Pakistan, evidence is required of internal elections before parties can register (Suri 2007). In East Asia, government regulation of the internal functioning of parties has gone furthest in Thailand and South Korea (Thornton 2002), these both being polities that traditionally have particularly suffered democratically from weak party organization. Africa lags behind these regions, although Ghana's 2000 Political Parties Act states that parties' internal organization should conform to democratic principles (Wiafe-Akenten 2004).

However, such requirements, and parties' own governing rules, are not necessarily a reliable guide to practice. In reality, there are few parties with significant levels of internal democracy. Most outstanding has been the Workers' Party (PT) in Brazil, with a pyramid of internal party representative bodies from the local level to the centre, operating in accordance with explicitly democratic rules (Samuels 2004).

There are several parties, including the African National Congress in South Africa, the United Malays National Organization (UMNO) in Malaysia and the Congress Party in India, which are to some degree based on a historical movement, and whose internal structures feature ascending tiers of at least formally representative bodies. These bodies meet and conduct their business with a reasonable degree of regularity and without everything being totally controlled from the top: upsets are possible. There are also parties such as the National Action Party (PAN) in Mexico (Mizrahi 2003) and the Democratic Progressive Party (DPP) in Taiwan (Rigger 2001), which, emerging in opposition, have retained a strong commitment to internal party democracy, even if the mechanisms for ensuring this are somewhat rudimentary. There are even movements to promote internal democracy within established former ruling parties, including the KMT in Taiwan, which in 2005 held the first direct election contest for the position of party Chair, and the Institutional Revolutionary Party (PRI) in Mexico.

Despite these instances, internal party democracy is mostly noticeable by its absence. At the far extreme we hear of parties in the Democratic Republic of Congo whose leaders 'reign like absolute monarchs' (Ngoy-Kangoy and Kabungulu 2006). And authors of a report on Bolivia's parties were told: 'Parties are built on the father-son accession processes, not ideology'; and also heard references to parties 'belonging' to particular individuals (Mandaville 2004: 21–22).

To summarize, party representation is a complex concept but, beyond a minimal contribution almost by definition entailed in party participation in competitive elections, it seems that typically parties in developing democracies do little to further substantive representation. So, what can be said about their contribution to democratic socialization? Popkin, cited by Dalton and Wattenberg (2000: 9), has characterized elections as courses in civic education, where political parties are the teachers of democratization. In short, it could be said that simply by offering a means of participation in competitive elections, parties help to induct citizens into democratic habits.

But the extent to which they do more than this is generally questionable. We have seen that internal democratic-party processes are distinctly underdeveloped. There are some parties, such as the MDC in Zimbabwe or the DPP in Taiwan, whose raison d'être in a sense has been campaigning for democracy. More typically, the overt messages of party leaders and, still more the implicit messages contained in their conduct, often do little to promote democratic values. On the one hand, there is the example of post-Pinochet Chile's longstanding cooperation or *concertao* between centre-left parties that embodied a commitment to protecting democracy. We can also note recent trends in Ghana, where Abdulai and Crawford (2010: 30) are impressed by the manner in which, following the 2008 general election, 'an incumbent party handed over power to the opposition after having taken the lead in the first round of an election, and after having lost the presidential run-off by a margin of less than 0.5%'. On the other hand, for instance, in his report on Lesotho, Olayele (2003: 1) refers to the damaging consequences of that country's parties' 'inability to transcend adversarial politics and accept the verdict of elections'. During elections in Bangladesh, violent clashes orchestrated by *mastaans* or party hoodlums, between supporters of the Awami League and the Bangladesh Nationalist Party (BNP), are a regular occurrence (Sobhan 2002). Even in the relatively established democracy of Jamaica, such clashes between adherents of the two main parties, associated in particular with the formation of local 'garrisons', have become an established feature of electoral politics (Figueroa and Sives 2002; Sky News Sunday September 2, 2007).

The third democracy-building function I have identified as providing a means of vertical accountability. To be sure, by the sheer fact of taking part in competitive elections, assuming these to be broadly free and fair, parties do help to give voters the chance to 'get the rascals out'. The value of this ultimate sanction, a powerful if blunt weapon, should never be underestimated and ruling parties, even Africa's 'predominant' parties, for all their superior resources, are not immune. Even so, the discussion so far has highlighted the typically very constrained representation of popular interests and voices through parties, other than within a clientelistic framework, and frequent absence of meaningful choice between contesting parties.

Parties can also promote horizontal accountability of the executive to the legislature, especially perhaps through providing effective legislative opposition. We have noted the potential dangers of having too strong and uncompromising an opposition early in the process of legislative institutionalization. Opposition needs to be responsible and respectful of parliamentary procedure. Thus, in Bangladesh, two relatively strong parties, the Awami League (AL) and BNP have been alternating in power since the early 1990s. However, the tendency has been for the party in opposition to deny the legitimacy of the ruling party, to boycott parliamentary sessions or stage numerous walkouts, as well as organizing anti-government strikes *(hartals)* and rallies 'seeking the premature overthrow of an elected government' (Sobhan 2002: 23).

But a much more common problem is the ineffectiveness of opposition. While contributory factors may include the prevalence of powerful presidential executives, a weakly developed committee system, and elected members' lack of technical competence or access to necessary information, equally relevant are the characteristics of parties themselves and the pattern of incentives typically associated with party politics. Opposition parties may be weak; specifically in reference to sub-Saharan Africa, Rakner and van de Walle (2007) note that they are often very small and further challenged by the growth in the number of independent candidates. Levels of discipline within parties' parliamentary wing vary considerably but are often low. In Latin America, for instance, they are relatively high in Chile, Mexico and in Brazil's PT but have traditionally been much lower in Ecuador and Colombia (Siavelis and Morgenstern 2008).

In addition, legislatures in developing countries are particularly prone to party 'hopping' or 'switching'. Deputies switch from one party to another for a range of reasons, but very often opposition deputies switch to the actually or imminently ruling party because it offers better prospects of office and resources. This has been reported, for example, in a succession of south Asian countries, as well as in the Philippines, Bolivia and Ecuador. In Brazil, around one-third of legislators in the Chamber of Deputies switch party during every four-year term (Desposato 2006). In many African countries such defections are endemic. In Senegal, as electoral competition became more meaningful in the 1990s, opposition leaders regularly showed themselves willing to be included in the government (Gavan 2001). In Mali, we are told that following the 2002 legislative elections, not only did many former opposition party members defect to the ruling party but 'all the incumbents claim to side with the ruling majority, which lends a monochrome hue to the current Malian parliament. No opposition to the current regime has a seat in Parliament' (IDEA country report 2005). Whilst increasingly regulations have been introduced to constrain this behaviour, their impact is often limited. In Malawi, for instance, Rakner and van de Walle (2007: 99) suggest that new constitutional restrictions on party switching may simply have led to an increase of the number of independent candidates: 'MPs may leave their party group and declare themselves "independent", and MPs elected as 'independents" may join an existing party group. Thus, standing as an independent provides individual MPs with, incentives in terms of striking bargains with the main party.'

Explaining parties' disappointing performance

To the extent that these specific contributions of parties and party systems to processes of democratic consolidation in developing countries are typically quite limited, this implies that their further contribution to the institutionalization of democracy and democratic regime legitimacy is similarly modest. In light of the democracy-building functions that parties are expected to perform, this might seem a very disappointing outcome. How do we explain it? The reasons are undoubtedly complex and, moreover, clearly vary in their precise character from case to case. Some have been alluded to earlier but, here, two very general contextual features will be emphasized.

First is the typical context of widespread poverty, economic insecurity and inequality in developing countries. The incidence of poverty obviously varies. It has the most crippling consequences for party organization in many sub-Saharan African countries, where, for instance, opposition parties faced with slender resources and difficulties of communication often largely restrict their organizational base to the main urban areas (Olukoshi 1998; Smith 2001). Across the developing world, economic insecurity impacts on the motives and conduct of party politicians, as in the widespread legislative practice of party-hopping. Poverty and inequality foster the clientelistic relationships that permeate political parties subverting formal party procedures.

Second is what could be called the timing factor. The process of democratization can be seen as an aspect of and against a backdrop of accelerated globalization. As Burnell (2005) has succinctly observed, 'the context which globalization now provides to the development of parties and party systems all around the world, and in new democracies specifically differs profoundly from the international environment that faced political parties in the formative days of today's long estab-lished democracies'. Put simply, globalization manifests itself in the changing global economic context, in pressures to democratize and in the development of communications technology. For this reason, as Carothers (2006) points out, although there are notable exceptions most political parties in developing democracies are very young and, in comparison with established Western parties, have experienced an extremely compressed process of development. Whereas, in theory at least, Western parties have gone through successive phases as mass parties, to catch-all, cartel and electoralist parties, those in developing democracies must move rapidly into the electoralist phase, in which winning elections is the overriding concern.

I suggested earlier that in discussing parties and democratization, one needs to be conscious of the impact of democratization on parties as well as that of parties on democratization. Especially when it has been to a degree imposed by external agents, the process of transition can arrive abruptly with little notice given before founding elections. A recurrent observation has been the very large number of parties registering for these elections, many of which then rapidly disin-tegrate – one of the more recent examples is in Afghanistan, where in 2005 more than 80 parties registered for elections to the House of the People (*Wolesi Jirga*). Typically, such parties are vehicles for ambitious individuals with minimal organizational or programmatic elaboration. In addition, in many parts of the developing world, including much of Latin America and Asia, multiparty competition has emerged or re-emerged in a transformed mass media context, reinforcing the focus on the party leader at the expense of policy issues or the party as such. Exploiting these media is often incredibly expensive, escalating the costs of electoral campaigns and thus enhancing the appeal of dubious funding sources.

Parties as the problem?

We have reached the point where we have to ask: if parties' contribution to democracy-building has in general been so deficient, does it make more sense to regard them as part of the problem rather than of the solution? In many cases, it seems that it is not simply that parties do not perform their democratic functions very well but that they are in their own right an obstacle to democracy.

In numerous developing countries, parties and corruption are perceived as almost synonymous. We have seen the pressures on parties fighting competitive elections, and in the absence of substantial membership dues or state funding, to raise adequate campaign finance. Increasingly they have recourse to what Kitschelt (2000) calls 'reverse clientelism', receiving funding from wealthy, or even semi-criminal, patrons in return for implicit future favours. A particularly scandalous example of corrupt campaign finance was in Kenya in 2001, where the funding for the 'Rainbow Coalition' under former vice-president, Mwai Kibaki, was facilitated by Anglo-Leasing, 'an entirely fictitious company whose only business was to receive funds from lucrative government contracts, then channel them back to those who dreamt up the scheme' (Mwangi 2008: 276). Party representatives within legislatures are also often perceived to use their office to their own material advantage. Parties furthermore often seek in different ways to 'buy' votes, although voters' attitudes are understandably more ambivalent regarding this arguably corrupt form of political behaviour.

In these and other ways, parties may lose voters' trust. Although survey findings vary between and within developing regions, they generally find that confidence in political parties is low, as compared for instance with other political institutions. Logan (2008) reports Afrobarometer findings for 18 African countries, observing that: 'many Africans hold political parties in relatively low esteem', while Corral (2008), writing about the Americas as a whole, finds levels of trust in political parties particularly low in Paraguay, Ecuador, Nicaragua, Peru and Bolivia (it must be said that the United States itself does not fare especially well in this survey). There is evidently widespread citizen disillusion with parties, which could feed into a loss of faith in democracy itself, although this does not automatically follow.

Another way in which parties actively inhibit democratization is where 'predominant' parties find ways to limit or even reduce their competitors' scope for manoeuvre. UMNO in Malaysia and the ANC in South Africa (Butler 2005) are familiar instances. Manning (2010) describes such a process currently occurring in Mozambique where the most recent elections, held in October 2009, were the least democratic thus far. Alhough some of the explanation lies in the incompetence of the main opposition party, RENAMO, it is also clear that 'the ruling party's dominance over state institutions has ever more severely curtailed the opposition's ability to compete' (152). The ruling party, FRELIMO, has not resorted to force or 'heavy-handed' civil liberties violations but proceeded more subtly, manipulating the legal institutions that govern elections and making use of its own superior access to state resources.

International democracy assistance and parties

It is partly this sense that parties are indeed often the 'weakest link' in the process of democratization that has in recent years led to a renewed interest on the part of the international community in providing support to parties in democratizing countries. Such assistance can come directly from bilateral or multilateral donors, often as part of general democracy assistance, but it appears that funds involved are modest. Moreover, this form of assistance can be problematic: if it appears to favour one party this may seem like unwarranted political intervention, but, on the other hand, if all relevant parties are supported, it can seem to encourage party fragmentation and polarization. Alternatively assistance comes from NGOs, intergovernmental agencies and private firms.

But by common consent some of the most significant players are party-based foundations and institutes (Kumar 2005). These provide assistance for parties in other countries, traditionally those identified as being within the same or similar ideological 'family', although this is no longer always the case. According to Amundsen (2007), there are at least 32 such bodies in the US and Europe. Probably the best known are Germany's *Stiftungen*, especially the FES (*Friedrich Ebert Stiftung*) closely linked to the Social Democratic party, and the KAS (*Konrad Adenauer Stiftung*), linked with the Christian Democrat Party (see Erdmann 2006); and, in the US, the International Republican Institute (IRI) and National Democratic Institute for International Affairs (NDI). Though such activities go back at least to the 1970s they have extended significantly from the 1990s.

Whilst there is some variation in the objectives of such assistance, commentators report that certain items tend to recur. Assistance is designed to develop organizational capacity, enable parties to participate in elections more effectively, improve parties' ability to participate in the legislature, promote internal democracy and increase the participation of groups such as women and youth. According to the objective, assistance can take different forms – for instance grants towards building party organization; technical assistance such as aid with book-keeping, media and outreach, and polling; and training through workshops, handbooks and even foreign tours.

So far, assessments of what has been achieved tend to be very qualified in their praise. The author of perhaps the most comprehensive review of this topic to date, Carothers (2006: 162) observes soberly that democratic party assistance 'rarely has transformative impact ... both because of the difficulty of the task and the inadequacies of much of the assistance'. Although Kumar (2005: 508) suggests that help with election campaigns has been more useful – 'It has enabled many nascent political parties to better participate in elections by teaching them skills and techniques they could put to use immediately' – his tone, like others, is generally more critical. There is broad agreement that approaches adopted in party assistance tend to be excessively standardized, relying too much on an outdated Western party model and failing to take into account contextual specificities.

This does not mean that such programmes should be abandoned. Carothers in particular remains convinced of the ultimate value of what they are seeking to accomplish. Nonetheless, if these programmes are to have stronger and better impact they need to be more tailored to the local political context. The initiative needs to come from party leaders not those providing the assistance, so that there is more sense of local ownership and more chance that what is provided is of genuine use. Finally, all such party assistance needs to be part of a wider project of democratic political reform, for instance of electoral processes and the operation of the legislature, if political parties are to make a more substantial contribution to democracy.

Conclusion

There is by now a substantial literature concerned with parties in emerging democracies. Much is on a case-by-case basis and not necessarily aiming to arrive at more general conclusions about the role of parties in democratization. As suggested, there have been relatively few attempts to pinpoint the precise potential contribution of parties and party systems to democracy-building. Even so, there is a growing realization that parties may not simply be failing to deliver on their democratic potential, they may actually be obstructing the process of democratization and helping to bring about democratic stagnation or backsliding. Partly as a consequence, international democracy assistance has directed increasing attention to political parties, though to date with little transformative impact.

Occasionally, the possibility is aired of democratization without parties, or where parties are largely marginal to the real democratic action (see, for instance, Enyedi and Toka 2007). But, more typically, the view continues that parties are essential as well as being, to use Carothers' term, 'inevitable'. For instance, it is increasingly accepted that civil society organizations do not provide an adequate substitute (Doherty 2001). We should, moreover, remember both that most political parties in emerging democracies are relatively young and that they are operating in a context far less conducive to stable democratic development than that surrounding the growth of the Western democratic parties with which they are so often unfavourably compared.

References

Abdulai, Abdul-Gafaru and Gordon Crawford (2010) 'Consolidating Democracy in Ghana: Progress and Prospects?', *Democratization*, 17 (1), pp. 26–67.

Amundsen, I. (2007) *Donor Support to Political Parties: Status and Principles*. Christian Michelsen Institute: Bergen, Norway.

Birch, A. H. (1972) *Representation*. Basingstoke: Macmillan.

Burnell, Peter (2004) *Building Better Democracies: Why Political Parties Matter*, Westminster Foundation for Democracy.

—— (2005) 'Globalising Party-based Democracy: Political Parties, Globalisation, and International Democracy Assistance', Centre for the Study of Globalisation and Regionalisation Working Paper, Coventry: University of Warwick.

Butler, Anthony (2005) 'How Democratic is the African National Congress?', *Journal of Southern African Studies*, 31 (4), pp. 719–736.

Carothers, Thomas (2006) *Confronting the Weakest Link: Aiding Political Parties in New Democracies*. Washington, DC: Carnegie Endowment for International Peace.

Coleman, J. and C. Rosberg, eds (1964), *Political Parties and National Integration in Africa*. Berkeley, CA: University of California Press.

Corral, Margarita (2008) '(Mis) Trust in Political Parties in Latin America', *AmericasBarometer Insights*, No. 2; available at http://www.vanderbilt.edu/lapop/ (accessed 6 May 2011).

Dalton, Russell and Martin Wattenberg (2000) 'Unthinkable Democracy: Political Change in Advanced Industrial Democracies'. In *Parties without Partisans: Political Change in Advanced Industrial Democracies*, ed. Russell Dalton and Martin Wattenberg. Oxford and New York: Oxford University Press.

Desposato, Scott W. (2006) 'Parties for Rent? Ambition, Ideology and Party-Switching in Brazil's Chamber of Deputies', *American Journal of Political Science*, 50 (1), pp. 62–80.

Doherty, Ivan (2001) 'Democracy Out of Balance: Civil Society Can't Replace Political Parties', *Policy Review*, April/May, pp. 25–35.

du Toit, Pierre (1999) 'Bridge or Bridgehead? Comparing the Party Systems of Botswana, Namibia, Zimbabwe, Zambia and Malawi'. In *The Awkward Embrace: One-Party Domination and Democracy in Industrialising Countries*, ed. Hermann Giliomee and Charles Simkins. Newark, NJ: Harwood Academic Publishers.

Enyedi, Zsolt and Gabor Toka (2007) 'The Only Game in Town: Party Politics in Hungary'. In *Political Parties in New Democracies*, ed. Paul Webb and Stephen White. Oxford: Oxford University Press, pp. 147–178.

Erdmann, Gero (2006) 'Hesitant bedfellows: The German *Stiftungen* and Party Aid in Africa'. In *Globalising Democracy: Party Politics in Emerging Democracies*, ed. Peter Burnell. London: Routledge.

Figueroa, Mark and Amanda Sives (2002) 'Homogenous Voting, Electral Manipulation and the "Garrison" Process in Post-Independence Jamaica', *Commonwealth and Comparative Politics*, 40 (1), pp. 81–108.

Gavan, Dennis (2001) 'Political Turnover and Social Change in Senegal', *Journal of Democracy*, 12 (3), pp. 51–62.

Gunther, Richard and Larry Diamond (2003) 'Species of Political Parties: A New Typology', *Party Politics*, 9 (2), pp. 167–199.

Hood, Steven J. (1997) *The Kuomintang and the Democratization of Taiwan*. Boudler, CO: Westview Press.

Janda, Kenneth (2005) *Political Parties and Democracy in Theoretical and Practical Perspective: Adopting Party Law*. Washington, DC: National Democratic Institute for International Affairs.

King, Anthony (1969) 'Political Parties in Western Democracies: Some Sceptical Reflections', *Polity*, 2, pp. 111–141.

Kitschelt, Herbert (2000) 'Linkages between Citizens and Politicians in Democratic Polities', *Comparative Political Studies*, 33 (6/7), pp. 845–879.

Kumar, Krishna (2005) 'Reflections on International Party Assistance', *Democratization*, 12 (4), pp. 505–527.

Lawson, Kay (1994) 'Conclusion'. In *How Political Parties Work*, ed. Kay Lawson. Westport, CT: Praeger.

Lipset, Seymour Martin (2001)'Cleavages, Parties and Democracy'. In *Party Systems and Voter Alignments Revisited*, ed. L. Karvonen and S. Kuhnle. London: Routledge.

Logan, Carolyn (2008) 'Rejecting the Loyal Opposition? The Trust Gap in Mass Attitudes toward Ruling and Opposition Parties in Africa', *Afrobarometer Working Paper*, No. 94, February.

Mainwaring, Scott and Timothy Scully, eds (1995) *Building Democratic Institutions: Party Systems in Latin America*. Stanford CA: Stanford University Press.

Mandaville, Alicia Phillips (2004) *Bolivia's Political Party System and the Incentives for Pro-Poor Reform*, Washington, DC: National Democratic Institute for International Affairs.

Manning, Carrie (2010) 'Mozambique's Slide into One-party Rule', *Journal of Democracy*, 21 (2), pp. 151–165.

Michels, Robert (2001) *Political Parties: A Sociological Study of the Oligarchical Tendencies of Modern Democracy*. Kitchener, ON, Canada: Batoche.

Mizrahi, Yemile (2003) *From Martyrdom to Power: The Partido Accion Nacional in Mexico*. Notre Dame, Indiana: University of Notre Dame Press.

Mwangi, Oscar Gakuo (2008) 'Political Corruption, Party Financing and Democracy in Kenya', *Journal of Modern African Studies*, 46 (2), pp. 267–285.

Ngoy-Kangoy, H. K. and V. Kabungulu (2006)'Parties and political transition in the Democratic Republic of Congo'. Electoral Institute for the Sustainability of Democracy in Africa Research report, No. 20, Johannesburg, South Africa.

Olayele, Wole (2003) 'Democratic Consolidation and Political Parties in Lesotho'. Occasional Paper No 15, Electoral Institute of Southern Africa, Johannesburg, South Africa.

Olukoshi, Adebayo O. (1998) 'Economic Crisis, Multipartyism and Opposition Politics'. In *The Politics of Opposition in Contemporary Africa*, ed. Adebayo Olukoshi. Uppsala: Nordiska Afrikainstitutet, pp. 8–38.

Phillips, Anne (1995) *The Politics of Presence*. Oxford: Oxford University Press.

Pridham, Geoffrey, ed. (1990) *Securing Democracy. Political Parties and Democratic Consolidation in Southern Europe*. New York: Routledge.

Rakner, Lise and Nicolas van de Walle (2007) 'Opposition Parties in Sub-Saharan Africa'. In *Globalization and Democratization: Challenges for Political Parties*, ed. Siri Gloppen and Lise Rakner. (Essays in Honour of Lars Svåsand), Bergen, Norway: Fagbokforlaget.

Randall, Vicky (2007) 'Inner-Party Democracy and Democracy-Building'. In *Globalization and Democratization: Challenges for Political Parties*, ed. Siri Gloppen and Lise Rakner. (Essays in Honour of Lars Svåsand), Bergen, Norway: Fagbokforlarget.

—— and Lars Svåsand (2002a) 'Introduction: The Contribution of Parties to Democracy and Democratic Consolidation', *Democratization*, 9 (3), pp. 1–10.

—— and —— (2002b) 'Party Institutionalization in New Democracies', *Party Politics*, 8 (1), pp. 5–29.

Rigger, Shelley (2001) *From Opposition to Power: Taiwan's Democratic Progressive Party*. Boulder, CO: Lynne Rienner.

Samuels, David (2004) 'From Socialism to Social Democracy: Party Organization and the Transformation of the Workers' Party in Brazil', *Comparative Political Studies*, 37 (9), pp. 999–1024.

Sartori, Giovanni (1976) *Parties and Party Systems: A Framework for Analysis*, vol. 1, Cambridge: Cambridge University Press.

Scarrow, Susan (2005) *Implementing Intra-party Democracy*. Washington, DC: National Democratic Institute.

Sherlock, Stephen (2004) 'The 2004 Indonesian Elections: How the System Works and What the Parties Stand For', Centre for Democratic Institutions, Canberra: The Australian National University.

Siavelis, Peter M. and Scott Morgenstern (2008) 'Candidate Recruitment and Selection in Latin America: A Framework for Analysis', *Latin American Politics and Society*, 50 (4), pp. 27–58.

Smith, Zeric Kay (2001) 'Mali's Decade of Democracy', *Journal of Democracy*, 12 (3), pp. 73–79.

Sobhan, Rehman (2002) *Bangladesh in the New Millennium: Between Promise and Fulfillment*. Dhaka: Centre for Policy Dialogue; available at www.cpd-Bangladesh.org

Suri, K. C. (2007) 'Political parties in South Asia: the challenge of change', Stockholm: International IDEA; available as free pdf download at: http://www.idea.int/publications/pp_south_asia/index.cfm (accessed 21 December 2010).

Tan, Alexander C. (2002) 'The Transformation of the Kuomintang Party in Taiwan', *Democratization*, 9 (3), pp. 149–164.

Thornton, Laura L. (2002) 'Political Party Strategies to Combat Corruption' (NDI and CALD) See National Democratic Institute website: http://www.ndi.org/.

van de Walle, Nicolas (2003) 'Presidentialism and Clientelism in Africa's Emerging Party Systems', *Journal of Modern African Studies*, 41 (2), pp. 297–321.

—— and Kimberley Butler (1999) 'Political Parties and Party Systems in Africa's Illiberal Democracies', *Cambridge Review of International Affairs*, 13 (1), pp. 14–28.

Wanjohi, Nick (2003) 'Sustainability of Political Parties in Kenya'. In *African Political Parties*, ed. M. A. Mohamed Salih. London: Pluto Press.

Wiafe-Akenten, Charles (2004) *Ghana: Country Report based on Research and Dialogue with Political Parties*. Stockholm: International IDEA; available at www.idea.int/parties/upload/Ghana%20laid%20out.pdf (accessed 7 May 2011).

15

Civil society

David Herbert

> Probably the only proposition about civil society that few would contest is that over the last ten to fifteen years interest in the subject has been enormous and the literature about it has grown exponentially.
>
> *(Burnett and Calvert 2004: 1)*

Thus begins a recent collection on the role of civil society in democratization, a much discussed but highly contested topic. In the 1990s discussion mushroomed as commentators sought to grasp the reasons for the wave of democratization that swept the globe in the last quarter of the twentieth century, which placed a focus on the role of civil society in democratic transition. Since 2000, the slide of some of those new democracies back into autocracy (Shlapentokh 2008) has placed new emphasis on the role of civil society in democratic consolidation and deepening; that is, on what might serve to anchor and stabilize not just democratic political institutions (consolidation) but also to embed democratic practices in society ('deepening', Heller 2009). These debates have proved contentious for several reasons. First, normative ideas about what civil society ought to do and be have sometimes obscured and dominated empirical enquiry into what actually existing (empirical) civil society actually is and does (Kopecký and Mudde 2003; Omelicheva 2009). This problem is present both in more theoretical and in more policy-oriented work. Thus as Tester comments on Keane (theory oriented):

> all too often it is simply asserted that civil society involves democratic pressures; the connection is never really deconstructed or interrogated.
>
> *(1992: 128)*

... so Mercer (2004) comments in a critical review of the policy literature:

> Of particular concern is the widespread embracing of NGOs as democratic actors that is discernible in much of this literature. This appears to owe more to ideological persuasion and assumption than to an engagement with wider debates about the politics of development.
>
> *(2004: 5)*

Second, there are definitional arguments about what civil society is – whether commercial organizations or the 'economic sphere' should be considered part of civil society, for example, or concerning the relationship with the state, with some commentators insisting on the independence of civil society from both (Cohen and Arato 1992), others that the shaping role of the state is vital to grasp its dynamics (Chandhoke 2001). Third, some influential political actors (Western governments and international non-governmental organizations, INGOs) may be seen to have a stake in emphasizing the role of civil society in democratization, the former to justify limiting state intervention (either to save money or for ideological reasons), the latter to promote their own agendas. Fourth, to these reasons may be added some methodological problems common to social scientific research, including those of causation (whether 'good' civil society is caused by 'good' democratic institutions, or vice versa, Schmitter 2010: 17), and how far the actions of civil society organizations (CSOs) rather than other social actors are responsible for particular outcomes in a complex social field (Omelicheva 2009).

Fifth, and particularly pertinent as at the time of writing (May 2011) with the 'Arab Spring' turning into a hot summer of conflict in Syria and Libya, smouldering opposition in the Gulf (Yemen, Bahrain), and with Egypt and Tunisia looking to be on the path to democracy having overthrown authoritarian regimes, we may note that the role of religion in civil society as a factor in democratization is a contested one. Since Huntington's (1993) 'clash of civilizations' thesis, much opinion in the West has seen Christianity (at least in its Western, Protestant and (later) Catholic forms) as broadly supportive of democratization, but Islam, conversely, as an inhibiting factor – witness, for example, the lack of Arab democracies until at least 2011 (Diamond 2010). On the other hand, democracy has proved sustainable in Muslim majority societies beyond the Arab world (e.g. Turkey, Indonesia), while if one looks for evidence of public attitudes, which may be more indicative of civil society than looking at regimes, survey evidence indicates stronger support for democracy in Muslim majority societies than in the (mostly Christian/post-Christian) post-communist world (Norris and Inglehart 2004: 154). Therefore, the final substantive section of this chapter will examine the relationship between religion, civil society and democratization, with particular reference to Islam.

Given these contexts it will be useful first to briefly trace the history of the uses of the concept of civil society, to examine how the field arrived at its current state, and then at how the concept may best be defined, before moving on to consider the nature of its relationship to democratization in more detail.

A brief history of the concept

In still the most comprehensive account of the development of the concept of civil society, Cohen and Arato (1992) trace its origins from Aristotle's *politike koinonia* (political community) through the Roman translation *societas civilis*, to the medieval city state (Cohen and Arato 1992: 84–86). But the modern history of the concept begins with Hobbes (1588–1679), Locke (1632–1704) and Montesquieu (1689–1755). Their early modern concept was introduced in opposition to their respective *ancien regimes* in the late seventeenth and eighteenth centuries. Each was convinced of the bankruptcy of the old patriarchal order of authority, but unsure how society could avoid degenerating into chaos without it (Tester 1992). Their solution was to reinvest the monarch's authority in the state, and to legitimize the state from the bottom up instead of the top down (Hobbes, Rousseau), so that 'horizontal networks of interdependencies' (Habermas) or 'relations of symmetric reciprocity' (Tester 1992), intermediate between the state and kinship networks, took centre stage in their thinking. This concept they called 'civil society', drawing on ancient precedents and constructed in opposition to the old aristocratic chains of dependence and obligation.

However, this Enlightenment deconstruction of hierarchy was limited: the 'horizontal networks' they saw replacing old hierarchies were composed of men like themselves – they did not include women or the lower orders. The patriarchal and elitist construction of the early modern concept of civil society therefore raises doubts about its contemporary relevance. Furthermore, the universality of the civil society they imagined was bounded by the emerging nation state, and religion tended to be framed in opposition to civil society, whereas the late twentieth century was marked by rapid globalization, and in recent use of the term (in East-Central Europe and Latin America for example), religion has sometimes emerged as a leading force in popular movements.

Writing a little later from a vantage point where it was possible to see that public religion could become decoupled from the ruling class of an *ancien regime*, Alexis de Toqueville (1805–59) did not see religion as a dangerous divisive force to be contained, but rather, based on his observations of America in the 1830s, as a key constituent of civil society. For him, the churches were important social institutions for the learning of civic virtues necessary for democracy to flourish. Yet de Toqueville was one of the last users of the idea in this early modern sense of 'an inclusive, umbrella-like concept referring to a plethora of institutions outside the state' (Alexander 1998: 3). This broad and idealistic use of civil society is described by Alexander as the first phase of the modern theory of civil society (CSI). It was brought to an end by the decisive intervention of Karl Marx.

Not long after de Tocqueville completed the second volume of *Democracy in America* (1840), Karl Marx began a series of writings (1842–5) that provided such a critical account of the naive sense of civil society (CSI), linking it so closely with capitalist domination that he virtually put the concept out of circulation for a century (Abercrombie *et al.* 1994: 429; Alexander 1998: 4–5). For Marx:

> Not only is civil society now simply a field of play of egotistical, purely private interests, but it is now treated as a superstructure, a legal and political arena produced as camouflage for the domination of commodities and the capitalist class.
>
> *(Alexander 1998: 4–5)*

This marks the beginning of the second historical phase (CSII) identified by Alexander (1998: 4–6). But Marx's deconstruction of civil society as a reification of particular interests (in Marx's case, class) can also be seen as setting the pattern for subsequent critiques of CSI, including those of its recent (1980s–2000s) revival. Michel Foucault, for example, shortly before his death in 1984, criticized use of the concept of civil society in relation to the emergence of the Solidarity movement in Poland:

> when one assimilates the powerful social movement that has just traversed that country to a revolt of civil society against state, one misunderstands the complexity and multiplicity of the confrontations.
>
> *(1988: 167)*

For Foucault, civil society obscures the complexity of social and political relations in a particular dualistic kind of way:

> it's … never exempt from a sort of Manichaeism that afflicts the notion of 'state' with a perjorative connotation while idealizing 'society' as a good, living, warm whole.
>
> *(Ibid.: 167–168)*

In the Marxist tradition, the rehabilitation of the concept of civil society began with Antonio Gramsci (1891–1937). Gramsci's nuanced understanding of the relationship between the state, civil society and popular, potentially revolutionary, movements, predates but to some extent provides a response to the kind of objection articulated by Foucault. This is because it recognizes the ambivalence of civil society as both permeated by state interests and at the same time a site for the articulation of resistance to the state. Gramsci's work forms part of a West European re-examination of Marxist thought, and especially the role of culture, which comes to be seen as more than mere superstructure. This understanding has been influential from Japan in the 1960s to Central America in the 1990s (Keane 1998: 12–14).

As indicated, Gramsci saw civil society as ambivalent: on the one hand it was the means by which the state secured authority through consent rather than coercion, but on the other hand it was also potentially the site of most effective resistance to the state. This is because where the state is entrenched in institutions and the minds of the population through a developed civil society, it cannot be moved by frontal assault – hence the failure of revolutions other than the Russian, where civil society was not well developed, during Gramsci's lifetime. However, the 'trenches' of civil society are also potentially sites of resistance to the vested interests that control the state – places where the proletariat can reflexively deconstruct the 'second nature' of existing arrangements (Tester 1992: 140–143). Gramsci's Marxist understanding of the proleteriat as the revolutionary class may be no longer relevant (Keane 1998: 16–18), but his understanding of the ambivalence of civil society – that it could become the site of resistance to a repressive state as well as the means of entrenchment of the state – remains a useful analytical insight.

The revival of CSI by activists in Eastern Europe in the 1980s, followed by its rapid worldwide dissemination to the Middle East (Therborn 1997), Africa (Hearn 2000), China (Strand 1990) and South America (Hudick 1999) gave new impetus to the concept, which became a powerful source of mobilization against repressive states. The idea of the spontaneous self-organization of society also appealed in a Western context in which the limits of state intervention, especially of the welfare state, seemed to be increasingly exposed. But a combination of the difficulties of post-communist reconstruction (Skapska 1997), the limitations of Western strategies to promote civil society in developing societies (Hearn 2000) and the problems of applying the concept cross-culturally (Hann 1996), together with criticisms of the CSII kind, have left many disillusioned with the analytical value of the concept.

Defining civil society

Responding to this situation, White (1994, 2004) provides a definition of the concept – stripped of the presumption that civil society necessarily involves democratic pressures – which enables the connections between civil society and democratization to be critically examined. Thus he defines civil society as:

> an intermediate associational realm between state and family populated by organizations which are separate from the state, enjoy autonomy in relation to the state, and are formed voluntarily by members of society to protect and extend their interests or values.
>
> *(2004: 10)*

However, for critics such as Chandhoke (2001) this definition remains highly problematic, because by defining civil society in opposition to the state ('separate from … enjoy autonomy in relation to') White neglects the critical role of the state in shaping civil society. Chandhoke illustrates this shaping role using the example of the 'Mandalization' (and reactive 'Mandirization') of India in the 1990s: here, government enforcement of the recommendations of Mandal commission, designed to increase equality for marginalized social groups (Mandalization), led to a massive and ongoing Hindu nationalist backlash (Mandirization, from the Hindi *mandir*, 'temple'), which, while deeply rooted in civil society, also contained profoundly uncivil elements.

But if the state shapes civil society, can it nonetheless be distinguished from it in terms of its 'governing logic'? This is how Cohen and Arato (1992) and Habermas (1996) distinguish civil society from the state and also the economy. As Heller summarizes, they:

> distinguish political and civil society by their distinct modes of social action. Political society is governed by instrumental-strategic action and specifically refers to the set of actors that compete for, and the institutions that regulate (in a democratic system) the right to exercise legitimate political authority. Civil society refers to non-state and non-market forms of voluntary association that are governed by communicative practices.
>
> *(2009: 124)*

However, as the emergence of Hindu nationalist politics from organizations (such as the VHP and RSS) that fit White's definition of civil society as 'intermediate associational realm between state and family' suggests, 'civility', in the sense of oriented to communication is not necessarily a property of all organizations in this realm; rather, it is a contingent emergent property.

This point is underlined by the observation that simply having a high density of civil society organizations – that is, 'intermediate associational realm between state and family' – does not relate in a straightforward way to the prospects for democratization. Thus, the former East Germany boasted a dense network of civil society organizations, in line with north European norms, and in excess of those found in southern European societies (Therborn 1997: 47). Yet this was one of the more repressive communist regimes. In fact, one may even argue that the very density of networks of civic association facilitated the police state, for it was via these networks that informants worked. Moreover, informants did so without necessarily compromising the autonomy or purposes of such organizations (Spülbeck 1996). Thus same dense civil networks, which in some circumstances enable society to organize against a repressive state, can work against democratization by enabling the surveillance state.

Conversely, a repressive state can sometimes sponsor organizations that, over time, develop some autonomy, and can end up providing a basis for mobilization against the state. For example, following the coup of 1981 Turkey's military government encouraged the growth of Islamic groups to counter the perceived threat of communism. It has been argued that such groups tend to replicate the patterns of state authoritarianism in their organizational structures and hence lack the 'horizontal' component taken to be characteristic of civil society (Çaylak 2008). Nonetheless, even though they may be characterized by internal divisions and tend not to cooperate with each other, there is now substantial evidence over time that they also perform a democratizing function by encouraging alternative perspectives and providing public milieux for discussion (White 1996; Çaylak 2008).

So, associations intermediate between state and kin (though likely shaped by the former and sometimes by the latter, and by economic relationships) sometimes (but not always) provide space where discussion about social, cultural and political issues takes place. And even critics of normative conceptions of civil society such as Chandhoke agree that:

> democracy requires as a precondition a space where various groups can express their ideas about how society and politics should be organised.
>
> *(2004: 162)*

and that this stratum of intermediate organizations that White identifies as civil society provides the prime social location where such debates take place. Even in the Indian case, which

Chandhoke uses as an example of both state penetration of civil society and of uncivil movements arising from it, she nonetheless (2001: 21) argues that this stratum still provides space for discussion and mobilization that is critical for the development of (at least participative modes of) democracy, and for the articulation of resistance to exclusionary forms of identity:

> if the project of Hindutva hegemonized civil society to some extent, civil society also provides a space for communal groups to struggle against this particular formation, howsoever unequal the battle may seem to be at the present moment.
>
> *(Ibid.: 21)*

So, in defining civil society it seems reasonable to retain White's basic idea of 'organizations intermediate between state and family' as providing the kind of social space where pre- or micro-political mobilization and debate can take place, depending on context, and especially on the relationship between the state and such organizations. To exercise this democratic function, they need some autonomy from the state, but autonomy alone does not guarantee that they will become agents of democratization.

One response to the contingency of civil society's democratizing influence and to the reality of uncivil elements within it, is to redefine civil society as an ideal state or condition, only ever partially achieved. Thus Alexander (1998) argues that:

> Civil society should be conceived ... as a solidary sphere in which a certain kind of universalising community comes gradually to be defined and to a certain degree enforced. To the degree that this solidary community exists, it is exhibited by 'public opinion', possesses its own cultural codes and narratives in democratic idiom, is patterned by a set of peculiar institutions, most notably legal and journalistic ones, and is visible in historically distinctive sets of interactional practices like civility, equality, criticism, and respect. *This kind of community can never exist as such; it can only exist 'to one degree or another'.*
>
> *(Ibid.: 7, emphasis added)*

Bringing together the foregoing discussion of the history of the concept with this discussion of definition, we can see that Alexander's concept represents an improvement on the vague breadth and confusion of normative and empirical elements we noted above in CSI: his normative concept recognizes the contingency of the democratizing effects of empirical – or 'actually existing' – civil society. It also overcomes the negative narrowness of CSII, pointing to the potential modes through which civil society can exercise its democratic effects. However, by making civil society an emergent property, a quality or condition rather than a social location, Alexander flies in the face of common uses, which tend to talk about civil society in a concrete (if not very well defined) way. Better, we suggest, to stick with a definition of civil society as a social location (as White does, above), but to stress in doing so the contingency of civil society's democratizing influence, and that it also is likely to give rise to uncivil, as well as civil, elements (Kopecký and Mudde 2003).

A further problem with Alexander's definition is that it conflates civil society with the public sphere, which we suggest is better kept analytically distinct: civil society organizations channel private opinion into the public sphere, they do not constitute the latter (Cohen and Arato 1992; Habermas 1996). For the sake of clarity then, it seems better to reserve 'public sphere' for spaces of shared public discussion for the expression and formation of public opinion, and civil society for the range of organizations that channel private opinions into the public sphere, and serve as a forum for discussion for a more defined range of interests. Alexander's ascription of some institutions to civil society is also problematic. Journalistic institutions are appropriately located there (although they would not be if the state controlled the media); but law is more problematic, as at one level it is clearly a function of state, even though it needs legitimization from civil society.

A further definitional issue to introduce before looking more closely at the contingent relationship between civil society and democratization is the unfortunate tendency to conflate particular kinds of organization with civil society as such, as sometimes found in the literature on non-governmental organizations (NGOs). Thus Mercer argues in the context of a critical review of the literature on NGOs and democratization:

> It is often argued that NGOs aid democratization because they pluralize the institutional arena, expand and strengthen civil society, and bring more democratic actors into the political sphere. However, it is too simplistic to suggest that the mere existence of an NGO sector will lead to these outcomes. Such a position often rests on the *conflation of NGOs with civil society itself (and vice versa)*, so that sheer numbers of NGOs are taken as indicators of the existence or otherwise of a civil society in a given place.
>
> *(2004: 10)*

Rather, NGOs are just one of a range of types of organization intermediate between state and kin that populate civil society. Mercer understands NGOs to be:

> organizations that are officially established, run by employed staff (often urban professionals or expatriates), well-supported (by domestic or, as is more often the case, international funding), and that are often relatively large and well-resourced.
>
> *(Ibid.: 6)*

In contrast are grass-roots organizations (GROs), which are more locally based, less professionalized and:

> usually understood to be smaller, often membership-based organizations, operating without a paid staff but often reliant upon donor or NGO support, which tend to be (but are not always) issue-based and therefore ephemeral.
>
> *(Ibid.)*

In addition, there are INGOs (international NGOs), which are usually headquartered in the United States or Europe, normally with professional staff and well resourced. But alongside, and partly overlapping with GROs, civil society comprises a plethora of organizations, including sports clubs, religious and charitable organizations, and hobby-based groups. So, we have a concept of civil society that locates it institutionally, and which is oriented to assessing (rather than assume) its democratizing properties. But can we go further in spelling out the nature of the relationship between civil society and democratization?

Civil society and other factors in democratization: mapping the field

It is important to recognize the roles of other parts of society in contributing to democratization. Linz and Stepan (1996) do so in their comparative study of the conditions of democratic transition and consolidation in southern and post-communist Europe and South America. They suggest that five factors are of critical importance to democratization: a 'free and lively civil society'; a stable, uncontested territorial state with an effective bureaucracy; respect for the rule of law; political society; and economic society. Political society here refers to 'mechanisms such as political parties and interparty alliances, elections and electoral rules, political leaders and legislatures' (Keane 1998: 48). Economic society refers to a 'mixed system of legally crafted and regulated non-state forms of property, production, exchange and consumption' (ibid.: 49). At each level, the crucial element is the presence of institutions able to guarantee the 'integrity' – diversity and autonomy – of each sphere from state or other monopolistic control. Linz and Stepan also stress the importance of the form of pre-democratic regime, and of contingencies such as timing (of the onset of democratic revolutions) and prudent leadership (Keane 1998: 46–47).

Linz and Stepan's model shows features of each of the three types of theory of democratization outlined by Potter *et al.* (1997), in their major comparative study of democracy from the eighteenth to the late twentieth century. These types of theory are modernization, elite and structural theories. In brief, modernization theories of democratization hold that once a certain level of development (principally economic) is achieved, democratization will come about. Linz and Stepan give less attention to economic development per se than to the conditions for the development of a regulated market economy, and also stress the importance of political society. In this they reflect Potter *et al.*'s criticisms of overly deterministic economic models. For example, Lewis argues:

> It was the more socially and economically developed countries in Eastern Europe that democratised more rapidly, it is nevertheless difficult to identify any 'modernization theory' that actually explains this.
>
> *(Lewis in Potter et al. 1997: 414)*

Furthermore, only weak correlations between levels of social and economic development and democratization are found outside elsewhere in the world, and during other periods of history.

Transition theories argue that the actions of political elites at key moments or crises best explain democratization, and Stepan and Linz's emphasis on the role of leadership coincide with this. Again, Lewis finds more evidence in Central Eastern Europe than elsewhere to support this view (1997: 418–419), while stressing that under conditions of globalization international events play a larger role than either of these models permit, based around – as with much political and sociological theory – the analytic unit of the nation state. We shall develop this point further when we examine the concept of transnational civil society, below.

Structural theory emphasizes the importance of social, economic and political developments over a long period of time, and Stepan and Linz's emphasis on the stability of the territorial state through time, as well as on the development of political and economic society, fit well with this. It is possible to argue that structural theory in fact provides a more nuanced version of modernization theory, emphasizing the diversity of interacting factors in varying historical and cultural circumstances, rather than the linear trajectory with its possibly ethnocentric assumptions underlying unreformed modernization theory. As with Stepan and Linz, this can be usefully combined with elite theory to help understand why, given long-term historical conditions, democratic transitions occur at particular times.

In summary, democratization appears to depend on civil, economic and political society, and especially on the development of cultures of social trust allowing for freedom of development within these each of these notional spheres, a key aspect of which is respect for the rule of law. Without agreement on the basic political unit of the state, the development of such trust is extremely difficult. International factors also play a growing role in a global information economy, and the role of political actors at moments of crisis is likely to be influential. Civil society, then, is just one factor in the process of democratization. Disillusionment with civil society as failing to 'deliver democratization' may in part be due to the failure to recognize this multifactorial and multicontingent process. But in what ways does civil society influence democratization?

Civil society and democratization: democratic transitions

Writing in the immediate aftermath of the wave of democratic transitions in East-Central Europe and South Africa in the late 1980s and early 1990s, White (1994, 2004) outlines four ways in which civil society impacts on democratization. First, he argues that activity in civil society can alter the power balance between state and civil society, which can be a key factor in triggering democratic transition, as occurred in parts of Central and Eastern Europe such as Poland and Czechoslovakia in the late 1980s (2004: 12). Second, he argues that civil society may perform a disciplinary role in relation to the state, seeking to ensure, for example, that the state adheres to principles to which it is constitutionally bound (human rights groups, nationally and internationally located, are an example of this; for national examples see Dalacoura 1998 on Tunisia and Egypt; Kubiek 2005 on Turkey). Third, he argues that civil society may act as a channel of communication between society and the state (White 1994: 14). The role of the Lutheran Church during the democratic transition in East Germany is an example of this (Pollack 1995). Fourth, he argues that civil society can sometimes play a constitutive role, coming to redefine the rules of the political game in a more democratic way; the case of Charter 77 in Czechoslovakia coming to influence the new Czechoslovak constitution is a case of such constitutive influence.

Critics argue that those who stress the importance of civil society in democratic transition tend to focus on a rather narrow range of cases to support their argument. Thus, in the post-communist cases, Poland and Czechoslovakia are more often cited than, say, Latvia or Hungary, precisely because there were organized and internationally visible popular civil society elements involved in the transition. Such selectivity is also found in the context of the claims made for the role of NGOs, as Mercer argues:

> Taken as a whole, the empirical literature on NGOs, civil society and democratization is characterized by a rather selective geography ... Claims for the role of NGOs as important civil society actors pursuing democratic development are often backed up by reference to the experiences of several core countries: those most frequently referred to include Brazil, Chile and the Philippines; Bangladesh, India and (to a lesser extent) Kenya also feature frequently; while South Africa and Thailand have been mentioned more recently.
>
> *(2004: 12)*

This selectivity is significant and problematic not only because it tends to exaggerate the role of particular civil society elements, but because:

> first, what is taken to be an 'NGO given' – that is, the ability to foster an inclusive and democratizing development process – is on closer inspection the experience of only a handful of countries (and only a handful of NGOs and localities *within* those countries); secondly, these successes become the normative ideals to which other NGOs in other (mostly African) countries should aspire; and thirdly, countries whose NGO sectors are not able to replicate such experiences are labelled as having 'weak' and 'underdeveloped' civil societies in need of strengthening (usually through increased donor support to NGOs).
>
> *(Mercer 2004: 13)*

Thus it is important always to consider local and regional differences and contingencies before assuming that 'lessons' from one context can be readily applied in another, and to remember that any general understanding of civil society is always only an abstraction from particular existing instances. Nonetheless, large-scale comparative studies can be useful for putting the contingent effects of civil society on democratic transition into perspective.

Reflecting on a quarter of a century of comparative research on democratization processes, Philippe Schmitter writes:

> Civil society has figured prominently and favorably in the literature on democratic transition and consolidation, but it may be a mixed blessing.
>
> *(Schmitter 2010: 24)*

He argues that civil society actors played leading roles in six of fifteen cases that he studied (the Philippines, South Korea, Peru and Czechoslovakia, and later in the Georgian and Ukrainian 'colour revolutions'). This suggests that it has been a significant if not overwhelming factor in achieving democratic transition, and one that might be considered to be more influential if one considers the international effects of some transitions, for example those of Poland and Czechoslovakia on the rest of East-Central Europe. However, Schmitter concludes that most post-1974 ('third wave') transitions have been of the 'pacted' or 'imposed' kind, which is brought about through national or international elite negotiations, so that the role of civil society is less clear, although it may have played some role in pressuring individuals and factions towards the negotiating table.

On the debit side, he argues that the emergence of nationalist elements in civil society can be distinctly unhelpful in consolidating democracy, for example in the Yugoslavian case with emergent Serb and Croat nationalist factions. He expresses scepticism about the role of civil society in the democratic consolidation phase more generally, arguing that:

> Democratic theorists ... have tended to assume that democratic stability hinges on the flourishing of a 'civic culture' replete with ample intergroup tolerance, trust in institutions, and readiness to compromise. What we seem to be observing in new democracies today is a political culture that is less 'civic' than 'cynical'.
>
> *(Schmitter 2010: 22)*

Schmitter suggests that this prevailing cynicism may not matter so much as 'democratic theorists' have tended to assume: so long as ruling elites continue to judge that democracy is less of a threat to their interests than a return to authoritarianism, then democratic institutions should be reasonably safe.

On the other hand, while popular disillusionment (Norris and Ingelhart 2004) and elite cynicism (Shlapentokh 2008; Schmitter 2010) may present little serious threat to democracy as 'the only game in town' (Linz and Stepan 1996) in most post-communist societies, because few believe that their interests would be better served by a return to previous arrangements, in other contexts 'other games' may provide more of a threat, if not to a national democratic regime then to the effective power of the democratic state. Hence the role of civil society in stabilization and 'deepening' democracy again becomes urgent. Arguably, India and South Africa provide two such contexts, where Maoist and Naxalite insurgencies (India) and some version of one-party state dominated African nationalism (South Africa) provide possible alternative paths, already followed by some regional neighbours.

While the author of the next study we shall consider, Heller, believes that democratic institutions in South Africa and India are basically safe, he disagrees with authors such as Schmitter that popular disillusionment and elite cynicism are as a result relatively unimportant.

Rather, he refers to a further phase of democratic deepening beyond consolidation, which is necessary for democratic flourishing, but towards which progress in these societies is faltering.

Deepening democracy: India and South Africa

Heller (2009) provides a useful comparative study of the role of civil society in what he calls 'deepening' democracy in these two societies. He begins by arguing that these are two of the most striking cases of successful democratic consolidation:

> democracy has made a real difference. In India it has helped forge a nation from the most heterogeneous social fabric in the world. In South Africa, democratic politics and constitutional rule have managed a transition from white minority to black majority rule with minimal conflict. That this has been achieved against a social backdrop of extreme social exclusions (the caste system in India) and the worst maldistribution of wealth in the world (South Africa) only underscores the achievements at hand.
>
> *(Ibid.: 123)*

These are remarkable achievements, and democratic transition has been followed by a consolidation of democratic institutions such that 'the likelihood of democratic reversal or even destabilization … is remote' (ibid.). And yet, 'even as formal constitutional democracy has been consolidated, there is little evidence of an increased capacity of subordinate groups to have an effective role in shaping public policy' (ibid.: 124).

It is the process of 'closing this gap between formal legal rights in the civil and political arena, and the practical possibility of practising those rights that Heller calls 'democratic deepening' (ibid.: 125). He sees civil society as essential to this process, because it is the intermediate organizations of civil society, if they are allowed to form and operate freely and have access to sufficient resources, that can provide space for organization and the articulation of interests, and enable issues from marginalized groups to be channelled into mainstream public arenas and on to political agendas.

If the four roles of civil society in democratization outlined by White (1994) fit the transition phase of democratization, those outlined by Heller (2009) correspond to the deepening phase. He describes three roles associated with civil society in this phase of deepening, or, in established democracies, of maintenance:

> (1) provide a space in which citizens can meaningfully practise democracy on a day-to-day basis; (2) anchor the legitimacy of political practices and institutions in vigorous public debate; and (3) serve as a countervailing force to the power-driven logic of political society.
>
> *(123–124)*

Unlike some normative conceptions of civil society, he does not characterize political society as 'bad', because 'power-driven'. Rather, the instrumental logic of political society is needed to get things done, but this needs to be balanced by the communicative activities of civil society if political action is to respond to the needs of those outside the elites (ibid.: 125). Such activities need not necessarily be narrowly 'deliberative' as Heller, perhaps too closely following Habermas's terminology, describes; other forms of communication – such as symbolic protest and direct action – may also serve to give marginalized people and issues a voice (De Luca and Peeples 2002). But there need to be means through which all citizens have opportunities for self-organization, and ultimately formation and expression of political will. It is this kind of process, however, which is largely failing in India and South Africa.

The reasons for this are complex and somewhat different in each case. In India, one aspect of the problem is that the Congress Party's limited penetration in rural society meant that it was forced to govern through existing (and highly socially exclusionary) elites, which meant that legislation against such issues as caste abuses had little impact in practice. Since officials came largely from such elites, it has meant that contact with the state, for many, has largely been mediated through corrupt patronage networks or, worse, police brutality (Brass 1997: 324). As a result:

> the form of the local state and the mode of its interface is so institutionally weak and so thoroughly permeated by social power and extra-legal authority as to vacate the actual practice of citizenship.
>
> *(Heller 2009: 134)*

In South Africa, during the consolidation phase, the African National Congress rapidly moved into a position of mediating citizen and intermediate organizations' relationships to the state, a process that has been accompanied by a certain kind of professionalization: '[c]onditions for engagement with the State are increasingly set by complex standards for meeting performance targets and accounting practices that all but rule out community-based organizations' (ibid.: 140). As a result, civil society has become bifurcated between professionalized groups dominated by the middle classes and the urban poor:

> Business groups, professionalized NGOs and organized labour continue to be well positioned to engage with the State. But subaltern civil society, and especially the urban poor, has more or less been sidelined from the political process in South Africa.
>
> *(Ibid.: 139)*

Thus, although they are very different, the relationship between Indian and South African cases share some common features: in each, the problems can be seen to relate to an imbalance between political society and civil society, such that the former dominates the latter. In both, too, NGOs (and INGOs) have become significant, even dominant actors in civil society, but these groups may lack articulation with the grass roots . As Katzenstein and Ray conclude for India, but which equally applies to South Africa (Heller 2009: 140):

> Economic liberalization has been accompanied by the massive NGO-ification of civil society arguably crowding out some of the more protest oriented forms of organizing within the social movement sector.
>
> *(2005: 9)*

And if it is a problem in relatively stable societies such as India and South Africa, it is even more acute in societies affected by war, where whatever pre-conflict civil society existed is likely to have been greatly weakened by conflict. Thus, in Bosnia, early research (Chandler 1999) into the Organization for Security and Cooperation in Europe's civil-society-building strategy found that most NGO activists were mostly middle class urban intellectuals – those already conversant with the discourse of the international community – but who had little influence beyond their circle. As one of his respondents commented:

> The Citizen's Alternative Parliament, the Shadow Government and the coalition for return are basically the same 20 people when you scratch the surface. There is no depth to this.
>
> *(Ibid.: 87)*

Research conducted in 2007 came to similar conclusions:

> Although the rhetoric of the internationals is positive about the development of civil society, it is clear that a number of fundamental problems exist in the context of Bosnia. Not least among these are the lack of committed participation from both political elites and individuals, and the subversion of international assistance to create new local elites. While the NGOs and international community blame each other for the shortcomings of civil society, what is clear is the absence of a sustainable civil society.
>
> *(Richmond and Franks 2009: 32–33)*

International authorities in such postwar reconstruction contexts face the difficulty of, on the one hand, not wanting to hold on to power for too long, to avoid charges of neocolonialism and not respecting local democracy themselves; yet on the other they want to transfer power to leaders who will continue some form of liberal democracy, in which the rights of ethnic and religious minorities and women will be respected. Investing in developing civil society would seem to be a way of enabling the emergence of new leadership that might break the stranglehold of nationalist politicians on political society in Bosnia, for example; but so far this strategy does not seem to be working, at least in terms of democratic deepening. And if this is the case in Bosnia – where such strategies have been longest in place, international forces have not become bogged down fighting insurgents, and there was a pre-existing urban, industrial culture with strong links to other parts of Europe – the problems are likely to be even greater in more problematic countries such as Iraq and Afghanistan. Such situations raise questions about the relationship between culture, religion and civil society, to which we now turn.

Civil society, culture and religion: the case of Islam

The resurgence of religion as a political factor since the Iranian revolution of 1979, and especially since 11 September 2001, has led to much discussion of whether at least some kinds of religion are incompatible with democracy, and hence to questions about the role of religion as a factor in democratization processes. Debate around Huntington's (1993) well-publicized 'clash of civiliza- tion' thesis has thrown the spotlight on Islam in particular. Thus, while it is broadly accepted that Christianity in civil society can play a positive role in democratization (witness the role of Catholic symbols and discourses, and to an extent institutions, in Poland in the period leading up to democratic transition, Kubik 1994), even though it can clearly also play a divisive role (former Yugoslavia), the debate around Islam has had a much more negative and sceptical tone. As far as the relationship between religion, civil society and democratization goes, a key issue is the extent to which particular religions inhibit or boost the emergence of individualism, and hence the formation of the kind of individuals both equipped and inclined to form civil society organizations, and to participate in democracy.

Still the most fully articulated case to date for the incompatibility of Islam and civil society was presented by the late Ernest Gellner in his influential *Conditions of Liberty: Civil Society and its Rivals* (1994). Here, Gellner claimed that Islam is fundamentally 'unsecularisable', and he concludes from this that Islam is also incompatible with civil society, both normatively and empirically (1994: 15). Gellner understands secularization as the declining social significance of religion – 'in industrial or industrializing societies religion loses much of its erstwhile hold over men and society' (ibid.). While religion remains socially significant, argues Gellner, the development of individual auton- omy is constrained. This in turn constrains the development of civil society because, as one commentator explains:

Individuals, who are not able to act independently of the community of believers, cannot become the building-stones of the kind of intermediary organizations on which civil society is built.

(Özdalga 1997: 74)

However, each stage of Gellner's argument is contestable. First, Gellner neglects the different ways in which modernity has been mediated to different regions, and hence the consequences of this for reactions to modern institutional forms and discourses, including civil society. Second, Muslims have in fact generated a wide range of responses to the discourses of democracy, civil society and human rights (Halliday 1996; Goddard 2002). Third, the historical model on which Gellner bases his argument actually applies only to a minority of historic Muslim societies, while the historically predominant model of Muslim society has been characterized by institutional differentiation. Fourth, in practice in many parts of the Muslim world today, Islam has proven itself capable of mobilization as a public discourse without stifling democratic pluralism. Let us consider each of these arguments in more detail.

First, the impact of modernity on a region as a whole may be a key factor in shaping the reception and cultural embedding of modern ideas such as civil society. Therborn (1997) outlines four routes to modernity. First, the Western and Central European route in which both modernity and anti-modern movements were an internal development. Second, the route of the New Worlds in the Americas and Australasia, areas where European settlers came to constitute a majority of the population, and where opposition to modernity was principally perceived to lie in the Old (European) World. Third, the colonial zone, where modernity arrived from outside and resistance to modernity was domestic and suppressed, but where those of non-European origin nonetheless continued to constitute a majority of the population, for whom 'everyday life ... kept its own laws and customs, though often rigidified by colonial intervention or "indirect rule" ' (1997: 50). Fourth, countries characterized by 'Externally Induced Modernization', selectively imported by a ruling elite never overrun but pressured by European and American imperial powers, of which he gives as examples China, Japan, Iran, the Ottoman Empire/Turkey and the north African states most resistant to colonialism. Most Muslim majority societies fall into the third or fourth category.

Under these conditions, one might anticipate ambivalent attitudes to modern discourses, including civil society: certainly this has occurred with other modern discourses such as democracy and human rights. Indeed, normatively, Muslims have in fact taken up a full range of positions on the compatibility or incompatibility of the relationship between Islam and both democracy and human rights. Thus, Goddard (2002) outlines four positions on the relations between Islam and democracy, ranging from the view that democracy is anathema to Islam through to the view that democracy is essential for Islam. Similarly, Halliday (1996) outlines five positions that Muslims have taken up on human rights, again ranging from full compatibility through to outright rejection. Each position within both spectra seeks to justify itself in relation to the Qur'an and Sunnah, the primary textual sources of Islamic law.

This contemporary ideological pluralism corresponds to the diversity of historical forms of Muslim society. For example, Ira Lapidus argues that whereas Gellner, working principally from North African examples, sees just one Islamic blueprint for society, two have in fact been present from a very early stage of Middle Eastern history, with Gellner's model historically the less influential:

The Middle Eastern Islamic heritage provides not one but two basic constellations of historical society, two golden ages, two paradigms, each of which has generated its own repertoire of political institutions and political theory. The first is the society integrated in all dimensions, political, social, and moral, under the aegis of Islam. The prototype is the unification of Arabia under the leadership of the Prophet Muhammad in the seventh century ... The second historical paradigm is the imperial Islamic society built not on Arabian or tribal templates but on the differentiated structures of previous Islamic societies ... By the Eleventh century Middle Eastern states and religious communities were highly differentiated ... Thus, despite the common statement that Islam is a total way of life defining political as well as social and family matters, most Muslim societies ... were in fact built around separate institutions of state and religion.

(Lapidus 1992: 14–15)

Thus the Western history of social differentiation is not the only conceivable one, and historically most Muslim societies have been socially differentiated. Yet Gellner, as a sociologist, does not simply argue that Islam is normatively resistant to differentiation. Rather, he argues that this normative orientation coincides with structural features that render Islam 'secularization-resistant' (1994: 14). Drawing on north African examples, Gellner characterizes Muslim history until recent modernity as a cyclical process driven by relations between two versions of Islam: an urban, scripturalist 'High' version, and a rural, ritualistic, ecstatic and saint-mediated 'Low' version. The High version is prone to laxity and pragmatic compromise over time: but at just such times it has been reinvigorated by the zeal of discontented followers of the Low version, who appropriate the ideals of 'High' Islam and are powered by *asabiyya* (energy of tribal groups). But modernity broke this cycle:

Come the modern world however – imposed by extraneous forces rather then produced indigenously – and the new balance of power, favoring the urban centre against rural communities, causes central faith to prevail, and we are left with a successful Ummah at long last. This is the mystery of the secularization-resistant nature of Islam.

(Ibid.)

The centralized state, asserting its authority over rural areas and destroying tribal society, is able to sustain the reforming zeal of High Islam. Both versions of High Islam are compatible with instrumental aspects of modernity – industrialization, urbanization, etc. – and hence increasingly displace the popular saint-led Low Islam throughout an increasingly urbanized society, except for Westernised elites. Furthermore, it is the puritanical version of High Islam that triumphs over the lax variant, because only the latter has genuine local appeal (1994: 23).

But how does this picture of a triumphant, 'puritanical' Islam – successfully harnessed by the centralizing state, displacing Sufism and preventing the emergence of individualism – fit with the evidence in contemporary North African and Middle Eastern societies? The short answer is, not very well. Let us focus on the case of Egypt, the most populous Arab society, and highly influential in the region. To begin with the obvious, the recent sight of protesters tweeting away in Cairo's Tahrir Square, facing down a military that refused to back the president, leading eventually to his resignation, does not suggest either the failure of an individualist culture to emerge, nor the triumph of the centralized state. Of course, Gellner was writing in the early 1990s (also when Huntington's 'clash' thesis was formulated), so cannot be held responsible for not having anticipated the spread of mobile communication technologies amongst urban Arab populations a decade and a half later. But it is not just about Twitter. The idea that Islam somehow inhibits the formation of individualized cultures (and hence civil society and democracy) is inconsistent with a range of evidence running back to at least the late 1980s.

It doesn't fit well with much of what is known about the most influential political Islamic movements in Egypt, with their tendency to evolve from more revolutionary into more reformist and democratic forms (Abdo 2000; Stark 2005). It is inconsistent with the considerable growth of Islam-inspired private voluntary organizations performing health, welfare and entrepreneurial functions that have proliferated in Egypt since the late 1980s (Sullivan and Abed-Kotob 1999), and with the way that Islamic discourse is appropriated by individuals in their struggle for autonomy and economic and social improvement in a context of authoritarian government and poverty (Starrett 1998). It is also inconsistent with individual opinion-poll data, not only in Egypt but across the Muslim majority world, for example as collected by the World Values Survey (Norris and Inglehart 2004). This is true when one considers attitudes towards democracy in Muslim majority societies and the West:

> when political attitudes are compared (including evaluation of how well democracy works in practice, support for democratic ideals, and disapproval of strong leaders), far from a clash of values, there is minimal difference between the Muslim world and the West.
>
> ...
>
> Support for democracy is surprisingly widespread amongst Islamic publics, even among those who live in authoritarian societies.
>
> *(Ibid.: 154–155)*

It is also true when one considers a wide range of values associated with cultures of individualism. For example, Weber's Protestant work ethic notwithstanding, Muslim societies come out higher than Protestant societies on support for the intrinsic value of work (items including values attached to opportunities to use initiative, a job in which you feel you can achieve, and a job meeting one's abilities; ibid.: 164–165), in seeing the benefits of economic competition as outweighing the costs, and in favouring individual responsibility over state responsibility (ibid.: 171).

None of this is to say, of course, that there are not authoritarian forms of Islam (clearly there are: see Mukherjee 2009), nor that religion is not sometimes a major motivating factor in political violence (clearly, it is: see Glazier 2009), or even that the proliferation of 'horizontal' (many-to-many) communications media such as the Internet necessarily has a liberalizing effect. Rather, this is multiply contingent (Calfano and Sahliyeh 2008), and in fact studies of Islamic websites suggest that the opposite trend may even be predominant at present (Cesari 2004: 112). Nor is it to say, conversely, that the kind of religion is irrelevant to the formation of civil society. Rather, the World Values Survey suggests that on a range of gender (Norris and Inglehart 2004: 154) and ethical issues – such as abortion, euthanasia, suicide (ibid.: 174) – Muslim majority societies do differ significantly from Western and indeed other groups of societies, and this does have implications for the development of civil society and the kind of democracy that has (Indonesia, Turkey) and may (Egypt, Tunisia) emerge. But what it does mean is that when it comes to the formation of individualist cultures in a manner conducive to the formation of civil society and propensity to support democratic politics, the evidence suggests that there is no general effect attributable to Islam. In fact, Muslim majority societies do rather better than Orthodox Christian ones in this respect (Norris and Inglehart 2004: 154). Thus, the evidence reviewed suggests that Gellner's thesis on the incompatibility of Islam and civil society and Huntington's clash of civilization thesis are both wide of the mark. But, however inaccurate they may be, such views sadly remain widely influential, informing stereotypical media representations of Islam and Muslims across the West (Poole and Richardson 2006).

Conclusion

The associations intermediate between the state and kinship networks that we have identified as empirical civil society clearly play significant if contested roles in the various stages of democratization. They have played an important role in many, if not all, democratic transition and consolidation processes, and are critical if democratic deepening is to occur. While the importance of civil society in democratization has increasingly been recognized by governments and international bodies, this knowledge has proved difficult to turn into effective policy interventions. The combination of neoliberal economic policies and managerialist discourses on 'effectiveness' have produced an instrumentalization and professionalization of sections of civil society that have reduced its deliberative and demonstrative dimensions, and its articulation with grass roots and community groups. Finally, in spite of much rhetoric to the contrary, there is no essential incompatibility between Islam and civil society, although the discourse of civil society, like other Western originating discourses, is contested in many post-colonial contexts.

Bibliography

Abdo, E. (2000) *No God But God: Egypt and the Triumph of Islam*. Oxford: Oxford University Press.

Abercrombie, N. *et al.* (1994) *The Penguin Dictionary of Sociology*. 3rd ed. London: Penguin.

Alexander, J., ed. (1998) *Real Civil Societies: Dilemmas of Institutionalization*. London: Routledge.

Brass, P. (1997) *Theft of an Idol: Text and Contenxt in the Representation of Collective Violence*. Princeton, NJ: Princeton University Press.

Burnell, P. and P. Calvert (2004) *Civil Society in Democratization*. London: Frank Cass.

Calfano, B. and E. Sahliyeh (2008) 'Transmitting Reform? Assessing New Media Influence on Political Rights in the Middle East', *Critique: Critical Middle Eastern Studies*, 17 (1), pp. 63–77.

Çaylak, A. (2008) 'Autocratic or Democratic? A Critical Approach to Civil Society Movements in Turkey', *Journal of Economic and Social Research*, 10 (1), pp. 115–151.

Cesari, J. (2004) *When Islam and Democracy Meet: Muslims in Europe and the United States*. London: Palgrave Macmillan.

Chandhoke, N. (2001) 'The "Civil" and the "Political" in Civil Society', *Democratization*, 8 (2), pp. 1–24.

Chandler, D. (1999) *Bosnia: Faking Democracy After Dayton*. London: Pluto.

Ciprut, V. (2008) *Democratizations: Comparisons, Confrontations and Contrasts*. Cambridge, MA: MIT Press.

Cohen, J. and A. Arato (1992) *Civil Society and Political Theory*. Cambridge, MA and London: MIT Press.

Dalacoura, K. (1998) *Islam, Liberalism and Human Rights*. London: I. B. Tauris.

DeLuca, M. and J. Peeples (2002) 'From Public Sphere to Public Screen: Democracy, Activism and the "Violence" of Seattle', *Critical Studies in Media Communication* 19 (2), 125–151.

Diamond, L. (2010) 'Why Are There No Arab Democracies?', *Journal of Democracy*, 21 (1), pp. 93–104.

Foucault, M. (1988) *Politics, Philosophy, Culture: Interviews and Other Writings 1977–1984*. trans. A. Sheridan *et al.* London: Routledge.

Glasier, R. (2009) 'Religiously Motivated Political Violence in Iraq.' In *Religion, Conflict and Military Intervention*, ed. R. Durward and L. Marsden. Aldershot: Ashgate, pp. 53–70.

Goddard, H. (2002) 'Islam and Democracy', *Political Quarterly* 73 (1), pp. 3–10.

Goodhardt, M. (2005) 'Civil Society and the Problem of Global Democracy', *Democratization*, 12 (1), pp. 1–21.

Halliday, F. (1996) *Islam and the Myth of Confrontation: Religion and Politics in the Middle East*. London: I.B.Tauris.

Hearn, J. (2000) 'Aiding Democracy? Donors and Civil Society in Africa?', *Third World Quarterly*, 21 (5), pp. 815–830.

Heller, P. (2009) 'Democratic Deepening in India and South Africa', *Journal of Asian and African Studies*, 44, pp. 123–149.

Hudick, A. (1999) *NGOs and Civil Society: Democracy by Proxy?* Cambridge: Polity.

Huntington, S. (1993) 'The Clash of Civilizations?', *Foreign Affairs*, 72 (2), pp. 22–43.

Keane, J. (1998) *Civil Society*. Cambridge: Polity.

Kopecký, P. and C. Mudde (2003) 'Rethinking Civil Society', *Democratization*, 10 (3), pp. 1–14.

Kubiek, P. (2005)'The European Union and Grassroots Democratization in Turkey' *Turkish Studies* Vol. 6, No. 3, 361–377.

Kubik, K. (1994) *The Power of Symbols Against the Symbols of Power: The Rise of Solidarity and the Fall of State Socialism in Poland*. Philadelphia: Pennsylvania University Press.

Lapidus, I. (1992) 'The Golden Age: The Political Concepts of Islam', *Annals of the American Academy*, 524, pp. 13–25.

Luxmoore, J. and J. Babiuch (1995b) 'In Search of Faith, Part 2: Charter 77 and the Return to Spiritual Values in the Czech Republic', *Religion, State and Society*, 23 (3), pp. 291–304.

Mercer, C. (2002) 'NGOs, Civil Society and Democratization: A Critical Review of the Literature' *Progress in Development Studies*, 2 (1), pp. 5–22.

Mukherjee, K. (2009) 'Islamism and Neo-fundamentalism.' In *Religion, Conflict and Military Intervention*, ed. R. Durward and L. Marsden. Aldershot: Ashgate, pp. 17–32.

Norris, P. and R. Inglehart (2004) *Sacred and Secular: Religion and Politics Worldwide*. Cambridge: Cambridge University Press.

Omelicheva, M. (2009) 'Global Civil Society and Democratization of World Politics: A Bona Fide Relationship or Illusory Liaison?', *International Studies Review*, 11, pp. 109–132.

Pollack, D. (1995) 'Post Wende Citizens' Movements'. In *Between Hope and Fear: Everyday Life in Post-Unification East Germany, A Case Study of Leipzig*, ed. E. Kolinsky asst. by S. Wilsdorf. Keele: Keele University Press, pp. 101–122.

Poole, E. and J. Richardson, eds (2006) *Muslims and News Media*. London: IB Tauris.

Potter, D., D. Goldblatt, M. Kiloh and P. Lewis eds. (1997) *Democratization*. Cambridge: Polity.

Richmond O. and J. Franks (2009) 'Between Partition and Pluralism: The Bosnian Jigsaw and an "Ambivalent" Peace', *South-East European and Black Sea Studies* 9 (1–2), pp. 17–38.

Schmitter, P. (2010) 'Twenty-five Years, Fifteen Findings', *Journal of Democracy*, 21 (1), pp. 17–28.

Shlapentokh, V. (2008) 'Russian Civil Society: Elite versus Mass Attitudes to the Democratization of Russia'. In *Democratizations: Comparisons, Confrontations and Contrasts*, ed. J. Ciprut. Cambridge, MA and London, UK: MIT Press, pp. 165–196.

Stark, J. (2005) 'Beyond "Terrorism" and "State Hegemony": Assessing the Islamist Mainstream in Egypt and Malaysia', *Third World Quarterly*, 26 (2), pp. 307–327.

Starrett, G. (1998) *Putting Islam to Work: Education, Politics and Religious Transformation in Egypt*. Berkeley, Los Angeles and London: University of California Press.

Strand, D. (1990) 'Protest in Beijing: Civil Society and Public Sphere in China', *Problems of Communism*, 34, May–June.

Sullivan, D. and S. Abed Kotob (1999) *Islam in Contemporary Egypt: Civil Society vs. the State*. Boulder, CO: Lynne Rienner.

Tester, K. (1992) *Civil Society*. London: Routledge.

Therborn, G. (1997) 'Beyond Civil Society: Democratic Experiences and Their Relevance to the "Middle East" '. In *Civil Society and Democracy in the Muslim World*, ed. E. Özdalga and S. Persson. Istanbul: Swedish Research Institute, pp. 45–54.

White, G. (1994) 'Civil Society, Democratization and Development (I): Clearing the Analytical Ground', *Democratization*, 1 (3), p. 378.

White, J. (1996) 'Civic Culture and Islam in Turkey'. In *Civil Society: Challenging Western Models*, ed. C. Hann. London: Routledge.

16

Social capital

Bo Rothstein and Rasmus Broms

For the last two decades, the idea of social capital has been identified as a remedy for many, if not most, of the ills and woes of states and societies. The field of democratization is no exception. In 1993, Robert Putnam, whose book *Making Democracy Work* today has the status of a 'modern classic', showed how the concept of social capital could be successfully applied on a broad scale. He states:

> Democratic government is strengthened, not weakened when it faces a vigorous civil society. … without norms of reciprocity and networks of civic engagement, the Hobbesian outcome of the Mezzogiorno – amoral familism, cientilism, lawlessness, ineffective government, and economic stagnation – seems likelier than successful democratization and economic development.
>
> *(Putnam 1993: 182–183)*

Another 'modern classic' that has pointed to the importance of social capital is Elinor Ostrom's *Governing the Commons*. In this book, which analyses how local groups can organize themselves for the successful handling of common, pooled resources, thus overcoming the famous 'tragedy of the commons' problem, Ostrom states that 'shared norms that reduce the cost of monitoring and sanctioning activities can be viewed as social capital' (1990: 36). As these two major books collectively make clear, over the last two decades the link between social capital, along with its conceptual sibling, civil society, has been a 'hot button' topic among scholars, politicians and practitioners alike, working to analyse, and advance, both democratization and democracy.

Putnam's claim is, like all 'big' theories, straightforward and simple. He emphasizes the importance of interpersonal cooperation and civic spirit as a real force in society at large as well as an important component of the quality of democratic governance. This notion can be labelled as a neo-Toquevillian view of democracy after the French nineteenth-century philosopher Alexis de Toqueville, whose study of civic life in the world's first democratic nation, *Democracy in America* (2000 [1835]), has become a central work for understanding the prerequisites for democracy. As is well known, Tocqueville placed great emphasis on voluntary associations and their ability to enhance trust and cooperation between citizens, furthermore strengthening the quality of democracy on a political and institutional level. Putnam's *Making Democracy Work* updated and systematized these notions, and provided powerful quantitative and qualitative evidence to boost them.

Ever since the publication of Putnam's groundbreaking work, his claims have, like all influential theories, been criticized, mainly from two camps: first, by those who question the societal bottom-up causality inherent in the argument, and second by a strand of researchers who warn about the 'dark sides' of social capital and civil society. In addition, as the third and fourth waves of democracy have coincided with a huge increase of social capital research, the universality of the theory has come into question.

This chapter reviews the current research landscape investigating the relationship between social capital and democratization. It is organized along the aforementioned fault lines in the ongoing debate, beginning with a brief discussion of how social capital is conceptualized. Second, we present an overview of its place in contemporary democratization research. Third, we address the issue of causality: can it be proven that social capital affects democratic development in a bottom-up process, as Putnam argues, or is the relationship reversed so that it is democracy that brings about social capital? Or is it the case that the relationship is spurious? This query, in turn, relates to the fourth section: is there a universal relationship between social capital and democratization, or are there contextual cultural or even country specific variables that need to be considered before making such judgments? The fifth part relates to Putnam's other main postulate: the claim that the relationship between social capital and the quality of a given democracy is inherently positive.[1] We examine to what extent this claim is supported by empirical evidence. Finally, does social capital act in the same way in fully fledged democracies as in new democracies, autocracies and in the so called 'hybrid regimes'?

Social capital at a glance

In brief, social capital is considered to consist of a quantitative and a qualitative dimension: social networks and social trust (Rothstein 2005: chapter 3). The former aspect, which is closely linked to civil society, is usually measured in terms of membership in voluntary (or secondary) associations, which can span from church choirs and sport clubs to labour unions and political advocacy groups. These types of associations are often considered to function as 'schools of democracy'. The type of organization that is 'counted' varies, as many scholars argue that the mainstream view focusing on formal organizations is too Eurocentric, and argue for the inclusion of more informal familiar and communal networks (Krishna 2002: 4–5). Even amongst those favouring the formalized notion of associationalism, there is no real homogeneity in what kind of organization may be counted. Do we include political parties, for example? It can be noted that in his 1993 book about Italy, Putnam excluded the Catholic Church on the grounds that it was too hierarchic, while in his book about social capital in the US, published in 2000, churches were included.

Social trust (also 'interpersonal' and 'generalized' trust in the literature) and norms of reciprocity are generated, according to Putnam, within the associational sphere. They help citizens unite, deliberate and solve collective action-problems more efficiently. This is quite useful in the daily business of grass roots democracy, as it makes it easier to apply pressure on governments and institutions. As stated by Newton:

> Particularly important are attitudes and values relating to trust and reciprocity, because these are crucial for social and political stability and cooperation. Treated in this way, social capital focuses on values and attitudes involving the cooperation, trust, understanding, and empathy that enable citizens to treat each other as fellow citizens, rather than as strangers or potential enemies. It is a social force that binds society together by transforming individuals from self-seeking and egocentric calculators, with little social conscience or sense of mutual obligation,

into members of a community with shared interests, shared assumptions about social relations, and a sense of the common good.

(2001: 225–226)

Generally, these two assets are considered to be mutually reinforcing and necessary components of social capital. Putnam (1993: 23, 107) stresses that it is *horizontal* bonds (such as those formed in a church choir), as opposed to *vertical* relations of authority (formed within the [Italian] Catholic Church) that can be considered to generate 'true social capital'. Second, his notion of civic culture is seen in terms of consensus and cooperation, rather than conflict and struggle. In this line of reasoning, there is a complementary emphasis on *weak ties* and *bridging* social capital, where people from different groups and societal strata are made to interact in larger, loosely structured, interaction patterns, rather than *strong ties* or *bonding* social capital, where only homogeneous groups tend to interact internally, which would increase the likelihood of a more factionalized society (2000: 22–23). The former is exhibited in civic, and generally more social-capital-successful, northern Italy, while the latter characterizes southern Italy, plagued by a sense of 'amoral familism', a term Putnam borrows from Edward Banfield's (1958) study of a small town in the southern province of Basilicata (Putnam 1993: 88).

Social capital in democratization research

Most of the earlier research on social capital treated it in relation to already developed democracies, and thus mainly tested its abilities to deepen and enhance the quality and scope of an already democratic state. Nevertheless, as we shall see, over the last two decades there has been a good amount of interesting research on social capital and societies at earlier stages of the democratization process. Sometimes the concept of social capital itself is the theme of study, sometimes it is particular components such as interpersonal trust, or adjoining topics such as civil society.

As mentioned, a major inspiration for Putnam's research has been the work of Alexis de Tocqueville, who during the early nineteenth century made assiduous inquiries in America into what appears to create and sustain a new democracy. Still, while certainly deemed relevant, and of late, increasingly so, social capital has not been one of the centrepieces in democratization research, at least not explicitly (cf. Teorell 2011). Several closely relating topics have, however. Civil society was a key theme in the field well before the 'social capital explosion' (cf. Burnell and Calvert 2004) and, with the 'political culture' strand of research initiated by Almond and Verba in the 1960s, the importance of the 'masses', and their attitudes towards regime and democracy, has been canonical to the field. Regardless of whether researchers argue for a top-down or a bottom-up approach in their explanations, the main point that can be made regarding social capital in democratization research is that neither elite behaviour and strategizing nor strictly structuralist socio-economical (cf. Lipset 1959) factors can account for the whole truth when attempting to explain the mechanics of democratization. People's system of beliefs matter, too.

The issue of causality

A major issue in the scholarly debate regarding social capital in general is how to deal with causality. Not least when linking social capital to democratization, many other variables come into play at both ends. Here, the cultural, bottom-up centred, neo-Tocquevillian view – proclaiming that social capital, exhibited in a vibrant political culture (Almond and Verba 1963), and the efforts of 'ordinary citizens' (Welzel and Inglehart 2008), can foster and uphold democracy – is contrasted with the notion that it is rather state institutions and democratization that increase social capital (see Stolle 2003: 31–32 for an overview of the argument). Yet some argue that the link is much more indirect, spurious, or even non-existent. As causal claims tend to be hard to either prove or disprove, some respond by remaining explicitly 'agnostic' (Norris 2001: 16); or simply find the relationship to be 'interdependent' (Paxton 2002). Others, however, have taken on the difficult task of showing whether the egg or the chicken comes first.

Amongst those favouring the bottom-up approach, Larry Diamond (2008: 300) argues that the creation and strengthening of a vibrant, horizontally structured, civil society is the first step among a number of preconditions for overcoming the 'predatory state' in order to usher in democracy. John Dryzek (1996: 476) is equally confident regarding the causal nature of the mechanics of democratization: 'An examination of the history of democratization indicates that pressures for greater democracy almost always emanate from oppositional civil society, rarely or never from the state itself.' While Putnam's own conceived relationship is deriving from the bottom-up, from social capital to democracy, he emphasizes that the development ought to be viewed as a reciprocal 'virtuous circle' (see also Inglehart 1999: 104, 118n). Several institutionalists agree with the 'virtuous circle' argument, but identify democratization as the initial spark that creates fertile ground for social capital and a benevolent civil society to work its magic. While Sztompka (1999) appears to reason in terms of such a virtuous circle, he argues that institutionalizing democracy is most likely to be seen as a prerequisite for trust, as 'it is not only that democracy engenders trust, but also, once in place, the culture of trust helps to sustain democracy'.

This is remarkably similar to Michel Walzer's statement: 'only a democratic state can create democratic civil society; only a democratic civil society can sustain a democratic state' (cited in Whitehead 2002: 769). Gahramanova's (2009) historical case-study of civil society in Azerbaijan notes that the other side of the coin, i.e. a vicious circle, also can apply, where the absence of both turns into a catch-22: 'restrictive POS [political opportunity structures] lead to a resource-poor civil society, which in turn leads to a level of social capital that is too low to challenge the reduced POS' (790). Letki and Evans (2005) analyse the relationship in Central and Eastern Europe, and reach the conclusion that the initial democratization does affect trust, while subsequent democratization is not affected by trust, arguing against both the bottom-up approach, and perhaps also the virtuous circle argument.

Another line of reasoning is to see democratic institutions, for example the respect for the rule of law and the complicated apparatus needed to ensure the implementation of 'free and fair' elections, as a public good that all groups in society stand to gain from if the rules are respected by 'all' (Rothstein 2005). However, as is well known from theories about collective action, the temptation to tamper with such rules in order to gain an advantage can be very strong, especially if group A doesn't trust that group B will refrain from manipulating the rules once it gets a chance to do so. In the absence of trust that the rules will be respected, the democratic system may unravel. This problem, also known as the 'second-order collective action dilemma' (Ostrom 1998: 42), was emphasized by the philosopher John Rawls in his groundbreaking book *A Theory of Justice* in the following way:

> For although men know that they share a common sense of justice and that each wants to adhere to existing arrangements, they may nevertheless lack full confidence in one another. They may suspect that some are not doing their part, and so they may be tempted not to do theirs. The general awareness of these temptations may eventually cause the scheme to break down. The suspicion that others are not honoring their duties and obligations is increased by the fact that, in absence of the authoritative interpretation and enforcement of the rules, it is particularly easy to find excuses for breaking them.
>
> *(Rawls 1971: 240)*

Finally, some have found that the causality ultimately depends upon the wider context. In his study of autonomous civil society in Mexico, Fox (1996) identifies three main causal pathways for local social capital formation within an authoritarian environment. He notes how civil society 'thickens' in different ways, dependent upon its 'political construction'. It can either arise in concert with the political establishment, especially its more reform-oriented wing, through external civil society, either national or international, or entirely from below, independently of external allies. Fox's findings, at least in a non/semi-democratic context, appear to lend some support to both the top-down and bottom-up strands of the causality debate.

A universal relationship? Contextual factors at play

As Fox's study implies, the relationship between social capital and democratic transition can appear very different in different places. As the field of social capital research started out measuring the Western social context, much effort has been devoted to inquire whether or not this can be translated to other parts of the world, coincidently places that tend to have had a much weaker tradition of democracy. Regarding causality, Göran Hydén suggests that in some places the chicken may in fact come first, while in others it is the egg:

> Civil society has been both a cause and a consequence of [the third wave of democratization] process. In many places around the world, the rise of civil society has contributed to the emergence of democratic government. In others, its rise has been facilitated by the introduction of a democratically elected government. It has provided the political space in which new forms of social capital are being built. We must recognize, therefore, that the challenges of civil society are bound to vary from place to place.
>
> *(1997: 19)*

Several authors have emphasized other factors that come into play when dissecting the relationship at hand; while some argue for context to be a simple background variable, others appear to prefer to take social capital out of the equation as an essentially spurious factor. Some of the main contextual factors are presented below.

Institutions

Tarrow (1996) and Thörnquist (1998: 113) point to the fact that much of the social capital research conducted in the spirit of Putnam's works really haven't measured democratization as a dependent variable. Thörnquist states that 'on a closer look one finds that the dependent variable of the social capital analyst is neither democratization nor democratic practice (despite the titles of books and applications for funds) but *government performance* (ibid., our italics)'.

While democracy in general links to good government, the latter cannot be *equated* with democracy, either empirically (which Singapore and other Southeast Asian Tiger economies have potently demonstrated) or conceptually (as good government may, at best, capture aspects of the *output* component of democracy, while basically leaving out the *input* aspect). Hence, institutions of governance may matter as a causal force of their own. Encarnación, among other commentators, shows how the social capital/civil society-democracy relationship really is not as direct as many would like to see it:

> [I]t is generally expected that for civil society to realize its full democratizing potential political institutions must be reduced, restrained, or pushed out of the way. Largely ignored

by this perspective is the decisive role that political institutions, from the state to the government to the party system, play in shaping the nature of civil society, including its organizational composition and political coloring. In playing this role, political institutions determine not only whether civil society is weak or strong but also whether it works to the benefit or detriment of democracy.

(2006: 36, see also Grix 2001)

Armony (2004: 54–55) also emphasizes institutions, especially those ensuring rule of law for the promotion of a benevolent civil society. Whitehead (2002: 84–85) lists a number of factors with the potential to destroy a healthy civil society, such as an irresponsible mass media, a 'disoriented electorate', irresponsible financial speculation and organized crime, thus furthering the claim that institutions and structures matter for the relationship between social capital and democracy, and noting that in new democracies these tend to be underdeveloped, or simply in a state of flux and turmoil.

Inequality

Uslaner (2003: 171) pushes the contextual argument further, stating that while one can find correlations between social capital and democracy, the relationship is essentially spurious: 'democracy doesn't make people more trusting', rather it is economic inequality that *decreases* trust. Armony (2004: 214) also deems the relationship contingent upon societal preconditions such as inequality (both socio-economic and rights-based). This is hardly new information. Tocqueville himself opened his *Democracy in America* by pointing out that:

> Among the new objects that attracted my attention during my stay in the United States, none struck my eye more vividly than the equality of conditions. I discovered without difficulty the enormous influence that this primary fact exerts on the course of society; it gives a certain direction to public spirit, a certain turn to the laws, new maxims to those who govern, and particular habits to the governed.
>
> *(Tocqueville 2000 [1835]: 3)*

Time

On a global level, one main finding has been that if the relationship between social capital and democracy exists at all, it is not necessarily linear, nor does it occur instantaneously. Norris (2001) compares the level of democracy in 47 states at various stages of democratic and socio-economic development. Her findings show that, looking at a composite measurement of social capital, the relationship to democracy is curvilinear, with older democracies scoring significantly higher than the new democracies on social capital, while autocracies linger somewhere in-between.

Similarly, according to Uslaner's (2003: 178) quantitative analysis, '[i]t takes 46 years of continuous democracy to move a country from well below the mean on trust to above it' (see also Armony 2004: 212). Muller and Seligson (1994) also test, and refute, the civic culture–democracy hypothesis, while noticing that long-term democracy does appear to have a positive effect on interpersonal trust. Valkov (2009: 2), who studies the post-communist countries, claims that the 'Toquevillian pattern is not universal', and finds that while the link between democracy and voluntary associations is significantly positive in the West, the results do not hold in other regions of the world.

This runs contrary to Welzel and Ingleharts's (2008: 131) findings that 'the length of time a society has lived under democratic institutions in fact show no impact on self-expression values' (in which interpersonal trust is a central component; see also Inglehart 2005). Tusalem (2007) also reaches somewhat more optimistic findings when looking at third- and fourth-wave democracies, recording a deepening of civil liberties and political freedoms (Freedom House's two components in measuring 'democracy') where civil society, both before and after transition, is measured as strong.[2]

Trust as an interaction effect

Many of the authors emphasizing time as a factor also appear to identify that levels of generalized trust not only are more important than associationalism, but also function as a prerequisite for, that is, an agent of, democratization. Norris (2001) thus finds that generalized trust consistently outperforms the level of associational membership as a determinant of level of democratization, as well as on political culture and electoral participation. Muller and Seligson (1994: 646) note that while some Latin American and southern European countries, such as Argentina, Portugal and Spain, managed to democratize despite low levels of interpersonal trust, both Guatemala and Panama, with apparently higher levels of interpersonal trust, failed to do the same.

Paxton (2002: 272) attempts to synthesize findings regarding the two main aspects of social capital and democracy, and finds that the impact of associational activity is contingent upon the level of trust, summarizing: 'the impact of associations on democracy depends on the level of trust present in society. At low levels of trust, increases in association memberships have a negative impact on democracy'. Only when around half of the population can be considered 'trusters' in a society (which is quite rare), does associationalism start to become a positive influence.

Political capital

Researchers favouring a more bottom-up-focused analysis also question the initial link between social capital and democracy. Here, the main argument relies on the claim that *political* capital is what ought to be considered most conducive to democratization. Booth and Richard (1998: 785–787) show that political capital variables (operationalized in terms of democratic norms, voting behaviour, contacting public officials and campaign activism) outperform social capital regarding correlation to levels of democracy in Central America. For example, 'the attitudes and behaviors stimulated by organizational membership that most clearly shape state performance (in this case the level of democracy) are those with an explicit political referent or impact' (Booth and Richard 1998: 796; see also Booth and Richard 2001; Wood 2001). Putzel (1997: 947) and Thörnquist (1998: 127) reach similar conclusions, preferring a more direct, i.e. political, link between civil society and democratization.

In a similar vein, Schuurman (2003: 1008) concludes that it may be time to take a closer look into the interplay between social capital, political capital and institutions, and their potential 'politico-emancipatory' effects:

> Whatever the outcome of the quest to reconnect the social and the political, it seems certain that civil society organizations will play an important role. There is reason to believe that social capital research, focusing especially on issues like bonding and bridging social capital and trust, can deliver valuable insights in assessing the capability of societies (at global, national or local levels) to reconnect the political and the social.

Social capital – mixed blessing?

Nevertheless, it would be a great exaggeration to claim that social capital is inherently bad or irrelevant for democratization. Rather, research has come to show that context matters, both regarding the external political and social preconditions, as well as the nature of civil society as such. Regarding the prospects for democratization, Encarnación (2006: 260) dubs social capital:

> a double-edged sword; citizens can just as easily employ it to build democracy as to under-mine it. The same social trust that emerges in organizations that civil society enthusiasts celebrate (trade unions, boy scouts, choral societies, and, most famously, bowling leagues) can also be located in the ones they detest (cults, gangs, militias, and terrorist organizations).

Regardless of whether social capital or democratization is perceived to be the driver of change, the mainstream view has long been that there does exist a strong and positive correlation, as indicated above. Still, a rather sizeable body of research finds the social capital-democratization claim, in Armony's (2004) words, 'dubious', or at least contingent upon a range of other factors. Some of these are said to pertain to the internal mechanisms of the social capital under study, while others are seen as external, often institutional, variables (Rothstein and Stolle 2008). Armony (2004: 213) finds that civil society 'tend to potentiate dominant features in the broader socio-historical context!' in a rather neutral manner. Van Deth and Zmerli (2010), as well as Levi (1996) and Rothstein (2005), note that any type of organization can benefit from the social capital generated through popular involvement, regardless of people's attitude towards democracy. In order to further our understanding of how social capital and civil society may be interrelated to democratization, we must look into how different types and perceptions of the concepts in question may have different effect in different contexts.

Associations and democracy

Contextual factors that affect the impact of popular associations upon democracy, both external and internal to the framework of civil society itself, are dissected in a volume edited by Sigrid Rossdeutscher (2005). The concluding findings are tied into the notion that an underlying political culture in reality decides the effects of associationalism in a given society. The presence of a 'democratic memory' upon which the associations can rely, combined with the level of internal hierarchy in the structure of organizations, are important. In addition, this study points to the difficulty of externally constructing institutions and organizations to do the job, which in the end decide whether the 'associative elixir' can be expected to actually work its magic for democratization (Rossdeutcher 2005: chapter 12).

As we have seen, associations are a key element for both civil society and social capital. Warren (2001: 61), a member of the 'optimist' camp, finds three main contributions from associationalism to democracy: first, the *developmental effect* on individuals', by which the school of democracy is strengthened. Second, the *public sphere effects*, through a creation of a 'social infrastructure' that give citizens a place to deliberate and debate. Third, Warren points to an *institutional effect* that works either directly through organizing voice for the citizenry towards the formal political process, or indirectly, by facilitating for individuals to exert their rights with regards to institutions and the market.

Warren further notes that different types of associations may potentially have different types of democratic effects. The three most relevant factors are: 1) degree of voluntariness (i.e. ease/cost of exit); 2) sphere of interest, such as economic, social attachment or political power, and the associations' embeddedness in the respective medium (i.e. vested or non-vested, 'inside' or 'outside' groups); and 3) objectives and purpose (i.e. what type of individual or social goods they attempt to achieve, such as social status, material wealth or interpersonal identity) (Warren 2001: 94ff). He continues by cross-matching these ideal types with the potential democratizing effects and finds that different associations have different values for democracy, both in terms of quantity and quality. A mix of these types, in his opinion, is most conducive to democracy (ibid.: 208).

Paxton (2002) empirically compares the democratic impact of different types of associations, dependent upon whether they are connected to other associations, i.e. their level of isolation or connectedness, measured as the average number of *other* associations members belong to. The findings are that this matters, as membership in isolated associations (such as trade unions, sport clubs and religious associations) are detrimental to the level of democracy in a nation, while 'connected' associations (for example, peace groups and human rights organizations) have a positive effect (Paxton 2002: 269–270). This runs partly contrary to Putnam's argument, and may lend further support to the political capital supporters (see above) as the most democracy-promoting association appear to have an explicitly political bend. One problem in this line of research is that it is not clear whether it is the 'politic-ness' or connectedness that matters (as trade unions, too, can be considered political). The close connection between trade unions and other economic interest organizations have been put forward as a form of 'organized social capital' that is related to research about the impact of neocorporatist structures (Rothstein 2002). In this context, a large literature has pointed out that in many Western democracies, associations can turn into political pressure groups that serve 'special interests' that becomes detrimental to the possibilities for the democratic machinery to act for the 'common good' (Lewin 1994; Zakaria 2003).

Consensus vs conflict

The focus on a possible consensual effect of social capital in general, and civil society in particular, has not been spared its share of criticism. Foley and Edwards (1996: 39) see civil society in a broader light: on the one hand, they see a 'type I' civil society, where emphasis is put upon 'the ability of associational life in general and the habits of association in particular to foster patterns of civility in the actions of citizens in a democratic polity', which is very much in line with Putnam's description, and a sphere in which social capital is likely to thrive. Additionally, Foley and Edward note that it is equally plausible to see civil society as a more conflict-based sphere: 'a sphere of action that is independent of the state and that is capable – precisely for this reason – of energizing resistance to a tyrannical regime'. This is precisely what Fox (1996: 1098) discovers to be the case with the Mexican Zapatista movement of the early 1990s. While this type of civil society may in fact have little to do with social capital, at least in the harmonious-Putnamic sense, it will still be measured as such, at least when one focuses on associational membership rates.

These two very different forms of civil society may have very different effects, depending on the type of society in which they operate. While the latter variant may be a potent force against an undemocratic regime, 'there is no reason in principle why the 'counterweight' of civil society should not become a burden to a democratic as well as an authoritarian state' (Foley and Edwards 1996: 39). This conflictual-within-a-democracy-type, Booth and Richard (1998) prefer to sort under a separate 'type III' category of civil society.

Fung similarly notes how associations can be understood to enhance democracy in very different ways, depending on whether the regime itself already is a democracy, or if it is an autocratic regime yet to be democratized. Still, the need for a conflictual associational sphere may also extend to quite advanced democracies, where civil liberties are not yet fully advanced, such as the USA in the 1960s:

> This rift between those who favor tame as opposed to mischievous associations as agents of democracy may stem from differences in their assessments of political context. In tyrannical

contexts, most observers agree that voluntary associations capable of resisting authority are crucial to democratic advance. In mature democracies like those of North America and Western Europe, it may be that the proliferation of mischievous associations – social-movement organizations and other unruly groups – would indeed increase equality and inclusion but do so at too high a cost to social peace and civic sentiments.

(Fung 2003: 520)

Interestingly, as Putnam's bestseller *Bowling Alone* (2000) laments, the time of the civil rights reforms was also the starting point of the 'collapse' of American community and social capital. This, in turn, begs for more elaborate questions about what we prioritize when attempting to define 'democracy'.

The civic road to autocracy

One notable case of a 'technically' well-functioning democracy descending into its complete opposite is the Weimar Republic. Sheri Berman (1997) convincingly shows how the strength of civil society, coupled with weak political institutions during the Weimar era in the German 1920s enabled the National Socialist takeover. Nationalistic associations largely out-competed established parties, leaving room for the Nazis, who had heavily invested in civil society, to grow and spread their influence. Berman is counted as a particularly influential critic of neo-Tocquevillianism, stating, similar to Armony (2004) and Encarnación (2006: 427), that 'associationalism should be considered a politically neutral multiplier – neither inherently good nor inherently bad, but rather dependent for its effects on the wider political context'.

Similarly, Riley (2005) compares the fascist movements in Italy and Spain during the same era, the 1920s, and notes that where the Italian fascists succeeded in co-opting and politicizing the voluntary sphere to strengthen their rule on society, the Spanish counterparts only managed to hold a looser grip on it, paving the way for a period of democratization, albeit brief and unstable, in the 1930s. Interestingly, the most civic regions in the Italian north, according to Putnam's 1993 study, were also the same regions where fascism was strongest and first to take over (something that has not gone unnoticed by many of his peers and critics; see for example Riley 2005; Kwon 2004; Laitin 1995: 173; Putzel 1997: 943).

The beneficial effects of the social-trust side of social capital may be equally contingent upon the greater political context, as the 'type I' associationalism can be expected to create a generalized form of trust, which further tends to correlate closely to trust and confidence in state institutions. If this is the case within an undemocratic context, social capital can potentially rather work to placate a citizenry, which otherwise could be demanding democracy according to the mainstream 'demo-cratization from below' camp. Rossdeutscher (2010) empirically shows how, according to Putnam, conceptually 'good' social capital can become detrimental in terms of prospects for democratization:

Trust increases the stability of nondemocratic leaderships by generating popular support, by suppressing regime threatening forms of protest activity, and by nourishing undemocratic ideals concerning governance. The conclusions concerning the associative sector are only slightly brighter. Voluntary activity also increases confidence in governments of nondemo-cratic regimes; it undermines protest action, but – in contrast to trust – strengthens the belief in democracy as the best form of governing a political community.

(Rossdeutscher 2010: 752)

In line with the roman numeral-conceptualization of civil society, Rossdeutscher's findings suggest that, just as 'type II' civil society can transform into a malicious type III, once its job of democratization is done, the social capital-bearing 'type I' may similarly need to be complemented with a 'type IV' for authoritarian regimes, where little societal change occurs in a stable but dictatorial society. In the words of Tocqueville: 'I shall acknowledge without difficulty that public peace in a great good; but I nevertheless do not want to forget that it is through good order that all peoples have arrived at tyranny' (Tocqueville 2000 [1835]: 516). The claim that interpersonal trust can exist within autocracies is in no way an overextended claim; among the group of highest trusting populations in the World Value Surveys, we find, for instance China, Belarus and Iran.

... And back again

These studies point not only to the fact that there is a dark side to civil society and social capital, but also that the composition of voluntary associations, and with them, civil society in general, is not static, but can change over time. Just as Riley's and Berman's examples of fascism colonizing the civic sphere show how associations can change for the negative, authors such as Haddad (2010) demonstrate how Japanese volunteer fire-fighters post-Second World War gradually have transformed from a traditional, militaristic and undemocratic organization to one more in accord with today's democratic society. In Pérez-Diaz's (2002 see also Whitehead 2002: 78) historic survey of the development of social capital in Francoist Spain, a similar transition took place. Here, the initially radical and rather 'uncivil' associational sphere in the war-torn society of the 1930s and 40s was eventually 'tamed' (ibid.: 285) during the latter and 'softer' part of Franco's tenure. This indicates that a 'type II' civil society, with time, can morph into a more peaceful 'type I' variant, alongside gradual political liberalization. When, following Franco's death, democratization did take place:

> we find that a stock of social capital of the civil kind had already been accumulated. This was a reservoir of goodwill on which the political and social leaders of the late 1970s would draw in order to make the democratic transition and consolidation successful.
>
> *(Ibid.)*

Diamond (2008: 53) accredits civil society as one of the main contributors to the 'third wave of democratization', and alludes to Inglehart's thesis of socio-economic development–cultural shift– stable democracy (see Inglehart 1999: 97), while noting that an increased notion of self-expression and emancipation from authority generates higher levels of 'peaceful protest activities', which lasts 'even well after the surge of mass mobilization to bring down dictatorship has subsided'. Tusalem (2007: 371) contrasts Putnam's major findings regarding civil society and democracy with the 'Berman (2009) critique' in the third- and fourth-wave democracies, and finds enough evidence to vindicate Putnam, demonstrating 'that a strong civil society before and after transition is, in fact, strongly correlated with a positive effect on deepening political freedoms and civil liberties'.

New and struggling democracies

Sztompka (1999) gives a theoretical account of the many unexpectedly complicated relationships between trust and democracy. In his opinion, democracies are based upon a view that people in general can be trusted, and thus, paradoxically, institutionalizes distrust, i.e. the possibility to dissent, as demonstrated in the system of checks and balances built into most democratic constitutions (see also Cook *et al.* 2005). Autocracies, on the other hand, operate under a diametrically different notion. Here, the citizenry is essentially an enemy not to be trusted, and thus the leadership attempts to institutionalize trust, giving it life-support on their own terms. While the 'spontaneous' and organic form of trust in the former mode of governance is in the end to be preferred, Sztompka argues, the most detrimental condition for a culture of trust might in fact not be an outright autocracy, but when a democracy or autocracy falters and reserves of either spontaneous or institutionalized trust become depleted, resulting in passive prebendalism, corruption and social fractionalization.

Several empirical studies have given this outlook support. Apart from the quantitative findings mentioned above, time is very much a factor in the link between social capital and democratization. Uslaner and Badescu (2003), who look at generational differences in various social capital-relevant variables in post-communist Romania and Moldova, find that people who became adults after democratization, while having a greater satisfaction with life overall, are less trusting in their peers as well as the political system, while showing a lower rate of civic organization. This indicates that democratization in these countries has effectively decreased the level of social capital over the course of a single generation. These findings thus lend no support to the democratization-social capital argument, but rather the reverse. Rose and Weller (2003: 214) reach similarly problematic, if slightly different, conclusions in a study of late 1990s Russia, finding that while generalized trust has a weak, but positive influence on democratic values, 'Russians involved in social capital networks tend to be less supportive of democratic values'.

In a study of contemporary Palestine, Jamal (2007: 130) finds that, while the link between interpersonal trust and confidence in the regime (political trust) is positive, in such a polarized and dubiously democratic context, it was the supporters of the undemocratic regime who displayed higher levels of interpersonal trust. Members of anti-regime associations were, in turn, low on interpersonal and political trust but high on democratic values. Jamal paints an enlightening picture of how context matters:

> Because democrats tended to fall outside of the PNA [Palestinian National Authority], they could not rely on government institutions to sanction those who might sever relationships based on trust. Because they – for good reason – had little faith in the government and believed that all citizens should work together to overcome the abuses of the regime, they sought the help of their fellow citizens, expecting them to be as disappointed and frustrated with the inadequacies of government as they were. But when more and more citizens became part of the PNA's clientilistic regime, democrats were dealt a serious blow, and their levels of trust plummeted. Democrats saw those who involved themselves in patron-client relations as communal sellouts. Levels of interpersonal distrust, then, are a positive indicator when we consider whether citizens desire, demand, and work for democratic reforms in a nondemocratic polity. Just as levels of trust can be good in some polities, so too can levels of distrust.
>
> (Ibid.: 134–135)

Whitehead (2002) mirrors Sztompka's claim of the threats to trust, noting that civil society is under fire from two main directions, traditional particularism and an intrusive state, both of which we can exemplify in the history of Italy, with Mussolini's fascism colonizing the north, and amoral familism still being a problem in the south. However, civil society could be threatened not so much from statism or traditional familism, but from a majoritarian incivility generated by democratization itself. This could arise out of the gap between civil society and the emerging citizenry, something the experiences of many emerging democracies tend to confirm.

Change is not an easy thing, neither accomplishing it, nor dealing with its repercussions. Even in more successful cases of democratization, where social capital and civil society are perceived to be an element of positive change, the link is not necessarily linear. Pickvance (1999: 367; see also Diamond 1999; Encarnación 2006; Seligman 2009) shows how voluntary associations tend to increase in numbers during the liberalization phase of an autocratic rule, only to decline once democratization has been carried through. This, he believes, is due to a 'crowding out' effect from parties and other more institutionalized actors, such as political parties, now legal and thriving. Albeit the sample of cases is restricted to Spain, Hungary and Hong Kong, the author refers to similar findings across Latin America.

The problematic and at times confusing findings regarding the influence of social capital in different stages of democratization and de-democratization can perhaps best be explained as either 'rocking the boat', through a more conflictual (and, according to some, ridden with unsocial capital) 'type II' and 'type III' civil society, while its 'type I' and possible 'type IV' counterparts rather stabilizes the situation at hand, disregarding whether the said situation, from a democratic point of view, is good or bad.

Conclusion

The relation between social capital and democratization is as fascinating as it is complex. On the one hand, democracies, along with other 'good' factors (such as economic development, control of corruption, gender equality) are generally higher on social capital than non-democracies. On the other hand, social capital has been deteriorating in many established democracies, especially in the US. Moreover, while social capital's link with democracy appears to be positive, its relationship to the actual process of democratization appears to be either non-existent or, in some cases, even negative. Furthermore, while the hypothesis of the need for associations following initial liberalization may hold true, this does not explain the low levels of interpersonal trust in many transitional countries. In general, while we believe that social capital as a concept has been of great value for understanding 'what makes democracy work', many if not most of the causal mechanisms are still unclear, and will probably be so until longer time-series data are being gathered, and the sensitivity towards geographic- and historically specific differences increases. Still, then, the reciprocal circle argument may be hard to refute.

Notes

1 It should be noted, however, that Putnam later has acknowledged the existence of negative, darker shades of social capital (2000: 350–363). Nevertheless, he remains very much an optimist in the matter.
2 http://www.freedomhouse.org/.

References

Almond, Gabriel A. and Sidney Verba (1989 [1963]) *The Civic Culture: Political Attitudes and Democracy in Five Nations*. Newbury Park: Sage.

Armony, Ariel C. (2004) *The Dubious Link: Civic Engagement and Democratization*. Stanford, CA: Stanford University Press.

Berman, Sheri (1997) 'Civil Society and the Collapse of the Weimar Republic', *World Politics*, 49 (3), pp. 401–429.

Berman, Sheri (2009) 'Re-integrating the Study of Civil Society and the State'. In *Is Democracy Exportable?*, ed. Zoltan Barany and Robert G. Moser. Cambridge: Cambridge University Press.

Booth, John A. and Patricia Bayer Richard (1998) 'Civil Society, Political Capital and Democratization in Central America', *Journal of Politics*, 60 (3), pp. 780–800.

—— and Patricia Bayer Richard (2001) 'Civil Society and Political Context in Central America'. In *Beyond Toqueville: Civil Society and the Social Capital Debate in Comparative Perspective*, ed. Bob Edwards, Michael W. Foley and Mario Diani. Hanover, NH: University Press of New England.

Burnell, Peter J. and Peter Calvert, eds (2004) *Civil Society in Democratization, Democratization Studies*. London: Frank Cass.

Cook, Karen S., Russell Hardin and Margaret Levi (2005) *Cooperation without Trust?* New York: Russell Sage Foundation.

Diamond, Jared (1999) *Developing Democracy: Toward Consolidation*. Baltimore, MD: Johns Hopkins University Press.

Diamond, Jared (2008) *The Spirit of Democracy: The Struggle to Build Free Societies Throughout the World*. New York, NY: Times Books/Henry Holt & Co.

Dryzek, John S. (1996) 'Political Inclusion and the Dynamics of Democratization', *American Political Science Review*, 90 (3), pp. 475–487.

Encarnación, Omar G. (2006) 'Review: Civil Society Reconsidered', *Comparative Politics*, 38 (3), pp. 357–376.

Foley, Michael W. and Bob Edwards (1996) 'The Paradox of Civil Society', *Journal of Democracy*, 7 (3), pp. 38–52.

Fox, Jonathan (1996) 'How Does Civil Society Thicken? The Political Construction of Social Capital in Rural Mexico'. *World Development*, 24, pp. 1089–1103.

Fung, Archon (2003) 'Associations and Democracy: Between Theories, Hopes and Realities', *Annual Review of Sociology*, 29, pp. 515–539.

Gahramanova, Aytan (2009) 'Internal and External Factors in the Democratization of Azerbadjan', *Democratization*, 16 (4), pp. 777–803.

Grix, Jonathan (2001) 'Social Capital as a Concept in the Social Sciences: The Current State of the Debate', *Democratization*, 8 (3), pp. 189–210.

Haddad, Mary Alice (2010) 'From Undemocratic to Democratic Civil Society: Japan's Volunteer Fire Departments', *Journal of Asian Studies*, 69 (1), pp. 33–56.

Hydén, Goran (1997) 'Civil Society, Social Capital, and Development: Dissection of a Complex Discourse', *Studies International Development*, 32 (1), pp. 3–30.

Inglehart, Ronald (1999) 'Trust, Well-being and Democracy' In *Democracy and Trust*, ed. Mark E. Warren. Cambridge: Cambridge University Press.

—— (2005) 'Inglehart-Welzel Cultural Map of the World', *World Values Survey*; available at worldvalues-survey.orgwvs/articles/folder_published/article_base_54.

Jamal, Amaney A. (2007) *Barriers to Democracy: The Other Side of Social Capital in Palestine and the Arab World*. Princeton, NJ: Princeton University Press.

Krishna, Anirudh (2002) *Active Social Capital: Tracing the Roots of Development and Democracy*. New York, NY: Columbia University Press.

Kwon, Hyeong-Ki (2004) 'Associations, Civic Norms and Democracy: Revisiting the Italian Case', *Theory & Society*, 33 (2), pp. 135–166.

Laitin, David D. (1995) 'The Civic Culture at 30', *American Political Science Review*, 89 (1), pp. 168–173.

Letki, Natalia and Geoffrey Evans (2005) 'Endogenizing Social Trust: Democratization in East-Central Europe', *British Journal of Political Science*, 35 (3), pp. 515–529.

Levi, Margaret (1996) 'Social and Unsocial Capital: A Review Essay of Robert Putnam's "Making Democracy Work" ', *Politics & Society*, 24 (1), pp. 45–55.

Lewin, Leif (1994) 'The Rise and Decline of Corporatism', *European Journal of Political Research*, 26 (1), pp. 59–79.

Lipset, Seymour M. (1959) 'Some Social Requisites of Democracy: Economic Development and Political Legitimacy', *American Political Science Review*, 53 (1), pp. 69–105.

Muller, Edward N. and Mitchell A. Seligson (1994) 'Civic Culture and Democracy: The Question of Causal Relationships', *American Political Science Review*, 88 (3), pp. 635–652.

Newton, Kenneth (2001) 'Social Capital and Democracy'. In *Beyond Toqueville: Civil Society and the Social Capital Debate in Comparative Perspective*, ed. Bob Edwards, Michael W. Foley and Mario Diani. Hanover, NH: University Press of New England.

Norris, Pippa (2001) 'Making Democracies Work: Social Capital and Civic Engagement in 47 Societies', John F. Kennedy School of Government, Harvard University Working Paper Series 01–036.

Ostrom, Elinor (1990) *Governing the Commons: The Evolution of Institutions for Collective Action*. New York: Cambridge University Press.

—— (1998) 'A Behavioral Approach to the Rational Choice Theory of Collective Action: Presidential Address, American Political Science Association 1997', *American Political Science Review*, 92 (1), pp. 1–22.

Paxton, Pamela (2002) 'Social Capital and Democracy: An Interdependent Relationship', *American Sociological Review*, 67 (2), pp. 254–277.

Pérez-Díaz, Víctor (2002) 'From Civil War to Civil Society: Social Capital in Spain from the 1930s to the 1990s'. In *Democracies in Flux: The Evolution of Social Capital in Contemporary Society*, ed. Robert D. Putnam. Oxford: Oxford University Press.

Pickvance, Christopher G. (1999) 'Democratisation and the Decline of Social Movements: The Effects of Regime Change on Collective Action in Eastern Europe, Southern Europe and Latin America', *Sociology*, 33 (2), pp. 353–372.

Putnam, Robert D. (1993) *Making Democracy Work: Civic Traditions in Modern Italy*. Princeton, NJ: Princeton University Press.

Putnam, Robert D. (2000) *Bowling Alone: The Collapse and Revival of American Community*. New York: Simon & Schuster.

Putzel, James (1997) 'Accounting for the "Dark Side" of Social Capital: Reading Robert Putnam on Democracy', *Journal of International Development*, 9 (7), pp. 939–949.

Rawls, John (1971) *A Theory of Justice*. Oxford: Oxford University Press.

Riley, Dylan (2005) 'Civic Associations and Authoritarian Regimes in Interwar Europe: Italy and Spain in Comparative Perspective', *American Sociological Review*, 70 (2), pp. 288–310.

Rose, Richard and Craig Weller (2003) 'What Does Social Capital Add to Democratic Values?' In *Social Capital and the Transition to Democracy*, ed. Gabriel Badescu and Eric M. Uslaner. London: Routledge.

Rossdeutscher, Sigrid (2005) 'The Associative Elixir: Lure or Cure?' In *Democracy and the Role of Associations: Political, Organizational and Social Contexts*, ed. Sigrid Rossdeutscher. London: Routledge/ECPR studies in European political science series.

—— (2010) 'Social Capital Worldwide: Potential for Democratization or Stabilizer of Authoritarian Rule?', *American Behavioral Scientist*, 53 (5), pp. 737–757.

Rothstein, Bo (2002) 'Sweden: Social Capital in the Social Democratic State'. In *Democracies in Flux: The Evolution of Social Capital in Contemporary Society*, ed. Robert D. Putnam. Oxford: Oxford University Press.

—— (2005) *Social Traps and the Problem of Trust*. Cambridge: Cambridge University Press.

—— and Dietlind Stolle (2008) 'The State and Social Capital: An Institutional Theory of Generalized Trust', *Comparative Politics*, 40, pp. 441–467.

Rudebeck, Lars and Olle Thörnquist (1998) 'Introduction'. In *Democratization in the Third World*, ed. Lars Rudebeck, Olle Thörnquist Virgilio Rojas. Basingstoke, UK: Macmillan.

Schuurman, Frans J. (2003) 'Social Capital: The Politico-Emancipatory Potential of a Disputed Concept', *Third World Quarterly*, 24 (6), pp. 991–1010.

Seligman, Adam B. (2009) 'Democracy, Civil Society, and the Problem of Tolerance'. In *Is Democracy Exportable?*, ed. Zoltan Barany and Robert G. Moser. Cambridge: Cambridge University Press.

Stolle, Dietlind (2003) 'The Sources of Social Capital'. In *Generating Social Capital: Civil Society and Institutions in Comparative Perspective*, ed. Marc Hooghe and Dietlind Stolle. New York, NY: Palgrave Macmillan.

Sztompka, Piotr (1999) *Trust: A Sociological Theory*. Cambridge: Cambridge University Press.

Tarrow, Sidney (1996) 'Making Political Science Work across Space and Time: A Critical Reflection on Robert Putnam's Making Democracy Work', *American Political Science Review*, 90 (2), pp. 389–397.

Teorell, Jan (2011) *Determinants of Democratization: Explaining Regime Change in the World, 1972–2006*. Cambridge: Cambridge University Press.

Thörnquist, Olle (1998) 'Making Democratization Work: From Civil Society and Social Capital to Political Inclusion and Politization–Theoretical Reflections on Concrete Cases in Indonesia, Kerala and the Philippines'. In *Democratization in the Third World*, ed. Lars Rudebeck, Olle Thörnquist and Virgilio Rojas. Basingstoke, UK: Macmillan.

Tocqueville, Alexis de (2000 [1835]) *Democracy in America*. Chicago: University of Chicago Press.

Tusalem, Rollin F. (2007) 'A Boon or a Bane? The Role of Civil Society in Third- and Fourth-Wave Democracies', *International Political Science Review*, 28 (3), pp. 361–386.

Uslaner, Eric M. (2003) 'Trust, Democracy and Governance: Can Government Policies Influence Generalized Trust?' In *Generating Social Capital: Civil Society and Institutions in Comparative Perspective*, ed. Marc Hooghe and Dietlind Stolle. New York, NY: Palgrave Macmillan.

—— and Gabriel Badescu (2003) 'Legacies and Conflicts: The Challenges to Social Capital in the Democratic Transition'. In *Social Capital and the Transition to Democracy*, ed. Gabriel Badescu and Eric M. Uslaner. London: Routledge.

Valkov, Nikolay (2009) 'Membership in Voluntary Organizations and Democratic Performance: European Post-Communist Countries in Comparative Perspective', *Communist & Post-Communist Studies*, 42 (1), pp. 1–21.

van Deth, Jan W. (2008) 'Part II: Democratic Politics – Introduction: Social Capital and Democratic Politics'. In *The Handbook of Social Capital*, ed. Dario Castglione, Jan W. van Deth and Guglielmo Wolleb. Oxford: Oxford University Press.

—— and Sonja Zmerli (2010) 'Introduction: Civicness, Equality and Democracy – A 'Dark Side' of Social Capital?', *American Behavioral Scientist*, 53 (5), pp. 631–639.

Warren, Mark E. (1999) 'Conclusion'. In *Democracy and Trust*, ed. Mark E. Warren. Cambridge: Cambridge University Press.

—— (2001) *Democracy and Association*. Princeton, NJ: Princeton University Press.

Welzel, Christian and Ronald Inglehart (2008) 'The Role of Ordinary People in Democratization', *Journal of Democracy*, 19 (1), pp. 126–140.

Whitehead, Laurence (2002) *Democratization: Theory and Experience*. Oxford: Oxford University Press.

Wood, Richard L. (2001) 'Political Culture Reconsidered: Insights on Social Capital from an Ethnography of Faith-Based Community Organizing'. In *Beyond Toqueville: Civil Society and the Social Capital Debate in Comparative Perspective*, ed. Bob Edwards, Michael W. Foley and Mario Diani. Hanover, NH: University Press of New England.

Zakaria, Fareed (2003) *The Future of Freedom: Illiberal Democracy at Home and Abroad*. New York: W. W. Norton & Co.

Part III
Democratization and international relations

17

The third and fourth waves of democracy

Fabrice Lehoucq[1]

Democratization refers to the shift from non-democratic to democratic forms of government. It involves expanding the size of the electorate, typically by lifting the property, literacy, or gender requirements that keep the poor, the uneducated or females from voting. Democratization improves protection for individual rights by restricting the ability of state officials to jail or otherwise harass their critics. It amplifies the power of elected officials by curtailing the authority of unelected officials, especially those of monarchs and military officers. And it makes citizens, at regularly scheduled intervals, responsible for selecting executives and legislatures in relatively free and fair elections.

This chapter concentrates on the last two dimensions of democratization and it seeks to identify and examine what was distinctive about the third wave of democratization (Huntington 1991), while also commenting on what some call the fourth wave of democratization. The first and longest wave of democratization started in 1828 with the elimination of property requirements for voting in many states of the United States, which thus expanded the franchise to nearly half of (white male) voters. The first wave ended in 1926 with fascist takeovers in several European countries, including Germany and Italy, by which time most democracies had universal suffrage rights. The second wave was much shorter, lasting less than two decades between 1943 and 1962, during which a number of countries, once again including Germany and Italy, either democratized or redemocratized. The third wave began with a revolution in Portugal in 1974, which saw the military take office in 1974 before democratic elections – and European Union membership, in that order – followed. The third wave continued with the decline and removal of military government in Latin America during the 1980s. It sought to create new, democratic states in the wake of the Soviet Union's collapse in 1991, and also had an impact in other world regions, including Sub-Saharan Africa and Asia. Some argue that the transition away from communism in Eastern Europe and the former Soviet Union constitutes a fourth wave of democratization (McFaul 2002). In this chapter, I discuss these trends under the rubric of the third wave for the sake of simplicity, while highlighting the distinctive features of the transitions of the post-communist world.

This chapter identifies, first, the distinctive traits of the third and fourth waves of democracy. Second, it will review the causes of the marked increase in the absolute and relative number of democracies and semi-democracies since 1980. It suggests that international events, including the collapse of the Soviet Union and the increase in global interest rates, triggered changes that often (but not always) led to transitions to some form of – often limited – democracy. When these changes weakened incumbents, opposition movements were often able to negotiate fundamental changes to political systems. Third, it surveys some of the key challenges faced by new democracies: all too many third- and fourth-wave democracies suffer from citizen apathy, institutional sclerosis and low rates of economic growth. This chapter is largely a work of synthesis and interpretation: it summarizes key findings and trends necessary to make sense of the historical significance of the third and fourth waves of democracy. It relies upon comparative politics datasets (including Polity IV and the Economist Intelligence Unit ranking of political systems) to document key claims.

The third and fourth waves: basic facts

The data in Figure 17.1 depict trends in regime developments since the mid-twentieth century, which approximates the dates mentioned by Huntington (1991). It uses Polity IV's classification of regimes, which is based upon a quantitative scale running from −10 to 10 (Polity IV 2011). Until the mid-1970s, most political systems were autocratic, a trend that started after the Second World War, even as Huntington's second democratic wave came to an end in the early 1960s. The number of countries with democratic political systems began to increase from the mid-1970s. Both the proportion of countries with democratic *and* semi-democratic systems – the latter refers to regimes with both democratic and non-democratic features – increased notably by the late 1980s. By semi-democratic, Polity IV refers to political systems it rates between −5 to 5 on its 20-point scale. By 1991, 47 per cent and 26 per cent of polities were, respectively, democratic and semi-democratic. By the mid-1990s, more than half the world's national political systems were characterized as 'democratic', a figure to which we can add one-quarter of the world's countries that had 'semi-democratic' political systems. In sum, the third wave of democracy was a two-decade period, from the mid-1970s to the mid-1990s, which saw many new democracies and semi-democracies come into being.

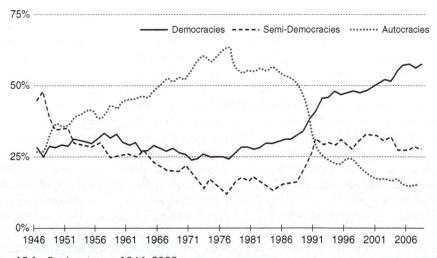

Figure 17.1 Regime types, 1946–2008

Notes: Semi-democracies (or anocracies) are regimes with scores between –5 and 5. Autocracies score between –10 and –6 and democracies rate between .6 and 10.

Source: Polity IV.

Where did regimes change? Figure 17.2 shows the results of a systematic classification of regimes in 2010, approximately some 35 years after the start of the third wave of democratization in 1974. This effort, which is broadly consistent with Polity IV's findings, indicates that political landscapes have changed, often dramatically, in Eastern Europe, Latin America (including the Caribbean) and in Asia-Pacific. More than 60 per cent of the regimes in the 80 countries in these regions are democratic, whether of the 'fully' or 'flawed' sort. On the eve of the third wave, the vast majority of these countries had unelected governments. While many countries in sub-Saharan Africa underwent regime change in the 1990s, around 60 per cent of the region's 44 countries had unelected governments in 2011. Regimes did not change in North America/Western Europe and in the Middle East/North Africa, though for very different reasons, although very recent events in Egypt, Tunisia and elsewhere may change regime types in the future. The vast majority of the 20 regimes in the Middle East (including the Arab countries of North Africa) were authoritarian at the time of writing (April 2011), even if the overthrow of long-term presidents in Tunisia and Egypt in early 2011 suggests that social movements in some countries are spearheading what may turn out to be far-reaching political reforms. Finally, democracies exist in all 23 Western European countries, as well as Canada and the United States; note, however, that all these countries had democratic regimes in place at the start of the third wave.

The classification in Figure 17.2 is produced by the Economist Intelligence Unit (EIU), the sister company of *The Economist* magazine. I use this classification because it, first, improves upon Polity IV's classification by being more explicit about the criteria it uses to measure the various dimensions of democracy. Second, it adds data about the quality of democratic institutions – that is, about how well governments function – to the conventional list of defining criteria of democracy emphasizing competitive and regularly scheduled elections, universal suffrage rights, and a robust and comprehensive system of civil liberties. Third, it also modifies these last two features by adding rating systems on how democratic (and satisfied) their citizens are, and the extensiveness and quality of citizen participation in politics. On the basis of these five criteria – free, fair and competitive elections; civil liberties; well-functioning government; democratic political culture; and political participation – the EIU produces a fourfold classification of regimes: full democracies, flawed democracies, hybrid regimes and authoritarian systems.

Unlike full democracies, flawed democracies have poorly functioning governments, often ones with corrupt elected officials and officials otherwise unaccountable to the citizenry. Flawed regimes lack the institutions of horizontal accountability that can check the arbitrary behaviour

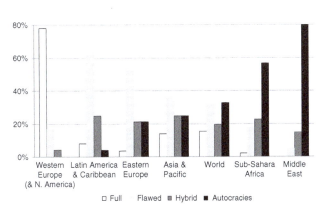

Figure 17.2 Types of democracy, by region, 2010
Source: Economist Intelligence Unit (2010).

of state officials, especially of the elected branches of government. They are also likely to have a large number of apathetic voters, who express little support for democracy and do not all turn out to vote on election day. Long-established democracies that the EIU categorizes as flawed suffer from these ailments. Israel is on this list because of restrictions on the civil liberties of some of its (Arab) citizens. Italy is on it because Prime Minister Silvio Berlusconi's (2008–present) huge media empire, when added to public television, restricts critical coverage of the government. And France has become a flawed democracy because public confidence in parties and the state has recently fallen dramatically. Most of Polity IV's democracies are what the EUI labels full and flawed democracies, though some of the latter are characterized as semi-democracies by Polity IV. Hybrid regimes are systems with low scores on several of the five dimensions, but high enough not to be called autocracies. These are systems that Andreas Schedler (2009) calls electoral authoritarian regimes. They have popularly elected executives, which typically maintain themselves in office by restricting political competition and deactivating the checks and balances of genuinely democratic constitutions.

This classification generates two sobering conclusions about the third and fourth waves of democracy. First, the EUI's classification suggests that the extent of democratization in the world can be exaggerated. Not only are half the political systems in the world hybrid or authoritarian regimes, but two key parts of the world – sub-Saharan Africa and the Middle East – remain largely unaffected by democratization. And only about half of the political systems of Asia-Pacific are democracies of one type or another. Second, a lot of these regimes are low-quality democracies. While the normative superiority of flawed democracy over hybrid or authoritarian regimes is hard to deny, many of the problems of the autocracies of yesteryear – especially that of unaccountable governments – have become the ailments of many of today's democratic systems.

Why do autocracies democratize?

Why (and how) dictatorships become democracies is a perennial question. Modern responses to this question begin with the claim originally made by Seymour Martin Lipset (1959) that development is associated with political and economic changes. This became known as modernization theory because of its emphasis on value changes – 'modernization' – that are said by Lipset to lead to societies that are supportive of democracy. Other approaches, ones that underscore the importance of the strategic calculations, identify the political conditions that lead autocrats to relinquish power to democratically elected officials.

Modernization theory and the third and fourth waves

Lipset (1959) was the first to draw systematic attention to the relationship between economic development and democracy, a relationship that he investigated through a simple classification of 48 political systems and a host of economic and social variables. Countries that had been democratic since the end of the First World War were wealthier, more industrialized, educated and urbanized. Lipset's pioneering study concluded that development inculcated the values of modernity among individuals and thus support for democratic systems. His findings also sparked a debate aiming to determine whether the empirical relationship is robust and whether higher incomes lead to democracy because development changes social values. This debate was fundamental to judgments about the democratic impact of the third and fourth waves.

Four decades of cross-national research, on balance, indicates that higher gross domestic product (GDP) per capita levels does not cause political systems to democratize. Adam Przeworski and his colleagues (2000) use a database of 135 countries to conclude that between 1950 and 1990 increases in levels of development did not boost the probability that a political system will become democratic. Daron Acemoglu and his co-authors (2008), using a database of 120 countries between 1960 and 2000, agree that the relationship between economic development and regime type is unproven. They argue that the beneficial effects on development of democracy disappear once statistical models use country-fixed effects (that is, statistical models that control for the effects of unexplained or omitted variables in cross-national regression equations). They suggest that the relationship between both factors is a product of how long countries have been independent, as well as how many checks and balances exist on executive authority and religious freedom.

But there is evidence for Lipset's claim that democracies are more likely to exist at higher levels of development. Przeworski and his co-authors (2000) argue that democracy is less likely to collapse at higher levels of development, which they argue explains why wealthier countries are more likely to be democratic than poorer countries. This relationship may be a product of the fact, as Carles Boix and Susan Stokes (2003) contend, that older democracies emerged in countries that were industrializing. After the Second World War, development does not generate democracy. So, the existence of a large number of democracies in the most developed parts of the world – Western Europe and North America, along with Australia, Japan and New Zealand – upholds this relationship. David Epstein and his co-authors (2006) are the most supportive of modernization theory. But their findings are contingent upon a threefold classification of regimes: while development does not encourage non-elected regimes to become democracies, departures from autocracy into partial democracy and transformations from this hybrid regime into democracy are highly contingent upon the dynamics of partial democracies.

There are several implications of existing cross-national, statistical research on our understanding of transitions to democracy. First, cultural attitudes – tolerance for minority opinions and interpersonal trust – do not appear to change with development. They are not the transmission belt of economic development, assuming that such a relationship exists in the modified forms suggested by the analysts cited in the previous paragraph. Edward Muller and Mitchell A. Seligson (1994) argue that in a sample of European and Central American countries they analyse, attitudes to democracy do not increase levels of democracy (but, see Inglehart and Welzel [2005] for a statement in support of the values change thesis). Second, political factors appear to be likely candidates to explain the shift to democratic regimes, especially in the contemporary world during the third and fourth waves. Boix and Stokes's paper, in fact, implies that non-economic factors significantly account for particular political developments in the larger number of countries that come into existence following decolonization of Africa and Asia during the 1950s and 1960s, and the breakup of the Soviet Union during the early 1990s. Finally, the study by Epstein and colleagues makes the point that the structure of intermediate regimes – political systems with democratic and authoritarian features – is central for their subsequent trajectory. Understanding how and why semi-democratic regimes become democracies is an area of active research; perhaps their openness allows incumbents to negotiate reforms with the opposition that leads to a broadening of the regime. Before identifying how political factors shaped different routes to democracy in the third and fourth waves, I discuss the inherently strategic nature of any transition from authoritarian rule and why some transitions lead to a fundamental break with the past.

Strategic calculations

To understand why, in some countries but not others, democracy replaced dictatorship during the third wave requires focusing upon the relationships between governments and their opponents, a point made long ago by Robert Dahl (1966). In control of the military, the decisions made by incumbents, whether they be lifting press restrictions or allowing opposition candidates to run for select offices, are the initial steps that shape, first, whether political liberalization occurs and, second, whether this is followed by democratization and, in some cases, a consolidated democracy.

The decision to liberalize and then democratize presents both autocrats and opposition movements with a strategic dilemma. Its resolution determines both the pace and final outcome of liberalization and democratization. Przeworski (1991) contends that hardliners – political actors perhaps willing to use violence to accomplish their objective of no change to the current regime – on both sides of this divide have no incentives to negotiate with their rivals because neither wants to share state power. Incumbent hardliners stick with the status quo because they do not want to share the spoils of office and/or because they consider the opposition to be dangerously subversive, in the sense that they would fatally undermine the current regime, if successful. For their part, opposition hardliners want nothing less than the dictatorship to capitulate, both because they distrust the regime and because they are fed up with the lack of democratic rights. Neither will back the actions of moderates, that is, those who are willing to share power with their adversaries. Knowing this, hardliners try to exercise their veto to prevent encounters between pro- and anti-government moderates from reaching concrete agreements. The dictatorship, as a result, continues.

Przeworski (1991) identifies three scenarios that lead to democracy. First, regime moderates disguise their true intentions and gain the assent of military hardliners to negotiate a mere broadening of the regime's support coalition. Once negotiations have reached a certain point and the opposition is able to mobilize large sectors of society, regime moderates show their true colours and democratic forces win the showdown with incumbent hardliners. Second, the dictatorship begins conversations with the opposition and discovers that it cannot repress its opponents. It updates its preferences and negotiates an agreement to democratize government. Third, contacts between the regime and its opponents teach both sides to trust each other. Hardliners conclude that regime change will not endanger their core interests because accords can be reached with their opponents that limit the impact of democratization on their interests.

In each of these outcomes, I would emphasize, it is the behaviour of the regime – especially of its security forces – that is pivotal. If the regime stays united, there is no opening, there is no liberalization. If the military splits, the strength of its opponents shapes the outcome of the bargaining between government and opposition. This is why only the first of these paths leads straightforwardly to democracy. Alongside street protesters, regime moderates seek to mobilize other resources – including, in some cases, organized groups of followers – against the incumbent regime. Situations where the opposition is stronger than anticipated may well lead to bloodbaths if regime moderates are neutralized. For example, the Algerian military's decision to annul the 1992 election results, one that the Islamist opposition party, the *Front Islamique de Salut*, was very likely to win, is a good example of regime moderates closing ranks with regime hardliners. The 1989 destruction of the youth movement in Tiananmen Square in Beijing, China is another example of this outcome. After several days of apparent disagreement, the Chinese Communist Party decided to quash the pro-democracy movement (Nathan and Link 2001).

In the second scenario, a dictatorship decides to crush the opposition, even if a fair reading of events suggests that it is unlikely to succeed. El Salvador's civil war (1979–94) is a good example of an aborted democratization. In October 1979, military reformers overthrew a hardline regime. They created a junta with civilian moderates that began conversations with mass movements. By early 1980, hardline officers, aided by US foreign policymakers, reasserted their control over government because military hardliners continued to gun down opposition protesters. Civilian moderates abandoned the junta and the rural insurgency intensified (Bonner 1984).

Mexico and South Africa are examples of the third scenario that ends in democratization, that is, where incumbents and the opposition negotiate and build trust over long periods of time. This route involves a long series of tiny reforms, ones that produce lengthy transitions to, first, democratization, and later, in some cases, to a recognizable democracy. For negotiations to prosper, there must be a commonality of interests, ones that encourages leaders to bargain and thus to conclude that compromise is preferable to conflict. In Mexico, a key sector of the opposition, led by the National Action Party (PAN), and presidents Carlos Salinas (1988–94) and Ernesto Zedillo (1994–2000) of the incumbent Institutional Revolutionary Party (PRI) wanted economic liberalization. Technocratic presidents of the PRI believed that dismantling a state-centred model of development would reactivate an economy that was instrumental in encouraging growing numbers of citizens to oppose the government. PAN wanted a better business climate, one that would allow capitalists to reap the returns on their investments (Thacker 2000). And PAN, as well as the Party of the Democratic Revolution (PRD), wanted a level playing field to wrest power from the long-standing incumbents, the PRI. By 2000, the Mexican people obliged by electing Vicente Fox of PAN, the first opposition president in Mexico (Domínguez and Lawson 2004): a clear case of democratization by gradual agreement.

In South Africa, the common interests between the black majority and the white minority regime were harder to fathom (Sparks 1995). Regime moderates, especially in the business community, wanted international sanctions to end. They also wanted an end to extensive civil unrest. While the black African majority wanted a swift end to an oppressive government, Nelson Mandela and other nationalists concluded that making South Africa democratically stable and economically vibrant would require the cooperation of the business community, largely in white hands. Long-term negotiations and endless meetings allowed both sides to fix upon the institutional compromises that would protect their core interests (Sisk 1995).

Note that conflict is intrinsic to democratic transitions. Since Dankwart Rustow (1970), students of democratization have highlighted this point. The main thrust of Charles Tilly's work, especially in the last decade of his life, was that authoritarian regimes rarely give up without a fight (Tilly 2006; also, see Markoff 1996); mass mobilization is an indispensable part of creating political systems that respect civil rights and are responsive to citizens. A central implication is that electoral competition within well-defined institutional boundaries is hard to construct, even if it appears to be well entrenched in 30 or so countries with full democracies. A related implication is that political conflict in the context of democratization should not shift the balance of power decisively in favour of one set of interests. Conflict among a network of forces encourages them to turn agreements into institutions that can turn a democratic transition into a consolidated democracy.

Triggering events and trends

The scenarios that can lead to democratization and then democracy can be a result of endogenous change. Modernization theory, for whose claims the evidence is mixed, is one version of how domestic change can lead to a gradual shift from authoritarianism to greater democracy. The third and fourth waves of democracy, however, have largely been products of non-economic changes, and typically of exogenous change. In this section, I discuss three types of events or trends that can lead members of the ruling body to shift decisively in favour of a transition to democracy, each of which overlaps with changes in the parts of the world that experienced the most political transformation during the last two decades of the twentieth century.

Economic Crisis. Much of Latin America began the 1980s with economic collapse, caused by the decline in the region's terms of trade and, most importantly, the global rise in interest rates (Devlin 1993). Both trends reduced incomes, especially among the poor, and led many regional countries to experience a dramatically declining economic situation. The outcome was that many governments cut their expenditures and raised taxes, decisions that encouraged citizens in many countries to mobilize in pursuit of regime change. In many countries, these events led to incumbent governments beginning to negotiate with opposition leaders.

Research shows that autocracies are more likely to crumble in the face of economic adversity than are democracies (Geddes 1999). During the third wave, military regimes, from Peru to Brazil and from Ecuador to Chile, began to bargain with adversaries. Such conversations typically led to a freer press, reductions in martial law, and constitutional reforms, often after voters chose members of Constituent Assemblies. Agreements were struck to turn power over to democratically elected presidents once leaders of governments and opposition movements were able to build the necessary trust to take forward negotiations. In Argentina and Chile, it took mass mobilization to force the hand of regimes that remained unified around hardliners. Stimulated by the Argentine generals' 1982 decision to invade the Falkland Islands and the subsequent defeat by Britain in the Falklands/Malvinas conflict, the incumbent non-democratic regime collapsed, followed by democratic elections in 1983. In addition, in 1989, a majority of Chileans voted for the end of the Pinochet regime, a referendum that forced the regime to honour its promise to hold competitive elections for both presidency and legislature.

In sub-Saharan Africa, the political consequences of economic decline were more ambiguous. Though this trend was 'the impulse to reform', to cite Robert Bates (1994), many non-elected regional governments were able to settle for little more than the liberalization of the harshest aspects of authoritarianism, which produced a lively debate about the extent and significance of political change (Gibson 2002). Quite a few held reasonably free and fair elections, which was a novel development in most cases (Bratton and Van de Walle 1997; Lindberg 2006). Few autocracies, however, have been replaced by democratically responsive governments overall in sub-Saharan Africa, as the data in Figure 17.2 reveals. By 2010, 80 per cent of the political systems in these countries had governments characterized more by their authoritarian than their democratic aspects.

The End of the Cold War. The security concerns of the superpowers, the US and the Soviet Union, helped shape their relationships with states large enough to threaten their existence, while sometimes encouraging democratic forces in smaller states, including ones that had long been disinclined to hold competitive and non-fraudulent elections. The Cold War widely affected the contours of state design and democratic politics in the post-Second World War era. The impact of the Cold War appears to have been considerable in Eastern Europe, where the Soviet Union helped to cement the power of communist regimes. American backing for undemocratic regimes in Latin America, sub-Saharan Africa, the Middle East and Asia were also commonplace during the Cold War (Schmitz 2006), although perhaps only in Central America did the end of the Cold War have as much of an impact on political systems as it had in Eastern Europe.

Three events helped to trigger political transformation in Soviet-dominated Eastern Europe. The first was perestroika, interactive economic and political reforms undertaken under the leadership of Mikhail Gorbachev, the general secretary of the Communist Party of the Soviet Union, during 1985–91, which fatally undermined the unity and continuity of the Soviet regime. Regime moderates such as Gorbachev took over the Communist Party and began to unravel its political and economic monopoly. Second, Gorbachev's decision not to block the 1989 historic elections in Poland, elections that saw parties aligned with the Solidarity labour union capture all open seats, signalled the end of Soviet support for regimes in Eastern Europe. One by one, mass mobilization forced dramatic concessions from the communist regimes of Eastern Europe. In 1990, political change began to threaten the integrity of the Soviet Union itself. Nationalist leaders in the three Baltic states – Estonia, Latvia and Lithuania – declared their independence, which the Soviet Union recognized one year later.

Third, the collapse of the Soviet Union led to the rapid formation of a number of new states, a trend that a number of scholars suggest constitutes a 'fourth wave' of democratisation (Bunce, McFaul and Stoner-Weiss 2010). The breakup of the Soviet Union was itself the result of gradual economic decline, and especially of infighting within the Communist Party and mass mobilization in Russia and throughout the federated republics of the Union itself (Beissinger 2002). Perestroika and glasnost ('opening up') did not, however, go uncontested within the Communist Party. The allied policy of *demokratizatsiya*, quite literally democratization, led to multi-candidate elections in March 1989, where reformers won all 300 open seats to the Congress of People's Deputies, elections that nevertheless preserved 87 per cent of the total seats for regime-sanctioned members of the Communist Party (most remained in the hands of appointed deputies). In 1991, hardliners failed to overthrow the incumbent government. The aborted coup led not only to a rapid transition away from totalitarianism in Russia, but also a breakup of the Soviet Union itself as street protesters joined regime moderates to call for fundamental changes.

The collapse of the Soviet Union dramatically undermined the ability of incumbent communist regimes elsewhere in the Soviet bloc to crush the opposition. Regional communist regimes could no longer count upon Soviet troops to overthrow putative reformers, as they did in Hungary (1956) and in Czechoslovakia (1968). Like the government of the Soviet Union, communist regimes elsewhere in the Soviet-led bloc had become incapacitated as a result of economic mismanagement and political repression (Kotkin 2009). Unable to repress their adversaries, these regimes were forced to negotiate with members of the opposition, who demanded either a return to pre-Second World War parliamentary systems (where they had existed as in the Baltic states) or to democratize for the first time. This helps to explain why democratization happened swiftly in much of Eastern Europe (Ash 1993) and why, for the most part, incumbent communist regimes collapsed surprisingly easily. Once a relatively small number of citizens defied these regimes, much larger numbers of citizens lost their fear and regime change became possible (Kuran 1991). In the constituent republics of the Soviet Union itself, changes were even more abrupt than elsewhere in the bloc. But where opposition movements were weak or simply did not exist, as in Belarus, the old communist rulers reasserted themselves, leading to regimes with few if any genuine democratic characteristics (McFaul 2002).

Changes in the Soviet sphere help explain why there were subsequent political changes in both Latin America and, to an extent, in sub-Saharan Africa. The fall of the USSR robbed the Left of its revolutionary project and thus its threat to conservative forces in much of the developing world. The international repercussions of the Cold War's conclusion encouraged the Bush administration to encourage autocracies to liberalize. For example, it pushed its clients in El Salvador to negotiate with left-wing guerrillas and to withdraw support from the Sandinistas in Nicaragua. It also encouraged pro-Soviet regimes in Africa to liberalize. Note, though, that it did little to end the dictatorships in Cuba, North Korea or throughout the Middle East.

Civil War. Another route to democratization and, in some cases, democracy was via armed conflict between incumbent regimes and opposition insurgents. This path is not contemplated within Przeworski's scenarios, though it is akin to the second route, that is, where the regime negotiates with the opposition because it cannot suppress it. But this route can be expanded to include other scenarios, such as when the government decides to fight, either because it under-estimates the opposition's strength or it prefers to fight a war it could very well lose, perhaps because it expects to improve its bargaining position. Alternatively, there might be violence because the armed opposition itself prefers defeating the dictator than reaching an agreement with him. However it starts, a civil war can become what Elizabeth Jean Wood (2000) calls an 'insurgent path to democracy', one in which war forces contending sides to accept democracy or to impose a version of it upon the vanquished.

These internal wars include a wide variety of struggles. Such wars could pit a colonial European power against a liberation movement. Civil wars in Central America during the 1970s and early 1990s involved Marxist guerrillas fighting right-wing dictatorships (Lehoucq forthcoming). Finally, armed looters attacking weak governments also turned in some cases into civil wars, ones that often produced 'failed states', following the collapse of incumbent govern-ments in, for example, Liberia and Sierra Leone (Bates 2008). This was a common occurrence in sub-Saharan Africa, especially in the wake of the end of the Cold War, when US support for friendly dictators declined with the disintegration of the Soviet Union. The cheap availability of weapons also fuelled insurgencies in many African and Asian countries (Collier and Hoeffler 2004).

Systematic research on civil war outcomes concludes that civil war, strangely enough, may actually improve the quality of government – an outcome that surprises observers of Central America, especially those watching since at least the 1970s. The research on the effects of civil war consistently demonstrates that new regimes tend to be more open or at least less autocratic than their predecessors (Gurses and Mason 2008; Toft 2010: 64–65). The argument is that a civil war so shakes a dictatorship in many underdeveloped countries that just about any new government is an improvement – albeit in some cases not for long – over the previously existing regime.

Civil wars that end with internationally supervised negotiations between governments and insurgents have the highest rate of regime improvement (Toft 2010). Of the 130 civil wars in the world between 1940 and 2000 (and excluding 13 continuing as of 2003), 19 per cent (or 22 civil wars) involved a ceasefire as part of an extensive agreement on a range of political and socio-economic issues. Most cases – 37 per cent (or 48 civil war) ended because the government won. Insurgents defeated the government in one-quarter of all (or 33) civil wars. Within five years of the signing of a comprehensive accord, the Polity IV regime index rates the average post-civil war system as democratic, even the quality of its political system decays with time. None of the other outcomes of a civil war – a ceasefire/stalemate or victor by the government or rebels – does much better than lead to semi-democracy, even if an insurgent victory outperforms a negotiated settlement 20 years after the war is over.

Third and fourth waves: an assessment

The extraordinary accomplishment of replacing dictatorships with elected governments was not followed in most cases by democratic consolidation. The vast majority of political systems that have shed autocracy remain democratically flawed, to use the EIU's useful character-ization of these systems. These are democracies with poorly functioning political institutions and/or apathetic citizens. Often, such institutions do only a poor job in holding elected officials accountable, which often replaces trust in democracy with distrust of its institutions.

Nearly 40 years after the start of the third wave of democratization, only a handful of countries outside of Western Europe, North America, Japan, Australia and New Zealand have become consolidated democracies. Of the 26 countries that the EIU classified as full democracies in 2010,

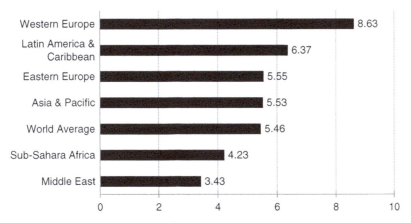

Figure 17.3 Democracy index averages, by region, 2010
Source: Economist Intelligence Unit (2010).

only a handful of countries are third-wave consolidated democracies, including: the Czech Republic, South Korea, Mauritius and Portugal. In addition, Uruguay did become democratic by 1985, but its transition was more of a recovery than the establishment of democracy. Prior to the 1973 coup, politicians and citizens in Uruguay had been constructing democratic institutions since the second decade of the twentieth century. Costa Rica, a late first-wave democracy, is the only full (and long-term) democracy in Latin America.

Figure 17.3 shows the EIU's 2010 democracy index for the major regions of the world. On a 10-point scale, the average for Western Europe (and North America) is 8.63, with Norway scoring the highest at 9.8 and Portugal scoring the lowest at 8.02 among full democracies. The political systems of Latin America and the Caribbean have an average of 6.37, almost a one-quarter drop from the mean of the established and long-term democracies. Part of this reflects the fact that the political systems of Bolivia, Honduras, Nicaragua and Venezuela have become hybrid – that is, a mixed democratic/non-democratic – system. This score, however, is mostly a product of the fact that only Costa Rica and Uruguay are full democracies; nearly all of the elected governments of Latin America and the Caribbean preside over flawed democracies. The democracy index average for Eastern Europe and Asia and the Pacific is approximately 5.5, which is very slightly above the global mean. In both regions, relatively low scores are a result of the existence of just a handful of full democracies, slightly more highly ranked 'flawed' democracies, and an assortment of hybrid and authoritarian governments. The index scores for the Middle East (and North Africa) and sub-Saharan Africa are 3.43 and 4.23, respectively. Autocracies in both regions largely resisted the wave of democracy that so changed Latin America and Eastern Europe.

The unimpressive scores for Latin America, Eastern Europe, and Asia and the Pacific reflect the existence of large numbers of flawed democracies. These systems mostly hold relatively free and fair, competitive elections and largely respect the civil rights of their citizens, which is why their scores rise above the lower scores of countries with less or non-democratic systems. Unlike full democracies, flawed democracies have lower rates of political participation, either because sizable numbers of citizens do not bother to vote at all or only occasionally vote. They are also political systems where: (1) citizens frequently express little satisfaction with democracy, and (2) where elected officials and bureaucracies typically ignore citizen demands for decent public services and/or honest government.

Conclusions and implications

The third wave of democracy, which started in the early 1970s, gradually swept away a large number of dictatorships. By the end of the 1990s, most political systems had become democratic, to use Polity IV's classification of regimes since 1946. By 2000, the 40 or so democracies in existence in 1980 had doubled. The number of semi-democracies also doubled in these two decades; their number increased from 23 to slightly more than 50. This, perhaps, is the single most important way to summarize the central political change of the contemporary world.

What caused this transformation? While industrialization may be responsible for the shift from monarchical to parliamentary authority in Western Europe – and, more importantly, the adoption of democratic forms of government in the Americas and Australia and New Zealand – during the first wave of democracy, the cause of regime change during the third wave of democracy does not really seem to be economic development. The statistical evidence is inconclusive, with different groups of researchers coming to divergent conclusions about the impact of GDP per capita growth on political system change. And it is almost certain that the alleged change in values ushered in by growth in economic productivity is not the mechanism that accounts for the fact that democracies seem to thrive with economic development.

The story of democratization instead is about the crumbling of autocratic rule. It is about why dictators liberalized their regimes enough to allow freely elected politicians to become executives and legislators. The evidence reviewed in this chapter suggests that it was a series of exogenous events – ones external to the societies these autocrats ruled – that in many cases kick-started democratization. Without these changes, there was little incentive for autocracies to split and provide the openings for anti-regime forces.

The first of these exogenous trends was the global rise in interest rates by the late 1970s, along with a decline in the international terms of trade, which undermined the economic stability of Latin American authoritarian governments. In response, military dictatorships hesitantly liberalized and, even more unwillingly, began a process of democratization, which led to drawn-out negotiations and in most cases gradual transitions to democracy. The other global trigger, which was the end of the Cold War, reshaped the domestic politics of Eastern Europe and the former republics of the Soviet Union. The collapse of the Soviet Union was in part a result of long-term economic decline. Most importantly, it was a product of infighting in the Communist Party about how to address the Soviet Union's economic mismanagement and mass mobilization.

The third mechanism I analyse in this chapter is more domestic in orientation. It is about autocrats refusing to negotiate with their adversaries. In response, opposition movements turned to violence to evict dictators from high office. This is the pattern we see from Central America to parts of Africa (e.g. South Africa) and in some Asian countries. In most of sub-Saharan Africa, there were conflicts between incumbent governments and armed bandits. In some of these countries, insurgents were able to overwhelm governments weakened by years of economic mismanagement and political cronyism, which unleashed an implosion so severe that it led to state failure and anarchy. In some of these cases (e.g. El Salvador and Ghana), civil war laid the basis for political reform and even democratization.

Note

1 I thank Jeff Haynes for numerous comments. Philip Freeman assembled the list of references, for which I am grateful.

References

Acemoglu, D., S. Johnson, J. A. Robinson and P. Yared (2008) 'Income and Democracy. *American Economic Review*, 98 (3), pp. 808–842.

Ash, T. G. (1993) *The Magic Lantern: The Revolution of '89 Witnessed in Warsaw, Budapest, Berlin, and Prague.* New York: Vintage Books.

Bates, R. H. (1994) 'The Impulse to Reform in Africa. In *Economic Change and Political Liberalization in Sub-Saharan Africa*, ed. J. A. Widner. Baltimore, MD: Johns Hopkins University Press, pp. 13–28.

—— (2008) *When Things Fell Apart: State Failure in Late-Century Africa.* New York: Cambridge University Press.

Beissinger, M. R. (2002) *Nationalist Mobilization and the Collapse of the Soviet State.* Cambridge: Cambridge University Press.

Boix, C. and S. C. Stokes (2003) 'Endogenous Democratization', *World Politics*, 55 (4), pp. 517–549.

Bonner, R. (1984) *Weakness and Deceit: U.S. Policy and El Salvador.* New York: Times Books.

Bratton, M. and N. van de Walle (1997) *Democratic Experiments in Africa: Regime Transitions in Comparative Perspective.* New York: Cambridge University Press.

Bunce, V., M. McFaul and K. Stoner-Weiss, eds (2010) *Democracy and Authoritarianism in the Postcommunist World.* New York: Cambridge University Press.

Cheibub, J. A. (2007) *Presidentialism, Parliamentarism, and Democracy.* New York: Cambridge University Press.

Collier, P. and A. Hoeffler (2004) 'Greed and Grievance in Civil War', *Oxford Economic Papers*, 56 (4), pp. 563–595.

Dahl, R. A. (1971) *Polyarchy: Participation and Opposition.* New Haven, CT: Yale University Press.

—— , ed. (1966) *Political Oppositions in Western Democracies.* New Haven, CT: Yale University Press.

Delvin, R. (1993) *Debt and Crisis in Latin America: The Supply Side of the Story.* Princeton, NJ: Princeton University Press.

Domínguez, J. I. and C. Lawson, eds (2004) *Mexico's Pivotal Democratic Election: Candidates, Voters, and the Presidential Campaign of 2000.* Stanford, CA: Stanford University Press.

EIU (Economist Intelligence Unit) (2010) *Democracy Index 2010: Democracy in Retreat.* London: EIU.

Epstein, D. L. *et al.* (2006) 'Democratic Transitions', *American Journal of Political Science*, 50 (3), pp. 551–569.

Geddes, B. (1999) 'Authoritarian Breakdown: Empirical Test of a Game Theoretic Argument'. In APSA (American Political Science Association), Annual Meeting of the American Political Science Association. Atlanta, 2–5 September 1999.

—— (2003) 'What Do We Know About Democratization After Twenty Years?', *Annual Review of Political Science*, 2 (1), pp. 115–144.

Gibson, C. G. (2002) 'Of Waves and Ripples: Democracy and Political Change in Africa in the 1990s', *Annual Review of Political Science*, 5 (1), pp. 201–221.

Gurses, M. and T. D. Mason (2008) 'Democracy Out of Anarchy: The Prospects for Post-Civil-War Democracy', *Social Science Quarterly*, 89 (2), pp. 315–336.

Huntington, S. P. (1991) *The Third Wave: Democratization in the Late Twentieth Century.* Norman: University of Oklahoma Press.

Inglehart, R. and C. Welzel (2005) *Modernization, Cultural Change, and Democracy.* New York: Cambridge University Press.

Kalyvas, S. N. and L. Balcells (2010) 'International System and Technologies of Rebellion: How the End of the Cold War Shaped Internal Conflict', *American Political Science Review*, 104 (3), pp. 415–429.

Kotkin, S. (2009) *Uncivil Society: 1989 and the Implosion of the Communist Establishment.* New York: Modern Library.

Kuran, T. (1991) 'Now Out of Never: The Element of Surprise in the East European Revolution of 1989', *World Politics*, 44 (1), pp. 7–48.

Lehoucq, F. (Forthcoming) *Civil War, Democratization, and Underdevelopment in Central America.*

Lindberg, S. I. (2006) *Democracy and Elections in Africa.* Baltimore, MD: Johns Hopkins University Press.

Lipset, S. M. (1959) 'Some Social Requisites of Democracy: Economic Development and Political Legitimacy', *American Political Science Review*, 53 (1), pp. 69–105.

McFaul, M. A. (2002) 'The Fourth Wave of Democracy and Dictatorship: Noncooperative Transitions in the Postcommunist World', *World Politics*, 54 (2), pp. 212–244.

Markoff, J. (1996) *Waves of Democracy: Social Movements and Political Change.* Thousand Oaks: Pine Forge Press.

Muller, E. N. and M. A. Seligson (1994) 'Civic Culture and Democracy: The Question of Causal Relationships', *American Political Science Review*, 88 (3), pp. 635–652.

Nathan, A. J. and P. Link, eds (2001) *The Tiananmen Papers*. New York: Public Affairs.

Polity IV, Political Regime Characteristics and Transitions, 1800–2009; available at http://systemicpeace.org/polity/polity4.htm (accessed 3 March 2011).

Przeworski, A. (1991) *Democracy and the Market: Political and Economic Reforms in Eastern Europe and Latin America.* New York: Cambridge University Press.

——, M. Alvarez, J. A. Cheibub and F. Limongi (2000) *Democracy and Development: Political Institutions and Well-Being in the World, 1950–1990.* New York: Cambridge University Press.

Robinson, J. A. (2006) 'Economic Development and Democracy', *Annual Review of Political Science*, 9 (1), pp. 503–527.

Rustow, D. A. (1970) 'Transitions to Democracy: Toward a Dynamic Model', *Comparative Politics*, 2, pp. 337–363.

Schedler, A. (2009) 'Electoral Authoritarianism'. In *The SAGE Handbook of Comparative Politics*, ed. T. Landman and N. Robinson. Los Angeles: SAGE. Ch. 20.

Schmitz, D. F. (2006) *The United States and Right-Wing Dictatorships, 1965–1989.* Cambridge: Cambridge University Press.

Sisk, T. D. (1995) *Democratization in South Africa: The Elusive Social Contract.* Princeton, NJ: Princeton University Press.

Thacker, S. C. (2000) *Big Business, the State, and Free Trade: Constructing Coalitions in Mexico.* Cambridge: Cambridge University Press.

Tilly, C. (2006) *Regimes and Repertoires.* Chicago: University of Chicago Press.

Toft, M. D. (2010) *Securing the Peace: The Durable Settlement of Civil Wars.* Princeton, NJ: Princeton University Press.

Wood, E. J. (2000) *Forging Democracy from Below: Insurgent Transitions in South Africa and El Salvador.* Cambridge: Cambridge University Press.

18

Democratic conditionality

Richard Youngs

When the democracy-promotion agenda began to take shape in a more systematic fashion after the Cold War the concept of 'political conditionality' gained currency. What might more specifically be termed 'democratic conditionality' referred to the notion of Western relations with other countries, varying in accordance with regimes' degree of plural democracy. In countries where authoritarianism persisted or deepened, punitive sanctions were considered. Conversely, where democratic advances were forthcoming, benefits such as financial aid would flow. In the 1990s, Western states and several international institutions introduced formal measures and policy instruments of both the carrot and stick variety of democratic conditionality. It seemed that the principle of democratic conditionality was set to become a core feature of international democratization.

In practice, democratic conditionality has not been deployed in a significant or consistent fashion. In recent years, its use has almost disappeared from Western foreign policies. As the international context has become more turbulent and uncertain, Western governments have reverted to attaching high priority to deepening political engagement with autocratic regimes. Western governments' use of sanctions as a means of prompting democratic reform is now extremely sparing. The rewards and incentives they offer for democratic reform remain partial and unevenly distributed. Democratic conditionality has been superseded and undermined by other types of conditionalities attached to more immediate, short-term security goals.

Should this move away from democratic conditionality be celebrated or mourned? Many would proclaim a welcome good riddance to the end of democratic sanctions. Many analysts were initially alarmed at the prospect of conditionality being used to prioritize democracy promotion. It was widely seen as a Trojan horse for aid reductions and market liberalization convenient for Western commercial interests. Criticisms have grown over the ineffectiveness of sanctions as a tool for incentivizing political reform. A striking degree of consensus has taken shape among analysts and policymakers: sanctions are too blunt a tool to help engineer democratization and are appropriate as a response only to the most egregious of rights abuses. While positive conditionality enjoys firmer support, much doubt exists that Western governments today possess incentives sufficient to have anything other than a marginal impact.

So, is it time simply to relinquish the whole notion of trying to press and cajole non-democratic regimes towards political openness? Is all effort to be invested in unconditional engagement, assisting modernization and socialization in a way that, it is hoped, spills over eventually into meaningful democratization?

This chapter argues that engagement with non-democratic regimes, underpinned by the assumptions of modernization theory, is desirable, but that political leverage is also needed to unblock the potential of liberalizing reform. For a variety of reasons, in today's environment punitive sanctions cannot be considered a pre-eminent tool for democracy promotion. More positive incentives, such as financial rewards in return for regimes introducing reforms, can still be used to greater effect, but must also be conceived as part of a broader range of policy instruments. Western governments concerned with advancing democracy internationally need to move from narrowly conceived conditionality to a broader set of means of exerting political leverage. This chapter suggests a number of ways in which they should make this move.

Analytical doubts

Academic studies weigh heavily against sanctions. Over the last decade, analysts have on balance concluded against the widespread use of political conditionality. Few studies extol the virtues of democratic conditionality; many point to its limitations. For the purposes of this chapter, space precludes a comprehensive review of the academic literature; suffice it to summarize here the range of problems with political conditionality that has been catalogued:

- It is increasingly difficult to make sanctions watertight due to the explosion in international commerce and the technologically complex forms in which it is carried out.
- The very fact that the targeted political elite is generally not accountable and mostly able to protect its own privileges means that it has little need to heed strictures on the need for greater accountability. The catch-22 is that sanctions tend to work in countries that already have a functioning multiparty system; they may work for other aims but not democratization.
- Strongly recalcitrant states may be backed even further into a corner, while in cases where soft- and hard-liners are beginning to converge around a 'pacted' plan for transition, tough punitive measures will be likely to unsettle this fragile alliance.
- Counterproductive backlash is more likely to the extent that punitive measures will inevitably be selective – they cannot be imposed in response to every case of democratic imperfection without fundamentally undermining the West's own capacity to influence those same concerns over democracy – and will therefore lead to charges of 'double standards'.
- To the extent that sanctions bring about general hardship, they are likely to encourage political elites to rely even more heavily on opaque and corrupt means of hoarding a bigger share of the smaller pool of resources: scarcity will discourage elites even further from opening up procedures of governance. Indeed, sanctions may hit hardest at the incipient entrepreneurial class, precisely the group whose prosperity is most likely to lead to pressure for political change. Sanctions actually make citizens more dependent on their government for economic provisions and less independent in basic means.
- The feasibility of targeting sanctions to affect only the hardline, that is, unwilling to reform, government elite is widely doubted. Selecting particular companies as subjects of targeted measures can produce anomalies, and a frequent complaint is that the more international actors delve into choosing particular businesses and individuals for sanction the more the limits of their local knowledge are tested.
- In most states, the quantity of aid flows is too limited for threats to remove development assistance to have a significant impact. What may hurt more are measures such as sporting bans (and their symbolic impact), rather than the actual impact of a loss of revenue or transfers.

- Governments can easily 'dupe' donors, by implementing only cosmetic reforms that do little to disperse effective power: conditionality will then encourage 'empty shell' democracy with a few showpiece practices to satisfy donors.
- Encouraging democracy properly entails building widespread and strongly embedded consent for democratic norms. Political liberalization adopted as a result of external pressure, reluctantly and in the absence of positive consent, will rarely be sustained for a long period of time. Indeed, the isolation of a non-democratic or weakly democratic regime is likely to undermine rather than generate such consent.
- Aggressive coercion imposed by Western countries in the name of democracy weakens democracy's moral appeal in the developing world. There is a real danger of democratic values being associated with, and tainted by, the developed world's heavy-handed domination of international politics.
- The implementation of punitive measures cuts off the possibility of an ongoing partnership and dialogue, which is the only way of helping to build-up consent and gain leverage over the series of challenges confronting incipient democracies. Punitive measures might actually hinder the accumulation of potential democratic 'capacity'. If sustainable democracy requires the generation of equitable growth, social capital, increased literacy and education levels, it might over the longer term simply be delayed by the interruption of trade preferences and development funds, even if such conditionality succeeds in forcing through a few institutional modifications.

In sum, analysts tend to argue that conditionality and sanctions are appropriate only in very specific circumstances: where internal reformers themselves seek tough international pressure; in moments of acute economic crisis when a tough policy on the part of international actors might help hasten the end of an already-weakened authoritarian regime; or in response to fundamental reversals from established democracy to authoritarianism.[1] After summarizing the academic debate on restrictive measures, Michael McFaul suggests the policy lesson is clear: 'Sanctions must never be enforced alone as a policy for supporting democratic development' (McFaul 2010: 163). In general, the use of sanctions denotes the failure of policy signals sent by both the imposer and the target state; if the point is reached where sanctions are actually implemented, it is, strictly speaking, too late for them to have any effect (Hovi, Huseby and Sprinz 2005: 482).

Democratic sanctions in practice

Policy has moved in line with these analytical doubts. In 2005, the World Bank noted a general retraction from any form of governance conditionality that was predicated on the 'micromanagement of reform programs', along with an emerging feeling that in the delivery of aid it was necessary to 'respect domestic decision-making processes' (World Bank 2005). The Paris and Accra agendas have put the onus on 'local ownership' in the use of development aid. These international policy frameworks have given impetus to the use of direct budget support – whereby donors channel increasing amounts of their aid directly into the treasury accounts of recipient governments, without stipulation regarding the use of these funds. More broadly, United Nations sanctions have not been aimed at supporting democracy: their use has self-evidently been curtailed not only by non-democratic regimes but also by many emerging democratic powers.

The Obama administration has repudiated the punitive approach to national security policy of its predecessor. Out of inertia some sanctions remain, but the conceptual approach has tilted decidedly against their use. The 2010 US National Security Strategy pivots around a section headed 'Pursuing Comprehensive Engagement' (US Government 2010). Caveats are added about the propriety of 'principled engagement', but the tone of US policy since Obama's accession to power in January 2009 has been to downplay punitive diplomacy. The 're-setting' of relations with Russia is only the highest-profile example of this general trend. Of course, many would point out that by his second term President George W. Bush had himself already reverted to realpolitik engagement with autocrats, including Saudi Arabia, Egypt and Pakistan. Regardless of where we situate the inflexion point, however, the drift away from a belief in the systematic use of democratic conditionality in US foreign policy is clear (Piccone 2010).

Despite the fact that the European Union (EU) has been imposing sanctions for the past two decades, their use was only formalized in 2005, with a narrowing of the focus to 'smart' sanctions, that is, measures aimed specifically at senior members of the regime in question (Hellqvist 2010). Many European governments and the EU institutions have elaborated principles for the use of sanctions that effectively circumscribe their use. These principles establish that sanctions must not impact negatively on ordinary citizens; they must be contemplated only as a very last resort, and only in response to massive rights abuses; they must be accompanied by a clear and easily implemented exit strategy for their removal; and the focus must be on targeted rather than general sanctions (House of Lords 2007). While the EU increased its use of human rights sanctions during the 1990s, this trend is now reversing (Kreutz 2005; Portela 2005). Moreover, there is in practice little consistency in their deployment (Brummer 2009). In nearly all cases, the preference is now for targeted restrictions on admission, the freezing of funds and arms embargoes – and invariably with review clauses that limit their application to relatively short periods of time.

The EU includes a human rights and democracy clause in all its international agreements that explicitly provides for punitive measures. But this clause has been used no more than a handful of times. Many European diplomats would now like to see the clause removed; many of them argue unreservedly that the clause has no impact, but merely complicates security and economic objectives, and persists simply as a sop to the European Parliament. The EU very rarely uses sanctions that are not tightly targeted on regime officials. There have been very few cases where sanctions have been designed in a way that has disrupted European trade and investment flows with autocratic states. Even the Nordic states now question the potential of conditionality, and they are the countries traditionally seen as the most committed supporters of democracy, often labelled pejoratively as 'hardliners' on this issue by other EU member states.

The EU agreed a new democracy support strategy at the end of 2009, which states that 'no new political conditionality is needed' (Council of the European Union 2009). Several member states – Germany, France and all southern member states – had indicated they would not sign such a strategy if it were seen to give a green light to the greater use of democratic conditionality. A 2009 EU strategy document expressed caution even over the use of sanctions narrowly targeted at regime officials responsible for the most serious of human rights abuses (Council Secretariat 2009).

Sanctions have been used in a small number of 'really bad cases'. Even here, however, the trend is away from a conviction in pure isolation. To demonstrate this, it is instructive to look at four examples of particularly repressive regimes where punitive measures have been adopted. Each case demonstrates the way in which Western strategy is conditioned by a balance of policy calculations, with the United States retaining only a slightly firmer position on sanctions than European governments.

In Belarus, targeted sanctions have been imposed against members of the Lukashenka regime, and the EU removed special trade preferences in 2007. But European governments did not break off relations with the continent's 'last dictator'. And, recently, sanctions have been diluted, travel restrictions eased and aid increased. Even Sweden – for a long time one of the firmest advocates of a hard line – has increased engagement through a new aid programme and the opening of an embassy in Belarus. In contrast, in 2007 and 2008 the United States imposed new sanctions targeting government entities, as well as officials responsible for human rights abuses and repression. However, following the release of political prisoners in 2008, the United States suspended sanctions against two subsidiaries of state-owned petrochemical conglomerate Belneftekhim. This suspension was extended in November 2009.

In the wake of Russia's invasion of Georgia in 2008, Lukashenka is seen as a potential ally to be courted against Russian expansionism. There is a general feeling that with Belarus isolation has not worked. The country's opposition, which was denied a single seat in parliament in the 2008 elections, supported the EU offer of new dialogue but not the removal of targeted sanctions. Belarus is now included in the EU's Eastern Partnership and a new Commission aid package was made available to Belarus in June 2009. In March 2009 sanctions were waived for another nine months. Conditionality is switching more to the EU's desire that Belarus not recognize South Ossetia and Abkhazia rather than internal democratic reform (Jarabik 2009).

European sanctions imposed on Uzbekistan in response to the 2005 Andijan massacre, when Uzbek troops fired into a crowd of protesters in Andijan, Uzbekistan on 13 May 2005, were retained in full for only 12 months before being incrementally removed. Germany led a campaign to have these sanctions overturned. The regime of President Karimov released two identified political prisoners as justification for European governments to remove sanctions. It then immediately imprisoned two others, once relations with the EU had been normalized. The only remaining measure imposed against Uzbekistan, an arms embargo, was removed in October 2009. The US also holds a de facto aid programme and a set of trade preferences for Uzbekistan.

In Burma, the EU has had a relatively wide range of sanctions in place since the mid-1990s, including an arms embargo, aid reductions, a ban on high-level visits, asset freezes and prohibition on funding going to state enterprises. Trade preferences were also removed. A ban on the import of timber, metals and precious stones from Burma has more recently been added to the list of EU punitive measures – products representing about 1 per cent of Burma's total exports.

The Obama administration has carried out a review of US-Burma policy and decided that the US would engage in direct, senior-level dialogue with Burmese authorities. The first senior-level meeting between the United States and Burma under the Obama administration's new policy took place in September 2009. However, prohibitions remain on investment in Burma by US persons (regardless of whether the activities are 'grandfathered' or not). Also prohibited are imports, exports and purchasing shares in third-country companies whose activities derive form resources located in Burma. The US Congress has renewed the Burmese Freedom and Democracy Act (BFDA), most recently in July 2010.

Within Europe a big division now exists on Burma. A majority of EU member states now want an easing of sanctions. The retention of sanctions is supported by only a small minority of states (the United Kingdom, Czech Republic, Netherlands, Ireland and Denmark). Pleas by the main opposition party in Burma, the National League for Democracy, for stiffer sanctions have gone unheeded. Overall it is widely perceived that the EU has relaxed its position on Burma because of the growing importance of unblocking relations with the Association of Southeast Asian Nations (ASEAN). Those arguing for a softening of sanctions suggest that the social ties of tourism would be particularly beneficial in opening up Burma. They also point out that EU sanctions have actually prejudiced suppliers in neighbouring Thailand more than the Burmese junta.

Zimbabwe remains to some extent an exception. The US and EU imposed sanctions a decade ago, but even here these are selective and targeted rather than comprehensive. In 2009 the US and EU reluctantly backed a power-sharing deal between President Robert Mugabe and the opposition. But sanctions have not yet been lifted. The US's Zimbabwe Democracy and Economic Recovery Act, containing a similar range of targeted restrictive measures, also continues in force.

The then UK foreign secretary, David Miliband, said in early 2010 that the functioning of the coalition government and general human rights situation were still too precarious to lift sanctions, and that punitive measures should 'be lifted only in a calibrated way, as progress is made'. Even here, however, some donors, such as the European Commission have increased engagement and support through humanitarian aid that goes beyond the strict confines of the non-political. Moreover, Mugabe has been welcomed by France and Portugal at their respective hosting of EU-Africa summits.

Beyond Zimbabwe, the EU has invoked its democracy clause to impose sanctions on a dozen occasions in Africa over the last decade. Here, sanctions have been used mainly in response to military coups in various countries, including: the Central Africa Republic, Guinea-Bissau, Togo, Niger and Mauritania. Measures have invariably taken many months to be introduced, as the EU undertakes rounds of formal consultations with the offending regime; and they have generally been removed before anything resembling genuine democracy is (re)installed. Member states do not always adopt the same critical measures in their bilateral relations with the same regimes. EU sanctions against Cuba were lifted in 2005; Spain has restarted a full development programme on the island.

In 2009 the EU did decide to remove Generalized System of Preferences (GSP) for Sri Lanka, in response to human rights abuses committed in the government's campaign against the Tamil Tigers. But this again represents a relatively modest and symbolic move. Sri Lanka was permitted several months to engage in dialogue and take 'corrective' measures, such that trade preferences were not actually withdrawn until the summer of 2010. The effect on trade and investment was widely expected to be modest.

An arms embargo remains in place against China, but this is a minor measure set alongside the plethora of new cooperation agreements between the EU and Beijing; moreover, this embargo only remains in place because a small minority of member states have been able to block the French, German and Spanish-led campaign to have it revoked. In general, the EU's relatively weak code of conduct on arms sales has not prevented massively increased sales of weaponry to various non-democratic countries, including China and Gulf states.

The disinclination to exert pressure for reform through critical measures is even more striking in countries that are not so politically closed but which are still moving in an anti-democratic direction. A large number of non-democratic countries have in recent years won from the EU new agreements and/or more generous trade and aid benefits, even as repression has increased and elections have been patently manipulated. A select, illustrative list of such beneficiaries would include (pre-Arab Spring) Libya, Syria, Egypt, Tunisia, Armenia, Azerbaijan, Kazakhstan, Russia, Ethiopia, Rwanda, Kenya, Nigeria, Uganda and the Côte d'Ivoire. For the purposes of this chapter, space precludes entering details on each of these cases, but the list suffices to demonstrate a clear conclusion: there are many, many more instances of democratic regression that the EU has met with policy upgrades than with sanctions.

Sanctions *have* been used in relation to security aims. The best known examples are sanctions related to the real or imagined development of weapons of mass destruction. The flip side of these sanctions is that when deals are struck on nuclear and chemical weapons programmes – as with Libya, Syria, North Korea and, for a period, Iran – punitive measures are invariably lifted without any improvements in democratic rights. In Syria, concern over democracy is not absent – especially from the US Syria Accountability Act of 2004 – but in practice is of secondary concern and not in itself the barrier to engagement. The US has had more of a focus on regime change in Iran, but even here has increasingly sought to maintain the nuclear and democracy agendas separate from one another. This was evident is the extremely cautious US response to the violence surrounding Iran's 2009 elections (Sadjapour 2010).

Sanctions have been imposed against al-Qaida affiliates, and on the question of terrorist financing more generally. However, regarding both US and European access bans, more names are banned from entry by virtue of being on terrorist lists than on lists of officials from non-democratic countries. The much-lauded Kimberley Process is related to diamond sales used to finance rebel insurgency, and is not attentive to democratic governance standards. Because these kinds of security-related measures are used mostly against non-democratic regimes, analysts often confuse them for democracy-related conditionality and thus conclude that this represents a heavy use of the latter. This is not precisely the case.

Incentives conditionality

In light of the limits to coercive pressure, rewards-based conditionality is widely touted as a more productive policy option. It appears to offer the prospect of encouraging democratic reform without counterproductive intervention from the outside. However, what is presented as incentives-based political conditionality often crosses the line into largely unconditional engagement – rewards are invariably granted on the basis of no more than vague promises of future reforms. Conversely, the difference between positive and negative conditionality is not always perceived to be that great by many in target states: denial of an expected reward is not always seen as qualitatively different from the removal of an existing preference.

Established by the Bush administration in 2004, the Millennium Challenge Corporation (MCC) is formally based on the principle of *ex-post* rewards for proven achievements. Countries are selected to apply for MCC assistance based on their performance on 16 policy indicators in three areas: ruling justly, investing in people and promoting economic freedom. Indicators are used from several independent sources. The 'ruling justly' criterion includes indicators on civil liberties and political rights; voice and accountability; corruption; the rule of law; and government effectiveness. Selection for eligibility initiates a multi-year partnership dedicated to pursuing economic growth and poverty reduction through the development and implementation of a compact. If a country suffers a significant policy reversal, the MCC may issue a warning, suspension, or termination of eligibility and/or assistance.

In practice, some non- or only partially democratic countries have received sizeable amounts of MCC aid. These include Armenia, Madagascar, Senegal, Uganda, Jordan, Morocco and Nicaragua – although, in the case of Armenia and Madagascar, aid was belatedly cut. Some of these are included on development grounds, some seemingly on security grounds – the democracy indicators seem to get squeezed from both these sides. A host of non-political indicators are thrown into the mix.[2]

Some states have been subject to measures prohibiting them from receiving US development partnerships on political grounds – including China, Cuba, Venezuela, Burma and the Côte d'Ivoire. But the list of the top ten recipients of mainstream US aid includes Egypt, Ethiopia, Kenya and Uganda. Reflecting the perceived policy trade-offs, US aid officials argue that Ethiopia is making good progress on health issues so cannot have its aid diverted to better democratic reformers even after patently unfree elections in 2005 and again in 2010.

EU enlargement continues to be the clearest case of positive democratic conditionality, but it is not quite the cut and dried example it is often assumed to be. Extensive work on the conditionality deployed by the EU in the context of eastern enlargement has concluded that incentives played a secondary role and were linked mostly to second-phase governance reforms not the big, over-arching choices in favour of democracy (Schimmelfenning and Wagner 2004; Schimmelfennig and Scholtz 2007).

In the Balkans, a twin dynamic exists, both elements of which cloud the clarity of incentive conditionality attached specifically to democracy. The EU's group of 'friends of the Balkans' increasingly insists that even positive conditionality should be toned down to get countries from the region admitted as soon as possible. Conversely, those member states more sceptical over future enlargement now find it convenient continuously to raise the hurdle of reform conditionality as a convenient delaying tactic. Policy outcomes reflect an ad hoc mixture of these dynamics.

So, for example, diplomats argue that conditionality has failed in the case of Serbia, and that the fragility of this country's fledgling democracy requires more engagement than external pressure. The Dutch government unblocked Serbia's association agreement before key war-crimes suspects were apprehended. In Bosnia and Herzegovina (BiH) the EU has been more cautious in pushing for democracy-deepening constitutional reform. Bosnia's Stabilization and Association Agreement was held up until 2008 over the issue of police reform; after this failed to incentivize far-reaching reform of the police, most member states concluded that positive conditionality should be used in a less heavy-handed fashion in the future. Conversely, Macedonia complains that the EU has added more and more conditions beyond the Copenhagen criteria. And some technical aspects of entry talks with Croatia are being held up by the condition that fuller cooperation with the International Criminal Tribunal for the former Yugoslavia (ICTY) is still required (Sebastian 2009).

Outside the sphere of accession candidates, the new Eastern Partnership introduced in 2008 – that includes Belarus, Ukraine, Moldova, Georgia, Armenia and Azerbaijan – offers new association agreements conditional upon progress in democracy and human rights. 'Deep free trade' is proposed and the carrot of visa-free travel is waved. At the same time, the notion of 'graduated membership' has gained currency, with debates over how states can participate in an ad hoc range of EU policies without full membership (Schmidt 2008). However, reformers in aspirant states see this as a rebuff more than incentives-based engagement. One expert notes that governments of the former Soviet space continue to use engagement with the EU as a lever against Russian influence, not as a tool for modernization (Popescu 2008). In some sectors, Russia's own neighbourhood policy actually offers more immediate gifts than the EU's Eastern Partnership.

Since the Orange Revolution, Ukraine has expressed bitter disappointment at being denied a 'membership prospect', arguing that the EU has failed to reward it for its 2004 democratic transition. The EU has sought to compensate by offering Ukraine a range of new policy initiatives. Under the mandate for the new association agreement being negotiated are plans to develop 'deep free trade' and incorporate Ukraine into the EU energy market. But all this is still interpreted in Ukraine as a dereliction of the EU's commitment to help consolidate democracy.

Elsewhere, the use of positive conditionality exhibits similar limitations. It has been found that no statistical link exists between aid allocations and improvements in governance standards (Girod, Krasner and Stoner 2009). Lists of the top ten recipients of European development assistance include some notably non-democratic countries. For Germany these include Cameroon, China, Egypt and Morocco; for the UK they include Nigeria, Ethiopia, Sudan and China (although the last of these is set to decline in importance under the conservative-liberal government); for Spain they include Morocco, China and Senegal; for France, included are Cameroon, Morocco, Tunisia, China, Congo and Senegal.[3] Suggesting that President Sarkozy has failed in his promise to close down *La Françafrique*, the shadowy network of French-African elites that has long run France's Africa policy, the list of top recipients of French aid is still dominated by *La Francophonie*. After Gabonese dictator Omar Bongo died in spring 2009 France helped his son to power.

In Africa, the biggest aid increases have not gone to the most reformist states. The European Commission insists it has added significant amounts to European Development Fund allocations for good reformers. But many African democrats berate EU donors for inflating the reformist grades of many states as they need to show 'successes'. Countries such as Mali, Mozambique and Ghana have attracted sizeable increases in aid from major European donors on the basis of commitments to political reform. But overall the correlation between European aid and recipients' democratic quality remains low in Africa. Three billion euros of the budget for the 10th European Development Fund (out of a total €22 billion for 2008–13) were set aside to reward those African, Caribbean, Pacific (ACP) states cooperating with the EU on governance reforms. But this Africa Governance Facility has been distributed among 70 states and this governance tranche represents less than 1 per cent of countries' aid receipts. Member states explicitly say they are unwilling to push beyond African regime's own reform plans in allocating this governance tranche, while stating that the latter 'is not a form of conditionality' (Council of the European Union 2009b).

From conditionality to leverage

The calculations of how to mix engagement and pressure judiciously are extremely difficult. The challenge of getting this balance right is reflected in the fact that Western governments and international institutions are criticized from both directions. Some critics berate them for overdoing the use of sanctions, because ministers have to be seen to be 'doing something' to assuage domestic public opinion. Conversely, other observers lament that the West unduly eschews democratic conditionality due to strategic self-interest. Debate becomes confused: Western powers are widely criticized for their unethical engagement with dictators; then as soon as they do adopt sanctions they are slammed for the neo-imperial imposition of their own values. Some commentators see the use of sanctions as unadulterated self-interest; but groups such as Human Rights Watch and Amnesty International tend to see the lack of sanctions as rendering hollow the stated commitments to human rights – rather than as a legitimate tactical calculation (Wood 2009).

This chapter has stressed the highly circumscribed way in which both negative and positive conditionality have been deployed in support of democratic reforms. In formal terms, the commitment to political conditionality has not disappeared altogether. The Swedish development minister has, for example, stated: 'the implementation of both negative and positive conditionality has been weak. If democratic development is to take place, we must dare to implement the tools we have at hand. While there is a need to recognise the diversity of democratic practices at country level, firmness on principles is still necessary' (Carlsson 2007). Sweden's aid programme for 2009–11 commits to sharpening up the use of conditionality. Other states often make similar statements of intent.

In practice, however, political conditionality looks set to decline in importance. The challenge for Western governments is to move beyond conditionality to fashioning a more widely cast, effective leverage. Amongst Western policymakers the conviction is now strong that disengaging from authoritarian regimes is rarely helpful for democratic reform. Compounding a paucity of faith in democracy-related sanctions, the feeling is also that short-term policy challenges are today so complex and myriad in nature that it is simply not feasible to vary relations only in accordance with other countries' degree of democratic-ness. Given security and developmental objectives, few diplomats are prepared to tighten the correlation between depth of engagement and recipient countries' degree of commitment to democracy. Add to this the West's declining relative power and the case against conditionality would appear overwhelming.

Does this confluence of factors render obsolete all forms of pressure in favour of human rights and democracy? Not quite. But bearing in mind the patchy evidence on the effectiveness of punitive sanctions and governments' reluctance to compromise engagement, it does mean that a number of policy questions present themselves as pertinent.

First, the pressing policy challenge is to consider how pressure can be exerted within a framework of positive engagement. The advocates of deeper engagement with non-democratic regimes argue that this can assist rather than negate the possibility of greater pressure for political reform. There is certainly logic in this argument. After all, there needs to be engagement and interdependence for a non-democratic regime to have some stake in cooperation continuing. But, this 'dual track' approach, the central pivot of the Obama administration's post-Bush values-based re-engagement with the world, must still demonstrate tangible results. Evidence is required that it can indeed be distinguished from unconditional engagement.

A number of policy options should be pursued in this vein. Where Western governments have built-up or consolidated diplomatic, government-to-government partnerships with authoritarian regimes, they should use such relations as leverage to negotiate access for a much deeper 'track two' civil society component to engagement. Support for independent civic organizations should be raised as a quid pro quo for the security cooperation that authoritarian regimes really like. At present, the international community is still too ready to forego this dimension. Western governments must at least resist the imposition of reverse conditionality: autocratic regimes pushing for such civic links to be downgraded as a condition for security cooperation. They should also point out that economic engagement aimed at increasing investment and economic modernization implies more commitment to the rule of law. And opaque political dialogues must begin to hone in on more concrete and tangible reform aims – at present many see such dialogues as a cover for inaction.

Second, 'smart' sanctions may still be useful at the margins, but the way in which they are crafted needs to be re-examined. To date, smart sanctions have not shown themselves to be that smart. Targeted sanctions are now the most common form of measure adopted. But their popularity with policymakers has not yet been fully justified. There is a danger that targeted sanctions end up being neither one thing nor the other: they do enough to stifle a country's full integration into the modernizing potential of international linkages, but do not do enough to impose costs on elites that are sufficient to effect a change in their repressive behaviour. Few assessments are yet available on whether smart sanctions live up to their name.

Indeed, smart sanctions have clearly failed to dislodge some very repressive regimes. Is this a failure of external pressure per se? Or is it a result of sanctions being too narrowly and selectively targeted? Systematic review is required of the way in which targeted sanctions have impacted upon political dynamics within different states. Asset freezes would appear to have been too restricted in scope and would, at a minimum, need extending down to mid-level officials in order to stand any chance of being effective.

Two issues need to be distinguished from each other more clearly. One problem is where punitive pressure by its very nature impacts prejudicially on the democratic dynamics of the society in question. Another problem is where Western governments deploy different policy instruments that cancel each other out. Sanctions hit the people. Western powers compensate for this through humanitarian provision; they take with one hand, and give with the other. This reverts to the same point: the need for policy to be defined in its broadest totality.

This leads us on to a third policy challenge: the relationship between pressure for democratic reform and conditionalities imposed in other areas of policy. There is some truth in the complaint that Western offers of new agreements have become overloaded with conditionalities. But most of these are conditionalities other than democracy-related conditionality. Arguably, they reduce the negotiating capital available to push for political reform. Democratic conditionality is increasingly crowded out by other forms of conditionality. Today, conditionality is used more for security containment than democracy. Where sanctions have been used against autocratic regimes it has most commonly been due to security concerns and not those regimes' lack of democracy per se.

It must be considered how these various conditionalities now relate to one another: how far do they undercut each other? Which should be prior? Why is it assumed that punitive pressure can work for some policy aims but not democracy? The US and EU have to re-examine the way in which they prioritize their different policy aims. Ostracizing regimes for security-related purposes may cut across the kind of engagement required to assist the kind of political reforms that would render those same security aims more achievable. Conversely, offering rewards to regimes purely for agreeing 'hard security' cooperation is likely to undercut pressure relevant to more enlightened rights-based security approaches over the longer term.

One lesson from academic studies is that sanctions must be legitimate in the eyes of the broader population. For this reason, it is untenable to separate out the use of sanctions for security aims while concern for human rights is allowed to wallow in insubstantiality (Shen 2008). Western arms embargoes have been crafted with loopholes sufficient to allow increased sales of weapons to the world's most repressive regimes (Yanik 2006). At present there is a dramatic lack of joined-up thinking between defence and human rights policy units. Arms embargoes at least must be tightened up.

All this leads to a crucial observation: efforts to press for and incentivize democratic reform must be formulated in a less stand-alone fashion. If international leverage is to be retained it must be through more systematic incorporation of the democracy agenda into trade, development, security and energy policy as well as into multilateral diplomacy. More innovative ways must be found of intersecting incentives and pressure between the 'silos' of different policy domains. One example of such new measures is found in current efforts on the part of the US and some European states to build into post-crisis financial sector regulations the requirements for banks to report more transparently on their dealings in overseas markets. More such innovation and lateral thinking is required.

A fourth consideration is how Western governments incorporate the views of local stake-holders. How far are they really willing to take a lead from local actors? Most Western governments now make a point of stressing that their democracy support policies must be driven by local demands. But, what happens when local actors ask for more not less democratic conditionality? If donors have already decided against conditionality, their commitment to following the lead of local actors may appear rather cosmetic. The evidence is that civil and political society organizations in non-democratic or weakly democratic states are divided over the use of conditionality on the part of external actors. Better local consultation and awareness-raising is urgently needed on this question. Western governments can still be shockingly unaware of what local democrats actually want from them. And where local actors do ask them not to completely override pressure for democratic reform, the Western commitment to listen to local voices can suddenly dissipate. A pressing challenge is to align the forms of political leverage and pressure that are used to the specific demands of local actors and circumstances.

In sum, to the extent that some genuine commitment does remain to support democracy, Western governments and international institutions must move away from deliberating policy choices purely in terms of stark choices between engagement and ostracism. The era of imposing sweeping conditionalities is over – for both practical and normative reasons. Engagement with non-democratic regimes is proper and does not in itself denote a lack of commitment to encourage political reform. But engagement can and should be more effectively leveraged to ensure that such broader partnerships facilitate, more than they undercut, democratic potential.

Richard Youngs

Notes

1 Select references on political conditionality, from a large literature, include Gottemoeller (2008); Moll and Zimmerman (2008); Marinov (2004); Lavin (1996); Hendrickson (1994); Sorenson (1993); Stokke (1995).
2 All information on the MCC can be obtained at www.mcc.gov, especially under the sections on Selection Criteria and Countries and Country Tools.
3 Aid figures are from 2008, the latest figures available from the OECD DAC statistics database. www.oecd. org/dataoecd (accessed 20 September 2011).

References

Brummer, Claus (2009) 'The Not So "Normative Power Europe" ', *European Foreign Affairs Review*, 14 (2), pp. 191–207.
Carlsson, G. (2007) 'Supporting Democracy – Highlighting the Political Dimension of International Development Cooperation', Speech, 28 May; available at http://www.sweden.gov.se/sb/d/8812/a/ 83076 (accessed 20 September 2011).
Council of the European Union (2009) 'Draft Council Conclusions on Support to Democratic Governance – Towards an Enhanced EU Framework', 9047/09, Brussels: European Council, 27 April.
Council of the European Union (2009) 'Council Conclusions on Democracy Support in the EU's External Relations', 17 November.
Council Secretariat (2009) *Guidelines on Implementation and Evaluation of Restrictive Measures (Sanctions) in the Framework of the EU Common Foreign and Security Policy*, Doc 17464/09.
Girod, D., Stephen Krasner S. and Kathryn Stoner-Weiss K. (2010) 'Governance and Foreign Assistance: the Imperfect Translation of Ideas into Outcomes. In *Promoting Democracy and the Rule of Law*, ed. M. A. McFaul, Magen and T. Risse. Basingstoke: Palgrave Macmillan.
Gottemoeller, R. (2008) 'The Evolution of Sanctions in Practise and Theory', *Survival*, 49 (4), pp. 99–110.
Hellqvist, E. (2010) *Success and Credibility in EU's Sanctions Policy*, Paper presented at the ISA Annual Convention, New Orleans, February.
Hendrickson, D. (1994) 'The Democratist Crusade: Intervention, Economic Sanctions and Engagement', *World Policy Journal*, 11 (4), pp. 18–30.
House of Lords Select Committee on Economic Affairs (2007) 'The Impact of Economic Sanctions', May.
Hovi, J., R. Huseby and D. Sprinz (2005) 'When do (Imposed) Sanctions Work?', *World Politics*, 57, pp. 479–499.
Jarabik, B. (2009) 'Belarus: Are the Scales Tipping?', FRIDE policy brief no. 6, Madrid: FRIDE, March.
Kreutz, Joakim (2005) 'Hard Measures by a Soft Power? Sanctions Policy of the European Union 1981– 2004', Bonn International Center for Conversion (BICC), Paper 45.
Lavin, F. (1996) 'Asphyxiation or Oxygen? The Sanctions Dilemma', *Foreign Policy*, No. 104, pp. 139–54.
Marinov, N. (2004) 'Do Sanctions Help Democracy? The US and EU's Record 1977–2004', Stanford University, Centre on Democracy, Development and the Role of Law, working paper 28, November.
McFaul, M. ed. (2010) *Advancing Democracy Abroad: Why We Should and How We Can*. Lanham, MD: Rowman and Littlefield.
Moll, A. and F. Felix Zimmerman (2008) 'A Farewell to Policy Conditionality', OECD Development Centre Policy Insight, August.
Piccone T. (2010) *Around the Halls: A New National Security Strategy*. Brookings, 27May; available at http:// www.brookings.edu/opinions/2010/0527_halls_clinton.aspx (accessed 20 September 2011).
Popescu, N. (2008) *The EU's Sovereign Neighbours*. London: European Council on Foreign Relations.
Portela, C. (2005) 'Where and Why Does the EU Impose Sanctions?', *Politique européenne*, 3 (17), pp. 83–111.
Sadjapour, K. (2010) 'Iran: One Year Later', *CSpan Washington Journal*, 17 June; available at www.carne-gieendowment, org (accessed 20 September 2011).
Schimmelfennig, F. and C. Wagner (2004) 'Preface: External governance in the European Union', *Journal of European Public Policy*, 11 (4), pp. 657–660.
Schimmelfennig, F. and H. Scholtz (2007) 'EU Democracy Promotion in the European Neighborhood: Political Conditionality, Economic Development and Transnational Exchange', National Centre of Competence in Research Challenges to Democracy in the 21st Century, Zurich, Switzerland, Working Paper 9.
Schmidt, V. (2008) 'A "Menu Europe" will Prove Far more Palatable', *Financial Times*, 22 July.

Sebastian, S. (2009) 'No Time to Wind Down in Bosnia', Madrid, FRIDE Policy brief no. 17, August.

Shen, D. (2008) 'Can Sanctions Stop Proliferation?', *The Washington Quarterly*, 31 (3), pp. 89–100.

Sorenson, G., ed. (1993) *Political Conditionality*. London: Frank Cass.

Stokke, O., ed. (1995) *Aid and Political Conditionality*. London: Frank Cass.

United States National Security Strategy (2010) Available at http://www.whitehouse.gov/sites/default/files/rss_viewer/national_security_strategy.pdf (accessed 20 September 2011).

Wood, S. (2009) 'The European Union: A Normative or Normal Power', *European Foreign Affairs Review*, 14 (2), pp. 113–128.

World Bank (2005) *Conditionality Revisited – Concepts, Experiences and Lessons*. Washington, DC: World Bank.

Yanik, Lerna K. (2006) 'Guns and Human Rights: Major Powers, Global Arms Transfers and Human Rights Violations', *Human Rights Quarterly*, 28 (2), pp. 357–386.

19

The United Nations and democratization

Martin Slann

This chapter argues that the United Nations (UN) has done little effectively to promote or sustain a process of democratization in failed and at-risk states. I use the Israeli-Palestinian conflict as an important point of reference. The chapter further suggests that, if the world is devoted to democratic peace theory, then there is a need for greater attention to the various ways in which the United Nations actually undermines the development of democracy. I argue that democratization itself is an unreliable process that does not always lead to the establishment of a full-blown and viable, that is, consolidated democracy. Failed, failing, and at-risk states may in fact contain political and overall cultures that are unsuitable for, or are even opposed to, democracy. The notion that democracy itself can promote international peace is a viable one as long as the peace being promoted is between and among democracies. However, the fact that at any given time there are as many as 50 or 60 wars on the planet, and that the overwhelming majority of them are within rather than between states, suggests a lack of a widespread 'democratization' environment. In a typical conflict, it seems highly likely that neither side is overtly committed to, or in some cases even has hopes for, the creation of democratic regimes. Instead, ethnic, tribal and religious-rival affiliations and goals tend to predominate in such conflicts. In the Palestinian areas, for example, Hamas and the Palestinian Authority are nearly as much at odds with one another as either is with Israel.

The primary reference in this chapter is the Israeli-Palestinian conflict, which most clearly illustrates the moral duplicity and hypocrisy of the United Nations. Israel is the most frequently condemned and challenged member of the United Nations and has been throughout its history as an independent state. I shall argue that the anti-Israel bias of the United Nations exemplifies a serious level of antipathy to a country that is actually a good example of a Western-style democracy. Indeed, Israel is the only clear-cut democracy in the Middle East – with the partial exception of Turkey. Further, it is the only democracy in the world that is consistently under siege – from Arab and Muslim militants – determined to end its existence. At the same time, Israel's economic and technological success, mostly because of the country's emphasis since the 1980s on the free market and technological innovation ('Beyond Start Up Nation' 2009), is both hated and envied by the same neighbours that fervently want Israel destroyed. This chapter suggests that the Israeli–Palestinian conflict is symptomatic of the United Nations' predisposition against democracy and in favour of a non-Western world it considers to be exploited and victimized by the West.

The democratic constellation in the post-Cold War era

With the collapse of the Soviet empire in the late 1980s, the emerging assumption that democracy no longer faced serious predators was both celebrated and taken for granted (Fukuyama 1992; although see Huntington 1991 for a counterview). A strong belief prevailed that the demise of communism in Eastern Europe, following the apparent demise of fascism after the Second World War, appeared to some scholars to mean that there was now nothing to prevent entire nations from quickly embracing and adopting political democracy. To some extent, this phenomenon did in fact occur. Several Eastern European states quickly and, for the most part, peacefully removed their totalitarian dictatorships, installed democratic or quasi-democratic regimes, and successfully resuscitated free market economies. Doing so qualified several of them to join the North Atlantic Treaty Organization (NATO) and/or the European Union, and most became members at the earliest opportunity. The total number of real democracies in the world did in fact grow, and more people than ever before began to live under democratic governments that guaranteed individual rights. There was no need or desire for any United Nations effort here.

It is important to note, however, that even in Europe there were setbacks. Most of the former Soviet republics did not evolve into full or even partial democracies and illustrate little promise they will do so in the foreseeable future. Pleasant if infrequent exceptions include Poland and the Baltic states. By the middle 1990s Yugoslavia had completely deteriorated into a three-sided civil war among Muslim Bosnians, Catholic Croats and Orthodox Serbs that, while relatively quiet at the time of writing, could again explode at any time. Only Slovenia was actually able to successfully disengage from the turmoil that afflicted southeast Europe during the 1990s, to become and remain a peaceful and prosperous country, enjoying an impressive level of democratization. Slovenia is overwhelmingly Slovene and Catholic, and it may be that the relative ethnic and religious homogeneity provides the country with an important cohesion that is seriously lacking elsewhere in the former Yugoslav federation.

At this time, the mid-1990s, there was also widely expressed hope for other regions in the world to democratize. After all, by this time much of Latin America had already begun the transformation from dictatorship to democracy. The effort by the Castro regime in Cuba to spread its brand of revolution to the region had completely failed. Instead, Cuba had become relatively isolated and ignored. Once its Soviet patron was removed from the equation, Cuba's ostracism was fairly complete and its formerly iconic leader, Fidel Castro, was paid little attention compared with the past.

None of this progress removed or blunted the determination of many, but by no means all, United Nations member states to remain steadfastly undemocratic. In some cases, there was an ideological suspicion of democracy, especially if it was regarded as the liberal, individualistic, Western variety in general or the Americanized version in particular. In fact, the United States became in the minds of numerous member states an international pariah because of its status as the unequalled global superpower, although paradoxically the US government was also the single greatest source of funding for United Nations activities and agencies (Babbin 2004). By contrast, several Eastern Europe countries had earlier developed political infrastructures that, somehow enduring despite German Nazi and Soviet communist occupations, were relatively conducive to democratization with relative ease after the demise of European communism.

Of course, all of this was actually the easy part. Many – but not all – non-Western democracies are fragile affairs. Most have yet to demonstrate that they have staying power, though Japan and India, among others, are clearly exceptions. In addition, it appears that some societies are culturally and traditionally very resistant to the concept of democratic governance, including such developed countries as Singapore. Although Singapore is a unified nation, not all such societies are either coherent or unified. In some cases, failed states are the result of having been fake or fraudulent from their beginning. There are illustrative examples: Saudi Arabia is essentially the largest family estate in the world. The country has been completely dominated by the Saud clan since its inception during the 1930s. Its government, bureaucracy, military and economy are controlled by members of the royal family or their retainers. Most of the remaining 27 million inhabitants appear to be politically subdued and subservient while at all times given to understand that neither the United Nations nor any other power on the planet possesses either the will or the ability to 'democratize' the country (Glazov 2009).

In retrospect, we need to at least consider the proposition that societies deeply scarred by ethnic and religious conflicts may be far away from even a glimmer of democratic governance; a situation that the United Nations has neither the will nor the ability to change. Indeed, some such countries may actually be effectively non-governable – except perhaps by military fiat, although even this non-democratic solution may be less viable in some cases than previously thought: witness, for instance, the Arab Spring revolutions (May 2011) extant in Bahrain, Syria, Egypt, Libya, Tunisia and elsewhere in the Middle East and North Africa. Previously run by authoritarian means, countries such as Somalia, for example, have recently deteriorated into what is essentially a series of fiefdoms dominated by warlords; the idea of a nation state seems to be an elusive goal and democracy practically unachievable in the country. And all this has occurred in a country that has a population in which the overwhelming majority of people belong to one overall ethnic group. Of Somalia's total population (10 million) around 85 per cent is Somali (The World Factbook 2010). Somalia is a member state of the Arab League, though the actual Arab community is less than 1 per cent of the total population (ibid.). Moreover, such law that prevails is either sharia law per se or at least based on sharia law. This is a legal code that, it can be argued, does not sit easily with much current international law and Western interpretations of individualistic human rights.

The Universal Declaration of Human Rights (1948), sponsored by the United Nations, declares in Article 18 that:

> Everyone has the right to freedom of thought, conscience and religion; this right includes freedom to change his religion or belief, and freedom either alone or in community with others and in public or private, to manifest his religion or belief in teaching, practice, worship and observance.

This statement appears contradictory to the Qur'anic injunction, frequently interpreted by Islamic scholars, that it is necessary to kill apostates: 'Those among you who revert from their religion, and die as unbelievers, have nullified their works in this life and the Hereafter. These are the dwellers of Hell, wherein they abide forever' (Qur'an 2: 217, cited in Warraq 2005: 429).

Human rights are the cornerstone of any democracy worth its name. In Western democracies, human rights are protected primarily by secular law. Large portions of secular law, of course, are based on or are derived from religious or quasi-religious doctrines. But pertinent aspects of spiritual injunctions are incorporated as determined by a government that has constitutionally or culturally distinguished between church and state authority or has clearly, as in France and the United States, confirmed that religious laws must be compatible with secular law or must remain inapplicable.

The 1990 Cairo Declaration insists that Islamic law (sharia) is superior to and must supersede all other legal codes. This document, the Universal Declaration of Human Rights in Islam, effectively places sharia, at least in Islamic societies, first over any other rival human rights interpretation, including those endorsed by the United Nations. It is, in fact, a statement of Islamic superiority and a stark contradiction of the Declaration of Human Rights in that it calls for the death penalty for apostasy ('Apostasy and the Islamic Nations' 2009).

Non-Western societies have quite reasonably formulated democracies that are compatible with their own political cultures. Most have done this without the assistance of the United Nations, although there are examples of the United Nations playing a useful and constructive role. For example, the United Nations Transitional Authority in Cambodia (UNTAC) was instrumental in bringing the country out of the remarkably violent, and mercifully brief, dark age imposed on it by the Khmer Rouge during 1975–9. In addition, the United Nations was instrumental in helping enable East Timor to establish its sovereignty during the period of time that this small country separated itself from Indonesia during the 1990s.

One region in particular, however, reveals all of the conditions that work against democratization and that the United Nations is simply ill-equipped to do much about. Until the current 'Arab Spring', it was widely believed by Western scholars that the Arab countries were overall very unlikely candidates for democratization. Some suggest that this situation is linked to poor developmental situations, a position captured in *The Arab Human Development Report 2009*, which suggests very significant developmental shortfalls, a situation that has got worse since the rather dismal first report issued in 2002 (*Arab Human Development Report 2002*). In great part, this phenomenon is the result of a variety of socio-economic, political and environmental challenges that would seriously confront even those societies that are consciously working to move in the direction of democracy. Water scarcity, desertification and the highest population increases in the world contribute to what can be referred to as a democracy deficit. While demographic pressures are decreasing in the advanced industrial democracies of Western Europe and North America as well as Japan, they are accelerating in the Arab region. By 2015, the total Arab world's population is expected to reach 400 million, a 167 per cent increase from 1980 (United Nations Development Programme 2009: 2). This will be perhaps the most youthful region in the world with a median age of only 22, well below the median age of 28 for the planet overall (ibid.: 3). The largest Arab state, Egypt, is indicative of the serious nature of the issue of underdevelopment. As many as half a million people are added to the workforce annually. Even with a high economic growth rate that is currently around 5 or 6 per cent, it is not possible to create and sustain the additional jobs that are needed for a very young and dramatically increasing workforce.

Such problems are present in Egypt and elsewhere in the region: scarcity of resources, over-population and institutionalized corruption. These are not matters that the United Nations is equipped, let alone authorized, to deal with. Absent also, however, is the basic ingredient of the rule of law. More appropriately, there is at present a competition between the essential bodies of international law and sharia law that the United Nations in general and the UN Human Rights Council in particular have not resolved and apparently have no desire to do so. The Council, for example, attempted in 2008 to offer criticism of the rite of female circumcision and was quickly and rather successfully challenged by the Egyptian and Pakistani delegates, who took the criticism to be an attack on Islam ('Muslim countries win concessions' 2008). A few months earlier, the United Nations had already banned the controversial documentary *Fitna*, produced in the Netherlands, as an attack on Islam ('U.N.'s Ban Condemns Dutch' 2008). Secretary-General Ban Ki-moon enthusiastically agreed that *Fitna* was 'offensively anti-Islamic' (ibid.). These episodes suggest that the dedication to democratization on the part of the United Nations is suspect. The (in)famous cartoons that were published in 2005 by a Danish newspaper produced violent demonstrations in several Islamic countries and led to the violent death of one Catholic nun and numerous injuries to other non-Muslims. Instead of apologizing on behalf of the Islamic community, the Organization of the Islamic Conference (OIC) adopted a resolution that called on the United Nations to adopt a position that, in effect, condemned any criticism of Islam as bigotry and Islamophobia (Abrams 2009). Of course, the Human Rights Council is not the only United Nations agency to cater to or collapse from pressures by the OIC or individual Islamic states, but it is probably the most flagrantly consistent. For example, the United Nations Relief Works Agency for Palestinian Refugees in the Near East (UNRWA) supports 600 schools and 200,000 children throughout the Gaza Strip. In September 2009, the Hamas regime there informed UNRWA that it did not want the history of the Holocaust taught in schools, denying that the Holocaust was a fact and claiming that it was a fabrication of Zionists to gain sympathy for Israel. UNRWA immediately responded by cancelling any mention of the Holocaust in its curriculum.

Freedom of speech and expression, highlighted in the United Nations Declaration of Human Rights, a basic cornerstone of any democracy, is obviously and dangerously being compromised here. Article 19 stipulates that: 'Everyone has the right of freedom of opinion and expression; this right includes freedom to hold opinions without interference and to seek, receive and impart information and ideas through any media and regardless of frontiers.' Many members of both the United Nations and the Commission on Human Rights also flagrantly violate Article 18: 'Everyone has the right to freedom of thought, conscience and religion; this right includes freedom to change his religion [apostasy in most Islamic states can be and frequently is punishable by death] or belief, and freedom, either alone or in community with others and in public or private to manifest his religion or belief in teaching, practice, worship and observance.' Moreover, several Muslim states, both Arab and non-Arab, consider themselves to be within the Islamic tradition that insists on the Qur'an as the ultimate source of law and social behaviour. For example, Sura 2:28 stipulates that men are superior to women, a clear contradiction of the Declaration's Article 16, which states that 'men and women are entitled to equal rights'. In addition, Sura 4:11 follows through by maintaining that women should only receive half of what men receive in any inheritance from their parents.

In contrast, neither the United Nations nor any of its agencies has seriously or continuously condemned anything in the electronic or print media that is anti-Buddhist, anti-Christian, anti-Semitic, anti-Sikh or anti-Hindu. These biases are regularly present in much of the press in Arab and other Islamic countries. There is clearly a double standard at work that is unhealthy and debilitating for the democratization process. No successful democracy has ever been constructed by agreeing to place one community, whether economic, social, ethnic or religious, in a category that is considered immune from criticism or removed from the open marketplace of ideas. In a very real sense, the United Nations is contradicting its own initiative, goals and stated policy because, in fact, one community is considered by the UN to be at least supremacist and, by others, as misunderstood or as victimized by a rapacious, insensitive and exploitive West (Brown 2008).

In its pretence of objectivity, the United Nations usually cautions Israel and its Arab antagonists to end their 'cycle of violence'. Ken Levin argues, however, that there is no real cycle of violence to end: some see the situation as one of unprovoked attacks on Israel and Israeli responses to them (Levin 2005: 468).

The United Nations and self-destructive democracy

Since its inception, the UN has officially pursued the realization of the concept of individual freedom. However, the failure of this initiative has been obvious for some time. In fact, the failure began at the beginning of the UN's history. However, many UN member states – including many in Africa, Central Asia and the Middle East – are not free by most measurements, although some are more authoritarian than others. In its debates and adopted resolutions, the UN has frequently ignored the notion of 'free' for a notion of an 'equality' of sovereign states. This cannot be considered a step forward. Sovereignty of the state became a sufficient condition for membership; popular sovereignty was dismissed as impractical. The latter is a notion that is not geographically restricted to the West, but is found elsewhere, though in a rather haphazard fashion. Huntington notes the post-Cold War disparity between Western states and the 'Asian-Islamic grouping' that had serious disagreements on where human rights begin and end (Huntington 1996: 195–196).

It is disingenuous to suggest that the United Nations is a collection of free states. Non-free member states still remain a decisive majority in the UN General Assembly, while 'incompletely free' states, Russia and China, can wield the veto in the Security Council. In fact, it may very well be that non-free states such as Saudi Arabia and Iran, because of the precious natural resources of oil and natural gas, have in the past successfully pressurized free states to do their bidding. One of the most notorious examples of such pressure may be the 1975 General Assembly resolution that equated Zionism with racism and that was passed overwhelmingly. This resolution, number 3379, endured for 16 years. Again, most full democracies voted against the resolution. The tally was 72 to 35 and 32 abstentions. The General Assembly repealed the resolution in 1991 (#4686), though the Arab states and remaining communist countries such as the Democratic Peoples' Republic of (North) Korea, Vietnam and Cuba voted against the repeal.

In addition, non-free states often combine to ensure that no resolution is directed against them. Arab states, for example, are very protective about Sudan and are determined to thwart any resolution that condemns and holds responsible the Sudanese government for genocidal acts against the population of Darfur. The Arab League has yet to condemn Sudan or take any measures to relieve the rape and slaughter of hundreds of thousands of Sudanese citizens. And the Arab states can be and frequently are joined by other Islamic countries, and even by the Castro and Chavez regimes in Cuba and Venezuela, as well as occasionally by the Democratic Peoples' Republic of (North) Korea. In practice, nearly one-third of the General Assembly is filled by countries in the 'Islamic bloc', represented by the 57-member Organization of the Islamic Conference (OIC). The outcome is that it is sometimes relatively easy to proceed from one-third to an absolute majority because of the alliances forged with many other non-democratic and autocratically governed states, such as China and Cuba.

Another resolution, passed by the UN Commission on Human Rights on 24 December 2007, by a vote of 29 to 16, with 7 abstentions, was entitled 'Combating defamation of religions' (Barak 2009). The resolution was sponsored by the Islamic Republic of Pakistan, with the support of the OIC. Interestingly, it was opposed by most of the Western democracies on the Commission but endorsed by all the non-democratic states, with a very few democratic exceptions such as Costa Rica. Islam was the only religion that was named in the resolution, which 'noted with deep concern the intensification of the campaign of defamation of religions, and the ethnic and religious profiling of Muslim minorities in the aftermath of the tragic events of 11 September 2001'. There was no direct or indirect reference to or mention of the many instances of persecution, in Pakistan and elsewhere, of non-Islamic minorities, and the murder or attempted murder, sometimes by their own families, of former Muslims who had converted to Christianity (Trifkovic 2002: 77). Nor is the OIC or the Commission (or, for that matter, the Arab League) in any apparent hurry to condemn the slaughter of more than 200,000 people and the hundreds of thousands of others driven from their ancestral homes in Darfur and forced to live at a subsistence level during the early years of the twenty-first century by military units of the pro-Islamist government in Khartoum.

Article 51 of the United Nations Charter very precisely recognizes the intrinsic right of member states to national self-defence. The democratic peace thesis claims that most democracies, most of the time, do not become aggressive actors on the international scene and are inherently reluctant to do so because of their democratic status and proclivities. They do react, however, frequently in a concerted and massive effort, against attackers, who are almost uniformly autocratic or totalitarian regimes (Maoz and Abdolali 1989; Fukuyama 1992). However, it should be noted that democracies can also be very severe critics of one another. The European Union (EU), for example, usually finds fault with Israel and sometimes the United States when there is any violence that involves Israeli armed forces and Palestinian terrorist organizations, especially if there are Israeli military incursions into the Gaza Strip.

Despite the UN's recognition of the right to national self-defence, the then UN Secretary-General Kofi Annan urged Israel to work for a ceasefire with its attacker, while appearing to condemn the Israelis merely for defending themselves against external attack. During its 2008 session, the General Assembly 'directed 68 percent of its condemnatory resolutions and other strictures against Israel' and the secretary-general continually called for a worldwide boycott of Israel (Gilder 2009: 235). The condemnations mostly came after Israel retaliated against Hamas or other terrorist organizations that threatened or terminated Israeli lives on Israeli soil. Two-thirds of condemnatory resolutions directed against one small country suggests an unhealthy as well as bigoted obsession on the part of the United Nations, one that borders on the grotesque. It is at the very least counterproductive, if only because it goes against the United Nations Charter that upholds a country's right of national self-defence.

The Israeli/Palestinian conflict is not the only inconsistency in what can justifiably be regarded as a politicized United Nations. The occupation of Tibet by China is certainly another. Since China, a growing economic superpower with fast-growing international influence, is a veto-wielding member of the UN Security Council, there is little likelihood this situation will change. In fact, China has so diluted the indigenous population in Tibet that the recently arrived Han Chinese outnumber the indigenous Tibetans by at least two million. China's presence in Tibet began in 1951 when it invaded and occupied the country, but in nearly six decades the United Nations has neither condemned China nor seriously considered sanctions against it. In contrast, Israelis living in the West Bank currently constitute perhaps one-tenth of the total population there, about 275,000 out of approximately 2.6 million inhabitants in 2009. Israel, of course, is regularly condemned by various agencies and committees of the United Nations, especially the General Assembly, for retaining settlements in the West Bank, thus ignoring the inconvenient fact that 1.5 million Palestinian Arabs, more than 20 per cent of the total Israeli citizenry, reside in Israel with full citizenship rights that include a free press, the ability to vote by secret ballot in regular elections, and to criticize the government with impunity. The starkness of this double standard is noteworthy: Israel has been a practising democracy since 1949; China still is not.

The United Nations record on North Korea and Iran is hardly better, although theoretically there is some room to deal effectively with them should the United Nations in general, and the Security Council in particular, develop the will to do so. Neither of these states can exercise any sort of veto power, and neither apparently has more than a handful of reliable allies. Iran's membership in the OIC is, of course, helpful to it because of a built-in bloc of Islamic states in the United Nations General Assembly, as is the fact that the country exports substantial amounts of oil. North Korea, however, is devoid of valuable natural resources and natural allies and must rely on China as well as one or two other pariah states such as Myanmar for any diplomatic support.

The United Nations as a menace to democratization and democracy?

The United Nations does many productive and useful things, and these should not be ignored or discounted. In the areas of health care and relieving the impact of disease and hunger, for example, there is certainly a reasonable record. For the most part, the United Nations Children's Fund (UNICEF) and the World Health Organization (WHO) have distinguished records. The real good that is done, however, rarely or only ineffectively obtains at the political level. The United Nations culture is one that seems to emphasize and cater to engagement with some regimes that are both thuggish and ideologically motivated against democracy. It seems that only when a government is led by those who are clearly sociopathic does the United Nations resort to sanctions and international ostracism. North Korea is a case in point. The activities and speeches of its mercurial leader are too much even for a lot of the United Nations membership. Of course, the North Koreans, unlike Iran or Saudi Arabia, do not have any significant deposits of natural gas and oil. Thus it is safe to condemn the North Korean regime since the government only has the capacity to make life endlessly miserable for its own unfortunate citizens.

However, the current secretary-general of the UN, Ban Ki-moon, is outdoing his predecessor in efforts to placate dictators who have demonstrated the capacity to commit egregious and violent outrages, mostly against their own nations. This approach is being overdone even by UN standards. The Norwegian permanent representative to the UN, Mona Juul, has referred to Ban as a secretary-general who is 'spineless and charmless', a remarkably harsh criticism in a normally staid organization that is also generally polite (Lynch 2009). Since his installation as secretary-general, there has been no indication that the UN is about to improve on its record of hypocrisy.

The UN could also live up more to its own charter by ridding itself of bizarre political ironies that defy reason and human decency. In 2003, Libya – never in its history known for championing individual liberties – was selected to chair the Human Rights Commission. During the 2009–10 session, the General Assembly presidency was occupied by a former Libyan foreign minister and Qaddafi confidant.

One solution that has been proposed in various forums, and is usually received with substantial scepticism, is American withdrawal from the United Nations. If the US was to leave the UN, this would mean that the organization would lose nearly one-quarter of its annual budget (Babbin 2004: 86–91). It has also been suggested that, short of overall withdrawal from the UN, the United States might wish to retain active membership on selected agencies. Some have contended that the US government is capable of working with other important and free societies to establish an international organization – in effect, a rival to the UN – that would work on the premise that only solidly democratic states would be accepted as members. The argument is that democratic countries such as India, Israel and Australia could easily qualify to become charter members, while other democracies might be persuaded to withdraw from the United Nations – as the organization becomes increasingly irrelevant without American membership and dues. For some countries, including but not restricted to Israel, the United Nations is actually a global menace that wouldn't be missed or lamented if reduced to irrelevance.

The basis of such concerns is the wide perception that the United Nations has not turned out how it was intended when founded nearly seven decades ago. This point has been made quite cogently by Walid Phares (2009), who has argued that the 'United Nations…has completely abandoned its principles' by essentially establishing itself as neutral between terrorism and the war on terrorism. This is reflective of a position that contends that the UN's continued usefulness to the pursuit of democracy and human rights is at best questionable. Indeed, it is sometimes contended that the UN is gradually becoming an ally or at least an enabler of institutionalized Islamist terrorism, or of terrorism sponsored by Islamic regimes. Such a view is underpinned by events such as those in 2009 and 2010 when Colonel Muammar Gaddafi of Libya and President Ahmadinejad of Iran were featured speakers in those years respectively at the UN's opening sessions in New York. Gaddafi is known as *Fata alk Majnun*, the crazy man, even in the Arab

Middle East, while the latter has regularly threatened to destroy Israel, a member state of the United Nations.

It is widely agreed that since its inception the UN's main organs and most agencies have been relentlessly corrupted by member states who are neither peace-loving nor democratic. In a remarkable irony, the United Nations Environmental Programme (UNEP) refers to Egypt as 'a western-democracy' (despite the fact that the main opponent to the candidacy of now-deposed, six-term, president Hosni Mubarak spent the campaign in 2009 in prison), and the United Nations International Protection Workshop (UNIPW) continues to call for 'a boycott of Israeli goods' (Solway 2009). The consequence of these developments is that, overall, the UN may well be doing more harm than good to the Kantian goal of global peace and harmony between nations. Many now assert that neither democracy nor human rights can be adequately extended or protected by an organization that appears powerless to affect the sometimes inhumane activities of leaders – such as, Ahmadinejad, Gaddafi and Chavez – who enthusiastically seek to use the UN as a forum to express their anti-Western and, many would contend, anti-democratic ideas.

Conclusion

It is worth recalling that the League of Nations failed miserably to stop or even confront aggression from totalitarian regimes in Germany, Italy, Japan and the Soviet Union prior to the Second World War. The United Nations is following a dreadfully similar course. Tens of millions of lives were destroyed because of policies that were tragically mistaken because of the weakness, appeasement or accommodation of the League of Nations. It may very well be that the UN more actively abets horrific regimes than its predecessor did and, in doing so, undermines the security of democratic states. In any case, it seems safe to assume, granted the current membership and credibility provided to tyrannical regimes and their leaders, that little or nothing will change for the better in the foreseeable future. Democracy and the process of the democratization are better off and have a much improved chance of success without the United Nations.

References

Abrams, F. (2009) 'UN-acceptable Censorship: The United Nations Tries to Outlaw Criticism of Islam', *New York Daily Times*, 14 January; available at http://www.nydailynews.com/opinions/2009/01/14/2009-01-14_unacceptable_censorship_the_united_natio.html (accessed 21 April 2011).

'Apostasy and the Islamic Nations' (2009) available at http://www.american thinker.com/printpage/?url=http://www.americanthinker.com/2009/09 (accessed 22 September 2009).

Babbin, J. (2004) *Inside the Asylum: Why the UN and Old Europe are Worse Than You Think*. Washington, DC: Regnery Publishing, Inc.

Barak, E. (2009) 'At the U.N., Terrorism Pays', *The Wall Street Journal*, 25 September.

Brown, S. (2008) 'The United Nations: Islam's Gestapo', 11 April; available at http://archive.frontpagemag.com/readArticle.aspx?ARTID=30567 (accessed 21 April 2011).

'Beyond start up nation' (2011) *The Economist*, 1 January, p. 60

Fukuyama, F. (1992) *The End of History and the Last Man*. New York: Free Press.

Gilder, G. (2009) *The Israel Test*, Minneapolis, MN: Richard Vigilante Books.

Glazov, J. (2009) *United in Hate: The Left's Romance with Tyranny and Terror*. Los Angeles, CA: WND Books.

Huntington, S. (1991) *The Third Wave: Democratization in the Late Twentieth Century*. Norman: University of Oklahoma Press.

—— (1996) *The Clash of Civilizations and the Remaking World Order*. New York: Simon & Schuster.

Levin, K. (2005) *The Oslo Syndrome: Delusions of a People Under Siege*. Hanover, NH: Smith and Krause, Inc.

Lynch, C. (2009) 'U.N. Chief's 'Quiet' Outreach to Autocrats Causing Discord', *The Washington Post*, 1 September.

Maoz, Z. and N. Abdolali (1989) 'Regime Types and International Conflict, 1816–1976', *Journal of Conflict Resolution*, 33 (March), pp. 3–35.

'Muslim countries win concessions regarding religious debates' (2008) Associated Press, 19 June.

Phares, W. (2009) 'Message to The U.N. – Support Democracy Not Dictators'. Foundation For The Defense of Democracies; available at http://www.defenddemocracy.org/index.php?option=com_content&task=view&id=11786793&Itemid=0 (accessed 21 April 2011).

Rosett, C. (2009) 'The U.N. Kicks Off Another Session of Bedlam' , *Forbes Magazine*, 20 August; available at http://www.forbes.com/2009/08/19/united-nations-bribery-muammar-gaddafi-opinions-columnists-claudia-rosett.html (accessed 21 April 2011).

Solway, D. (2009) 'UN Report'; available at http://www.frontpagemag.com/Printable.aspx?ArtId=36405, 25 September (accessed 21 April 2011).

The World Factbook (2010) Washington, DC: Central Intelligence Agency.

Trifkovic, S. (2002) *The Sword of the Prophet*. Boston: Regina Orthodox Press.

'U.N.'s Ban condemns Dutch film as anti-Islamic' (2008) Reuters, 28 March.

UNDP (United Nations Development Programme) (2002) *Arab Human Development Report 2009*. New York: UNDP.

UNDP (United Nations Development Programme (2009) *Arab Human Development Report 2009*. New York: UNDP.

Warraq, Ibn (2005) 'Apostasy, Human Rights, Religion, and Belief—New Threats to the Freedom of Opinion and Expression: A General Overview of Apostasy'. In *The Myth of Islamic Tolerance: How Islamic Law Treats Non-Muslims*, ed. R. Spencer. Amherst, New York: Prometheus Books.

20

The European Union and democratization

Michelle Pace

A key assumption underlying the European Union's democratization policy is that democratization requires political institutions and processes. In particular: regular, free, fair and transparent elections; a thriving civil society; a growing middle class; and proper civic education.

This chapter builds on intensive interviews that the author carried out with various European Union (EU) actors across EU institutions in Brussels, during March and April 2009, in order to unravel the self-understanding of EU actors and what they think they are doing by promoting democracy in the case of a specific region: the Middle East. Supplemented by discourse analysis of key EU documents, this chapter investigates significant paradoxes and contradictions in the EU's 'democracy promotion' efforts in the cases of Palestine and Egypt. It argues that since there is no working definition of which type of democracy the EU is actually attempting to export, the meaning of democracy can only be inferred from policy documents, and conflates various policy areas including human rights, development, security and trade. Moreover, the chapter contends that there is no coherent EU strategy or a well-articulated democratization policy in practice, which would bring together the various EU instruments at hand. It explores how, during 2006, a discussion ensued in Brussels about the need to define a more general strategy on democracy promotion: the need arose when the US wanted to discuss this policy area with EU officials! This brief debate did not materialize into any concrete EU stances on democratization but, in 2009, there was a renewed attempt by the Czech and Swedish presidencies to define a common, overarching EU framework on 'democracy support/building'. The Council Conclusions of 2009 aimed at reaching a European consensus on democracy by 2010. This chapter further highlights limits and constraints on the EU's democratization agenda, including too much a focus on procedural democracy.

In the 1990s, EU member states found an opportunity to project the European Community's role as a global actor. In the context of the collapse of communist rule in Europe, the EU opted for the promotion of democracy as another key foreign policy instrument in its external relations.

The European Commission set out the strategic and funding priorities of the EU in the area of democracy and human rights assistance in the report on *The EU Role in Promoting Human Rights and Democratization in Third Countries* (European Commission 2001). The EU's approach to democracy promotion is marked not by a military posture, but by a predisposition to promoting its preferred values – highlighting democratization, democracy and associated human rights – through its interaction with and the socialization of political actors in other, non-democratic countries. This is known as the EU's 'partnership-based approach'. The document indirectly sent a message to the targets of the EU's democracy promotion efforts that the EU was somewhat different from the United States in the manner in which it was proposing to encourage political reform in other, non-democratic countries and regions.

As a key institution of the EU, the European Commission has primary responsibility for developing and implementing democracy-related programmes in the framework of the EU's external relations. Since the decentralization reform of 2000, its delegation offices in the Middle East have had an increased role on the ground, including the management of the former Mesures d'Accompagnement (MEDA) programme,[1] the European Neighbourhood and Partnership Instrument (ENPI), human rights and civil society projects as well as European Instrument for Democracy and Human Rights (EIDHR) microprojects. The delegation offices also report on political developments and human rights in the region. However, the Commission is far from an autonomous actor. EU member-state governments are represented through the Council of the European Union, which sets the general political orientation of EU policies, and more specifically through the High Representative of the Common Foreign and Security Policy (CFSP) – the second pillar of the EU system covering the political and security dimension. Democracy and human rights are core objectives of the EU's CFSP (Treaty on European Union, article 11.1). Making the assumption that economic development leads to political reform, the EU commits itself 'to contribute to the general objective of developing and consolidating democracy and the rule of law, and to that of respecting human rights and fundamental freedoms' (Treaty establishing the European Community, articles 181a and 177.2). The European Parliament emphasizes the importance of supporting democratization processes, particularly 'EU measures to support the electoral process and to allow comprehensive and effective election monitoring' (European Parliament 1998). In 1999, the Commission granted the Swedish International Development Agency €990,000 to implement common European standards for electoral observation. Members of the European Parliament exercise their limited power through regular resolutions, parliamentary exchanges in the Euro-Med Parliamentary Assembly, reports, hearings, oral and written questions and missions during elections in the area. There is a European Parliament delegation to the Euro-Med Parliamentary Assembly. According to Chris Patten, formerly European commissioner responsible for foreign affairs, in the implementation of measures intended to promote observance of human rights and democratic principles in the EU's external relations 'the pivotal role of the European Parliament is in both the development of policy and the expansion of available resources' (Commission of the European Communities 2000).

It has long been acknowledged by diplomats, academics and journalists that when it comes to the EU's external relations with the Middle East, the lack of a coherent and unitary voice is a key constraint on its effectiveness (MacShane 2008). This institutional constraint is not limited to differences between the positions of the Council of the European Union, the European Commission and European Parliament. It extends to differences within and between EU member states. A second factor, which adds to the EU's malaise, is its failure to deal with the real political causes of the Middle East conflict, which include a settlement of the long-running Israel-Palestinian issue. In this context, 'malaise' refers to the EU's tendency to react in the Middle East and North Africa (MENA) via a series of empty – often rhetorical – gestures. I would argue that the EU needs instead to try to address the adverse effects that undemocratic regimes in the region have on the core conflict – between Israel and the Palestinians – as well as to revisit the overly narrow policy parameters of its conflict-resolution efforts and seek to develop, in relation to the region, an overall strategy that actively promotes democracy through its own example. Moreover, a major limitation on the EU's identity as a global actor, particularly in the Middle East, is that the EU is often a spectator as events unfold, waiting for the US to give its green light.[2]

Use of the term 'global actor' refers to how the EU performs as an actor in world politics, particularly in the MENA region. The Middle East conflict between Israel and the Palestinians is, of course, one of the core areas of the EU's foreign policy. Yet, despite its apparently strong economic and diplomatic influence, the EU often appears powerless in this context, merely a hand-wringing bystander. No other area highlights these constraints more than democracy-building in Egypt and Palestine, the two cases considered in this chapter.

In the first section, this chapter gives a brief outline of the EU's key objectives and instruments in its democratization agenda. The next section highlights the *raison d'être* behind the EU's agenda in this policy area. In a separate section, this chapter analyses key challenges for the EU in the democratization arena as well as any lessons learnt from past EU experience in this field. It concludes by arguing that only a clear and effective EU political reform agenda in the MENA can save the region from further de-democratization.

European Union democracy promotion efforts

As noted above, EU democracy promotion efforts have, so far, mainly focused on improved human rights and better, more transparent elections. Two key pillars of the EU's efforts are human rights education and an emphasis on institution-building. The adoption of the legal basis for the EIDHR in December 2006 paved the way for the first Strategy Paper covering the period 2007–10 (which was adopted by the European Commission in August 2007). The concrete implementation of EIDHR activities only came underway, however, in the second half of 2008. The Strategy Paper highlights five key objectives, namely:

1) Enhancing respect for human rights and fundamental freedoms in countries where they are most at risk;
2) Strengthening the role of civil society in promoting human rights and democratic reform, in supporting the peaceful conciliation of group interests and, in consolidating political participation and representation;
3) Supporting actions on human rights and democracy issues in areas covered by EU guidelines, including on human rights dialogues, on human rights defenders, on the death penalty, on torture, on children and armed conflict, on the rights of the child, on violence against women and girls and combating all forms of discrimination against them, on international humanitarian law and on possible future guidelines;
4) Supporting and strengthening the international and regional framework for the protection and promotion of human rights, justice, the rule of law and the promotion of democracy;
5) Building confidence in and enhancing the reliability and transparency of democratic electoral processes, in particular through election observation (EIDHR Strategy Papers 2007–10 and 2011–13).

These same five objectives reappear in the revised EIDHR Strategy Paper for the period from 2011–13.[3] Thus, EU democracy-building efforts have also prioritized relations with civil society and non-governmental organizations (NGOs), as the main implementing partners for projects such as those under the EIDHR. It is a key stated aim of the EU to strengthen the development of a pluralistic civil society in its neighbouring countries and regions, i.e. including in Central and Eastern Europe, the MENA. Linked to this aim are the declared objectives of the EU's democracy promotion activities: to develop and consolidate the principles of liberty, democracy, respect for human rights and the rule of law in its neighbouring countries through the development of cooperative activities under association agreements in the case of Mediterranean partners, including Egypt, or, in the case of Palestine, an interim agreement. Article 2 of each association agreement stipulates that respect for democratic principles and human rights is an essential element. This clause is legally binding on both parties to the agreement, with the possibility of suspension of the agreement in cases of violation.[4]

The EU seeks to achieve these aims primarily through a number of instruments ranging from political dialogue, diplomatic demarches and specific human rights dialogues to various tools of financial and technical cooperation such as funding projects or democracy assistance packages for particular target groups, including women and victims of torture. Rather than directly challenging the strategies used by authoritarian regimes to suppress and silence opposition voices in the MENA, the EU prefers to offer assistance for 'countering the abuse of prisoners and detainees, empowering survivors of torture and developing capacity in the area of forensic medicine' (Commission of the European Communities 2000: 53). One of the fastest growing areas of EU support is the wider governance agenda. Under the EIDHR the key objective of the EU's assistance has been to assist in meeting differentiated human rights and democracy objectives at international and national levels, complementing action within the EU's various national and regional cooperation programmes and the Instrument for Stability (IfS).[5] In the case of the Middle East region, these programmes include bilateral relations between the EU and individual countries in the south, the Euro-Mediterranean Partnership or Barcelona Process, the European Neighbourhood Policy and the Union for the Mediterranean. Over and above its support for civil society organizations, the EU also offers support for international human rights instruments and mechanisms, and the international criminal justice system, including the International Criminal Court (ICC) and other ad hoc international criminal tribunals. The EU has also developed its role as a leading actor in election observation, based on the principles and procedures outlined in the 2000 Commission Communication on EU Election Assistance and Observation, endorsed by the Council in 2001.[6] In its 2003 European Security Strategy, the EU reiterated its interest in a peaceful resolution of the Middle East conflict between Israel and the Palestinians and, more generally, a democratized Mediterranean neighbourhood, stating that 'it is in the Union's interest that countries on our borders are well governed. Our task is to promote a ring of well-governed countries to the east of the European Union and on the shores of the Mediterranean with whom we can enjoy close and cooperative relations. Resolution of the Arab-Israeli conflict is a strategic priority. Without this, there will be little chance of dealing with other problems in the Middle East.'[7] In the 2009 Council Conclusions on 'Democracy Support in the EU's External Relations' (2009) there is an emphasis on the need for increased coherence and effectiveness of EU policies and instruments for democratic support in EU external action.[8]

Raison d'être behind the EU's democratization agenda

So what is the raison d'être behind the EU's democracy promotion approach? It is often argued in EU documentation that the processes of political liberalization and democratization have brought about peaceful coexistence in Europe and that such successful processes can be emulated else-where (see e.g. European Commission 2001). Thus, the model of democracy that the EU attempts to push for emulation in neighbouring countries is that of liberal democracy. However, the term liberal democracy as such is rarely used in EU rhetoric and texts, as it is in US democracy-promotion documents. Liberal and liberalization are used more in the economic sense, that is, referring to the diminishing and eventual breakdown of tariff and non-tariff barriers to trade. On the other hand, some exceptional explicit references to liberal democracy may be found, for instance, in the debates of the European Parliament:

> The European Union has become a global player, always on the basis of its principles such as respect for peace, the quest for compromise, plus the defence of human rights and of liberal democracy. In particular, it is engaged in an effort to promote democracy in countries in North Africa, the Middle East, the Caucasus and Eastern Europe.
>
> *(Józef Pinior, 2006)*[9]

Otherwise, the notion of liberal democracy is merely implied in EU presentations, programmes and publications. This may reflect a further assumption: democratic freedoms are something very specific to the European experience.

In addition to the EU's discourse, there is a vibrant academic literature on the merits and legitimacy of liberal democracy as an instrument for the achievement of progress and equality. Some argue that liberal democracy is the best political system for ensuring Immanuel Kant's *perpetual peace*. Kantian scholars assume that democratic states do not engage in wars against each other, although this theory was severely challenged during the Balkan wars of the 1990s.

Underpinning this idea in an ethical sense is the notion that 'liberal' in liberal democracy denotes visions of a society made up of individuals, where defence of their individual rights is a – perhaps *the* – primary social good. The origins of liberal democracy are to be found in eighteenth-century Europe, during the Age of Enlightenment. At this time, it was argued that human affairs should be guided by reason and the principles of equality and liberty. By the nineteenth century, the idea and model of liberal democracy was also widely believed to include encouragement of a free market economy and free trade. However, over time the relation between liberalism and democracy has been widely contested. Liberalism is considered individualistic and concerns itself with limiting state power. In theory at least, democracy is concerned with the power of the people and is a collectivist ideal. Fareed Zakaria (1997), for example, has argued that constitutional liberalism and democratic government are not necessarily connected. Winston Churchill famously argued that democracy is the worst form of government except for all the other forms that have been tried from time to time. Thus, there is an inherent disposition not to question liberal democracy: this model of democracy is not perfect as a political system but it is widely held, often implicitly, to be the best available.

For the EU, this predisposition to liberal democracy is extended and put into practice through a strong focus on elections and election-observation missions, which worldwide form a vital component of its activities to promote democracy, human rights and the rule of law (European Commission 2000). Therefore, the EU bases its democracy-promotion agenda on an overall optimism with regard to the liberal peace paradigm,[10] yet without creating the necessary flexibility to make strategic adjustments in cases of pending state-building projects, persisting conflict and frustrated national identities as can be found, for example, in several countries in the MENA.[11] This, Kurki (2008) argues, is more akin to *electoral* democracy than *liberal* democracy. It follows that the EU frames a cornerstone of its foreign and security policy – the promotion of democracy – in a *procedural* manner. For the EU, the organization of elections goes hand in hand with the consolidation of institutions, but there is very little by way of detail on how such institutions can be secured on a long-term basis in particular contexts (see e.g. Council of the European Union 2005). Nor is there much reflection on whether or not European models of institution-building fit political, social, cultural and historic contexts elsewhere. This complacency helps reinforce a widely held view that the EU has become comfortable with its technical approach to external relations and external governance, with the resulting danger of an overly procedural conception of democracy.

EU democracy promotion policies are not alone in placing this emphasis on free and fair elections. Statements from other external actors, including the United States and international organizations such as the International Institute for Democracy and Electoral Assistance (IDEA), highlight an embedded belief in the power of elections to transform the political landscape worldwide. Thus, the promotion of democracy is conceived as operating through processes familiar in a reality (the European context) that is external to the core roots of political configurations in the Middle East, specifically that of occupation in the case of Palestine and, for example, of authoritarianism in the case of Egypt. This EU framing of democracy promotion in procedural terms has been severely challenged in the case of Palestine. As Rami Nasrallah puts it:

> We cannot talk about elections as tools for democratic transformation – elections in Palestine have nothing to do with democratic values. In reality they are either to support a political agreement like the elections in 1996,[12] or an election is held to build a new political landscape and to integrate factors that are not part of the [Palestine Liberation Organization] PLO as when Hamas won in the 2006 election.[13]

In the academic debate, there are those who move beyond the procedural view of promoting liberal democracy and argue instead for a broader perspective that takes account of diverse contexts and cultural values. Zakaria's work (1997) shifts the discussion to the promotion of the gradual *liberalization* of societies. In practical terms, according to Haitham Arar, '[T]his means especially rights, the right of freedom of movement, the right of freedom of expression and of thought, and other rights. You cannot just import a model from the outside – one has to check if ideas are useful for Palestinian society or not'.[14]

The so-called cultural turn in the democratization literature is further developed by David Chandler (1999), Cox *et al.* (2000), Larry Diamond (1999), Nagel and Mahr (1999), Ottaway and Carothers (2000) and Youngs (2001). In the context of Egypt, for instance, this would entail addressing the authoritarian nature of the regime and external actors' political will to adopt strong sanctions against such governments (Brownlee, 2002). As Kamal Khalil (2008) argues:

> Change will come from outside the regime, because the government's interest goes in line with oppressing freedoms … starting from the middle class to the poor classes, because even 10,000 intellectuals won't make a difference unless followed by millions. And the way I see it, Gamal [Mubarak's son] or whatever military successor will be a dictator as well and won't care for a *real* democracy. So the core of change comes from inside – yet, we cannot deny the supporting role of our worldwide friends in the struggle for freedom.[15]

Although the cultural turn in International Relations debates on democracy attempted a move away from a focus on procedures, institutions and elections, it did little to contest the liberal model of democracy at a deeper level. There has been no such reflexive move in the EU for a long time. For instance, in the run-up to the Annapolis Conference in December 2007, Javier Solana and Benita Ferrero-Waldner (Solana and Ferrero-Waldner 2007) focused on what they called Palestinian state-building as a key pillar for a new momentum in the peace process, stating under 'Comprehensive institution-building and good governance' that: 'For over a decade the EU has been at the forefront of efforts to empower the Palestinian Authority (PA) via institution building and its work in the Jerusalem based "Governance Strategy Group". The EU foresees intensifying these activities, in areas which complement PA plans, for example health, education and the judiciary.'

But this statement was without any mention of *how* the EU would engage with the democratically elected Hamas government in the Gaza Strip. In fact, the EU representatives spoke almost as though Hamas-in-government did not exist, despite the fact that the movement and complementary government is a crucial aspect of the Palestinian political landscape. Whether the EU likes it or not, Hamas controls the Gaza Strip.

Such shortcomings in the philosophy and practice of democracy promotion take us back to the academic literature in search of broader ideas that might open up the possibility of alternative models. Peter Burnell (2000) is a strong advocate of thinking beyond the limitations of a liberal conception of democracy and refers to the use of the notions of democracy in such contexts as 'political constructs'. He calls for the inclusion of ideas from *social* and *economic* democracy and for a reflection on *communitarian* as opposed to individualistic notions of society, which in the end contribute to the ideal of a *sustainable* democracy. According to Haitham Arar:

> Here people struggle because they think that democracy is a way of having influence on the political. This is very important. Having a democratic awareness relates to the economic situation because if you have a democratic system you have a good economic situation with employment and thereby less poverty and hunger. It is about ensuring that Palestinian laws are in line with international standards … the rights of refugees.[16]

It appears that the EU prefers to work on the basis of a model of democracy that protects perceived stability, on occasion by retaining authoritarian regimes in power and maintaining the status quo in conflict situations, at the expense of taking bold moves to deal with the reality on the ground for the very targets it seeks to influence through its democracy-promotion packages. However, to solidify and advance its democracy agenda in neighbouring non-democratic countries and regions may well require the EU to move towards what might be called a 'social' or 'welfare model' of democracy. This would require some reflexivity on the part of EU actors over what exactly they seek to advance in promoting a European model of democracy, particularly in the context of the Middle East, where democratization/democracy has proved to be a particularly elusive goal.[17]

Reality check: challenges and lessons learnt

Most EU officials are fully aware that there is no working definition of democracy in EU documents:[18] rather, the meaning of democracy can be inferred from some policy documents where one can find a mix of policy areas ranging from human rights to development, and from democracy promotion to security and trade. There is thus no coherent strategy or well-articulated policy in practice that brings together the various instruments at hand. It should, therefore, come as no surprise that a key area of the EU's external relations – democratization of its southern periphery – continues to pose severe challenges for the EU. As the above brief overview illustrates, the EU is not short of a range of instruments, particularly economic levers, for influencing democratization in the Middle East. The main reasons for the EU's lack of success in this policy domain are therefore beyond the simple argument of lacking the right instruments. First, and most basic, the EU is lost in its own politics of empty gestures. The EU remains the key paymaster of various projects aimed at democracy-building in the MENA,[19] yet has very few monitoring procedures in place to evaluate the effectiveness of its financial assistance. Some analysts argue that the EU simply puts money in the wrong pockets, particularly in the hands of corrupt elites who pose as civil society representatives but are in reality accomplices with Middle Eastern authoritarian regimes (Pace 2010). Second, the EU's lobbying to friendly Arab governments has made no clear headway towards the democratic changes that the EU claims to want to see take place in the region. Third, past EU policies have not been successful because the basic policy parameters, in particular regarding the stakeholders to be included in democratization efforts, have not been seriously addressed. Fourth, the EU lacks an overall strategy towards the MENA that incorporates the active promotion of democracy through its own example.[20] Addressing this requires a clear strategy of how to convince the US that the EU can play a constructive role in the Middle East, and to reassure Arab partners that the EU is serious about its role. One way for the EU to show it is serious is to have a robust policy of criticizing Arab governments for failing to live up to their reform commitments. The EU should also create more opportunities for democratic reformers from southern neighbouring countries to come together and share experiences, including, where appropriate, Islamists. In addition, the EU should also support civil society organizations (CSOs) on the basis of projects focused on real reform and change rather than CSOs endorsed and underpinned by regional authoritarian governing regimes.

Has the EU extracted any lessons from its experience thus far in attempting to promote a particular model of democracy in the Middle East region? Following the January 2006 elections in Palestine, EU officials acknowledge having learnt a number of lessons.[21] It was, in fact, during 2006 that a discussion ensued in Brussels about the need to define a more general strategy on democracy promotion: the need arose when the US wanted to discuss this policy area with EU officials! While this brief debate did not clearly materialize into any concrete EU stances on democratization, in 2009 there was a renewed attempt by the Czech and Swedish presidencies to define a common, overarching EU framework on 'democracy support/building'. EU officials who I interviewed were quick to emphasize that the EU is not trying to impose democracy in its neighbourhood: it has to grow from within, and only then can the EU offer its support. During their presidency, the Swedes interpreted the EU's democratization policy through a development prism.[22] The Council Conclusions of 2009 aimed at reaching a European consensus on democracy by 2010. When interrogated about which principles the EU's democracy promotion policy has been built on, officials in Brussels agree that there is an inherent belief across EU institutions that democracy and a free market economy is what the EU itself is all about and that it is therefore only 'natural' for the EU to promote this system of governance in neighbouring regions. Moreover, EU officials insist that only democracy can effectively guarantee the enjoyment of full human rights across the globe, including economic, social and political rights. They also emphasized their belief in a linkage between (economic) development and democracy (political pluralism), and perceive democratization as an instrument to an end.

EU officials acknowledge, however, that in practice democratization in the MENA creates tensions between different policy areas. For example, in January 2008, the European Parliament issued a critical resolution on the situation of human rights in Egypt.[23] The Egyptian government responded by claiming that the European Parliament had no right to interfere in Egypt's internal affairs.[24] In spite of vowing not to yield to Egyptian pressure, just a few weeks later, EU lawmakers went ahead and signed a Memorandum of Understanding agreement regarding the National Indicative Programme (NIP, 2007–10) with Egypt. This 'assistance' package totals €558 million. Thus, it appears that there is a clear tension between the EU's stated objective of, on the one hand, promoting democracy and human rights in the MENA, and, on the other, ensuring 'security' (that is, economic security in terms of oil and gas supplies, and political security in terms of relations with familiar authoritarian regimes rather than a key opposition group in Egypt of an Islamist nature, the Muslim Brotherhood). Similarly, in the case of Palestine, EU officials acknowledge that they had promoted the parliamentary elections of January 2006 and even sent their own observation mission, which deemed the result of the elections to be fair, free and transparent. But their limited interpretations of liberal democracy were seriously challenged when Hamas won the majority of parliamentary seats. Thus, following the electoral victory of Hamas in the Palestinian elections of January 2006, the EU had to rethink its democratization discourse approach. Officials from Brussels could not disguise their boycotting of a democratic government.

Despite its best intentions in the region, the EU came across as supporting the liberal (party) – Fatah – at the expense of supporting the democratically elected party: Hamas. EU officials argue that they had no choice since Hamas had been included on the EU's list of proscribed terrorist organizations, and that once they had included Hamas on this list it was very difficult to remove it. This decision led the EU to be perceived as supporting those who lost the elections in Palestine (Fatah) because they claim to be liberal in the Western sense. This major event in the Middle East has led to a rethinking process in Brussels about the democratization discourse in the EU.[25]

Conclusion

Several EU institutions now acknowledge that a mistake was made in not recognizing the Hamas victory in the Gaza Strip in the Palestinian elections of 2006. Moreover, many EU officials agree that too much focus on procedural democracy leads to severe limitations and constraints on the EU's democratization agenda. Most officials I interviewed in Brussels also agree that the EU needs to become more pragmatic and flexible if there is to be any potential for reinvigorating the democratization process both in Palestine and more widely in the MENA: 'Today we understand more than before how crucial Palestinian reconciliation is to the democratisation process in Palestine.'[26] In other words, many EU officials now acknowledge the lack of democratic legitimacy of the Fatah administration in the West Bank.

More broadly, most EU officials interviewed agree that they have not reflected well enough on the implications of the EU's efforts at promoting liberal democracy in the MENA, primarily through encouraging periodic elections – procedural democracy. Substantial EU support to Palestinian, Israeli, Egyptian and regional civil society organizations arguably supports a more grounded approach to democracy. Yet the EU's focus on a selective core of civil society groups has so far resulted in little or no clear progress in political reforms on the ground, and has demonstrated that there is nothing inherent in civil society that attaches it to a democratizing project. Representatives of civil society across the MENA admit that once they learnt how to speak the EU's language and prepare funding applications accordingly, they have had no problem in getting funding for 'civil society projects' from the EU. Thus, the EU needs to reach out to grass-roots reformers by changing its funding rules and regulations.[27] EU officials, on the other hand, also admitted that the funding procedure for democracy-related civil society projects is very technical and bureaucratic and does not leave enough time for EU officials to monitor exactly what EU funds are achieving through the projects that are funded.[28]

Without a clear strategy on what exactly it is trying to achieve by promoting democracy-building in the Middle East, the EU has very few choices left for future policy in this domain. On the Palestinian reform front, EU actors have already acknowledged that they missed a golden opportunity to encourage Palestinian unity and should therefore prepare themselves for the eventual resuscitation of such unity and should actively encourage it.

EU democracy assistance and aid programmes should also be monitored and revised carefully to ensure that money goes to grass-roots reformers who can make a real difference on the ground in the Palestinian territory, Egypt and elsewhere in the MENA. Dealing with 'the usual suspects' – i.e. those in power – is no longer a policy the EU can afford to follow in this regard. Only a truly political reform agenda in the Middle East can save the further de-democratization of the region.

Notes

1 MEDA was a major financial instrument of the EU to support economic and social reforms in the Mediterranean region, providing finance for bilateral and multilateral cooperation. For example, MEDA

involved projects relating to the education, health and environment sectors as well as to the improvement of infrastructure and restructuring of administrations. Until 31 December 2006, EU assistance to the countries of the Middle East was provided under geographical programmes including MEDA, as well as thematic programmes such as the European Instrument for Democracy and Human Rights (EIDHR). Launched in 2006, the EIDHR replaces and builds upon the European Initiative (2000–6). For the budgetary period 2000–6, available funding amounted to approximately €5.3 billion for MEDA, as well as approximately €2 billion in European Investment Bank lending for MEDA beneficiary countries. See http://ec.europa.eu/world/enp/funding_en.htm for more information.

2 Author's interview with Dr Diaa Rashwan, Al Ahram Centre, Cairo, 26 March 2008.

3 European Commission 2010. 'European Instrument for Democracy and Human Rights. Strategy Paper 2011 – 2013'. April 21, C(2010)2432. Available at http://ec.europa.eu/external_relations/human_ rights/docs/eidhr_strategy_paper_2011–2013_en.pdf (accessed 31 October 2010).

4 The EU has not thus far suspended any agreement with any Mediterranean partner. This may be difficult as such a suspension would require a consensual agreement between all 27 EU member states.

5 Council Regulation (EC) No 1717/2006, 15.11.2006.

6 Commission Communication EU Election Assistance and Observation COM(2000) 191 final of 11 April 2000; Council conclusions of 31 May 2001; Resolution of the European Parliament of 15 March 2001.

7 Council of the European Union, 2003. 'A Secure Europe in a Better World.' European Security Strategy, Brussels, 12 December.

8 Recommendations on how to increase the visibility and public diplomacy on the EU's external human rights work. Draft paper by the Council Secretariat and the Commission services of 7 July 2009 (11867/09).

9 Pinior is a Polish Member of the European Parliament.

10 This paradigm, predicated on a number of normative assumptions regarding the economic, political and institutional prerequisites necessary to achieve peace in situations of conflict, has been influential in post-conflict state-building operations since the early 1990s. It assumes that the transformation required to peace, democracy and market economy is a self-strengthening process leading to sustainable development.

11 Natalia Mirimanova, (2010). 'Civil Society Building Peace in the European Neighbourhood: Towards a New Framework for Joining Forces with the EU'. MICROCON Policy Working Paper 10, March. Available at http://www.microconflict.eu/publications/PWP10_NM.pdf (accessed 31 October 2010).

12 The Oslo Agreement was signed by the PLO and Israel in 1993. It was renegotiated in 1995 as Oslo 2, partly because there were several unclear elements in the first agreement.

13 Author's interview with Mr Rami Nasrallah, Head of International Peace and Cooperation Center (IPCC), East Jerusalem, 3 September 2007.

14 Interview by the author with Haitham Arar, Ministry of Interior, Democracy and Human Rights Division, Ramallah, 5 September 2007.

15 Author's confidential interview with Kamal Khalil, Cairo, 24 March 2008. See also http://www. amnesty.org/en/library/asset/MDE12/005/2003/en/dom-MDE120052003en.html on Kamal Khalil's incommunicado detention during February 2003 (accessed 9 February 2009).

16 Interview by the author with Haitham Arar, Ministry of Interior, Democracy and Human Rights Division, Ramallah, 5 September 2007.

17 According to Aletta Norval (2007) such reflexivity requires moving away from what she terms aspect blindness to aspect dawning, aspect learning and eventually aspect change. See also Pace (2008).

18 The EU documentation on democracy promotion analysed by this author from the 1990s to date include European Parliament debates, Council conclusions and European Commission reports. For more information see www.birmingham.ac.uk/research/activity/government-society/eumena/ index.aspx.

19 In 2005, for example, EU governments allocated €10 million to the European Commission-managed European Initiative on Democracy and Human Rights (EIDHR) for democracy-promotion projects in the region. See Richard Youngs, 'Survey of European democracy promotion policies 2000–2006', Fundación para las Relaciones Internacionales y el Diálogo Exterior, 2006a.

20 Various interviews conducted by the author in Brussels in the European Parliament, Council and Commission. February – March 2009.

21 Author's interviews with various officials from the European Parliament, Commission and Council, February – March 2009, Brussels.

22 See International IDEA (2010). 'Democracy in Development – Global Consultations on the EU's role in democracy building'. Stockholm: International IDEA. Available at http://www.idea.int/publications/democracy_in_development/index.cfm (accessed 31 October 2010).

23 Available at http://www.europarl.europa.eu/sides/getDoc.do?pubRef=-//EP//TEXT+MOTION+P6-RC-2008-0023+0+DOC+XML+V0//EN (accessed 31 October 2010).

24 See, for example, Cairo Institute for Human Rights Studies, available at http://www.cihrs.org/English/NewsSystem/Articles/141.aspx (accessed 31 October 2010).

25 See Council Conclusions, November 2009. Available at http://www.consilium.europa.eu/uedocs/cms_data/docs/pressdata/en/gena/111250.pdf (accessed 1 December 2010).

26 Author's interview with an official from the Council of the European Union, Brussels, February 2009.

27 Richard Youngs (2006b). 'Europe's flawed approach to Arab democracy'. London: Centre for European Reform, October.

28 Author's interviews with civil society representatives in Jerusalem, September 2007 and November 2009 and with an EU official from EuropeAid section (EIDHR instruments and implementation) of the Commission, March 2009.

Bibliography

Brownlee, J. (2002) 'The Decline of Pluralism in Mubarak's Egypt', *Journal of Democracy*, 13 (4), pp. 6–14.

Burnell, P. (2000) *Democracy Assistance: International Co-operation for Democratization*. London: Frank Cass.

Chandler, D. (1999) *Bosnia: Faking Democracy After Dayton*. London and Sterling, VA: Pluto Press.

Council of the European Union, European Security Strategy of 12 December 2003 *On a Secure Europe in a Better World*.

Council of the European Union, Document 10255/1/05 of 16–17 June 2005 *Presidency Conclusions*.

Council of the European Union Regulation 1717/2006 of 15 November 2006 *Establishing an Instrument for Stability*.

Council Secretariat and the Commission services Draft paper 11867/09 of 7 July 2009 on *Recommendations on How to Increase the Visibility and Public Diplomacy on the EU's External Human Rights Work*.

Cox, M. G., J. Ikenberry and I. Takashi (2000) *American Democracy Promotion: Impulses, Strategies and Impacts*. Oxford: Oxford University Press.

Diamond, L. (1999) *Developing Democracy: Toward Consolidation*. Baltimore, MD: Johns Hopkins University Press.

European Commission Communication COM (2000) 191 final of 11 April 2000 *Concerning EU Election Assistance and Observation*.

European Commission Communication COM (2001) 252 final of 08 May 2001 concerning *The EU Role in Promoting Human Rights and Democratisation in Third Countries*.

European Commission Egypt Country Strategy Paper 2007–2013; available at http://ec.europa.eu/world/enp/pdf/country/enpi_csp_egypt_en.pdf (accessed 6 June 2011).

European Commission COM (2010) Strategy Paper 2432 of 21 April 2010 concerning *European Instrument for Democracy and Human Rights 2011–2013*.

European Council (2001) The Council Conclusions on Election Assistance and Observation of 26 June (9990/01).

European Council 2009 Council Conclusions on *Democracy Support in the EU's External Relations*.

European Parliament (1998) *Resolution on Human Rights in the World 1997–1998 and the European Union Policy in the Field of Human Rights* (A4-0410/98, para. 93)

European Parliament (2008) Joint Motion for a Resolution on *The situation in Egypt*. [online] Available at http://www.europarl.europa.eu/sides/getDoc.do?pubRef=-//EP//TEXT+MOTION+P6-RC-2008-0023+0+DOC+XML+V0//EN (accessed 31 October 2010).

European Union (2006) Consolidated Versions on *The Treaty on European Union and Treaty establishing the European Community*, Official Journal of the European Union, C321 E/1 Available at http://eurlex.europa.eu/LexUriServ/LexUriServ.do?uri=OJ:C:2006:321E:0001:0331:EN:PDF (accessed 31 October 2010).

International IDEA (2010) Democracy in Development–Global Consultations on the EU's role in democracy building. [online] Available at http://www.idea.int/publications/democracy_in_development/index.cfm (accessed 31 October 2010).

MacShane, D. (2008) 'Europe needs to speak with one voice', *The Independent*, 29 June 2008. Available at http://www.independent.co.uk/opinion/commentators/denis-macshane-europe-needs-to-speak-with-one-voice-850964.html (accessed 1 June 2009).

Mirimanova, N. (2010) 'Civil society building peace in the European Neighbourhood: towards a new framework for joining forces with the EU'. MICROCON Policy Working Paper 10, Brighton: MICROCON.

Nagel, J. D. and Mahr, A. (1999) *Democracy and Democratization: Post-Communist Europe in Comparative Perspective* London: Sage Publications.

Norval, A. (2007) *Aversive Democracy: Inheritance and Originality in the Democratic Tradition.* Cambridge: Cambridge University Press.

Ottaway, M. and Carothers, T. (2000) *Funding Virtue: Civil Society Aid and Democracy Promotion*, Washington DC: Carnegie Endowment.

Pace, M. (2010) 'Interrogating the European Union's Democracy Promotion Agenda: Discursive Configurations of 'Democracy' from the Middle East'. In European Foreign Affairs Review, 15, Special Issue, pp. 611–628.

Pinior, J. (2006) 'European Neighbourhood Policy', European Parliament Debates, 18 January 2006, http://eur-lex.europa.eu/LexUriServ/LexUriServ.do?uri=OJ:C:2006:287E:0101:0102:EN:PDF (accessed 11 May 2010).

Rushd Salon, I. (2008) 'Cairo Institute for Human Rights Studies'; available at http://www.cihrs.org/English/NewsSystem/Articles/141.aspx (accessed 31 October 2010).

Solana, J. and Ferrero-Waldner, B. (2007) 'Statebuilding for Peace in the Middle East: An EU Action Strategy', Document S378/07, http://www.consilium.europa.eu/ueDocs/cms_Data/docs/pressdata/en/reports/97949.pdf (accessed 9 February 2009). See also http://www.amnesty.org/en/library/asset/MDE12/005/2003/en/dom-MDE120052003en.html on Kamal Khalil's incommunicado detention during Feb 2003 (accessed 9 February 2009).

University of Birmingham (2010) Paradoxes and Contradictions in EU Democracy Promotion Efforts in the Middle East. [online] Available at http://www.birmingham.ac.uk/research/activity/government-society/eumena/index.aspx (accessed 6 November 2010).

Youngs, R. (2001) *The EU and the Promotion of Democracy* Oxford: Oxford University Press.

—— (2006a) *Survey of European democracy promotion policies 2000–2006.* Madrid: Fundación para las Relaciones Internacionales y el Diálogo Exterior.

—— (2006b) *Europe's flawed approach to Arab democracy.* London: Centre for European Reform.

Zakaria, F. (1997) 'The Rise of Illiberal Democracy', *Foreign Affairs* 76 (6) pp. 22–43.

List of Interviews

Rashwan, D., 26 March 2008. Held at Al Ahram Centre, Cairo.

Nasrallah, R., 3 September 2007. Held at International Peace and Cooperation Center (IPCC), East Jerusalem.

Khalil, K., 24 March 2008. Undisclosed location, Cairo.

Official from the Council of the European Union, 23 February 2009. Held at the Council of the European Union, Brussels.

Civil society representatives during September 2007 and November 2009. Jerusalem.

EU official from EuropeAid section (EIDHR instruments and implementation) of the Commission, 23 March 2009. Held at the European Commission offices, Brussels.

21

The African Union and democratization

Charles Manga Fombad

The establishment of the African Union (AU) in 2002, to replace the Organization of African Unity (OAU), which had proven too weak, unresponsive and incapable of addressing contemporary African problems, especially the abuses inflicted by the continent's dictators on their people, appears to have marked a new phase in the political arrangements of the region. The establishment of the AU raised hopes that it may be a significant actor in helping to arrest – and even reverse – the faltering democratic transitions and growing threats of authoritarian resurgence in Africa. Perhaps the most significant, and certainly unexpected, development that came with the creation of the AU is the special mandate it was given to promote democracy and good governance. Coming from the very leaders who, individually and collectively, have in many respects been responsible for wrecking their countries' economies and suppressing the people for so many years, there were reasons for scepticism.[1]

Whilst many welcomed the AU and its ambitious agenda for promoting democracy and good governance, there are others who see it as a decorative blueprint drawn up by desperate dictators, anxious to obtain new resources from an increasingly sceptical international community under the hegemonic domination of the United States – which is preoccupied with fighting international terrorism, rebuilding a war-ravaged post-Saddam Iraq and promoting the increasingly shaky Israeli-Palestinian roadmap (Mulikita 2003: 105–115). The challenge of promoting democracy in Africa, some argue, represents a historical novelty in the process of building democracies – comparable only to that of Latin America. Never before, it is said, has it been necessary to build democracy under extreme conditions of poverty and inequality and at a time of global recession (Caputo n.d.: 17).

This chapter attempts to see the extent to which the AU democracy agenda provides a credible framework within which genuine democracy can at long last be entrenched in African political and constitutional theory and practice. The critical question is whether this provides an imaginative and innovative new international regional mechanism for promoting and enforcing democracy and good governance or is just one ingenious pragmatic device to seduce an increasingly apathetic international community. The first section examines the basic framework for the AU's democratization agenda. The second section assesses how this agenda has been implemented, its challenges and future prospects. The critical issue is whether or not there is a real will to see the democracy agenda implemented. Can the AU overcome the credibility deficit that had rendered its predecessor an irrelevance? Can it effectively bring pressure to bear on African leaders to mend their democratic ways or hold them accountable for failures? The conclusion to this chapter will argue that, in spite of the challenges, the AU and African leaders have now recognized and accepted the fact that democracy and good political governance constitute a prerequisite for successful political stability and economic recovery on the continent.

The AU's democracy and good governance framework

The basic framework for promoting democracy and good governance amongst member states of the AU is laid down in the Constitutive Act setting up the Union and a number of treaties, declarations and other agreements. As an international treaty, the Constitutive Act is binding on member states and is governed by the rules of the 1969 Vienna Convention on the Law of Treaties, as well as the 1986 Vienna Convention on the Law of Treaties between states and international organizations or between international organizations. Although the AU, as an international organization, possesses the capacity to make legal agreements and other acts that are necessary for the fulfilment of its purposes, it is important to note that not all of these are legally binding on member states (Klabbers 2002: 278–299). A distinction needs to be made between acts adopted as treaties and protocols (which are binding on those member states that have signed and ratified them) and other acts, such as declarations, decisions, recommendations and resolutions (which although aimed at influencing the conduct of member states, are not necessarily legally binding). In this regard there are five major agreements that contain the basic democratic principles on the AU democracy agenda, namely the Constitutive Act itself; the Declaration on the Framework for an OAU (AU) Response to Unconstitutional Changes of Government; the Declaration Governing the Democratic Elections in Africa; the Declaration on Election Observation and Monitoring; and the African Charter on Democracy, Elections and Governance.

The principles contained in the AU act

The transformation of the OAU into the AU completed the emergence of a new organizational focus for this continental body. Unlike in the Charter of the OAU, the preamble of the Constitutive Act emphasizes the important place given to democracy when it affirms the determination of member states to 'promote and protect human and peoples' rights, con-solidate democratic institutions and culture, and to ensure good governance and the rule of law'. The basic democratic tenets of the Constitutive Act are carefully developed in the objectives and principles, which are far more elaborate and more radical than those that were contained in the Charter of the OAU. Insofar as democracy and good governance is concerned, Article 3 dealing with the objectives of the Union states that it shall, inter alia:

(g)   Promote democratic principles and institutions, popular participation and good governance;
(h)   Promote and protect human and peoples' rights in accordance with the African Charter on Human and Peoples' Rights and other relevant human rights agreements.

These objectives define the goals and are directly linked to the principles contained in Article 4, which indicate what shall inform the attainment of these goals. For our purposes here, the most relevant guiding principles contained in Article 4 include:

(g)   Non-interference by any member state in the internal affairs of another;
(h)   The right of the Union to intervene in a member state pursuant to a decision of the Assembly in respect of grave circumstances, namely war crimes, genocide and crimes against humanity

as well as a serious threat to legitimate order to restore peace and stability in the member state of the Union
upon the recommendation of the Peace and Security Council;

(j)   The right of member states to request intervention from the Union in order to restore peace and security;

(m) Respect for democratic principles, human rights, the rule of law and good governance;

(o)   Respect for the sanctity of human life, condemnation and rejection of impunity and political assassination, acts of terrorism and subversive activities;

(p)   Condemnation and rejection of unconstitutional changes of governments. (emphasis added)

These two provisions can be considered to be the legal basis of the AU's present democracy agenda. Their significance will be seen as we proceed throughout this chapter, but a number of preliminary observations are in order here. First, it is important to note that the democracy and good governance clauses in the Constitutive Act are not a novelty. Similar clauses had begun to appear in the constituent agreements of international organizations such as the Organization of American States (OAS), the European Union (EU) and the Commonwealth. Sanctions are often provided against member states that violate this commitment (Magliveras and Naldi 2002). A commitment to democracy by member states of regional international organizations has now become an established pattern and, through this, peer pressure can be brought to bear on states to democratize. Most of the literature on the democracy-promoting role of regional organizations suggests that democracy is now a basic human right (Franck 1992; Baracani 2004; Crawford 1994; MacMahon; Roth 2000; Udombana 2003).

Second, whilst the Constitutive Act, like the OAU Charter, reaffirms the principles of sovereignty and non-intervention as well as prohibits the use of force or the threat of the use of force amongst member states, this is now very heavily qualified. The AU, unlike the OAU, can now intervene under the circumstances defined in Article 4 (h) in respect of grave circumstances, specifically defined as amounting to 'war crimes, genocide and crimes against humanity' and, a bit controversially, where there is a serious 'threat to legitimate order'. Africa has seen the blood of its people being spilled by sadists such as Idi Amin, Jean-Bédel Bokassa and Macias Nguema at a time when the OAU was too weak and had no mandate to speak or act. With the present Article 4 (h), there should be no excuse for the AU not acting, but the ongoing atrocities by the Sudanese government, acting through its proxies, the Janjaweed militias, in Darfur, shows that fine words will not on their own solve any problem without a concerted political will. Perhaps more worrying is the fact that this provision was amended in a rather controversial manner during the AU's first extraordinary summit in February 2003. The amendment (highlighted above in italics) appears to shift the emphasis in the original Article 4 (h) from ensuring human security, as a means of advancing human rights, democracy and good governance, into ensuring the security of incumbent regimes (Baimu and Sturman 2003). There is an assumption here that all incumbent regimes are legitimate and that a 'serious threat' to them may provoke the AU into intervening. The danger with such a vague stipulation is that this could be used to intervene in situations where there is a legitimate uprising against an incumbent who wants to impose himself on his people, for example, through rigged elections. This observation is particularly true in respect of Article 4 (j), which allows a member state to request intervention from the Union in order to restore peace and security. Again, this is another provision that can be used not to promote but rather frustrate the cause of democracy. It is doubtful whether these two provisions are lawful, considering the powers given to the Security Council under the UN Charter to determine whether any particular incident can be characterized as a threat to or breach of international peace in order to warrant measures of a forcible or non-forcible nature being considered or taken (Magliveras and Naldi 2002; Baimu and Sturman 2003).

Be that as it may, the Constitutive Act does nothing more than provide a broad framework of objectives and principles to guide more concrete action that is expected to be taken by the different institutions created under it. Action has now been taken to operationalize some of these objectives and principles through a number of declarations as well as protocols, which confer specific powers to some institutions of the Union. Let us now briefly look at these workings.

The declaration on the framework for an AU response to unconstitutional changes of government

As noted above, this declaration was actually adopted by the OAU during its Lomé Summit in 2000 but is now one of the many OAU agreements that have been taken over by the AU. This declaration provides an interpretation for the vague wording of Article 4 (p), which condemns and rejects unconstitutional changes of government. The presence of this provision, as well as the amendments made to Article 4 (h) and the Lomé Declaration, underscore the concern by African leaders with the security of their hold on power at a time of momentous and sometimes violent changes. However, the declaration, although ostensibly dealing with 'unconstitutional changes of government' – an obvious euphemism for coup d'états – covers four important issues, namely:

(i)   a set of common values and principles for democratic governance;
(ii) a definition of what constitutes an unconstitutional change of government;
(iii) measures and actions that the AU would progressively take to respond to an unconstitutional change of government; and
(iv) an implementation mechanism.

In defining the common values and principles for democratic governance, the declaration makes it clear that the objective is to elaborate a 'set of principles on democratic governance to be adhered to by all member states'. The belief is that 'strict adherence to these principles and the strengthening of democratic institutions will considerably reduce the risks of unconstitutional change on the continent'. The declaration contains an elaborate set of provisions that articulate an agreed set of common values and principles for democratic governance. It then goes further, to define an unconstitutional change of government as consisting of any of the following situations:

(i)   Military coup d'état against a democratically elected government.
(ii) Intervention by mercenaries to replace a democratically elected government.
(iii) Replacement of democratically elected governments by armed dissident groups and rebel movements.
(iv) The *refusal by an incumbent government to relinquish power to the winning party after free, fair and regular elections* (emphasis added).

It is significant that the declaration repeatedly refers only to action taken against a 'democratically elected government', or one that refuses to relinquish power after losing elections.

Although it provides a series of measures that the AU can progressively take to respond to the unconstitutional change of government as well as an implementation mechanism, the interpretation of these defined and specified types of unconstitutional changes of government may give rise to difficulties in some situations. Since the declaration specifically prohibits coups against a democratically elected government, it is therefore inapplicable to a coup conducted against a military regime. This leaves a loophole that can be easily exploited by military juntas, with one member purporting to overthrow the other and therefore bringing the new regime outside the ambit of the declaration. The declaration also attempts in a rather timid and unrealistic manner to deal with incumbents refusing to concede defeat in elections. A simple way to pre-empt the application of this provision is for the incumbent to declare himself winner, as Paul Biya of Cameroon did in 1992, and the Côte d'Ivoire military dictator General Robert Guei did in 2002. This has also happened with bloody consequences in Kenya and Zimbabwe in 2008, where incumbents simply declare themselves winner when the electoral tide turns against them. Is this an unconstitutional change of government within the terms of this declaration?[2]

Be that as it may, what can be considered to be one of the most positive developments reflected in the declaration is what it refers to as the 'common values and principles of democratic governance' that all African governments are now expected to adhere to. It is particularly significant in that it amounts to an unreserved acceptance by all African countries of the Western liberal democracy as the only legitimate form of governance. There is no attempt anywhere in these principles to give democracy an African flavour, if indeed there is any such thing.

The AU declaration on the principles governing democratic elections in Africa

This declaration was adopted in Durban in July 2002 during the final summit of the OAU and the inaugural assembly of the AU. The declaration is quite innovative and its main thrust centres around five points:

(i)   An agreed set of principles of democratic elections.
(ii) A definition of the responsibilities of member states.
(iii) A definition of the rights and obligations under which democratic elections are conducted.
(iv) The role of the AU in election observation and monitoring.
(v)   The role and mandate of the AU commission.

These must be seen as reinforcing the agreed common values and principles for democratic governance, some of which are actually repeated in this declaration. In dealing with the principles of democratic elections, the declaration views regular elections as: the basis of the authority of any representative government; as a key element of the democratization process and hence good governance; as the rule of law, the maintenance and promotion of peace, security, stability and development; and as an important dimension in conflict prevention, management and resolution. It then defines the circumstances under which democratic elections should be conducted.

The responsibilities to which member states commit themselves make very interesting reading and there is no doubt that, if most of these responsibilities were implemented, one of the major sources of electoral problems in Africa would be eliminated. The declaration also contains elaborate provisions defining the rights and obligations that guide these democratic elections, the guidelines for the AU observing and monitoring elections and the role that the AU Commission will play.

The major challenge confronting the AU in giving effect to this declaration, particularly with respect to observing and monitoring elections, is the cost involved. Besides the fact that this declaration, like all the others is not strictly binding but merely provides a guide for member states, too many of the matters that it deals with are left to be determined within the national regulatory framework, many of which are not always consistent with the liberal democratic regime that the AU framework seeks to establish. This scope for variations makes effective monitoring difficult.

The AU guidelines on election observation and monitoring

These guidelines are premised on the fact that electoral observation and monitoring has become an integral part of the democratic and electoral processes in Africa. It also recognizes the fact that electoral observation and monitoring missions can play a role in diminishing conflicts before, during and after elections. The potential impact of the guidelines is considerably weakened by the fact that no member state is compelled to invite an AU observation and monitoring mission. The guidelines define the criteria for determining the nature and scope of AU electoral observation and monitoring; the mandates, rights and responsibilities of observation and monitoring missions; the codes of conduct for election observers and monitors; and virtually reproduce the declaration on principles governing democratic elections in Africa.

There is just one point that may raise some eyebrows. The involvement of the AU depends initially on a formal invitation being made to it by the country organizing the elections in accordance with what it refers to in its clause 3.2 as 'democratic legal framework', whatever this might mean. But even where it receives an invitation, the guidelines provide that the AU should only respond where it is satisfied that it can meet certain conditions, namely adequate lead-time for preparations; availability of essential planning information; availability of professional expertise; and financial and other resources. The guidelines make it clear that the AU reserves the right not to send or to withdraw observers in certain circumstances when the conditions in the country do not meet the AU guiding principles for organizing free and fair elections. It is submitted that a strict application of these rules may defeat the overall objective of putting peer pressure on countries to conform to universally agreed standards and practices of conducting elections. A better approach, which is consistent with the spirit of the AU democracy and good governance agenda, is for the AU to observe and monitor such elections and issue a frank report outlining the different instances where the state concerned has fallen short of the common standards.

The African Charter on Democracy, elections and governance

It appears to have been concerns about the effectiveness of the AU's democratic agenda that led to the adoption of the African Charter on Democracy, Elections and Governance in January 2007. Apart from the Constitutive Act, this Charter is probably the most radical and potentially most far-reaching instrument adopted by the AU as part of its democratization project. Its preamble refers to and reiterates all the commitments undertaken in all previous instruments. It is no surprise that in spite of the fact that the Charter requires only 15 ratifications to come into effect, only eight states (Burkina Faso, Ethiopia, Mauritania, Sierra Leone, Ghana, Guinea, Lesotho, and South Africa) out of the 53 countries of the AU have ratified it. It is also noteworthy that only 37 states have signed it, and whilst many of the countries with a poor record such as Cameroon, Libya and Egypt have not signed it, there is the surprising case of Botswana which has also not signed. Botswana may feel that it has nothing to gain from the Charter but the rising threats to democracy under the leadership of President Ian Khama suggests that there is no reason for it to be complacent.

Be that as it may, the Charter goes even further than all the previous AU agreements in its attempts to make certain aspects of democracy and good governance fundamental human rights. It contains detailed provisions that provide for the recognition and protection of democracy – rule of law and human rights; a culture of democracy and peace; democratic institutions; democratic elections; sanctions in cases of unconstitutional changes of government; political, economic and social governance – and detailed provisions that contain mechanisms for its application at individual state party, regional and continental level. Although this Charter tries to introduce its own implementation mechanisms, the AU democratization agenda largely depends on several organs of the AU for their implementation. Before assessing how these different agreements have been implemented, something needs to be said about the organs that have been put in place to implement this agenda.

The AU and democratization: challenges and future prospects

The history of Africa is littered with failed institutions and initiatives, and numerous broken promises. The AU democracy agenda is today one of the boldest and most daring initiatives that the leaders of the continent have ever embarked on. Whilst the agreements and institutions that are designed to implement it appear to underscore the determination to succeed of both individuals and the collective, the challenges that lie ahead are formidable. Any examination of this agenda cannot be complete without a consideration, however brief, of the obstacles that lie ahead and their possible implications.

One of the first problems is the existence within and outside the AU system of too many institutions with possibly conflicting functions. For example, the Constitutive Act created far many more institutions than the OAU ever had, and at a time when most African countries' economies are in crisis. Some have overlapping roles and functions, including in relation to the implementation of the democracy and good governance agenda.

Directly related to the problem of the proliferation of too many institutions is that of cost. One of the major problems of the OAU was the failure of many member states to pay their contributions. It is going to be extremely difficult for the AU, with its many ambitious structures and programmes, to squeeze money from many of the member states that are in dire financial straits. In spite of donor assistance, finding the money to manage all the new institutions and programmes will remain a major challenge that could impact on how the AU implements the democracy and good governance agenda.

Although some of the fairly serious commitments undertaken under the democracy agenda are contained in binding agreements, whilst others are in non-binding declarations and decisions, it is submitted that there may at the end of the day be little practical difference between the two. The organs that will determine whether or not there has been a violation by a state of its commitments are political bodies that decide issues not on their legal merits but rather on the instructions received from the member state. Peer solidarity will obviate against the finding of a violation of an obligation in anything but blatant cases such as coup d'états.

A look at the composition of one of the key organs of the AU, the Peace and Security Council (PSC), since its first members were elected on 15 March 2004, raises serious questions. What type of 'peace and security' or 'democracy and good governance' can authoritarian states that occupy seats on the PSC – such as Zimbabwe, Libya, Equatorial Guinea, Cameroon, Kenya, Mauritania, Gabon, Chad, Rwanda, Swaziland, Uganda and Burkina Faso – promote?. Do these countries even fulfil the criteria for membership of the PSC set out in Article 2 of the Protocol? (Williams)

Looking at arguably the most crucial and possibly contentious requirement, 'respect for constitutional governance, in accordance with the Lomé Declaration as well as the rule of law and human rights', it is clear that these countries fail this test. To the extent that the AU's democracy and good governance agenda has depended on its implementation on a PSC, which in many instances has been composed of authoritarian states that have in many respects made a mockery of democracy and good governance and regularly violate the human rights of their citizens, it is no surprise that it has not played the lead role that it was supposed to play. But perhaps more worrying for the future is the fact that the AU agenda depends on some notorious leaders such as Paul Biya of Cameroon, Mugabe of Zimbabwe, Gaddafi of Libya, Mswati III of Swaziland

and Hosni Mubarak of Egypt, who can do more than pay lip service to democracy and many of whom have contrived to rule for life. In fact, much like the OAU, in 2009 Gaddafi was elected as chair of the AU. He did not only use this platform to express his distaste for democracy but tried, unsuccessfully, to secure a second term as chair of the organization.

Another key element in the AU democratization project is the New Partnership for Africa's Development and the African Peer Review Mechanism (NEPAD/APRM). Peer review mechanisms work best when they are part of a wide range of assessments but the first problem with the NEPAD/APRM peer review mechanism is that it operates within the same organization, the AU. What initially made the NEPAD/APRM very attractive to foreign donors, who have consistently argued that lack of political accountability and bad governance was the root cause of Africa's problems, was the fact that the political and governance review of African states was to be carried out by the United Nations Economic Commission for Africa (UNECA), which was considered independent, experienced and credible (Cilliers 2000). Africa's development partners, especially the G8, were disappointed when political and governance review was removed and lodged within the heavily politicized structures of the AU (Cilliers). Second, NEPAD attempts to do too much within a short period of six months and hopes, rather unrealistically to repeat this exercise within two to four years (Kanbur). The military promised to organize elections within the shortest possible time, and only did so a year later after pressure from the AU and the international community. Even then, Mohamed Ould Abdel Aziz who had led the 2008 coup won the elections and therefore cynically transformed himself from a military dictator into a civilian democratically elected leader. Third, it is not clear what pressure it intends to bring to bear on recalcitrant states. The description of the whole review process becomes immediately obscure when it comes to discussing the so-called 'appropriate measures'[3] that should be collectively taken against a recalcitrant state that fails to take any corrective measures to remedy shortcomings exposed in the team report submitted at the end of the review process. Fourth, to perhaps counter the criticism that the whole process is too top-down driven to be credible, civil society in the different countries under review should have been given the resources to do an assessment of their own. Five, since not all AU members are necessarily part of the APRM, why should the final report be tabled before AU bodies such as the Economic, Social and Cultural Council (ECOSOCC) and the PSC, which may have states that are not parties to the review mechanism. Finally, the failure to base the NEPAD/APRM on a legally binding document, such as a protocol, which all African countries are obliged to sign undermines the attempts to project this review mechanism as an implementation of the commitment to democracy and good governance under the AU Constitutive Act. A good number of countries, whose standards of governance has regularly been questioned, remained conspicuously absent from the 29 countries that have acceded to the APRM process. Besides this, the NEPAD/APRM operates like a closed state to state process with no room for non-state, independent critical voices[4] who could contribute constructively to make the process more productive, effective and credible.

The AU's record so far in dealing with one of Africa's most recurrent problems, electoral malpractices that often provoke violence, coup d'états and political instability, has not been encouraging. It is worthwhile pointing out again here that to the extent that the African Charter on Democracy, Elections and Governance in Africa is a binding agreement, which contains various provisions that seek to entrench a culture of democracy that reflects many of the political realities of the African situation (with an emphasis on protecting the rights and interests of people rather than that of regimes), it goes further than all the other agreements adopted by the AU and even other regional organizations such as the European Union and the Organization of American States. However, as noted above, most African states have not ratified the Charter, and the chances of it coming into effect any time soon are not good. The AU democratization process on many critical issues therefore depends on a number of non-binding ambivalent agreements.

On the issue of elections, the AU depends on its guidelines on election monitoring and observation. With respect to election monitoring, the guidelines are quite vague and depend too much on the goodwill of member states; this has been compounded by the lack of funds and professional expertise. Even when the AU sends observers, as it has done in elections in countries such as Cameroon, Kenya, Malawi, Nigeria, Sudan and Zimbabwe, the organization has been happy to quickly declare them free and fair, as compared with most international election observers and monitors, who have generally been critical of these elections, therefore raising doubts about the interpretation of what it actually means by 'free and fair' elections. The failure by the organization to react firmly and decisively where there have been blatant electoral irregularities has often resulted in unnecessary post-electoral violence and bloodshed as occurred in countries such as DR Congo, Kenya and Zimbabwe.

The African Charter discourages any constitutional amendments or revisions that infringe on the principles of democratic change of government. A good number of presidents have removed one of the major constitutional innovations of the post-1990 constitutional rights revolution – the presidential term limit – and thus have virtually gone back to the pre-1990 life-presidency syndrome. As a result, many of the present leaders are guaranteed to rule for life since, increasingly, no African leader organizes an election in order to lose.[5]

On the very contentious issue of unconstitutional changes of government, the AU has often responded very slowly and in an ambivalent and inconsistent manner. The obscure wording of the relevant provisions in the Constitutive Act and the Declaration on the Framework for an AU Response to Unconstitutional Changes in Government has not helped. Nor have sanctions had a strong dissuasive effect. The frequency of coups, a phenomenon described by Keith Somerville as 'Africa's virulent military virus', one that has ravaged the continent from the time of independence, remains a potent threat to the democratization process (Cited in Ngoma 2004: 93). The assumption has usually been that increased democratic practices should lead to fewer incidents of coups or coup attempts (Ngoma 2004: 93). Since the Egyptian revolution in 1952, until 1998, Africa has experienced at least 85 coups, with 78 of these taking place from 1961 to 1997 (Adeyanju 1997; Van der Linde 2001: 127–128). From 1990 to 2010, there have been 20 successful and 8 unsuccessful coups in Africa.[6] There has, therefore, been no dramatic reduction in the incidences of coups. This apparently challenges the assumption that democratization would bring about a more stable political and socio-economic environment that will discourage military adventurism. In fact, Ngoma argues that the 'belief in a direct relationship between democracy and the likelihood of military coups or coup attempts does not appear to be necessarily true to the African continent' (2004: 93). This can only be so on the assumptions that these coups have occurred in countries where democracy has not yet taken root, yet the reality is that this has often not been the case. Even in some African countries that are considered to be making tremendous progress in good governance and democracy, such as Ghana, the threat of coups continues to exist.[7] But what is critical here, for the purposes of this chapter, is the way the AU has reacted to these coups in the light of its clear anti-coup and anti-unconstitutional changes in governments' stance.

The reaction of the organization over coups has sometimes been confusing, as was the case over the coups in Guinea-Bissau, Central African Republic and Madagascar. In the latter, the problem arose over the recognition of the government of Ravalomanana in 2002. Ravalomanana had declared himself president after the incumbent, who was widely regarded to have lost the elections, had attempted to declare himself as winner. This not only led to divisions within the AU but also to the absurd situation in which several African countries such as Mauritius, Burkina

Faso, Libya and even Senegal (which had been negotiating on behalf of the AU, as well as the regional body, COMESA), and the UN itself ignored an AU decision not to recognize the Ravalomanana government (Cornwell 2003).

Both the Rules of the PSC and the Constitutive Act indicate a range of sanctions that may be imposed against any state that violates the prohibition against unconstitutional changes of government; and Rule 37(5)(e) even gives the PSC powers to recommend any additional sanctions. This does not, therefore, rule out military intervention by the AU if the perpetrators of the coup remain intransigent. One could therefore see in this light the invasion of Anjouan, an island that is part of the Union of Comoros, (under what was codenamed 'Operation Democracy in Comoros'), on 25 March 2008. It was an amphibious assault, led by the Comoros but backed by AU forces, including troops from Sudan, Tanzania and Senegal, with logistical support from Libya and France. The goal was to topple Colonel Mohamed Bacar. The latter had refused to step down after a disputed 2007 election, in defiance of the federal government and the AU. It was clear here that the AU felt there was little risk of failure involved, and was hoping to earn some international prestige to offset the failures of its struggling peacekeeping missions in Sudan and Somalia. This was certainly an important step to show that the AU was determined to promote a culture of democracy – but why was it only in this one case? It must be remembered that this all took place the same year that Robert Mugabe and Mwai Kibaki both lost elections in Zimbabwe and Kenya respectively, but refused to concede defeat and, because of their intransigence, thousands of lives were needlessly lost. This suggests that the willingness of the AU to act decisively will depend on which country is violating the Constitutive Act rather than the nature or effects of the violations. The problem of inconsistency in enforcing compliance with the democracy agenda is often made worse by the obscure language in which some of the commitments are worded.

A potentially damaging ambiguity that runs through both the Declaration on the Framework for an AU Response to Unconstitutional Changes of Government, into the Rules of the Assembly, is that whilst it urges a 'speedy return to constitutional order', there are no provisions designed to ensure that the perpetrators of the coup do not eventually become the beneficiaries of their illegal and unconstitutional action by staging sham elections at the end of which they declare themselves winners. There seems at the moment to be no way that the AU can prevent this. Such elections, whilst certainly complying with the requirement that there is a 'return to constitutional order', in reality defeat the whole objective, since the new order would have been achieved principally through the barrel of the gun rather than through the ballot box. This is exactly what happened in Togo. President Faure Eyadéma was installed by the military after his father's death in 2005. After pressure from the AU and the international community, he briefly handed over power to an interim leader from 25 February 2005 but was sworn in on 3 May 2005 after winning elections held to 'democratize' him. The AU and the Economic Community of West African States (ECOWAS) had negotiated a deal that allowed elections to be organized hastily under circumstances that preserved the massive advantages that the ruling party and Faure had, making his victory easy and predictable. Alas, it was a hollow victory for the AU (Cornwell 2005: 2–5; Quist-Arcton 2005: 20–23). In Mauritania, President Cheikh Abdallahi, the first democratically elected president, was overthrown by the military in 2008. The military promised to organize elections within the shortest possible time, yet as of May 2010, in spite of sanctions imposed by the AU, are yet to respect this promise. Similarly, the AU has failed to persuade Andry Rajoelina of Madagascar, who seized power in 2009, to accept a peace deal calling for a government of national unity and fresh elections. Again, under the present legal framework, the incumbents or their appointees will certainly win any elections that are eventually organized, once again allowing the coup plotters to benefit from their adventure, even if not directly. The sanctions have proven weak and ineffective but perhaps the major weakness of the AU democracy agenda is that it only allows the organization to react to crisis rather than pre-empt potential crisis or adopt a proactive policy that will prevent such. An example of this inability to pre-empt a crisis is the recent coup that took place in Niger. Former president Mamadou Tandja of Niger tried but failed to pressurize parliament to amend the constitution in order for him to secure a third term in office. He then proceeded to organize a referendum through which the presidential term limit in the constitution was removed; he ignored a supreme court decision declaring this illegal and disregarded strong opposition to the change from within and outside the country. As a direct result of the political crisis that this provoked, he was overthrown in a military coup in February 2010.

Some of the ugly cleavages and divisions that helped to render the OAU impotent are gradually emerging; regional, racial, linguistic and other forms of mutual self-interest solidarity alliances and bonds. For example, the Arab countries have been instrumental in blocking any decisive action being taken against the Sudanese government's action in Darfur. The AU in general, and South Africa in particular, has gone to absurd limits to block the issue of democracy and human rights abuses in Zimbabwe being discussed within the AU.

Perhaps one of the boldest innovations of the Constitutive Act is the right it gives the Union to intervene in certain clearly defined circumstances in a way that the OAU would never have done. This is predicated on a decision of the Assembly and the PSC. As a practical matter, unless where invited to do so under Article 4(j), it is doubtful whether the present leaders, many of whose human rights records are not to be envied, will easily support a decision to intervene under Article 4(h), except under the rather dubious pretext of preventing 'a serious threat to legitimate order'. Beyond these practical political imponderables, there are, as we have seen, doubts as to whether or not some of these grounds of intervention can be reconciled with the UN Charter, particularly the powers conferred on the Security Council to maintain international peace and security. The AU might well make a valuable contribution to promoting international peace and security, provided it uses its powers to genuinely advance the course of democracy and good governance as well as human rights, and not merely to protect vulnerable dictators who have ran out of favour with their people.

In looking at the future, one can say that the prospects for democracy will be considerably enhanced when most African countries ratify the Charter on Democracy, Elections and Governance, and the NEPAD/APRM processes and mechanism become a compulsory rather than a voluntary commitment. Second, the regime of sanctions needs to be completely over-hauled. More often than not, the sanctions provided hurt the population more than the impostors who seize power. The AU processes presently pay too much attention to addressing the effects of bad governance and pay little attention to dealing with the root causes. Many coups are caused by incumbents who rig elections or do not want to concede defeat. Unless the AU is ready to deal with these root causes, there will remain serious problems with the democratization process. There is even need to go further. Leaders who rig elections or refuse to concede defeat after losing elections are as problematic as those who come to power by coups. They must be considered outlaws who, in every African country, should be subject to prosecution.

The future success of the AU agenda will also depend on the willingness of the international community to assist it. The problem of intervention by foreign powers still looms large in Africa, in spite of the fact that the end of the Cold War has led to a massive devaluation of Africa as a sought-after ally. The issue of democratization and good governance in Africa, as the June 2005 Gleneagles G8 Summit shows, has to compete for the attention of the industrialized countries with more pressing problems such as terrorism, HIV/AIDS, climate change and globalization. Individually, the attitude of some Western countries towards the democratization process in Africa raises doubts as to whether the Cold War mentality, which led some countries to back repressive and undemocratic dictators doing their bidding, has changed in Africa. A typical example is

France, which has selectively supported the democratization process according to criteria pertaining more to its own core foreign-policy interests in Africa than anything else (Martin 1995; Schroeder 1995). By way of contrast, US policy, for reasons relating to history and particular American idealism, has always advocated some form of democracy as part of its foreign policy. However, the low priority that Africa has on the American political agenda generally, even under the Obama administration, has limited the US in its will to actively support and influence positive changes on the continent. However, the situation in Zimbabwe and Sudan in the last few years, and the way this has been handled by the AU, has reinforced US misgivings about the democracy and good governance agenda and the role of NEPAD/APRM in implementing it.

The burden to make the democracy and good governance agenda for Africa actually work, depends as much on the Africans themselves as it depends on their leaders. As Gerald Caiden has observed, people usually get the government they deserve. If they are diligent, demanding, inquisitive and caring, they will get good government. If they allow themselves to be intimidated, bullied, deceived and ignored, then they will get bad government (1986). Having said this, it must be recognized that the deteriorating economic situation has robbed the streets of the angry but resolute agitators and demonstrators of the early 1990s, who are now too busy trying to irk out a living. With the opposition parties being progressively weakened, the increasingly confident but arrogant ancient regimes have sufficiently regained their poise and, in many places, appear ready to stop at nothing to maintain their stranglehold on power. Much as one may criticize the AU framework for failing to adequately involve civil society, and even the present Pan-African Parliament (PAP) as being constituted of members most of whose election victories are questionable, ECOSOCC provides a big window of opportunity for more active civil society involvement in putting pressure on the AU.

Conclusion

Moving from the rhetoric of democracy and good governance to concrete acts that will give effect to this was never going to be easy. More than two decades of democratization had only brought about some modest gains. Nevertheless, the Constitutive Act and the various instruments that attempt to implement its democracy agenda provide a better framework for more robust engagement than the OAU ever had. There are now more democrats at AU summits than the OAU ever had, and the West is now more willing to support genuine democratic efforts than it has ever been willing to do in the past.

What the future holds for genuine democracy in Africa is something about which one can only afford to be cautiously optimistic. The legal framework is not the best but it is a good starting point. Peer pressure must continue to be applied. However, the behaviour of some of Africa's most powerful and prominent leaders who had driven the AU agenda in the past, such as Olusegun Obasanjo of Nigeria[8] and Thabo Mbeki of South Africa[9] has not helped. However, the countertrends and counterforces against dictatorship, misrule, repression, greed and corruption are too strong to resist. Some of the 'sit tight' leaders who are still holding out, such as Biya of Cameroon, Mugabe of Zimbabwe, Teodoro Nguema of Equatorial Guinea, Yoweri Museveni of Uganda, Blaise Campoare of Burkina Faso and Idriss Deby of Chad are fighting a lost cause. Neither their likes, nor the extremes such as Jean-Bédel Bokassa, Idi Amin or Marcia Nguema are likely to surface again. A more disciplined and united opposition backed by civil society is needed to put the pressure on the African leaders still resisting change.

The evolution of international law and recent developments in certain Western countries such as Britain and Belgium suggests that, in the future, present or former rulers who have committed what amounts to crimes against humanity in their attempts to hang on to power, can expect to be arrested and tried under international law.[10] If it is a crime to kill half a million people in Rwanda in 1994, it should also be a crime to cause millions of innocent people, especially the most vulnerable such as children and elderly people, to die of hunger and malnutrition, or through lack of adequate health care through misrule and corruption. All that remains now is to recognize the unacceptability, bestiality and inhumanity of dictatorship for what it is, a crime that should be included in the crimes against humanity. There is, therefore, a need for the creation of an economic crime against humanity to try rulers who have caused their people to die needlessly through bad governance.[11]

A civil society demonstration poster in Mali says: 'Another Africa is possible.'[12] The challenges that the AU faces are enormous but not insurmountable. Like the proverbial dog that danced on its hind legs, the significance lies less in how well it danced and more on the fact that it could dance at all. The mere recognition by African leaders that democracy and good governance is critical to the continent's recovery and survival is a giant step in the right direction. Whilst it is certain that the AU will never become as impotent, ineffective and unresponsive as the OAU, its ability to compel African leaders to deliver on their commitments must not be taken for granted. With pressure from civil society and foreign donors, the AU's democracy agenda would ultimately gather a momentum of its own.

Notes

1 There are many sceptics who find it difficult to bring themselves to believe that these very corrupt African dictators could miraculously bring themselves to implement a programme that will destroy the very basis of their power. See, I. Taylor, 'Why NEPAD and African politics don't mix', http://wwwfpif.ofrg/commentary/2004/0402nepad_body.html (accessed 20 May 2010).

2 The definition of unconstitutional changes in government that appears here is only part of a much broader, and some claim more reasonable, definition that had been recommended by a sub-committee of the Central Organ of the OAU Conflict Resolution Mechanism constituted in 1995 to look into this matter. In the report they submitted in 2000, besides the four categories that were eventually adopted, the sub-committee had also included: the refusal by a government to call for general elections at the end of its term of office; any manipulation of the constitution aimed at preventing a democratic change of government; any form of election rigging and electoral malpractice; systematic and persistent violation of the common values and principles of democratic governance; and any other form of unconstitutional change of government as may be defined by the OAU policy organs. See OAU, Report of the Sub-Committee of the Central Organ on Unconstitutional Changes in Africa, paras 25(v)–(iv) (2000).

3 See, 38th Ordinary Session of the Assembly of the Heads of State and Government of the OAU: African Peer Review Mechanism. http://www.au2002.gov.za/docs/summit_council/aprm.htm (accessed 19 May 2010).

4 For example, African leaders and the independent experts who are supposed to be running the programme were at loggerheads in March 2004 because of disagreement over when the experts' report should be published. The experts wanted the report published soon after it was released in order to preserve its credibility, whilst the leaders say the report will only be published after it has been discussed and possibly edited by them. See, 'NEPAD: African Leaders and Experts at Loggerheads'. http://www.ghanaweb.com/GhanaHomePage/NewsArchive/artikel.php?=53222 (accessed 10 May 2010).

5 Examples of rulers who removed presidential term limits are: President Abdelaziz Bouteflika of Algeria (in 2008), President Paul Biya of Cameroon (in 2008), President Yoweri Museveni of Uganda (in 2006), President Idriss Deby of Chad (in 2006), after bloodily suppressing opponents of the change, President Idriss Deby of Chad (in 2005), President Blaise Compaore of Burkina Faso (in 2005) and President Zine el-Abidine Ben Ali of Tunisia (2002). The list could have been longer but for the fact that attempts by others was successfully repelled by a combination of a robust civil society, opposition parties and international pressure. Such is the case of former presidents Frederick Chiluba of Zambia in 2001, Bakili Muluzi in Malawi a year later, and Olusegun Obasanjo in 2006. One might even add Thabo Mbeki, whose abortive attempts to retain the presidency of the African National Congress with an automatic right to stand as presidential candidate could only be interpreted as an attempt to seek a third

term. Perhaps the most recent case, which ended tragically, is that of Niger's President Mamadou Tandja, who had just won a referendum allowing him to extend his term in power by three years but was overthrown in a coup within months.

6 The successful coups are as follows: Liberia (1990), Somalia (1991), Ethiopia (twice in 1991), Gambia (1994), Sierra Leone (1997), Burundi (1996), DR Congo (1997), Sierra Leone (1997), Comoros (1999), Côte D'Ivoire (1999), Guinea Bissau (1999), Central African Republic (2003), Mauritania (2006), Madagascar (2006), Mauritania (2008), Guinea (2008) and Niger (2010). The following coup attempts were unsuccessful: Mauritania (2003), DR Congo (twice in 2004), Chad (2004), Côte D'Ivoire (2006) and Guinea Bissau (2010).

7 For example, on 5 November 2004, just before, the Criminal Investigations Department announced, not for the first time since a democratically elected government took over in 2000, that another coup plot had been foiled and five persons had been arrested. See, Comment. Another supreme test for Ghana. http://www.africaweekmagazine.com/news/commnet.php?pageNum_r_comm=5&totalRo. (accessed 15 May 2010).

8 Nigeria still has to convince many that its democracy is on a sound footing and that it has shed its image of a regional bully boy. For example, it is only after considerable pressure that it has started to implement an International Court of Justice judgment that awarded the Bakassi peninsula, which it occupied more than a decade ago, to Cameroon. See http://www.icj-cij.org/icjwww/idocket/icn/icnjudgment/icn_judg ment_20021010.PDF (accessed 20 March 2010).

9 Although South Africa alone accounts for about 40% of sub-Saharan Africa's GDP, Thabo Mbeki appears to have put the country's economic interest first in his reaction to the numerous abuses of Robert Mugabe in Zimbabwe.

10 See, C. M. Fombad and J. B. Fonyam (2004) 'The Social Democratic Front, the Opposition, and Political Opposition in Cameroon'. In *The Leadership Challenge in Africa: Cameroon under Paul Biya*, ed. J. M. Mbaku and J. Takougang (Trenton, NJ: Africa World Press), p. 484.

11 See, similar idea put forward by the Kenyan environmentalist and human rights activist, and 2004 Nobel Peace laureate, Wangari Maathai, 'Bottle-necks of Development in Africa'. http://gos.sbc.edu/m/ maathai.html (accessed 15 March 2010). Also see, C. J. Bakwesegha (1998), 'The Organization of African Unity and the Democratization Process in Africa: Lessons Learned', http://www.un-ngls.org/ documents/publications.en/voices.africa/number8/3bakwese.htm (accessed 15 March 2010).

12 See, 'African Union: A Dream under Construction', http://www.un.org/ecosocdev/genifo/afrec/ vo116no1afrun.htm (accessed 15 March 2010).

References

Adeyanju, D. (1997) 'African Records 78 Coups in 30 Years', *The Guardian*, 9 February 1997.

Baimu, E. and K. Sturman (2003) 'Amendment to the African Union's Right to Intervene: A Shift from Human Security to Regime Security?', *African Security Review*, 12 (2), pp. 37–42.

Bakwesegha, C. J. (1998) 'The Organization of African Unity and the Democratization Process in Africa: Lessons Learned', http://www.un-ngls.org/documents/publications.en/voices.africa/number8/3bakwese. htm (accessed 15 March 2010).

Baracani, E. (2004) 'The European Union and Democracy Promotion: A Strategy of Democratization in the Framework of the Neighbourhood Policy?', http://www.fscpo.unict.it/EuroMed/baracani.pdf (accessed 10 May 2010).

Caiden, G. (1986) 'Public Maladministration and Bureaucratic Corruption'. In *Fraud, Waste, and Abuse of Government: Causes, Consequences and Cures*, ed. J. Mackinney and M. Johnston. Philadelphia: PA.ISHI Publications.

Caputo, D. (n.d.) 'Remarks by Organization of American States'. In Democracy Bridge: Multilateral Regional Efforts for the Promotion and Defense of Democracy in Africa and America, http://www. oas.org/sap/docs/BRIDGE_20-12-07_completo.pdf (accessed 15 May 2010).

Cilliers, J. (2002) 'NEPAD African Peer Review Mechanism,' *ISS Paper No. 64*, http://www.iss.co.za (accessed 10 March 2010).

—— 'Peace and Security through Good Governance. A Guide to the NEPAD African Peer Review Mechanism', http://www.iss.co.za/Pubs/Papers/70/Paper70.html (accessed 15 March 2010).

Columbus, F., ed. (2002) *Politics and Economics of Africa*, vol. 3. New York: Nova Science Publishers Inc., pp. 43–69.

Cornwell, R. (2003) 'Madagascar: First Test for the African Union', *African Security Review*, 12, http://www. iss.co.za/pubs/ASR/12no1/AWCornwell.html (accessed 10 May 2010).

—— (2005) 'Togo: Family Matters', *News from the Nordic Africa Institute*, 2, pp. 2–5.

Crawford, J. (1994) 'Democracy and International Law', *British Yearbook of International Law*, 64, pp. 113–130.

Diamond, L. 'Developing Democracy in Africa: African and International Perspectives', Paper presented at the Workshop on Democracy in Africa in Comparative Perspective, at Stanford University (27 April 2001), available at http://democracy.stanford.edu/Seminar/DiamondAfrica.htm (accessed 12 March 2010).

—— (1996) 'Is the Third Wave Over?', *Journal of Democracy*, 7, pp. 20–21.

—— et al., eds (1997) *Consolidating the Third Wave of Democracies*. Baltimore, MD: Johns Hopkins University Press.

Fombad, C. M. (2006) 'The African Union, Democracy and Good Governance', *Current African Issues*, 32, pp. 9–38.

—— and J. B. Fonyam (2004) 'The Social Democratic Front, the Opposition, and Political Opposition in Cameroon'. In *The Leadership Challenge in Africa: Cameroon under Paul Biya*, ed. J. M. Mbaku and J. Takougang. Trenton, NJ: Africa World Press.

Franck, T. (1992) 'The Emerging Right to Democratic Governance', *African Journal of International Law*, 86, pp. 46–91.

Huntingdon, S. (1991) *The Third Wave: Democratization in the Late Twentieth Century*. Norman, OK: University of Oklahoma Press.

Ihonvbere, J. and T. Turner (1993) 'Africa's Second Revolution in the 1990s', *Security Dialogue*, 24 (4), pp. 349–352.

Kanbur, R. (2004) 'The African Peer Review Mechanism (APRM): An Assessment of Concept and Design', www.people.cornell.edu/pages/sk145 (accessed 30 March 2010).

Kingsbury, B. (1997) 'The Concept of Compliance as a Function of Competing Conceptions of International Law'. In *International Compliance with Nonbinding Accords*, ed. E. B. Weiss. Washington: American Society of International Law, pp. 49–80.

Klabbers, J. (2002) *An Introduction to International Institutional Law*. Cambridge: Cambridge University Press.

Lemarchand, R. (1992) 'African Transitions to Democracy: An Interim (and Mostly Pessimistic) Assessment', *African Insight*, 22, pp. 178–185.

Maathai, W. (2009) 'Bottle-necks of Development in Africa', http://gos.sbc.edu/m/maathai.html (accessed 15 March 2010).

McGowan (2003) 'African Military Coup d'Etat, 1956–2001: Frequency, Trends and Distribution', *Journal of Modern African Studies*, 41 (2), pp. 339–359.

MacMahon, E. R. (2009) 'The African Charter on Democracy, Elections and Governance: A Positive Step on a Long Path', http://www.afrimap.org/english/images/paper/ACDEG&IADC_McMahon.pdf (accessed 20 May 2010).

Magliveras, K. D. and G. J. Naldi (2002) 'The African Union – A New Dawn for Africa?', *International and Comparative Law Quarterly*, 51, pp. 417–435.

Martin, G. (1995) 'Continuity and Change in Franco-African Relations', *Journal of Modern African Law*, 33, pp. 1–20.

Mulikita, N. (2003) 'A False Dawn? Africa's Post-1990 Democratization Waves', *African Security Review*, 12, pp. 105–115.

Ngoma, N. (2004) 'Coups and Coup Attempts in Africa: Is There a Missing Link', *African Security Review*, 13 (3), pp. 83–94.

Roth, B. R. (2000) *Governmental Illegitimacy in International Law*. Oxford: Oxford University Press.

Schedler, A. (2002) 'The Menu of Manipulation', *Journal of Democracy*, 13 (2), pp. 36–50.

Schroeder, P. (1995) 'From Berlin 1884 to 1989: Foreign Assistance and French, American, and Japanese Competition in Francophone Africa', *Journal of Modern African Studies*, vol. 33, pp. 539–567.

Szasz, P. C. (1997) 'General Law-making Processes'. In *The United Nations and International Law*, ed. C. C. Joyner. Cambridge: Cambridge University Press.

Taylor, I. 'Why NEPAD and African Politics don't Mix,' http://wwwfpif.ofrg/commentary/2004/0402nepad_body.html (accessed 20 May 2010).

Quist-Arcton, O. (2005) 'Togo: Fall of the Grand Baobab', *Focus on Africa*, April–June, pp. 20–23.

Udombana, N. (2003) *Human Rights and Contemporary Issues in Africa*. Lagos: Malthouse Press.

Van der Linde, M. (2001) 'Emerging Electoral Trends in the Light of Recent African Elections', *African Human Rights Law Journal*, 1, pp. 127–140.

Williams, P. D. 'Autocrats United? The Peace and Security Council of the African Union', http://csis.org/blog/autocrats-peace-and-security-council-african-union (accessed 18 March 2010).

22

The Organization of American States and democratization

Monica Herz

A regional norm of international protection of and responsibility for democratic regimes and institutions has been established in Latin America during the last 20 years. This has led to the engagement of regional actors in both crisis management and institution-building. This chapter analyses the process of the construction of this reality.

The new weight given by the Organization of American States (OAS) to the defence of democracy marked the international landscape in the region in the 1990s. The concept of democracy is present in the OAS's founding document and has played a role in inter-American affairs for the last 60 years. But only in the 1990s was the norm of representative democracy generated as a condition for participation in the OAS inter-American system. The idea of democracy as a domestic norm was wedded to the idea that the countries of the region should collectively defend it. A norm of regional disapproval of authoritarian regimes or the disruption of democratic regimes was established; the OAS was crucial in shaping this new environment.[1]

The OAS has developed a set of practices involving assistance for and legitimatization of elections, debates, educational activities, the dissemination of information on democratic governance, and possible collective intervention when political crisis occurs. These practices have established a strong link between the OAS and regional domestic political processes and, as a result, the norm of non-intervention in domestic affairs has become more flexible because of its commitment to the principle of regional democracy.

Democratization in Latin America

This section examines three important historical processes in order to understand the emergence of what I shall call the 'democratic paradigm' in Latin America: the transition to democracy in most countries of the region, the incorporation of democratic governance to the international agenda, and the building of the inter-American human rights regime.

The wave of democracy that began in 1978 in Latin America (Huntington 1991), ended in the 1990s when virtually all regional countries had an elected government. A region that in the late 1970s was overwhelmingly under the control of authoritarian rulers, where only Costa Rica, Colombia and Venezuela stood out as liberal democracies, had become almost entirely democratic. Cuba is the notorious exception. Elections were held in the Dominican Republic in 1978, and democratic procedures followed in Brazil, Chile, Peru, Uruguay and Argentina at the beginning of the next decade. In the 1980s, the wartorn societies of Central America moved towards peaceful conflict resolution and began their own systematic experiences with liberal democracy involving democratic stabilization.

Now, democracy is the norm in the Americas, in line with the globalization of this form of political organization (Muñoz and D'Leon 1998; Schnably 2000; UNPD 2004; Hagopian and Mainwaring 2005). The transfer of presidential office by the ballot box became commonplace, although in some cases this was accompanied by constitutional crisis, such as in Bolivia in 2008. The universal right to vote was recognized in all regional countries, which held legitimate general elections between 1990 and 2009. The competitive elected regimes survived social and egregious economic inequalities, economic crises, ethnic divisions and even the lack of support for the institutions of democracy (UNDP 2004).

Regarding human rights, the conditions have changed gradually but significantly since the 1970s. Most countries in the region have ratified international treaties protecting human rights, and enacted legislation guaranteeing equality under the law: civil, political and social rights. Although police brutality, inhuman prison conditions, violations of economic and cultural rights and impunity for human rights violations are still widespread – and disappearances, extra-judicial executions and torture still occur – the human rights discourse and practice has been gaining relevance and impact in the societies of Latin America.

At root, these changes are linked to the development of social and political movements in each of the regional countries. In addition, both international and regional environments favoured the sustainability and comprehensiveness of this process. Contributors to this scenario include the flow of information; the role of transnational relations, such as the part played by non-governmental organization (NGOs) and social movements; international assistance; changes in international culture; the pressure exerted by the United States after Jimmy Carter's administration human rights policy took shape; and, finally, the role played by the OAS. Conversely, the transition to democracy in each country of the region added new governments that were overall able to live comfortably with the idea of democracy as a norm and thus contribute to politic-building efforts.

After the end of the Cold War, the United Nations (UN) Security Council treated failures to guarantee democracy and human rights or to protect individuals and groups against humanitarian abuses as threats to peace and security. There was also at this time a significant increase in international democracy promotion (Weiss *et al.* 1994; Burnell 2000). The then UN Secretary General Boutros-Ghali was important in this new focus, articulating links between democracy, sovereignty, peace and development (Gali 1992, 1996; Duffield 2001). The association between the concept of democracy and the prospect of a peaceful and prosperous international system was now at the centre of diplomacy, foreign policy and the debate on the international agenda (see, for example, Huth and Alle 2002; Doylr 2006). A greatly institutionalized human rights regime was one of the building blocks of this process (Risse *et al.* 1999; Donnelly 2003).

By the beginning of the 1990s there was agreement about the desirability, under some circumstances, of the principle of multilateral intervention, reflecting shared values and increasing interdependence between societies under the rubric of 'international'. The locus of legal authority shifted and criteria for evaluating governance broadened to include democratic institutions and respect for human rights. In a nutshell, good governance associated to democracy emerged as the political rationale at the UN (Gali 1996; Burnell 2000; Zanotti 2005).

Regional organizations such as OAS and the Organization for Security and Cooperation in Europe played an important role, as their membership became conditional on a candidate's democratic credentials. The process of incorporation of Eastern European countries by the European Union also reinforced this development.

The idea of democracy became central to OAS, the oldest regional organization. The 1948 OAS Charter mentions representative democracy as one of the guiding principles of the organization. The link between democracy and human rights is acknowledged in the OAS Charter and addressed in the American Convention on Human Rights. The 1948 American Declaration of Rights and Duties of Men launched the inter-American human rights regime even before the UN General Assembly approved the Universal Declaration of Human Rights, the first declaraion in May 1948 and the second in December 1948. In addition, the Declaration of Santiago (OAS 1959) issued by the fifth meeting of foreign ministers in 1959, explicitly mentions the importance of free elections, freedom of the press, respect for human rights, and effective judicial procedures. During that meeting, the Inter-American Commission on Human Rights (IACHR) was created. The commission receives petitions from states, individuals and NGOs affected by a violation.

But at this time, defence of democracy became secondary in the context of the Cold War. Although the view that the US had complete control over the OAS is misleading (Shaw 2004), the defence of democracy was framed in terms of the bipolar rivalry between the Western block and the communist world.

The OAS resolution to condemn 'communism' in Guatemala in 1954 was the first attempt to make the connection between the defence of democracy and the Cold War confrontation in the context of a political crisis. But there are other clear examples of the US strategy. When Cuba was suspended in 1962, the link between the defence of democracy within the OAS and the organization's involvement in the fight against communism was reaffirmed. There is a contrast to be noted between the decision to suspend Cuba in 1962 and the lack of reaction regarding Latin America's 'anti-communist' authoritarian regimes in the 1960s and 1970s. Paradoxically, however, a regional pro-human rights movement was contemporaneously growing

The American Convention on Human Rights was adopted in 1969, coming into force in 1978. Today, it is ratified by 25 members of OAS, although not by either the United States or Canada. The Inter-American Court of Human Rights was established in San José, Costa Rica in 1979; the jurisdiction of the court is recognized by 22 members of OAS. Although the court does not produce legally binding decisions, and OAS does not use enforcement to deal with human rights violations, the availability of public information and legal procedures has had a very significant impact in the region. Civil, political, economic, social and cultural rights are laid down in the documents, although so far their effectiveness has been limited.

IACHR was able to play a crucial role during the 1970s and 1980s, adopting positions critical to systematic and mass violations of human rights by Latin American dictatorships, in particular forced disappearances in, for example, Argentina. This organization also addressed the situation of specific victims, although it did not have a mandate to do so, requesting information from member states, carrying out on-site visits and producing reports (Conzalez 2001; Duhaime 2007). The Inter-American Court of Human Rights issued rulings that set standards regarding abduction, arbitrary detention, torture, extrajudicial executions, the need to prosecute those responsible for human rights violations, and the responsibility of states regarding the protection of citizens' human rights. The Protocol of San Salvador of 1999, which has been ratified by 15 OAS member states, introduced 'country reporting' as a monitoring mechanism. Nevertheless, only in 1979, did OAS collectively begin seeking to legitimize and support democratic consolidation in the Americas, manifested in a resolution condemning the human rights record of the Anastasio Somoza regime in Nicaragua. After a report on a visit to Nicaragua was issued by IACHR, the seventeenth meeting of consultation approved a resolution that, for the first time in the history of OAS, withdrew the legitimacy of an incumbent government of a member state of the organization, because of its gross human rights violations against its own population. This resolution was passed by a number of OAS members where non-democratic governments were in place. It can be considered an important benchmark as it established that the organization could have a say regarding the responsibilities of governments towards their citizens.

The 1985 Cartagena Protocol, which entered into force in 1988, established the promotion and consolidation of representative democracy as an 'essential purpose'. It did not create mechanisms to introduce sanctions against non-democratic behaviour but was still a crucial step in building democratic norms. Thus when General Manuel Noriega staged a coup d'état in Panama in 1989, there was a legal and normative basis for a resolution defending the democratic legitimacy of the incumbent government. A mediating mission, headed by Ecuadorian Foreign Minister Diego Cordovez, tried to promote a political solution with no success, although OAS did adopt a resolution calling for the peaceful transition of power 'to a democratically elected government' (OAS 1991). Thus, for a second time, an undemocratic process was delegitimized by OAS.

The presence of a tradition of human right protection, therefore, along with the transition to democracy in most Latin American states, and the possibility of generating a norm regarding domestic politics in an international context, has led to a sustained effort by OAS to help build regional democracy (Cooper and Legler 2001; Massote de Moura de Sousa 2007).

The construction of the democratic paradigm in the 1990s

Apart from the developments analysed above, the new multilateral approach of the US administration regarding Latin America and policies adopted by important regional countries, such as Canada, Mexico, Argentina and Brazil, was strongly supportive of the idea of democracy as a regional norm. At the beginning of the 1990s, the United States sought to implement its policy of support for democratic regimes in the hemisphere partly through OAS.

The 1991 declaration on the collective defence of democracy passed by the OAS General Assembly in June 1991, often referred to as the Santiago Declaration, called for a prompt reaction from the region's countries to a threat to democracy in a member state. Resolution 1080, passed at the same time, determined that the OAS permanent council should be summoned in case of the suspension of the democratic process in any member state, followed within 10 days by a meeting of foreign ministers and potentially economic and diplomatic sanctions. Resolution 1080 enabled OAS to react collectively in the case of a serious threat to democratic breakdown, as occurred in Haiti, Peru, Guatemala and Paraguay.

Following a coup d'état that took place in Haiti in September 1991, Resolution 1080 was applied with an ad hoc meeting of foreign ministers. This event was particularly important not only in establishing parameters for the application of the Resolution but also in underlining the role of OAS in condemning and acting against a breakdown of constitutional and democratic government.

The second crisis in which OAS was put to the test occurred in Peru. President Alberto Fujimori, elected in 1990, dissolved congress, closed courts, suspended the constitution and assumed emergency powers. In accordance with Resolution 1080, the OAS Permanent Council called an emergency meeting of foreign ministers. This body then created three fact-finding missions, putting pressure on Fujimori for the restoration of democracy. When elections were called for a new constitutional congress that would rewrite the country's constitution, OAS sent an observation mission. Significant pressure from several governmental, intergovernmental and non-governmental actors had an impact on the country's road back to formal democracy. A close analysis of the political process reveals that Fujimori emerged from the crisis more powerful, and that both the elections and the rewriting of the constitution were controlled by the president to a level that contradicts basic democratic principles. Furthermore, between 1992 and 2000,

Peru's political system became increasingly authoritarian and the limited capacity of the regional actors to influence the process beyond crisis management became clear (Coletta 2000). The Inter-American Court of Human Rights did, however, produce several rulings critical of the prosecution processes against insurgents, again playing a role in support of democracy in the region. Partly as a result, the Peruvian government withdrew in 1999 from the jurisdiction of the Court.

In 2000 the OAS electoral mission, led by Eduardo Stein, the former foreign minister of Guatemala, played a role in the demise of the Fujimori regime. The mission issued a report stating that the electoral process had not met international standards and the government's legitimacy was seriously damaged (Cooper and Legler 2001, 2006). A resolution issued by the Windsor OAS General Assembly created a high-level mission, led by Lloyd Axworthy, Canada's foreign minister, and Cesar Gaviria, the secretary general of the OAS, which played a part in changing the Peruvian political landscape. They made 29 propositions in order to strengthen democracy in Peru, including: the need for an independent judiciary, wider access to the media, the establishment of an independent human rights commission, the returning of a television network to an owner who had been stripped of his property, the removal of the chief of intelligence Vladimiro Montesinos, and civilian control over the intelligence service. Leaders of the opposition, civil society representatives, and the government formed a dialogue roundtable (*mesa de diálogo*). Although the process was controversial and criticized by many actors involved in the Peruvian political process, it did provide a forum for the generation of a non-violent way out of the crisis after the Montesinos affair, leading ultimately to a new election, a partial reform of the Peruvian political system and the end of the Fujimori era (Cooper and Legler 2006: 72–83). (A video broadcast on national television showed Vladimiro Montesinos bribing an opposition congressman; he was dismissed and the National Security System was deactivated. He finally was granted asylum in Panama.)

In 1993, the OAS Secretary General João Clemente Baena Soares led a fact-finding mission to Guatemala in the context of a political crisis. President Jorge Serrano had suspended basic rights, shut down congress and the courts and, with the support of the army, locked up members of the opposition. Eventually, however, following pressure exerted from Washington, the country's congress elected a new president.

The Inter-American Court of Human Rights (IACHPR) and the Inter-American Commission on Human Rights (IACHR) also played a significant role in the development of regional democratic norms, especially links between human rights, democracy and freedom of expression. In 1997, the court created the office of the special *rapporteur* for freedom of expression, which generated relevant information regarding this aspect of the democratic agenda. The Alberto Fujimori government in Peru, for instance, was criticized repeatedly for violation of human rights: in particular, the manipulation of the judiciary. Thus the human rights court and the commission played a role in one of the cases that established the OAS practice of monitoring democratic institutions (Bicudo 2002).

The 1994 Miami Summit of the Americas set the tone for the growing commitment of OAS to help maintain regional democratic regimes. Earlier, a reform of the OAS Charter had taken place through the ratification of the 1992 Protocol of Washington, an amendment to Article 9 of the charter, which took effect in September 1997. It established that a country may be suspended from participation in the workings of the organization if a 'democratically constituted' government is overthrown by force. The agreement strengthened representative democracy by creating a condition for participation in OAS. In fact, this was the first case of a regional organization allowing for suspension of a member whose democratically constituted government was overthrown by force.

Finally, in 2001, the Inter-American Democratic Charter was adopted, further institutionalizing the democratic paradigm. The charter created both procedures for situations when democracy is at risk and for cases of serious democratic disruption. It was first formally applied when a coup d'état was attempted against President Hugo Chávez of Venezuela in 2002.

The 2001 Charter established a clear link between the inter-American human rights regime and efforts to combat poverty, promote development, act against discrimination and improve representative democracy. It also laid down criteria for the definition of a functioning representative democracy. Articles 3 and 4 were a vital contribution, defining the practices that need to be in place if a country is to be considered democratic.

In addition, the charter treats as equal the 'unconstitutional interruption of the democratic order' and the 'unconstitutional alteration of the constitutional regime that seriously impairs the democratic order' (Article 19), thus dealing with the problem of democratic backsliding by elected governments.

Article 20 provides for the suspension of the membership of a state: 'In the event of an unconstitutional alteration of the constitutional regime that seriously impairs the democratic order ...' by a 2 to 3 majority vote. This procedure is in contradiction with the norms of consensus decision-making present until this moment, thus expressing a paradigmatic shift in the history of the organization.

In this context, the OAS Unit for the Promotion of Democracy (UPD), now the Department for the Promotion of Democracy, was established in 1991. As Andrew Copper and Thomas Legler (2001: 103) note: 'the creation of this agency signals a more embedded institutional concern with the process of democratization'. Its mandate includes assistance for the development of democratic institutions and for conflict resolution, involving democratic institution-building, educational activities, electoral and technical assistance, and exchange of information on democratic institutions. During the first years of its activities, the UPD concentrated on the area of electoral observation, and later became involved in programmes to support regional peace processes and, more generally, development of regional democratic norms, with the last named under the auspices of the Secretariat for Political Affairs.

The Department for State Modernization and Governance is involved in institutional reform: aiding in the improvement of representative mechanisms, promoting transparency, access to public information, public financing, technological modernization and, crucially, building universal civil registration mechanisms. Civil registry improvement projects are in place in Haiti, Paraguay, Honduras, Peru, El Salvador, Guatemala, Bolivia and Peru.[2] Training and educational programmes geared towards the generation of a democratic culture are considered central to this endeavour. The modernization and internationalization of legislative bodies is also important for this agenda, and OAS has been involved in several projects that seek to disseminate and organize knowledge and generate contact between members of the legislatures of the countries in the region.[3]

Links were also established between OAS and country civil services, legislative institutions, local governments, political parties and civil society, with the goal of increasing the organization's influence. The Inter-American Political Parties Forum fosters debate and research on issues pertaining to the political system of states, such as campaign financing and confidence in the political system.

The focus on transparency and public access to information is connected to the fight against corruption, in line with the 1996 Inter-American Convention against Corruption. For OAS, local level governance is a key focus, as it is believed to encourage improved overall supervision of government bodies.

OAS is most visibly involved in crisis-related activities. The Department of Sustainable Democracy and Special Missions deals with crisis prevention, management and resolution. In situations of crisis, OAS can have an important role in establishing a framework for the solution of the disputes in question and generating a forum for dialogue. Special missions are sent to countries that seek support for a democratic process in crisis. Thus, in the context of a deep political crisis in 2005 in Bolivia, OAS observers monitored elections, provided technical assistance and established contact with different sectors of society, allowing for a peaceful transition. That same year, missions supported the process of selection of supreme-court judges in Ecuador, and mediated the negotiations between the executive and legislative branches of government in Nicaragua, again in the midst of a political crisis. Fact-finding missions to crisis-ridden countries are also employed.

The regional democratic paradigm is geared towards negotiating improved democracy. OAS has promoted national dialogue in countries where political institutions have faced a crisis, such as Guatemala, Haiti, Nicaragua, Peru, Suriname, Bolivia, Venezuela and Honduras. Intra-elite negotiations are often encouraged by OAS through the establishment of a 'mesa', as was the case in Peru, Venezuela and Honduras. The most recent contribution in this field took place on 5 July 2009. OAS invoked Article 21 of its charter, suspending Honduras from active participation in the hemispheric body. The unanimous decision was adopted as a result of the coup d'état on 28 June that expelled President José Manuel Zelaya from office.

As Table 22.1 indicates, in the following instances Resolution 1080 or the Inter-American Democratic Charter were invoked:

Table 22.1 Instances when Resolution 1080 or the Inter-American Democratic Charter were invoked

Dispute	Date	Action taken by OAS
A coup d'état takes place in Haiti	1991	The council condemns the coup based on resolution 1080 and sends a mission to Haiti beginning the process that would lead to President Aristide's reinstatement in 1994, after an American-led intervention authorized by the security council.
In April 1992, President Alberto Fujimori of Peru shut down the courts, suspended the constitution and assumed special emergency powers.	1992	For the second time, resolution 1080 was invoked. A meeting of foreign ministers was called and a mission was sent to Lima. OAS exerted pressure, which added to positions of many other actors, and elections were held for a constitutional congress. The Fujimori regime was strengthened and stability was maintained. OAS has been criticized frequently for allowing a regime without proper democratic credentials to be stabilized.
Institutional crisis in Guatemala when President Jorge Serrano suspended basic rights, shut down congress and the courts, and detained members of the opposition. This happened in the context of the civil war that only ended in 1996.	1993	The Secretary General João Baena Soares headed a fact-finding mission. The president resigned and the Guatemalan congress elected a new president that served until the January 1996 elections.
Paraguay: attempt to overthrow the government	1996	OAS condemns the coup and democratic stability is restored after negotiations involving Brazil and the United States.

(continued on the next page)

Table 22.1 (Continued)

Dispute	Date	Action taken by OAS
Venezuela: coup d'état against President Hugo Chávez, who returns to power after 48 hours	2002	The permanent council condemns the coup based on the Inter-American Democratic Charter. A fact- finding mission of the secretary general is sent to Venezuela. OAS's secretary general aids the mediation between the government and the opposition.
Institutional instability in Belize	2005	The permanent council supports the country's constitutional government.
President Carlos Mesa of Bolivia in the context of political and social upheaval	2005	The permanent council declares its support for the democratic process in Bolivia, sends a mission and provides support for the strengthening of democratic institutions. Ambassador Horacio Serpa of Colombia was designated special representative of the secretary general and facilitated political dialogue and then headed the OAS mission that observed the electoral process. On 18 December 2005, President Evo Morales was elected, through a process considered free and fair.
Institutional instability in Ecuador	2005	A permanent council resolution supports democratic institutions. A mission is sent to the country. OAS supported the establishment of the Supreme Court of Justice. José Miguel Insulza appointed two jurists as his special representatives to observe the selection process. Members of Ecuador's new supreme court were sworn in November 2005.
Political instability that marks the end of the Fujimori period in Peru	2000	Elections in Peru are not considered free and fair by the OAS mission. Resolution 1753 created the OAS high-level mission to Peru, which mediated negotiations to strengthen Peruvian democratic institutions between the government, civil society and the opposition within the context of the 'dialogue roundtable'. Fujimori leaves Peru and new elections take place.
Coup in Honduras, the president is removed by force from office	2009	OAS sends a mission that is unsuccessful in trying to negotiate a way out of the crisis, and a resolution suspends Honduras from the organization

The support for democratic norms is also related to efforts in the field of peacekeeping. Rolland Paris (1997) has suggested that the peace-building efforts of international agencies are guided by a paradigm of liberal internationalism that champions liberal democracy and market-oriented economics. As Yasmine Shamsie (2007) argues, the OAS approach to peace-building has been informed by assumptions and prescriptions based on this perspective. Representative democracy, civil society building and good governance allied to market-oriented reforms are the model for conflict prevention and avoiding violence.

Finally, civilian control over the military is one important dimension of democratic regimes and it is particularly relevant in Latin America, where in the past the overthrow of governments by military coups was common in the context of political polarization and crisis. OAS has played a role in this area, generating norms of transparency and putting forward an agenda of political control over military strategy, as seen in the publication of documents on defence strategy and policies.

Support for electoral processes

International monitoring of elections (IEM) has improved the integrity of the electoral process and is a potent expression of the interconnection between domestic and international politics in the context of emerging global governance. As one subject expert puts it: 'IEM is one way through which the meaning of sovereignty has gradually changed' (Santa-Cruz 2004: 189).

After a decade of developing rules and methods, the Declaration on Principals for International Election Observation was approved in 2005, establishing international standards for this activity. Electoral monitoring has become more intrusive, more frequent and based on techniques put forward as neutral and scientific. Sharon Lean (2009: 204) refers to this as the new 'transnational election-monitoring field'.

Although a few election observation missions did take place before the 1990s, this was the period when they became a cornerstone of the activities of OAS, were legalized and were associated with the wider process of constitution of the norm of democratic governance After the OAS mission to Nicaragua in 1989 in particular, a new phase was inaugurated, with increasingly more complex and more frequent missions. The OAS secretary general would also play a more important role, sometimes joining the mission (Soares 1994).

The UPD took part in several electoral observation missions on national and municipal levels, supporting training, educational, research and information programmes (Therien and Gosselin 1997). Since 1990 OAS has set up nearly 100 electoral observation missions in 20 different countries.[4] The Department for Electoral Cooperation and Observation (DECO) is in charge of supporting regional electoral systems and institutions as well as promoting democratic elections. It is responsible for electoral observation, technical assistance in this area, training, research and the organization of seminars. According to OAS, the operational principles of the work done in this field are neutrality, respect for national legislation, respect for national actors, application of standardized criteria, methodologies in electoral observation and the incorporation of gender perspectives.[5]

The 2000s have seen changes to the format of OAS electoral missions. During the 21 May 2000 elections in Haiti and during the Peruvian presidential elections in April and May of that same year, the OAS missions in place adopted an 'active observation stance' having openly criticized these countries' procedures (Cooper and Legler 2006: 58).

An analysis of the recommendations made by the electoral missions organized between 1999 and 2008 allows us to conclude that their focus was the generation of a standard array of relevant procedures. The rapid consolidation of results is a crucial concern of OAS missions and many recommendations are geared towards the crucial moment when results become available, are legitimated and permit a government to be formed. The legitimacy and efficient management of the process is sought and expressed in recommendations regarding access to the media, access to information on rules to all involved, particularly public access to electoral laws, clarity regarding the meaning of the rules in place, and transparency on financial matters.

Finally, in the context of post-conflict peace-building, OAS also monitored elections. Support for electoral processes in context of peace operations was carried out in Nicaragua and Guatemala in 1996 and in Haiti in 1994 and 2008.

Conclusion

The Latin American democratic deficit has been widely debated in academic literature, focusing on design and functioning of democracy and governance including electoral processes, political parties and political culture, the lack of a fair judicial system, interference of the executive with judicial procedures and problems of accountability (O'Donnell 2003; UNDP 2004). However, the rule of law remains the biggest democratic problem area, while corruption and lack of transparency and increasing political polarization are also serious issues.

Broad popular disillusionment with democracy has been systematically detected by recent public opinion surveys. Social and economic inequality and social exclusion of the poor and minority groups is a hallmark of most Latin American countries (Morley 2001), affecting citizen's civil, political and social rights. State capacity to reach objectives and fulfil functions, particularly guaranteeing the rule of law and the monopoly of the use of force, is limited in many countries. In this context, the cost of the overthrow of constitutional governments may not be very high, and regional and international input is a very positive step forwards, significantly changing the costs/benefits in each country. But they may, and have, been criticized. Critics have raised the issue of tension between the concept of sovereignty and the building of democracy. A debate about the relation between the principle of non-intervention and democracy promotion, as well as the use of preventive mechanisms has been continuous since the 1990s (Gindin 2005; Sacasa 2005). As Hurrell (1998: 135) states, 'while democratic values are indeed widely shared throughout the Americas, the dangers of abuse of hegemonic power have led, and will continue to lead, Latin American states to try to limit the scope for 'democratic interventionism' and to place continued emphasis on the principle of non-intervention'.

OAS has focused on government as a managerial activity, concentrating on the organization of political life, in particular on procedures to generate desirable outcomes. The emphasis on electoral processes results from the treatment of the construction of democracy as the institutionalization of a political regime as similar as possible to the Western liberal democratic model, including its norm of limited political participation. As a result, OAS assistance has been aimed primarily at governments and political parties rather than civil society.

The pattern of recommendations made by OAS electoral missions expresses a core concern: how to build efficient democratic mechanisms that allow for predictability and legitimacy. Thus, the organization of the population, and control over information and time, are stressed. The production of a constituency for any government in the making, acknowledged by the media, the wider population and by other states and international organizations is the aim of the process. According to OAS advice, citizens need to understand the rules involved in order to accept the legitimacy and authority of the electoral process as the main channel for expression of political ideas and projects. The state, on the other hand, needs to acquire the necessary techniques for control over the process, in particular accurate registration of individuals.

Leonardo Avritzer's (2002: 5) observation regarding the academic approach to Latin American democracy applies well to the line chosen by OAS: 'Despite this powerful presence of popular collective action at the public level, democratization in Latin America continues to be analyzed by the most well-established democratization theories … as the restoration of political competition among elites.'

Thus, if we understand democracy in terms of equal social, political and civil rights, and in terms of citizen participation in decision processes and political debates, OAS has contributed in a marginal way to the development of this form of social and political organization by reinforcing a limited vision of democracy as a system of government centred on electoral mechanisms.

An improved human rights regime, as we have seen, is a significant pillar in the process of consolidation of liberal democratic regimes in Latin America. Nevertheless, it is not a universal system, since only 22 regional states recognize IACHR's jurisdiction, and no more than 25 OAS member states have ratified the Convention. Moreover, governments often do not implement decisions by the court (IACHPR) and the commission (IACHR) (Duhaime 2007: 143).

OAS is not effective in dealing with authoritarian regression by incumbent democratically elected governments, a growing problem in the region. After President Alberto Fujimori began the process of undermining democratic institutions in 1992, and throughout the following eight years, the organization was unable to make a difference in this respect. The curtailment of free expression and the balance of power between instances of government in Venezuela during the last five years has not met with a significant response from OAS.

Although it may be argued that the regional documents on democracy do not specify what constitutes a violation of the principles and norms of this regime (see for example Cameron Maxwell 2003; Boniface 2009), the option of dealing with authoritarian regression will always be political. Critics point out that the OAS Charter has rarely been invoked in defence of democracy and that there is no 'clear set of benchmarks' that determine when OAS should act (Legler 2007). The concepts in the OAS Charter allow for interpretation and will inevitably be only part of the political process.

In addition, there is tension as different countries in the region evolve in different directions, and as many of the social change parameters being discussed in countries such as Ecuador, Venezuela, Bolivia and Nicaragua seem to go against norms present in the representative democratic paradigm. On the other hand, the existence of forums where the process of construction of the democratic norm differs, and is framed in distinct manners, has a positive effect, allowing for alternative forms of interaction between the domestic and international political processes.

Benefits from the complex process linking international, domestic and transnational political processes can only succeed if based on concepts strongly embedded in social practices over time. Another option involves the use of power resources. We are in fact dealing with the classic relation between legitimacy and power. It will take time to build a mechanism that can deal with authoritarian regression efficiently. Moreover, the model of political participation put forward by OAS is in itself a limitation for the process of deepening the understanding of democracy within this multilateral context. We can see that the multilateral experience in the Americas and in Latin America in particular has been intertwined with the development of a regional norm establishing democracy as the regime for domestic governance. OAS reinforces the discourse on the legitimacy of the democratic regime prevalent in the region. This does not imply a universal and homogeneous concept of democracy or the same level of conceptualization of the regime. The debate will continue in the context of this plural architecture. A trend is well established, but predictions regarding the medium or long-term future will always be extremely difficult, as complexity and predictability do not necessarily balance each other.

Notes

1 OAS was founded in 1948 and was the first regional organization created after the Second World War according to the logic present in Chapter VIII of the UN Charter. The organization has played a role in peaceful conflict resolution, crisis management and domestic governance assistance.
2 For details, see http://www.oas.org/sap/english/cpo_modernizacion_puica_projects.asp#B.
3 For details, see http://www.oas.org/sap/publications/2004/pafil/doc/doc_pafil_12_04_spa.pdf.
4 For details, go to: http://www.oas.org/electoralmissions (accessed 20 September 2001).
5 For details, go to http://www.oas.org/sap/english/default.asp (accessed 20 September 2001).

References

Arrighi, Jean Michel (2004) *Organização dos Estados Americanos*. São Paulo: Manole.
Atkins, G. Pope (1999) *Latin America in the International Political System*. Boulder, CO: Westview Press.

Avritzer, L. (2002) *Democracy and the Public Space in Latin America*. Princeton, NJ: Princeton University Press.

Berenson, W. M. (1996) 'Joint Venture for the Restoration of Democracy in Haiti: The Organization of American States and United Nations Experience: 1991–1995', Igloo Library; available at http://www.igloo.org/library/edocuments?id=%7B3B025173-1514-4279-9438-E87357280730%7D&view=full (accessed 19 September 2009).

Bicudo, Helio (2002) 'The Inter-American Commission on Human Rights and the Process of Democratization in Peru', *Human Rights Brief*, 9 (2), p. 18.

Boniface, D. S. (2002) 'Is there a Democratic Norm in the Americas? An Analysis of the Organization of American States', *Global Governance*, 8 (3), pp. 365–381.

—— (2009) 'Dealing with Threats to Democracy'. In *Which Way Latin America? Hemispheric Politics Meets Globalization*, ed. Andrew Cooper and Jorge Heine, pp. 182–202.

Boutros-Ghali, B. (1992) *An Agenda For Peace: Preventive Diplomacy, Peacemaking and Peace-keeping*, Doc. A/47/277 - S/24111, New York; available at http://www.un.org/Docs/SG/agpeace.html (accessed 19 September 2009).

—— (1996) *An Agenda for Democratization*. New York: United Nations, Dept. of Public Information.

Burnell, P. (2000) *Democracy Assistance: International Co-operation for Democratization*. London: Routledge.

Cameron, Maxwell (2003) 'Stregthening Checks and Balances: Democracy Defence and Promotion in the Americas', *Canadian Foreign Policy*, 10 (3).

Carter, A. B., W. J. Perry and J. D. Steinbruner (1992) *A New Concept of Cooperative Security*. Washington, DC: Brookings Institution.

Castaneda, J. (2006) 'Latin Americas Left Turn', *Foreign Affairs*, 85 (3), pp. 28–43.

Centeno, Miguel Angel (2002) *Blood and Debt: War and the Nation-State in Latin America*. University Park, PA: Penn State University Press.

Cooper, A. and T. Legler (2001) 'The OAS Democratic Solidarity Paradigm: Questions of Collective and National Leadership', *Latin American Politics and Society*, 43 (1), pp. 103–126.

—— (2005) 'A Tale of Two Mesas: The OAS Defense of Democracy in Peru and Venezuela', *Global Governance* (11), pp. 425–444.

—— (2006a) *Intervention Withoug Intervening? The OAS Defense and Promotion of Democracy in the Americas*. New York: Palgrave Macmillan.

—— (2006b) *Intervention Without Intervening? The OAS Defense and Promotion of Democracy in the Americas*. New York: Palgrave Macmillan.

Domingues, Jose Mauricio (2008) *Latin America and Contemporary Modernity. A Sociological Interpretation*. New York and London: Routledge.

Duhaime, B. (2007) 'Protecting Human Rights: Recent Achievements and Challenges'. In *Governing the Americas Assessing Multilateral Institution*, ed. Gordon Mace, Jean-Philippe Thérien and Paul Haslam. Boulder, CO: Lynne Rienner.

Esteves, Paulo (2009) 'A paz democrática e a normalização da sociedade internacional'. In *Os conflitos internacionais em múltiplas dimensões*, ed. Reginaldo Mattar Nasser. São Paulo: UNESP, pp. 35–46.

Farer, T. (1996) *Beyond Sovereignty Collectively Defending Democracy in the Americas*. Baltimore, MD: Johns Hopkins University Press.

Fawcett, L. (2003) 'The Evolving Architecture of Regionalization'. In *The United Nations and Regional Security: Europe and Beyond*, ed. Michael Pugh, and Waheguru Pal Singh Sidhu. Boulder, CO: Lynne Rienner.

—— and M. Serrano, eds (2005) *Regionalism and Governance in the Americas: Continental Drift*. London: Palgrave Macmillan.

Flemes, D. (2004) 'Institution Building in Mercosul's Defence and Security Sector (II).The Common Containment of Transnational Security Threats', *Working Paper no. 22*, Hamburg: Institute for Iberoamerican Studies.

Francisco Rojas Aravenas (2000) *Multilateralismo: Perspectivas latinoamericanas*. Santiago: FLACSO-Chile.

Galvão, Thiago Ghere (2009) America do Sul: Construção pela reinvenção (2000–2008) *Revista Brasileira de Política Internacional*, n. 2.

Gaviria, C. (1995) *A New Vision for the OAS*. Washington, DC: OAS.

Gindin, J. (2005) *Whose Democracy? Venezuela Stymies US (again)*, Available at http://alia2.voltairenet.org/article125718.html (accessed 20 September 2009).

González, F. (2001) 'La OEA y los derechos humanos después del advenimiento de los gobiernos civiles: expectativas (in)satisfechas', *Derechos Humanos y Interés Público. Cuaderno de Análisis Jurídico*, Special Issue 11, Santiago: Escuela de Derecho, Universidad Diego Portales.

Hagopian, F. and S. Mainwaring, ed. (2005) *The Third Wave of Democratization in Latin America: Advances and Setbacks.* Cambridge: Cambridge University Press.

Heine, Jorge (2006) 'Latin America and Multilateralism'. In *Multilateralism Under Challenge Power International Order, and Structural Change,* ed. Edward Newman, Ramesh Thakur and John Tirman. Tokyo: United Nations University Press.

Hoffman, Andrea Ribeiro (2007) 'Political Conditionality and Democratic Clauses in the EU and Mercosur'. In *Closing or Widening the Gap? Legitimacy and Democracy of Regional International Organizations,* ed. Andrea Ribeiro Hoffmann and A. Vleuten. Hampshire: Ashgate Publishing Group.

—— (2009) 'Democracia e Integración Regional: el caso del Mercosur'. In *Integración suramericana a través del derecho? Un análisis interdisciplinario y multifocal,* ed. A. C. Bogdandy Arroyo, and M. Antoniazzi. Madrid: Heidelberg & Madrid – Max Planck Institute for Comparative Public Law and International Law & Centro de Estudios Políticos y Constitucionales de Madrid.

Huntington, S. P. (1991) *The Third Wave: Democratization in the Late Twentieth Century.* Norman: University of Oklahoma Press.

Hurrell, A. and L. Fawcett, eds (1995) *Regionalism in World Politics: Regional Organization and International Order.* Oxford: Oxford University Press.

Inter–American Democratic Charter, September (2001) OAS http://www.educadem.oas.org/documentos/dem_eng.pdf.

Inter-American Dialogue Study Group on Western Hemisphere Governance (1997) *The Inter-American Agenda and Multilateral Governance: The Organization of American States.* Washington, DC.

Legler, T. (2007) 'The Inter-American Democratic Charter: Rhetoric or Reality?'. In *Governing the Americas: Assessing Multilateral Institutions,* ed. Gordon Mace, Jean-Philipe Thérien and Paul Haslam. Boulder, CO: Lynne Rienner, pp. 113–130.

Lincoln, Jennie and César Sereseres (2000) 'Resettling the Contras: The OAS Verification Commission in Nicaragua'. In *Peacemaking and Democratization,* ed. Tommie Sue Montgomery. Miami: North South Center, pp. 17–36.

Mackenzie, M. (2001) 'The UN and Regional Organizations'. In *The United Nations and Human Security,* ed. Edward Newman, and Oliver Richmond. Basingstoke: Palgrave Macmillan.

Malamud, A. (2007) 'Are Regional Blocks Leading from Nation States to Global Governance? A Skeptical View from Latin America'. In Iberoamericana, *Nordic Journal of Latin American and Caribbean Studies,* 37 (1), pp. 115–134.

Michael, Pugh and Waheguru Pal Singh Sidhu, ed. (2003) *The United Nations and Regional Security: Europe and Beyond.* Boulder, CO: Lynne Rienner.

Morley, Samuel (2001) *The Income Distribution Problem in Latin America and the Caribbean ECLAC Books.* Mexico.

Muñoz, Herald and Mary d'Leon (1998) 'The Right to Democracy in the Americas', *Journal of Interamerican Studies and World Affairs,* 40 (1), pp. 1–8.

OEA (2004) Programa de Apoyo al Fortalecimiento de las Instituciones Legislativas—UPD/OEAhttp://www.oas.org/sap/publications/2004/pafil/doc/doc_pafil_12_04_spa.pdf

Oliveira, M. F. (2008) 'União Sulamericana de Nações: democracia, oportunidades para o desenvolvimento econômico e entraves políticos'. In ANPOCS, *32nd ANPOCS Annual Meeting,* Brazil: Caxambu, 27–31 October 2008.

Organization of American States (OAS) (1959a) *Declaration of Santiago de Chile.* Fifth Meeting of Consultation of Ministers of Foreign Affairs, Doc. OEA/Ser.C/II.5: 4–6.

OAS (Organization of American States) (1959b) *Final Act.* Fifth Meeting of Council of Ministers of Foreign Affairs, Doc. OEA/Ser.C/II.5.

OAS (Organization of American States) (1960) *Declaration of San José, Costa Rica;* available at http://avalon.law.yale.edu/20th_century/intam13.asp (accessed 19 September 2009).

OAS (Organization of American States) (1985) *Protocol of Amendment to the Charter of the Organization of American States, Protocol of Cartagena de Indias.* Fourteenth Special Session of the General Assembly.

OAS (Organization of American States) (1991) *Santiago Commitment to Democracy and the Renewal of the Inter-American System.* Fifth Plenary Session of the General Assembly, Resolution 1080, Doc. OEA/Ser.P/XXI, O.2.

OAS (Organization of American States) (1993) *Support for a New Concept of Hemisphere Security: Co-operative Security.* Permanent Council of the Organization of American States, Special Committee on Hemisphere Security, Doc. OEA/Ser.G, GE/SH-12/93 rev. 1, 17 May 1993.

OAS (Organization of American States) (2001) *Inter-American Democratic Charter, Resolution of San José,* General Assembly, Doc. AG/ RES. 1838 (XXXI-O/01); available at http://www.oas.org/charter/docs/resolution1_en_p4.htm (accessed 13 September 2009).

OAS (Organization of American States) (2003a) *Declaration on Security in the Americas* OEA/ser.k/xxxviii ces/ Dec. 1/03 rev.1, 28 October 2003. P.5 http://www.oas.org/en/sms/docs/DECLARATION% 20SECURITY%20AMERICAS%20REV%201%20-%2028%20OCT%202003%20CE00339.pdf (accessed 1 February 2010).

OAS (Organization of American States) (2003b) *Rules of Procedure of the Permanent Council*, Doc. OEA/Ser.G CP/doc.1112/80 rev. 4 corr. 1.

OAS (Organization of American States) (2007a) *Program Budget of the Organization for 2008*, Doc. OEA/Ser.P AG/doc.4755/07.

OAS (Organization of American States) (2007b) *Working Groups that Completed their Work*, Committee on Hemispheric Security; available at http://www.oas.org/csh/english/Workinggroupspast.asp (accessed 19 September 2009).

OAS (Organization of American States) (2007c), available at http://www.oas.org/key%5Fissues/eng/ KeyIssue_Detail.asp?kis_sec=6 (NÃO EXISTE MAIS, REVER O LINK) (accessed 19 September 2009).

OAS (Organization of American States) (2008a) *Charter of the Organization of American States*, Department of International Law; available at http://www.oas.org/juridico/English/charter.html (accessed 19 September 2009).

OAS (Organization of American States) (2008b) *Rules of Procedures of the General Assembly*; available at http:// www.oas.org/juridico/english/agres_1737_xxxo00.htm (accessed 19 September 2009).

Santa-Cruz, Arturo (2004) 'Redefining Sovereignty, Consolidating a Network: Monitoring the 1990 Nicaraguan Elections', *Revista de Ciência Política*, V (XXIV) n 1.

Santa-Cruz, Arturo (2005) *International Election Monitoring Sovereignty and the Western Hemisphere: The Emergence of an International Norm*. London: Routledge.

Schnably, Stephen (2000) 'Constitutionalism and Democratic Government in the Inter-American System'. In *Democratic Governance and International Law*, ed. G. Fox and B. Roth. Cambridge: Cambridge University Press.

Secretaria Geral de La OEA (2008) *La Seguridad Publica En Las Américas: Retos e Oportunidades* OEA/ Ser.D/ XXV.2, Washington DC.

Seresere, C. (1996) 'Case Study: The Regional Peacekeeping Role of the Organization of American States: Nicaragua, 1990–1993'. In *Managing Global Chaos*, ed. Chester Crocker, Fen Hampson and Pamela All. Washington, DC: United States Institute of Peace Press.

Shaw, C. M. (2004) *Cooperation, Conflict and Consensus in the Organization of American States*. New York: Palgrave Macmillan.

Smith, Brian D. and William Durch (1993) 'UN Observer Group in Central America'. In *The Evolution of UN Peacekeeping*, ed. William J. Durch. New York: St. Martin's Press, pp. 436–462.

Soares, Baena (1994) *Síntese de uma gestão, 1984–1994, Organização dos Estados Americanos*.

Stoetzer, C. (1993) *The Organization of American States*. Westport, CT: Praeger.

Thérien, J. P. and G. Gosselin (1997) 'A democracia e os direitos humanos no hemisfério ocidental: um novo papel para a OEA', *Contexto Internacional*, 19 (2), pp. 199–220.

Thomas, C. R. and J. T. Magloire (2000) *Regionalism Versus Multilateralism: The Organization of American States in a Global Changing Environment*. Boston: Kluwer.

Tickner, J. Ann. (1995) 'Re-visioning Security'. In *International Relations Theory Today*, ed. Ken Booth, and Steve Smith. Oxford: Polity Press.

United Nations Development Programme (UNDP) (2004) *Report on Democracy in Latin America: Towards a Citizen's Democracy*; available at http://democracyreport.undp.org/Informe/Default.asp?Menu=15& Idioma=2 (accessed 3 September 2009).

United Nations Office on Drugs and Crime (2008) Coca Cultivation in the Andean Region: A Survey of Bolivia, Colombia And Peru; available at http://www.unodc.org/documents/crop-monitoring/ Andean_report_2008.pdf (accessed on 20 September 2009).

Villa, Rafael Duarte (2008) 'Avaliando o sistema de governança da OEA:capacidade de concertação intra-estatal e fragilidades inter-estatais'. In *Governança Global*, Rio de Janeiro: Fundação Konrad Adenauer, pp. 181–199.

Villagran de Leon, F. (1992a) *The OAS and Democratic Development*. Washington, DC: United States Institute of Peace.

Violante, Caterina (2007) *El Papel de La Orgnización de Estados Americanos em La Resolución Pacífica Del Conflicto Armado em Colombia (2004–2006)*. Bogota: Master Dissertation University of Los Andes.

Wentges, Taylor (1996) 'Electoral Monitoring and the OAS/UN International Civil Mission to Haiti', *Peacekeeping & International Relations*, 25 (6), November/December.

Zanotti, L. (2005) 'Governmentalizing the Post-Cold War International Regime: The UN Debate on Democratization and Good Governance', *Alternatives: Global, Local, Political*, 30 (4), pp. 461–489.

Part IV

Democratization and development

23

Democratization, poverty and inequality

Gordon Crawford and Abdul-Gafaru Abdulai

This chapter explores the linkages between democratization and socio-economic development, focusing on the impact of democracy on poverty and inequality. It does so with a slant towards relatively new democracies in the developing world, raising the question of whether or not they have delivered anticipated developmental outcomes. Although democracy has historically been viewed as desirable in itself, most notably with regards to the expansion of political freedoms and civil rights, the trend towards democratization associated with the 'third wave' (Huntington 1991) was also influenced by instrumental expectations that democracy would be the means to developmental outcomes such as faster economic growth, poverty reduction and a more equitable distribution of income. Such ideas were promoted in particular by international bilateral and multilateral development agencies in the post-Cold War period. For example, while the Swedish Foreign Ministry asserted in 1991 that 'Democracy is one of the prerequisites for making advances in development' (cited in Kirdar and Silk 1994: 102), the UK government's Department for International Development (DfID 2000: 7) subsequently claimed that: 'Healthy democracies ... are far more likely to deliver economic growth for their citizens.' Yet this conventional wisdom is questionable. While democracy is based on the principle of political equality, most notably 'one citizen, one vote', it does not follow that democracy will necessarily lead to a reduction in poverty levels and socio-economic inequalities. It also has to be acknowledged that poverty and inequality are conceptually distinct and have their own dynamic, such that there is the possibility of rising income inequality amidst poverty reduction, as happened for instance in the UK during the early years of the Labour government from 1997 onwards under Prime Minister Tony Blair.

Therefore, in order to examine the interrelationship between democracy, poverty and inequality, this chapter poses two separate questions: to what extent has democracy led to poverty reduction? To what extent has democracy led to a decrease in economic inequality? We address these questions in the following two substantive sections, examining the theoretical and empirical evidence concerning the impact of democracy on poverty and on levels of socio-economic inequality respectively. Our findings are that there is no clear and unambiguous evidence of democracy leading to reductions in poverty and inequality, and therefore that the anticipated developmental outcomes have often not been realized. In concluding, we provide some reflections on why this is so, exploring two lines of explanation: sustained elite control and differing forms and degrees of democracy.

Democracy and poverty

Theoretical perspectives

Why does conventional wisdom perceive that democracies, compared with other political regimes, are best suited to improving the welfare of the poor? Theoretically, a number of causal mechanisms are purportedly at play in the democracy-poverty nexus, but we focus here on two well-developed and interrelated ones. First, democracy is often held to be a powerful stimulus for enhancing the well-being of the poor because the democratic principle of elections makes governments more responsive and accountable. In theory, it is anticipated that the selection of leaders through competitive elections creates an environment in which public office holders, concerned with possible future electoral sanctions, find it compelling to respond to the needs of the wider citizenry rather than focusing on satisfying the interests of a narrow section of society. In other words, since democratically elected leaders tend to be chosen by a larger 'selectorate' and require a larger 'winning coalition' than their non-democratic counterparts (Bueno de Mesquita *et al.* 2003), democratic rulers 'have the incentive to listen to what people want if they have to … seek their support in elections' (Sen 1999: 152). This necessity of appealing to a wide range of supporters, it is claimed, in turn results in greater provision of public goods, including education and health services, more than in authoritarian systems where the provision of such services depends overwhelmingly on the benevolence of political elites. In principle, while publicly provided goods are of benefit to the entire population, low-income groups tend to derive the most benefit from such goods as, in contrast to upper-income classes, they are less capable of securing such services privately (Carbone 2009: 132).

The second argument is associated with Nobel laureate Amartya Sen (1999), who argued convincingly that democracy serves the interests of the poor by working as an early warning mechanism that helps to avert famines and other major social disasters associated with severe deprivation. Multiparty democracy, he maintains, has a 'protective role' for the poor in which political incentives generated by elections and competitive politics compel political leaders to act strategically in order to prevent famine and other devastating crises that would tend to undermine their electoral fortunes. Thus, to the extent that 'there has never been a famine in a functioning multiparty democracy' (Sen 1999: 178), this is in large part because the fear of being thrown out in elections make the prevention of such calamities an inescapable priority of every democratic government. Moreover, the availability of a free press and uncensored investigative journalism associated with democratic polities serve as significant famine-preventative mechanisms, both by functioning as channels of information to government about food scarcity and enabling citizens to demand appropriate public action from government. In this respect, even when both democratic and non-democratic regimes are equally committed to famine prevention, the lack of a free press system in the latter means that well-intentioned autocrats devoted to the cause of the poor are still less likely to know when appropriate action is required.

Empirical studies

But to what extent are these theoretical expectations realized in practice? Several empirical studies have tried to establish a link between democracy and some measures of poverty, with the evidence pointing to a more complex relationship than the theoretical literature assumes. For example, Moore and Putzel (1999), in their background paper for the World Bank's *World Development Report 2000/2001: Attacking Poverty*, point to the intricacy of the democracy-poverty linkage. As well as highlighting that three of the studies prepared for the background paper conceptualized 'pro-poorness' in a significantly different way, they noted that 'all concluded that there was no consistent connection between pro-poorness and democracy' (Moore and Putzel 1999: 8–9).

One poverty indicator that has been employed extensively in assessing the democracy-poverty nexus has been infant mortality. It is widely claimed to be especially appropriate because of its concentration in the lowest income quintile, as well as its close relationship with other welfare measures such as nutritional quality, medical and sanitary conditions, and female education and literacy rates (Navia and Zweifel 2000). Based on this indicator, substantial empirical evidence suggests the existence of a positive relationship between democracy and levels of poverty. For example, in a pair of studies covering 138 countries over the period 1950–97, Navia and Zweifel (2000, 2003) find that 'fewer children die in democracies than in dictatorships' (2000: 99). Similar positive assessments were made by Przeworski et al. (2000) and Bueno de Mesquita et al. (2003), with the latter's findings leading them to claim that: 'Infants have a vastly better prospect of surviving and going on to live a long, prosperous life if they are born in a democratic ... society than if they are born anywhere else' (2003: 194). Lake and Baum (2001) have been more specific in their influential study of 92 countries, concluding that as 'democracy moves from its lowest to highest values, the rate of infant mortality declines by nearly five deaths per 1,000 live births' (2001: 616). Albertus's (2010) recent study also affirms the existence of a positive impact of democracy on infant mortality. Utilizing data on infant mortality from 1950–2002 for 167 countries in conjunction with the Polity IV dataset,[1] he finds that: 'If a state moved across half the range of the Polity interval to democracy, infant mortality rates would drop by about 1.3% per year, or 12% in the span of a decade' (2010: 11). Thus, taking levels of infant mortality as proxy for poverty, he concludes that not only are 'democracies... generally better than autocracies at improving the welfare of the poor', but also 'the effect of democracy on poverty reduction is not small' (ibid.: 21).

It has been pointed out, however, that many empirical studies of democracy's impact on poverty have been plagued by significant methodological shortcomings, inclusive of data quality and coverage as well as selection bias. Ross's (2006) review of the literature reveals the exclusion of wealthy and high-performing authoritarian states in most so-called 'global' studies, a gap that he argues has the tendency of leading to a 'false inference that democracies outperform nondemocracies' (2006: 865) in reducing poverty. Accounting for these shortcomings, his own estimation of the impact of regime type on infant and child mortality utilized a dataset that included all 168 states with populations of more than 200,000 between 1970 and 2000. Of the 44 countries amongst these states that transited to democracy over the period 1970–99, he found that whereas the infant mortality rate of these countries collectively fell by 10.7 per cent during the immediate five years prior to their transition, it fell by only 7.4 per cent during the first five years after their transition. The answer to the question he posed at the outset – as to whether democracies necessarily produce gains for the poor – is, therefore, that 'in general they do not' (ibid.: 860).

Regarding the impact of democracy on the provision of social services, extant empirical research has focused mainly on two key questions. First, do democratically elected leaders spend more on social service provision than their non-democratic counterparts? Second, and if so, to what extent do poor people benefit from the increased social spending associated with democracies? As regards the former, the empirical evidence appears strikingly consistent with the view that democratic governments do expend more on social sectors than their authoritarian counterparts. For example, Lindert (2004, cited in Remington 2008: 2) found democratization in Europe and the United States to have resulted in dramatic increases in spending on public education and social transfers. Similarly, work by Kaufman and Segura-Ubiergo (2001) and Brown and Hunter (2004) in Latin America has found that democracies tend to spend more on social services such as health and education than do autocracies. However, Avelino et al.'s (2005) study of 19 countries in the region made a more nuanced observation. While they found democracy's impact on increased expenditures for education to have been so robust as to warrant the conclusion that, overall, 'democracy has a strong positive association with social spending' (Avelino *et al.* 2005: 625), they also show that 'democracies do not increase spending on health or social security' (ibid.: 634). Additionally, Stasavage (2005) employed time-series data to analyse public spending of 44 African countries over the period 1980–96. His findings demonstrated that 'when they are subject to multiparty competition, African governments have indeed tended to spend more on education, and more on primary education in particular' (Stasavage 2005: 344). Therefore, overall, there is some evidence of a positive correlation between democracy and poverty reduction through social service provision, most clearly in respect to education, though less so regarding health and social security.

Nonetheless, there is hardly any conclusive evidence that the increased social sector spending associated with democracies necessarily translates into poverty reduction and improved living standards for the poor. Nelson (2007) reviewed 22 cross-national empirical studies that examined the impact of democracy on social sector spending and improved social sector outcomes. Although these studies varied significantly in several respects, inclusive of the periods and number of countries covered, it is striking to note that 'all but one find that democracy is associated with higher relative spending on social sectors' (Nelson 2007: 81). Regarding the more critical question as to whether more money necessarily results in enhanced service delivery for poor people, however, the evidence was found to be at best 'inconsistent and weak' (ibid.: 80). Further, considerable evidence on this weak democracy-service delivery nexus has been provided in the United Nations Development Programme's (UNDP) *Human Development Report 2002*, which found, for instance, that Mali had done no better in spreading primary schooling, raising literacy or reducing infant mortality than Togo, despite the former's relative progress in stabilizing its democratic structures. Similarly, autocratic Bahrain and Syria were shown to have done as much in the spread of primary education to the poor as democratic Jordan (UNDP 2002: 60).

How, then, do we explain this disjuncture between increased social expenditure by democracies and a lack of corresponding benefits for the poor? One reason is that despite the rhetoric of equal citizenship embodied in democratic regimes, there is often an inherent bias of satisfying the needs of elite groups, largely because of the political weakness of the poor in competing for power and demanding responses to their needs (Luckham *et al.* 2003: 29–30). Thus, as Ross (2006) has powerfully argued, more money may be spent on health in democracies without infant and child mortality actually falling, because the increased social sector spending may only amount to subsidizing the budgets of middle- and upper-income groups, while leaving the poor hardly affected and thus making little impact on poverty reduction. This is compounded by the fact that policies aimed at resource reallocations away from privileged groups often attract significant bureaucratic and social opposition, as redistributive policies are assumed to have a zero-sum character whereby gains for the poor come at the expense of elite groups (Nelson 1989, cited in Luckham *et al.* 2003: 30). Unsurprisingly, empirical research in both authoritarian and democratic regimes has shown that 'public spending is often skewed in favour of rich people in such critical areas as basic health and education' (UNDP 2002: 59).

Indeed, a cursory glance at the experiences of real-world democracies in fighting poverty provides good reasons to believe that democratization is no panacea for reducing poverty, with Hickey (2006: 9–10) reminding us that 'chronic poverty and destitution remain visible phenomena [even] in long-standing democracies'. In Africa, the world's poorest continent, the developmental expectations that accompanied the wave of democratization during the 1990s has mainly turned out to be a paradox of 'growth without prosperity' (Lewis 2008: 97), with improved economic growth largely failing to foster broad-based poverty reduction and equitable development. While

India, the largest democracy in the world, may have succeeded in averting famines in its post-independence history, because of its democratic structures (Sen 1999), it has persistently failed to address the continuing problem of abject poverty, with the Asian Development Bank (2008, cited in Ghosh 2010: 19) estimating the number of poor in India in 2005 at between 622 to 740 million, based on a poverty line of US$ 1.35 per day per person.

According to Alex de Waal (2000: 13), the reason why poverty and homelessness persist even in so-called advanced democracies such as the United States is that these forms of deprivation have rarely achieved a comparable political saliency to famine in the history of any country. Moreover, the rather simplistic assumption that the conduct of periodic democratic elections means that the poor will vote out those who fail to alleviate their poverty does not always hold true. There are a number of other issues that imply greater complexity, and we have already noted the problem of elite control and elite bias. In many developing countries, forms of identity such as ethnicity and religion may be as significant in shaping voters' electoral choices as poverty and other socio-economic needs. And in countries where electoral outcomes are determined largely by candidates' ethno-regional identities, politicians may resort to playing the ethnic card in attempts to win elections, rather than appealing to a broader mass of citizens. In many sub-Saharan African countries in particular, such ethnic-based politicking has triggered violent conflicts, ones that in turn can exacerbate levels of poverty. The election-related violence in Kenya in late 2007, for example, is reported to have resulted not only in the loss of more than 1,000 lives, but also in the internal displacement of some 255,000 persons who had been deprived of their various means of livelihood (Centre for Rights Education and Awareness 2008: 2, 26). In such circumstances, the claim that democracy reduces poverty by enhancing domestic peace (Landman 2006: 17) becomes highly questionable.

But defenders of liberal democracy tend to explain the democracy-poverty reduction disconnect differently, often attributing the problem to 'democratic deficits', rather than to democracy per se. They insist, for example, that democracy's failure 'to improve the lot of the poor … derives not from the intrinsic limitations of democracy as a political system, but rather from the fact that democracy functions in a limited, shallow, illiberal fashion' (Diamond 2004: 9). It is argued that the critical missing link between democracy and poverty reduction is due in particular to the lack of effective institutions of accountability and to inadequate checks and balances in the operation of state institutions. In such illiberal or hybrid regimes, individual liberties are hardly protected, while the abuse of governmental power for private gain often becomes rampant, with significant adverse implications for addressing the welfare needs of the poor (see Diamond 2004).

Yet, one shortcoming of these arguments is that they neglect the fact that the 'East Asian Tigers' – Singapore, South Korea, Taiwan and Hong Kong – almost entirely eliminated poverty under authoritarian political settings. Additionally, Indonesia achieved significant poverty reduction during 1971–91 under the dictatorial rule of Suharto, while Malaysia made enormous strides in poverty reduction under a regime that was less than democratic (Quibria 2003: 8). Indeed, the superior economic performance of these East Asian economies, coupled with the more recent spectacular poverty-reduction record of China, has led some to suggest the possibility of an 'authoritarian advantage' (Lewis 2008: 95) in economic prosperity, in which some degree of insulation from self-interested pressure groups may be necessary in enabling public officials to implement economic policies that result in rapid poverty reduction. On a global scale, however, the record of non-democratic regimes in poverty reduction is as ambiguous as that of their democratic counterparts. Indeed, the fact that authoritarian regimes in both Latin America and Africa have driven many countries to economic ruin has been so well documented that 'it is difficult to escape the association between non-democratic rule and economic failure' (Lewis 2008: 95) in these continents. Nonetheless, while these varied historical experiences would seem to suggest that regime types by themselves do not necessarily reduce poverty, it remains largely undisputed that 'democracy does provide some kind of safety net' (Moore and Putzel 1999: 8–9) in preventing the worst kinds of human tragedies, including famine. Accordingly, whereas democracies may not have achieved the spectacular economic performance of the East Asian autocracies, there is little doubt that democratic regimes are also not the worst economic performers, and tend to cluster in the middle (UNDP 2002: 56; Quibria 2003: 8).

Democracy and inequality

The question of the interrelationship between democracy and inequality has provoked considerable interest amongst social scientists over the past 50 years, resulting in a substantial literature on the topic. While the democracy-inequality relationship can be looked at in two ways – i.e. whether and how democracy affects inequality and how inequalities affect democracy and democratization – we focus here on the former, with inequality as the dependent variable. The section first looks at competing theoretical perspectives regarding democracy's impact on inequality, before turning to examine the empirical evidence on this relationship.

Theoretical perspectives

Given that 'the advance of democracy entails, by definition, a decrease in political inequality' (Bermeo 2009: 23), there are expectations that democratization is likely to result in a decline in other forms of inequality, notably economic inequality. This has been a long-held view, one that Bollen and Jackman (1985: 438) claimed can be traced back to Aristotle and John Stuart Mill. In more modern times, they noted that it is a view put forward by Lipset (1959) and Lenski (1966). Lipset (1959) thought that the extension of the franchise led to elections that served as an expression of democratic class struggle in which citizens vote for parties that represent their class interests, shifting politics to the left, with the classic example being the rise of the British Labour Party in the first half of the twentieth century (cited in Bollen and Jackman 1985: 439). Similarly, Lenski (1966) argued that democracy entailed a major redistribution of political power to the majority of relatively disadvantaged people in a society, which is in turn expected to lead to more social equality due to the electoral demand on political elites for a more egalitarian distribution of material goods (cited in Bollen and Jackman 1985: 439). Such views continue to be expressed on the basis that democracy is 'pro-majority'. For example, Peter Lewis (2008: 96) recently noted that since democratic systems rest on accountability to voters, they 'reinforc[e] pressures on leaders to improve the economy and better popular welfare'.

A degree of sophistication has been added to such expectations by the 'theories of economic redistribution' that have stemmed from economic historians such as Justman and Gradstein (1999), Bourguignon and Verdier (2000) and Acemoglu and Robinson (2006). Such theories are based on the evolution of democracy in Western Europe and its effect on income distribution, central to which is an inverse U-shape relationship between democracy and inequality, known as a Kuznets curve.[2] This suggests that, as the voting franchise is extended, income inequality may worsen initially before it starts to improve. In studying historical processes of economic development in nineteenth-century Britain, Justman and Gradstein (1999) noted that income inequality peaks at the point of democratization and radical political reform, but that the institutional changes introduced by democratization, including the extension of educational provision, subsequently encouraged redistribution and a decline in income inequality. Acemoglu and Robinson (2006) also regard economic inequality as an influential factor that leads to demands for democratization, but in a context where the impact, in turn, of democratization on reducing inequality may be limited. Their interpretation suggests that under conditions of industrialization and capital accumulation by the capitalist elite, income inequality intensifies to such an extent that there is the threat of revolution. But instead of resisting political reform, the elite may acquiesce in democratization, perceived as a means of protecting their wealth through avoidance of violent confrontation and possible confiscation of their property (Acemoglu and Robinson 2006). Therefore, although income inequality may decline somewhat with democratization, the degree of redistribution may be less than the elite feared would occur in more revolutionary circumstances. In such a way democratization becomes a means to sustain elite rule in the context of a threat of greater political upheaval.

Despite the overall predominance of the perspective that democracies lessen inequalities, Beitz (1982) put forward a counter view that authoritarian regimes were more likely to pursue egalitarian policies (cited in Sirowy and Inkeles 1990: 135). He questioned the majoritarian assumption built into the democratic model, suggesting that poorer sections of developing countries in particular may not be able to take advantage of available political rights, and contended that authoritarian governments may actually be more capable of protecting the interests of the poor and working classes than democracies (cited in Sirowy and Inkeles 1990: 135). This view has been given empirical credence by the real world developments in East Asia, notably South Korea and Taiwan, where high rates of economic growth have been achieved from the 1960s onwards, and where the benefits of growth have also been distributed relatively equitably (Birdsall *et al.* 1995). A key factor in explaining the success of East Asian developmental states is their 'embedded autonomy', in other words their institutional capacity and autonomy to promote developmental goals without being 'captured' by particularistic interests (Evans 1995), an explanation that is reminiscent of that of Beitz.

Although not supportive of an authoritarian model, Bollen and Jackman (1985: 440) also noted that the argument that democracy reduces inequality is predicated on majoritarianism, yet in the real world 'few democracies adhere rigorously to majoritarianism'. The democratic model also assumes that low-income voters feel a sense of injustice and demand income redistribution, whereas they may lack class consciousness or be insufficiently well organized to do so (ibid.). More than a quarter of a century ago, Bollen and Jackman were essentially pointing to the ability of elites to manipulate democratic institutions in their own interests and hence undermine any expectations of democratic accountability to the majority, a point that we will return to.

Empirical studies

Do the empirical studies confirm the dominant theoretical expectation that democratization results in reductions in economic inequality? Fortunately, a useful survey of empirical studies that addresses the links between democracy and inequality was published in 2004 by Gradstein and Milanovic. They note two main groups of studies, distinguished by their definition and measurement of democracy. One strand takes the extension of the voting franchise as its proxy for democracy (i.e. electoral democracy), while the other associates democracy with the protection of civil liberties and political rights, in other words what is termed 'liberal democracy' in the literature. We look first at these two groups of studies, based on Gradstein and Milanovic's (2004) survey article, and then at other studies published subsequently.

The first strand of research is more historical in nature and examined the expansion of the voting franchise in Western Europe and the United States in the late nineteenth and twentieth centuries and the subsequent trends in income inequality. However, as Gradstein and Milanovic point out, the extent of the franchise is now of 'limited value as a proxy for democracy' (2004: 525), given that universal franchise formally exists in most of the contemporary world.

The second strand of research is more voluminous in nature and looks at the links between civil and political rights, as a proxy for democracy, and income inequality. It mostly entails cross-national quantitative studies, undertaken with a larger sample of countries over a more contemporary time period. Earlier work of this nature was usefully reviewed by Sirowy and Inkeles (1990). However, their survey of 12 (now rather dated) studies only enabled them to conclude somewhat downbeat that 'political democracy does not widely exacerbate inequality' and that 'the existing evidence suggests that the level of political democracy as measured at one point in time tends not to be widely associated with lower levels of income inequality' (1990: 151). Six of the studies did find what is described in statistical terms as a 'negative relationship', in other words that higher levels of democracy did *lessen* income inequality, while six others either found a 'positive relationship', meaning that higher levels of democracy were associated with *increased* income inequality, or could find no significant association.

Gradstein and Milanovic (2004) also provide us with a review of more recent cross-national quantitative studies that have investigated the links between civil and political rights and income inequality. These studies are said to be based on three methodological improvements. One is the utilization of a better quality dataset on income inequality, the Deininger-Squire dataset created by World Bank researchers. The second is the use of a different index of civil liberties and political rights, the Gastil index (based on Freedom House data) instead of the Bollen index, as a proxy for political democracy, though the similarity between the two reduces the significance of this. Finally the number of countries included in the data samples is generally higher. The review in the following paragraph is based on information in Gradstein and Milanovic (2004: 527–528).

Rodrik (1999) focused on the wages received by workers as a key measure of income inequality, and found a statistically significant association between the extent of democratic rights and workers' wages as a share of gross domestic product (GDP), one that existed both across countries and over time within countries. Li *et al.* (1998) explore two channels that were likely to impact on levels of inequality: the political-economy channel (a measure of political freedom and secondary schooling), and the imperfect capital-markets channel. Their results indicated that all their variables were significant determinants of inequality, inclusive of a reduction in income inequality through an expansion of political liberties. However, the variables associated with market imperfections were more significant and had the opposite effect of increasing inequality. In contrast, Lundberg and Squire (1999) did not find a significant relationship between democracy and aggregate measures of inequality, although they did find that expansion of democracy benefits the lowest quintile of income distribution, thus reducing poverty. Importantly, this latter study was the first to include post-communist countries from Central and Eastern Europe in their sample, where economic inequality increased significantly following democratic transitions.

In summary, Gradstein and Milanovic (2004: 528) conclude that this more recent set of studies, based on improved data sets and bigger data samples, does 'cautiously suggest existence of a negative relationship between the two [democracy and inequality]'. In other words, these studies do provide some evidence that increased levels of democracy lead to decreases in income inequality, though with the obvious exception of Central and Eastern Europe. In particular, some studies have indicated that the length of democratic experience, referred to as 'accumulative democracy', is a crucial factor for inequality-reducing policies.

Not included in Gradstein and Milanovic's (2004) survey article, two further empirical studies have also affirmed a positive impact of democracy on income inequality. First, Reuveny and Li (2003) undertook a cross-national study comprising 69 countries during the period 1960–96, inclusive of both developed countries and less-developed countries. They statistically investigated the effects of both economic openness and democracy on income inequality. Their findings confirmed that 'a higher level of democracy reduces the level of income inequality within countries' (2003: 593).

The effect of democracy on income inequality was statistically significant for the samples for both developed countries and less developed countries. Second, Alberto Chong (2004) re-examined the idea of a political Kuznet's curve by looking at more recent trends. Undertaking simple cross-country regressions for the period 1960–97, his main findings were twofold. The first finding was of a non-monotonic link between democracy and inequality, i.e. that inequality does *not* constantly increase or decrease with democratization, but is variable over time. Relatedly, the second finding supports the existence of a political Kuznets curve, in that inequality increases as political liberalization commences, but then decreases as democratic government becomes more established (Chong 2004: 204).[3]

Therefore, it appears that later studies have not only provided more evidence than earlier ones that democracy leads to reductions in income inequality, but also provided findings that are methodologically more robust due to the improved quality of the data (Deininger-Squire). However, there is a major sting in the tail, with the robustness and quality of data continuing to be questioned. Timmons (2010) revisited the recent findings of, amongst others, Li *et al.* (1998), Reuveny and Li (2003) and Chong (2004). He utilized the updated and revised version of the Deininger-Squire dataset (WIID, Version 2), which gave him the benefit of an additional decade of data, and ran very similar tests as previous studies. However, his conclusions were very different. He states that: 'Our finding is clear: the updated WIID does not indicate a systematic relationship between democracy and inequality' (2010: 755). He explains these contrasting findings by the persistent problem of the quality of data, stating that:

> The WIID data is, arguably, the best source for comparisons along the lines of those executed here, but it is still thin for reliable inferences: With just an additional decade of data, we obtained considerably different results using the same countries and nearly identical specifications.
>
> *(2010: 755)*

Therefore, in his view: 'Whether, and how, democracy decreases economic inequality remains an open question' (Timmons 2010: 741). Further: 'Democracy has many virtues, but reducing inequality may not be one of them' (ibid.: 755). This questioning of the findings of cross-national quantitative research due to the crucial issue of data quality, leads us to the next subsection.

Democratization wave and rising inequalities

Timmons (2010: 753) states that one reason for reconsidering recent statistical studies was that their conclusions – that democracy reduces inequality – seemed incongruent with individual country experiences. And, indeed, the widely acknowledged reality is that economic inequalities within countries have grown throughout the world in the past three decades, with such upward surges in inequalities associated in particular with the implementation of neoliberal economic policies.

A review by Cornia and Court (2001) of the experience of 73 countries covering 80 per cent of the world's population in the post-1945 period established two key trends. The first was an overall fall in income inequality from 1950 to the mid-1970s, and the second was a sharp rise in inequality in the 1980s and 1990s, as the effects of the introduction of neoliberal policies took hold. This overall pattern was found throughout the globe: in developed countries, in developing countries and in transitional countries, although most pronounced in the (then) 21 transitional countries, all of which experienced a sharp rise in income inequality in the post-communist period. Similarly, Raphael Kaplinsky, in his book *Globalisation, Poverty and Inequality*, concludes that 'the overwhelming evidence is that inequalities have risen, particularly within countries, and on a range of dimensions' (2005: 233) during the 1980s and 1990s.

Thus it would seem that the third wave of democratization, usually dated from 1974 until the late 1990s, and the rise of income inequality have occurred simultaneously, though the extent to which they are linked remains a separate question. In Latin America, initial optimism about welfare benefits stemming from (re)democratization in the 1980s and 1990s gave way to a growing pessimism as gross economic and social inequalities intensified (Green 2003: 224). Similarly in Africa, as noted above, Lewis (2008: 97) talks of the democratization wave having led to 'growth without prosperity', and its failure to achieve broad-based prosperity and equitable development.

It is in Central and Eastern Europe, however, where simultaneous democratic transition and rising inequalities have been especially evident. With the fall of communism in the late 1980s, these transition countries all experienced a marked rise in income inequality and a fall in living standards, with life expectancy declining sharply in some cases (Kaplinsky 2005: 238). As well as the transition to market economies, such rises in inequalities coincided in most cases with the introduction of democratic reforms. Gradstein and Milanovic (2004) refer to this outcome as an 'enigma', contrary to the theoretical expectations that democratization would reduce inequalities, as well as running counter to the predominant findings of recent empirical literature. They acknowledge that this 'enigma' indicates that 'the real relationship between democracy and inequality is a more complex one than most of the literature, based on cross-sectional analysis, has led us to believe' (Gradstein and Milanovic 2004: 529), and attempt to understand it. Two main explanations were put forward. First, simply, insufficient time has passed and that 'in order for democracy to "work" on inequality through various redistributive mechanisms, sufficient "democratic time" needs to elapse' (ibid.). This relates to the point above about 'accumulative democracy'. However, although it is possible that the consolidation of democracy in post-transition countries could lead to a reduction in current high levels of economic inequality, it would seem inconceivable that the relative egalitarianism of the communist period will be returned to in the foreseeable future. Second, transition countries are exceptional given their starting point of low levels of income equality that existed pre-transition, stemming from socialist values and ideology (Gradstein and Milanovic 2004: 532). This point may be more pertinent, suggesting that democracy's impact on inequality is dependent on the pre-existing situation, with different outcomes in contexts where there are gross inequalities – with possible redistributive effects – compared with those with relatively low income inequality, where inequalities are likely to widen. But perhaps transition countries are, in fact, less of an enigma or riddle than suggested. Transition countries experienced a sharp rise in income inequality due to the nature of the neoliberal 'shock therapy' implemented in the early 1990s to enforce a rapid transition from a command economy to a free market economic model, notably through the deregulation of state controls, trade liberalization and privatization of publicly owned assets. Similarly, many developing countries experienced a rise in income (and other forms of) inequality during the 1980s and 1990s due to the implementation of similar neoliberal economic policies as part of World Bank and International Monetary Fund-imposed structural adjustment programmes. This suggests that the chosen economic model is the key determining factor in accounting for rises and falls in inequality, indicting the relative independence of economic and political pathways and that democracy can be quite compatible with economic inequality.

Conclusion

Contrary to some theoretical expectations, we have found that there is no clear and unambiguous evidence of positive linkages between democracy, poverty and inequality. Democracy's record in reducing poverty is at best mixed, with some dimensions of poverty reduced but not others. Evidence is strongest with regard to falls in infant mortality rates and primary education, though more questionable in terms of other aspects of service delivery, with the increased public expenditure associated with democratic politics at times providing greater benefits to middle- and upper-income groups. Regarding democracy and inequality, the findings of cross-national statistical studies have increasingly suggested an association between democratic regimes and falls in income inequalities, though recent research (Timmons 2008: 25) again questions the quality and reliability of the data, an issue that has bedevilled such studies for a considerable time (see UNDP 2002: 56). Such positive findings also seem to fly in the face of the evidence from country case-studies and other sources that indicate that democratization and a surge in socio-economic inequalities have occurred simultaneously in different regions of the world in recent decades, though the key cause of rising inequality is usually identified as neoliberal economic policies. Therefore, why have the performance of democratic governments often not matched the theoretical expectations? In concluding, two lines of explanation are explored, the first pertaining to elite control, and the second to the issue of forms and degrees of democracy. Then, finally, we reverse the linkage and briefly address the implications of persistently high levels of poverty and economic inequality for democracy.

Sustained elite control within many democracies means that the majoritarian assumption explicit in theoretical expectations of pro-majority outcomes has proved to be misconceived. Acemoglu and Robinson (2006) have noted the initial context in which democratic transitions often occurred, where economic and political elites conceded democratic reforms in the face of radical opposition movements precisely as a means of mitigating the potential loss of wealth and status associated with the threat of greater social upheaval. Post-transition, elite control of democratic institutions has frequently continued by various means. While country case-studies are needed to illustrate the detailed ways by which such control is maintained, a few indications can be given here. Most obvious is the use of private wealth to tilt the electoral playing field and influence electoral outcomes. This is seen in so-called advanced democracies, for instance in the private funding of US presidential election campaigns and British political parties, often by business elites, as well as in newer democracies, for example the 'money politics' of Southeast Asia (McCargo 1996), and the neopatrimonial politics, characterized by patron-client relations, in Africa (see Lockwood 2005). The concentration of media ownership in a small number of private hands is another key means of achieving disproportionate influence over citizens' choices and voting patterns. Elite manipulation can also take more devious forms, such as 'playing the ethnic card' and the exploitation of ethno-regional identities in attempts to win elections, at times with violent and bloody consequences. Additionally, political equality in terms of the universal franchise may mean little to those 'equal citizens' who are denied the basic necessities of life, an essential condition for the effective exercise of citizenship (Beetham and Boyle 1995: 113). Therefore, by various means, democratic government can remain in the hands of an elite ruling class. And as the UNDP (2002: 3) notes, 'when a small elite dominates economic and political decisions, the link between democracy and equity can be broken'.

Additionally, in the era of globalization, elite control extends beyond national elites and takes on an international dimension. It can be argued that economic policy sovereignty has been removed from national governments, especially in low-income countries, both directly by IMF/World Bank economic conditionality and indirectly through the ideological hegemony of neoliberalism as propagated by the same international financial institutions and the Western governments that control them. As Mkandawire (2004: 143) trenchantly notes: 'the first victim of globalisation has been the state's power to intervene in the economy to ensure certain social outcomes, such as equity and poverty alleviation'. Such outcomes are characterized as a 'hollowing out of democracy' as policy choices are determined externally and state intervention-ism is subject to disapproval and censure from international institutions and from the dominant ideological discourses that they have effectively propagated.

A second line of explanation to account for the lack of a positive impact by democracy on poverty and inequality pertains to the *type* and *degree* of democracy. One methodological short-coming of many of the cross-national statistical studies is their failure to differentiate beyond a crude binary distinction of democracies and non-democracies. One consequence in some studies can be the inclusion in the 'democracies' category of minimal or electoral democracies, and perhaps even illiberal democracies or hybrid regimes where formal democratic procedures are combined with authoritarian characteristics. Instances of such limited democracy are often characterized by elite fractions competing for political control, with notions of 'majority rule' becoming relatively meaningless. Even with the fuller version of liberal democracy, characterized by greater protection of civil and political rights, we noted that democracy was still limited to 'a system of political authority, separate from any social and economic features' (Diamond 1996: 21). As such, democratic processes are solely a *means* for political decision-making, but the *substance* of policy content remains an open question. When combined with elite control of such democratic mechanisms, the likelihood of economic and social policies that favour a poor majority remains highly unlikely. In contrast with Fukuyama's (1989) claim that liberal democracy was becoming universalized and that we had reached the end of history, we assert here that the concept of democracy has always been contested and will remain so in future. Therefore, an important research task is to examine the relative success of different *forms* of democracy in reducing poverty and inequality. We would posit that social democracies in parts of Western Europe in the post-1945 period are one type of democratic government that has addressed poverty and inequality more successfully through substantial market regulation and intervention, economic redistribution and welfare state measures.

Finally, the intention of this chapter has been to examine the impact of democracy and democratization on poverty and inequality, and it has become evident that democratic polities can be equally associated with rising poverty and inequality. But, reversing the direction of influence, what are the implications of socio-economic inequalities for democracy? It would take a separate chapter to fully address this question. But suffice to note here that persistent and rising socio-economic inequalities can have adverse effects on political equality and on the quality of democracy. As Beetham and Boyle (1995: 111) point out: 'The greater the economic inequal-ities in a society, the more difficult it becomes to have effective political equality, since accumula-tions of wealth can be used as a significant resource to determine political outcomes.' Nancy Bermeo perceived the possible implications more dramatically, stating that: 'High levels of poverty and inequality not only lower the quality of democracy, but may pave the way for the emergence of authoritarian populists and democratic backsliding' (cited in Network of Democracy Research Institutes 2009: 6). In some respects, such possibilities are contained within the current predomi-nance of 'hybrid regimes' and various types of 'pseudo-democracies' and 'electoral autocracies'. In the specific context of Latin America, Terry Lynn Karl (2000: 156) similarly warns against: 'Inequality's pernicious undermining of democratic aspirations, institutions, and rules', stating that this is 'the greatest threat facing democracy in the Americas today'. It becomes evident that the failure of democracy to address issues of poverty and inequality could lead to the compromising of democratic political regimes themselves.

Therefore, in conclusion, it is clear that democracy brings no guarantee of a reduction in either poverty or income inequality, and a democratic polity may continue to display high levels of both. Thus it may seem that we should simply value democracy for its own intrinsically positive values, notably the protection of political freedoms and civil rights, rather than generating high expectations of developmental benefits. However, poverty and inequality do matter. They matter in themselves and they matter in terms of being in conflict with the very ethos of democracy. As articulated powerfully by Guillermo O'Donnell (1996: 15): 'Extended poverty and deep inequality [are] deeply offensive to the values on which democracy is grounded.'

Notes

1 Polity IV codes how democratic each country is on a scale from -10 (most autocratic) to 10 (most democratic).
2 The Kuznets curve was originally developed by Simon Kuznets (1955) as a graphical representation of the process of economic development in which economic inequality initially increases during early industrialization and then starts to decrease as industrialization becomes more advanced. This hypothesis of rising and then falling inequality has also been applied to democratization processes as a 'political Kuznets curve'.
3 Chong is careful to state that his research does not provide 'absolute evidence' on the existence of a political Kuznets curve, and that there remains the issue of data quality (2004: 209).

References

Acemoglu, D. and J. Robinson (2006) *Economic Origins of Dictatorship and Democracy*. Cambridge: Cambridge University Press.

Albertus, M. (2010) *Political Institutions and the Well-Being of the Poor*, available at http://www.stanford.edu/~y/index_files/RegimePoverty_May10.pdf (accessed 11 June 2010).

Avelino, G., D. S. Brown and W. Hunter (2005) 'The Effects of Capital Mobility, Trade Openness, and Democracy on Social Spending in Latin America, 1980–1999', *American Journal of Political Science*, 49 (3), pp. 625–641.

Beetham, D. and K. Boyle (1995) *Introducing Democracy: 80 Questions and Answers*. Cambridge: Polity Press in association with UNESCO Publishing.

Beitz, C. R. (1982) 'Democracy in Developing Societies'. In *Freedom in the World: Political Rights and Civil Liberties*, ed. R. Gastil. New York: Freedom House, pp. 145–166.

Bermeo, N. (2009) 'Does Electoral Democracy Boost Economic Equality?', *Journal of Democracy*, 20 (4), pp. 21–35.

Birdsall, N., D. Ross and R. Sabot (1995) 'Inequality and Growth Reconsidered: Lessons from East Asia', *The World Bank Economic Review*, 9 (3), pp. 477–508.

Bollen, K. and R. W. Jackman (1985) 'Political Democracy and the Size Distribution of Income', *American Sociological Review*, 50 (4), pp. 438–457.

Brown, D. S. and W. Hunter (2004) 'Democracy and Human Capital Formation: Education Spending in Latin America, 1980 to 1997', *Comparative Political Studies*, 37 (7), pp. 842–864.

Bourguignon, F. and T. Verdier (2000) 'Oligarchy, Democracy, Inequality, and Growth', *Journal of Development Economics*, 62, pp. 285–313.

Bueno, de Mesquita, B. A. Smith, R. M. Siverson and J. D. Morrow (2003) *The Logic of Political Survival*. Cambridge: MIT Press.

Carbone, G. (2009) 'The Consequences of Democratization', *Journal of Democracy*, 20 (2), pp. 123–137.

Centre for Rights Education and Awareness (CREW) (2008) *Women Paid the Price!!!: Sexual and Gender-based Violence in the 2007 Post-Election Conflict in Kenya*; available at http://www.creawkenya.org/pdf/2009/women_paid_the_price2.pdf (accessed 11 June 2010).

Chong, A. (2004) 'Inequality, Democracy, and Persistence: Is There a Political Kuznets Curve?', *Economics & Politics*, 16 (2), pp. 189–212.

Cornia, A. C. and J. Court (2001) 'Inequality, Growth and Poverty in the Era of Liberalization and Globalization', *Policy Brief No. 4*. Helsinki: WIDER.

De Waal, A. (2000) 'Democratic Political Processes and the Fight Against Famine', *IDS Working Paper* 107. Brighton, UK: Institute of Development Studies.

Department for International Development (DfID) (2000) *Realising Human Rights for Poor People*. London: DfID.

Diamond, L. (1996) 'Is the Third Wave Over?', *Journal of Democracy*, 7 (3), pp. 20–37.

Diamond, L. (2004) 'Moving Up Out of Poverty: What Does Democracy Have to Do With It?', *CDDRL Working Paper* No. 4. Stanford University: Center on Democracy, Development, and the Rule of Law.

Evans, P. (1995) *Embedded Autonomy: States and Industrial Transformation*. Princeton, NJ: Princeton University Press.

Fukuyama, F. (1989) 'The End of History?', *The National Interest*, Summer, pp. 3–18.

Ghosh, J. (2010) 'Poverty Reduction in China and India: Policy Implications of Recent Trends, *DESA Working Paper No. 92*, United Nations Department of Economic and Social Affairs

Gradstein, M. and B. Milanovic (2004) 'Does Liberté = Egalité? A Survey of the Empirical Links between Democracy and Inequality with Some Evidence on the Transition Economies', *Journal of Economic Surveys*, 18 (4), pp. 515–537.

Green, D. (2003) *Silent Revolution: The Rise and Crisis of Market Economics in Latin America*. 2nd ed. London: Latin America Bureau.

Hickey, S. (2006) 'The Politics of What Works in Reducing Chronic Poverty', *CPRC Working Paper 91*. University of Manchester, UK: Chronic Poverty Research Centre.

Huntington, S. P. (1991) *The Third Wave: Democratization in the Late Twentieth Century*. Norman, OK and London: University of Oklahoma Press.

Justman, M. and M. Gradstein (1999) 'The Industrial Revolution, Political Transition, and the Subsequent Decline in Inequality in 19th Century Britain', *Explorations in Economic History*, 36, pp. 109–127.

Kaplinsky, R. (2005) *Globalization, Poverty and Inequality*. Cambridge: Polity.

Karl, T. L. (2000) 'Economic Inequality and Democratic Instability', *Journal of Democracy*, 11 (1), pp. 149–156.

Kaufman, R. R. and A. Segura-Ubiergo (2001) 'Globalization, Domestic Politics, and Social Spending in Latin America', *World Politics*, 53 (4), pp. 553–587.

Kirdar, U. and L. Silk eds (1994) *A World Fit for People*. New York: New York University Press.

Kuznets, S. (1955) 'Economic Growth and Income Inequality', *American Economic Review*, 45, pp. 1–28.

Lake, D. A. and M. Baum (2001) 'The Invisible Hand of Democracy: Political Control and the Provision of Public Services', *Comparative Political Studies*, 34 (6), pp. 587–621.

Landman, T. (2006) 'Democracy and Human Security: Essential Linkages'. In *Democracy, Conflict and Human Security: Further Readings*, ed. International Institute for Democracy and Electoral Assistance. Sweden: Stockholm, pp. 13–24.

Lenski, G. (1966) *Power and Privilege: A Theory of Social Stratification*. New York: McGraw Hill.

Lewis, P. (2008) 'Growth Without Prosperity in Africa', *Journal of Democracy*, 19 (4), pp. 95–109.

Li, H., L. Squire and H. Zou (1998) 'Explaining International and Intertemporal Variations in Income Inequality', *Economic Journal*, 108 (446), pp. 26–43.

Lipset, S. M. (1959) 'Some Social Requisites of Democracy: Economic Development and Political Development', *American Political Science Review*, 53, pp. 69–105.

Lockwood, M. (2005) *The State They're In: An Agenda for International Action on Poverty in Africa*. Warwick: ITDG Publishing.

Luckham, R., A. M. Goetz and M. Kaldor, (2003) 'Democratic Institutions and Politics'. In *Can Democracy be Designed? Politics of Institutional Choice in Conflict-Torn Societies*, ed. S. Bastian and R. Luckham. London: Zed Books.

Lundberg, M. and L. Squire (1999) 'Growth and Inequality: Extracting the Lessons for Policy-makers.' Mimeo, World Bank.

McCargo, D. J. (1996) 'Vote-buying in Thailand's Northeast: The July 1995 General Election', *Asian Survey*, 36, pp. 376–393.

Mkandawire, T. (2004) 'Disempowering New Democracies and the Persistence of Poverty'. In *Globalisation, Poverty and Conflict*, ed. M. Spoor. Kluwer Academic Publishers, pp. 117–153.

Moore, M. and J. Putzel (1999) *Politics and Poverty: A Background Paper for the World Development Report 2000/1*; available at http://siteresources.worldbank.org/INTPOVERTY/Resources/WDR/DfID-Project-Papers/synthes.pdf (accessed 3 June 2010).

Navia, P. and T. D. Zweifel (2000) 'Democracy, Dictatorship, and Infant Mortality', *Journal of Democracy*, 11 (2), pp. 99–114.

Navia, P. and T. D. Zweifel (2003) 'Democracy, Dictatorship, and Infant Mortality Revisited', *Journal of Democracy*, 14 (3), pp. 90–103.

Nelson, J. M. (2007) 'Elections, Democracy, and Social Services', *Studies in Comparative International Development*, 41 (4), pp. 79–97.

Network of Democracy Research Institutes (NDRI) (2009) 'Poverty, Inequality and Democracy'. Conference report, Bratislava, Slovakia, 26–28 April 2009.

O'Donnell, G. (1996) 'Poverty and Inequality in Latin America: Some Political Reflections'. *Working Paper No. 225* – July 1996, Helen Kellogg Institute for International Studies, University of Notre Dame.

Przeworski, A., M. E. Alvarez, J. A. Cheibub and F. Limongi (2000) *Democracy and Development: Political Institutions and Well-being in the World 1950–1990*. Cambridge: Cambridge University Press.

Quibria, M. G. (2003) 'Growth and Poverty Reduction: Does Political Regime Matter?' Paper presented at the FAISD-GRIPS Symposium – Can Japanese and Asian Experiences be Applied to Other Countries?, Tokyo, Japan.

Remington, T. F. (2008) 'Democracy, Governance, and Inequality: Evidence from the Russian Regions'. Paper prepared for conference on New Frontiers in Political Economy Higher School of Economics and New Economic School Moscow, Russia, 30–31 May 2008.

Reuveny, R. and Q. Li (2003) 'Economic Openness, Democracy, and Income Inequality: An Empirical Analysis', *Comparative Political Studies*, 36 (5), pp. 575–601.

Rodrik, D. (1999) 'Democracies Pay Higher Wages', *Quarterly Journal of Economics*, 114, pp. 707–738.

Ross, M. (2006) 'Is Democracy Good for the Poor?', *American Journal of Political Science*, 50 (4), pp. 860–874.

Sen, A. (1999) *Development as Freedom*. Oxford: Oxford University Press.

Sirowy, L. and A. Inkeles (1990) 'The Effects of Democracy on Economic Growth and Inequality: A Review', *Studies in Comparative International Development*, 25 (1), pp. 126–157.

Stasavage, D. (2005) 'Democracy and Education Spending in Africa', *American Journal of Political Science*, 49 (2), pp. 344–358.

Timmons, J. T. (2010) 'Does Democracy Reduce Economic Inequality?', *British Journal of Political Science*, 40 (4), pp. 741–757.

UNDP (United Nations Development Programme) (2002) *Human Development Report 2002: Deepening Democracy in a Fragmented World*. New York and Oxford: Oxford University Press.

24

Democratization and security

Vincent Boudreau

An inconsistency undercuts much thinking about the relationship between democracy and security. Among the world's established democracies, and particularly in the United States and Western Europe, national security concerns are often described as existing in tension with democracy. Following the terrorist attacks on September 11, 2001 in the United States, and later attacks in Spain and England, democratic rights and freedoms were mainly conceived as providing operational space for terrorists and other subversive forces. Similar concerns about trade-offs between open societies and security also inform debates on immigration in places such as the United States and France. At the same time – and herein lies the inconsistency – the application of *more* democracy has often been invoked as an antidote to security threats in places without functioning democratic systems. In such places, typically located in underdeveloped areas of the world, the empowerment of populations – the distribution of political voice, rights and freedoms – is conceived of as contributing to a more robust security situation.

What explains this apparent inconsistency? Does democracy quell security threats in some places, but enflame them in others? Are security problems confronting developed and under-developed nations so different? Is democracy so variegated a concept that advocates mean different things in relationship to the two contexts? Or, is the discourse about democracy's relationship to security politicized and analytically unreliable?

In this chapter, I develop some answers to these questions by explicitly establishing how differences in security-threat structures (i.e. interstate, domestic, civil and transnational) influences the relationship they have with democracy. To find answers, I look to causal mechanisms linking specific kinds of security concerns to specific elements of democratic processes and systems; in this way, I hope to avoid the conceptual murkiness of attempting to associate democracy and security with one another *tout court*. In what follows, I assume that democracy and security are multi-faceted, and so implicate one another in complex ways. Moreover, I will separate arguments about international security from those more concerned with the security of domestic societies, since different traditions colour how we think about democracy and security in these different realms. Starting the discussion around key causal mechanisms allows us to make some generalizations across the boundaries of international and domestic politics, or so I shall argue.

From the basic discussion about causal connections between security and democracy, I move to a consideration of democracy assistance policy. Analysts often disagree about the importance of democratic outcomes *versus* democratic processes in this policy: are goals of democracy and security best served by promoting democratic processes, or democratic outcomes and candidacies? I will argue that although the ends of democracy are generally better served by close attention to process, as security concerns grow more salient, policymakers frequently regard democratic processes as unreliable and insufficient guarantees on security. In a pinch, that is, the broad relationship between democracy and security that captured such attention among policymakers fails to generate sufficient confidence when it would seem to matter most.

Structures of security and their implications for democracy

Analysts have considered how three broadly different security structures influence and are influenced by democracy. First, security can be compromised across international borders, in wars between states, or between states and non-state actors; in such security threats, democratic peace theorists contend that since democracies seldom fight one another, the promotion of democracy should help call into existence zones of international peace. Second, those engaged in insurgencies and/or civil conflict seek to withdraw from or overthrow those in power. In the face of such threats, points for political access and participation established through democratic governance are thought to prevent or dilute the appeal of rebellion; where successful and legitimate, democratic governance provides a framework that aims to maintain citizens' support, including those who have been disappointed in government policy decisions or electoral outcomes. Finally, transnational threats, which I will describe mainly in terms of terrorist networks and attacks, reach across borders, often from very distant recruitment grounds, to stage attacks. The relationship between recruitment grounds and what has been called terrorist venues poses distinct puzzles for security. Democracy and democratization processes can be expected to influence these different security conditions in different ways.

Democracy and international security

The observation that democratic states do not (or seldom) wage war against one another – the so-called democratic peace theory – arises primarily from a robust empirical observation. Since large-scale statistical examinations of the factors leading states to go to war, scholars have recognized the rarity with which democratic nations take up arms against one another. Despite some sustained debate about the robustness of the findings, after Michael Doyle attached some broad Kantian principles to the observation (Doyle 1983a, b), the idea of something called a democratic peace was fairly well established. This is not to say that all analysts accept the premise. For some, points on a democracy's developmental trajectory work different influences on its foreign policy. Snyder, in particular, has argued that the democratization process is particularly likely to produce warlike foreign policies because new state leaders so often rely on bellicose populist ideologies (Snyder 2000). Others see the correlation between democracy and peace – and even between democratization and peace – as more robust (Ward and Gleditsch 1998).

Among those who accept the basic premise that democracy produces some form of pacific international relations, at least with other democracies, two main points of disagreement persist, one primarily driven by methodological concerns, and the other by disagreements over causal mechanisms. On the methodological side of things, scholars argue about whether the most robust empirical association between democracy and peace is monadic or dyadic. That is, does democratic peace describe a relationship among democracies only (that they do not wage war on one another) or between liberal, democratic states and the rest of the world? If the former, the study of democratic peace should take dyadic relations (between two states) as its unit of analysis, and expect to see more peace among democratic dyads than among mixed or non-democratic dyads (Doyle 1983). If the relationship is monadic, then democracies can be expected more generally to be pacific (Rummel 1983; MacMillan 2003). The complexity of the data on wars – associated with questions about what counts as a war, what counts as a democracy, and whether only states or both state and non–state actors are included – renders this discussion inconclusive; frequently, where one stands on the issue often has depended on definitional preferences.

But the methodological matters also influence the two causal considerations that analysts most often applied to the puzzle of the democratic peace. Those in the so-called normative camp argue that democratic norms and values promote peaceful international engagement – but this argument plays out differently in dyadic and monadic approaches to the subject. Dyadic approaches emphasize the fact that democracies share norms and values that promote mutual understanding and pacific conflict resolution. Indeed, some have seen a missionary arrogance in democracies that allow state leaders to mobilize democratic values as a way of justifying war on non-democracies (Forsythe 1992). Monadic approaches see pacifism as more inherent to democratic states, and some even expect to find particular care in the conduct of democratic states towards weaker or more vulnerable nations.

Structural explanations for the democratic peace look instead to the constraints that democratic institutions allow pacific publics to impose on decision-makers (Reiter and Stam 2002). Whether or not structural arguments vary across dyadic or monadic interpretations of the argument is a bit of an open question at the moment. If pacific publics are pacific *generally*, they may not much care whether adversaries are democratic or non-democratic. On the other hand, where pacific publics are selectively pacific – in ways guided by democratic norms and values – we would expect their pacifism to be most insistent in relationship to other democratic states (and, in this way, some arguments blend structural and normative explanations). But the ambiguity of the question has led some to argue for a far closer analysis of precisely how public opinion impinges on state leaders in different settings (Ravlo *et al.* 2003).

These different arguments have undergone substantial criticism (Rosato 2003) and currently face rival explanations, such as those centring on relationships between winning coalitions in domestic elections and the propensity to wage war (Bueno de Mesquita *et al.* 1999). In this alternative explanation, democracy itself matters less than the scope of popular support in producing a politics of belligerence or restraint. Still, the conversation largely continues to involve considerations of how robust normative and structural arguments are, and what possible relationship may exist between the two (Zinnes 2004).

In fact, when one looks more closely at causal mechanisms, normative and structural arguments require one another. Public restraint on the war-making inclinations of elected officials stand at the heart of the structural approach – but in what ways do publics restrain elected officials? And, when elected officials succeed in whipping their citizenry into a posture of support for war, how does that occur? Democracy provides a range of norms and values to animate the conversation – from the necessity of protecting and spreading this 'best of all systems' to the need to approach politics in ways that lean more heavily on diplomacy than on force. Indeed, as Ravlo *et al.* note, national and state leaders demonstrate a fairly consistent ability to make the case for war to their publics, and appeals to democracy have often been part of that appeal (Ravlo *et al.* 2003). In order to fully explain how publics restrain foreign policy officials, or how those officials persuade publics of certain policies, we need some theory concerning the interests and norms that guide those interactions – and the simple equation of democracy and pacifism seems more the stuff of propaganda than analysis. Similarly, while norms and values could temper the inclination to war in state leaders and publics, the way these perspectives interact with one another – as proponents of two level games argue – depend on the structure of that interaction.

As we will see, a great deal of the policy discussion generated by the democratic peace literature assumes that pacific democracies can be produced by democratizing non-democracies. But can we assume that dynamic democratization processes, no less than stable democratic systems, will restrain militarism and enhance security? In an early study, Oneal and Russet found that democratization processes and regime transitions did not really influence levels of military conflict (Oneal and Russett 1997). If one controlled for level of economic interaction, they argue, regime type ceases significantly to influence the propensity to war. Over the last decade, however, our criteria for what counts as a full transition to consolidated democracy grew more stringent. Working with these newer, tighter criteria, Mansfield and Snyder found that incomplete transitions to democracy were more likely to engage in military activity, but more thorough and fully consolidated democratic transitions were less likely to fight (Mansfield and Snyder 2002). As we will see, these findings follow patterns that also emerge in relation to questions of domestic security, findings that associate high insecurity with incomplete democratization or with transitional periods between autocracy and democracy.

Moreover, empirical questions continue to nag. Scholars over the past decade have realized that the core empirical finding that triggered the entire democratic peace debate, so compelling in its simplicity (liberal states do not go to war with other liberal states) has substantial holes in it. How, for instance, do we account for covert operations that one democracy visits on another? When colonial powers invaded pre-modern societies with democratic decision-making structures, does that count, or not? If democracies are disinclined to fight one another, but more motivated to make war on non-democracies, does that, in the end, make them pacific, or not? As more nuanced empirical presentations of the record have replaced simpler, early versions, the puzzle has evolved into more open-ended questions about the kinds of situations in which liberal societies will more likely fight and the kinds of wars they will likely pursue. In this more sophisticated presentation of the empirical record, whether democracies promote or endanger security remains an open question.

Democracy and domestic security

Bruce Magnusson introduces a useful principle for distinguishing among four different varieties of domestic security challenge (Magnusson 2001). In his scheme, we distinguish between the sources of a security challenge, and the location of that challenge – and combine the two to describe one of four ideal security-threat types. Security threats may originate or may play out either in society or in the state's institutional environment. A coup d'état, for instance, originates in the state's institutional fabric, and plays out there as well. Intercommunal conflicts both originate and occur in society. Other kinds of threats have institutional origins and social arenas, or social origins and institutional arenas. These different security threats destabilize democracy in different ways, and draw attention to the two mechanisms by which democracy, when it stabilizes, is thought to do so. First, democracy stabilizes procedurally, by establishing rules that operate fairly and transparently, particularly those that select government officials, mediate conflict and limit the power of public authorities. Second, democracy is thought to stabilize politics by safeguarding the interests and freedoms of society: providing voice, civil rights and a mechanism by which public authorities, rather than private offices, are trusted to resolve disputes and distribute resources.

In both spheres, the stabilizing power of democracy is thought to lie in its ability to inspire a diffuse sense of legitimacy. Transparency and clearly institutionalized procedures limiting political power should mean that no branch of government grows so strong as to introduce tyranny into the system, and ample procedural checks exist to push back those who overstep their bounds (Foweraker and Krznaric 2002; Mainwaring and Welna 2003; Dodson and Jackson 2004). Democracy assures those on the short end of an election or a policy dispute that they will have other opportunities to express their grievances, or to make claims on the system. Beyond working to resolve disputes or reconcile populations to political disappointments, democratic systems draw strength from the liberal claim that a fair process defines the fairness of outcomes. In this sense, the normative components of democracy counterbalance the friction of political conflict, and so can be thought to have a pacific civil impact that compliments its affect on international relations.

It is, however, a very different thing to mediate the disputes that arise in a settled democratic system and to use democratization to solve security questions in transitional settings. One of the initial and still most consistently robust empirical findings about the relationship between democracy and development has been that democracy is strongly associated with increased development and prosperity (Lipset 1959; Burkhart 1997). But developed and prosperous settings (those with the strongest democracies) also produce relatively weak distributional conflicts. The pacific effects of democracy in such settings are overdetermined and difficult to disentangle from the peace that accompanies the general satisfaction of social need. Arguments about democratic stability that arise from the study of established democracies emphasize the diffusion of legitimacy, and conditions, such as cross-cutting cleavages and strong institutions, that convince citizens to evaluate their government over the long term, rather than at the turn of every political decision. What happens when we examine the impact of democracy and democratization in places that figure more prominently in contemporary security concerns: in places moving through regime transitions, faced with problems of poverty and insurgency, and moving from recent histories of unrest or civil war? Can democracy exert a pacific effect in places where things have not been pacified?

In some ways, the institutional side of Magnusson's insecurity typology presents less interesting questions than the civil side, because the relationship between security challenges created by the state – repression, for instance, and violent inter-institutional conflicts such as coups d'état – exist in a definitional, rather than causal relationship to democracy. It makes less sense, that is, to ask whether democracies are more or less repressive than to question whether one can call a repressive government, past a certain point, democratic. Similarly, when state actors embroiled in institutional conflicts begin to disregard formal limits on their power, they put distance between themselves and democracy.

Nevertheless, there is evidence that democratic processes actually do work over time to reduce institutionally based sources of instability – but these processes may also have a clearer impact in more stable democracies, presiding over more developed socio-economic formations. Consider repression. Those who write about repression in transitional or underdeveloped settings (as well as in formal democracies grappling with the enfranchisement of formerly excluded populations) often describe the important operation of threat perception in helping authorities make decisions about who to repress and how (Boudreau 2007). In such situations, the survival of a regime may cause state leaders who perceive strong threats to fall back on repression, whatever the costs to democracy. Recent writing about hybrid regimes, in which democratic and authoritarian attributes exist side by side, captures important elements of this situation. In such settings, the key questions may not be whether or not democracy moderates security threats, but what conditions convince state leaders that democracy alone will not hold challengers at bay, and repression may be necessary. In such settings, domestic authorities and international agencies may continue to evoke democracy, but use the term in its bare procedural sense: a government that holds relatively free and fair elections. But such limited democracy does not seem to produce strong pressures that limit repression (Carothers 2002).

Many authors writing in and about more established democracies concern themselves more with processes of technique and learning. For example, for Della Porta and her collaborators, the evolution of repression in Western democracies hinges on security-force lessons about the consequences of different policing styles – and many instances of repression consist in individual acts that break ranks with established policy in the heat of the moment (Della Porta and Reiter 1998). In civil rights struggles, the conflict between protecting and excluding populations often reflects electoral dynamics, and these dynamics can eventually be decisive in moderating repression (Polletta 2000). At the same time, arguments about the emergence of 'social movement societies' in the industrialized and liberal global north indicate that, over the long haul, the easy access that democracy opens for claim-making may routinize and domesticate protest, even frequency of demonstrations tends to increase (Meyer and Tarrow 1998). Over time, in an established democracy, the often relatively minor sources of internal disturbance tend to grow even more minor, in consequence of meaningful and continuous democratic representation that involves the vast majority of citizens.

Far more hangs in the balance, both for policy and academic analysis, in societies with unsettled distributional conflicts, faltering economies, daunting social need, and recent histories of conflict – places that seldom have long or consolidated democratic histories. In such cases, the initial absence of security (often associated with transitional crisis) makes democracy's pacific potential more pressing. Moreover, the belief that democratization can remedy domestic insecurity has moved democratization higher up the foreign policy agendas of many countries. But are there strong reasons to believe that democracy can help tamp down domestic security threats? To seek an answer, we return to a closer consideration of the causal mechanisms by which democratization is said to work its effect on security issues.

While the spatial and substantive character of insurgencies differ from place to place, all attempt to take power away from state authorities. In this sense, all differ from more communicative forms of political contention and protest, aimed at making claims and raising the costs associated with ignoring those claims. A good deal of counterinsurgency and democratization theory assumes that insurgent challenges will falter where participatory avenues are open and undermine insurgent recruitment efforts. In this view, the key element in the relationship between democracy and insecurity lies in the extent and character of what Charles Tilly has called 'protected consultation' (Tilly 2000). In Tilly's terminology, protected consultation describes the capacity of the democratic state to consult with, and act upon, the desires of the public. The expansion of protected consultation will diminish the scope of popular support for challenges to government, and will reorient societies away from non-state authorities. In this view, democracy is part of a strategy to state power: protected consultation makes states more powerful by cultivating consent, and can help insulate governments from challenges and insurgent claims. Indeed, where violence emerges in democracies, it often is regarded as criminal rather than political. The democratic system is thought to turn violence into discourse, institutionalized participation, or passivity in the face of fair procedures that are difficult to challenge. Still, democracy per se may not be responsible for this stability, for many observe that civil war is rare in both established democracies and in more authoritarian governments (DeNardo 1985; Francisco 1995).

Many have also argued that democracy has potential to tame security threats in periods of democratic transition; in general, analysts make one of two arguments defending this position. The first argues that the institutionalization of democratic politics, including both people's normative preference and systemic functioning, turn people away from supporting security challenges. Even in new democracies, many argue that citizens have strong affinities for fair and open political participation – either inherently or in consequence of internationally diffused and programmatically supported democratic norms. Struggles against tyranny produce a preference for democracy: if people can come to trust in the even-handedness of the new system, in its transparency and participatory character, they will entrust their interests to democratic deliberation. In its starkest form, this approach to democratization takes on neoconservative garb: as the most obviously superior form of government, the march of history pushes democracy forward, and in that march, democracy solves domestic problems (Fukuyama 1995). Even those unburdened by the teleology of neoconservatism often approach unruly post-transition democracies as requiring institutional diagnostics – as if democracy should, other things being equal, capably steward citizen interests and displace alternative modes of conflict resolution. Such approaches cast persistent security threats in democratizing climates (rather than democratization itself) as in need of explanation. Finding democracy stalled or security threats more intractable, analysts look for democratic deficits: corruption, unreconciled security dilemmas, or remnant authoritarian practices (Barnes 2001; Horovitz 2003). But functioning and appropriately designed democracy should, they seem to say, work to quell violence and moderate social conflict.

Others pay less attention to normative support or institutional outcomes, and focus instead on how democratic processes change how people engage with the political system. Democracy, they argue, may indeed appeal to a broad enthusiasm for fairer and more participatory politics, but real changes in behaviour (including an embrace of more civil political modes) emerge over time through engagement with democratic processes. Democracy, in this view, is a political process that gradually influences and reinforces new behaviour, and does not carry the day in the transition's first blush. A vibrant discussion, for instance, has opened up about the relationship between the electoral arena and parties that have espoused sectarian platforms or violent modes of struggle. In this argument, the practice of democracy itself democratizes politics, and in the process moderates security challenges. As political operatives run for office, or seek to accumulate a winning electoral coalition, they must also broaden their message and moderate their tactics (Ottaway *et al.* 2009; Phillips 2009). In office, pressures to meet constituent needs force former radicals towards compromise, and pull attention from radical objectives towards the more mundane administrative tasks of running a government. Elections, moreover, require different skills than insurgent fighting and, over time, may provoke the rise of new leaders within a party, leaders more equipped to argue and negotiate than to direct military attacks (Manning 2002). From this perspective, democratic pacifism does not require a prior commitment to democracy or to peace. Hence, in some measure, analytical difference between normative and institutionalist arguments about the international democratic re-emerge among those interested in explaining democracy's influence over domestic security threats.

Arguments that associate democracy with increased domestic security, however, have trouble accounting for the fact that transitions to democracy often produce dramatic increases in violence and increased security threat. Waves of ethnic violence and separatism followed transitions in places as diverse as Eastern Europe, Indonesia and Iraq. Elections often occasion great violence and instability, even in places that had enjoyed relative stability, as Kenya had before the waves of post-election violence in 2007 and 2008. Following Snyder's work linking elections and increased violent conflict in transitional settings (Snyder 2000), analysts have begun exploring how democratic participation (and voting in particular) can destabilize a government. In this discussion, something like consensus emerged around the finding that democracy is most precarious when it is mixed or unconsolidated. Two main explanations for this observation have emerged.

The first lies rooted in the study of social movements, and approaches security challenges as rival political forces, rather than as unaccommodated interests. Insurgent groups often predate the transition to democracy, and participate in those transitions as dictatorships stumbled and the opposition expanded and diversified. Such movement organizations enter the democratic era with a programme to acquire power, and may evaluate democracy less as an objective than as a new political arena, structured by new opportunities and constraints. Activists will search a newly democratic system to discover how best to recruit support, what tactics will resonate in the new context, or how sharply they can oppose authorities (Bohara *et al.* 2006). From this standpoint, semi-democracy looms as a time of particular promise. During unconsolidated transitions, state authorities may still substantially rely on repression, but espouse liberalized rules of democratic participation that allow more frequent mobilization and protest. The juxtaposition of increased resources and opportunities for unrest with a persistently repressive state produces incentives to insurgency. From this perspective, the fact of democracy does not itself explain fluctuations in security threats – but a whole range of factors, including the availability of appropriate forms of cover – can influence the security situation.

At the same time, democracy may limit the power for movement organizations by carving off a flank of support most committed to democratic, rather than substantive or economic, reform. The last days of a dictatorship, or an expanding democracy movement, often builds on the earlier efforts of movements with broad-ranging reform agendas – but recruits those more fixed on the idea of reforming a closed and repressive political system. Large sections of the democracy movement may gladly abandon their activism when elections take place, or a new constitution comes into effect. The democratic system itself, with its emphasis on participatory fairness rather than specific outcomes, drives wedges among comrades formerly united in the democracy movement, separating those committed only to process from those with more fixed commitments to what a just outcome should look like. These separations impose hardships on movements, forcing them to choose between radical tactics with diminishing support or a more moderate approach to politics.

In fact, the opportunity structure perspective on the relationship between democracy and security can be conceptualized as an inverted U-shaped curve (reminiscent of a curve that Tilly (1978) introduced decades ago to describe the relationship between mobilization and resources). The curve illustrates the robust finding that strong authoritarian government and established democracy are both associated with rather low levels of security threat – but that intermediate settings (transitions to democracy or hybrid regimes wherein democratic and authoritarian elements coexist) typically experience the strongest security problems. The logic here is familiar: where democracy is absent, repression restricts the opportunities challengers have; where democracy is robust, systemic challenges attract limited support. In the intermediate range, however, liberalized political rules allow greater challenge to the system, and the weakness or uncertainty of democracy inspires support for those challenges. In fact, hybrid regimes or weakly consolidated democracies may allow regime opponents to mobilize around ideas of the system's failed promise. If (as seems partly true) the enthusiasm for democracy as a way of solving security problems is currently on the wane, it may reflect our re-evaluation of which post-transition regimes are, in fact, democratic: analysts have only recently recognized various forms of non-democratic governments that had, for several decades, been misclassified as democratic (Collier and Levitsky 1997; Hood 1998; Carothers 2002; Volpi 2004).

A second perspective recognizes that different democracies face highly variable levels of ambient conflict. Virtually the entire first half of Huntington's 'third wave' transitions occurred in the context of weakening Cold War dictatorships, where democracy movements mainly sought to open up participatory avenues where narrow, externally supported dictatorships had closed them down (Huntington 1993). In such cases, democratization provided a more just and equitable framework for social and economic development than narrowly based Cold War dictatorships, which allowed state leaders to lavish largess and advantage on their close political cronies, leaving many in poverty. Repression and authoritarian control (rather than intercommunal rivalry) seemed the main obstacle to more generalized prosperity, and so increased participatory democracy appeared a more relevant and effective solution to a broad range of social problems. Initial social pressures brought to bear on the system were also relatively manageable, and successfully concluded elections did much to assure everyone that progress was under way. Even if liberalization and broader participatory opportunity did not resolve all problems, they provided breathing room for the new system's institutions to settle in and attract support.

Since the early 1990s, however, post-transition regimes have more frequently needed to shoulder a more immediate burden of conflict. The multi-ethnic societies of the Soviet Union's successor states produced deep distributional conflicts and persistent security dilemmas. Elsewhere, particularly as the idea of democracy's conflict-resolving efficacy spread, democratic exercises were brought in as a way of resolving conflict – an approach that was especially salient in US policy in Iraq and Afghanistan. Increasingly, democratic exercises encamped atop the unstable ground of hot, shooting wars, on the expectation that the political conflict would displace armed struggle. But time and again this expectation has been disappointed. Elections have enflamed more violent forms of conflict, and that conflict has undercut the freedom of fairness of the electoral exercise.

The problem should not excite too much surprise, if we set aside the ill-conceived idea of democracy as a political endpoint at which most serious conflicts have been resolved. At best, democracy drives conflict into formally regulated institutional arenas, but does not eliminate it. Levels of moderation and civility probably have as much to do with a society's state of conflict as with democracy's domesticating influence. Viewed from only a slightly different angle, democracy is a periodic and general invitation for social actors to mobilize their claims and grievances, and hurl them against one another. To be sure, where the grievances and the level of conflict are limited, democracy can proceed in temperance and comity. But where democratic institutions are weak, are emergent, or have a reputation for unreliability or unfairness, people will be sorely tempted to fall back on self-help. Where conflict remains fresh or a matter of recent memory, security dilemmas may convince populations to retain their arms, to resist efforts to disband their militia, and to regard the electoral arena and the rule of law with substantial suspicion. Where language policy, educational opportunity, and the distribution of social goods reflect electoral outcomes, people may bring their weapons onto the campaign trail, or use those weapons when elections fail to reflect their position (Manning 2004). The juxtaposition of democracy's invitation to moderated, domesticated conflict and the inability of democratic institutions to quell suspicions or reassure popular fears present abundant tinder for the spark of political conflict and instability. Moreover, if new democratic institutions need time to develop standing and attract confidence, early post-transition conflict may derail that process. Such factors suggest that we exercise extreme caution in our regard for democracy (or democracy alone) as a solution to extant or recent conflict or insecurity.

Democracy and transnational security threats

Much current democracy assistance policy, at least since the terrorist attacks of 9/11, has been based on the assumption that democratization and democracy assistance policy are clear avenues to undercutting terrorist movements. Yet the relationship between terrorism and democracy is not clearly established and, in fact, debates still persist about whether democracy undercuts terrorism by reducing its appeal (Crenshaw 1981; Eubank 1994), or promotes terrorism by providing terrorists greater freedom of movement (Eyerman 1998). A great deal of the confusion currently lies in questions of what counts as transnational terrorism, and whether one measures violent incidents, terrorist organizations, or something else. But the category of transnational terrorism also often lumps together different relationships between the source of threat, the venue for violence, and the political system to which both relate – relationships that I have here identified as responsible for key differences in the causal relationship between democracy and security threat (Li 2005). It may be necessary to distinguish spatially between different venue-source dyads in the analysis of how international terrorism responds to democracy (and, to be clear about whether we are talking about democracy at the terrorist venue, or in its recruitment base).

Transnational security threats differ from domestic security threats in one important respect: while a domestic insurgency both targets and recruits in the same geopolitical space, a transnational threat recruits support in one theatre, and applies violence in another. This spatial separation has important implications for the relationship between democracy and security. As we have seen, democracy works two general influences over domestic security threats: it provides greater freedom for those who wish to adopt violence, but it also works generally to narrow the social support for violent or radical challenges. The balance between operational freedom and social support tends, other things being equal, to move in an inverse relationship to one another: a state that grows more repressive may narrow a movement's space to act freely, but draw new support to movements looking to challenge the system. In general, the evolution of democracies moves towards the provision of broad freedom, on the expectation that aggrieved populations and unmet social demands will, in general, fall. For this reason, Sidney Tarrow (1998) associated the radicalization of protest with that phase of a movement when mass support begins to fall away: the resort to violence in democratic society has often been seen as a desperate, last-ditch effort, taken when participants begin to adopt other moderate and routine political modes.

Transnational security challenges, however, pose particular problems for democracy because of the potential spatial separation between its recruits and targets. As technologies for transportation and communication have grown more advanced, terrorists (as well as less violent social movement forms) have become more and more able to coordinate activity across borders. This distance, however, sharply alters the effects of democracy on transnational terrorist movements. In the theatre where terrorist networks recruit, democratic systems are a distant and often irrelevant political phenomenon: they cannot, except through less direct demonstration effects, serve to undercut recruitment to terrorism. Hence, the key mechanism by which democracy may pacify domestic politics – by inspiring support and a sense of legitimacy – will not work. Terrorists may not 'hate' the freedom of distant democracies (in the populist phrasing of post-9/11 America) – but that freedom is largely irrelevant to the populations among whom they recruit. But neither is distant democracy entirely irrelevant to terrorist recruitment: when explicit democratic ideologies are set to naught by state action, in human rights violations or the denial of due process, terrorist groups can use that news to recruit support. Set against these ambiguous effects of democracy on terrorist recruitment, democratic freedoms do certainly allow security threats greater operational latitude in venue states – and this equation renders the pacific effect of democracy on transnational terrorism particularly problematic. Such considerations have reinvigorated questions about how foreign policy can work to promote or support democracy, and what impact this has on transnational terrorism.

Democracy assistance policy and security

All of this brings us back to the initial inconsistency we noted in the relationship analysts see between democracy and security. Faced with transnational terrorist threats, venue states tighten security at home (even at the expense of democracy) to reduce the latitude for terrorist operations – but seek to expand and promote democracy abroad, as a way of undercutting the recruitment base for terrorism. But can democracy assistance policy be effective – either in promoting democracy itself, or in reducing security challenges, and if so, how? Analysts and policymakers have generally moved away from strong, early assertions about the efficacy of democracy promotion efforts (Allison and Beschel 1992). Today, more analysts make carefully qualified claims about what democracy assistance policy can do, and often warn that these policies may also have important unintended consequences (Goldsmith 2008). Others, while perhaps adopting some general notes of caution, warn against specific varieties of democracy promotion (Carothers 2006), recommending, for instance, long-term and incremental efforts to bolster capacities for democracy, short-term efforts to impose democratic systems.

I have argued elsewhere that democracy promotion policy has generally adopted one of two perspectives (Boudreau 2007). One attempts to promote democracy by identifying democrats and providing them with support. The policy draws on some of the early work of transitologists, who saw regime transitions as conjunctural contests between hardliners and softliners; from this perspective, democracy promotion was a matter of supporting democrats and constraining the actions of those more set against democratic reform. Eric McGlinchey has argued that resources contributed to the candidacy of democrats provides them socially exogenous resources that operate to relieve the ties of democratic accountability to constituents (McGlinchey 2007). In this sense, democracy assistance can act like oil wealth (Ross 2001) – and, in the process, encourage purported democrats down the road towards more authoritarian practices. A second kind of democracy assistance policy enters the local arena with a greater sense of agnosticism about who should win a contest, or who would rule democratically, if elected. From this perspective, democracy emerges from a pattern of institutional constraint and systemic design, rather than from the hearts of men and women in electoral competition. Patient democracy promotion policy focuses less on the immediate consequences of one or another election, but instead works to insure democratic processes in the belief that, in time, democratic processes will constrain state and regime officials to rule in democratic ways.

The difference between these two varieties of democracy assistance policy is particularly striking in situations that seem strongly to threaten democracy assistance providers. In the case of Hamas in Palestine, Hizballah in Lebanon, or even the Taliban in Afghanistan, pressing security threats may convince democracy assistance providers that electoral outcomes cannot be left to democratic processes – that democracy demands that professed democrats win office, and the enemies of democracy not. There are several problems with this approach. First, following McGlinchey, exactly this kind of support can drive the beneficiary of democracy assistance away from democratic governance. Second, if Thomas Carothers (2006) is correct in his observations about a backlash against democracy promotion, then we can expect intervention designed to favour one or another side in a political contest to undercut support for democracy, rather than the reverse. Finally, the evidence tracing the operation of democratic systems, much of it reviewed in the preceding pages, suggests that by short-circuiting a democratic process, policy replaces the prospect of a gradual consolidation of democracy – accomplished as people acquire stronger and stronger trust in the operation of democratic institutions – with a short-term victory of uncertain character and weak long-term prospects.

For those particularly interested in democracy as a way of moderating security threats, these cautions carry a particularly important freight. Recall that both in international and domestic arenas, some of the most dangerous regimes are those that are only partially democratic. Democracy assistance policy that is only partially successful – that produces, in Enterline and Grieg's (2005) evocative terminology, dim rather than strong beacons – is likely not merely to fail to reduce security threats but to actively push nations towards that intermediate position between democracy and authoritarian rule, one that we can expect to be most dangerous and prone to producing violence.

References

Allison, G. T., Jr. and R. P. Beschel, Jr. (1992) 'Can the United States Promote Democracy?', *Political Science Quarterly*, 107 (1), pp. 81–98.

Barnes, S. H. (2001) 'The Contribution of Democracy to Rebuilding Postconflict Societes', *American Journal of International Law*, 95 (1), p. 86.

Bohara, A. K., N. J. Mitchell, *et al.* (2006) 'Opportunity, Democracy, and the Exchange of Political Violence: A Subnational Analysis of Conflict in Nepal', *The Journal of Conflict Resolution*, 50 (1), pp. 108–128.

Boudreau, V. (2007) 'Security and Democracy: Process and Outcome in a New Policy Context', *Democratization*, 14 (2), pp. 313–330.

Bueno de Mesquita, B., J. D. Morrow, *et al.* (1999) 'An Institutional Explanation of the Democratic Peace', *The American Political Science Review*, 93 (4), pp. 791–807.

Burkhart, R. E. (1997) 'Comparative Democracy and Income Distribution: Shape and Direction of the Causal Arrow', *The Journal of Politics*, 59 (1), pp. 148–164.

Carothers, T. (2002) 'The End of the Transition Paradigm', *Journal of Democracy*, 13 (1), pp. 5–21.

—— (2006) 'The Backlash Against Democracy Promotion', *Foreign Affairs*, 85 (2), pp. 55–68.

Collier, D. and S. Levitsky (1997) 'Democracy with Adjectives: Conceptual Innovation in Comparative Research', *World Politics*, 49 (3), pp. 430–451.

Crenshaw, M. (1981) 'The Causes of Terrorism', *Comparative Politics*, 13 (4), pp. 379–399.

Della Porta, D. and H. Reiter (1998) *Policing Protest: The Control of Mass Demonstrations in Western Democracies.* Minneapolis: University of Minnesota Press.

DeNardo, J. (1985) *Power in Numbers: The Political Strategy of Protest and Rebellion.* Princeton, NJ: Princeton University Press.

Dodson, M. and D. Jackson (2004) 'Horizontal Accountability in Transitional Democracies: The Human Rights Ombudsman in El Salvador and Guatemala', *Latin American Politics and Society*, 46 (4), pp. 1–27.

Doyle, M. W. (1983a) 'Kant, Liberal Legacies, and Foreign Affairs', *Philosophy and Public Affairs*, 12 (3), pp. 205–235.

—— (1983b) 'Kant, Liberal Legacies, and Foreign Affairs, Part 2', *Philosophy and Public Affairs*, 12 (4), pp. 323–353.

Enterline, A. J. and J. M. Greig (2005) 'Beacons of Hope? The Impact of Imposed Democracy on Regional Peace, Democracy, and Prosperity', *The Journal of Politics*, 67 (4), pp. 1075–1098.

Eubank, W. and Weinberg, L. (1994) 'Does Democracy Encourage Terrorism?', *Terrorism and Political Violence*, 6 (4), pp. 145–165.

Eyerman, J. (1998) 'Terrorism and Democratic States: Soft Targets and Accessible Systems', *International Interactions*, 24 (2), pp. 151–170.

Forsythe, D. P. (1992) 'Democracy, War, and Covert Action', *Journal of Peace Research*, 29 (4), pp. 385–395.

Foweraker, J. and R. Krznaric (2002) 'The Uneven Performance of Third Wave Democracies: Electoral Politics and the Imperfect Rule of Law in Latin America', *Latin American Politics and Society*, 44 (3), pp. 29–60.

Francisco, R. A. (1995) 'The Relationship between Coercion and Protest: An Empirical Evaluation in Three Coercive States', *The Journal of Conflict Resolution*, 39 (2), pp. 263–282.

Fukuyama, F. (1995) 'Reflections on the End of History, Five Years Later', *History and Theory*, 34 (2), pp. 27–43.

Goldsmith, A. (2008) 'Making the World Safe for Partial Democracy? Questioning the Premises of Democracy Promotion', *International Security*, 33 (2), pp. 120–147.

Hood, S. J. (1998) 'The Myth of Asian-Style Democracy', *Asian Survey*, 38 (9), pp. 853–866.

Horovitz, D. L. (2003) 'Electoral Systems: A Primer for Decisions Makers', *Journal of Democracy*, 14 (4), pp. 115–127.

Huntington, S. P. (1993) 'The Third Wave Democratization in the Late Twentieth Century'; available at http://www.netlibrary.com/urlapi.asp?action=summary&v=1&bookid=15342, an electronic book accessible through the World Wide Web; click for information.

Li, Q. (2005) 'Does Democracy Promote or Reduce Transnational Terrorist Incidents?', *The Journal of Conflict Resolution*, 49 (2), pp. 278–297.

Lipset, S. M. (1959) 'Some Social Requisites of Democracy: Economic Development and Political Legitimacy', *The American Political Science Review*, 53 (1), pp. 69–105.

McGlinchey, E. (2007) 'Foreign Assistance and Domestic Power: Aiding Political Parties in Central Asia and the Caucasus', *Conference Papers – International Studies Association*, pp. 1–30.

MacMillan, J. (2003) 'Beyond the Separate Democratic Peace', *Journal of Peace Research*, 40 (2), pp. 233–243.

Magnusson, B. A. (2001) 'Democratization and Domestic Insecurity: Navigating the Transition in Benin', *Comparative Politics*, 33 (2), pp. 211–230.

Mainwaring, S. and C. Welna (2003) *Democratic Accountability in Latin America.* Oxford; New York: Oxford University Press.

Manning, C. (2002) 'Conflict Management and Elite Habituation in Postwar Democracy: The Case of Mozambique', *Comparative Politics*, 35 (1), pp. 63–84.

—— (2004) 'Elections and Political Change in Post-War Bosnia and Herzegovina', *Democratization*, 11 (2), pp. 60–86.

Mansfield, E. D. and J. Snyder (2002) 'Incomplete Democratization and the Outbreak of Military Disputes', *International Studies Quarterly*, 46 (4), pp. 529–549.

Meyer, D. S. and S. G. Tarrow (1998) *The Social Movement Society: Contentious Politics for a New Century.* Lanham: Rowman & Littlefield Publishers.

Oneal, J. R. and B. M. Russett (1997) 'The Classical Liberals Were Right: Democracy, Interdependence, and Conflict, 1950–1985', *International Studies Quarterly*, 41 (2), pp. 267–293.

Ottaway, M., A. Hamzawy, *et al.* (2009) *Getting to Pluralism: Political Actors in the Arab World*. Washington, DC: Carnegie Endowment for International Peace.

Phillips, D. L. (2009) *From Bullets to Ballots: Violent Muslim Movements in Transition*. New Brunswick, NJ: Transaction Publishers.

Polletta, F. (2000) 'The Structural Context of Novel Rights Claims: Southern Civil Rights Organizing, 1961–1966', *Law & Society Review*, 34 (2), pp. 367–406.

Ravlo, H., N. P. Gleditsch, *et al.* (2003) 'Colonial War and the Democratic Peace', *The Journal of Conflict Resolution*, 47 (4), pp. 520–548.

Reiter, D. and A. C. Stam (2002) *Democracies at War*. Princeton, NJ: Princeton University Press.

Rosato, S. (2003) 'The Flawed Logic of Democratic Peace Theory', *The American Political Science Review*, 97 (4), pp. 585–602.

Ross, M. L. (2001) 'Does Oil Hinder Democracy?', *World Politics*, 53 (3), pp. 325–361.

Rummel, R. J. (1983) 'Libertarianism and International Violence', *The Journal of Conflict Resolution*, 27 (1), pp. 27–71.

Snyder, J. L. (2000) *From Voting to Violence: Democratization and Nationalist Conflict*. New York: Norton.

Tarrow, S. G. (1998) *Power in Movement: Social Movements and Contentious Politics*. Cambridge, UK; New York: Cambridge University Press.

Tilly, C. (1978) *From Mobilization to Revolution*. Reading, MA: Addison-Wesley.

—— (2000) 'Processes and Mechanisms of Democratization', *Sociological Theory*, 18 (1), pp. 1–16.

Volpi, F. (2004) 'Pseudo-Democracy in the Muslim World', *Third World Quarterly*, 25 (6), pp. 1061–1078.

Ward, M. D. and K. S. Gleditsch (1998) 'Democratizing for Peace', *The American Political Science Review*, 92 (1), pp. 51–61.

Zinnes, D. A. (2004) 'Constructing Political Logic: The Democratic Peace Puzzle', *The Journal of Conflict Resolution*, 48 (3), pp. 430–454.

25

Democratization and human rights

Convergence and divergence

David Beetham

The first part of this chapter will look at the relation between democracy and human rights considered as *constants*, and will seek to identify the main points of convergence and divergence respectively between them. Establishing the character of their relationship will be a necessary precondition for understanding the different ways in which it plays out in the course of democratization, considered as a *process*. This will form the subject of the second part of the chapter.

Convergence

Three different ways in which democracy and human rights converge will be considered here: conceptual, justificatory and empirical. I take each of these in turn.

Conceptual

Although there have been many different ways in which democracy has been defined, most definitions involve an appeal, directly or indirectly, to two core principles. First is the idea that the people are the rightful source of political authority, reflected in their free choice of government; that government should be responsive to their views and promote their interests; and that they are entitled to take an active part in the common affairs of their society at every level. The famous slogan 'government of the people, by the people, for the people' offers a succinct expression of this principle of people power or popular control. The second principle is that of political equality: all voices are entitled to an equal hearing, and all persons should be given equal consideration in the formulation and delivery of public policy. Historically, struggles for democracy or 'democratization' have been struggles to give the people more influence over their government, and to make that influence more equal and inclusive. We can call institutional arrangements 'democratic' in so far as they embody or help to realize these two core principles. The fact that actually existing democracies may not measure up to these principles, and may fall short in different respects, does not itself invalidate the principles, or justify dismissing them as merely utopian (Beetham 1999: 1–6).

Defining democracy in terms of its core principles, rather than as a set of institutional mechanisms that are derivative from these principles, leads us directly to the language of rights. If democracy requires that the people *should* have a controlling influence over their collective affairs, and over the government that rules in their name, then this is the same as saying that they have a *right* to do so, and have rights to those things necessary to make that influence effective. And these are precisely the basic rights and freedoms enshrined in the human rights civil and political rights conventions. These include the familiar rights and freedoms of expression, association and assembly, without which people cannot communicate and organize freely to identify and solve their common problems, or influence the course of government, or hold it effectively to account. Although these rights have to be guaranteed to people as *individuals*, their significance derives from the *collective* and *public* context in which they are exercised, which is that of a democracy. By the same token, when the standard international human rights conventions come to define the permissible restrictions that may be imposed on these rights, they use the phrase 'which are prescribed by law and which are necessary *in a democratic society*'. Moreover, the right to take part in the conduct of public affairs, to vote and be elected to public office, is itself defined as a basic human right (Brownlie and Goodwin-Gill 2002: 189). So, democracy and the basic rights and freedoms of the human rights conventions are not only complementary, but mutually entailing.

The same applies to other human rights that at first sight may not so obviously relate to democracy. The rights to security of the person and freedom of movement may be denied to candidates in the process of electoral campaigning, or to investigative journalists in the course of their work. The right to due legal process may be denied to members of opposition movements or parties through trumped-up charges or preventive detention without charge. It was the frequent experience of such abuses under authoritarian regimes of the eighteenth century that led to the simultaneous demand for popular government and the formulation of the first human rights charters in the American (1776) and French (1789) revolutions.

If, then, it is evident that democratic principles entail the typical rights of the United Nations International Covenant on Civil and Political Rights (ICCPR), more contestable is whether or not they also require the rights of the International Covenant on Economic, Social and Cultural Rights (1966) for their realization. Democratic principles certainly require *some* economic and social rights. The possibility of making a contribution to the collective affairs of one's community or society is hardly realizable for those suffering from chronic disease or malnutrition, those lacking basic literacy or civic education, or those denied the right to contribute in their own mother tongue (Sen 1999: 87–110). Beyond this point, however, the full list of economic and social rights should be seen more as the possible *product* of a democratic process than as the *precondition* for it.

Justificatory

At the conceptual level, then, democracy as defined in terms of the two key principles of popular control and political equality entails a set of basic rights and freedoms guaranteed equally to all, such as those specified in the international covenants on civil and political rights. A second point of convergence follows from the first one. This lies in the character of the justification given respectively for democratic principles and for human rights. Both of these are now so widely accepted they are often treated as self-evident, and not requiring any considered justification. However, all it needs is a significant challenge to this self-evidence, whether from cultural or philosophical relativists, from defenders of traditional morality, or from elite guardians of the national security state, to require more considered justification (Beetham 2011). A key point of contention typically centres on the claim that people have an *equal* right, whether to take part in the collective affairs of their society, or to enjoy the rights and freedoms necessary thereto – an equality that is typically challenged on the grounds that some class of people is better suited by nature, education or social position to have a determining influence over public affairs, while others should legitimately be restricted in their rights if not excluded altogether.

The challenge for both democracy and human rights is to show in what respect, and by virtue of what characteristics, people can be shown to be equal, sufficient to justify an equality in their rights: to decide on their own way of living, to express their ideas freely and publicly, to associate with others for common interests, and to take part in public affairs. The justifications given in the standard human rights charters and conventions turn out to be insufficient for this purpose. The Universal Declaration of Human Rights (UDHR 1948) states that all are 'equal in dignity', and the ICCPR (1966) that the rights 'derive from the inherent dignity of the human person' (Brownlie and Goodwin-Gill 2002: 18–19, 182). The possession of dignity certainly requires that we treat people with equal respect, but it does not follow from that alone that all are capable of effective *agency* in the public domain. The same applies to the statement of the UDHR that all are 'endowed with reason and conscience', which is entirely compatible with people fulfilling their allotted role in a hierarchical or paternalist social order, in which the guidelines for their lives are laid down by others.

To justify an equal right of *public agency* to all, which is central to both democracy and the civil and political rights conventions alike, we have to show that the possession of the capacities necessary to its exercise is a potentially universal human characteristic. Having an 'activity right' as we could call it, entails possessing the capacities necessary to its exercise. What are these capacities that all are potentially capable of developing? They include: the capacity to make considered choices about what is good for one's life, and the life of the communities of which one is a part; to contribute to collective discussion about these choices and priorities; and to treat other contributors with respect when doing so. Certainly these capacities are ones that require developing, and that is the reason why we do not allow children to enter into binding contracts, to sit on juries, to vote or stand for public office, until they have reached a certain age. Only by the time that they have gained sufficient experience of making considered judgments in lesser matters will it imply that they can be entrusted with larger ones. It will also indicate that they have enough experience of the world to appreciate what the typical consequences of different choices or courses of action might be (Beetham 2009).

Historically, every attempt to justify the exclusion of a given adult group from public activities – whether on grounds of class, race, gender or whatever, and the 'natural' incapacities that supposedly attend that status – has fallen down by virtue of its circularity. First, a given group is legally or socially prevented from participating in a given activity. As a result it is discouraged from developing the capacities necessary for such an activity. Then the resulting incapacity or unsuitability is deemed to be 'natural' or 'inborn', thus justifying the original exclusion. Only when the excluding barrier is broken through does it become evident that the supposed incapacity is socially constructed, rather than naturally given.

In opposition to every such circularity of argumentation, the human rights conventions noted above make clear that all the rights specified apply 'to everyone', and all make an anti-discrimination declaration central to their programme, most explicitly in the European Convention on Human Rights (1953): 'The enjoyment of the rights and freedoms set forth in this Convention shall be secured without discrimination on any ground' (Brownlie and Goodwin-Gill 2002: 403). By the same token, democracy requires not only a right for the people to take part in their governance, but an explicitly *equal* right, most obviously in the equal value of each person's vote. In the words of Jeremy Bentham, 'everyone should count for one, and none for more than one', whether this be as objects of public policy, or as subjects in the electoral process. 'The happiness of the most helpless pauper,' he wrote, 'constitutes as large a part of the universal happiness as does that of the most powerful, the most opulent member of the community' (Bentham 1843: 95–100). So we can conclude that the participatory expectations entailed in democratic citizenship, and the corresponding activity rights of the civil and political rights conventions, share a common grounding or justification in a universal human capacity for considered choice and deliberation about collective as well as individual affairs.

Empirical

So far, the convergence between democracy and human rights has been considered at a purely theoretical level, and as a matter of intrinsic connectedness. But what about the record of actual practice? Do democracies in practice protect human rights more effectively than non-democratic regimes? In the main they do, though we need to take some care over how we define a democracy 'in practice', and which rights we are talking about. If we exclude the so-called 'façade' or 'illiberal' democracies, which may have elections for governmental office but no freedoms of association, movement or expression that would allow such elections to be genuinely open and competitive, and so provide a reasonable expression of the popular will, then democracies have been shown to be more effective at protecting the whole range of civil and political rights than non-democratic regimes. This range includes personal physical security, freedom from arbitrary arrest or detention, and due legal process as well as the more directly democratic rights (Landman 2005).

The greater protection that democracies provide is hardly surprising. Censorship-free media can readily bring gross human rights violations to public attention before they become chronic. Human rights organizations are free to engage in advocacy work and mobilization campaigns. Law-enforcement agencies are publicly accountable, both for their actions and for their failures to act. And executives, for their part, are subject to a variety of legislative and non-legislative constraints. Authoritarian regimes, by contrast, are rarely subject to such forms of accountability or constraint. And their innate tendency is to suppress or pre-empt all political opposition by force or the threat of it, and by collusion in extra-legal violence. The result is a record of persistent human rights violations under such regimes.

However, not all democracies emerge with a clean bill of health in the matter of human rights protection. This is particularly the case with regard to governments facing insurgency or civil war. While these situations give them the right to declare states of emergency and to derogate from their obligations under human rights conventions in the interest of 'public security', they also compromise or remove many of the constraints and accountability mechanisms that are typical of democratic systems in normal times and places. Moreover, a condition of armed conflict is one where human rights violations are endemic, on the part of all parties to the conflict (Regan and Henderson 2002; Carey 2010).

Even long-established democracies have not been free from unjustified human rights violations in the name of national security. The definition of the struggle against terrorism after 9/11 as a state of war, rather than as a legal or policing issue, allowed governments to circumvent the normal obligations under human rights conventions, including prohibitions against torture or collusion in torture, detention without trial and other due process requirements (Wilson 2005; Goold and Lazarus 2007).

These exceptions aside (and others considered in the next section), democratic systems of government have a better record of protecting the civil and political rights of their populations than non-democratic regimes. What of economic, social and cultural rights? Here the record is more mixed. There is little evidence that democracies are better at promoting economic growth than non-democratic systems, growth being seen by many as a necessary condition for raising populations out of poverty. On the other hand, there is evidence that they perform better in promoting human development, as defined by the United Nations Development Programme in a wide range of indicators, including life expectancy, literacy and educational achievement (Przeworski et al. 2000; Halperin et al. 2010). This is presumably because democracies are more responsive to the basic welfare needs of their electorates. And, at a negative level, Amartya Sen has argued that the massive famines that disfigured countries in the nineteenth and twentieth centuries would have been impossible under democratic governments, since they would have been widely publicized at an early stage, and governments would have been held accountable for their alleviation (Sen 1981).

In conclusion, then, democracy and human rights show a clear pattern of convergence at all the three levels considered: conceptual, justificatory and empirical. While the first of these can be seen as a relationship of entailment, and the second as a family likeness or common derivation, the third is one of contingent probability.

Divergence

On the other side of the equation are three ways in which democracy and human rights can be seen to diverge, involving their respective subjects, institutions and academic modes of analysis.

Subjects

The typical subjects of democracy are *citizens*, whereas the subjects of human rights are *human beings*. Citizenship is by definition an exclusivist category, distinguishing those who are members of a given 'polity' or 'demos' from those who do not belong. Even though, as we have seen, democratic principles make universalizing claims about human capacity and agency, in practice democracies are territorially limited and assign rights to their members that outsiders do not enjoy. Governments, in their policies and respective treatment, also give priority to their citizens over foreigners. Human rights conventions, in contrast, make no such distinction, since their subjects are the global-wide category of human beings, who qualify for the rights assigned to them simply by virtue of their membership of the human species.

This distinction is evident in the way democracies treat aliens both at home and abroad. Even where foreign migrants are legally resident in a country, their admission is discretionary and may be subject to conditions of time and permissible activity; their families may be prevented from joining them; they may be restricted in their welfare rights; they are typically not allowed to vote in national elections; if they leave the country they may not have an automatic right to return; and if they break the law they may be subject to deportation. It can be argued that the human rights conventions recognize the category of state membership, and therefore give legitimacy to the differentiation of treatment between citizens and aliens (Medjouba and Stefanelli 2008: 57–70). However, political pressure from domestic populations may create conditions where even legal migrants come to be denied basic human rights.

As regards illegal immigrants and asylum seekers, the situation in most countries is much worse. Illegal immigrants are often subject to gross exploitation, in some cases involving virtual slavery and/or sexual abuse. Governments for their part are less keen at stamping out these violations than they would be if their own citizens were subject to them. Conditions for asylum seekers are often made intolerable in order to discourage further entrants. Denied either welfare or employment, they may be kept in detention centres, and subjected to bureaucratic procedures that make it difficult to prove their former victimization.

However, the distinction between citizens of a democracy and aliens is at its sharpest in the record of democratic citizens abroad, especially in the case of imperial and post-imperial powers. The wars of decolonization in the 1950s and 1960s involved massive human rights abuses by European democracies, of which those involving Algeria and Kenya are only the most notorious. Similar abuses took place in the many wars, proxy wars and insurgencies, which the US was involved in around the globe, either directly or indirectly, in the struggle against communism from the 1960s to 1980s. And the most recent 'wars of choice' in Iraq and Afghanistan have involved huge displacements of population and enormous civilian casualties, not to mention torture, while only the dead of the invading and occupying forces have been properly counted and given serious attention by the public back home. Nowhere is the distinction between the rights of citizens and human rights brought more sharply into focus. And because foreigners in such conflicts do not count for as much as citizens, foreign policy is rarely subject to the same degree of scrutiny, accountability or constraint as democratic governments are subject to in their domestic policy.

Institutions

A second point of divergence between democracy and human rights concerns the distinctive institutions through which they are given expression. Democracy as the 'will of the people' finds expression in the policies of a popularly elected government, in the legislation of a representative assembly and, in some countries, in the direct mandate of a referendum or citizens' initiative. Individual rights, by contrast, whether those of citizens or human rights more widely, are sustained by the protection of the courts and the basic principles of the rule of law: that no one, whether private citizen or public official, is above the law; and that the judiciary should be both institutionally and personally separate and independent of parliament and the executive. It is only through the establishment of this principle that the courts are able to defend the basic rights of a population against possible encroachments or restrictions initiated by a popularly elected government or legislature, or the direct vote of a referendum (Bingham 2010).

It should be said, also, that the rule of law is a central feature of democracy. The legislation of a popularly elected assembly is of little worth if it cannot be enforced throughout the territory, and the courts are an essential agent in this process. Moreover, as we have already seen, the institutions of electoral democracy presuppose at least some basic rights and freedoms. In practice, however, the courts often find themselves at odds with elected governments, and even legislatures, when a popularly endorsed measure infringes individual rights prescribed either in a constitution or an international human rights convention, or indeed both together, to which the state is a signatory. Then a clear tension or division emerges between the institutions of a representative democracy and the courts; between the actions of a popularly elected government and the rule of law; and between the collective will of the people and individual rights.

Examples of this tension are easy to enumerate. Necessary and democratically sanctioned public construction projects may be challenged in the courts in the name of individual property rights or means of livelihood. Measures to protect public security may be challenged as excessive in the name of the right to due legal process or right to privacy. Prohibitions on modes of dress may be challenged in the name of the right to manifest one's religion. And all manner of popularly endorsed discriminations may be challenged on the principle of equality before the law, or the rights of minorities. Such issues form the everyday business before the courts in most democratic jurisdictions, and serve to demonstrate that, however much democracy and human rights may complement one another, in practice they also often diverge. The divergence is given added sharpness when judges are criticized as 'undemocratic', due to the fact that their office is typically an unelected one.

Modes of analysis

Democracy and human rights diverge, finally, in their respective modes of analysis. The study of democracy belongs in the discipline of political science, which is concerned with the struggle to influence and control the exercise of political power, and the often messy processes and compromises through which public office and policy outcomes are arrived at. Its analysis of democracy is necessarily an analysis of *imperfection*: in the processes through which it is developed, in the manner in which it operates, and in the people who practise it.

The study of human rights, on the other hand, has traditionally belonged to the academic study of law, and in particular human rights law. This discipline concerns itself with the increasingly rigorous process of standard-setting of human rights articles by UN and other international agencies, and their adjudication in international committees and regional and national courts. It sets itself the task of assessing the quality of particular jurisdictions and their judgments against the most developed standards available in the international human rights treaties. And even as it recognizes the reality in many places of gross human rights abuses, it always looks to an *ideal of impartial justice* central to the concept of law, rather than at the struggles and compromises involved in power relations. This distinction between the perspectives of power and justice is reflected in many of the real-life tensions evident in the course of democratization (Beetham 1995).

What we find, in conclusion, is a two-sided process of both convergence and divergence between democracy and human rights. There is some ground for saying that, over the last 20 years or so, the divergences have become less pronounced as democracy has become a globally recognized norm enjoying a similar status to human rights, and the two have become inseparably linked in the agendas of international development agencies and programmes. Yet, in practice, the tensions between the two sides of this conjuncture still remain, and have been particularly evident in the processes of democratization that will be discussed in the second half of this chapter.

Human rights and the process of democratization

This second part of the chapter will build on the first by considering aspects of convergence and divergence between democracy and human rights in the *process* of democratization. It will begin with episodes of transition to democracy, defining 'transition' here broadly as including both the struggle against authoritarian rule and the establishment of a new or restored system of democratic government. The final section will consider the relation between democracy and human rights in the process of democratic consolidation.

Human rights in the transition to democracy

The region where issues of human rights first took central place in the struggle against authoritarian regimes and the subsequent transition to democracy was Latin America in the 1970s and 1980s. The military dictatorships of Argentina, Brazil, Chile and elsewhere had been responsible for widespread human rights abuses against political opponents and former activists, involving torture, murder, 'disappearance', arbitrary imprisonment, forced deportation and assassination abroad. The sheer scale of these abuses made agitation for human rights the main focus of public opposition to the military regimes, and one they could not readily dismiss or suppress because it did not directly challenge their positions of power. A number of other factors contributed to making human rights, rather than democratization per se, the main arena of political struggle:

- Human rights provided a unifying element for otherwise disparate social and political groups, and brought in new social actors, of whom women were particularly prominent.
- Human rights constituted an internationally recognized discourse that gave added legitimacy to demands for information about the 'disappeared' and an end to further abuse.

- International human rights organizations played an important role in raising external awareness about the level of human rights violations in Latin America, as well as supporting refugees, many of whom later returned to their countries.

This combination of internal and external exposure of human rights abuses, and public mobilization around them, served over time to delegitimize the military regimes and weaken public support for them. And it was a short step from agitation over violations of personal physical integrity to demand the full range of civil and political rights, including freedom of expression, association and assembly, and a type of government in which these would all be protected in the future. In this way we can see a clear convergence between a human rights agenda and the process of democratization across the region (Garreton 1994).

However, in many countries the actual transition itself produced a sharp tension or divorce between the two. This took the form of a disagreement over whether or not, and how far, military officers should be brought to trial for past human rights abuses. Those who argued that they should not be, pointed to the difficulty of deciding how far down the command chain responsibility should rest, and that trials lasting years would further polarize public opinion, which was already divided over the record of the military regimes. Above all, in those countries – and these were the great majority – where the transition was a result of negotiation between the military and opposition forces, public trials would destabilize the new democratic arrangements, by alienating those whose cooperation or at least acquiescence remained important to their success. The military were still a potentially powerful force, and demands for justice had to be subordinated to the requirement of consolidating fragile democratic processes and institutions.

On the other side, it was argued that the punishment for human rights crimes was necessary not only to secure justice and restitution for the victims and their families, but as a deterrent to prevent such abuses in the future. In particular, if the attraction of a democratic system was that it would ensure respect for civil and political rights in the future, it would convey a deeply ambiguous message if the new democracies started out by overlooking past crimes (Panizza 1995).

In the event, only in Argentina did it prove possible to bring military officers to trial for past human rights abuses, albeit only to a limited extent. Scholars explain this by the fact that Argentina was a rare example in the hemisphere of what O'Donnell calls 'transition by collapse', through the complete discrediting of the regime as a result of defeat in the Falklands/Malvinas war. The other countries were examples of 'transition by transaction' or negotiation, in which the armed forces were able to impose certain conditions for surrendering power, not least that their members would enjoy immunity from prosecution (O'Donnell 1989).

Nevertheless, the demands of the victims and relatives of the dead and disappeared could not be ignored. To compensate for the denial of justice, a number of countries set up so-called 'truth commissions', to establish the precise fate of those who had been tortured, executed or simply 'disappeared'. The first was the Argentine National Commission on Disappeared Persons (CONADEP), whose 1984 report *Never Again* catalogued nearly 9,000 cases of unresolved disappearances. This was followed by a similar though unofficial report by the archdiocese of São Paulo in Brazil in 1985, and an officially appointed Commission for Truth and Reconciliation in Chile, which reported in 1991. An international Commission appointed by the UN was set up in El Salvador in 1992 to report on human rights abuses committed by both sides in the country's protracted civil war. These truth commissions were concerned not only with establishing what had happened, but with making recommendations for preventing its recurrence in the future. They served as a model for resolving the tension between justice and power in the democratization process, which was widely copied, both in Latin America and beyond. In the phrase quoted by Francisco Panizza, they offered a way of 'turning the page without closing the book' (1995: 176).

However, with the passage of time and a much greater confidence in the stability of democracy, some of the amnesties and immunities granted for human rights abuses during the transition process have recently started to unravel, and the page has begun to be 'turned back'. This has coincided with the evolution of human rights law at the international level, culminating in the establishment of the International Criminal Court in 2002 to try war crimes and crimes against humanity. At the same time, there has evolved the concept of 'universal jurisdiction', whereby charges of torture and other crimes against humanity can be brought in any jurisdiction outside where they were committed. Against these most serious charges domestically granted immunities are now held to be invalid (Robertson 1999: 219–24, 300–341).

The first and most notorious case under this new conception involved the arrest of General Augusto Pinochet while on a visit to London in 1998, on an extradition warrant lodged by the Spanish magistrate Baltasar Garzón, concerning the torture and assassination of Spanish citizens under Pinochet's dictatorship (Robertson 1999: 342–373; Sands 2005: 23–45). Although Pinochet was allowed to return to Chile on health grounds, this action and the international interest it aroused led eventually to his domestic immunity being lifted and to his standing trial in 2006 for kidnap, torture and disappearances, from which only his death relieved him. In 2009 Baltasar Garzón turned his attention to the Spanish transition to democracy, and began investigating the fate of more than 100,000 disappearances on the Republican side during and after the Spanish Civil War, in so doing challenging an amnesty law of 1977 that shielded members of the Franco regime from legal prosecution. This led to his subsequent suspension from legal office by a judicial court, which he is currently (2011) challenging at the European Court of Human Rights.

In the light of these and other similar developments, even if future democratic transitions were to require compromise with human rights abusers at the expense of justice, it is far from clear that such arrangements would be recognized internationally; or that they would not eventually begin to unravel domestically once full confidence in the stability of democracy was assured. It may be for this reason that the use of judicial proceedings over human rights abuses became more frequent from the late 1990s onwards.

The concept of 'transitional justice'

The experience of so many transitions since the Latin American ones of the 1980s – in Eastern Europe and the former Soviet Union, in Asia and sub-Saharan Africa – and the many different mechanisms developed for reconciling political imperatives with the demands of justice, has led to the emergence of a whole academic sub-discipline devoted to the study of what is called 'transitional justice'. This embraces not only transitions from a variety of different types of authoritarian regime, but also the establishment of democracy after armed conflict, insurgency and civil war (McAdams 1997).

Transitional justice has been defined as a 'response to systematic or widespread violations of human rights and to promote possibilities for peace, reconciliation and democracy. Transitional justice is not a special form of justice, but justice adapted to societies transforming themselves after a period of human rights abuse' (International Center for Transitional Justice 2010). The concept embraces a variety of different mechanisms, each with its own strengths and limitations, and often used in combination with one another according to the context (Andrieu 2010). These mechanisms include:

- *Judicial trials*, held in normal or special courts, at national or international level, or more recently in local traditional courts (as in Rwanda). They serve a retributive purpose, though often it is only a few 'big fish' who are actually brought to trial, and many lesser perpetrators escape justice.

- *Truth and Reconciliation Commissions*, whose purpose is to arrive at the truth about past crimes and to discover the precise fate of their victims. Often perpetrators are given immunity from prosecution in return for confessions and evidence. They are intended to serve a reconciliatory purpose, but many victims' families are made to relive their suffering and feel denied of justice, even though their 'right to truth' may be satisfied. After the early Latin American examples, the Truth and Reconciliation Commission under Archbishop Desmond Tutu in South Africa became the most famous, and has served as a model for such commissions subsequently elsewhere (Wilson 2001).
- *Vetting procedures*, or 'lustrations' as they are technically known, which prevent those suspected of human rights abuses from taking or retaining positions in sensitive areas of public life. They serve as both a symbolic and a practical means for ensuring abuse-free public services in the future. However, the criteria for such exclusions may not always meet the requirements of impartial justice.
- *Reparations* are intended to compensate victims and their relatives for their past suffering, and to acknowledge the state's own accountability for it, whether directly or indirectly. They aim to put an end to a cycle of 'victimhood', although putting a monetary price on suffering can seem mercenary and incommensurate to the scale of past abuses.
- *Commemorations* of all kinds including museums, memory sites, national days of remembrance, and so on, the purpose of which is to confirm a nation's determination not to allow abuses to return.

Much of the recent research in the literature on transitional justice has been concerned to establish, on the one hand, which of these mechanisms or which combination is most effective, and against what criteria; on the other hand, it is interested in explaining why particular mechanisms have been used or ignored in a given context. In regard to the latter, there is now considerable comparative research on the former communist countries of Eastern Europe and the former Soviet Union, to explain the variations between them in the opening up of former intelligence files and the extent to which vetting procedures were adopted after the transition to democracy. In countries where the former elites were able to retain power, or there was substantial electoral support for the successor communist parties, the opening of secret files was resisted, and vetting procedures were either delayed or proved much less extensive (Stan 2009).

Once again, we can see that the early history of 'transitional justice' in Latin America has been repeated subsequently. Although the experience of human rights abuses has everywhere provided a major impetus in the struggle for democratization, the process of transition itself has often demonstrated a tension between considerations of power and justice. Where substantial compromise has had to be made with former elites in order to secure their cooperation or acquiescence in a new democratic order, then either the investigation or the retribution for past human rights abuses may have been less than thorough. But, by the same token, the quality of the subsequent democracy may itself be compromised where past abuses have not been adequately addressed.

Human rights in the process of democratic consolidation

One familiar version of 'consolidation' holds that a democracy is consolidated when it becomes accepted by all potential contenders for power, that elections for public office constitute 'the only game in town', and an illegal seizure of power becomes unrealistic. On its own, however, this is a very thin conception, even if we limit ourselves to a purely electoral idea of democracy. And it is particularly thin where the electoral process is not underpinned by a guarantee of basic civil and political rights.

To begin with, the very fact that elections are 'the only game' encourages existing power-holders to do whatever they can to manipulate the electoral process, so that they can remain in office and enjoy its benefits. It is to minimize this possibility that robust international standards for 'free and fair elections' have been developed, together with the practice of involving international election observers or monitors to determine how far these standards have been met. Much of the content of these standards requires ensuring that basic civil and political rights are guaranteed to all voters and candidates during the electoral process. As one expert on free and fair elections, Goodwin-Gill, writes, 'the essentially human rights dimension to many political and electoral rights should not be ignored'. He goes on to say:

> Specifically, national and international observers will need to know whether freedom of movement, assembly, association and expression have been respected throughout the election period; whether all parties have conducted their political activities within the law; whether any political party or special interest group has been subjected to arbitrary and unnecessary restrictions in regard to access to the media or generally in regard to their freedom to communicate their views; whether parties, candidates and supporters have enjoyed equal security; whether voters have been able to cast their ballots freely, without fear or intimidation.
>
> *(Goodwin-Gill 1994: 62)*

In the second place, even where elections are declared by observers to be broadly free and fair, these standards relate only to a narrow period of the election process itself, from the registration of voters to the counting of ballots and any subsequent appeals. Yet, in between elections, opposition movements and parties may be subject to harassment, their access to the media be restricted and their meetings banned or disrupted, any of which may compromise their chances in a subsequent election. For this reason we should conclude that even an 'electoral democracy' cannot be considered as consolidated without an ongoing guarantee of the fundamental freedoms of the human rights canon, including the freedoms of expression, association and assembly.

If, then, the guarantee of basic human rights is necessary for the electoral process to result in a fair reflection of the popular will, then we need to examine in turn what is required if these basic rights are to be guaranteed in practice, rather than merely announced in a written constitution or the text of an international treaty. Fundamental here is what has already been referred to as the 'rule of law': that no one, whether private citizen or public official, is above the law; and that the judiciary should be both institutionally and personally separate and independent of parliament and the executive. We should add to these an effective individual right of appeal and redress where basic rights have been infringed or violated (Bingham 2010).

In practice, these necessary features of the rule of law turn out to be much more difficult to establish than a functioning electoral system. Many societies have a long tradition of rulers and their officials considering themselves to be above the law, and their actions as not being constrained by it. Judges may be appointed on the basis of their deference to the government of the day, or for their partisan sympathy or membership, such that any distinction between the institutions of the state and those of the ruling party becomes blurred. As a result, individuals may have little confidence that, in the event of a serious rights violation, appeals will be fairly treated, or they may simply lack the resources to initiate them. Such deviations from the rule of law may particularly hinder the normal activities of opposition parties or political movements, and become especially critical in the context of a closely fought election.

It turns out, then, that even if we understand 'democratic consolidation' to mean that elections for public office are regularly conducted in conditions that are 'free and fair', this criterion requires an extensive range of guaranteed civil and political rights to realize, underpinned by the principles and practices of the rule of law. And these everywhere prove more difficult to achieve than the technicalities of the electoral process itself.

Electoral democracy and minority rights

So far, then, a clear convergence between human rights and the establishment of a stable electoral democracy can be identified, in that a guarantee of basic freedoms is necessary for elections to be 'free and fair', and therefore to be widely accepted as legitimate because they broadly reflect the will of freely organizing citizens. The word 'broadly', however, conceals a relatively common way in which electoral democracy may in practice result in jeopardizing if not infringing significant rights – and that concerns the rights of minorities. Electoral democracy involves the rule of the greater number, and hence privileges majorities over minorities. This can be particularly damaging to minorities that are distinguished from the majority by relatively permanent characteristics such as language, religion, ethnicity or nationhood. Here, the process of democratization can give political leaders an incentive to mobilize an electoral majority and organize political parties along these basic divisions in order to achieve or consolidate political power, as happened in many countries of the former Soviet Union and Yugoslavia and sub-Saharan Africa. In such situations minorities can find themselves permanently excluded from a share in power, and see their basic rights unprotected from majority-endorsed infringement; in effect they become second-class citizens in their own country. These exclusions readily sow the seeds of civil strife, secessionist demands and terrorism, if not outright civil war (Beetham 2009: 291–294).

In this context, it is hardly surprising that the UN and some regional bodies have sought to give special protection to minority rights within the human rights agenda. Before 1990 the only protection for minorities lay in the anti-discrimination provisions of the two International Covenants and the specific Convention on the Elimination of All Forms of Racial Discrimination, where 'race' is defined to include distinctions of 'national or ethnic origin'. There is one article in the 1966 Covenant on Civil and Political Rights devoted to minorities (no. 27), but its wording is hardly resounding: persons belonging to ethnic, religious or linguistic minorities, it states, 'shall not be denied the right to enjoy their own culture, to profess and practise their own religion, or to use their own language' (Brownlie and Goodwin-Gill 2002: 190).

In 1992, however, a UN Declaration on the Rights of Persons Belonging to National or Ethnic, Religious and Linguistic Minorities was passed without a vote by the General Assembly, giving much more explicit and comprehensive protection to minorities. Its provisions include: the protection and promotion of their distinctive identities; the right to learn their mother tongue, to be educated in their own traditions and to express their culture publicly; to maintain their own associations, and to participate effectively in public life and in decisions affecting them and the regions where they live; and to maintain contact with members of their community across state borders. These provisions, if fully implemented by states, would go a long way to remedying the disadvantages suffered by minorities under the rule of a different majority group (Brownlie and Goodwin-Gill 2002: 59–62).

However, this 1992 Declaration, while setting an international standard for minority rights, has never been codified in a binding treaty or convention for individual state ratification. The only region where this has happened has been in Europe, through the Council of Europe sponsored Convention for the Protection of National Minorities, which came into force in 1998 with a full compliance monitoring system. Although the term 'national minority' is not defined in the convention, it is clearly intended to cover minorities defined by language, religion and ethnicity as well as nationhood. The convention offers similar protections to those included in the UN Declaration, on which it is indeed modelled. Both the UN Declaration and the 1998 Convention have proved important practically, in setting standards of conditionality for the admission of applicant states to membership of the European Union. And, given that the vast majority of European states have ratified the 1998 Convention, it constitutes a vital ongoing bulwark for the defence of minority rights across the European political space (Brownlie and Goodwin-Gill 2002: 518–525).

For all the robustness of this more recent standard-setting for minority rights, it must be doubted whether or not a human rights approach can be effective *on its own* in resolving the disadvantages suffered by minorities within an electoral democracy. This is because many of the divisions are so deep-rooted and require a political rather than a legal process to resolve. What is most needed is an inclusive political dialogue around the creation or modification of constitutional arrangements in a way that guarantees minorities a share in power, from which they would otherwise be permanently excluded. Possible solutions will vary according to the circumstances and the nature of the minority or minorities, but can include: autonomy for self-governing regions where the minorities are territorially concentrated; electoral rules that prevent single-party majorities, and facilitate changing governing coalitions; special representation for minorities; second chambers constructed on pluralist lines; veto rights where matters specifically affecting a given minority are at issue; formal power-sharing executives; and other devices with similar effect. None of these solutions may be perfect, but all are preferable to the threat of secession, civil war or forcible suppression by the central state.

Conclusion

Despite the fact that, in general, human rights and democracy support one another, we have seen a number of points in the process of democratization where they in practice diverge: in the centrality of the appeal to internationally endorsed human rights rather than democracy in undermining the legitimacy of an authoritarian regime; conversely, the priority often given to establishing consensus around new democratic institutions over judicial proceedings against past human rights abusers; in the relative ease and strong international support with which a functioning electoral process comes to be established, in contrast to the basic elements of the rule of law on which the protection of human rights depends; and, finally, in the way in which a majoritarian electoral democracy may be neglectful or even oppressive in respect of disadvantaged minorities.

Most of these divergences could be seen to be matters of temporal rather than intrinsic priority – to do with democratization as *process* – which can be diminished over time. The last is a question of how democracy itself is to be configured: whether as a primarily electoral process for securing a government that enjoys majority support; or as a system that ensures effective equality of citizenship to all, and an equal chance to influence the decisions on which one's well-being depends. While even the first, thinner, account of democracy requires a guarantee of basic freedoms, as we have seen, the latter requires a fuller incorporation of human rights in what might be termed a 'rights-based democracy'. Here is how the legal philosopher Ronald Dworkin puts it:

> True democracy is not just *statistical* democracy, in which anything a majority or plurality wants is legitimate for that reason, but *communal* democracy, in which majority decision is legitimate only if it is a majority within a community of equals. That means not only that everyone must be allowed to participate in politics as an equal, through the vote and through freedom of speech and protest, but that political decisions must treat everyone with equal concern and respect, that each individual person must be guaranteed fundamental civil and political rights no combination of other citizens can take away, no matter how numerous

they are or how much they despise his or her race or morals or way of life. That view of what democracy means is at the heart of all the charters of human rights.

(Dworkin 1990: 35–36)

If this more comprehensive and inclusive conception of democracy remains something of an ideal, nonetheless it is one towards which actually existing democracies can meaningfully strive. Moreover, the fact that many long-established democracies fall short of it suggests that the process of democratization is never fully complete, or even irreversible, but that it is always a work in progress.

References

Andrieu, K. (2010) 'Transitional Justice: A New Discipline in Human Rights', *Online Encyclopaedia of Mass Violence*; available at http://www.massviolence.org (accessed 20 September 2010).

Beetham, D. (1995) 'Human Rights in the Study of Politics'. In *Politics and Human Rights*, ed. D. Beetham. Oxford: Blackwell, pp. 1–9.

—— (1999) *Democracy and Human Rights*. Cambridge: Polity Press.

—— (2009) 'Democracy: Universality and Diversity', *Ethics and Global Politics*, 2 (4), pp. 281–296.

—— (2011) 'Universality, Historical Specificity and Cultural Difference in Human Rights. In *Strategic Visions for Human Rights*, ed. G. Gilbert, F. Hampson and C. Sandoral. London and New York: Routledge.

Bentham, J. (1843) *Works*. vol. 9. Edinburgh: William Tait.

Bingham, T. (2010) *The Rule of Law*. London: Allen Lane.

Brownlie, I. and G. S. Goodwin-Gill, eds (2002) *Basic Documents in Human Rights*. 4th ed. Oxford: Oxford University Press.

Carey, S. C. (2010) 'The Use of Repression as a Response to Domestic Dissent', *Political Studies*, 58 (1), pp. 167–186.

Dworkin, R. (1990) *A Bill of Rights for Britain*. London: Chatto and Windus.

Garreton, M. A. (1994) 'Human Rights in Processes of Democratization', *Journal of Latin American Studies*, 26, pp. 221–234.

Goodwin-Gill, G. S. (1994) *Free and Fair Elections: International Law and Practice*. Geneva: Inter-Parliamentary Union.

Goold, B. J. and L. Lazarus, eds (2007) *Security and Human Rights*. Oxford and Portland OR: Hart Publishing.

Halperin, M. H, J. T. Siegle and M. M. Weinstein (2010) *The Democratic Advantage: How Democracies Promote Prosperity and Peace*. 2nd ed. New York: Routledge.

International Center for Transitional Justice (2010) *What is Transitional Justice?*; available at http://ictj.org/en/tj/.

Landman, T. (2005) *Protecting Human Rights: A Comparative Study*. Washington DC: Georgetown University Press.

McAdams, A. J. (1997) *Transitional Justice and the Rule of Law in New Democracies*. Notre Dame: Notre Dame University Press.

Medjouba, F. and J. N. Stefanelli (2008) *The Rights and Responsibilities of Citizenship*. London: The British Institute of International and Criminal Law.

O'Donnell, G. (1989) 'Transitions to Democracy: Some Navigation Instruments'. In *Democracy in the Americas: Stopping the Pendulum*, ed. R. A. Pastor. New York and London: Holmes and Maier, pp. 62–75.

Panizza, F. (1995) 'Human Rights in the Process of Transition and Consolidation of Democracy in Latin America'. In Beetham (1995), pp. 168–188.

Przeworski, A., M. E. Alvarez, J. A. Cheibub and F. Limongi (2000) *Democracy and Development: Political Institutions and Well-being in the World 1950–1990*. Cambridge and New York: Cambridge University Press.

Regan, P. M. and E. A. Henderson (2002) 'Democracy, Threats and Political Repression in Developing Countries: Are Democracies Internally Less Violent?', *Third World Quarterly*, 23 (1), pp. 119–136.

Robertson, G. (1999) *Crimes against Humanity*. London: Allen Lane.

Sands, P. (2005) *Lawless World*. London: Allen Lane.

Sen, A. (1981) *Poverty and Famines: An Essay in Entitlement and Deprivation*. Oxford: Clarendon Press.

—— (1999) *Development as Freedom*. Oxford: Oxford University Press.

Stan, L., ed. (2009) *Transitional justice in Eastern Europe and the Former Soviet Union: Reckoning with the Communist past*. London: Routledge.

Wilson, R. A. (2001) *The Politics of Truth and Reconciliation in South Africa: Legitimising the Post-Apartheid State*. Cambridge: Cambridge University Press.

—— , ed. (2005) *Human Rights in the 'War on Terror'*. Cambridge: Cambridge University Press.

26

Democratization and gender

Wendy Stokes

The term – and practice – of democratization is most often applied to less developed or post-socialist countries, and is often strategic and coloured by ideology. It may mean no more than the creation of electoral and party systems and the conduct of (relatively) free elections. However, if democratization means the creation of a democracy, a lot more than free and fair election processes is needed, and a lot more time has to be spent on the question that lies at the heart of politics: who gets what and how?

When applied to women, the answer very often is: not much and only after a struggle. Women have been excluded from public life for much of history. Their concerns have been designated private or personal and therefore not political. Yet without women taking responsibility for care and reproduction, along with subsistence farming and low-paid work, neither politics nor the economy could carry on. Until recently, women have been invisible in democratization, yet the gendering of social relations means that democratizing processes are not gender neutral. Rather, if democratization does not explicitly consider women, then it disadvantages them. Women comprise a minority of politicians and chief executive officers (CEOs), but a majority of the poor and low-paid. Therefore, it is necessary to make women visible and to press for their rights through a range of democratizing institutions: voting rights, political representation, public policy and welfare.

When we associate democratization with less developed and post-socialist countries, we imply that more developed, or Western countries, are democracies and have no further need of democratization. In doing so, we dissociate from the term democracy the gross inequalities and injustices in the West, and dismiss the considerable literature that is critical of Western models. Depending on how democracy is defined, we could argue that it has barely been achieved anywhere in the world. In places where democratic mechanisms are recent introductions, it is apparent that the creation of elections by internal elites or foreign powers has had very mixed results – and a tendency to turn into benevolent one-party domination. Meanwhile, in long-standing democracies analysts and commentators talk about elected dictatorships, where power is concentrated in the hands of a small group of politicians between elections, and are aware that the persistence of elites, inequalities, and voter apathy qualifies the claim of these countries to be self-governing.

The state is not neutral; it actively engineers social roles, relationships and the distribution of social goods through laws and policies. Therefore, this chapter is not going to look at the processes of democratization per se, rather it seeks to measure how democratization is working out for women. In doing so, it takes two approaches. The first, and perhaps the more in keeping with an interpretation of democracy as governance, is to look at women's political participation; the second adopts a more critical view of democratic outcomes and considers broader socio-economic measures of citizen equality.

In order to do this, the chapter first introduces a critical perspective on democratization, using different conceptions of democracy. In particular, the radical and feminist critiques that assert a fully functioning democracy should extend beyond the realm of formal politics and into economic and private spheres. This grows out of the notion that equal citizenship depends on the absence of gross inequalities of socio-economic power. Women's representation in elected assemblies is referred to increasingly as a measure of both democratization and gender equity; therefore, the second section looks at women's participation in formal politics (voting and holding elected office). However, counting women in this way presents a very narrow and possibly deceptive picture, so the discussion extends to a consideration of what women *do* in office. Taking the view that democratic equality demands more than representation in peak organizations, the third section examines measures of sexual equality, including education, income and occupation, as well as political representation, in a range of countries, using data from Gender Gap surveys. This data illuminates the intimate connection between socio-economic inequalities and political inequalities. These gender gaps around the world are not accidental; they may originate in historical practices, but they are perpetuated through poorly designed public policy. Women's budget initiatives, which have sprung up in some 60 countries, examine national budgets for gender balance and use their findings to raise awareness of policies and their outcomes. In view of this, the final section discusses women's budget groups and initiatives, looking in particular at the United Kingdom Women's Budget Group's analysis of the 2010 Budget and its challenge to the government.

Democracy and democratization

The view that democracy is a device for delivering responsible, responsive, accountable and legitimate government, popularized by writers such as Schumpeter (1966), remains potent in the twenty-first century, but trust in governments is now often in short supply. Equality is central to democracy; while Rousseau's model of popular sovereignty has little place in a modern, mass society, his claim for the damaging effects of inequality among citizens holds true. Equal political and civil rights are fundamental to democracy, but are not enough. Without wider and deeper social and economic equality there is radically unequal *access* to those fundamental rights, and thus unequal citizenship. Equality – particularly that between men and women – often gets confused with sameness. The problem of clarifying the distinction has therefore exercised feminist writers. It is not differences between individuals per se that are the issue but, rather, differences that define a group. And even then, not all differences are important, but only those that map on to disadvantage. So, the biological fact that women can give birth and men cannot would not matter if it were not that this biological capacity maps on to a range of exclusions and subordinations that have persisted through history – thus becoming inequality rather than just difference. Hence the claims not only that complex equality – comprising both legal and substantive elements – must extend to women, but also that the quality of a democracy might be assessed from the quality of women's lives.

Assessing whether a community is democratic or not might be quite a simple business: answering 'yes' to the questions of whether it has regular elections, and whether there are political parties and an elected government free to govern, is often regarded as an adequate rule of thumb. From this perspective, democratization is fulfilled once a community has political parties; free, fair and regular elections; and effective government. While such an achievement is no bad thing, including women as full and equal citizens forces us to challenge the adequacy of the measure from both practical and theoretical perspectives.

Enabling democratization and deepening democracy entails adding respect for human rights to the equation; introducing human rights adds layers of complexity by making explicit the connection between civil and social rights. It also explicitly adds women. The passing of the United Nations Convention on the Elimination of All Forms of Discrimination Against Women (CEDAW) in 1979 defined women's rights as human rights. A general claim of equality between men and women had been made in the Universal Declaration of Human Rights (1948) but this was now augmented by CEDAW which outlawed: '[a]ny distinction, exclusion or restriction made on the basis of sex which has the effect or purpose of impairing or nullifying the recognition, enjoyment or exercise by women, irrespective of their marital status, on a basis of equality of men and women, of human rights and fundamental freedoms in the political, economic, social, cultural, civil or any other field.' Thus, any assessment of successful democratization must include respect for women's – human – rights.

Assessing democratic practice is not, therefore, a straightforward matter. And it gets even more difficult. Underlying an assessment of the achievement of democracy there has to be an understanding of what democracy is. Analysis of the concept 'democracy' has been popular sport among political theorists. The instrumental definitions of writers such as Joseph Schumpeter (1966) and Robert Dahl (1971) remain influential despite the challenges posed by participatory, deliberative and radical alternatives. A very new addition to the debate is what John Keane (2009) is calling 'monitory democracy': a concept that draws on several existing approaches in order to argue that, in addition to the mechanisms of political representation and popular organization, modern democracy requires an active culture of 'monitory' – watchdog – institutions to protect it from corruption, by constantly monitoring the state and calling its institutions to account. This fits very well with feminist concerns that the impact of policies and institutions must be monitored for outcomes that turn out to be different for men and women.

Feminist interventions range from rejection of democracy as a concept that has been built on the subordination of women, to reconstructions of alternatives that can accommodate both women and men. Influential among these is Anne Phillips's 1991 text *Engendering Democracy*. She describes sexual inequality as:

> something built into the very foundations of both classical and contemporary thought … the tasks of reconstruction are more major than most (male) theorists had hoped. Politics has to be reconceptualised without the blind spots of gender, and democracy rethought with both sexes written in. Old concepts must be fashioned anew.
>
> *(Phillips 1991: 3)*

Phillips draws attention to the polarity of 'universal values and sexually differentiated experience' and demands a reconfiguration of political concepts and practices. Just as Phillips points to the shortcomings of democratic theory, Georgina Waylen (2007: 15) underlines the gendered weakness of democratization scholarship when she writes: 'Despite the long-standing critiques of feminist scholars, the mainstream democratization literature has remained largely gender-blind.'

It is often argued that a true democracy only exists when all citizens are equally able to access and exercise their civil rights. Societies have generated many ways to structure power: class and race have proved very effective, but, arguably, none has been as effective or ubiquitous as sex/gender. Often compared with class and race, the power structures of sex and gender are proving more tenacious; while we have found convincing ways to argue that societies have constructed class and race, we can't quite escape the feeling that sex/gender is a 'natural' distinction and, therefore, that whatever grows from it must itself be natural. This may be a fair argument when thinking about giving birth, but is a little strained when applied to an ability to operate a vacuum cleaner, decide on a level of taxation, or own the land you work on. There are, of course, two sides to this: women's disadvantage in the public world, and that of men in the 'private'. While not dismissing the plight of men who want to play a greater role in parenting, or to be nursery teachers, cleaners or care assistants, the weight of comparative disadvantage rests on women, and they are the focus in this chapter.

Women and political participation: enfranchisement and voting

Since Saudi Arabia gave women the vote in 2011, women around the world, with the exception of parts of the Middle East and Brunei in Southeast Asia, have access to the vote on pretty much the same legal terms as men. Almost without exception, women around the world were enfranchised later than men. Most industrialized countries had extended the vote to women by the end of the 1920s, although the first country to do so was New Zealand in 1893, followed by Australia in 1902, and Norway in 1913. At the other end of the spectrum, France only allowed women the vote in 1946, and Liechtenstein in 1984.

Away from the more economically developed regions, some colonized countries in Africa gave women the vote at the same time as the colonizing nation did. Thus, francophone Cameroon, Niger, Senegal, Seychelles and Togo extended the franchise to women in the 1940s, when it was happening in France. Other African countries gave women the vote at the time of independence. As a result, women in some 40 African states were enfranchised between 1952 and 1989. Across Asia, gaining access to the vote spanned some 50 years, with women in Mongolia getting the vote in 1924, while those in Bangladesh waited until 1972. Arab countries have been slow to include women. Women in Djibouti were enfranchised in 1946, Oman in 2003, Kuwait in 2005, while access to the vote for women in UAE is somewhat qualified.

Having gained the vote, women started to use it. By the end of the twentieth century, women in more economically developed countries were voting in pretty much the same proportions as men – and catching up in other parts of the world (Norris 2002). Women and men from the same socio-economic group do not, however, always vote for the same parties. Data suggests that in some circumstances gendered differences in values over such issues as the welfare state, defence and the environment may shape the votes of women and men differently (Conover 1994; Inglehart and Norris 2003).

So, when looking at the most basic measures of democratic citizenship – having a vote and going to the polls – we find that differences between men and women are diminishing, although what they do with their votes may differ.

Women and political participation: elections and office

Since the 1980s there has been considerable pressure internationally to increase the numbers of women elected to office locally, nationally and to international governmental organizations such as the European Union Parliament. This arose in parallel with the movement of politically active women from pressure groups to political parties, along with an awakening in those parties to the need to seek out new constituencies. The election of women, and discussion of the relevance of their numbers, has become a preoccupation with feminist researchers. However, there is an emerging awareness that measuring women's political participation only by the number of women in parliament is unlikely to produce a true or full understanding of their political influence – let alone the democratization of the wider community. Nevertheless, the number of female legislators does tell us about changes in political practices and provides a starting point from which to consider the gendering of democracy.

The proportions of women elected to parliaments around the world vary hugely. Ranging from 56.3 per cent in Rwanda and 42.1 per cent in the Nordic countries, to 11.1 per cent in Arab states and zero in nine countries including Belize, Oman, Micronesia, Qatar and the Solomon Islands; the international average is 19.2 per cent. There is no universally consistent pattern reflecting economic development, women's access to education or the development of a welfare state. The strongest predictors are the electoral system and the existence of an electoral quota of some sort. Generally speaking, all systems of proportional representation (PR) facilitate the election of more women than single-member majoritarianism (first past the post). The explanation of this has been extensively pursued and summarized by, for example, Darcy *et al.* (1994); Lovenduski and Norris (1993); and Goetz (2003). Despite the greater friendliness of PR towards the election of women and members of minority groups, this alone has not delivered a sea change in the membership of elected assemblies. Therefore quotas have been introduced in a large number of countries as a measure to correct what was understood as a democratic deficit.

A quota can be voluntary or compulsory. They are instituted for women more often than for any other group in society, and can be found in some 70 countries. However, there are also quotas for religious, ethnic or other groups – notably in India – where there are a number of different quotas in the parliament. Quotas are never uncontroversial, but they appear to be more acceptable in social democracies (such as the Nordic countries) and in less developed countries than in liberal democracies (such as the UK, USA and Australia). Heated debates both for and against have taken place in academic literature, political parties and the media, which can be found in the work of Drude Dahlerup (1998) and others. What is clear is that where there are quotas there are more women, and those women cannot easily be dismissed universally as unqualified tokens. Although the legitimacy of women elected using a quota is questioned in India and Pakistan, where systems of reserved seats in legislatures are used, systems that focus on selecting women as candidates, rather than electing them to reserved seats, cause less disquiet (Goetz 2003).

Female representatives once elected do not make it into government in large numbers: in 2008 women held only 16 per cent of ministerial portfolios around the world (Ballington 2008: 15). It is in the Nordic countries that the largest numbers of women can be found routinely in charge of departments. In 2008, Finland, Grenada and Norway had women in at least half of all ministerial posts (and, since then, we can add Iceland, Switzerland and Spain); in 22 countries in Europe and the Americas women held 30 per cent or more of the ministerial posts. At the other end of the scale, 8 countries had less than 5 per cent women ministers, and in 13 countries there were no women in cabinet positions (Ballington 2008: 15).

When we come to the highest political office, there have not been many female heads of government: in 2008 only 8 of the world's 192 governments (4.2 per cent) were led by women (Ballington 2008: 15). In October 2010, there were 12 counties with women as political leaders (Argentina, Australia, Bangladesh, Costa Rica, Croatia, Finland, Germany, Iceland, Liberia, Lithuania, Trinidad and Tobago, and Slovakia) and 13 when Brazil elected Dilma Roussef in January 2011. The first country to elect a female head of government was Sri Lanka, where Srimavo Badaranaike was in office from 1960–5; the most recent were Slovakia's election of Iveta Radicova in July 2010 and the 2011 election of Roussef in Brazil.

This represents considerable change in the demography of parliaments, and progress for women with political ambitions, but it does not necessarily amount to democratization in favour of women. Simply having women in parliament – especially if those women are from the same socio-economic elites as their male colleagues – does not of itself advance democratic change in the wider society. An examination of what female parliamentarians do in office may help with this.

What do female parliamentarians do?

There has always been ambivalence about female officeholders, deriving, no doubt, from broader assumptions about gender. On the one hand, women in office are expected to represent their constituencies and parties just as their male colleagues do; while on the other there is an expectation that, as women, they will behave differently. For critics, 'differently' might mean less effectively; for others, it might mean adopting different policies from men, or working in a different way. Whatever focus is trained on them, it is rare for the position or policy of a female legislator to be analysed without her sex entering into the discussion. In some countries, women in office continue to be regarded with unease, as illustrated by the negative media coverage of 'Blair's Babes', 'Cameron's Cuties', and the election of the first female Australian prime minister. Other countries, such as Brazil, Iceland, Liberia and Rwanda are electing women in the expectation that they will spearhead change.

There is an underlying assumption in discussions of female politicians that getting more of them elected matters because they are going to behave differently from men – hence a fair bit of rather inconclusive research into what women *do* in parliaments. As the presence of women in elected office in significant numbers is still new, and not that common, there is not a large amount of material for analysis. The idea of 'critical mass' – that a group will be able to exert influence once it reaches a certain proportion of the organization, usually around 30 per cent – has been cited with respect to women more than it has been researched, and has been much criticized of late (Childs 2004; Waylen 2007).

Concern with the political interests of female politicians tends to take two overlapping paths. First, do the women have a different perspective (and thus support different policy directions) from their male colleagues? Second, do they have a special commitment to what might be termed 'women's interests'?

Party loyalty and voting discipline within parliamentary parties make it very difficult to discern gendered patterns. However, research from the US, where party discipline is comparatively lax, suggests that US congresswomen tend to be slightly more liberal than their male colleagues in their voting patterns (Burrell 1994: 154–159; Norris and Lovenduski 1995: 211; Thomas and Wilcox 1998). There is also some evidence of different behaviour in the UK (Childs 2001, 2002) and in the Nordic countries (Wangnerud 2000; Skjeie 2003). Moreover, research in South America and Norway has found women taking the unusual step of cooperating in parliaments across parties in support of particular policies (Skjeie 2003; Waylen 2008).

It is easier to identify the promotion of policies focused on specifically women's interests. Not only do female parliamentarians in a number of countries agree that they have a particular commitment to representing women in their constituencies (Skjeie 1991; Thomas 1998: 70–78; Waring et al. 2000: 133; Childs 2001: 187; Sawer 2002: 8) but their advocacy of specific policies can be demonstrated. For example, in Australia Marion Sawer (2002: 9) found that female senators were five times more likely to raise issues of domestic violence than men; Sarah Childs describes how, in the UK, female parliamentarians presented bills attempting to prohibit female circumcision and abolish taxation on sanitary products (Childs 2001).

The Nordic countries are generally recognized as having family, employment and welfare legislation that enhances sexual-equality. However, taking policymaking into other aspects of what might be women's interests, since 2006 all public limited companies in the private sector in Norway have been legally obliged to follow the example of state-owned companies (2004) and the cabinet, and have a minimum of 40 per cent representation of both men and women. Similar legislation was proposed in Sweden in 2006 but did not go ahead owing to a change in government (there is, however, ongoing debate about its introduction). Icelandic legislation in

2008 followed the Norwegian example of 40 per cent on all public committees, boards and councils, and, according to the records of the Council of Europe, is likely to extend this to the private sector in the present parliament (Council of Europe 2010). Moving to a different aspect of gender relations, in 1999 Sweden decriminalized prostitution, while making the purchase of sexual services an offence. This novel approach was also adopted by Norway and Iceland in 2009. In Iceland, where there was a new female prime minister, Jóhanna Sigurðardóttir, this was followed by legislation abolishing other aspects of the sex-industry, such as lap-dancing clubs. The politician behind the bill, Kolbrún Halldórsdóttir, argued: 'It is not acceptable that women or people in general are a product to be sold' (Clark-Flory 2010).

Much of the research into female politicians' difference from men relies on their claims and goals rather than on policy or voting analysis. The Inter-Parliamentary Union (IPU) undertakes large surveys of parliamentarians. The IPU found in 2008 found that:

> The views of politicians in this research show that women have concerns that are different to men's. These concerns stem from a range of experiences shared by women and which they tend to prioritize: 'It's the women in politics who put women's rights and violence against women and children on the political agenda' and 'women are normally more focused on women, family and social welfare issues and men more focused on the economy and the sciences'. […] The concerns identified in this research as being those that women tend to prioritize include:
>
> - Social issues: childcare, equal pay, parental leave and pensions
> - Physical concerns: reproductive rights, physical safety and gender-based violence
> - Development: human development, poverty alleviation and service delivery.
>
> *(Ballington 2008: 33)*

So, to conclude this discussion of women's political participation: at the base-line level of participation – voting – women are equalling men in numbers, while showing some small propensity towards different values that are on occasion expressed through the ballot box. As elected representatives, women lag far behind men in most countries, tending only to catch up where and when electoral and quota systems counteract political culture. Women make up a small proportion of cabinet members around the world, and an even smaller proportion of political leaders. As legislators, there is some evidence that they may, when the conditions are right, support different policies from their male colleagues and may adopt a different political style, but the numbers are too small and the history too short to make strong claims.

Thus we can see that the peak institutions of democracy – parties, parliaments and governments – are democratizing their inclusion of women (although this is highly variable) and female politicians are influencing policy, particularly with regard to what are considered to be women's issues. The next area of concern is democratization in a wider sense: is public policy achieving greater equality between women and men in democratic societies? Examination of policies and their impact on women is a huge project, so the following discussion uses equality of wealth as a proxy for the equalizing impact of public policy. Picking up on the theme introduced earlier – that political equality depends on, and is inseparable from, a reasonable level of socio-economic equality – this discussion leads on to an assessment of how well women have been served by processes of democratization thus far.

Democratization and socio-economic equality

Active citizenship is not just voting or holding office, as described above, it is fully engaging in the society – economically, socially and politically. The term 'empowerment' has been used a lot in recent years with reference to both women and minorities but it is important to remember that money (and the status and power that it brings with it) matters. Economic independence (or at least access to the means of economic independence) is vital to other forms of independence and thus to equal citizenship. If we look at the high end of the economy, only 3 per cent of the companies in the US Fortune 500 have females CEOs (Globewomen 2010). According to a report from Corporate Women Directors International, analysing the Fortune Global 200 in 2009, although the percentage of seats on the board of the 200 largest companies around the world held by women increased to 12.2 per cent in 2009, 45 of them still did not have a single woman on their board of directors, and only 58 of them had 2 women board members (Globewomen 2010). Such claims as 'women own only 1% of the world's wealth, have only a 10% share of global income, and occupy only 14% of leadership positions in the public and private sector' are common (World Trade Organization 2009). The data is complicated, but the truth is not so far removed: hence the term 'the feminization of poverty'.

The phrase 'feminization of poverty' is often used, but the reality is complex. To summarize: there are a lot of poor people and there are more poor women than men, but part of this is simply demographics, i.e. there are more women in some poor groups – notably the very elderly – than there are men. However, there are occasions of women becoming poorer than similarly situated men. In more economically developed countries this tends to occur where social cohesion is weak, employment structures disadvantage women, and there is no comprehensive welfare state (Mclanahan and Kelly 2006); whereas in less developed countries it tends to be connected to tradition. Traditional land rights, in particular, reinforce power and economic inequalities. For example, Kenyan women have the right to use land, but usually do not have the right to transfer (by sale or any other means) the land. While transfer rights are legally protected, use rights are not, so women's access to land is vulnerable (Adhiambo-Oduol 2001: 6). It is not surprising that since women do the vast majority of agricultural labour, but only own around 1 per cent of the land, their ability to borrow money to finance a business is limited by lack of capital. The concentration of income and wealth in the hands of men around the world is not just a historical, social or economic fact: it is evidence of political failure.

There are many different ways of measuring income and wealth in order to make comparisons. Different pictures emerge from looking at average or median weekly, monthly or annual incomes, and whether or not bonuses, overtime and benefits are included. Recently, the creation of a Gender Index has become a popular way of collating and analysing differences. Indices include the African Gender and Development Index introduced by the United Nations Economic Commission for Africa in 2004; the Global Gender Gap Index, devised by the World Economic Forum in 2006; and the Social Institutions and Gender Index (SIGI) produced by the Organization for Economic Cooperation and Development (OECD) in 2009, which introduces a range of social indicators including age at marriage, domestic violence, freedom of movement and access to land and credit.

The Global Gender Gap Index is a tool for capturing the size and scope of differences between men and women, and keeping an account of how these change and develop. The Index tracks the gender gaps in the economy, politics, education and health within nations, producing country rankings that facilitate meaningful comparisons across regions and income groups, and over time (Hausmann *et al.* 2008: 3). The 2008 *Global Gender Gap Report* describes how the Index is applied to four broad areas of life: political empowerment, economic participation, educational attainment, and health and survival, and summarizes the results. In the report, male status is taken as the base and expressed as 1.0, and the status of women is expressed as a fraction of male status. Thus the index does not comment on absolute conditions, only on the relation between women and men. Universally, while women are not much worse off than men in education, and health and survival, they are significantly worse off in political empowerment, at just over 0.1 of the male score, and economic participation, at 0.6 of men's achievement (Hausmann *et al.* 2008: 26).

In 2008, the overall gender gap was greatest in the Middle East and North Africa, where women's overall score was just 0.6 that of men; and least in Oceania, where women's score was more than 0.8 that of men. For example, in Chad women's score was 0.53 of the male, whereas in New Zealand it was 0.79 (Hausmann *et al.* 2008: 28). While these differences matter everywhere, they are probably most damaging in countries where the majority of the population is poor, since the largest part of the difference is made up of the economic participation and political empowerment factors.

The picture that emerges is illuminating, surprising and disappointing. The research that underlies *The Global Gender Gap Report* demonstrates that despite levels of enrolment in tertiary education that frequently matchor even exceed those of men, and similar levels of professional or technical occupation, women's wages remain noticeably lower than those of men, both on average and in similar jobs, everywhere. At the same time, women's achievements in education and the professions are rarely reflected in their access to elected office. While there are absolute differences between countries, the patterns are similar in both less and more developed countries.

For example, in Bangladesh there are more women than men in tertiary education and among professional and technical workers; the literacy rate for women is nearly 80 per cent that of men, yet women earn only an estimated 34 per cent of the male wage. It may be relevant that only 8 per cent of members of parliament and 11 per cent of ministers are women (Hausmann *et al.* 2008: 47). Similarly, in Australia there are more women than men in tertiary education and among professional and technical workers, male and female literacy rates are the same, and yet women's wages are only 70 per cent of the male wage, while just over one-third of members of parliament and ministers are women (ibid.: 43).

These data seem to confirm what Anne-Marie Goetz found in 2003, that while a high level of education correlates strongly with political success for men, the same is not true for women: 'even when women's educational levels approach parity with those of men, formal political institutions remain relatively closed to women. Simply put: women's participation in formal politics does not appear to increase in step with advances in their educational status in comparison with men' (2003: 6). Similarly, the conclusions of *The Gender Gap Report* suggest that women's achievements in education, the professions and even politics are not reflected in economic rewards. Goetz argues that although women are matching men in key areas, they lack the means to translate this into political power. She cites Anne Phillips's explanation of what 'everyone knows to be the case: that the extent to which individuals become involved in politics and thereby gain access to decision-making channels is directly correlated with the resources they have at their command; that all else being equal, those who have everything else get political power as well' (Phillips 1991: 79). Hence the importance of the social variables introduced by the OECD to its Index (SIGI); in order fully to understand the distribution of power at the highest levels, we need to see how it is established at the underlying levels of family and society. Economic policy is only an approximate way to get at this, but the distribution of money and access to collective goods matter, so we need to see whether or not government policies aimed at maximizing the common good are affecting men and women differently. Women's budget initiatives present an opportunity to consider this.

Women's budget initiatives and groups

If a just and democratic state is one that treats its citizens equally – not the same, but equally, taking account of difference – then the accumulation and distribution of state funds should have equal impact. Since 1984, when Australia first put the implementation of women's budgets into practice, it has become increasingly common around the world. Although some women's budget initiatives are run from within government, typically a women's budget group is an independent, voluntary organization bringing together people from academia, non-governmental organizations (NGOs) and trades unions; its purpose is to assess the impact of a national budget on women and children. Thus, a women's budget is not a budget in its own right but a critical commentary, from the perspective of women, on a country's budget. A seemingly unobjectionable project, women's budgets have in fact proved controversial and, on occasion, radical.

Following the Australian example, there have been gender budget groups and initiatives in more than 60 countries around the world (United Nations Platform for Action 2010). The Australian initiative – like those in the Philippines and Rwanda – was directed from within government. The Offices on the Status of Women at the various administrative levels were, for 12 years, charged with the responsibility of examining the budgets of federal, state and territorial governments, until a change of government discontinued it in 1996. South Africa's Women's Budget Initiative (WBI) was started by the post-apartheid government in 1995 and involved NGOs, parliamentarians and a wide range of researchers and advisers. Piloted in 1996, the WBI covered housing, education, welfare and work – and the crosscutting themes of public sector employment and taxation, which affect all sectors (Budlender 1996: 16). The NGO-led initiatives in Tanzania (1997) and Uganda (1999) examined the impacts of structural adjustment programmes in these countries and specifically focussed on education and health. Within Europe, there are women's budget groups in Austria, Belgium, France, Germany, Ireland, Italy, Norway, Russia, Spain, Switzerland and the United Kingdom.

Government backing gives force to the findings of a women's budget, but it is argued that a top-down approach is less effective than one driven by NGOs (Budlender and Hewitt 2003). According to Warren Krafchik (2001: 70), 'the involvement of civil society organizations in the analysis of budgets has grown in tandem with the trend towards democratization ... they share an agenda that acknowledges the value of an inclusive budget process' (ibid.). The value of the initiatives is confirmed by the United Nations Development Fund for Women (UNIFEM), which has been supporting women's budget projects in 20 countries since 2001 (Sharp 2003).

Many of the early gender budget initiatives were focused primarily on the gendered effects of government expenditure. Recently, however, they have been looking more closely at the sources of revenue as well (taxes), and emphasizing the practice of performance-oriented budgeting: 'performance oriented budgeting in principle demands that budgetary intentions for the next financial year ... be assessed against what actually occurred' (ibid.: 71). Thus, not only do the groups look at the budget plans and analyse how the policies will play out; they also compare budget pledges with what actually happens.

The United Kingdom Women's Budget Group

With regard to projecting and analysing the impact of a Budget, we can look at the example of the UK, where a Women's Budget Group (WBG), formed by individuals from a range of sectors, including academia, has been active since the early 1990s (Fawcett Society 2010; Women's Budget Group 2010). In June 2010, according to the Fawcett Society:

> [t]he Women's Budget Group has produced a preliminary analysis of how the Coalition Government's Emergency Budget will impact on the individual incomes of women and men and shows that while the budget has a few individual measures that help to offset gender inequality, taken as a whole the budget is unfair in its impact on women as compared to men. The analysis reveals that the Budget seems more supportive of an out-dated "male bread-winner, dependent female carer" model of relations between women and men, than an egalitarian "dual earner, dual carer" model and therefore runs the risk of fostering, in the long

run, a fall in women's participation in the labour market, and the loss of the talents of many women to the economy.

(Fawcett 2010)

Having analysed the 2010 Budget, the WBG issued *A Gender Impact Assessment of the Coalition Government Budget, June 2010*, claiming that the UK government is failing in its duty, established by the 2006 Gender Equality Act, to be proactive in eliminating gender discrimination and promoting equality of opportunity between women and men. The report goes on to say that: 'The Gender Equality Duty applies to all public bodies ... It applies to taxation, the benefits system and to public services. There is thus a positive duty to examine the impact of the budget (and the spending review) on women as compared with men' (Women's Budget Group 2010).

The WBG claims that their analysis shows that women will be disadvantaged by several measures. Part of their criticism is that the government analysis has failed to take account of structural differences in the population. Therefore, they argue that since women earn less than men, are more reliant on transfer payments (welfare benefits etc), make up the bulk of lone parents and carers, figure disproportionately among the elderly poor, make more use of public services than men, and are employed in large numbers in the lower-paid jobs in the public sector, the proposed cuts and changes will impact more detrimentally on women than men.

In the report, proposed changes to both the welfare state and taxation are assessed. The report concludes that women will be harder hit than men by: the decision to link increases in benefits to the Consumer Price Index (CPI) rather than the Retail Price Index (RPI) (since the CPI is usually lower than the RPI); increasing the age of eligibility for the state pension; freezing of child benefit for three years; elimination of the Health in Pregnancy Benefit and restriction of the Sure Start Maternity Grant; changes in the tax credit system and benefits for lone parents; and reductions to housing benefit and Disability Living Allowance. The two-year freeze on public-sector employment and pay will hit women harder than men as they tend to predominate in the lower-paid ranks of public service, and cuts to public services will affect women more than men since they are the primary users of many of these.

Changes in taxation, on the other hand, will benefit men more than women, as they earn and own more; the benefit to women from reduction in income tax is outweighed by increased VAT and loss of welfare benefits and services (Women's Budget Group 2010: 5). Quoting an impact assessment undertaken by the House of Commons library at the request of Yvette Cooper MP, the report points out that of the £8 billion that the budget aims to raise by changes in direct taxes and benefits '£5.8 billion will be paid by women and only £2.2 billion by men' (p. 2). The report closes on the following note: 'on the whole women will be made worse off by the budget than men ... This is not a gender-neutral budget. Nor is it a fair one' (p. 12).

Conclusion

The work of women's budget initiatives and groups illuminates how gender-blind policymaking and execution perpetuates inequalities between men and women. Economic inequality is not incidental to citizenship. It has profound implications for the quality of life and capacity to participate in the social and political life of the community. The output from gender gap indices has shown correlation between income/wealth equality and women's representation in legislatures around the world. Advance in the political inclusion of women is a valuable, but inadequate, measure of gender democratization. Gender gap indices and women's budgets have appeared around the world to address a need: the failure on the part of governments to take account of the different situations of men and women and the need for equal (rather than 'same') consideration of differently situated groups in planning the generation and expenditure of revenue, and the execution of legislation. Gender gap indices and women's budgets are, therefore, performing a role in democratization by pushing governments to acknowledge their role in both perpetuating and addressing gendered inequalities.

This goes beyond pluralism. These are not simply groups competing for a share of power, or even for influence over government, nor do they fit very well into conceptions of social movements. Women's budget initiatives and groups are better understood in terms of Keane's (2009) 'monitory' model: as bodies with the explicit and active goal of monitoring the performance of government over time and holding it to account. Such organizations are clearly needed if democratization is to approach the gendered democracy described by commentators such as Anne Phillips. This kind of democracy takes account of the whole life of citizens, including care and reproduction alongside power and production, as the proper domain of equal citizenship. The evidence introduced above suggests that there are mechanisms in existence around the world both to prompt governments into action and to monitor the results, but that progress is slow and sometimes contradictory.

References

Adhiambo-Oduol, J. (2001) *Transforming Tradition as a Vehicle for Women's Empowerment: A Critical, Dimension of Poverty Eradication*. UN Division for the Advancement of Women, Expert Group Meeting November 2001, New Delhi.

Ballington, J. (2008) *Equality in Politics: A Survey Women and Men in Parliaments*. Lausanne, Switzerland: Inter-Parliamentary Union.

Budlender, D. (1996) 'South Africa: The Women's Budget', *Southern Africa Report*, SAR, 12 (1), p. 16.

Burrell, B. C. (1994) *A Woman's Place is in the House*. Ann Arbor, MI: University of Michigan Press.

Budlender, D. and G. Hewitt (2003) *Engendering Budgets: A Practitioner's Guide to Understanding and Implementing Gender-Responsive Budgets*. London: Commonwealth Secretariat.

Childs, S. (2001) 'In Their Own Words: New Labour Women and the Substantive Representation of Women', *British Journal of Politics and International Relations*, 3 (2), pp. 173–190.

—— (2002) 'Hitting the Target: Are Labour Women MPs 'Acting for' Women?', *Parliamentary Affairs*, 55, pp. 143–153.

—— (2004) 'A Feminized Style of Politics? Women MPs in the House of Commons', *British Journal of Politics and International Relations*, 6 (1), pp. 3–19.

Clark-Flory, T. (2010) available at http://www.salon.com/life/broadsheet/2010/03/26/iceland_bans_stripping_strip_clubs (accessed 10 September 2010).

Conover, P. J. (1994) 'Feminists and the Gender Gap'. In *Different Roles, Different Voices: Women and Politics in the United States and Europe*, ed. M. Githens, P. Norris and J. Lovenduski. New York: Harper Collins.

Council of Europe (2010) *Increasing Women's Representation in Politics through the Electoral System*; available at http://assembly.coe.int/Main.asp?link=/Documents/Records/2010/E/1001271500ADD3E.htm (accessed 3 October 2010).

Dahl, R. (1971) *Polyarchy: Participation and Opposition*. New Haven, CT: Yale University Press.

Dahlerup, D. (1998) 'Using Quotas to Increase Women's Political Participation'. In *Women in Parliament: Beyond Numbers*, ed. A. Karam *et al*. Stockholm: International Institute for Democracy and Electoral Assistance, pp. 91–106.

Darcy, R., S. Welch and J. Clark (1994) *Women, Elections and Representation*. Lincoln: University of Nebraska Press.

The Equality and Human Rights Commission (EHRC). *Gender Equality Duty*; available at http://www.equalityhumanrights.com/advice-and-guidance/public-sector-duties/what-are-the-public-sector-duties/gender-equality-duty/ (accessed 4 October 2010).

Fawcett Society (2010) *The Women's Budget Group response to Emergency Budget*; available at http://www.fawcettsociety.org.uk/index.asp?PageID=1164 (accessed 26 August 2010).

Globewomen (2010) *Corporate Women Directors International 2010 Report: Women Board Directors of the 2009 Fortune Global 200*; available at http://www.globewomen.org/cwdi/2010%20Global/Key.Findings.html (accessed 4 September 2010).

Goetz, A. (2003) 'Women's Education and Political Participation', Background paper prepared for the Education for All Global Monitoring Report 2003/4, *Gender and Education for All: The Leap to Equality*, UNESCO, 2003, p. 4.

Hausmann, R., L. D. Tyson and S. Zahidi (2008) *The Global Gender Gap Report 2008*, World Economic Forum, Geneva, p. 3.

Inglehart, M. L. and P. Norris (2003) *Rising Tide: Gender Equality and Cultural Change Around the World*. Cambridge: Cambridge University Press.

Inter-Parliamentary Union; available at http://www.ipu.org/wmn-e/classif.htm (accessed 23 August 2010).

Keane, J. (2009) *The Life and Death of Democracy*. London: Simon and Schuster UK Ltd.

Krafchik, W. (2001) 'Can Civil Society Add Value to Budget Decision-Making?' In *Gender Budget Initiatives: Strategies, Concepts and Experiences*. Brussels: UNIFEM.

Lovenduski, J. and P. Norris (1993) *Gender and Party Politics*. London: Sage Publications.

Mclanahan, S. S. and E. L. Kelly (2006) *The Feminization of Poverty: Past and Future*. Princeton, NJ: Network on the Family and the Economy, Office of Population Research; available at http://apps.olin.wustl.edu/macarthur/working%20papers/wp-mclanahan3.htm#top (accessed 4 September 2010).

Norris, P. (2002) 'Women's Power at the Ballot Box'. In *Voter Turnout Since 1945 A Global Report*, ed. L. Pintor and M. Gratschew; available at http://www.idea.int/publications/vt/upload/Voter%20turnout.pdf (accessed 22 August 2010).

—— and J. Lovenduski (1995) *Political Recruitment: Gender, Race and Class in the British Parliament*. Cambridge: Cambridge University Press.

OECD. *Social Institutions and Gender Index: The Social Institutions Variables*; available at http://genderindex.org/content/social-institutions-variables#family (accessed 13 September 2010).

OECD (2007) *Sample Presentation of Selected GID Indicators*; available at http://www.oecd.org/dataoecd/57/19/36338556.pdf (accessed 13 September 2010).

Phillips, A. (1991) *Engendering Democracy*. Cambridge: Polity.

Sawer, M. (2002) 'The Representation of Women in Australia: Meaning and Make-Believe', *Parliamentary Affairs*, 55 (1), pp. 5–18.

Schumpeter, J. A. (1966) *Capitalism, Socialism and Democracy*. London: Unwin University Books.

Sharp, R. (2003) *Budgeting for Equity: Budget Initiatives within a Framework of Performance Oriented Budgeting*. New York: United Nations Development Fund; available at http://www.unifem.org/materials/item_detail.php?ProductID=3 (accessed 26 August 2010).

Skjeie, H. (1991) 'The Rhetoric of Difference: On Women's Inclusion in Political Elites', *Politics and Society*, 19, pp. 233–263.

—— (2003) 'Credo on Difference- Women in Parliament in Norway'. In *Women in Politics Beyond Numbers: Women in Parliament Beyond Numbers*. Stockholm: International Institute for Democracy and Electoral Assistance.

Thomas, S. (1994) *How Women Legislate*. Oxford: Oxford University Press.

—— and C. Wilcox, (1998) *Women and Elective Office*. Oxford: Oxford University Press.

United Nations Platform for Action (2010) *Gender Budget Project: What is a Gender Budget?*; available at http://www.unpac.ca/gender/whatis.html (accessed 23 August 2010).

Wangnerud, L. (2000) 'Testing the Politics of Presence', *Scandinavian Political Studies*, 23, pp. 67–91.

Waring, M., G. Greenwood and C. Pintat (2000) *Politics: Women's Insights*. Geneva: Inter Parliamentary Union.

Waylen, G. (2007) *Engendering Transitions: Women's Mobilization, Institutions and Gender Outcomes*. Oxford: Oxford University Press.

—— (2008) 'Enhancing the Substantive Representation of Women: Lessons from Transitions to Democracy', *Parliamentary Affairs*, 61 (3), pp. 518–534.

Women's Budget Group; available at http://www.wbg.org.uk/ (accessed 23 August 2010).

—— (2010) *A Gender Impact Assessment of the Coalition Government Budget, June 2010*; available at http://www.fawcettsociety.org.uk/index.asp?PageID=1164 (accessed 26 August 2010).

WTO (World Trade Organization) (2009) *Trade Finance: Make it Work for Women*; available at http://www.wto.org/english/news_e/news09_e/fac_10mar09_e.htm (accessed 4 September 2010).

27

Democratization and war

Wolfgang Merkel

The complex relation between democracy and war requires a consideration of at least three strands of related research: the empirical, the legal and the ethical. The first strand is the empirical research associated with the 'democratic peace' thesis, which has thus far been addressed almost exclusively by International Relations scholars. Although this research uses, at least in part, sophisticated statistical methods, it often relies on a rudimentary understanding of democracy and the inter-dependent workings of democratic institutions. While these researchers specialize in questions of war and peace, they are hardly democracy scholars.[1] The second strand of research concerns the juridical-normative questions of legality, which belong primarily to the sphere of international law. The third strand belongs to political ethics and concerns moral–philosophical questions about 'just' war. This chapter intends to couple the statistical analysis of the democratic peace research with a theoretically substantive comparative democracy research focus, and to connect these to the normative debates occurring in law and philosophy. Thus, following Immanuel Kant, three interlinked questions are addressed: (1) Empirics: What do we know?; (2) Law: What are we allowed to do?; (3) Ethics: What *should* we do?

Empirics

In his seminal writing, *The Perpetual Peace*, Immanuel Kant ([1795] 2005: 24) formulated three 'definitive articles' for perpetual peace: the civil constitution of every state should be republican; the law of nations shall be founded on a federation of free states; and national rights should be transformed into a cosmopolitan right of world citizenship, a universal right of humanity. Only when states find themselves ever more closely approaching the realization of these three maxims can we 'flatter' ourselves with thinking that we are on the path towards perpetual peace.

The discipline of International Relations often takes Kant's theses as a point of departure to study empirically the following questions about the relationship between democracy and war:

- Do democracies fight fewer wars than autocracies?
- Do democracies wage wars against other democracies?
- Are wars midwives to the birth of democracies?
- Does an increasing quantity and quality of democracies reduce the likelihood of war?

Do democracies fight fewer wars than autocracies?

The answer is: no. Almost all studies come to the conclusion that democracies do not fight fewer wars than non-democracies. When we further ask whether democracies involved in conflict tend more often to be the aggressor or the defender, the statistical results are not flattering – democracies do wage wars of aggression (Small and Singer 1976: 50–69; Russett and Oneal 2001; Hasenclever and Wagner 2004: 465–471). But these voter- and cost-sensitive democracies can be comforted by the fact that high-tech foreign wars hardly ever lead the democracy's domestic population to suffer, as Kant ([1795] 2005: 12–13) had assumed they would. Statistically, democracies generally win the wars they fight (1816–1992: 81 per cent to 19 per cent), create collective war and defence alliances, choose their wars more wisely, tend to win them and suffer fewer casualties, are less likely to initiate crises, and rarely fight preventive wars (Mansfield and Snyder 2002: 300).

Nevertheless, there are considerable differences among democracies in terms of their willingness to go to war and to be involved in military conflicts. Thus, it was not the small democracies such as Switzerland, Sweden or Austria that waged the post-1945 wars, but the former colonial powers such as France and Great Britain, and especially the hegemonic USA (Brock et al. 2006: 6). In the period from 1946 to 2002, the USA engaged in 13 military interventions, France in 8, and Great Britain in 6. The development of modern high-tech weapons, the strategy of surgical strikes, and the increasing use of private military contractors have made the costs of intervention for democracies easier to calculate and to convey. Given these developments, the Kantian argument that republics would only reluctantly carry the damage and costs of war is proving to be ever less constraining on the war willingness of large democratic states. In this light, Johan Galtung's (1996: 49–59) dictum that democracies are especially 'self-righteous and belligerent' may indeed stand the test of time. This applies, however, almost exclusively to wars between democratic and authoritarian regimes.

Do democracies wage wars against other democracies?

The Kantian proposition that democracies ('republics' in Kant's terms) do not wage war against one another has shown itself in statistical analyses to be exceptionally robust (see e.g. Rummel 1983; Doyle 1986, 2005; Russett 1993; Russett and Oneal 2001). Democratic peace research refers to this as the 'dyadic peace phenomenon' (Kinsella 2005). The argument that this result is simply an artefact of the bipolar East-West confrontation has proven untenable since 1989. Even after 1991 there have been no armed conflicts between liberal constitutional democracies. There are some occasionally cited examples of post-1945 wars between democracies, but these do not convincingly disconfirm the democratic peace thesis, since the aggressor states were not fully developed constitutional democracies, rather belonging to 'defective democracies' (Merkel 2004). This is as true of the racist, apartheid 'democracies'[2] of South Africa and Rhodesia and their interventions in Botswana, as it is of the military conflict between India and Pakistan. The latter is a case of conflict between the defective democracy of India and the sometimes semi-democratic, sometimes 'soft' authoritarian regime in Pakistan.[3] The only remaining cases are the border skirmishes between Ecuador and Peru (1981, 1984), in which Peru was a defective democracy and Ecuador could just barely be classified as liberal.

The normative argument that war between democracies is incompatible with fundamental democratic values (Müller and Wolff 2006: 68), and the structural argument that democracies have greater institutional controls and procedural barriers to war initiation (Mansfield and Snyder 2002: 300) are both compelling. These two arguments merge into an especially persuasive explanation for the absence of purely 'democratic wars' in a sense not so far removed from Kant, when we supplement them with the observations that democracies are generally more inclined to bargain and compromise, that they are economically interdependent and members of the same international organizations, and that they have a common basis of trust.[4] The argument that it is, above all, the democratic institutions, procedures and deep-seated democratic values that keeps war between democracies off the political agenda, indicates that the democratic peace thesis must apply only to consolidated democracies, because only in these do democratic institutions work in the described war-inhibiting way. Institutions in regimes in transition, in defective and unconsolidated democracies, do not develop a comparable restraining power (Merkel 2004). For this reason, too, the examples of wars between 'democracies' occasionally mentioned as evidence against the democratic peace thesis are misleading and reveal a conceptual misunderstanding of what constitutes democracy.

Are wars midwives to the birth of democracies?

The escalating growth of democracy after the First and Second World Wars suggests an empirical, if not causal, relationship (see Figure 27.1). The spectacular democratization successes after the Second World War seem to especially suggest this. The murderous dictatorships of Nazi Germany and Japan were, after war and defeat, rapidly transformed into stable, constitutional democracies. The authoritarian regime in fascist Italy and the (even pre-1938) authoritarian-corporatist regime in Austria offer further examples of the possibility to democratize dictatorships after military defeat. The fall of the Greek Junta in 1974 after the Cyprus adventure, and the defeat of the Argentinian generals in the 1982 Falklands War also support this thesis. Empirically, it cannot be dismissed that the two world wars contributed to the diffusion of democracy, even if they were not fought to reach this goal and even if they were not fought on these grounds.[5] At the same time, counterexamples certainly exist: Panama in 1989; Haiti in 1994; perhaps even Bosnia in 1995; Afghanistan and Iraq at present. For the identification of causes of successful and failed democratization, these cases are suggestive. But from a statistical perspective, they offer only anecdotal evidence.

Figure 27.1 Development of democracies, 1800–2009
Note: The data was very slightly smoothed out to present a clearer figure. Figures have to be interpreted cautiously because the total number of states covered by Polity IV steadily rose from 22 in 1800 to 163 in 2009.
Source: Marshall and Jaggers (2009).

More democracies and fewer wars?

Using sophisticated statistical methods, a Scandinavian study did indeed show that military interventions led by democracies lead to a moderate increase in democracy scores on the Polity IV autocracy-democracy scale (Gleditsch *et al.* 2004: 26ff.). This result can be explained by the fact that democracies tend to win the wars that they wage. Autocratic regimes, however, are more prone to lose. Military defeat, in turn, destabilizes autocratic regimes and this often opens the way for democratic regime change. In contrast, when democracies are defeated in war, they tend to experience a change of government, but not a change in the basic character of the political regime. Thus, the statistical result provides evidence for the proposition that wars successfully fought by democracies against autocracies contribute to an increase in the worldwide level of democracy. When we add to this the fact that democracies do not fight against other democracies, the apparent paradox that an initial increase in wars can later lead to their decline is resolved. That this is in no way a legitimation for 'democratic wars of aggression', wars intended to bring about democracy, will become clear later in this chapter.

How valid are these statistical analyses? Do democratic interventions indeed lead to more democracy and finally to more peace? At least three additional questions must be answered in order to come to a rigorous conclusion:

- How stable are these imposed democracies?
- What type of democracy is at stake?
- Are these democracies, in fact, more peace-loving among one another than with other regime types?

Leaving aside the model cases of Japan and Germany, statistically representative studies (Gates and Strand 2004) show that democracies that are externally imposed and that follow military defeat are less stable and less durable than those political regimes that experience internal democratization. The new institutionalism can explain this by pointing to the mismatch between the domestic context and the new institutions[6] and the dearth of complementary informal social and formal political institutions (North 1990; Lauth 2004). A swift external overthrow of a government cannot, then, lead to a stable political order if strong domestic actors in the country itself do not support the democratization process. Only an elite settlement that includes the strongest political forces can provide formal democratic institutions with validity (Burton *et al.* 1992: 13ff.). Over time, repetitive rule compliance leads to a de facto transformation of informal rules into formal institutions. In the positive case, informal institutions and elite and popular attitudes change and adapt themselves to the operating mode of formal institutions. In this respect, democratic elites under international supervision can contribute to the institutionalization of democracy, but democracy is in no way a predetermined outcome. Democratic interventions often lead to short-lived successes. Over the long term, stable democratic regimes following armed intervention remain the exception rather than the rule (Gleditsch *et al.* 2004: 33).

Most commonly, postwar orders shed their openly autocratic character and become hybrid, semi-democratic regimes; but only rarely do they become consolidated democracies. Two important implications for the democratic peace thesis follow from this observation. First, institutionally inconsistent hybrid regimes are less stable than autocratic regimes and even less stable than democratic regimes. Second, from a statistical viewpoint, such hybrid regimes are significantly more prone to violence, susceptible to war, and in danger of civil war than mature democracies or stable autocratic systems (Mansfield and Snyder 1995, 2002, 2005).

The most important distinction, then, is between consolidated democracies and democratizing states. This distinction is often decisive for war and peace. In precarious transitional regimes, the threatened former autocratic elite find themselves in a new political game and often seize on political strategies that promise to deliver the quickest electoral victory and the most power. These are typically nationalist and ethnic mobilization or aggressive foreign policies, which are risky but domestically popular. The Greek's Junta occupation of Cyprus in 1973 and the Argentinian generals' war in the South Atlantic Falklands/Malvinas make clear the hazards of using foreign policy as a strategy of legitimation. The Balkan wars of the 1990s and the religious power struggle in Iraq show the perils of mobilizing people on the basis of primordial beliefs. Such strategies are hardly moderated by the now obsolete old institutions and the still insufficiently influential new institutions. The double-edged sword of increasing social mobilization, on the one hand, and weak political institutions, on the other (Huntington 1968), results not infrequently in short-sighted, reckless, violent political acts. This is made even easier by the fact that accountability mechanisms that exist between the government and voters are still unfamiliar and ineffective. Overall, democratizing regimes face a 60 per cent higher chance of being involved in war than states that are not undergoing democratic regime change (Mansfield and Snyder 1995: 13). The danger of military conflict is especially pronounced in the first phase of democratization. Transitional regimes that do not rapidly consolidate are not only almost by definition less stable than democracies or autocracies, but also find themselves much more often involved in civil war than other regimes. Hybrid regimes have to be distinguished from transitional regimes; hybrid regimes are not necessarily transitional. Although they have an inconsistent set of political institutions, they can be more stable than the traditional regime research has, for a long time, assumed. Figure 27.2 shows the three different types of political regimes and their involvement in civil wars.

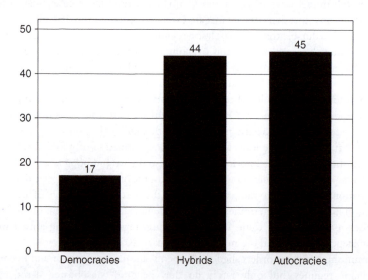

Figure 27.2 Regimes participating in civil wars (intrastate), 1945–2007
Note: Included are all regime types that participated in at least one civil war between 1945 and 2007. The data were collected from the Correlates of War (COW) Project (Sarkees and Wayman 2010). COW defines a civil war as an ongoing violent conflict between central government forces against an insurgent force capable of effective resistance, and resulting in at least 1,000 battle deaths per year. The classification of democracy, hybrid and autocratic regimes is based on Polity IV data (Marshall and Jaggers 2009). Polity IV codes different states according to different regime characteristics on a scale from 10 to –10. States with scores at or greater than 7 are classified as democracies, states between 6 and –6 are classified as hybrids, and states with scores at or lower than –7 are classified as autocracies.
Sources: Sarkees and Wayman (2010); Marshall and Jaggers (2009).

The central conclusion of Kant's democratic peace argument, then, must be rendered more precisely. *Mature* democracies do not wage war against one another. The mainstream of democratic peace studies neglects this critical analytical differentiation. It concentrates geographically on democracies and autocracies. Democratic regions such as Europe, North America and, increasingly, also Latin America are contrasted against almost purely autocratic regions such as the Arab Islamic belt of the Maghreb, the Middle East and Central Asia. Democracies support democracies, just as authoritarian regimes in regional clusters can better immunize themselves against regime change.

Taking these empirical observations into consideration, then, three relevant consequences must follow for actors engaged in 'democratic intervention':

1. Interventions that only set out to force an autocratic leader from power promise near-term success neither for democracy, nor for peace. Such 'democracies' threaten to remain incomplete and unstable and this, in turn, increases the danger of war.
2. Intervening democratic powers should support the new regime until it has climbed far enough up on the democracy scale that it is out of the zone of the violence-prone hybrid regime. The extent to which such willingness on the part of the intervener exists needs to be verified before any armed intervention is undertaken. If this willingness does not exist, then a military intervention cannot legitimately claim liberation and democratization as grounds for just war.
3. We know that regionally isolated democracies can in some cases survive, but that their average lifespan is significantly lower than it would be if they were surrounded by stable democracies. There is no evidence for the idea that establishing a shining example of democracy in a deeply autocratic region will create a domino effect among the other autocracies. The opposite is true; as a general rule, these 'democracies' remain unstable, crisis-prone, violent and short-lived. It could even be the case that the threat to regional peace, and the gravity of human rights violations, which had been the legitimate occasion for intervention in the first place, could actually increase.

One conclusion from the empirically based analysis thus far is that the world will become more democratic when democratization is not only initiated but when its consolidation is successfully set on course. Thus, intervention is not just about toppling the dictator and introducing democracy, but most importantly it is about supporting processes of democratic consolidation. Only then will both intrastate conflict and interstate conflict decrease over the long term.

Considering these important empirical and conceptual qualifications to the democratic peace thesis, could an informed 'democratic jihad' (Gleditsch *et al.* 2004) bring the world closer to Kant's perpetual peace? The answer is no. This is because evidence of a moderate but global increase on the democracy scale is not decisive; rather, the critical issue is whether autocratic regimes can transform into stable constitutional democracies. As we have seen, small advances towards democracy can move a stable autocracy into the conflict-prone zone of the hybrid regimes. Above all, it would be reasonable to object that good ends (democracy and peace) do not justify bad means (war). Since David Hume, we know that the unconditional derivation of 'ought' from 'is' presents a naturalistic fallacy. That is, the mistaken identification of moral properties with natural properties. 'Democratic wars of aggression', i.e. democratic interventions against dictators, cannot be legitimated solely on grounds of the vague statistical conclusion that an increase in consolidated democracies leads to a decrease in military violence. Indeed, the statistics of the twentieth century show that intrastate violence at the hands of murderous regimes has produced more victims than the two world wars put together (Rummel 1994; Gleditsch *et al.* 2004: 13). Even if we do not follow the crude utilitarianism of numbers, the possibility of preventing massive massacres can be an empirical and normative argument to allow the lifting of the Westphalian barrier to military intervention in a sovereign state. Is a community based on democratic values allowed to do this? And, when yes, under what circumstances? What could be the costs of allowing this?

Law

Defensive war

The modern law of nations, which in contrast to its name originally referred to the domestic law of state (Preuß 2000), underwent a transformation through the influence of Grotius (1625) and the Peace of Westphalia (1648). Under these influences, the medieval doctrine of *bellum justum* changed into the modern doctrine of *jus ad bellum*. Each sovereign state could decide for itself whether or not war was an appropriate tool of self-preservation. In the famous words of Prussian General Carl von Clausewitz, war was considered to be the 'continuation of politics by other means'.[7] With the 1928 Kellogg-Briand Pact, 'recourse to war for the solution of international controversies' was for the first time renounced by international treaty. But only the traumatic experience of the Second World War led to a universal proscription of the use of force in Article 2, Number 4 of the United Nations Charter. Using war to continue politics 'by other means' was made internationally illegal (Preuß 2000: 118). The only exception allowed for was individual and collective self-defence against the aggressions of a third state. As with individual self-defence, collective self-defence was designated as 'naturally given' and therefore an inalienable right. As Article 51 of the Charter makes clear, however, the Security Council's duty is not to vouchsafe this right but to limit it when necessary (Merkel 2009).

Humanitarian intervention

At least since NATO's attacks on Yugoslavia during the Kosovo War (1999), a new debate has been raging in international law. The 'humanitarian intervention' aimed at stopping Serbia's massacre and ethnic cleansing of the Kosovar population. A Security Council mandate did not exist. Even without it, *jus ad bellum* – and therefore also NATO's war involvement – can be justified within narrow normative bounds. Such a justification was provided by, among others, the Hamburg criminal lawyer and law philosopher, Reinhard Merkel, on the basis of the legal principle of 'emergency assistance'. Just as self-defence is a natural right, in criminal law emergency assistance on behalf of unlawfully threatened third parties is an undisputed fundamental norm. Article 51 of the UN Charter declares this principle to be applicable to states as well. International law today increasingly recognizes ethnic and religious communities, and even individuals, as bearing legal standing beyond the state. This standing applies to such rights as the right to life, the right to physical inviolability, and the protection from displacement. A state's unlawful attacks on its citizens' core group of negative human rights are breaches not only of objective international law, but also of the internationally recognized subjective rights of those affected. As such, the legal position of victims makes them eligible for emergency assistance. This opens up the 'theoretical possibility of the international community's right to pierce through the sovereign state's legitimating foundations' (Merkel 2000: 81).

The objection, incidentally, that an intervention so justified always requires the authorization of the Security Council, is misled. This is because 'just as the Security Council cannot establish non-existing state rights, neither can it eliminate existing ones' (ibid.: 79). The Security Council lacks the competence to set and deny rights. Emergency assistance rights are self-help rights and, as such, they are by definition asserted beyond the international legal order: 'That every resolution of the Security Council can be prevented by a simple, unjustified, purely egoistically motivated veto of each of its five permanent members' means that a right whose existence would depend on such a resolution would be made patently worthless and thereby nonexistent' (ibid.). Although this might be controversial in the sometimes unclear deductive positivist international law, if we follow the stricter subsumption logic of legal principles, then no doubt can remain about the so-called right to 'international emergency assistance'.

In extreme cases of grave human rights violations, the third party has a right to emergency assistance. What counts as 'grave human rights violations', however, is admittedly ambiguous in international law. What is clear is that such violations must have both a qualitative and a quantitative dimension of exceptionality and enormity and they relate to the core of human rights such as the right to life, physical inviolability, and the protection against displacement. These are universal human rights that enjoy global consensus. It is the dominant view that only the small core of fundamental negative defensive rights can be protected by humanitarian intervention. What remains unclear is the quantitative criterion. Are the historically rather unremarkable number of expulsions and massacres in Kosovo enough? Is it necessary to murder 400,000 citizens, as Saddam Hussein is alleged to have done?[8] Or do we need to think on the scale of Cambodia, Rwanda or even the Holocaust?

It makes sense to argue that the boundary of intervention is there where the state itself harms its primary legitimating function, namely the guarantee of internal peace. When the state undermines internal peace, it shows itself to no longer be *protector* but *hostis populi* (enemy of the people). But even though this thoroughly Hobbesian argument is plausible in the abstract, difficult questions regarding the precise details remain. Most importantly, when exactly is the boundary crossed, when the Leviathan itself instigates the violent creation of the state of nature, in this case the *bellum unius contra omnes* (war of all against all)? Where such boundaries can be neither substantially nor arithmetically determined, then they are proceeded in law and politics and handed over to an arbitrating authority. When, however, this authoritative body (such as the UN Security Council) is occupied by veto players who are themselves flagrant human rights violators, then such decisions become a normative farce.[9]

In sum, there are legally accepted reasons for humanitarian interventions, which can suspend the Westphalian state sovereignty. This can be considered as opposed to the dogmatization of state sovereignty, to be one of the most – if not the most – important humanitarian advance from an international law of states to a cosmopolitan right of world citizenship (Höffe 1999: 352ff.).

Democratic intervention

Humanitarian interventions can be justified by the flagrant violation of core negative human rights. This justification is increasingly accepted in international law. Is this also the case for 'democratic intervention'? That is to say, for intervention aimed at establishing a democratic political order in cases of massive violation of positive human rights? Does it apply to the case in which those subjected to the state are in whole or in part denied the right to vote or other important political, civil or social rights on the basis of their race, ethnicity or gender? The answer is no. Positive human rights (that is, participatory rights) do not possess the same legitimating weight as negative rights of protection (see e.g. ibid.: 79). This is consensus among legal philosophers or international lawyers. Would anyone have seriously thought of marching into Switzerland in 1970 before the introduction of the right to vote for women? Or to intervene in Singapore's well-ordered authoritarian regime? Armed intervention in South Africa and Rhodesia at the time of apartheid was never even debated. Also, the severe political and civil rights discrimination against women in Saudi Arabia would not be taken as grounds for intervention. Naturally, the threshold for any military intervention must be set very high. This is not just because of the danger of military conflict spreading or the unavoidable 'collateral victims' of such interventions, but more importantly it is because of the need to preserve individual state sovereignty as a generally war-preventing legal good in international relations. Nevertheless, state sovereignty is not an end in itself, but it must be permanently legitimated by the state's own citizens.

'Democratic interventions' can never be justified solely with the argument of establishing democracy. Democratic intervention can only be accepted and legitimated in connection with the (successful) termination of a humanitarian intervention, or after the defeat of a dictatorial regime that initiated a war of aggression (Germany, Japan and Italy in 1945). The prevention of new massacres or of further wars of aggression is the legitimating legal basis for democratizing protectorates. Democratic intervention in order to secure humanitarian goals following a huma-nitarian intervention is plausible, legitimate and – within bounds – also legal. To intervene democratically, then, means being willing to construct a legal system and democracy through something like a protectorate, with or without legitimate and un-incriminated representatives. The clearest examples of this in the last 20 years are doubtlessly Bosnia, Afghanistan and Iraq. In all three interventions, democratization is anything but guaranteed. A look at all cases of democratizing protectorates since 1945 is only slightly more optimistic.

Of the 14 cases of peace and democracy protectorates, the only successes that can be reported, in addition to Germany, Japan and Austria, are the relatively insignificant cases of Panama and Grenada. The cases of Bosnia-Herzegovina, Kosovo and East Timor are still too new to be diagnosed with any certainty as democratic successes or failures. Afghanistan and, even more, Iraq are far from the goal of being stable democracies, constitutional states, or even having secure statehood. But even if historical hindsight cautions firm restraint from 'democratic crusades', strict opponents will have to justify why it would be better to *not* protect populations threatened by mass murder and brutal violations of human rights and to *not* secure this protection over the long run through the establishment of constitutional democracy. Beyond national egoism and a dogmatic belief in Westphalian sovereignty, it is hardly possible to find consistent reasons.

Ethics

Just interventions: What should we do?

Humanitarian intervention can be justified by modern international law. However, the interna-tional laws do not stipulate a *duty* to intervene. Can such a duty even exist? And if it exists, does humanitarian intervention demand the fulfilment of specific duties not only *before* and *in* war, but also *after* war? Would such duties go beyond what we know to be the commandments of 'humanitarian international law'?

International law has thus far not delivered sufficient answers to these questions. Hans Kelsen's view that international law is a 'primitive law' seems to still hold; it is primitive because it possesses neither the possibility of enforcement and punishment, nor the completeness and subtlety of national criminal or civil law. Therefore, it is necessary to turn to political ethics to search for arguments that can help fill this gap.

Jus ad bellum

To intervene or not to intervene – this is the first question in modern moral theory of just war (Walzer 1977, 2003, 2005). Massacres, ethnic cleansing and state terrorism – whether in the former Yugoslavia, in the Caucasus, in the Middle East or in Africa – justify a moral right, and occasionally even duty, for armed intervention. This is one of the fundamental conclusions of just war theory (ibid.). Overall, in most areas of political ethics there are fewer restrictions against humanitarian intervention than in international law, because in political ethics external sovereignty is not inextricably linked to internal state sovereignty. Only a state that has not become a *hostis populi,* and therefore possesses a certain amount of internal legitimation, can also claim external sovereignty for itself.[10] Because external legitimacy is dependent on internal legitimacy, it follows that fundamental human rights have superiority over the sovereign state as an object of legal protection. In the case of blanket violations against humanity, finding a balance between protection of state sovereignty and protection against genocide or democide usually leads to a clear conclusion: when in doubt, intervene.[11]

In the ethics debate over just war, international multilateral interventions, ideally mandated by the UN Security Council, are clearly preferred. But the ever present question is what happens when multilateral solutions do not appear or are even prevented by the Security Council? What happens when France sends symbolic but harmless troops to Rwanda? What if Western Europe could not agree to interfere in the former Yugoslavia to end ethnic killings? What if the human rights-violating member of the Security Council, China, uses its veto? What if UN troops observe but do not prevent the deportation and eventual execution of 7,000 men, women and children in Srebrenica? Those who do not interfere, regardless of whether it is out of political calculus, cynical disinterest, or conscientious objection on pacifist grounds, get their hands dirty nevertheless. Michael Walzer refers to that quandary as the 'dilemma of dirty hands'. To escape from this dilemma he concludes: 'As long as we cannot rely on the ability and willingness of the UN, we must search for one-sided interventions' (Walzer 2003: 96). Humanitarian interventions are ethically (and also legally) justifiable, even despite a Security Council veto.

However, beyond the reason of massive violations against humanity, the ethic of *jus ad bellum* requires two additional legitimating reasons. First, there must be a reasonable prospect of success; and second, there must exist the willingness to stay in the country of intervention for as long as it takes to leave behind a 'well-ordered people' (Rawls 2002) so that the chances of state-sponsored massacres or civil war sprouting anew are made unlikely (Bass 2004: 386, 406). John Rawls's two legitimating conditions create a number of empirical problems. This morally justifiable duty calls for an intervention that is risk-accepting, blind to costs, and that is enormously patient. In contrast, democratic publics are sensitive to casualties, risk-averse and cost sensible. The citizens and voters of a democratic intervening state tend, therefore, to reject long-term occupations when the costs, in terms of their own resources and lives, are high.[12] A government that contradicts these preferences runs the danger of being voted out of office. As a result, democracies have a built-in institutional limit on their ability to intervene. Of course, this reality check does not mean that we can disavow the moral norm of what should be done. But every rational democratic government must take this limitation into consideration each time it decides whether or not to intervene.

Jus in bello

As in international law, in political ethics there are two categorical conditions for the 'law in war': the distinction between combatants and non-combatants and the use of proportional means. Just as these principles are consented to in theory, they are often ignored in practice. The most obvious breach occurs with the deliberate or – in the case of high-tech warfare – unintended but unavoidable 'collateral deaths' of civilians. The law's own binary distinction between legal and illegal is of limited help in clarifying whether or not a humanitarian intervention is completely impermissible because of a breach of *jus in bello.* The legal norm that no innocent actors may be killed is beyond question and must remain so. As a norm, it is untouchable. But if the norm were to be elevated to an absolute command in every situation, it would lead to a de facto prohibition against any humanitarian intervention. Such a legal absolutism would, in a way similar to pacifism, annul the moral duty to eliminate mass murder and mass forced displacement.

Utilitarians argue differently. They succumb to the temptation to weigh human life. The collateral death of hundreds of civilians is acceptable when it can save hundreds of thousands. This would apply to the bombing of Serbia during the war in Kosovo, just as it would justify the targeted bombing of Baghdad during the second Iraq war. But is this reasoning convincing? It does not. Machiavelli's strategic formula 'where the deed incriminates, the result forgives', does not allow itself to be legitimated as a humanitarian-utilitarian maxim.

Is there a middle way between the 'absolutism of the theory of rights' and the 'radical flexibility of utilitarianism' (Walzer 2003)? Michael Walzer attempts to pave such a path. 'How can we,' he writes, 'with our principles and proscriptions, stand aside and watch as the moral world in which these principles and proscriptions have their foothold is destroyed? How can we, the opponents of murder, not oppose mass murder – even when opposition means that we … get our hands dirty' (ibid.: 66). Walzer calls such situations moments of 'supreme emergency', a term he borrows from Winston Churchill. 'Supreme emergencies' are situations in which an imminent catastrophe threatens the foundations of humanity and devalues morality itself; situations in which immoral acts are necessary, even if that includes the killing of innocents. The Holocaust would have been such a supreme emergency. Walzer (2003) and Rawls (2002) also argue, incidentally, that the bombing of German cities up until 1943 was not justified, but could be morally defended as long as a victory of the immoral Nazi-regime could not be ruled out. The bombing of German cities in 1944 and 1945, at the end of an already decided war, can neither be justified, nor morally defended.

What also must be rejected on moral grounds is the manner in which the wars in Kosovo and Iraq were conducted. The risk-free use of force – namely, dropping bombs from a safe height and thereby accepting more collateral deaths in order to spare one's own soldiers – is politically understandable but morally reconcilable with neither Walzer nor *jus in bello*. In addition, from Kosovo we know that the airstrikes led to the intensification of the Serbian massacres and expulsions on the ground. The Milošević regime is unquestionably responsible for these victims. But the way in which NATO chose to conduct the war drove the number of victims higher. This is the kind of humanitarian intervention that threatens to renounce its own rightful grounds of intervention.

Jus post bellum

Humanitarian interventions demand a different ending than defensive wars. The *jus ad bellum* must be more closely tied to the *jus post bellum*. This has consequences, especially for the duties of the intervener and the international community at large. And it is here that democracy comes back into the game. With Rawls and Walzer, one can argue that forced regime change to rule of law and democracy are not only permissible, but also necessary after humanitarian interventions. This is because the law of just war, namely the elimination of grave violations against humanity, is only fully complete when it is complemented by 'justice after war'. This means that the intervening forces are obliged to ensure that the prevention of grave human rights violations will be enduring. As we have seen from the empirical findings of the democratic peace literature, this is most likely to occur when the rule of law and democracy are established. In humanitarian interventions, *jus ad* and *jus post bellum* are normatively and logically inextricably linked.[13] Humanitarian interventions must be complemented by democratic interventions so that they can thereby be brought to their final conclusion (Keohane 2003: 275ff.). Hybrid regimes do not fulfil this goal because, as we have already seen, they have the greatest tendency towards war and violence.

This maxim is not covered by prevailing international law. Even the mainstream of just war theory would reject this as too deep an interference with national sovereignty and a population's right to self-determination. Precisely, Brian Orend (2000: 217–263) has named five conditions for a moral *jus post bellum*: an end to the war when its goals have been achieved; just intentions, meaning above all no revenge; cooperation with a legitimate local authority, at least one that respects human rights; no collective punishment; and the proportional use of means.

From Rawls to Walzer, the same precept applies: victorious forces should leave the country as soon as possible. The defeated country's right to political self-determination requires it. Thus, according to the principle of assistance, the victor has a duty to the defeated 'that the burdened societies may arrange their own affairs in a reasonable and rational manner so that they can ultimately join the society of well-ordered peoples' (Rawls 2002: 137). This can hardly be contradicted. However, Rawls's and Orend's remarks are insufficient. What happens when such a demos does not exist, but only peoples, ethnicities or religious communities? That is, only fragments of a nation state, who are deeply inimical towards one another and who, in the absence of an occupying force, would sink into civil war? What happens when the dominant culture in a country is inclined to the gross suppression of minority ethnicities, religious communities or women? Is one then not allowed to, in Rawls's words, 'reconstruct' the society? Was 're-education' appropriate in post-Nazi Germany, while external involvement in other countries or civilizations with culturally based suppression is illegal? What would be the arguments?

According to Walzer, Rawls and others, it is not legitimate to force regime change on a 'normal' dictatorship. Exceptions apply only to cases of genocide (Walzer 1977: 107). In those cases, political and even social reforms are considered to be legitimate acts of humanitarian intervention. On this basis, Walzer holds that externally forced and supervised democratization was justified in Germany, but unjustified in post-1945 Japan. Even if the cruelties of the Japanese occupation of Nanjing (1937–8) cannot be compared with the extent of the murderous depravity of the Holocaust, Japan's barbarous massacre of the Chinese is also beyond all reason. In general, connecting the legitimate restructuring of a political system almost solely to the cruelties of a violent regime misses the point; namely, the prevention of *future* human rights violations and the outbreak of civil war, and the prospect of leaving behind a peaceful society and a fair political system. Understood in this way, *jus post bellum* is an integral part of the grounds for just war (Bass 2004: 412). Since democratic societies and elected regimes often shy away from such long-term costs, the criterion of *jus post bellum* raises the threshold for just wars and lowers their number. In closing, I will discuss this set of problems through the example of the war against Iraq.

Conclusion

The US's official reason for the war against Iraq – the presence of weapons of mass destruction – proved to be self-deceptive, if not (and much supports this view) the hegemonic power's fraudulent deceit of the world per se. If there had been an ethically durable reason for the second war against Iraq, then it would have had been the fact that Saddam Hussein was one of the bloodiest dictators of the twentieth century and that future victims had to be prevented. According to Amnesty International estimates, 400,000 Iraqi citizens were murdered by their own government: Kurds, Shiites, political and also personal enemies. About one million deaths resulted from Saddam's attack against Iran, waged with support from the US. These deaths weigh heavily. At the same time, one could argue that this was in the past and that after the massacre of Marsh Arab Shiites (1991), Saddam's actions were contained by the international air campaign,

Table 27.1 External supervision of democratization after military intervention, post-1945

Country	Period	Most important external actors	Type of administration	Polity IV[2]	Freedom House[3]	Democracy[4]
					After 10 years	
Germany (West)	1946–9	US, GB, F	Multilateral administration	10 (10)	(1.1)	Yes
Austria	1945–52	Allies	Multilateral administration	10 (10)	(1.1)	Yes
Japan	1945–52	US	US administration	10 (10)	(1.2)	Yes
Dominican Republic	1965–6	US	Local administration under US supervision	–3 (8)	7.7 (2.2)	No
South Vietnam	1964–73	US	Local administration under US supervision	–7 (–7)	7.6 (7.6)	No
Cambodia	1970–3	US	Local administration under US supervision	–66 (2)	7.7	No
	1991–3	UNO	Local administration under US supervision	2	6.5 (6.5)	No
Grenada	1983	US	Local administration under US supervision	–	1.2 (1.2)	Yes
Panama	1989	US	Local administration under US supervision	9 (9)	2.3 (1.2)	Yes
Haiti	1994–6	US, UN	Local administration under US supervision	–2 (–2)	6.5 (7.6)	No
Bosnia-Herzegovina	1995–?	NATO	NATO/EU/UNO administration	–66 (–66)	3.5 (3)	No
Kosovo[1]	1999–?	NATO/UN	NATO/EU/UNO administration	8 (–)	4.5 (5)	No
East Timor	1999–2002	UN	UN administration	7 (6)	3.5 (3)	No
Afghanistan	2001–?	US, Allies	Local administration under NATO/UN supervision	–66 (–66)	6.6 (5.6)	?
Iraq	2002–?	US, Allies	US administration	–66 (–66)	7.5 (7.5)	?

Notes:
1 The territorial status of Kosovo is not yet determined; therefore it remains unrated by Polity IV and Freedom House.
2 Polity IV values 10 years after the end of intervention. The values for Haiti, Bosnia-Herzegovina, Kosovo, East Timor, Afghanistan and Iraq are from 2002; and from 2003 in parentheses when available.
3 Freedom House: political rights, civil liberties. Freedom House ratings are available since 1973. Ratings are for 10 years after the end of intervention. The values for Haiti, Afghanistan and Iraq are from 2004; Bosnia-Herzegovina, Kosovo and East Timor are from 2010: in parentheses are political rights and civil liberties from the 2005 edition of Freedom House.
4 Polity IV considers a country to be democratic when it has a score of at least 6 points (out of 10). Freedom House designates a country as 'free' when it has an average score of 2.5 or better (with 1 being free and 7 being unfree).
Source: Marshall and Jaggers (2003, 2009), own research.

and therefore his ability to repress his people was limited. Nevertheless, every easing of the air-containment regime gave rise to the fear and the opportunity for renewed repression, torture, and when politically opportune – mass murder. An easement of the air-containment regime would have breached the *jus post bellum* of the first Gulf War.

The *jus ad bellum* for the attack against Iraq remains, from the perspective of just war theory, contested. The *jus in bello*, however, was clearly violated by the style of bombardments. But this does not excuse us from having to reflect on the postwar situation – not least because the war against Iraq can serve as a paradigmatic case of the victor's duties for a 'just occupation' after humanitarian intervention.

A premature withdrawal of American, British and the other symbolic partners of the war coalition would amount to a flagrant violation of the victors' postwar duties. Iraq is a deeply divided country. Kurds mistrust Arabs, Shiites mistrust Sunnis, moderates mistrust radicals, clerics mistrust secularists, and followers of the Baath regime mistrust everyone. The violations of the past, primarily begun by the Sunni, now predestine their entire group to be the target of revenge, discrimination and repression. The Kurds have, for long, begun to build a para-state. All three fundamental elements of a state are contested in today's Iraq: the nation, territory and power. The creation of a centralized monopoly on force, which is the beginning of every state, lies beyond reach. The same is true of nation-building. In comparison, the redemocratization of Germany after 1945 was child's play, since there was at least a nation and a state. Both are missing in postwar Iraq. In the absence of a trusteeship protectorate, Iraq is more likely to face Hobbes's state of nature than it is Rawls's 'well-ordered peoples'. An American withdrawal would not put an end to an unjust war. To the contrary, it would make a war that was already hardly justified even more unjust. If there is any other humanitarian significance beyond the toppling of a human rights-violating dictatorship, then it is that one cannot abandon Iraq to a Shiite-Sunni civil war. This thesis is also based on the robust empirical finding of Mansfield and Snyder (2002: 334) – that political regimes undergoing democratization are particularly vulnerable to war when the central state institutions are weak. Iraq seems to be a model example of this thesis.

Notes

1 Edward D. Mansfield and Jack Snyder (2002) are a notable exception.
2 Linz (1975) calls South Africa and Rhodesia 'racist democracies'.
3 Compare the Indian interventions in Pakistan in 1965–6, 1971–2, 1981, 1984–7.
4 Doyle (1997) argues that it is this fact that democracies trust other democracies and not autocracies that, above all, makes war unlikely between democracies but not between democracies and dictatorships.
5 Nevertheless, both Wilson and Roosevelt based their justifications for US entry into the two world wars on democracy arguments.
6 March and Olsen's 'logic of appropriateness', see March and Olson (1984).
7 Quoted from Preuß (2000: 118).
8 Not counted here are around one million deaths that followed from Saddam's illegal attack on Iran.
9 This applies especially to China, but also to Russia and occasionally even to the democratic US.
10 This position is not recognized by international law positivists. State sovereignty is a sufficient end in itself. According to this legal positivist view, even murderous totalitarian regimes do not lose their sovereignty.
11 Compare this to the Memorandum written by 58 American intellectuals, including Huntington, Fukuyama, Rorty, Walzer and Etzioni, in which they speak out in favour of defending universal (negative) human rights with armed violence in extreme cases. In contrast, the open letter of 'second tier' German intellectuals rejects this with specific reference to the war against Iraq.
12 This has been the situation in the US since at least 2006 after the number of casualties as a result of the American occupation in Iraq increased, *a fortiori*, the same occurred during the last years of the Vietnam War.
13 Walzer (1977: 123): 'The theory of ends in war is shaped by the same rights that justify the fighting in the first place.'

References

Bass, G. J. (2004) 'Jus post bellum', *Philosophy and Public Affairs*, 32 (4), pp. 384–412.

Brock, L., A. Geis and H. Müller (2006) *Democratic Wars. Looking at the Dark Side of Democratic Peace*. Houndmills: Palgrave Macmillan.

Burton, M., R. Gunther and J. Higley (1992) 'Introduction: Elite Transformations and Democratic Regimes.' In *Elites and Democratic Consolidation in Latin America and Southern Europe*, ed. J. Higley and R. Gunther. Cambridge: Cambridge University Press, pp. 1–37.

Doyle, M. W. (1986) 'Liberalism and World Politics', *American Political Science Review*, 80 (4), pp. 1151–1169.

—— (1997) *Ways of War and Peace*. New York: Norton.

—— (2005) 'Three Pillars of the Liberal Peace', *American Political Science Review*, 99 (3), pp. 463–466.

Freedom House (2005) *Freedom in the World. Country Ratings 1972–2005*; available at http://www.freedom house.org/uploads/fiw/FIWAllScores.xls (accessed 22 January 2006).

Galtung, J. (1996) 'Democracy: Dictatorship = Peace: War?' In *Peace by Peaceful Means: Peace and Conflict, Development and Civilisation*, ed. J. Galtung. London: Sage, pp. 49–59.

Gates, S and H. Strand (2004) *Military Intervention, Democratization, and Post-conflict Political Stability*, Ms. Montreal.

Gleditsch, N. P., L. Siljeholm Christiansen and H. Hegre (2004) 'Democratic Jihad? Military Intervention and Democracy', Ms. Oslo, pp. 26–27.

Grimm, S. (2008) 'External Democratization after War: Success and Failure', *Democratization: War and Democratization: Legality, Legitimacy and Effectiveness*, special issue, ed. S. Grimm and W. Merkel, 15 (3), pp. 525–599.

Hasenclever, A. and W. Wagner (2004) 'From the Analysis of a Separate Democratic Peace to the Liberal Study of International Conflict', *International Politics*, 41 (4), pp. 465–471.

Höffe, O. (1999) *Demokratie im Zeitalter der Globalisierung*. München: C.H. Beck.

Huntington, S. P. (1968) *Political Order in Changing Societies*. New Haven, CT, and London: Yale University Press.

Kant, I. ([1795] 2005) *Zum ewigen Frieden*. Stuttgart: Reclam.

Keohane, R. O. (2003) 'Political Authority after Interventions: Gradations in Sovereignty'. In *Humanitarian Intervention: Ethical, Legal, and Political Dilemmas*, ed. J. L. Holz-grefe and R. O. Keohane. Cambridge: Cambridge University Press, pp. 275–298.

Kinsella, D. (2005) 'No Rest for the Democratic Peace', *American Political Science Review*, 99 (3), pp. 453–458.

Lauth, H.-J. (2004) *Demokratie und Demokratiemessung, eine konzeptionelle Grundlegung für den interkulturellen Vergleich*. Wiesbaden: VS Verlag für Sozialwissenschaften.

Linz, J. (1975) 'Totalitarian and Authoritarian Regimes'. In *Handbook of Political Science, vol. 3: Macropolitical Theory*, ed. F. Greenstein and N. Polsby. Reading, MA: Addison-Wesley, pp. 175–411.

Mansfield, E. D. and J. Snyder (1995) 'Democratization and the Danger of War', *International Security*, 20 (1), pp. 5–38.

—— and J. Snyder (2002) 'Democratic Transitions, Institutional Strength, and War', *International Organization*, 56 (2), pp. 297–337.

—— (2005) *Electing to Fight. Why Emerging Democracies Go to War*. Cambridge/London: MIT Press.

March, J. G. and J. P. Olson (1984) 'The New Institutionalism: Organizational Factors in Political Life', *American Political Science Review*, 78 (3), pp. 738–749.

Marshall, M. G. and K. Jaggers (2003) *Polity IV Country Reports 2003*; available at http://www.cidcm.umd. edu/polity/country_reports/report.htm (accessed 20 July 2005).

—— (2009) *Polity IV Project: Political Regime Characteristics and Transitions, 1800–2009: Polity IV Dataset Version 2009* <p4v2009 and p4v2006d>; available at http://www.systemicpeace.org/inscr/p4v2009.xls (accessed 29 December 2010).

Merkel, R. (2000) 'Das Elend der Beschützten. Rechtsethische Grundlagen und Grenzen der sog. Humanitären Intervention und die Verwerflichkeit der NATO-Aktion im Kosovo-Krieg'. In *Der Kosovo-Krieg und das Völkerrecht*, ed. R. Merkel. Frankfurt a. M.: Suhrkamp, pp. 66–98.

Merkel, W. (2004) 'Embedded and Defective Democracies'. *In Special Issue of Democratization: Consolidated or Defective Democracy?*, ed. A. Croissant and W. Merkel. *Problems of Regime Change*, 11 (5), pp. 33–58.

—— (2009) 'Basic Principles of Law as Normative Foundations of, and Limits to, Military Enforcement of Human Rights Across State Boundaries'. In *War and Democratization: Legality, Legitimacy and Effectiveness*, ed. W. Merkel and S. Grimm. Abingdon: Routledge, pp. 16–30.

Müller, H. and J. Wolff (2006) 'Democratic Peace: Many Data, Little Explanation?' In *Democratic Wars. Looking at the Dark Side of Democratic Peace*, ed. L. Brock. London: Palgrave, pp. 41–73.

North, D. C. (1990) *Institutions, Institutional Change and Economic Performance*. Cambridge: Cambridge University Press.

Orend, B. (2000) *War and International Justice: A Kantian Perspective*. Waterloo, ON: Wilfried Laurier University Press.

Preuß, U. K. (2000) 'Der Kosovo-Krieg, das Völkerrecht und die Moral'. In *Der Kosovo-Krieg und das Völkerrecht*, ed. R. Merkel. Frankfurt a. M.: Suhrkamp, pp. 115–137.

Rawls, J. (2002) *Das Recht der Völker*. Berlin/New York: deGruyter.

Rummel, R. J. (1983) 'Libertarianism and International Violence', *Journal of Conflict Resolution*, 27 (1), pp. 27–71.

—— (1994) 'Focus on: Power, Genocide, and Mass Murder', *Journal of Peace Research*, 31 (1), pp. 1–10.

Russett, B. M. (1993) *Grasping the Democratic Peace: Principles for a Post-Cold-War*. Princeton, NJ: Princeton University Press.

—— and J. Oneal (2001) *Triangulating Peace: Democracy, Interdependence, and International Organizations*. New York: W.W. Norton.

Sarkees, M. R. and F. Wayman (2010) *Resort to War: 1816–2007*. Washington, DC: CQ Press.

Small, M. and J. D. Singer (1976) 'The War-proneness of Democratic Regimes, 1816–1965', *The Jerusalem Journal of International Relations*, 1, pp. 50–69.

Walzer, M. (1977) *Just and Unjust Wars: A Moral Argument with Historical Illustrations*. Harmondsworth: Penguin.

—— (2003) *Erklärte Kriege – Kriegserklärungen*. Hamburg: Europäische Verlagsanstalt.

—— (2005) *Arguing about War*. New Haven, CT, and London: Yale University Press.

28

Democratization and conflict resolution

Sonja Grimm

In its 2009 issue, the Heidelberg Conflict Barometer counts 365 political conflicts worldwide. Among those are seven wars and 24 severe crises, amounting to 31 conflicts fought through the use of massive violence (HIIK 2009: 1). Obviously, all of the countries involved need durable solutions to address their deep-rooted conflicts after violence has come to an end, with a truce or peace agreement. However, after the devastating experiences of failed peacekeeping during the 1990s, for example in Somalia, Rwanda or Bosnia-Herzegovina, one thing became very clear for the international community: one-dimensional operations focusing only on peace-enforcement through the use of force, or peacemaking by manipulating peace agreements, alone cannot produce a stable and durable positive peace in a crisis country. Having brought war or genocide to an end, conflict resolution requires a more comprehensive approach, including the development of stable and widely supported institutions from above and the empowerment of communities to build peace from below (Ramsbotham *et al.* 2005: 215). Thus, the international community of states has increasingly sought the use of 'democratization' as a tool to balance conflicting interests of warring factions, to offer institutional solutions for peaceful political decision-making, to constrain elite behaviour, and to educate a broader public in human rights and civil values. As a consequence, democratization *should* contribute to solving the root causes of conflict, and thereby produce a sustainable peace.

However, not all good things go – timely and conceptually – together. In most cases, democratization is not as successful as originally assumed, in either scope or pace of implementing democratic institutions, and elites playing according to the new democratic rules (Grimm 2010). Furthermore, democratization can be challenged by equally important goals such as security, stability and economic liberalization (Grimm and Leininger 2012). And, finally, the universal ideas of self-administration and local responsibility may clash with the Western democracies' wish for quick democratization by following their role models and thereby bypassing the right of local population's self-administration (Carothers 1999; Chandler 2006; Grimm 2010). Thus, the main questions that recent conflict studies and transition research try to answer are the following: To which extent is democratization an adequate tool for conflict resolution? Are there any alternatives to democratic rule in a post-conflict society? How and to what extent can democratization in a post-conflict society be successfully supported from the outside? Is this 'external democratization' legitimate?

This chapter seeks to offer an overview of the 'state-of-the-art' in the field, considering literature from conflict and peace research as well as comparative transition studies. First, I will give an introduction on what the terms of 'conflict resolution' (section 2) and 'democratization' mean and to what extent they go hand in hand (section 3). Second, I will discuss to what extent democratization is an endogenous process and how it can be supported by external actors (section 4). Considering the negative balance of post-1990 efforts to implement democratization from the outside for the sake of conflict resolution (section 5) I will continue with reflections on the dilemmas (section 6) and the overall legitimacy of externally induced democratization (section 7). I will conclude with some prospects for further avenues of research on post-conflict societies (section 8).

Before I begin, a word on the term 'post-*conflict* society', which is in a way misleading. It does not mean that the conflict is solved and violence has completely ceased. By convention, 'post-conflict' usually denotes societies affected by armed conflicts, where parts of the conflict are dealt with when the warring parties agree upon a ceasefire or a peace-treaty. Nevertheless, the root causes of the conflict still need to be addressed, and some parties may even continue to use violence in order to push their interests through. To avoid the misnomer problem, some authors use the term 'post*war* society' to refer to situations where the major warfare has ceased, but where incompatible issues may remain unsolved (Jarstad 2008: 20, fn. 3). However, the term 'postwar' only includes types of war with regular warfare as in the case of *interstate* or *intrastate* war, but excludes large-scale atrocities including genocide against unarmed civilians, which is, in many of the investigated societies here, the type of violent conflict we are talking about. Thus, I prefer the term 'post-conflict society'; keeping in mind that the root causes of violent conflict in these societies still have to be addressed in order to prevent renewed violence.

Conflict resolution

Following Ramsbotham *et al.* (2005: 13), conflict is 'an intrinsic and inevitable aspect of social change. It is an expression of the heterogeneity of interests, values and beliefs that arise as new formations generated by social change come up against inherited constraints.' In the case of a *violent conflict*, the parties involved use violent means to forward their interests. This may occur as interstate war, intrastate war, genocide and large-scale one-sided violence of combatants against unarmed civilians. The task of conflict resolution in the face of clashing interests is defined by Ramsbotham *et al.* as helping parties to overcome the conflict and to change the perception of a zero-sum game, where one party's gain is the other's loss, to a non-zero-sum game in which both may gain or both may lose (ibid.: 15). In general, one can distinguish between conflicts over positions, needs and values. In the case of conflicts over positions (such as access to resources or power) and basic needs (such as security or survival), one can clarify each opponent's interests and find a solution to their demands that satisfies both, in particular when these interests are not subject to relative scarcity (e.g. security for one part is reinforced by security for the other). Solution-finding may be more difficult if the conflict is over values that are often non-negotiable (ibid.: 18). But as long as one can translate a conflict into the language of needs, on outcome acceptable for both sides can be found.

A spiral of hostility and escalation that is typical for violent conflict may be altered by a third-party intervention. Such a third party may offer positive feedback, allow a different pattern of communication, help to negotiate resilient agreements, oversee the agreement's implementation, and give guarantees that secure the compliance of all parties (Walter 1999, 2002). The international community acting as a third party in conflict resolution can refer to the strategies of peacemaking, peacekeeping, peace-enforcement and peacebuilding, including post-conflict reconstruction to support conflict resolution from the outside (Durch 1996; UNO 2000; Bellamy *et al.* 2004). Peacemaking equals classical conflict mediation. Prominent persons into whom all warring parties put confidence bring to bear information about the interests involved, give all sides a chance to be heard in the negotiations, test their perceptions on the other side's commitment and exchange ideas on different institutional solutions. Thereby, they change communication structures and open a window of opportunity for voluntary compromise (Stedman 1996: 358–363; Stedman et al. 2002). In case of successful consensus-building, third parties can continue their engagement in peacekeeping. It includes deployment of troops mandated to separate the belligerents and to oversee the implementation of the agreement, with the consent of the conflict parties. Recently, the international community has also begun to implement peace using forceful measures, which allow troops to use force against the warring parties if the conflict parties fail to achieve or maintain peace. Furthermore, external actors can continue their engagement at the negotiating table by forcing the conflict parties to sign a peace agreement (Durch et al. 2003). This was, for example, the case with the 'Dayton General Framework Agreement for Peace in Bosnia-Herzegovina' signed in 1995.

Peacebuilding underpins the work of peacemaking, peacekeeping and peace-enforcement by addressing structural issues and the long-term relationships between conflicting parties (Ramsbotham et al. 2005: 30). Peacebuilding from above aims to resolve conflicts over institutional designs, the balancing of interests of the conflicting parties and their main representatives, and the regulation of the access to political power (Stedman et al. 2002; Paris 2004). Peacebuilding from below focuses on the empowerment of communities that have been torn apart by war (Galama and van Tongeren 2002; Lund 2003). In the literature on peacebuilding, the former is interchangeably called 'postwar reconstruction' whereas the latter also appears under the names of 'civil society formation', 'trust-building' or 'reconciliation' (see also Ramsbotham et al. 2005: chapter 8 and Lederach 1997: chapter 9).

In total, once again following Ramsbotham et al. (2005: 30), conflict resolution is 'to transform actually and potentially violent conflict into a peaceful process of social and political change'. This is where *democracy* comes into play. In earlier approaches to conflict resolution, external actors simply sought to assist the rehabilitation of the shattered system and to restore the status quo that existed before the conflict (Kumar and Zeeuw 2006: 3). The focus was on relief operations and, when possible, on rehabilitation of shattered physical infrastructure (Kumar 1997). With the paradigmatic shift to an 'emerging right to democracy' (Franck 1992) and to forms of good governance that should regulate the internal relations of a society based on the universal protection of human rights (Fox 2000, 2003), these approaches changed fundamentally. Non-interference in domestic state affairs was no longer the sole accepted norm in international politics, as the international community also began to consider a 'responsibility to protect' individuals from authoritarian states' arbitrariness (International Commission on Intervention and State Sovereignty 2001; Evans 2008).

Nowadays, when external actors are confronted with the task of assisting post-conflict recovery, besides supplying developmental aid, they also seek to build a new and legitimate post-conflict political system. And because this new system should be based on the will of the people, guarantee the people's lives and integrity, and prevent the reoccurrence of violent conflict, this new system cannot be authoritarian, but must be democratic (Burnell 2000, 2008; Newman and Rich 2004).

To summarize the complex history of democracy theory (see for example Held's seminal book, *Models of Democracy* (1996)) and link it to conflict resolution, one can state that a democratic political system offers the means for *legitimately regulating* change (and thus hopefully preventing the reoccurrence of violent conflict). 'Legitimately regulating' means the following: first, a democratic system provides rules for the selection of political representatives aiding the formation of a legitimate and representative government, thereby removing the need for costly armed fighting for access to political power. Second, it entails fixed procedures for non-violent decision-making supported by all parties. Consequently, undesired decision-making outcomes become acceptable – under the condition that the same party does not always lose (for the first two points see Dahl's *Polyarchy* (1971)). Third, a liberal democratic political system is based on the protection of political rights and civil liberties. In the sense of negative rights, a democratic system protects the life and property of each individual inhabitant who lives under a political regime. In the sense of positive freedoms, it allows for participation in preference-formation, interest-aggregation, decision-making, as well as for the selection of political representatives. It therefore acts as a channel for making different voices equally heard and considered (Holmes 1995; Berlin 2002). Finally, liberal democratic rule allows the people to hold political representatives accountable. In a consolidated democracy, decision-makers are peacefully selected, but also deselected by means of democratic elections. Furthermore, in constitutional forms of democracy, horizontal linkages (such as the checks and balances system of tripartite executive, judicative and legislative power) and vertical linkages (such as the subdivision in federal, regional and communal administrative levels) strengthen the mechanism of mutual control (Schmitter and Karl 1991; Ratner 2000; Schmitter 2004).

Democratization can be defined as the process of: (1) drafting and implementing democratic rules, or in other words democratic institutions, and (2) changing the attitudes and behaviour of decision-makers and voters constrained by these rules (O'Donnell and Schmitter 1989; Huntington 1991; Whitehead 2002). What democratization means in a post-conflict society is highlighted in the next section.

Democratization in conflict-ridden societies

During democratization, fair and transparent institutions replace authoritarian, clientelistic or solely rent-seeking behaviour. However, the structural and institutional challenges faced by a society ridden by violent conflict are manifold. First, failed security and state structures need to be rebuilt after violent conflict and must include demobilization, disarmament, reintegration of former combatants and the training of a new military and police. Second, war-economy structures need to be transformed into peace-economy structures as a basis for socio-economic recovery. Third, corruption needs to be fought and a functioning rule of law system to be installed. Fourth, the political system needs to be reorganized and a basis for future cooperation and compromise needs to be found. Fifth, in societies where violent conflict has exacerbated political, ethnical, religious or socio-economic cleavages, intercommunity trust must be built (Grimm 2008: 538–544).

Faced with these problems, conflict-ridden societies need substantial reforms and transformations. Adapted from transition research (Stepan 1986: 66–72; Merkel 2010: 95), I distinguish three phases of transformation for postwar societies: stabilization, institutionalization and consolidation. On this model, 'proper' democratization is embedded in the parallel transition of the five areas requiring reform after war over the three identified phases of transition (see Figure 28.1). Please note, one should view this model as an analytical concept to differentiate reform areas and reform pace, but it does not intend to argue that democratization is a linear process without setbacks and dead ends, as some prominent experts may misleadingly claim (see for example Carothers 2007).

Constitutional reform and democratic founding elections form the nucleus of institutionalizing democracy. By drafting a new democratic constitution, representatives of the formerly warring factions negotiate a compromise on the design of the future political system, the protection of civil and political human rights, and on checks and balances for mutual control. Through democratic

Phases Areas	Stabilization	Institutionalization	Consolidation
Security	Control of armed groups, disarmament, demobilization	Training of national army and police, transfer of military and police sovereignty	Consolidating a demilitarized polity, internal and external security
Rule of Law	Control of judiciary, application of transitional law	Training of judiciary, building of courts, prosecution of war criminals, war crime tribunal, transfer of judicial powers	Consolidating civil and political rights, impartial judiciary
Economic Prosperity	Humanitarian aid, control of industrial facilities	Reconstruction of infrastructure (transport, education, health care), property law, reintegration of combatants, tax reform, currency reform, developmental projects	Consolidating economic prosperity, social justice, fair distribution of prosperity
Democracy	Interim administration, selection of functional and territorial representatives for constituent assembly	Reconstruction of administration, constitution drafting, negotiating power sharing institutions, founding elections, transfer of executive and legislative powers	Consolidating political institutions, permanent democratic decision-making, regular free and fair elections, peaceful change of government
Political Society	Protection of civilians, control of media	Reintegration of refugees, reconstruction of plural media, voters' trainings, transitional justice, trust building, reconciliation	Consolidating a participative citizenry

Figure 28.1 Phases and areas of reform in post-conflict societies
Source: Own compilation; phases adapted from Merkel (2010: 95) and Stepan (1986: 66–72).

elections, new representatives are selected and government coalitions legitimately formed. In many post-conflict societies, however, it is almost impossible to have free and fair elections immediately following war, as elections might overrule already threatened minorities and return to power the political elites who had plunged the country into conflict (Reilly 2004; Kumar and Zeeuw 2006: 4). Here, power-sharing trumps pure democratic selection by a consensually pre-arranged comprehensive representation of all conflict parties. Such power-sharing instruments include means for minority protection (e.g. political, social and cultural group rights and fixed participation ratios in parliament and government); the design of a consensus democracy instead of a majoritarian one (executive power-sharing, proportional representation, veto rights in legislature, and arbitral jurisdiction for the case of protracted interest conflict); and territorial solutions (such as federalism, autonomy or even state secession) (Horowitz 1994; Lijphart 1999; Schneckener 2002; Hoddie and Hartzell 2005; Roeder and Rothchild 2005; Jarstad and Nilsson 2008).

Beyond this institutional core, external actors also promote the actor-side of democratization. They support the empowerment of political actors, for example by promoting the development of political parties and the training of delegates to assemblies, and they invest in control organs. This includes the promotion of free media and civil society organizations at both local and national levels (Gershman 2004; Kumar 2005, 2006; Erdmann 2006).

These programmes are accompanied by the hope for a spread of democratic thinking and behaviour to all the other areas requiring reform in postwar societies. As shown in the transition model above, it is clear that the success of democratization is closely linked to success in other reform areas; otherwise substantial problems remain and place the emerging democratic regime under stress. This concerns, for example, the challenge of state- and nation-building. Linz and Stepan (1996) convincingly argue in their seminal contribution that, without clarifying (and certifying) who belongs to the state and is therefore allowed to vote and to be elected, one cannot rule a country democratically. The representativeness of the government will always be questioned and those who were defeated in an election will never accept the decision. The unsolved question of citizenship will constantly be brought to the table and, as the examples of Bosnia-Herzegovina (Gromes 2009) and Kosovo (Tansey 2007; ICG 2008) have already shown, this can even threaten state survival.

Practitioners regularly state that young democracies emerging from violent conflict are overwhelmed by the mere amount of reform tasks and challenges with which their ruling elites are confronted. Therefore, they ask for the prioritization of external efforts (Spanger and Wolff 2007). But what should come first: security, socio-economic development, nation-building or democracy? In my mind, it is almost impossible to give one area priority at the expense of another. One risks unintended negative spillover effects and, in the worst case, even the complete blockage of the process (Grimm 2008). These blockades occur, in particular, when important aspects are not clarified in an area that functions as a prerequisite for further development in another area. Take for example the case of the return and reintegration of refugees and displaced persons in Bosnia-Herzegovina (political community) after the 1991–5 Yugoslav secession wars that ended with the 1995 Dayton Peace Agreement. Without the guarantee of political and civil rights and the clarification of property rights (rule of law) most of the refugees and displaced persons could not and would not return to their home of origin. However, the incumbent parties delayed passing the necessary legal acts in the early post-conflict years. In turn, urgently needed workers did not return, which further retarded economic recovery (economy prosperity). The emerging democracy failed to produce socio-economic success, which undermined its legitimacy (democracy) and even challenged the survival of the federal state as a whole (security) (for more details on Bosnia-Herzegovina's difficult path to democracy see Manning and Antić 2003; Oellers-Frahm 2005; Divjak and Pugh 2008; Gromes 2009).

Third-party intervention as external democratization

Insofar as reforming a post-conflict society is such a challenging task, all major conflict-resolution enterprises after 1990 have been assisted from the outside. When Western donors coming from democratic political systems support conflict resolution, they combine their engagement mostly with a liberal democratic agenda as described above. However, their request to support – and in some cases even to impose democracy from the outside – is challenged by classical democratization theory. Building on the seminal work of Rustow (1970), renowned transition experts such as Higley and Burton (1989), O'Donnell and Schmitter (1989), Przeworski (1991, 1992) and Merkel (2004) see democratization foremost as an endogenous process driven by internal elite settlements and based on a comprehensive elite consensus on democratic institutions. Higley and Burton

(1989) argue that an elite consensus on decision-making procedures, basic values and the required reform programme is necessary for successful democratization. In the long run, such a consensus allows for cooperation, trust-building and the capacity to compromise what in turn guarantees the survival of democracy, or in other words, the permanent elites' compliance with new democratic rules of the game. And because the political elites follow the rules, it is claimed that the people will also accept democracy as a legitimate political system. Furthermore, Merkel (2004) states that the larger the elite consensus, the more stable and the less vulnerable democracy becomes. Without such an internal elite consensus, the country would risk falling back into authoritarianism or, at best, stabilize as a democracy with defects.

Przeworski (1991: 61–64) perceives democratization as a result of permanently changing strategic situations, where members of the old regime and their political opponents try to push through their interests. On this perspective, democratization is an outcome of rationally behaving actors who either consent to democracy *or* who misperceive their chances to maintain power or to obtain access to power and therefore accept democratic reforms. In the latter case, democratization results when the hardliners of the old regime overestimate their power and accept reform demands because they believe themselves able to manage the transition from above without the political cost of losing elections. Regime and opposition elites also negotiate pacts in order to reduce the uncertainty about their future political influence. Whichever approach one prefers, Higley/ Burton's and Merkel's empirical-descriptive, or Przeworski's deductive-analytical one, both strands agree that democratization must be an internally driven process. This opinion challenges the concept of successful external democratization. Therefore, recent analysis in transition and post-conflict studies seeks to answer the question of whether or not external actors can alter internal elites' interests and preferences in favour of democratization, and if external actors can successfully support (or even impose) the development of democratic institutions.

Before one can assess the effectiveness of external oversight, one needs to distinguish its means. The means that external actors actually use range from less intrusive to highly intrusive forms of external intervention in democracy-building. At the less intrusive pole of the continuum, external actors refer to mediation during peace negotiations as a window of opportunity to encourage the institutionalization of democracy. Expert advice, persuasion and promises for financial and personal aid seek to alter the preferences of the warring parties and make them accept the drafting of democratic institutions. This mediation is often followed by the monitoring of the initiated democratization process, whereby external actors respect local ownership of the institutionaliza- tion of democracy. Moderately intrusive is the supervision of the peace process, whereby external and internal actors equally share the responsibility for building democracy. The task of adminis- tering the country is temporarily performed as a joint venture. In its most common form, external actors take over the responsibility for security-building and the monopoly of force, whereas internal actors constitute the government and draft the reform programme in the above described reform areas. For the latter, external actors usually also offer expert advice and money – democracy assistance tools well known from the field of developmental cooperation. At the most intrusive pole of the continuum, the responsibility for administering the country and for taking reform decisions temporarily goes entirely to external actors. If the warring parties consent, the external engagement takes the form of an international trusteeship administration; if the conflicting parties do not consent, external actors use the framework of an occupational regime (Grimm 2010: 19). Examples for monitoring missions accompanying a military peace mission can be found in Mozambique (1992–4), Rwanda (1993–6), Haiti (1993–7, and again since 2004), Angola (1995–9), Sierra Leone (1999–2005), the Democratic Republic of Congo (since 1999), Macedonia (2001–3), Liberia (since 2003), the Solomon Islands (since 2003), Burundi (2004–6), and Côte d'Ivoire (since 2004). Supervision has taken place in Bosnia-Herzegovina since the

Table 28.1   Military intervention and external oversight of democratization, 1990–2010

Country	Duration of military mission	External oversight over political reorganization	Peace[1]	State of democracy in 2010		
				Elections have taken place[2]	Democratic institutions implemented[3]	Human rights protection guaranteed[4]
Cambodia	1992–3	Trusteeship Administration	–	✓	–	–
Mozambique	1992–4	Monitoring	✓	✓	–	–
Rwanda	1993–4	Monitoring	–	✓	–	–
Haiti	1993–7	Monitoring	–	✓	–	–
	2004–...	Monitoring	✓	✓	–	–
Angola	1995–9	Monitoring	–	✓	–	–
Bosnia-Herzegovina	1995–...	Monitoring, since 1997 supervision	✓	✓	–	–
East Timor	1999–2005	Trusteeship Administration, since 2002 supervision	–	✓	–	–
	2006–...	Monitoring	✓	✓	✓	–
Democratic Republic of Congo	1999–...	Monitoring	–	✓	–	–
Kosovo	1999–...	Trusteeship Administration, since 2008 supervision	✓	✓	✓	–
Sierra Leone	1999–2005	Monitoring	✓	✓	✓	–
Macedonia	2001–3	Monitoring	✓	✓	✓	–
Afghanistan	2001–...	Supervision	✓	✓	–	–
Iraq	2003–...	Occupation, since 2004 monitoring	–	✓	–	–
Liberia	2003–...	Monitoring	✓	✓	✓	–
Salomon Islands	2003–...	Monitoring	✓	✓	✓	–
Burundi	2004–2006	Monitoring	–	✓	✓	–
Côte d'Ivoire	2004–...	Monitoring	✓	✓	–	–

Source: Own research. '–' no, '✓' yes.
[1] State of peace according to UCDP (2009a, 2009b) at year of withdrawal of troops or in case of ongoing intervention in 2009.
[2] Presidential or parliamentary elections on national level.
[3] State of democratic institutions according to Polity IV (2009) 'polity2'-score ≥ 6.
[4] State of human rights protection according to Freedom House (2010) average of 'political rights-' and 'civil liberties-'scores ≤ 2.5.

granting of the 'Bonn powers' in 1997, after efforts to simply monitor the peace process through the office of the High Representative failed. Similarly, the original 'light footprint approach' of the international community in Afghanistan (since 2001) crept into an international supervision of peace-building. United Nations trusteeship administrations have been implemented in Cambodia (1992–3), East Timor (1999–2002; since 2006 monitoring) and Kosovo (1999–2008). Iraq is the only country since 1990 to be forced into an occupational regime (2003–4) after the 2003 military intervention of the so-called 'Multinational Forces' led by the US government. This list equals 19 military interventions followed by external democratization in 17 countries for the sake of conflict resolution in the period 1990–2010 (see Table 28.1).

Depending on the degree of intrusiveness, external actors became part of democratization during these missions. Democratization was no longer a solely 'endogenous process' as older transition theory states. However, despite an extensive deployment of troops and civil support missions, and the spending of US$113 billion as 'official development assistance (ODA)' by the member states of the Organization for Economic Cooperation and Development (OECD) in 1990–2006 (OECD 2007), the balance of peace-building and democratization in these cases is mixed.

Assessing success of conflict resolution by external democratization

In only three of nine intervention cases in which the military intervention is concluded was there a negative peace at the point of the withdrawal of military troops (which means in Galtung's terms (1990) the absence of war or violent conflict). In 10 cases the military interventions were continuing in 2010. In 7 of these 10 cases, intervening troops achieved a negative peace that is still stable, in contrast to the 3 remaining cases with ongoing interventions. In the Democratic Republic of Congo, one-sided violence still occurs against civilians, in Afghanistan war continues after nearly a decade and, in Iraq, more than seven years after the external interventions (see UCDP 2009a, 2009b).

Concerning democratization, by 2010 democratic elections had indeed taken place in all 17 selected countries. Democratic constitutions were drafted and entered into force. However, according to the Polity IV dataset (2009), only 7 out of the 17 countries had functioning democratic institutions available for daily use. Following the Freedom House (2010) scale that measures political rights and civil liberties, none of the countries has yet fulfilled the standards of human rights protection comparable to a consolidated democracy.

Obviously, formal institutions such as democratic elections and constitutions can relatively easily be installed with external help. However, the consolidation of these formal political institutions is much more difficult. Thus, the emerging democracy suffers from a constant risk of institutional failure, which in turn could provoke relapse into war and violent conflict. Furthermore, the majority of countries in crisis remain dependent on external help even after the withdrawal of military troops. However, despite these donor dependencies, external actors seem hardly able to guarantee in the long run a stable peace on the basis of a consolidated democracy, no matter which type of external oversight has been used. Nor can external actors completely compensate for deficits caused by self-interested internal elites with nationalistic or economic agendas, who profit more from an unstable insecure status of ongoing transition instead of a stable, rule of law-based consolidated democracy.

Dilemmas of external democratization

The mixed results of external democratization as a tool for conflict resolution can be explained, on the one hand, through the challenging process of democratization itself and, on the other hand, through the performance of external actors.

To begin with the challenging process of democratization itself, first one has to bear in mind that democratization targets, according to Dahl and others, the introduction of competition in the political arena, clearly an antipode to stability and thus a challenge for an unstable post-conflict society. Przeworski *et al.* (1996: 51) characterize democratic contestation as a process of *ex ante* uncertainty and *ex post* irreversibility. They state thereby that only the procedural means such as electoral suffrage and political decision-making are known, but not the ends. Thus, conflicting parties can never be sure if their interest will be respected in decision-making, and, once a decision is taken, they cannot reverse it. In conflict-ridden societies such open-endedness and insecurity can lead to the risk of renewing violent conflict. In this regard it is no wonder that experts in international relations show that countries in transition have a higher risk of violent conflict and that these countries can also become a source of destabilization for neighbouring countries. The combination of increasing mass political participation and weak political institutions may create the motive and the opportunity for both rising and declining elites to play the nationalist card in an attempt to rally popular support against domestic and foreign rivals (Snyder 2000; Mann 2005; Mansfield and Snyder 2005, 2009; Collier *et al.* 2008).

Second, democratic elections by definition legitimize the elected representatives, even when these representatives do not comply with a democratic agenda, but are, for example, nationalist, radical or authoritarian. They can even award factions preferring violent means of conflict resolution (Jarstad 2008: 22) or playing the double game of politics and violence (Höglund *et al.* 2009: 538). Electoral success of anti-democratic forces can thus reduce room for further democratic development; authoritarian backlashes and even the breakdown of democratic rule become both possible and realistic (Reilly 2002; Manning and Antić 2003). Third, power-sharing instruments may be good to begin the transition to democracy and peace. Mostly, such carefully balanced institutional arrangements are the only way out of conflict. According to Rothchild and Roeder (2005), the consensus of all warring factions becomes a powerful signal of committing to resolve future disputes peacefully. But the same power-sharing institutions may be unstable and produce incentives to escalate future ethnic conflicts to more destructive levels. Rothchild and Roeder (2005: 13) show that oversized all-party governments with mutual vetoes may erode the efficiency of government over the longer term and increase the likelihood of decision-making deadlock, while proportional representation rules in parliament may hinder interethnic cooperation, and autonomous regions may become states within the state with a potential to sabotage the central government. Even worse, in many cases civil society organizations that might moderate the political process are excluded from power-sharing (Jarstad 2008: 23). Finally, as mentioned above, democracy needs a decision as to who belongs to the citizenry. Unfinished nation-building can provoke constant struggle over 'belongingness' and participation rights, and sometimes even the very existence of the state is questioned (Rustow 1970: 351; Linz and Stepan 1996). And when the survival of the state is substantially questioned, democratic rules can hardly unfold to their full potential of conflict resolution.

Beyond the conflicting objectives of peace-building and stabilization on the one hand, and democratization on the other, poor performance of external actors can also worsen the situation in a post-conflict society. First, most peace- and democracy-building missions lack accountability to the citizens in the target state. External democratization as a form of external control often ignores the need for local ownership of institution-building. An intervention that is blind to local needs and fears, risks increasing support for extremism and problematic forms of ethno-nationalism (Caplan 2005b; Jarstad 2008: 24). Second, de Zeeuw (2005) argues convincingly that 'projects do not create institutions'. Following de Zeeuw, post-conflict democracy programmes of international donors consist mainly of technical, material and financial assistance as well as short-term project aid. This aid may have spurred the growth of training activities and non-governmental organizations that excel in organizing workshops and seminars, but proves unsustainable and largely insignificant in the wider process of democratization, in particular in sustainable institution-building. Mostly focusing on short-term stability, leadership may be legitimized during well-funded elections but, de Zeeuw (2005) accounts critically, key issues of political control and regulation often remain unaddressed. Third, the general 'democracy templates' used by Western donors are often ill-suited to local contexts. Mostly external actors follow general aid agendas and blueprints without adapting them sensibly to the local context and respecting local traditions for conflict resolution (Jawad 2008). Finally – and most frequently cited in the literature – donor programmes and activities often lack coherence and coordination despite declarations to the contrary, numerous meetings, and basket-funding arrangements. Too little is known about what the other donors do, and sometimes different donor agencies even support contradicting reforms and institutions (Jones 2002; Paris 2004: 228–232; Caplan 2005a: 230–250; Herrhausen 2007; Zeeuw 2007).

To sum up, the norm of external democratization seems not to be a perfect solution for a post-conflict society, and the way it is implemented often does not meet the high expectations donors and target societies develop when they opt for democratization in a post-conflict context. Nevertheless, I will argue in the next section that despite its flaws democratization remains without a legitimate alternative in a post-conflict society.

Legitimacy of external democratization

Is external interference in a transition and reform process after violent conflict legitimate considering the manifold dilemmas attending external democratization? Can people in a post-colonial world still be 'forced to be free' (Peceny 1999) as was the case for Germany and Japan (Montgomery 1957) after the Second World War? Many analysts today are sceptical. They regard post-conflict state-building and democracy-building from the outside – in particular the more intrusive forms – as a new variant of colonialism. In Paris's (2004: 151) view, international peace-builders have promulgated a particular vision of how states should organize themselves internally, based on the principles of liberal democracy and market-oriented economy. By reconstructing war-shattered states in accordance with this vision, peace-builders would have effectively transmitted standards of appropriate behaviour from the Western liberal 'core' of the international system to the failed states of the 'periphery'. Paris (2002: 637) states that this form of peace-building resembles an 'updated (and more benign) version of the "*mission civilisatrice*", of the colonial-era belief that the European imperial powers had a duty to "civilize" dependent populations and territories'. Others, such as Chandler and Ignatieff, assess post-conflict state-building and democracy-building as new methods of exercising Western power, of the needs of the market, or of 'empire'(Chandler 2006) and 'imperialism' (Ignatieff 2003). As Chandler (2006: 10) notes: 'On the surface, the post-Cold War UN framework of sovereign equality appears to be intact but, underneath the formal trappings of independence, non-Western state governments have been opened up to a wide range of external regulatory controls and direct intervention under the rubric of state capacity-building.' With regard to, for example, Bosnia-Herzegovina, Kosovo and Afghanistan, both authors state that American military power, European money and humanitarian motives have combined to produce a form of imperial rule for a post-colonial age. Most critical here is that, according to both authors, these new forms of 'empire' would officially deny any direct political control, and would formally reinforce the legal status of sovereignty. Chandler (2006: 15) also argues that these practices might be much more interventionist than those based on contractual relations enforced by market dependency: 'The hierarchy of power and external dependency of states on external aid or debt relief is not concealed, through the equality of legal

12th. Thanks for your services, doctor; it's lost labour.

Doctor Arnott, don't people die of weakness? How can a man live eating so little?

13th. [Antommarchi with pills.]

Are they well wrapped up, covered? They won't poison my mouth? Really? [To Marchand.] Well, here you are, rascal, swallow them. He needed medicine, didn't he, doctor, and my pills will do him good? Give him some more now; as for me, I won't touch them again.

15th. I have nothing but satisfaction to express with my beloved wife, Maria Louisa; I shall retain my tender sentiments for her till my last breath; I beg her to watch and protect my son from the pitfalls that still surround his young days.

I bequeath to my son the objects specified in the schedule hereto. I hope this slight legacy will be dear to him, as recalling the memory of a father whom the whole world will tell him of.

Marchand will keep my hair, and will have a bracelet made of it that is to be sent to the Empress Maria Louisa.

16th. I wish my ashes to rest by the banks of the Seine, in the midst of the people of France whom I loved so dearly.

I have written too much. Ah, what suffering! What oppression! I feel at the left end of the stomach a pain that is unbearable. – You ought to marry, doctor. Marry an Englishwoman, her ice-cold blood will moderate the fire that devours you; you will become less obstinate. – Give me the potion!

19th. You are not mistaken, my friends, I am better today; but none the less I feel the end drawing near. When I am dead you will all have the sweet consolation of returning to Europe. You will see your relatives, your friends there, while I shall meet the brave in the Elysian Fields. I will relate the last events of my life to them.

21st. I was born in the Catholic faith, I wish to carry out the duties it imposes and to receive the consolation it gives.

24th. I have written too much, doctor; I am collapsing, I can't go on.

25th. [To M. Lafitte.] Monsieur Lafitte: I handed you, in 1815, as I was leaving Paris, a sum of six millions for which you gave me a duplicate receipt; I have cancelled one, and I charge Count Montholon to present the other to you, in order that you may hand the said sum to him after my death.

28th. After my death, which cannot be far off, I want my body to be opened; I also want, I exact, that no English doctor shall touch me. I further wish you to take my heart, place it in spirits of wine, and take it to my dear Marie Louise at Parma. You will tell her that I loved her tenderly, you will relate to her all you have seen, all that concerns my situation here, and my death.

May 2nd, 2 A. M.:

Stengel! Desaix! Masséna! Ah, victory is ours; go, hasten, press home the charge; they are ours!

3rd, 3 P. M.:

You have shared my exile, you will be faithful to my memory, you will do nothing to injure it.

5th, 5.30 P. M.:

. . . head . . . army . . .

5.50 P. M.:

THE END

BIOGRAPHICAL NOTES

The following brief biographical notes concern some of the individuals mentioned in the main text.

Abbatucci, General Jacques-Pierre (1723–1813). This elderly Corsican general served under Napoleon in Italy, but as suggested by the latter's remarks (entry for 14 August 1796), he was retired later that year.

Abdallah-Aga. The Ottoman commander of Jaffa survived the massacre of the garrison after it surrendered to the French by pleading for mercy, but Napoleon had him beheaded in July 1799.

Abou-Bekr (AD 573–634). Napoleon's reference (entry for 15 June 1799) concerns the important place held in the Islamic world by the descendants of Abou-Bekr (father-in-law and companion of Mohammed, and the first of the Muslim Caliphs), and of Fatima, Mohammed's daughter.

Abrantes, Duke of: see Junot.

Albitte, one of the representatives 'en mission' with the French Army, who ordered Napoleon's brief arrest after the *coup* of Thermidor. Later he was implicated in the disturbances of 1st Prairial (20 May) 1795, but escaped the fate of most of the other Jacobin leaders, who were capitally convicted.

Alexander I, Tsar of Russia (1777–1825); successor to the throne of Russia in March 1801, following the murder of his father, Paul I, in which some suspected he was implicated. Alexander's youthful idealism and admiration for Napoleon faded, and Russia opposed the French until forced to accede to the Treaty of Tilsit. The subsequent breakdown in Franco-Russian relations culminated with Napoleon's invasion of 1812, after which Russia played a major role in the war against France. Despite his initial liberal inclinations, Alexander remained an absolute monarch.

Alexander, King of Macedon, known as 'the Great' (356–323 BC); mentioned by Napoleon (entry for 14 March 1814) in reference to the cutting of Gordian knots. This relates to a story concerning the city of Gordium, where there was a wagon or chariot said to have belonged to its founder, King Gordius, on which the yoke and pole were bound by a huge and complicated knot. It was said that whoever untied the knot would become the ruler of Asia, but Alexander simply cut it with his sword instead of attempting to unravel it.

Alquier, French diplomat, ambassador to the Pope in 1806 and subsequently to Sweden.

Alvintzy, Baron Josef (1735–1810). An experienced Transylvanian general of the Austrian Army, Alvintzy served in Italy against Napoleon, being defeated at Arcola and Rivoli. Subsequently, he attained the rank of *Feldmarschall* and served as governor of Hungary.

Amherst, William Pitt, 1st Earl (1773–1857). Sent on an abortive British mission to China, Amherst was shipwrecked and on his return journey to England he called at St Helena, where he met Napoleon. He is best-known for his service as governor-general of India (1823–8).

Andréossy, General Antoine-François (1761–1828). This French artillery general served with Napoleon in Italy and Egypt, and subsequently held a number of important diplomatic positions, including ambassador to Britain (1803), to Austria (1806–9) and to Turkey (1812–13).

Andromaque. Napoleon's references in the entries for 8 February and 16 March 1814, and 14 October 1818, concern the mythological Greek character Andromache, wife of Hector, and her son Astyanax, whose family were all slain by Achilles. In Homer's version she demonstrates noble resignation toward the tragedies that befall her family, but the story was also recounted by Euripides and Racine, and it must be to the latter's version that Napoleon refers. Evidently he was comparing the situation of Andromache, Hector and Astyanax to Marie-Louise, himself and his son.

Antommarchi, Francesco (1789–1838). A Corsican who had studied medicine at Pisa and Florence, Antommarchi was chosen by Cardinal Fesch to serve as Napoleon's physician at St Helena from September 1819. He performed the post-mortem and subsequently published an account of Napoleon's final years.

Antonio, Don ('the Infant'). The somewhat simple brother of King Charles IV of Spain, Antonio was briefly head of the Spanish Junta of Regency; he shared the virtual imprisonment of Charles IV and Ferdinand VII at Valençay, where he spent much of his time in the library, mutilating books by removing anything he considered immoral or irreligious.

Archimedes (287–212 BC). Napoleon refers to the great Greek mathematician and inventor in the entry for 4 August 1816 in relation to Archimedes' famous remark, 'Give me a firm spot on which to stand, and I will move the earth' (on the attributes of the lever), which Napoleon compared to his own ability to achieve what he had determined upon.

Arnott, Dr Archibald (1771–1855). Surgeon of the British 20th Foot, Arnott was the senior medical officer at St Helena and was consulted by Antommarchi on the subject of Napoleon's health. He first met the ex-emperor on 1 April 1821 and became so friendly with him that Napoleon gave him a gold snuffbox, on which he had scratched his initial, and left him £600. Arnott attended him to the end and was present at the post-mortem.

Artois, Charles-Philippe, comte d' (1757–1836). Son of Louis XVI and younger brother of Louis XVIII, Artois was one of the most ardent of the French Royalist leaders and lived in exile in Britain, hence Napoleon's remarks in the entry for 28 December 1802. After his brother's restoration, Artois led the ultra-Royalist faction and succeeded to the throne as Charles X, but he was deposed in 1830 and again found refuge in Britain.

Asturias, Prince of the: see Ferdinand VII.

Astyanax: see Andromaque.

Auerstädt, Duke of: see Davout.

Augereau, Marshal Pierre-François-Charles (1757–1816). One of Napoleon's oldest and most valued subordinates, Augereau served from the Italian campaign through to 1814. He was appointed a marshal in 1804, and in 1808 was ennobled as Duke of Castiglione, a title taken from the battle of that name, where he performed one of his greatest services (5 August 1796).

Augusta, Princess (Augusta-Amelia of Bavaria, 1788–1851). Despite being arranged by Napoleon, the marriage of this Bavarian princess to Eugène de Beauharnais was a genuine love match, and they were extremely happy. Napoleon's reference in the entry for 29 August 1806 concerns Augusta's pregnancy with Eugène's first child, although his recipe to ensure the birth of a son was unsuccessful: on 14 March 1807, she gave birth to a daughter, Josephine (1807–76) who, in 1823, married Bernadotte's son, later King Oscar I of Sweden.

Augustus, Emperor (63 BC–AD 14). Napoleon's reference in the entry for 3 October 1809 concerns the first Roman emperor, Gaius Octavius, known as Augustus.

Augustus, Prince of Prussia. In the 1806 campaign, Augustus commanded Hohenlohe's rearguard and was captured at the surrender at Prenzlau. The entry for 6 December 1807 describes him as among those captivated by Madame de Staël.

Austria, Emperor of: see Francis II.

Austria, Empress of. When mentioned by Napoleon (entry for 21 May 1812), the Empress of Austria was Francis I's third wife, Maria Ludovica Beatrix of Este, whom he had married in 1808. After her death, he married for a fourth time, to Carolina Augusta of Bavaria (1816).

Azara, Don José Nicholas de (1731–1804). Noted both as a diplomat and an antiquary, Azara was the long-serving Spanish ambassador to Rome, who had been instrumental in securing the election of Pope Pius VI. In 1796, he acted on behalf of the Pope, and on 24 June arrived in Bologna to confer with Napoleon, as noted in the entry for 26 June. Subsequently, he served as Spanish ambassador to Paris. Napoleon liked him and found him easy to influence, but although originally friendly toward France, Azara became somewhat disillusioned.

Bagration, General Peter (1765–1812). A fierce and indomitable Russian commander, Bagration was a very experienced general who led the Second West Army in the resistance to Napoleon's invasion of Russia in 1812. Mortally wounded at Borodino, he was a great loss to the Russian Army.

Baraguay d'Hilliers, General Louis (1764–1813). This French general occupied Venice in 1797 and subsequently served quite widely, including in the Peninsula and Russian campaigns. His conduct in command of a division in the latter led to his dismissal (9 November 1812); he died before an enquiry could be held.

Barbé-Marbois, François, marquis de (1745–1837). A diplomat of the *Ancien Régime*, Barbé-Marbois was employed by Napoleon as a councillor of state and as minister of finance (1802–5), hence Napoleon's instruction to him to 'reassure the financiers' (entry for 9 August 1805). Caulaincourt recorded how Napoleon regarded him as unprincipled and untalented, and so transferred him to head the court of accounts where he could do no damage!

Barbier, M., Napoleon's librarian. Rather more than half of the thousand books Napoleon requested (entry for 17 July 1808) concerned history, and he even specified the format: without margins to economise on space, and with loose backs so that they would open flat.

Barclay de Tolly, General Mikhail Andreas (1761–1818). One of the leading

Russian commanders of the period, born in Livonia of Scots ancestry, Barclay de Tolly served as war minister (1810–13), led the First West Army in 1812 and after Bautzen was appointed as Russian commander-in-chief. Although rather cautious, he was not a bad field commander, while his administrative reforms were very significant.

Barras, Paul-François-Jean-Nicolas (1755–1829). One of the most important political figures of the later Revolutionary period, Barras became friendly toward Napoleon, whom he encountered at Toulon. As a director, his notorious immorality and avarice did much to undermine the reputation of that body, thus facilitating the *coup* of Brumaire, which brought Napoleon to power. His political career ended with the fall of the Directory, whereupon he retired to enjoy his dubiously-accumulated wealth. Josephine was one of his mistresses prior to her marriage to Napoleon.

Barthélemy, François, later marquis de (1747 or 1750–1830). Nephew of the renowned writer and numismatist Abbé Jean-Jacques Barthélemy (1716–95), François Barthélemy occupied a number of diplomatic posts under the Revolutionary government. Elected a director in 1797, he was arrested and deported later that year, returning after the *coup* of Brumaire. He entered the Senate in 1800.

Bassano, Duke of: see Maret.

Bataille de Tancarville, Colonel Baron Auguste. The ADC criticised by Napoleon in the entry for 7 September 1807 was an artillery officer selected as a member of Eugène's closest staff; he remained a devoted member of Eugène's staff even after the end of the latter's military career.

Bathurst, Henry, 3rd Earl (1762–1834). One of Britain's leading politicians, Bathurst served briefly as Foreign Secretary (1809), and from 1812 until 1827 was Secretary for War and the Colonies, responsible for much of the material and moral support for Wellington's army in the Peninsula.

Bavaria, Elector, later King of: see Maximilian I.

Bavaria, Prince Royal of: see Ludwig.

Bavaria, Queen of. The queen who so impressed Napoleon (see entry for 30 November 1817) was the second wife of Maximilian I, Princess Caroline Fredrike of Baden, whom he had married in 1797.

Beauharnais, Eugène de (1781–1824). Napoleon's stepson (the child of Josephine and her first husband), Eugène de Beauharnais became one of

Napoleon's most loyal subordinates. Appointed Viceroy of Italy in 1805, he led the Army of Italy in the 1809 and 1812 campaigns, and continued to support Napoleon until 1814. His father, General Alexander-François-Marie, vicomte de Beauharnais (1760–94), who is mentioned in the entry for 30 June 1797, had been guillotined after condemnation by the Revolutionary Tribunal.

Beauharnais, Hortense (1783–1837), Josephine's daughter and thus Napoleon's stepdaughter. Hortense Beauharnais was unhappily married to Louis Bonaparte and consequently became Queen of Holland.

Beauharnais, 'citoyen Tascher' (entry for 11 March 1796): see Josephine.

Beaulieu, General Johann Peter (1725–1819). This experienced Austrian commander retired from active duty following his defeats by Napoleon at Montenotte and Lodi in 1796.

Beker, General Nicolas-Léonard-Bagert (1770–1840), a French cavalry officer, general from 1801, who served quite widely until disgraced in 1809 by his criticisms of Napoleon. He commanded the escort that took Napoleon to exile in 1815, hence the reference in the entry for 15 July 1815.

Bellegarde, Field-Marshal Heinrich Joseph Johannes, Count (1756–1845). An experienced Austrian commander, Bellegarde was Archduke Charles's deputy in 1796 and accompanied him to Italy in the following year. He played a leading role in the battles of Essling and Wagram.

Belliard, General Augustin-Daniel (1769–1832). Promoted to general after serving under Napoleon in Italy, Belliard was governor of Cairo during the Egyptian campaign and wrote a ten-volume history of that expedition. Subsequently, he served as chief of staff to Murat and Joseph Bonaparte, and when mentioned in the entry for 23 January 1814 was *aide-major-général* for the *Grande Armée*, having recovered from being shot in the left arm at Leipzig.

Belluno, Duke of: see Victor.

Bennigsen, General Levin August Theophil (1745–1826). A Hanoverian soldier who entered Russian service in 1773, Bennigsen commanded the Russian Army at Pultusk and Eylau; he served as Kutuzov's chief of staff in 1812 and commanded formations in 1813–14.

Berg, Grand Duke of: see Murat.

Bernadotte, Marshal Jean-Baptiste-Jules (1763–1844). A general by 1794, this remarkable man served under Napoleon in Italy and became allied to the

Bonaparte family by his marriage to Désirée Clary (Joseph's sister-in-law; hence Napoleon's remark to Joseph in the entry for 5 June 1806 that Bernadotte had been ennobled out of consideration for Joseph's wife). Appointed a Marshal of France by Napoleon in 1804, and Prince of Ponte Corvo, he was virtually dismissed by Napoleon for mishandling his corps at Wagram and, as a result, accepted the position of Crown Prince of Sweden in 1810. He led the Army of the North against Napoleon in 1813–14, and in 1818 succeeded to the Swedish throne as King Carl XIV Johan. His family still occupies that throne, so of all the Napoleonic dignitaries he was the only one to have founded an enduring dynasty, somewhat ironically as he had been among the most ardent of republicans.

Bernardin de St Pierre, Jacques Henri (1737–1814). An important French literary figure and friend of Rousseau, Bernardin de St Pierre was perhaps best-known for his *Etudes de la Nature* (1784), intended to prove the existence of God through nature, and *Paul et Virginie* (1789), which Napoleon mentions in the entry for 22 January 1816. At the time Napoleon remembered him pleading poverty, he was on a state pension, while in 1792 he had married a wife who had a considerable dowry.

Berry, Charles-Ferdinand, Duke of (1778–1820). Son of the comte d'Artois, Berry was one of the leading members of the exiled French Royalist movement, hence Napoleon's claim (entry for 19 March 1804) that had Berry been in Paris, even under the protection of the Austrian ambassador Cobenzl, he would have had him shot; presumably a comment intended to justify the seizure of the duc d'Enghien from neutral territory.

Berthier, Marshal Louis-Alexandre, prince de Neuchâtel (1753–1815), Napoleon's chief-of-staff who served him from 1796 until the abdication of 1814. Undistinguished as a field commander, Berthier was invaluable as a staff officer, and was appointed a marshal in 1804, Prince of Neuchâtel in 1806 and Prince of Wagram in 1809. Napoleon's comment of 'what I am doing for you' in the entry for 1 April 1806 refers to Berthier's appointment as Prince of Neuchâtel, but the rest of the message was probably less welcome. Instead of recognising Berthier's liaison with his mistress, Madame Visconti, Napoleon arranged a marriage for him in 1808 with Princess Marie-Elisabeth of Bavaria (1784–1849), which Berthier regretted.

Berthollet, Claude-Louis (1748–1822). A notable scientist, physician and chemist, Berthollet accompanied Monge to Italy to select works of art from the conquered regions for appropriation by France; he was also a member of the Egyptian Institute. Napoleon ennobled him as a count.

Bertrand, General Henri-Gratien (1773–1844). Originally an engineer,

Bertrand was one of the most loyal of Napoleon's subordinates, serving as his aide, as governor-general of Illyria (1811–12), and from January 1813 as commander of the corps of observation of Italy, later IV Corps of the *Grande Armée*. He accompanied Napoleon to both Elba and St Helena, and escorted Napoleon's body on its repatriation to France in 1840. Bertrand's half-English wife, Fanny, dutifully followed him, although she pleaded with Napoleon not to take her husband to St Helena.

Berwick, James Fitzjames, Duke of (1670–1734). Natural son of King James II of England, Berwick was a Marshal of France and one of the leading military commanders of his age. He was killed at Philipsburg.

Bessières, Marshal Jean-Baptiste (1768–1813). Originally commander of Napoleon's small escort of Guides, this renowned cavalry commander led the Guard cavalry at Marengo and was appointed a marshal in 1804. Acknowledged as an honest, worthy man, he became a close friend of Napoleon, who ennobled him as Duke of Istria in 1809. Perhaps too cautious to make an outstanding field commander, he remained a loyal subordinate until killed at Rippach in 1813.

Bianchi, General Vicenz Friedrich (1768–1855). When mentioned (entry for 19 February 1814), this Austrian general was commanding I Corps of the Austrian Army, but was not personally in command at Montereau, having left only one brigade in support of the Crown Prince of Würtemburg's IV Corps, which was the force defeated there. Later, Bianchi achieved fame for his defeat of Murat at Tolentino, for which he was awarded the Neapolitan dukedom of Casalanza.

Billon, M. In 1795, 'citoyen Billon', a middle-aged soap manufacturer from Aubagne, was a suitor for Pauline Bonaparte. He was rejected because of his lack of money.

Blake, General Joachim (1759–1827). Of Irish descent, Blake was one of the best Spanish commanders of the Peninsular War. As Captain-General of Galicia, in 1808 he was defeated at Espinosa (entry for 18 November 1808) and subsequently held other commands, without great success, until captured at the surrender of Valencia in January 1812.

Blücher, Field-Marshal Gebhard Leberecht von (1742–1819). One of Napoleon's most determined opponents, this fiery old Prussian was a leading member of the anti-French 'war party' in Prussia in 1806, and was one of the last to give up the fight after Jena. Field-Marshal from 1813, he was one of the senior Allied commanders in 1813–14, and in 1815 he led the Prussian Army that helped inflict the final defeat upon Napoleon. His nickname, '*Marschall Vorwärts*' ('Marshal Forward'), exemplified his favoured strategy.

Bon, General Louis-André (1758–99). A general from 1794, Bon served under Napoleon in Italy, being wounded at Arcola. He was mortally wounded in the attempted storming of Acre.

Bonaparte, Caroline (Maria-Annunciata-Caroline, 1782–1839), Napoleon's youngest sister. She married Murat in 1800 and became, in succession, Grand Duchess of Berg and Queen of Naples. Despite not being entirely faithful – she had a notorious affair with Junot – she was a capable woman who worked hard for Murat's advancement, which caused some conflict with Napoleon.

Bonaparte, Charles-Marie (Carlo, 1746–85), Napoleon's father. A lawyer and member of minor nobility in Corsica, his influence upon the family was probably quite limited, and he died when Napoleon was aged only 15.

Bonaparte, Eliza (Marie-Anne-Elise, 1777–1820), Napoleon's eldest sister. In 1797, she married Félix Bacciochi and was given the principality of Piombino and republic of Lucca by Napoleon. In 1808, he allocated her a larger territory as Grand Duchess of Tuscany. A much stronger character than her husband, she ruled independently and thus relations became somewhat strained with Napoleon. After the collapse of the empire, her family was allowed to settle near Trieste, Eliza having taken the title of Countess of Compignano.

Bonaparte, Jérôme (1784–1860), the youngest, most indolent and least talented of Napoleon's brothers. He had an undistinguished career in the French Navy and infuriated his brother by marrying Elizabeth Patterson of Baltimore. Napoleon had the marriage annulled, arranged for Jérôme to wed Princess Catherine of Würtemberg and appointed him King of Westphalia. Jéröme went home after an undistinguished command at the start of the 1812 campaign, and handled his troops poorly at Waterloo. In exile after the fall of the empire, he returned to France in 1847, becoming a marshal and president of the Senate.

Bonaparte, Joseph (1768–1844), the eldest of the Bonaparte brothers. He was appointed by Napoleon to the thrones of Naples (March 1806) and Spain (June 1808). He was never accepted as king by the majority of the Spanish population, and the Peninsular War was the consequence. After the Hundred Days, he lived abroad, in the America and at Florence, where he died.

Bonaparte, Letizia ('*Madame Mère*', 1750–1836), Napoleon's strong-willed mother, who exerted a considerable influence over his formative years. Frugal in habit, despite the riches showered upon her by Napoleon, she was the bedrock of the family, but played little part in the politics of the period.

Bonaparte, Louis (1778–1846), Napoleon's younger brother. He served as Napoleon's aide in Italy and Egypt. Napoleon arranged for him an unhappy marriage to Josephine's daughter, Hortense, and in 1806 pushed him, unwillingly, into the position of King of Holland. When Louis proved too independent, Napoleon annexed his kingdom. Louis abdicated and went abroad, using the title comte de Saint-Leu.

Bonaparte, Lucien ('Luciano', 1775–1840), Napoleon's younger brother. Initially, he was of considerable support, notably as president of the Council of Five Hundred at the time of the *coup* of Brumaire, and he served subsequently as minister of the interior. Relations between Lucien and Napoleon cooled, however, and the rift was completed by the affair mentioned by Napoleon in the entry for 9 June 1805. In October 1803, Lucien (whose first wife had died in 1800) married Marie-Alexandrine Jouberthon after she had borne him a son, but before it had been confirmed that her first husband had died (he had gone to San Domingo after becoming bankrupt). Napoleon was furious, having planned a diplomatic marriage for Lucien, and ordered him to leave French territory; he retired to his estate at Canino, near Rome, until, in 1810, he was captured by the British while en route to America. In 1814, he returned to Italy and accepted the papal title of Prince of Canino.

Bonaparte, Pauline (Marie-Paulette, 1780–1825), Napoleon's second, most beautiful, flirtatious and extravagant sister. In 1797, she married General Victor-Emmanuel Leclerc, and after his death in San Domingo in 1802, married Prince Camillo Borghese.

Bonet, General Jean-Pierre-François (1768–1857). A general from 1794, Bonet served at Hohenlinden and, most prominently, in the Peninsula. When mentioned (entry for 24 May 1813), he was commander of the 2nd Division of Marmont's VI Corps. He was captured at the surrender of Dresden in November 1813.

Bordesoule, General Etienne Tardif de Pommeroux, comte de (1771–1837). When mentioned (entry for 30 June 1812), this French cavalry general was commanding a light cavalry brigade of the corps cavalry of Davout's I Corps. His jaw was broken by grapeshot at Borodino, but he recovered to serve later in the year and in the campaigns of 1813–14. As mentioned in the entry for 18 April 1815, he remained loyal to the king during the Hundred Days, serving as the duc de Berry's chief of staff.

Borghese, Camillo Filippo Ludovico, Prince (1775–1832), Pauline Bonaparte's second husband. This somewhat indolent and frivolous Italian prince was appointed Duke of Guastalla by Napoleon in 1806, led the 1st Carabiniers in the *Grande Armée* in the campaign of that year, became a general in 1807 and in 1809 became governor-general of the *département au-delà des Alpes*. Despite an estrangement, eventually he and Pauline were reconciled.

Borghese, Pauline: see Bonaparte, Pauline.

Bourmont, General Louis-Auguste-Victor de Ghaisnes, comte de (1773–1846). A French Royalist *émigré* who was a leader of the Chouan insurrection in 1799, Bourmont made peace with Napoleon, but subsequently was arrested and escaped. Despite this record, he was admitted into Napoleon's service in 1808, served in the 1812 campaign and became a general in 1813. Perhaps predictably, he deserted from Napoleon's army at the beginning of the Waterloo campaign and joined the Allies. The Royalists rewarded him, and he became a marshal in 1830, but he was dismissed for his continuing support of Charles X after the 1830 revolution.

Bourrienne, Louis-Antoine Fauvelet de (1769–1834). A school friend of Napoleon, Bourrienne served as his assistant in Italy and secretary in Egypt. He held the position of French envoy to Hamburg (1805–10), but was dismissed for financial irregularities. He is best known as the author of *Memoirs of Napoleon Bonaparte*.

Boyer. The unfortunate Boyer, surgeon of the hospital at Alexandria, so condemned by Napoleon (entry for 8 January 1799), had been accused unjustly and the sentence was not carried out. Napoleon was criticised subsequently, by the wife of a naval officer, for equating women's clothes with cowardice!

Brueys d'Aigalliers, Admiral François-Paul (1753–98). This experienced naval officer commanded French forces in the Adriatic (1796–8), and subsequently was commander in the Mediterranean. He was killed aboard his flagship *L'Orient* at Aboukir Bay.

Bruix, Admiral Eustache (1759–1805). An admiral from 1797, Bruix served as minister of marine (1798–9) and led the unsuccessful attempt to relieve the French expedition to Egypt. He died in Paris in March 1805.

Brune, Marshal Guillaume-Marie-Anne (1763–1815). A general in the Revolutionary Wars, Brune served under Napoleon in Italy. Subsequently, he commanded French forces in Switzerland and Holland, and against the Chouan rebels in 1800. Although appointed a marshal by Napoleon in 1804, he was too inclined toward republicanism to be an ardent follower of Napoleon and was dismissed in 1807, only returning to service in 1815. After Napoleon's second fall, he was murdered by a Royalist mob.

Brunswick, Karl Wilhelm Ferdinand, Duke of (1735–1806). A Prussian field-marshal who had served under Frederick the Great, Brunswick was prevailed upon to take command of the Prussian Army in 1806, despite the interference of the king and his advisors in his strategical decisions. He was mortally wounded at Auerstädt and died on 10 November.

Brutus, Marcus Junius (c. 78–42 BC). Napoleon's reference in his questioning of the would-be assassin Friedrich Staps (entry for 12 October 1809) concerns this leading Roman, one of the principal murderers of Julius Caesar, to whom Napoleon was evidently comparing himself.

Bubna und Litic, General Ferdinand (1768–1826). This experienced Austrian general was sent on a diplomatic mission to Napoleon in 1813 (see entry for 1 June) to suggest a negotiated peace between France and Russia, employing Austria as an intermediary, on terms very unfavourable to Napoleon. The discussions between Bubna and Napoleon were somewhat difficult, the latter refusing to comply with the suggested terms. After Austria joined the coalition against Napoleon, Bubna reverted to his military role as a field commander.

Bülow, General Friedrich Wilhelm (1755–1816). One of the foremost Prussian commanders of the period, Bülow had been military tutor to Prince Louis Ferdinand and served with distinction in the war of 1806–7. His corps played an important role in 1813–14, and he took his title of Graf von Dennewitz from the victory at that place.

Buonaparte, the original spelling of Napoleon's family name: see Bonaparte.

Cacault, François. When mentioned (22 January 1797), Cacault was French ambassador at Rome, where he returned subsequently to supervise the financial demands made by the French. Joseph Bonaparte became ambassador later in that year.

Cadoudal, Georges (1771–1804). Sometimes styled just 'Georges', Cadoudal was a Chouan leader and committed Royalist who fought against the Republicans in the Vendée, and thereafter conspired against them and against Napoleon. In a personal meeting, Napoleon tried to convince him otherwise, but he continued to agitate, and in 1803 plotted to seize Napoleon; he was arrested and executed in Paris in June 1804.

Caesar, Gaius Julius (102–44 BC). Napoleon's references (*eg* entry for 3 October 1809) concern the great Roman statesman and general.

Caffarelli du Falga, General Louis-Marie-Joseph-Maximilien de (1756–99). This engineer general was one of Napoleon's closest companions during the Egyptian expedition. He had lost a leg campaigning on the Rhine and lost an arm at Acre, dying of fever two weeks later.

Caffarelli du Falga, General Marie-François-Auguste (1766–1849), brother of the foregoing. He acted as Napoleon's ADC in 1805, and when mentioned (entry for 28 November 1805) had just replaced the wounded General Baptiste

Bisson in command of the 1st Division of Davout's III Corps. Subsequently, he served on diplomatic duties and in the Peninsula.

Cagliostro, Alessandro, Count (1743–95). Napoleon's reference in the entry for 4 March 1806 concerns the Italian alchemist and charlatan, real name Giuseppe Balsamo, who had died in prison in Rome while serving a life sentence for heresy.

Calder, Admiral Sir Robert, Baronet (1745–1818). When mentioned (entry for 22 August 1805), this experienced British naval officer was in command of the fleet blockading Ferrol and Corunna; on 22 July, he had fought an indecisive action against Villeneuve, and in December 1805 was court-martialled and reprimanded for timidity.

Cambacérès, Jean-Jacques Régis de (1753–1824). A moderate among the politicians of the Revolutionary era, Cambacérès played an important role in Napoleon's career, supporting the *coup* of Brumaire. He became Second Consul, and Napoleon appointed him Arch-Chancellor of the Empire and president of the Senate. In 1808 he was ennobled as Duke of Parma. Napoleon always valued his opinions and advice.

Caprara, Cardinal. Papal legate in 1801, Caprara is perhaps best known as the clergyman who crowned Napoleon as King of Italy in 1805.

Carnot, Lazare-Nicolas-Marguerite (1753–1823). Known as 'the organiser of victory', Carnot was a military engineer who took almost complete charge of French military affairs during the early Revolutionary Wars and was responsible for many improvements. Appointed a director in 1795, he had to flee abroad in 1797, returning after the *coup* of Brumaire, but until 1814 he took little part in public life, favouring republicanism over Napoleon's empire. He returned to office, supporting Napoleon, during the Hundred Days as minister for the interior.

Casabianca, General Joseph-Marie (1742–1803). Despite the comment made by Napoleon (entry for 14 August 1796), this Corsican general continued to serve in Italy until his retirement in 1803.

Castaños, General Francisco Xavier (1756–1852). One of the leading Spanish commanders of the Peninsular War, Castaños forced Dupont's surrender at Baylen, but was defeated at the Tudela (23 November 1808). Subsequently, he held other important commands until replaced for political reasons in 1813.

Castiglione, Duke of: see Augereau.

Castlereagh, Robert Stewart, Viscount (1769–1822). One of the foremost

European statesmen, Castlereagh served as British Secretary for War and the Colonies under Pitt and Portland, and as Foreign Secretary from 1812 until his death, in the latter role playing a major part in the opposition to Napoleon. In April 1821, he succeeded his father as Marquess of Londonderry, but killed himself in the following year.

Catherine, Empress of Russia, known as 'the Great' (1729–96). Catherine ruled Russia following the deposition of her husband, Peter III, in 1762 until her death. Napoleon's entry for 1 July 1812 compares the way in which the Tsar had spoken to him with the manner in which she might have addressed the (much weaker) kings of Poland. Napoleon's reference in the same passage to the Caudine Forks concerns the disaster that befell the Roman Army of Spurius Postumius and Venturius Calvinus at the hands of the forces of Gavius Pontius in 321 BC, during the Second Samnite War, when the Romans were assailed both front and rear.

Catherine, Princess of Würtemberg (1783–1835). Catherine married Jérôme Bonaparte on 22 August 1807 and thus became Queen of Westphalia. She remained loyal to Jérôme and they had three children between 1814 and 1822.

Cattaneo, M., a Genoese diplomat whom Napoleon was attempting to deceive about the intentions of the French.

Caulaincourt, General Armand-Augustin-Louis (1773–1827). One of Napoleon's closest assistants and his master of horse (1804–13), Caulaincourt was not only his chief diplomatic aide, but also an experienced soldier. He succeeded Duroc as Grand Master of the Palace and was foreign minister from late 1813 until Napoleon's abdication, and again during the Hundred Days. In 1808, Napoleon ennobled him as Duke of Vincenza.

Caulaincourt, General Auguste-Jean-Gabriel (1777–1812), brother of the foregoing. He was serving as commandant of Napoleon's general headquarters when sent to take command of II Cavalry Corps upon Montbrun's death at Borodino. He was killed a short time later, leading the charge against the Raevsky Redoubt.

Cervoni, General Jean-Baptiste (1765–1809). This Corsican general, who served under Napoleon in Italy, was killed at Eckmühl while acting as Lannes's chief of staff.

Chabot, General Louis-François-Jean (1757–1837). A general from 1795, Chabot served under Napoleon in Italy and was employed thereafter in largely administrative posts until service in the Peninsula (1808–9).

Chabran, General Joseph (1763–1843). A general from 1796, Chabran served under Napoleon in Italy, then in Switzerland and the Peninsula. He retired in 1810.

Champagny, Jean-Baptiste de Nompère de (1756–1834). One of Napoleon's valuable subordinates, Champagny served as minister of the interior from 1804 until he succeeded Talleyrand as foreign minister in 1807. Replaced in 1811, he was ennobled as Duke of Cadore by Napoleon.

Championnet, General Jean-Etienne (1762–1800). Distinguished in Italy, notably with the Army of Rome, Championnet succeeded to the command of the Army of Italy in 1799, but died of fever at Antibes in January 1800.

Charlemagne (c. AD 762–814). Napoleon's references (entries for 18 May 1800, 7 January 1806) concern the great emperor, with whose achievements he compared his own.

Charles IV, King of Spain (1748–1819). The incompetent Charles IV was dominated by his queen, Maria Luisa of Parma, and by her favourite, Godoy, so was hardly responsible for the disaster that overtook the Spanish monarchy when it was deposed by Napoleon. From 1808, he was kept a virtual prisoner by Napoleon, and after the fall of the empire took no further part in affairs; his son, Ferdinand VII, headed the restored monarchy.

Charles VIII, King of France (1470–98). Napoleon's letter of 8 April 1797 makes reference to the ineffectual Charles VIII in comparison to his own powerful position: when Charles attempted to establish himself in Italy, he had to withdraw, despite his victory at Fornovo (1495).

Charles XII, King of Sweden (1682–1718). One of the greatest military commanders of his time, Charles XII's war against Russia led to his defeat at Poltava (1709), which might have served as a salutary warning to Napoleon (see entry for 19 December 1811).

Charles XIII, King of Sweden (1748–1818). Brother of King Gustavus III, Charles, Duke of Sudermania, acted as regent during the minority of his successor, Gustavus IV, and was elected king after the deposition of the latter on the grounds of insanity (March 1809). Charles was childless, so adopted Bernadotte as his successor, allowing him to take over the government as Crown Prince.

Charles, Archduke of Austria (1771–1847). The most notable Austrian commander of his era, Charles was the third son of Emperor Leopold II and brother of Francis II, and a field-marshal from 1796. In overall command of the Austrian forces in 1809, he inflicted the first serious reverse upon Napoleon at Aspern-Essling, but retired from field command after his defeat at Wagram.

Chénier, Marie-Joseph Blaise de (1746–1811). Napoleon's remark in the entry for 31 December 1806 concerns this poet and dramatist, younger brother of the better-known poet, André Chénier, who was guillotined in 1794. The younger Chénier served as inspector-general of public education (1803–6), although originally opposed to Napoleon, and in 1806 was disgraced temporarily for writing *Epître à Voltaire*. In 1808, however, at Napoleon's behest, he produced a history and criticism of French literature from 1789.

Chesterfield, Philip Dormer Stanhope, 4th Earl of (1694–1773). This English politician and statesman was perhaps best known for his *Letters to his Son*, published in 1774, which emphasised courtesy and good manners; hence Cockburn's remark in the entry for 18 April 1816.

Cincinnatus, Lucius Quinctius. Napoleon's reference in the entry for 10 October 1797 concerns this early hero of Rome, an example of virtue and humility, who was twice called from his farm to lead the defence of Rome, and each time returned to his plough after achieving victory.

Clarke, General Henri-Jacques-Guillaume (1765–1818). A French general of English descent, Clarke was one of Napoleon's most important ministers. More of a bureaucrat than a soldier, after some diplomatic duties he served as Napoleon's war minister (1807–14) and was ennobled as Duke of Feltre in 1809. He sided with the Bourbons in 1815, was appointed a marshal in 1816 and was their war minister until 1817.

Clary, Désirée (1777–1860). The daughter of a Marseilles banker, Désirée Clary was betrothed to Joseph Bonaparte until Napoleon persuaded him to marry her elder sister, Julie, who had a larger dowry, then became betrothed to Désirée himself. However, she married Bernadotte (August 1798) and thus became Queen of Sweden.

Clary, Julie (Marie-Julie, 1777–1845), Désirée's sister, who married Joseph Bonaparte in 1794.

Clausel, General Bertrand (1772–1842). This French general was esteemed highly by Napoleon (see entry for 11 April 1816) and is best known for service in the Peninsula (he became commander at Salamanca after Marmont's injury). In 1815, he was appointed to command on the Spanish frontier; he became a marshal in 1831.

Clovis (c. AD 466–511). Napoleon's reference in the entry for 1 March 1806 concerns this great king of the Franks.

Cobenzl, Count Johann Ludwig. This Austrian diplomat negotiated the Treaty of Campo Formio with Napoleon and served as foreign minister (1801–5). His elder brother, Count Philip, acted as ambassador to France (see entry for 19 March 1804).

Cockburn, Admiral George (1772–1853). A rear-admiral in the British Navy from 1812, Cockburn conveyed Napoleon to St Helena aboard HMS *Northumberland* and remained in charge until the arrival of Hudson Lowe. He behaved correctly toward Napoleon – addressing him as 'General Bonaparte', saying he knew no emperor – but without much sympathy, arousing complaints from Napoleon and his entourage.

Colbert, General Auguste-François-Marie Colbert de Chabanais (1777–1809). One of three brothers who were all distinguished French cavalry commanders, Colbert was entrusted with a diplomatic mission to Russia (see entry for 11 March 1803); he was killed at Cacabellos during the pursuit of Moore's army to Corunna.

Colli, General Michael, Austrian commander of the Piedmontese forces; defeated by Napoleon at Mondovi.

Colonna, Simeone. Ex-prefect of a Neapolitan province, Colonna was Letizia Bonaparte's chamberlain, who accompanied her to Elba in August 1814 and remained in her service in her retirement.

Conegliano, Duke of: see Moncey.

Consalvi, Cardinal Ercole (1757–1824). Prime minister of Pope Pius VII, this influential clergyman was responsible for negotiating the concordat between Napoleon and the Papacy. Conflict over relations with Napoleon led to his resignation in 1807, and for three years he was confined at Rheims, but after Napoleon's abdication he served as the Pope's representative at the Congress of Vienna.

Constantine (Flavius Valerius Constantinus, AD 288–337). Napoleon's reference in the entry for 1 March 1806 is to the Roman emperor Constantine the Great.

Corbineau, General Jean-Baptiste-Juvénal (1776–1848). An experienced French cavalry officer, Corbineau's most valuable service was his discovery of the ford over the Berezina, which permitted the *Grande Armée* to escape from Russia in 1812. When mentioned by Napoleon (entry for 20 August 1813), he was commanding the 1st (Light) Division of I Cavalry Corps.

Cornwallis, Admiral Sir William (1744–1819). 'Billy Blue' (or 'Billy-go-tight') Cornwallis was an experienced British admiral; when mentioned by

Napoleon (entry for 2 July 1804), he was commander of a British naval force in the English Channel.

Corvisart des Marets, Jean-Nicolas, Baron (1755–1821). One of the foremost figures in French medicine, Corvisart met Napoleon in 1801 and was appointed as his 'First Physician', in which capacity he attended the birth of the King of Rome.

Crassus. Napoleon's reference (entry for 17 July 1808) to campaigning in the Euphrates region concerns the Roman triumvir Marcus Licinius Crassus (c. 115–53 BC) who, having crossed the Euphrates to conquer Parthia, was defeated at Carrhae and killed by the Parthian general Surenas.

Cretet, M. When mentioned by Napoleon (entries for 3 and 17 September 1808), Cretet was minister for internal affairs.

Cuesta, General Don Gregorio Garcia de la (1740–1812). One of the best-known, if least-effective, Spanish commanders of the era, Cuesta was appointed Captain-General of Estremadura in 1808. Defeated at Medina del Rio Seco, he was roundly condemned by his allies for his inactivity and failure to co-operate in the Talavera campaign. He retired in August 1808, following a stroke.

Czartorivski, Prince Adam George (1770–1861). A member of a very distinguished Polish noble family, Czartorivski joined the Russian Army after the Third Partition of Poland and became a close confidant of Tsar Alexander I: foreign affairs were almost entirely in his hands between 1804 and 1807, and he was influential again during the Congress of Vienna. He never trusted Napoleon and opposed the existence of the Grand Duchy of Warsaw; ever a Polish patriot, he led the administration of that state during the 1830 revolution.

Dalesme, General Jean-Baptiste (1763–1832). A general from 1793, Dalesme was governor of Elba from October 1810, vacating that position upon Napoleon's arrival in May 1814.

Dalmatia, Duke of: see Soult.

Dandolo (entry for 15 May 1797). The Dandolos were one of the great ancient families of Venice; Girolamo Dandolo was the last admiral of the Venetian Republic before the French occupation.

Dantzig, Duke of: see Lefebvre.

Daru, Pierre-Antoine-Noël-Bruno (1767–1829). Originally head of the commissariat (1800–9), Daru became one of Napoleon's most valued subordinates and served as *Intendant-Général* of the imperial household. Loyal, hard-working and intellectual, he became secretary of state in 1811.

D'Audenarde, Charles-Eugène, comte de Lalaing (1779–1859). An equerry of Napoleon's, when mentioned (entry for 17 January 1810) d'Audenarde was a colonel in the 3rd Cuirassiers; he was promoted to general in December 1812.

Daunu, Pierre-Claude-François (1761–1840). A French historian and states-man, noted for his oratory and integrity, and originally a moderate Girondist, Daunu was largely responsible for the suppression of the insurrection of 13th Vendémiaire, and was the principal author of the 1795 Constitution. Later first president of the Council of Five Hundred, he co-operated with Napoleon at the *coup* of Brumaire and aided him in the composition of the Constitution of Year VIII (drawn up in December 1799).

Daure, M., Napoleon's commissary-general, mentioned in the entry for 8 February 1814.

Davout, Marshal Louis-Nicolas (1770–1823). One of the most capable and formidable of Napoleon's subordinates, Davout served in Egypt, was the youngest of those appointed marshals in the original creation of 1804 and was greatly distinguished as a corps commander, notably at Austerlitz, Auerstädt and Eckmühl, and in Russia in 1812. He was ennobled as Duke of Auerstädt and Prince of Eckmühl. His battlefield skills were lost to Napoleon while he was besieged in Hamburg in 1813–14, and he was appointed war minister in 1815.

Decrès, Admiral Denis (1761–1820). An experienced naval officer, Decrès was Napoleon's minister of marine (1801–14 and in 1815) and had considerable influence over maritime policy. He was killed by a charge of gunpowder laid under his bed, apparently by a valet.

Delort, General Jacques-Antoine-Adrien (1773–1846). A French cavalry gen-eral, Delort served in the Peninsula and in the 1814 campaign, and led the 14th Cavalry Division of IV Cavalry Corps in 1815. At Waterloo, he received a shot in the leg and a sabre wound in the arm.

d'Erlon, General Jean-Baptiste Drouet, comte (1765–1844). A general in the French Army from 1799, d'Erlon served in the Austerlitz and Friedland cam-paigns, and in the Peninsula, but is best known for commanding I Corps at Waterloo. He became a marshal in 1843.

Desaix, General Louis-Charles-Antoine (1768–1800). One of the most cele-brated of Napoleon's early subordinates, Desaix rose to prominence initially under Jourdan and Moreau. He conquered Upper Egypt during the Egyptian expedition, but was killed at Marengo as the arrival of his troops swung the tide of victory Napoleon's way. His dying words (see entry for 15 June 1800) were almost certainly apocryphal, as the injury he suffered was such that it was adjudged to have caused almost immediate death.

Désirée: see Clary, Désirée.

Despinoy, General Hyacinthe-François-Joseph (1764–1848). This French general served under Napoleon in Italy and was appointed commandant of Milan on 14 May 1796.

Detascher, Marie-Joseph-Rose (see entry for 9 March 1796): see Josephine.

Djezzar Pasha, Achmed (c. 1735–1804). Governor of Acre and commander of the Ottoman forces in Syria, Djezzar Pasha was known as 'the Butcher' because of the atrocities committed against his opponents. He defended Acre successfully against Napoleon.

Doge, the ancient office of chief magistrate of Venice, ended after the French occupation. The last Doge, Lodovico Manin (to whom Napoleon's letter of 9 April 1797 was addressed), abdicated on 12 May 1797.

Doktourof, General Dmitri Sergeivich (1756–1816). Although described as something of a courtier, this Russian commander was a brave and experienced soldier who commanded the 1st Column of the Allied Army at Austerlitz. When mentioned (entry for 30 June 1812), he was commanding VI Corps of the First West Army.

Dolgorouki, Princess Ekaterina. The entry for 22 May 1805 hints that scandals were associated with this woman; when in Berlin in 1804, as wife of the Russian military attaché, she supposedly had a liaison with Metternich.

Dombrowski (or Dabrowski), General Jan-Henryk (1755–1818). This experienced Polish soldier served under Kosciuszko, entered French service in 1796 and led the Polish Legion of the Cisalpine Republic. When mentioned (entry for 24 November 1812), he was commanding the 17th Division of Poniatowski's V Corps, and his inability to hold the bridge over the Berezina at Borisov, vital for the escape of the *Grande Armée*, could have been catastrophic. He returned to Poland after Napoleon's abdication.

Dommartin, Elzéar-Auguste Cousin de (1768–99). This French artillery general served under Napoleon in Italy and commanded the forcing of the gates of Pavia; he was mortally wounded in Egypt.

Drouot, General Antoine (1774–1847). A capable artillery officer who had served at Trafalgar when attached to the fleet, Drouot was appointed a general and one of Napoleon's ADCs in January 1813, when he was head of the Imperial Guard artillery. He commanded the Guard in the Waterloo campaign, having followed Napoleon to Elba.

Dubois, Baron Antoine (1756–1837). Surgeon to Napoleon's household, Dubois was official superintendent at the birth of the King of Rome.

Ducos, Pierre-Roger (1754–1816). Although not the most prominent of French politicians, Ducos became a judge and was one of the directors, thanks to the influence of his friend, Barras. He supported the *coup* of Brumaire and served as Third Consul behind Napoleon.

Dugommier, General Jacques-Coquille (1738–94). This Guadeloupe-born general assumed command of the French forces at Toulon in November 1793 and, as Napoleon noted, gained particular distinction on the 30th of that month when repelling a sortie. Esteemed by Napoleon, who assisted in his victory at Toulon, Dugommier was killed by a shell in the Pyrenees on 17 November 1794.

Duhesme, General Philibert-Guillaume (1766–1815). This French general, whose career spanned the entire Napoleonic period, served under Moreau and in the Marengo campaign; he was sent home from the Peninsula after displaying cruel conduct as governor of Barcelona. Despite a reputation for plundering, he was a brave commander and was recalled in 1814; in 1815, he led the Young Guard with his usual courage until mortally wounded at Plancenoit while attempting to hold Napoleon's flank at Waterloo.

Dulauloy, General Charles-François (1764–1832). An artillery general, in March 1813 Dulauloy was appointed to lead the artillery of the Imperial Guard, the post he occupied when mentioned in the entry for 18 October 1813.

Dumolard, M. A member of the Council of Five Hundred, Dumolard was a persistent critic of the Directory who, in June 1797, condemned the government's conduct in regard to Venice and Genoa, and thus implied criticism of Napoleon as well.

Dumoulin, General Charles (1768–1847). A brigade-commander in I Corps of the *Grande Armée* in late 1805, Dumoulin was suspended from duty after abducting a young Bavarian noblewoman, Catherine-Eugenie Eckhardt von Leonberg, whom he married on 11 December 1806. He was reinstated later that month.

Dumouriez, General Charles-François (1739–1823). One of the great heroes of the early Revolutionary Wars (he won the victory of Jemappes and shared that of

Valmy with Kellermann), Dumouriez had no sympathy for the extremism of the Revolution and defected to the Allies in 1793. Thereafter, he aided Royalist intrigues and became an advisor to the British government, hence Napoleon's anxiety that he be apprehended (entry for 10 March 1804). (He was not, in fact, with Enghien, as Napoleon had suspected; presumably, there had been some confusion between his name and that of the marquis de Thumery, who *was* there.)

Dupont de l'Etang, General Pierre-Antoine (1765–1840). Berthier's chief of staff in the Army of Reserve in the Marengo campaign and a divisional commander (1805–7), this general is best known for his surrender at Baylen in 1808, one of the French Army's worst reverses, after which he was disgraced and for a time imprisoned.

Dupuy, General Dominique-Martin (1767–98). *Chef de brigade* of the 32nd *Demi-Brigade* in Italy, Dupuy declined promotion initially to be able to stay with his unit, but he was given a provisional promotion to general in Egypt. He was mortally wounded during the Cairo insurrection.

Duroc, General Géraud-Christophe-Michel (1772–1813). One of Napoleon's greatest friends, Duroc was as skilled in diplomacy as in military affairs. In 1798, he became Napoleon's senior ADC, and he was appointed Grand Marshal of the Palace in 1805; Napoleon ennobled him as Duke of Friuli. He was mortally wounded at Bautzen, a devastating blow to Napoleon.

Durosnel, General Antoine-Jean-Auguste-Henri (1771–1849). This experienced cavalry officer, who had served as an aide to Napoleon, was commanding French garrisons in Saxony when mentioned (entry for 3 September 1813). He was taken prisoner at Dresden on 11 November 1813.

Durutte, General Pierre-François-Joseph (1767–1827). An early associate of Moreau (which tended to delay his advancement), Durutte held divisional commands in 1809–13 and served as governor of Metz; he was wounded severely at Waterloo.

Eblé, General Jean-Baptiste (1758–1812). An artillery general who had commanded Masséna's artillery in the Peninsula, Eblé led the *Grande Armée's* pontoon-train in the 1812 campaign. It was due entirely to his efforts, and those of his men, that the bridges were constructed over the Berezina, allowing the army to escape from Russia. His heroic exertions led to his death from fatigue on 30 December 1812.

Eckmühl, Prince of: see Davout.

El-Bekry, Sheikh, one of the leading dignitaries of Egypt, head of the sherifs, who accepted the French occupation. It was said that his daughter had an affair with Napoleon (after the French left, she was executed for consorting with them), and it was from El-Bekry that Napoleon received his Mameluke servant, Roustam, as a gift.

Elchingen, Duke of: see Ney.

Enghien, Louis-Antoine-Henri de Bourbon-Condé, duc d' (1772–1804). This French Royalist was the subject of one of the actions for which Napoleon was most criticised. Believing that Enghien was implicated in Royalist plots, notably that of Cadoudal and Pichegru (which, in fact, was not the case), Napoleon ordered that he be seized by a raid into neutral territory (Ettenheim in Baden) in March 1804. He was summarily tried and shot in the moat of Vincennes Castle.

Epaminondas (c. 418–362 BC). When writing of Greece (entry for 11 March 1816), it is not surprising that the soldier Napoleon should link the names of Homer and Plato with that of the great Theban general and statesman Epaminondas, one of the foremost Greek soldiers. A great tactical innovator, especially in the use of heavy infantry, he enjoyed marked success, but was mortally wounded in achieving the victory of Mantineia.

Etienne, Charles Guillaume (1778–1845). This French dramatist and author, perhaps best known for his comedy *Les Deux Gendres*, was editor-in-chief of the official *Journal de l'Empire*. As secretary to Maret, he accompanied Napoleon on campaign in Italy, Germany and Poland.

Eugène: see Beauharnais, Eugène de.

Faypoult, Guillaume-Charles. When addressed correspondence by Napoleon (entries for 1 May and 11 July 1796), this diplomat was serving as French ambassador at Genoa. In 1799, he attracted criticism for the seizure and sequestration of property in Naples.

Ferdinand III, Grand Duke of Tuscany (1769–1824), second son of Emperor Leopold II. He succeeded his father as Grand Duke of Tuscany when Leopold became emperor. Ferdinand was driven out by a popular revolt in 1799, but returned to Tuscany in September 1814 and was formally reinstated by the Congress of Vienna, remaining in power until his death. He was uncle to Empress Marie-Louise.

Ferdinand IV, King of Naples (1751–1825). An ignorant and somewhat coarse sovereign, Ferdinand IV was an opponent of the French Revolution and of Napoleon; he was expelled from the mainland part of his kingdom in 1806. He remained in Sicily under British protection until restored to his territories after the collapse of Napoleon's empire.

Ferdinand VII, King of Spain (1784–1833). Son and heir of King Charles IV of Spain, this ineffective and selfish prince was at odds with his parents and Godoy. Forced by Napoleon to surrender the Spanish crown to Joseph Bonaparte, during the Peninsular War he was kept a virtual prisoner at Valençay. He ruled without compassion or great success when restored to his throne in 1814. Before he became king, he was known as the Prince of the Asturias.

Ferdinand, Archduke (1781–1835) – referred to as 'Prince Ferdinand' in the entry for 11 October 1805. Ferdinand d'Este, brother-in-law of Emperor Francis II, was a capable commander of the Austrian Army and nominal commander-in-chief in Germany in 1805; he led a corps into Poland in the war of 1809.

Fesch, Cardinal Joseph (1762–1819), Napoleon's uncle. An important influence during the youth of the Bonaparte children, Fesch was involved in the negotiations for the Concordat, became archbishop of Lyons in 1802 and was appointed ambassador to Rome by Napoleon in 1804. Relations between them became strained following Napoleon's conflict with the Pope, and Fesch refused Napoleon's offer of the archbishopric of Paris. After the fall of the empire, he retired to Rome and cared for his sister, Letizia (Napoleon's mother), for the remainder of her life.

Flahaut de la Billarderie, General Auguste-Charles-Joseph (1785–1870). Believed to be a natural son of Talleyrand, Flahaut de la Billarderie became the lover of both Caroline Bonaparte and Hortense de Beauharnais. A general from 1812, he became an aide to Napoleon in the following year and undertook diplomatic missions on the emperor's behalf. His son by Hortense became the duc de Morny.

Forfait, Pierre-Alexandre-Laurent. French minister for the navy and colonies, Forfait was replaced in March 1801 by Decrès. In May 1803, he was appointed inspector-general of the National (later Imperial) Flotilla, responsible for its construction and maintenance; he was also known as a designer of ships.

Fouché, Joseph (1763–1820). Probably the most sinister personality in the Napoleonic administration, Fouché survived the Revolution despite being expelled from the Convention, ingratiated himself with the Directory and thereafter served as minister of police, in which role he exerted great influence and maintained a network of agents. Although Napoleon mistrusted him (with good reason) as an intriguer, he ennobled him as Duke of Otranto, and Fouché remained a useful tool until dismissed in 1810, when clandestine foreign negotiations came to light. He returned to his old ministry during the Hundred Days, but after the Second Restoration was forced to flee abroad, where he lived on his enormous and dubiously-acquired wealth.

Fourier, Jean-Baptiste-Joseph (1768–1830). This great French mathematician, best known for 'Fourier's Series' of equations, was an important member of the party of *savants* who accompanied Napoleon to Egypt. In addition to his scientific role, he performed important political duties and delivered Kléber's funeral oration.

Fox, Charles James (1749–1806). One of the leading political personalities of the age, Fox was an opponent of Pitt and unwilling to condemn the excesses of the French Revolution. Napoleon met him in 1802, admired and liked him, and stated that there would have been peace between France and Britain had Fox been Britain's chief minister. He became foreign secretary in Grenville's administration after Pitt's death, and tentative negotiations were begun with France, but he died in September 1806.

Francis I, King of France (1494–1547). The reference in the entry for 8 May 1796 concerning Pavia compared the military situation at that date with 1525, when Francis I badly mishandled his army at the Battle of Pavia (24 February 1525) and was defeated by the Imperial forces of Charles de Lannoy.

Francis II, later Francis I (1768–1835). The last Holy Roman Emperor, son of Leopold II, was sovereign of one of Napoleon's most persistent enemies, Austria-Hungary. After the defeat of 1805 and Napoleon's domination of Germany, he became Emperor Francis I of Austria. In 1810, he became Napoleon's father-in-law, but returned to opposing the French militarily from 1813.

Frederick I, King of Würtemberg (1754–1816). Succeeding his father in 1797, Duke Frederick II of Würtemberg continued the policy of opposition to France until compelled to make peace. Granted the title of Elector by Napoleon, in 1805 he joined France in a military alliance, and in 1806 was elevated to the rank of king as Frederick I. He remained loyal to Napoleon until November 1813, when he joined the Allies, thus securing his title and territories.

Frederick II, 'the Great', King of Prussia (1713–86). One of the greatest military leaders in history, Frederick II was often opposed to France and her allies; hence Napoleon's visit to Frederick's tomb (entry for 26 October 1806) and removal of trophies by way of asserting his own dominance over Prussia.

Frederick Augustus I, King of Saxony (1750–1827). Succeeding his father as Elector of Saxony in 1763, Frederick Augustus I resisted involvement in the early period of the Napoleonic Wars, but supported Prussia in 1806. After the defeat, he joined the Confederation of the Rhine and was accorded the rank of king. Thereafter, he supported Napoleon loyally, until his troops defected at Leipzig and he was taken prisoner by the Allies. Napoleon thought him the most honest of men, and such was his devotion to his subjects that he was known, deservedly, as 'the Just'.

Frederick William III, King of Prussia (1770–1840). Succeeding to the Prussian throne in 1797, with the assistance of his wife, Louise of Mecklenburg-Strelitz, Frederick William III opposed Napoleon in 1806 and was defeated catastrophically. For some years thereafter, Prussia was in the position of a client-state of Napoleon's empire, but popular sentiment propelled the nation into opposition, and the king and state played a vital role against Napoleon in the 'War of Liberation' (1813–14) and in 1815.

Friant, General Louis (1758–1829). Davout's brother-in-law, Friant served as a divisional commander under him until becoming colonel of the Grenadiers of the Imperial Guard in 1812; from July 1813, he led the Old Guard infantry, holding the same command in the Waterloo campaign.

Friuli, Duke of: see Duroc.

Frotté, Louis, comte de. One of the leaders of the Royalist Chouannerie (insurrection) in the Vendée (1799–1800), Frotté was arrested and summarily executed while in course of negotiating peace, on the evidence of captured correspondence, which implied that his overtures for peace were a sham. Bourrienne claimed that he had persuaded Napoleon to show clemency, but that Frotté and his staff had been shot before the pardon arrived.

Gallo, Count di, with Merveldt, one of the Austrian negotiators of the peace of 1797.

Ganteaume, Admiral Honoré-Joseph-Antoine (1755–1818). Brueys's chief of staff for the Egyptian expedition, Ganteaume survived the defeat of Aboukir Bay (which is the 'truly horrible' experience referred to in the entry for 15 August 1798); subsequently, he commanded the Brest fleet and in the Mediterranean.

Gardanne (or Gardane), General Charles-Mathieu (1766–1818). The entry for 12 April 1807 concerns this officer, who became an ADC to Napoleon in 1805. In 1807, perhaps because his family was known in the Near East, he was appointed as Napoleon's envoy to Persia in the hope of launching a collaborative attack on British India. Persia wanted French help against Russia, but when this was prevented by the Treaty of Tilsit, Gardanne returned to France in 1809, subsequently serving in the Peninsula.

Gardanne, General Gaspard-Amédée (1758–1807). The entry for 9 November 1797 concerns this general, who achieved distinction at Marengo and at the siege of Danzig in 1807; he died of fever later that year.

Gardner, Admiral Alan, Baron (1742–1809). When mentioned by Napoleon (entry for 18 July 1805), Gardner was thought to be in temporary command of the British Channel Fleet, following the indisposition of Cornwallis; unknown to Napoleon, however, Cornwallis had actually resumed command on 6 July.

Garnier, General Pierre-Dominique (1756–1827). Despite Napoleon's critical remarks (entry for 14 August 1796), Garnier continued to serve in Italy until 1800 and occupied a number of largely administrative positions thereafter.

Gaudin, Martin-Michel-Charles (1756–1841). Napoleon's minister of finance (1799–1814 and during the Hundred Days), Gaudin was one of his most valuable civil servants and was ennobled as Duke of Gaeta in 1809. He founded the Bank of France.

Gaultier, General Paul-Louis (1737–1814). Having been the Army of Italy's chief of staff until replaced by Berthier, as Napoleon commented (entry for 14 August 1796) Gaultier was more used to staff duties than combat and continued to perform basically administrative tasks until his retirement in 1807. Despite Napoleon's comment, however, he had experienced some active service, albeit some time previously: he had been wounded in action at Grenada in July 1779.

George III, King of Great Britain (1738–1820). Sovereign of Napoleon's most persistent enemy, George III enjoyed the longest reign of any British monarch, with the exception of Queen Victoria, succeeding to the throne in 1760. In 1811, his mental health deteriorated to the extent that his son (later George IV) had to assume his duties as Prince Regent.

'Georges': see Cadoudal, Georges.

Gérard, General Etienne-Maurice (1773–1852). A very competent subordinate commander, Gérard served as Bernadotte's chief of staff, fought in the Peninsula and led a division during 1812–13; in February 1814, he took command of II Corps. He served in the Waterloo campaign and vouched for Bourmont's loyalty, but was misguided, as the entry for 15 June 1815 demonstrates. He became a marshal in 1830.

Germanicus Caesar (15 BC–AD 19). Napoleon's reference (entry for 3 October 1809) concerns this famous Roman commander, son of the general Drusus and nephew of Tiberius. In AD 15–16, he avenged the defeat of Varus in the Teutoberg Forest (AD 9) and was a candidate for emperor; his early and unexpected death raised suspicions of poison.

Germany, Emperor of: see Francis II.

Girard, General Jean-Baptiste (1775–1815). This French general's most famous action was probably in the Peninsula (he was the commander defeated at Arroyo dos Molinos), but he served effectively in the 1812 campaign, and when mentioned by Napoleon (entry for 2 May 1813) was leading the 3rd Division of Ney's III Corps. He was wounded at Lützen, rallied to Napoleon in 1815 and was mortally wounded at Ligny.

Godoy, Manuel de (1767–1851). 'Favourite' of Queen Maria Luisa of Spain, this incompetent statesman virtually ruled the country with her from 1792 to 1808, with a brief hiatus between 1798 and 1801. His policy toward France fluctuated between hostility and alliance; for his role in negotiating the Peace of Basle (1795), he was awarded the title 'Prince of Peace' (as often quoted; strictly, it is more accurate to refer to 'Prince of the Peace' ['*Principe de la Paz*']). The incompetence of his ministry and of the monarchy led to the fall of both in 1808.

Gohier, Louis-Jérôme (1746–1830). An important politician of the Republican period, Gohier became the last president of the Directory. Despite professing admiration for Napoleon, he was too ardent a republican to accept the *coup* of Brumaire, so (having refused to resign) he was deposed. For some years thereafter, he acted as French consul-general in Amsterdam.

Gourgaud, General Gaspard (1788–1852). One of the most loyal of all Napoleon's subordinates, in 1811 Gourgaud joined the Imperial staff as an *officier d'ordonnance*, proved a valuable aide and accompanied Napoleon to his final exile. He fell out with Las Cases and Montholon (challenging the latter to a duel) and, in 1818, returned to France to agitate for an improvement in Napoleon's conditions. He was one of those who accompanied Napoleon's body when it was repatriated in 1840.

Gouvion St Cyr, Marshal Laurent (1764–1830). Distinguished under Moreau, Gouvion St Cyr's dislike of political involvement led to him declining to endorse Napoleon's elevation to emperor, so after service in the Peninsula it was not until he gained distinction in the 1812 campaign that finally he was appointed a marshal. An honourable, upright man, he was an able commander, but not an easy comrade.

Grand Master. Napoleon's reference (entry for 13 June 1798) concerns Baron

Ferdinand von Hompesch, Grand Master of the Knights of St John and thus ruler of Malta. He had become Grand Master in 1797, was deposed by the French occupation in 1798 and resigned his office in favour of Tsar Paul I in the following year.

Grand Seignior. The reference in the proclamation to the people of Egypt (entry for 2 July 1798) concerns the Sultan of the Ottoman Empire, the nominal overlord of Egypt. The Sultan at the time was Selim III, who ruled from 1789 to 1807.

Gravina, Admiral Don Federico Carlos de (1756–1806). A capable officer, Gravina was the senior Spanish commander of the Franco-Spanish fleet defeated at Trafalgar, who took command after Villeneuve was captured; Gravina's advice had been ignored, so he was not responsible for the defeat. A wound he received at Trafalgar proved fatal.

Great Britain, King of: see George III.

Grenville, William Wyndham, Baron (1759–1834). Foreign Secretary in 1791, this colleague of Pitt resigned with him in 1801, but declined office upon Pitt's return in 1804. When mentioned (entry for 4 December 1802), he was an important political figure in Britain, hence Napoleon's desire for any information to discredit him. He headed the 'Ministry of all the Talents' (1806–7), but held no further offices of state.

Grouchy, Marshal Emmanuel, marquis de (1766–1847). Although an aristocrat of the *Ancien Régime*, Grouchy served in the French Army as a general from 1792. Because he was an associate of Moreau, his advancement was not very rapid. When first mentioned (entry for 3 December 1812), he was commanding the 'Sacred Squadron' of mounted officers, which comprised most of the cavalry still operational in the retreat from Moscow; earlier in the campaign, he had commanded III Cavalry Corps. He was the last of Napoleon's appointments to the marshalate (April 1815) and led the right wing in the Hundred Days campaign.

Guatemozin (now more usually, Cuauhtemoc), Montezuma's son-in-law and the last emperor of the Aztecs, who was captured and executed by Cortés. He is mentioned by Napoleon in the entry for 18 August 1816 by way of comparing his own treatment by Hudson Lowe to the tortures perpetrated by the Spanish Conquistadors.

Guieu, General Jean-Joseph (1758–1817). A French general from 1793, Guieu served under Napoleon in Italy, but his active career ended when he left the Army of Italy in 1799.

Gustavus Adolphus, King of Sweden (1594–1632). One of the 'great captains' of all time, Gustavus Adolphus made an indelible mark on the Thirty Years' War. The account of the battle he fought, which Napoleon sent to Marmont (entry for 14 October 1813) to inform him of the terrain he occupied, must refer to the Battle of Breitenfeld, four miles north of Leipzig, where Gustavus Adolphus defeated Tilly on 17 September 1631.

Guyon, General Claude-Raymond (1773–1834). When mentioned (entry for 1 August 1812), this French cavalry general was leading a light brigade of corps cavalry in Eugène's IV Corps during the invasion of Russia.

Gyulai, General Ignaz, Count (1763–1831). *Feldmarschall-Leutnant* in the Austrian Army in 1805, this distinguished officer was one of those who participated in the negotiations of the Treaty of Presburg in 1805. Subsequently, he held an independent command in 1809 and led a corps in 1813–14, including at Leipzig.

Harel, M., governor of Vincennes at the time of the arrest of the duc d'Enghien.

Harville, General Louis-Auguste Jouvenal (1749–1815). After a long career in the French Army, usually in cavalry commands, Harville retired in 1801 and became equerry to Josephine.

Hatzfeld, Madame. As recounted in the entry for 6 November 1806, this was the wife of General Franz Ludwig, Prince Hatzfeld (1756–1827) who, as Prussian governor of Berlin, surrendered the city to Napoleon after Jena. He also sent an account to King Frederick William III, which included details of French dispositions; when it was intercepted, he was accused of espionage and arrested. His wife obtained an audience with Napoleon, during which she pleaded for his life; Napoleon handed her the letter and indicated the fire, allowing her to burn the evidence of his guilt. In fact, it is unlikely that there was anything important in the document, and it was suspected that the whole affair was a ploy to enhance Napoleon's reputation with the Prussians.

Haugwitz, Christian August Heinrich Kurt, Count von (1752–1831). One of the leading Prussian statesmen of his generation, Haugwitz was foreign minister during 1805–6, but procrastinated too long to allow Prussia to participate in the 1805 campaign, then had to accept unfavourable terms at the ratification of the Treaty of Schönbrunn. He retired after Jena.

Hautpoul, General Jean-Joseph Ange, comte d' (1754–1807). Renowned as a leader of French heavy cavalry, Hautpoul achieved great distinction at Austerlitz, served at Jena and was mortally wounded at Eylau, where he declined the amputation of a leg and succumbed to septicaemia as a result.

Hauterive, Alexandre Maurice Blanc de Lanouette, comte d' (1754–1830). This French diplomat and statesman served in the foreign ministry from 1798 (and continued after the Bourbon restoration). Having attracted Napoleon's attention, he was made a councillor of state in 1805 and, following a disagreement with Talleyrand in that year (he favoured an alliance, not war, with Austria), he was put in charge of the ministry's archives.

Hédouville, General Gabriel-Marie-Théodore-Joseph (1755–1825). When mentioned by Napoleon (entry for 13 February 1800), Hédouville was commanding part of the Army of the West, involved in suppressing insurrection. Subsequently, he served in a variety of military and diplomatic posts; when mentioned in the entry for 16 March 1803, he was acting as French ambassador to Russia.

Henry IV, King of France (1553–1610). Napoleon mentions this monarch in the entry for 22 March 1804 by way of comparing his methods of facing his enemies on the battlefield with the intrigues from abroad of the exiled Bourbons. Brought up as a Protestant, Henry converted to Roman Catholicism in July 1593, which virtually ended opposition to him (Paris gave way in March 1594), hence Napoleon's remark in the entry for 26 April 1816.

Henry, Prince of Prussia, commander of a brigade in the Jena campaign.

Hoche, General Louis-Lazare (1768–97). One of the leading French generals of the time, Hoche was intended to lead the abortive invasion of Ireland, which was abandoned because of bad weather. He died, perhaps of consumption, while in command of the Army of the Sambre & Meuse.

Hohenlohe-Ingelfingen, General Friedrich Ludwig, Prince of (1748–1818). This general commanded the Prussian left in the 1806 campaign, rallied part of the army after Jena, but surrendered at Prenzlau on 28 October 1806. After two years as a prisoner, he retired to his estates.

Holland, King of: see Bonaparte, Louis.

Hortense: see Beauharnais, Hortense.

Ibrahim Bey (1735–1817); with Murad Bey, one of the two Mameluke rulers of Egypt, Ibrahim being the Sheik al-Balad, the head of state. Defeated by Napoleon, he escaped the massacre of the Mameluke leaders, but was unable to resist the rise of Mehemet Ali and fled south to New Dongola, where he died.

Istria, Duke of: see Bessières.

Ivan (also Yvan), Alexandre-Urbain (1765–1839), Napoleon's personal surgeon from 1796 to 1814, only abandoning him after the abdication of 1814.

Joachim, Prince (or 'Joachim Napoleon, King of the Two Sicilies'): see Murat.

John, Archduke of Austria (1782–1859). Younger brother of Emperor Francis II and the Archduke Charles, John was defeated by Moreau at Hohenlinden and, in 1809, led the Army of Inner Austria. He had the better of Eugène at Sacile, but was defeated by him at Raab and was criticised for his slowness in joining Charles at Wagram.

Jomini, General Antoine-Henri (1779–1869). Although criticised by Napoleon (entries for 22 July and 16 August 1813), this Swiss officer was one of the great military writers and theorists of the age, despite being overshadowed ultimately by Clausewitz. He served with Ney for much of his career, from volunteer ADC to chief of staff, and when first mentioned by Napoleon was serving on the General Staff of the *Grande Armée*. In August 1813, he changed sides and became a general in the Russian Army.

Joseph: see Bonaparte, Joseph.

Josephine, Empress (Marie-Joseph-Rose De Tascher de la Pagerie, 1763–1814), Napoleon's first wife, whom he married in March 1796. At the age of 16, she had married Alexandre, vicomte de Beauharnais, who was the father of her children, Eugène and Hortense. Napoleon divorced her in December 1809.

Joubert, General Barthélemy-Catherine (1769–99). A notable French commander who served under Napoleon in Italy, Joubert later commanded in that region, but was killed at Novi (15 August 1799).

Jourdan, Marshal Jean-Baptiste (1762–1833). One of the generals of the early Revolutionary Wars, Jourdan's active career continued until the end of the empire. Although he was defeated at Stockach in 1799 and refused to assist in the *coup* of Brumaire, he was appointed a marshal in 1804 and served in the Peninsula until he became unemployed after the defeat of Vittoria. He was given a relatively minor command (Army of the Rhine) in 1815.

Julie (see entry for 6 October 1795): see Clary, Marie-Julie.

Jullien de Bidon, General Louis-François-Victor (1764–1839). This artillery officer served in Egypt as Reynier's chief of staff, and later as commandant of Rosetta; hence Napoleon's reference in the entry for 20 July 1799. He became a general in 1803, but saw no further active service.

Junot, General Jean-Andoche (1771–1813). One of the most colourful of Napoleon's generals, Junot was first encountered by Napoleon at Toulon and impressed him by his coolness under fire (when showered by earth from the impact of a roundshot, Junot merely remarked that he no longer had need of sand to blot the document he was writing). An early suitor of Pauline Bonaparte (see entry for 22 March 1795), he became a friend of Napoleon, who ennobled him as Duke of Abrantes after his successful occupation of Portugal (until defeated at Vimeiro). Both Junot and his wife irritated Napoleon, however, by their spendthrift behaviour; later, Junot's mental health broke down and he died after leaping from a window.

Kalitchy (or Kalitcheff), Count. Sent by Tsar Paul I to Paris to act as Russian ambassador and help cement Franco-Russian friendship, Kalitchy is mentioned in the entry for 26 April 1801 as having transmitted the official report of the death of Paul and the accession of his son.

Kant, Immanuel (1724–1804). Napoleon's somewhat dismissive reference in the entry for 4 March 1806 concerns this great German philosopher and author.

Kaunitz, Wenzel Anton, Prince von (1711–94). The great Austrian chancellor and statesman was one of the most important political figures of the age. Thus the occupation of the castle described by Napoleon (entry for 3 December 1805) takes on added significance.

Keith, Admiral George Keith Elphinstone, Viscount (1745–1823). When mentioned (entry for 9 November 1803), this officer was in command of the British fleet in the North Sea; at this stage of his career, he was Baron Keith, his viscountcy dating from 1814. In 1815, Napoleon had a closer encounter with him, as he conveyed the British government's instructions to the ex-emperor regarding his exile at St Helena.

Kellermann, Marshal François-Christophe (1735–1820). One of the senior commanders of the early Revolutionary Wars and the victor of Valmy (20 September 1792), Kellermann's front-line career ended in 1797, but he remained invaluable to Napoleon in a variety of administrative and second-line commands until 1814. He was appointed a marshal in 1804 and Duke of Valmy in 1808. The reference in the entry for 14 May 1796 was in a response to a proposal that he should be sent to Italy to share command with Napoleon.

Kellermann, General François-Etienne (1770–1835), son of Marshal François-Christophe Kellermann (see previous entry). The younger Kellermann achieved perhaps even greater fame than his father, as a cavalry commander: he made a decisive charge at Marengo and served at Austerlitz, in the Peninsula, and in the campaigns of 1813–14 and Waterloo. He was one of the French Army's more ardent plunderers.

Kilmaine, General Edward Saul (originally Jennings, 1751–99). This Irish-born cavalry general served under Napoleon in Italy, notably at the siege of Mantua. Subsequently, he declined the command of French forces in Switzerland on health grounds; he died of dysentery in December 1799.

Kirgener, General François-Joseph (1766–1813). This experienced engineer served at Marengo, Jena, Eylau and in the Peninsula. He was the army's commanding engineer when he was killed by the same roundshot that mortally wounded Duroc at Bautzen.

Kléber, General Jean-Baptiste (1753–1800). A distinguished commander of the early Revolutionary Wars, Kléber went into a brief voluntary retirement out of dissatisfaction with his lack of advancement. He returned to a divisional command under Napoleon for the expedition to Egypt, being promoted to the command of the army after Napoleon returned home. He was assassinated by a fanatic at Cairo on 14 June 1800.

Klein, General Dominique-Antoine (1761–1845). This French cavalry commander led the 1st Dragoon Division of the *Grande Armée* during the period 1805–7, seeing action at Jena and Eylau. His subsequent services were more administrative.

Kleist, General Friedrich Ferdinand Emil, Graf von Nollendorf (1762–1823). After service as a staff officer in 1806, this renowned Prussian commander led a corps during 1813–14, seeing action at Bautzen, Dresden and Leipzig.

Knobelsdorf. This diplomat was the Prussian envoy to Paris in 1806, succeeding Luccesini.

Koscziusko, General Tadeuz Andrej Bonawentura (1746–1817). This great Polish soldier and patriot, who had been wounded and captured in the defeat that preceded the third partition of Poland, lived in Paris from 1798. Napoleon tried to gain his support to facilitate the creation of a Polish client-state, but Koscziusko refused to comply unless Napoleon promised full independence, which he was not prepared to countenance.

Kotzebue, August Friedrich Ferdinand von (1761–1819). The German dramatist and writer of articles critical of Napoleon had moved to Russia, where he had become a councillor of state. In 1813, he and Stein were appointed Russian administrators of the territories in Germany liberated from Napoleonic control, hence the reference (entry for 24 May 1813) concerning the happiness of the inhabitants of Bautzen at being delivered from them and the Cossacks, the latter being infamous plunderers of civilian property.

Kourakine, Prince Alexander. This leading Russian diplomat was a negotiator of the Treaty of Tilsit.

Koutousoff (also Kutuzov), Field Marshal Mikhail Larionovich Golenishev (1745–1813). One of the most famous Russian commanders of the era, Koutousoff led the Russian forces at Austerlitz, but could not be blamed for the defeat. Not popular with the Tsar, he was recalled only with some reluctance in 1812 to assume overall command against the French invasion. Although he allowed Moscow to be occupied after the indecisive battle of Borodino, his continued strategy of withdrawal allowed the elements to destroy the *Grande Armée*. Revered by ordinary soldiers, although criticised by those higher in the chain of command, Koutousoff made a vital contribution to Napoleon's defeat in 1812; however, he was relieved of command shortly before his death in April 1813.

Kozietulski, Captain. Commander of the Polish *Chevau-Légers* who made the charge at Somosierra, Kozietulski served in the subsequent campaigns and became commandant of the 3rd *Eclaireurs* of the Imperial Guard in 1814. In the entry for 27 November 1808, a very common mistake is repeated, by describing the troops involved as 'Polish lancers': they did not receive lances until some nine months later and, at the time, were actually 'Light Horse' (*Chevau-Légers*).

La Bruyère, Jean de (1645–96). Napoleon's reference in the entry for 17 July 1796 refers to the writings of this French essayist, whose major work, *Les Caractères de Théophraste . . . avec les Caractères et les Moeurs de ce Siècle*, was published in 1688.

Lacretelle, Jean-Charles-Dominique de (1766–1855), writer of a series of works on the French Revolution and its sequels, of which he had been an eyewitness and participant (of Royalist sympathies).

Lacroix, General François-Joseph-Pamphile (1774–1841). Previously chief of general staff of the Army of Naples, Lacroix was given command of a brigade in Lauriston's corps in January 1813; as noted (entry for 8 April 1813), he left his command without permission, was arrested and was court-martialled. He was permitted to return to the service in 1815.

Lafayette, Marie-Joseph-Paul-Yves-Roch-Gilbert du Motier, marquis de (1757–1834). Perhaps most famous for his role in the American War of Independence, Lafayette commanded the Armies of the Centre and the North

during the early Revolutionary Wars, but disillusioned by the extremism of the Revolution, he fled to the Allies in 1792. In 1799, he was permitted to return to France, but lived in retirement, although he remained an unreserved opponent of Napoleon.

Lafitte, Jacques, Napoleon's banker, hence the reference in the entry for 25 April 1821. The receipt mentioned by Napoleon was evidently a letter of credit sent by Lafitte to Napoleon after the emperor had handed him all his decorations and money. At the time, Napoleon refused to accept a receipt lest its discovery compromised the banker, showing remarkable trust in his (correct) judgement of Lafitte's honesty.

Laforest, Antoine, comte de. French ambassador to Berlin in 1806 and negotiator of the Treaty of Valençay in 1813, Laforest was appointed as Louis XVIII's foreign minister in 1814.

Laharpe, General Amédée-Emmanuel-François (1754–96), a Swiss-born general who served under Napoleon in Italy; he was killed on 10 May 1796.

Lalande, Joseph-Jérôme LeFrançais de (1732–1807). The great French astronomer occupied the chair of astronomy at the Collège de France from 1762, and it was to him that Napoleon wrote of his own interest in astronomy (entry for 5 December 1796).

Langeron, General Louis-Alexandre-Arnault de (1763–1831). A member of an old French family, Langeron entered Russian military service under Suvarov, led the 2nd Column at Austerlitz, served valuably under Tchichagof in 1812, and commanded a corps of Blücher's Army of Silesia in 1813–14, achieving notable distinction at Leipzig.

Lannes, Marshal Jean (1769–1809). One of Napoleon's oldest friends and most valuable subordinates, Lannes was an able and brave field commander (although notably unsuccessful as ambassador to Portugal: see entry for 15 August 1802). A marshal from 1804, he was ennobled as Duke of Montebello in 1808, but was mortally wounded at Aspern-Essling. The Duchess to whom Napoleon wrote his letter of condolence (entry for 31 May 1809) was Lannes's second wife, Louise Guéhéneuc, whom he had married in September 1800, having divorced his first wife for adultery in the previous May. The Duchess became lady-of-honour to Marie-Louise.

Lanusse, General François (1772–1801). A brigade-commander under Napoleon in Italy, Lanusse was mortally wounded in Egypt.

Laplace, Pierre Simon, marquis de (1749–1829). This prominent French mathematician and astronomer was a supporter of Napoleon, and served six weeks as minister of the interior before his unsuitability for that position compelled his replacement by Lucien Bonaparte. The reference in the entry for 26 November 1802 concerns his declaration in the third volume of *Mécanique Céleste* that of all the truths therein, the greatest was his devotion to the European peace-maker Napoleon.

Las Cases, Emmanuel-Augustin-Dieudonné-Martin-Joseph, comte de (1766–1842). Coming to Napoleon's notice in 1810, this ex-French naval officer was appointed his chamberlain and accompanied him to St Helena. In the early part of Napoleon's exile, Las Cases was one of his closest confidants, but he was ordered to leave in 1816 after attempting to smuggle correspondence to Europe. He had taken notes of Napoleon's conversations, and his resulting book, *Mémoriale de Sainte-Hélène*, enjoyed considerable success.

Latouche-Tréville, Admiral Louis-René-Madeleine Levassor, comte de (1745–1804). When mentioned by Napoleon (entry for 2 July 1804), Latouche-Tréville was in command of the French Mediterranean fleet at Toulon. He died on 19 August 1804, aboard the warship *Bucentaure* in Toulon roads.

La Tour, General Sallier de, one of the Piedmontese representatives who negotiated the armistice of Cherasco, following the defeat of Piedmont (the other representative was Colli's chief of staff, Colonel Costa).

Latour-Maubourg, General Marie-Victor-Nicolas de Fay (1768–1850). This experienced French cavalry commander had returned from the Peninsula to lead IV Cavalry Corps in 1812, and when mentioned (entry for 24 May 1813), he was commanding I Cavalry Corps of the *Grande Armée*. He was wounded severely at Wachau in October 1813.

Lauderdale, James Maitland, 8th Earl of (1759–1839). A political opponent of Pitt, Lauderdale was appointed ambassador to France in 1806 to investigate the possibility of peace; the negotiations were fruitless and he returned home in September.

Lauriston, General Jacques-Alexandre-Bernard Law, marquis de (1768–1828). Of Scottish descent, this talented officer was a friend of Napoleon and served as his ADC in 1800. Later he was envoy to Denmark and Britain, and ambassador to Russia (1811–12); he sailed with Villeneuve's fleet in 1804–5 and was present in the action off Cape Finisterre. He served in the Peninsula, at Wagram and in the campaigns of 1812–13 until taken prisoner at Leipzig; the account of his death (entry for 19 October 1813) was very premature!

Lavalette, Antoine-Marie Chamans, comte de (1769–1830). Having served with Napoleon in Italy, Lavalette became a close friend and was even related, having married the daughter of Josephine's brother-in-law. He served Napoleon as a councillor of state and postmaster-general during the Consulate and Empire, and superintended the post again in 1815. In this role, he was a valuable source of intelligence (the information that could be gleaned by such an official is exemplified by Napoleon's remarks in the entry for 9 January 1817). He was condemned to death by the Bourbons, but it was said that this sentence was unpopular, even with the king, and it was never carried out, as Lavalette escaped from prison by changing clothes with his wife. He was smuggled out of France by three British sympathisers, one of whom was the mercurial Sir Robert Wilson. Lavalette was pardoned in 1822.

Lebrun, Anne-Charles (1775–1859), son of Charles-François Lebrun (see following entry). Lebrun served as Napoleon's ADC in a number of campaigns and became a general in 1807, but he is probably best known as Desaix's ADC, who caught that general as he fell mortally wounded at Marengo.

Lebrun, Charles-François (1739–1824), father of Anne-Charles Lebrun (see previous entry). This lawyer entered politics at the beginning of the Revolutionary period. After supporting Napoleon in the *coup* of Brumaire, he was appointed Third Consul and, in 1814, Arch-Treasurer of the Empire. Ennobled by Napoleon as duc de Plaisance, he accepted the Bourbon restoration, but rallied to Napoleon again in 1815, hence the entry for 15 May 1815.

Lecamus, M. Long-serving secretary and confidant of Jérôme Bonaparte, Lecamus was regarded as not entirely respectable, as Napoleon suggested (entry for 4 January 1808). He *was* presented with the Fürstenstein property and 40,000 francs a year, and even became (an ineffective) Westphalian foreign minister.

Lecourbe, General Claude-Jacques (1758–1815). A follower of Moreau, Lecourbe commanded the Army of the Rhine in 1799, and in the Marengo campaign was responsible for keeping open the routes to the Army of Italy. Disgraced along with Moreau, he received no further employment until 1815, when he rallied to the support of Napoleon.

Lefebvre, Marshal François-Joseph (1755–1820). An unpolished, simple-mannered Alsatian, Lefebvre assisted Napoleon in the *coup* of Brumaire and was appointed a marshal in 1804, and Duke of Dantzig in 1808. Brave and honourable, although his talents in independent command were limited, he proved to be a loyal subordinate to Napoleon.

Lefebvre-Desnouettes, General Charles (1773–1822). The reference to 'General Lefebvre' (entry for 16 June 1808) concerns Lefebvre-Desnouettes, one of Napoleon's most loyal subordinates. He served as Napoleon's ADC in the Marengo campaign and married the emperor's second cousin. Subsequently, he received the important appointment of colonel of the *Chasseurs à Cheval* of the Imperial Guard. Captured during the pursuit of Moore's army to Corunna, he escaped by breaking his parole and returned to serve in the campaigns of 1812–15. He fled to America after Waterloo, but was drowned when the ship in which he was returning to Europe sank.

Lefol, General Etienne-Nicolas (1764–1840). After service in the Peninsula, Lefol was wounded at Leipzig and returned to serve in the 1814 campaign; in 1815, he commanded a division of Vandamme's III Corps, notably at Ligny.

Legendre d'Harvesse, General François-Marie-Guillaume (1766–1828). This general served at Marengo and Austerlitz, in Prussia and Poland, but his career was blighted by his association with Dupont, for whom he acted as chief of staff at Baylen. Although he did serve subsequently, the stigma continued to haunt him and led to him being placed under arrest on more than one occasion.

Leibnitz, Gottfried Wilhelm (1646–1716). Napoleon's reference in the entry for 4 August 1803 concerns the German philosopher and mathematician, who was contemporary with King Louis XIV of France (1638–1715).

Liébert, General Jean-Jacques (1758–1814). Like Souham, Liébert came under suspicion because of his friendship with Moreau and was arrested in February 1804. He was re-employed on staff duties from 1806 until his retirement in 1813.

Liechtenstein, General Prince Johann. *Feldmarschall-Leutnant* and commander of the Austrian contingent of the Russo-Austrian Army at Austerlitz, Liechtenstein accompanied Francis II to the audience with Napoleon after the battle, which was the preliminary for Austria's withdrawal from the war.

Lille, Count of: see Louis XVIII.

Livingstone, Edward (1764–1836). The great American jurist and statesman is mentioned by Napoleon in the entry for 5 April 1804. He had been mayor of New York (1801–3) and was to serve as minister-plenipotentiary to France (1833–55).

Lobau, General Georges Mouton, comte de (1770–1838). Having achieved a reputation for courage and ability, Lobau was appointed a general and aide to Napoleon in 1805. Ennobled as comte de Lobau for his counterattack, with Rapp, as Essling, he was captured at the fall of Dresden, having commanded I Corps. He led VI Corps in 1815. Napoleon appreciated his blunt and honest manner, and made the well-known pun about him: '*Mon mouton est un lion*' ('My sheep is a lion').

Loison, General Louis-Henri (1771–1816). Perhaps best known for being hated by the local population for his conduct toward them in Portugal, Loison spent much of his career in the Peninsula, but joined the *Grande Armée* in 1812. On 31 March 1813, he was relieved of duty for being absent from his command, but subsequently was reinstated. He retired in 1815.

Louis: see Bonaparte, Louis.

Louis XVI, King of France (1754–93), the most prominent victim of the French Revolution and, in the opinion of some, one of its many causes. Louis XVI was guillotined on 21 January 1793, about seven months after he was mentioned by Napoleon, whose comment in the entry for 20 June 1792 was indeed prophetic.

Louis XVIII, King of France (1755–1824), brother of Louis XVI and known as the Count of Provence or of Lille. Recognised as the king-in-exile, Louis XVIII was a leader of the French Royalists throughout the Napoleonic era. He was restored to his throne in 1814 and again in 1815, after the brief hiatus of the Hundred Days.

Louis Ferdinand, Prince of Prussia (1773–1806). Referred to by Napoleon as 'Prince Louis', this nephew of Frederick William III was considered to be a potentially great commander. One of the Prussians most belligerent toward Napoleon (who claimed that he was one of the authors of the war of 1806: entry for 12 October 1806), he was killed at Saalfeld on 10 October 1806, in combat with Quartermaster Guindet of the French 10th Hussars.

Louis 'le Debonnaire' (Emperor Louis I, AD 778–840). Napoleon's reference (entry for 22 July 1807) contrasts the determined and successful reign of Charlemagne with that of his somewhat ineffectual son and successor. Louis I was also known as 'Louis the Pious' from his great generosity to the Church, which, in the passage quoted, Napoleon clearly intends not to emulate!

Lowe, General Sir Hudson (1769–1844). A British expert on Mediterranean warfare (he commanded the Corsican Rangers), Lowe was rejected by Wellington for a position on his staff in 1815, but became Napoleon's 'gaoler' as governor of St Helena. He was condemned by Napoleon and his entourage for his unsympathetic behaviour toward them, although he met Napoleon only four times during the entire period of his confinement.

Lucchesini, Girolamo, marquis (1751–1825). Although born in Lucca,

Lucchesini was a member of the Prussian diplomatic corps from 1779, acting as ambassador in Paris from 1800 until just before the war of 1806. He favoured Franco-Prussian friendship and received no further employment when the armistice that he had negotiated following Jena was not ratified by the king. Thereafter, he served Elisa Bonaparte in Tuscany.

Ludwig (Louis), Crown Prince of Bavaria (1786–1868). The remarks concerning the inexperience of 'the Prince Royal' (entry for 14 March 1809) relate to Napoleon's appointment of Lefebvre to command VII Corps (composed of Bavarians) instead of the Crown Prince, who instead led its 1st Division. Relations between him and Napoleon were not good – Napoleon was goaded into asking why he should not shoot a prince! – and as leader of the anti-French party, Ludwig was among those who supported Bavaria's change of allegiance in 1813. He succeeded his father as King Ludwig I in 1825.

Macdonald, Marshal Jacques-Etienne-Joseph-Alexandre (1765–1840). A product of the Jacobite emigration following the 1745 Rebellion, Napoleon's marshal of Scots descent was a general in the French Army from 1793, but his association with Moreau led to him only returning to command in 1809. Appointed a marshal for his conduct at Wagram, and ennobled as Duke of Taranto, Macdonald served in the Peninsula and in the campaigns of 1812–14. Having pledged his allegiance to the Bourbons in 1814, he remained loyal to them during the Hundred Days.

Mack von Leiberich, General Karl (1752–1828). This Austrian commander was outmanoeuvred by Napoleon and forced to surrender at Ulm. Napoleon once remarked that he was the most mediocre man he ever knew, yet in the entry for 3 August 1808 he used him as an example of just how inept was his own general, Dupont.

Macquart (or Macquard), General François (1738–1801). This elderly general, who served under Napoleon in Italy, left the army in January 1797 and went into retirement.

'Madame Joseph': see Clary, Marie-Julie.

'Madame Mère': see Bonaparte, Letizia.

Maison, General Nicolas-Joseph (1771–1840). An officer of extensive service, Joseph commanded I Corps from December 1813, but was one of those mentioned for having remained loyal to the king during the Hundred Days (entry for 18 April 1815). He became a marshal in 1829.

Maitland, Captain (later Rear-Admiral Sir) Frederick Lewis. Captain of the

British 74-gun ship-of-the-line HMS *Bellerophon*, Maitland received Napoleon's surrender, in Basque Roads, on 15 July 1815. He sailed immediately for Torbay, then Plymouth, arriving there on 26 July. On 7 August, Napoleon was transferred to HMS *Northumberland*, which sailed for St Helena on the following day.

Manscourt du Rozoy, General Jean-Baptiste-Félix de (1749–1824). This artillery officer was commandant of Alexandria when mentioned by Napoleon (entry for 16 October 1798). He retired upon his return to France in 1801.

Marbot, Colonel Jean-Baptiste-Antoine-Marcellin de (1782–1854). A cavalry officer who served on the staff of Augereau, Murat, Lannes and Masséna, and as a regimental commander (1812–15), Marbot is best known for his colourful reminiscences, one of the most famous of soldiers' accounts of the Napoleonic Wars. In his role as ADC, he had frequent contact with Napoleon, which accounts for his mention in the text of this work.

Marceau-Desgraviers, General François-Séverin (1769–96). One of the great French heroes of the early Revolutionary Wars, Marceau-Desgraviers served with distinction in the Vendée and in Germany. In September 1796, he was mortally wounded by an Austrian sharpshooter at Altenkirchen.

Marchand, Louis (1792–1876), Napoleon's senior valet at St Helena; his mother had been the King of Rome's nurse. A loyal servant, Marchand was one of those who returned to St Helena for the exhumation in 1840, and in 1869 he was ennobled as a count. Napoleon named him as one of the executors of his will and left him handsome legacies for having served him as a friend.

Maret, Hugues-Bernard (1763–1839). This lawyer became Napoleon's secretary in 1799, then editor of the official state journal *Le Moniteur*. A minister from 1804, Maret was involved in much important diplomacy and was Napoleon's foreign minister during 1811–13. Napoleon ennobled him as Duke of Bassano.

Maria Carolina, Queen of Naples. Daughter of the Empress Maria Theresa and sister of Marie Antoinette, Maria Carolina married King Ferdinand IV of Naples in 1768 and came to control both him and the state, being partly responsible for its involvement in hostilities against France. When the royal family had to flee to Sicily, her intrigues were such that she was exiled in 1813; she died in Austria in 1814.

Maria-Louisa, Archduchess of Austria (1791–1847), usually known by the French version of her name, Marie-Louise. The daughter of Emperor Francis II, Marie-Louise was chosen by Napoleon as his second empress, partly to cement relations between France and Austria (in preference to a Russian princess), but also to provide him with an heir. Napoleon became genuinely attached to her, but after the abdication of 1814, she returned to her father and he never saw her again. She was granted the duchies of Parma, Piacenza and Guastalla by the Congress of Vienna, and even before Napoleon's death she was living with Count Adam von Niepperg, whom she later married.

Maria-Luisa of Parma, Queen of Spain. Married to her cousin, King Charles IV of Spain, Maria-Luisa dominated him entirely, and with her lover, Godoy, virtually ruled in his stead.

Maria Theresa, Empress of Austria (1717–80). The great Austrian sovereign is mentioned by Napoleon (entry for 23 October 1813) in connection with an address presented to his own empress: Marie-Louise was Maria Theresa's great-granddaughter.

Marlborough, John Churchill, 1st Duke of (1650–1722). One of the greatest military commanders of all time, Marlborough is mentioned by Napoleon (entry for 9 November 1816) in respect of a challenge issued to him by Sidney Smith, Napoleon remarking that only Marlborough would have been a suitable opponent for him.

Marmont, Marshal Auguste-Frédéric-Louis Viesse de (1774–1852). A close friend of Napoleon from an early age, Marmont became his ADC and had risen to the rank of marshal by 1809, although Napoleon admitted that the honour had been bestowed more out of friendship than military ability. He was also ennobled as Duke of Ragusa, but their friendship ended when Marmont helped negotiate the truce that permitted the Allies to enter Paris in 1814.

Masséna, Marshal André (1758–1817). One of the earliest and best of Napoleon's subordinate commanders, Masséna served in Italy and through until Wagram with Napoleon, although he enjoyed less success in the Peninsula. A marshal from 1804, he was ennobled as Duke of Rivoli in 1808 and Prince of Essling in 1810, both titles taken from battles in which he had achieved particular distinction.

Mattei, Cardinal. Napoleon's reproach (entry for 26 September 1796) refers to the opposition of the Cardinal-Bishop of Ferrara to the anti-Papal revolt there. Later, Mattei represented the Pope in the negotiations that took place at Tolentino in February 1797.

Maximilian I, King of Bavaria (1756–1825). Elector of Bavaria from 1799, Maximilian Joseph of Zweibrücken became one of Napoleon's most loyal allies; when mentioned (entry for 13 September 1805), his forces were collaborating with those of Napoleon against Austria. His loyalty was rewarded by elevation to King of Bavaria in 1806, but finally he defected to the Allies in 1813 on the guarantee of the integrity of his kingdom.

Melas, General Michael Friedrich Benedikt (1729–1806). This experienced Austrian commander opposed the French in Italy during 1799–1800, compelling Masséna to surrender at Genoa, but he was defeated by Napoleon at Marengo.

Melzi d'Eril, Francesco, Count, one of Napoleon's early supporters in Italy, who welcomed him to Milan. Napoleon opposed the plan to elect Melzi as president of the Italian Republic and had himself appointed instead, but as King of Italy he created the Duchy of Lodi for him.

Méneval, Claude-François de (1780–1842), Napoleon's loyal, capable and hard-working principal private and cabinet secretary, appointed when he was First Consul. Subsequently, he served Marie-Louise in the same capacity.

Menou, General Jacques-François de Boussay, comte de (1750–1810). At the time of the insurrection of 13th Vendémiaire, Menou was commander of the Army of the Interior and was dismissed for his laxity in opposing it. Subsequently, he succeeded Kléber to the command of the army in Egypt, being defeated by Abercromby at Alexandria in 1801.

Merveldt, Maximilian, Count. This Austrian general represented the Emperor in the negotiations of the armistice in 1797. When mentioned in the entry for 16 October 1813, he was commanding II Corps of the Austrian Army at Leipzig, where he was captured. He was greeted warmly by Napoleon, who knew him well, and on 17 October he was sent back to the Austrians on parole, with the offer of an armistice, which was refused.

Metternich-Winneburg-Beilstein, Clemens Wenzel Lothar von, Prince (1773–1859). Later to become the dominant European statesman of the age, Metternich entered the Austrian diplomatic service while young, and in August 1806 became ambassador to France. Foreign minister from 1809 (although without responsibility for the humiliating Treaty of Schönbrunn), he was less hostile to Napoleon than many in Austria. He suggested the marriage to Marie-Louise, but after Napoleon's reverses in 1812 realised that Austria would profit from siding with the Allies. His reputation was cemented by the Congress of Vienna and he remained in office until 1848, exerting considerable influence throughout Europe.

Meunier, General Hugues-Alexandre-Joseph (1751–1831). As suggested by Napoleon's remarks (entry for 14 August 1796), Meunier's later career was spent largely in administrative posts.

Milhaud, General Edouard-Jean-Baptiste (1766–1833). This skilled cavalry officer served at Austerlitz, Jena, Eylau and in the Peninsula; when mentioned (entry for 29 July 1813), he was a cavalry commander under Augereau. Later in the year, he commanded V Cavalry Corps, and led IV Cavalry Corps in the Waterloo campaign.

Miloradovich, General Mikhail Andreivich (1770–1825). One of the bravest and most popular of Russian generals, Miloradovich fought with distinction in the campaigns of 1812–14, notably at Kulm. When governor of St Petersburg, he was killed attempting to talk to some of the Decembrist insurgents.

Miot de Melito, André-François (1762–1841). One of Napoleon's best-known diplomats (despite the opinion expressed in the entry for 14 March 1814), Miot de Melito had also served as Joseph Bonaparte's interior minister at Naples, and as head of his household in Spain.

Mirabeau, Honoré-Gabriel Riqueti, comte de (1749–91). One of the most important political figures in early Revolutionary France, who favoured a constitutional monarchy of British style, Mirabeau was elected to the Convention, but died on 2 April 1791, only shortly after Napoleon mentioned him.

Modena, Duke of. Hercules III d'Este (1727–1803) lost his state when Modena was transformed into the Cispadane Republic after the French invasion. He declined to accept the principality of Breisgau and Ortenau (Baden), offered at Campo Formio, and died in exile at Treviso. His successor, Ferdinand, took the title of Duke of Modena-Breisgau, but in 1805 the latter territory was split between Baden and Würtemberg. In 1814, Hercules's grandson, Francis IV, was restored to Modena.

Moellendorf, Field-Marshal Richard Joachim Heinrich von (1724–1816). This distinguished subordinate of Frederick the Great played an advisory role in the Jena campaign, and might have persuaded the commandant of Erfurt not to surrender as soon as he did (see entry for 16 October 1806) had not the consequences of a wound caused him to faint during the negotiations.

Mollien, Nicolas-François (1758–1850). Having served in the French finance ministry under the *Ancien Régime*, as head of the treasury, Mollien was one of Napoleon's most valued and longest-serving ministers. He returned to the job during the Hundred Days, but then retired, despite the fact that Louis XVIII wanted him to continue.

Moncey, Marshal Bon-Adrien-Jeannot de (1754–1842). One of the less well known of Napoleon's marshals, noted more for courage and honour than military genius, Moncey had retired from front-line service in 1801, but served in the Peninsula during 1808–9 before returning to largely administrative duties. He was ennobled as Duke of Conegliano in 1808.

Monge, Gaspard (1746–1818). This noted mathematician and scientist occupied a number of posts during the Revolutionary period, notably in Italy in 1796 as an advisor on the appropriation by the French of works of art; he was appointed to head the Egyptian Institute during Napoleon's eastern campaign. Monge was ennobled as Count of Pelusium.

Monnier, General Jean-Charles (1758–1816). After service under Napoleon in Italy, Monnier commanded a division at Marengo, but shortly after was retired as a consequence of his opposition to Napoleon. He returned to the service briefly after Napoleon's abdication.

Montalivet, Jean-Pierre Bachasson, comte de (1766–1823). When mentioned, Montalivet was Napoleon's minister of the interior; his son, Marthe-Camille (1801–80), occupied the same ministry for most of the decade 1830–40.

Montbrun, General Louis-Pierre (1770–1812). One of the best of Napoleon's cavalry generals, Montbrun served notably in the Peninsula and in the 1809 campaign; he led II Cavalry Corps in the invasion of Russia in 1812. He was killed at Borodino.

Montebello, Duke of: see Lannes.

Montesquieu, Charles Louis de Secondat, baron de (1689–1755). Napoleon's reference in the entry for 19 September 1797 is to the great French philosopher and man of letters, perhaps best known for *L'esprit des Lois*.

Montesquiou, comte de, successor to Talleyrand as Grand Chamberlain of Napoleon's court.

Montesquiou, comtesse de, wife of the comte de Montesquiou (see previous entry) and governess to the King of Rome until he and his mother went to Austria after Napoleon's abdication. The closeness of her relationship with the child may be gauged from the fact that he called her '*Maman Quiou*'.

Montezuma II (also Moctezuma, c. 1480–1520). Ruler of the Aztec empire in Mexico, Montezuma was forced to pay tribute to the Spanish Conquistadors led by Hernán Cortés. In the entry for 18 August 1816, Napoleon compared the treatment he received from Hudson Lowe to that experienced by Montezuma.

Montholon, Albine Hélène, comtesse de. The wife of Count Montholon (see following entry) accompanied her husband to St Helena. Their marriage had not been approved by Napoleon and it damaged her husband's career, but on St Helena it was believed widely that she became Napoleon's mistress. She left the island with her children in July 1819.

Montholon, Charles-Tristan, comte de (1783–1853). A staff officer of no great distinction, who fell out of favour with Napoleon and in 1814 was accused of embezzlement, Montholon volunteered to accompany Napoleon to St Helena. Napoleon had no doubts about his loyalty, but it has been suggested that he may have been implicated in Royalist plots to murder Napoleon. Subsequently, he wrote successful books about Napoleon's time on St Helena.

Moore, General Sir John (1761–1809). Commander of the British forces in Portugal in 1808, Moore deflected Napoleon's attention from completing the destruction of the main Spanish forces by advancing into Spain. Napoleon pursued him to Corunna, where Moore defeated Soult (16 January 1809), but was killed in the battle.

Morand, General Charles-Antoine-Louis-Alexis (1771–1835). This very proficient subordinate commander fought with distinction at Austerlitz and under Davout, until wounded at Borodino. He led IV Corps from November 1813, but from the following month until the end of the war, he was besieged in Mainz. He also served with distinction in the 1815 campaign.

Moreau, General Jean-Victor-Marie (1763–1813). One of the most able French generals of the Revolutionary Wars, Moreau won his greatest victory at Hohenlinden in 1800. He might have been a rival to Napoleon and disapproved of Napoleon's assumption of supreme power, but he was exiled following the Pichegru and Cadoudal plot. He returned to Europe from the America to serve as military advisor to the Tsar, but shortly after his arrival he was mortally wounded at Dresden.

Mortier, Marshal Edouard-Adolphe-Casimir-Joseph (1768–1835). One of Napoleon's generals who was among the first creation of the marshalate in 1804, Mortier was a steady, if not especially gifted, commander. Napoleon ennobled him as Duke of Treviso in 1808.

Moskowa, Prince of the: see Ney.

Moustache, a favourite courier employed by Napoleon.

Muiron, M., Napoleon's ADC, appointed in October 1796, who was killed protecting him at Arcola. Napoleon never forgot this act and left a legacy in his will for Muiron's relatives.

Murad Bey (1750–1801). An ex-Circassian slave who shared the Mameluke governance of Egypt with Ibrahim, Murad was the Amir al-Hajj, the leader of the annual pilgrimage to Mecca, and he commanded at the Battle of the Pyramids. Unwilling to submit to his Ottoman overlords, however, he agreed to change sides and join the French, but he died of plague in May 1801.

Murat, Marshal Joachim (1767–1815). The most flamboyant of all Napoleon's commanders, and his brother-in-law by virtue of marriage to Caroline Bonaparte in 1800, Murat became a marshal in 1804, and was appointed by Napoleon as Grand Duke of Berg (1806) and King of Naples (1808). He was a great cavalry commander, but too mercurial, and was executed by firing squad in Calabria in 1815 while attempting to regain his throne.

Mustapha Pasha. Seraskier (Ottoman general) of Rumelia, Mustapha Pasha commanded the Turkish Army at Aboukir. Captured in the battle, he remained with the French Army and served subsequently as an intermediary between Kléber and the Grand Vizier. When he died (he was an old man) at Damietta in 1800, before an exchange could be arranged, the French gave him a full military funeral.

Naples, King of: see Ferdinand IV. After February 1806, this title refers to Joseph Bonaparte, and after August 1808 to Murat.

Naples, Queen of: see Maria Carolina. After August 1808, this title refers to Caroline Bonaparte.

Narbonne-Lara, General Louis-Marie-Jacques-Amalric, comte de (1755–1813). Born in Italy of a noble family and raised at Versailles with the French royal children, Narbonne-Lara returned from abroad after the Revolution and was employed by Napoleon as a diplomat, notably as ambassador to Vienna. From 13 September 1813, he was governor of Torgau (see entry for 19 September, which concerns his report), but he died there from typhus on 17 November.

Nelson, Admiral Horatio, 1st Viscount (1758–1805). The great British admiral did more than most to frustrate Napoleon's strategy, notably through his great victories of Aboukir Bay ('Battle of the Nile'), Copenhagen and Trafalgar, where he was killed.

Neuchâtel, Alexandre, Prince of: see Berthier.

Ney, Marshal Michel (1769–1815). Known as 'the bravest of the brave', Ney was one of the most resolute of Napoleon's subordinates. A marshal from 1804, he was ennobled as Duke of Elchingen (from the action in which he had distinguished himself in 1806) and as Prince of the Moskowa, following his sterling conduct in the 1812 campaign, notably in commanding the rearguard during the retreat from Moscow. Although he advocated Napoleon's abdication in 1814, he rallied to him in 1815 and, as a result, was executed by the Bourbons.

O'Connor, General Arthur (1763–1852). The 'General O'Connor' from whom Napoleon sought advice about landing in Ireland (entry for 6 September 1804) was the exiled leader of the United Irishmen, who had been acquitted at his trial in Britain. Napoleon appointed him a general in February 1804, but he saw no active service. He married the daughter of the marquise de Condorcet, who was Grouchy's niece, and became a French citizen in 1818.

Olsuvief, General. One of Blücher's corps commanders in 1814, this Russian general was defeated and captured at Champaubert, having offered battle unwisely while smarting under criticism for poor performance at Brienne and La Rothière.

O'Meara, Barry Edward (1782–1836). A British naval medical officer, O'Meara encountered Napoleon aboard HMS *Bellerophon* and served as his physician at St Helena. In July 1818, he was removed, evidently because it was thought that he had become too close to the ex-emperor. His book, *A Voice from St. Helena*, was critical of Hudson Lowe and his treatment of Napoleon.

Orange, Prince of: see William Frederick.

Ordener, General Michel (1755–1811). Distinguished in Italy and commander of the *Grenadiers à Cheval* of the Imperial Guard, whom he led at Austerlitz, Ordener is perhaps best remembered as the commander of the force that violated neutral territory to seize the duc d'Enghien. He retired in 1806 as a consequence of the many wounds he had received during his career.

Orléans, Louis-Philippe, duc d' (1773–1850). A descendent of Louis XIV, Orléans was one of the most prominent of the exiled French Royalists, but one least involved in intrigues against the Republican and Napoleonic regimes. He was still a threat to Napoleon, however, hence the latter's remark (entry for 19 March 1804) that even if Orléans had been living in Paris with diplomatic immunity, he would still have had him shot, presumably an attempt to justify the seizure of the duc d'Enghien. Louis-Philippe succeeded Charles X as King of France in 1830, but was deposed in 1848.

Otranto, Duke of: see Fouché.

Ott, *Feldmarschall-Leutnant* Peter Carl (1738–1809). An experienced Austrian commander, Ott served under Suvarov in Italy in 1799, and under

Melas commanded the force that compelled Masséna to surrender Genoa. He led the left wing at Marengo, his last active command.

Otto, M. A diplomatic agent employed by Napoleon, Otto helped negotiate the Treaty of Amiens and later served as ambassador to Austria.

Oudinot, Marshal Nicolas-Charles (1767–1847). The most frequently wounded of all Napoleon's senior commanders, Oudinot won great distinction leading a composite division of grenadiers in the 1805 campaign. Further distinguished at Wagram, he was appointed a marshal and ennobled as Duke of Reggio. He performed valuable service in the campaigns of 1812–14, but remained loyal to the Bourbons in 1815.

Paër, Ferdinando (1771–1839). From 1803, this renowned Italian musician had been court composer at Dresden, until Napoleon took him to Warsaw and Paris, where he settled as conductor of the Italian opera, a position he held until retiring in favour of Rossini in 1823. His wife, mentioned in the entry for 12 December 1806, was the famous singer Riccardi.

Paine, Thomas (1737–1809). The English Radical and political writer, most famous for his *Rights of Man* (1791), had served in the French Convention, but was becoming a dubious asset, as Napoleon's comment of 5 April 1800 suggests. He went to America in 1802, although he had lost sympathy even there, despite having had a considerable influence in the American War of Independence (hence Napoleon's comment that it was 'his own country').

Pajol, General Claude-Pierre (1772–1844). An expert commander of light cavalry, when mentioned (entry for 29 July 1813), Pajol was leading the 10th Cavalry Division; in September 1813, he was promoted to command V Cavalry Corps, but in the following month had to relinquish this post due to injury after falling from his horse. He led I Cavalry Corps in the Waterloo campaign.

Palafox y Melzi, General José de (1780–1847). One of the most famous Spanish commanders of the Peninsular War, as Captain-General of Aragon, Palafox y Melzi organised resistance to the French in the region of Saragossa. He defended the city successfully during the first French siege of 1808, and held out in the second (1808–9) until disease and starvation compelled its surrender (21 February 1809). He was imprisoned in France for the remainder of the war.

Paoli, Pasquale (1725–1807). This great champion of Corsican independence was originally a friend of the Bonaparte family, although eventually they rejected the concept of an independent Corsica. Paoli briefly achieved a degree of independence with British assistance – he offered sovereignty to King

George III – but France repossessed the island, and from 1796 Paoli lived in exile in England.

Parma, Duke of. Ferdinand, son of Don Ferdinand, *infante* of Spain, succeeded to Parma in 1765. His state was overrun by the French in 1796, and he purchased a lifetime tenure from them for six million lire and twenty-five of the finest paintings in Parma. Upon his death in 1802, the territory passed to France.

Patterson, Elizabeth (1785–1879). This American woman married Jérôme Bonaparte in her native Baltimore in 1803, but Napoleon was violently opposed to the union (see entry for 22 April 1805) and refused her entry to his territory. She gave birth to Jérôme's son at Camberwell in England in 1805, before returning to America. Having had the marriage annulled, Napoleon arranged for Jérôme to marry Princess Frederica Catherina of Würtemberg in 1806. Elizabeth's child (to whom Napoleon refers in the entry for 18 November 1808), Jérôme Napoleon (1805–70), was the origin of the American branch of the Bonaparte family.

Paul I, Tsar of Russia (1754–1801), known as 'the Mad Tsar'. Son of Catherine the Great, Paul I succeeded her in 1796, but his eccentric policies led to his assassination on 23 March 1801. Originally opposed to the French, subsequently he showed more sympathy toward Napoleon, having been angered by the British occupation of Malta. His cause of death, mentioned in the entry for 12 April 1801, was that given initially.

Paulette: see Bonaparte, Pauline.

Perée, Admiral Jean-Baptiste-Emmanuel (1761–1800). This French naval officer commanded part of Brueys's fleet during the Egyptian expedition, notably leading a flotilla of light vessels on the Nile. When taking supplies to the French garrison on Malta, his ship was intercepted by the British Navy and he was killed in the ensuing action, on 18 February 1800.

Peyri, General L.C.B.P.L.M., an Italian general who commanded an Italian division in Bertrand's Corps in 1813.

Philip V, King of Spain (Philip of Anjou, 1683–1746). Napoleon's reference in the entry for 19 July 1808 concerns this disputed successor to King Charles II of Spain and the War of the Spanish Succession (1701–14).

Pichegru, General Charles (1761–1804). Although a hero of the French Revolutionary Wars, Pichegru's progressively Royalist stance caused him to go into exile, where he worked for the restoration of the monarchy. He returned to

France in 1803 as leader of a projected insurrection, but was arrested and later found strangled in his cell. Murder was suspected, but Napoleon thought the accusation absurd, and there was little to contradict the theory of suicide.

Pijon, General Jean-Joseph-Magdelaine (1758–99). This officer served under Napoleon in Italy, then in Switzerland, and upon his return to Italy was mortally wounded at Magnano (5 April 1799).

Piré, General Hippolyte-Marie-Guillaume (1778–1850). When mentioned in the entry for 30 November 1808, this well-known cavalryman was serving as ADC to Berthier. Promoted to general in March 1809, he served through the succeeding campaigns, including Waterloo.

Pitt, William (1759–1806). British Prime Minister during 1783–1801 and 1804–6, Pitt was perhaps the best-known and most influential of all France's political opponents.

Pius VI, Pope (Giovanni Braschi, 1717–99), ruler of the Papal States with whom Napoleon came into contact in the Italian campaign. He made concessions by the Peace of Tolentino (19 February 1797), following French victories, but the French still entered Rome in February 1798, taking him into custody when he refused to surrender his temporal powers. He died in August 1799.

Pius VII, Pope (Luigi Barnaba Chiaramonti, 1740–1823). Successor to Pius VI and elected Pope in March 1800, Pius VII concluded the Concordat with Napoleon, but relations between them collapsed following the French occupation of Rome and annexation of the Papal States. He was arrested and did not return to Rome until May 1814.

Piveron de Morlay, M. As mentioned in the entry for 14 April 1798, Piveron de Morlay had been French ambassador at the court of Mysore for many years, hence Napoleon's idea of using him again. In 1783, he had helped broker the armistice between Tippoo and the besieged garrison of Mangalore, although it was said that he had attempted to conceal from the latter news of the cessation of Anglo-French hostilities by the Treaty of Versailles, only for the French military commander, de Cossigny, to exhibit a greater sense of honour and withdraw his forces from the siege.

Pompey. References to 'Pompey's column' (entries for 2 July 1798 and 28 January 1799) concern a famous landmark that commemorated the Roman triumvir 'Pompey the Great' (Gnaeus Pompeius Magnus, 106–48 BC).

Poniatowski, Marshal Josef Anton, Prince (1763–1813). A noted Polish patriot, Poniatowski was a nephew of King Stanislaus II of Poland. His support was courted by Prussia and Russia, but after the defeat of the former in 1806, he saw Napoleon as the best chance of establishing an independent Polish state. Commander of the army of the Grand Duchy of Warsaw, he led V Corps of the *Grande Armée* with distinction in 1812, and despite his mistrust of Napoleon continued to serve him. Appointed a marshal on 15 October 1813, he was drowned while attempting to cross the River Elster during the Battle of Leipzig.

Pons l'Hérault, André. Manager of the mines on Elba, Pons l'Hérault was a trusted friend of Napoleon and one of the few who knew of his plan to return to France in 1815, where he accompanied Napoleon.

Ponte Corvo, Prince of: see Bernadotte.

Pope: see Pius VI (until 1799) and Pius VII (from 1800).

Portalis, Jean-Etienne-Marie (1746–1807). A lawyer and moderate opponent of the Directory, Portalis was appointed a councillor of state by Napoleon in 1800. He played a major role in the formulation of the Concordat and, notably, the Code Napoléon.

Potemkin, Prince Grigory Aleksandrovich (1739–91). The reference in the entry for 22 May 1805 concerns this Russian statesman, lover of Catherine the Great and at one time said to be the most influential individual in Russia.

Poussielgue, E. Secretary to the French legation at Genoa, Poussielgue was sent to Malta in November 1797 by Napoleon, ostensibly on commercial business, but actually to attempt to facilitate French designs on the island. He was Controller-General (chief financial officer) to the Egyptian expedition and was one of the negotiators of the abortive convention of El-Arich.

Préameneu, Bigot, comte de. Mentioned by Napoleon (entry for 12 August 1800) in relation to the formulation of the Civil Code, Préameneu is perhaps better known as Napoleon's minister for public worship.

'Prince of Peace': see Godoy.

Prince Regent of England (as in entry for 14 July 1815). George, Prince of Wales (1762–1830), eldest son of King George III, became Prince Regent in 1811 when the king's health deteriorated to the extent that he was unable to perform his constitutional duties. He succeeded as King George IV in 1820.

Provence, Count of: see Louis XVIII.

Provera, General Johann (1740–1804). This Italian-born Austrian general, who opposed Napoleon in Italy, was forced to surrender at Cossaria and subsequently at La Favorita when attempting to relieve Mantua.

Prussia, King of: see Frederick William III.

Prussia, Queen of: see Louise, Queen.

Ragusa, Duke of: see Marmont.

Rampon, General Antoine-Guillaume (1759–1842). Promoted to general after distinguishing himself at Montelegino (April 1796), Rampon served under Napoleon in Italy and Egypt, retired from active duty in 1802 and held a number of administrative commands thereafter.

Rapp, General Jean (1771–1821). Originally an aide to Desaix, Rapp served Napoleon in the same capacity and became a general in 1803. Perhaps the most famous of Napoleon's aides, he was wounded on numerous occasions (he reckoned that he suffered his twenty-second wound in Russia in 1812). In 1815, he commanded the Army of the Upper Rhine.

Raynouard, François-Juste-Marie (1761–1836), an important French dramatist and linguistic researcher. At the time Raynouard was mentioned by Napoleon (entries for 1 June 1805 and 31 December 1806), his *Les Templiers* had been produced to considerable acclaim (1805), although his subsequent work, *Les Etats de Blois*, gave some offence to Napoleon.

Réal, Pierre-François. This councillor of state under Napoleon had opposed the Directory and, as a magistrate and subordinate of Fouché, was involved in the arrest and interrogation of Pichegru. He also produced a report on the Malet conspiracy.

Reggio, Duke of: see Oudinot.

Régnier (more usually, Reynier), General Jean-Louis-Ebenézer (1771–1814). Despite a reputation for insubordination, this Swiss general proved to be a loyal subordinate to Napoleon. He commanded a division in Egypt, was defeated at Maida, and served in the campaigns of 1809 and 1812–13, and in the Peninsula. Captured after Leipzig, he was exchanged, but died, probably of fatigue, in February 1814.

Rémusat, Auguste-Laurenant, comte de (1762–1823), Napoleon's chamberlain. Rémusat's wife, Claire-Elisabeth-Jeanée Gravier de Rémusat (1780–1821), is perhaps better known by virtue of her memoirs, which describe the Napoleonic court.

Rivoli, Duke of: see Masséna.

Roize, General César-Antoine (1761–1801). Murat's chief of staff in Egypt, Roize was promoted provisionally to general by Kléber in April 1800, but was killed at Alexandria in the following year.

Romanzoff, Count. As suggested by Napoleon's reference (entry for 2 February 1808), Romanzoff had succeeded Baron Budberg in September 1807 as director of Russian foreign affairs.

Rome, King of (Napoleon-François-Joseph-Charles Bonaparte, 1811–32), Napoleon's only legitimate child, his heir by Marie-Louise, born at the Tuileries on 20 March 1811. After Napoleon's abdication, the child became Napoleon II in the eyes of Bonapartists. Marie-Louise took the boy to Austria, where he came under the guardianship of his grandfather, the Emperor Francis. The title given him by Napoleon – King of Rome – was replaced by that of Prince of Parma, and from July 1818 he was styled the Duke of Reichstädt, when it was decided that he should not inherit his mother's territory. He was never permitted to correspond with his father, and his early death was due to tuberculosis.

Rosen, Axel, Count. The Swedish ambassador is mentioned in connection with the adoption of Bernadotte as Crown Prince of Sweden.

Rousseau, Jean-Jacques (1712–78), the great French philosopher about whom Napoleon wrote in 1786, although his opinion changed, as indicated by the entry for 12 January 1803. Later, Napoleon remarked that his brother, Louis, had been spoiled by reading Rousseau!

Roustan Raza (or Roustam Raza, 1780–1845), Napoleon's Mameluke servant, Armenian by birth, whom he was given in Egypt in 1799. He became Napoleon's closest attendant and was recognisable instantly by virtue of the oriental costume that he always wore.

Ruchel, General Ernst Philipp von (1754–1823). Commander of the Prussian detached corps that supported Hohenlohe's army at Jena, Ruchel was severely wounded, but Napoleon's report of his death (entry for 15 October 1806) was premature. Although Soult ordered his own surgeon to attend him, Ruchel had made off before he arrived.

Russia, Emperor of: see Paul I and Alexander I (after March 1801).

Sacken, General Fabian Gottlieb von der Osten, Count (1752–1837). This Russian general of German descent commanded part of the 3rd West Army in

1812. During 1813–14, he was one of three corps commanders (with Langeron and York) in Blücher's Army of Silesia.

Sainte Croix, Colonel Charles-Marie-Robert (1782–1810). When his conversation with Napoleon was recorded (entry for 12 June 1809), Sainte Croix was Masséna's senior ADC. He was promoted to general in 1809, but was killed in Portugal in October 1810.

Saint-Cyr: see Gouvion St Cyr.

Saint-Hilaire, General Louis-Vincent-Joseph Le Blond (1766–1809). Described by Lejeune as 'the pride of the army, as remarkable for his wit as for his military talents', Saint-Hilaire served with great distinction in Italy, and at Austerlitz, Jena and Eylau. He was mortally wounded at Aspern-Essling and Napoleon felt his loss deeply. The wound mentioned in the entry for 13 November 1796 was presumably that suffered two months earlier, when he was shot in both legs.

Saint Marsin, M. When mentioned (entry for 10 February 1813), this diplomat was serving as French ambassador to Prussia.

Saliceti, Antoine-Christophe (1757–1809). A Corsican lawyer, with Augustin Robespierre, Saliceti was one of the representatives 'en mission' with the French Army at Toulon who appointed Napoleon to command the artillery, and who, after the *coup* of Thermidor, briefly placed Napoleon under arrest. Later, he supported Napoleon in his dealings with the Directory and served as a minister under Joseph Bonaparte at Naples. Despite the remarks in the entry for 1 April 1795, Napoleon came to hold him in high regard.

Santini, Jean-Natale. A Corsican, Santini was one of Napoleon's servants at St Helena ('usher of the cabinet') who resolved to shoot Hudson Lowe and then himself. He told another servant, who informed Napoleon, who quashed the idea, saying that it would be he, Napoleon, who received the blame if the plot were carried out.

Sardinia, King of. Victor Amadeus III (ruled 1773–96) was an incapable and decadent monarch who presided over a government of similar qualities, such that his country (Piedmont) was in no state to resist the French. Not long after he was mentioned by Napoleon (entry for 1 July 1795), he was defeated, acceded to the Treaty of Cherasco (28 April 1796) and abdicated.

Sauret, General Pierre-Franconin (1742–1818). After serving under Napoleon in Italy, Sauret retired in 1802.

Savary, General Anne-Jean-Marie-René (1774–1833). Although a soldier, it was as a diplomat that Savary was most valuable to Napoleon. He carried a message to the Tsar during the 1805 campaign, which aided Napoleon's tactical plan, and subsequently performed diplomatic duties in Russia and Spain. Ennobled as Duke of Rovigo in 1808, he succeeded Fouché as minister of police (1810–14).

Schérer, General Barthélemy-Louis-Joseph (1747–1804). Preceding Napoleon as commander of the Army of Italy, Schérer served as minister of war (1797–9) and was reappointed to command in Italy in 1799. However, he was unsuccessful and resigned in April of that year.

Schwarzenberg, Field-Marshal Karl Philipp, Prince of (1771–1820). One of the foremost Austrian commanders, Schwarzenberg achieved military prominence at an early age. After commanding a cavalry division at Wagram, he was sent as ambassador to Paris to negotiate Napoleon's marriage to Marie-Louise. He led the Austrian Reserve Corps during Napoleon's 1812 campaign, and in 1813–14 commanded the Army of Bohemia against Napoleon, notably at Leipzig.

Schwerin, Prince of. Duke Frederick Francis I of Mecklenburg-Schwerin (1756–1837) had remained neutral during the Revolutionary Wars, but his territory was overrun by the French in 1806 and he joined the Confederation of the Rhine. He was the first to renounce the French alliance, and in 1813–14 fought against Napoleon.

Sebastiani, General Horace-François-Bastien (1772–1851). This Corsican-born cavalry general was also an experienced diplomat, twice serving as envoy to Turkey. When first mentioned by Napoleon (entry for 15 July 1812), he was leading the 2nd Light Cavalry Division of Montbrun's II Cavalry Corps, to the command of which he succeeded after Montbrun's death at Borodino. Twice during the 1812 campaign he was seriously caught out, hence his nickname 'General Surprise', but he continued to lead cavalry in 1813–14.

Ségur, Philippe Henri, marquis de (1724–1801). A distinguished soldier who was appointed a Marshal of France in 1783, Ségur served as minister of war during 1780–87, in which capacity he received a request from Napoleon in 1786 for leave of absence. In 1800, he received a pension from Napoleon, a notable change in their respective positions in fourteen years. His grandson, the historian Philippe Paul, comte de Ségur, served as a general under Napoleon.

Selim III, Sultan. Successor to his father, Abd-ul-Hamid, in 1789 as Sultan of the Ottoman Empire, Selim encountered internal opposition to attempts at reform, and in 1806 conflicts arose with Russia over the provinces of Moldavia, Wallachia and Bessarabia. The Ottoman Empire declared war, with Napoleon's encouragement, hence the entry for 11 October 1806. In 1807, internal unrest led to Selim being replaced on the throne by his nephew, Mustapha IV, and he was murdered before he could be reinstated by the returning army, freed by the suspension of hostilities following the Treaty of Tilsit.

Serurier (spelled 'Serrurier' by Napoleon in these entries), Marshal Jean-Matthieu-Philibert (1742–1819). After serving with some distinction under Napoleon in Italy, Serurier's active service ended in 1799, but he was appointed a marshal in 1804, a largely honorific promotion.

Sicily, Queen of: see Maria Carolina, Queen of Naples (referred to as Queen of Sicily after she and Ferdinand IV were forced to flee there).

Sieyès, Emmanuel-Joseph (1748–1836). The Abbé Sieyès was more prominent in politics than the church, becoming a director in 1799. He disapproved of the Directory, however, and worked for its replacement, seeing Napoleon as the future. Having aided the *coup* of Brumaire, when what followed did not accord with his own ideas, he retired from the post of Consul to which he had been appointed.

Smith, Sir William Sidney (1764–1840). This most colourful British naval officer came to greatest prominence for his contribution to the successful defence of Acre against Napoleon. Subsequently, he concluded the convention of El-Arich with Kléber, but it was disowned by his commander-in-chief. His active service ended in 1814, but he became an admiral in 1821.

Souham, General Joseph (1760–1837). A general from 1793, Souham was arrested in February 1804 after coming under suspicion for his friendship with Moreau. He was released after spending forty days in prison, but received no further employment until 1807, after which he served in the Peninsula and in Germany.

Soult, Marshal Jean-de-Dieu (1769–1851). One of Napoleon's most capable subordinates, Soult had served in Germany and Switzerland before being named as a marshal in 1804. Greatly distinguished at Austerlitz, he had two important spells of command in the Peninsula, interrupted by service in Germany in 1813; he was ennobled as Duke of Dalmatia in 1808. In 1815, he served as Napoleon's chief of staff, although his great talents might have been better employed in a battlefield command.

Sorbier, General Jean-Barthélemot (1762–1827). When first mentioned by Napoleon (entry for 24 November 1812), Sorbier was commanding the Imperial Guard's artillery reserve. The instruction for Zayonchek to transfer as many horses as possible to Sorbier was an attempt to keep the guns moving, even at the expense of the army's baggage wagons. Sorbier acted as artillery commander of the *Grande Armée* in 1813–14.

Spain, King of: see Charles IV; after June 1808, Joseph Bonaparte was King of Spain.

Spain, Queen of: see Maria-Luisa of Parma.

Staël, Anne-Louise-Germaine, baronne de Staël-Holstein (1766–1817). 'Madame de Staël' was one of the great literary personalities of the period, daughter of the Bourbon finance minister, Jacques Necker, and married to a Swedish baron from whom she took her title. Her political views caused a feud with Napoleon, who eventually forbade her to live in France, so she spent much time at her family estate at Coppet, in Switzerland, and in England. Presumably, Napoleon's reference to her as an 'intriguing foreigner' (entry for 10 February 1803) relates to her Swedish husband and to the Swiss origin of her family, and that to the evils committed by her family concerns Necker's career.

Staps, Friedrich. The son of a Lutheran pastor, this would-be assassin was tried by court-martial and shot on 16 October 1809.

Stein, Heinrich Friedrich Karl (1757–1831). One of the most vehement opponents of Napoleon, after Tilsit Stein became virtually the chief minister of Prussia and instituted wide-ranging reforms that transformed the state. Knowing of his hostility to France, however, Napoleon demanded his removal. He sought refuge in Austria and Russia, and assisted in the formation of the coalition against France, which engaged in the 'War of Liberation'. Although his object of a federal Germany with a liberal constitution was unfulfilled in his time, his influence was immense.

Stengel, General Henri-Christian-Michel (1744–96). This French general was mortally wounded at Mondovi.

Stephanie, Princess of Baden (1789–1860). Napoleon's adopted daughter – actually the daughter of Eugène de Beauharnais's uncle, Claude – was married in 1806 to Prince Charles of Baden, who succeeded to the title of Grand-Duke of that state in 1811.

Suchet, Marshal Louis-Gabriel (1770–1826). One of the most capable of Napoleon's generals, Suchet defended southern France along the Var during the 1800 campaign, but thereafter served in subordinate positions until sent to the Peninsula, where he proved to be one of the best French commanders in that theatre. Napoleon appointed him a marshal in 1811 and Duke of Albufera in 1812.

Sulkowsky, Jozef (1770 or 1773–98). A Polish nobleman appointed as one of Napoleon's ADCs in Italy in 1796, Sulkowsky was thought to be a man of great potential, perhaps even an eventual rival to Napoleon. He was killed during a reconnaissance mission ordered by Napoleon in Egypt.

Sweden, Crown Prince of: see Bernadotte.

Talleyrand-Perigord, Charles-Maurice de (1754–1838). The greatest political survivor of the period, Talleyrand forsook the church (he had been Bishop of Autun) in 1791 to concentrate upon politics and diplomacy. Foreign minister under the Directory, he helped in the *coup* of Brumaire, and as Napoleon's foreign minister, from December 1799 to 1807, exerted considerable influence over foreign policy. Napoleon ennobled him as Duke of Benavente, although never liked nor trusted him, remarking that he was always in a state of treason, but no less useful for that! He remained an advisor while cultivating links with the Bourbons, and so prospered in the post-Napoleonic era, becoming one of Europe's most important diplomats.

Talma, François-Joseph (1763–1826). The greatest French actor of his time, Talma was a friend of Napoleon, who even took him to Erfurt in 1808 to meet the Tsar.

Taranto, Duke of: see Macdonald.

Tascher de la Pagerie, Louis Robert (1787–1861). This cousin of the Empress Josephine served as Eugène's ADC, in which capacity he is mentioned in the entry for 18 February 1814. His wife was Princess Amélie de la Leyen.

Tauenzien, General Bolesas Friedrich Emanuel (1760–1824). A general in the Prussian Army from 1801, Tauenzien commanded the left flank of Hohenlohe's army in the Jena campaign, but is perhaps best known for his success at Wittenberg in 1814, from which he took his title, Graf von Wittenberg.

Tchichagof, Admiral Pavel (1767–1849). This Russian officer served as navy minister (1808–12), but commanded the Army of the Danube (or Moldavia) in the 1812 campaign. His principal service – as mentioned in the entry for 29 November 1812 – was an attempt to block Napoleon's escape route over the Berezina, but the *Grande Armée* was able to fight its way through.

Themistocles (c. 514–449 BC). In his letter to the Prince Regent requesting sanctuary (entry for 14 July 1815), Napoleon compares himself to the great Athenian soldier and statesmen who, after being expelled from his own country, was allowed to settle in the territory of the Persians, despite having been their foe in previous years. Themistocles may have been regarded as a renegade, but clearly Napoleon felt himself as unwelcome in France as was the former in Athens.

Tippoo Sahib (1753–99). Sultan of Mysore, son of Hyder Ali, Tippoo Sahib was a persistent opponent of the British in India, and Napoleon hoped to make him an ally in his attempt to undermine British interests in the East. He was killed when the British stormed his capital, Seringapatam, in 1799.

Tolstoi, Peter, Count. When mentioned by Napoleon (November 1807–February 1808), Tolstoi was the Tsar's representative in Paris. The significance of Napoleon's remark that when receiving him (7 November 1807) 'I wore the ribbon of St. Andrew all day' is that, as a mark of respect to the Russian ambassador, and thus to the Tsar, Napoleon wore the ribbon of the Russian Order of St Andrew, the senior Russian decoration established by Peter the Great in 1698.

Tournon, M. de, an agent employed by Napoleon on a mission to Madrid (entry for 25 February 1808) to provide a source of information other than Murat and similar 'official' channels.

Trelliard, General Anne-François-Charles (1764–1832). A French cavalry commander who had seen much service in the Peninsula, Trelliard was recalled from that theatre to help Napoleon in January 1814, leading a dragoon division.

Treviso, Duke of: see Mortier.

Tronchet, François-Denis (1726–1806). A French jurist who had defended Louis XVI at his trial, Tronchet helped prepare the Civil Code and was the first senator of the Empire to be buried in the Pantheon.

Tschernitchef, General, Count. ADC to the Tsar, Tschernitchef had served as Russian military attaché at Napoleon's headquarters, and subsequently served with distinction in the 1813–14 campaigns.

Tuscany, Grand Duchess of: see Bonaparte, Eliza.

Tuscany, Grand Duke of: see Ferdinand III.

Tweeddale, George Hay, 7th Marquess of (1753–1804). An English civilian prisoner at Verdun, Tweeddale's release was ordered by Napoleon (entry for 30 July 1804). Unfortunately, the gesture was somewhat futile, as he died on 9 August while still at Verdun. His wife had died, also in captivity, on 8 May 1804.

Valmy, Duke of: see Kellermann, François-Christophe.

Vandamme, General Dominique-Louis-René (1770–1830). One of Napoleon's most loyal, brave and troublesome subordinates, Vandamme might have become a marshal (which he thought he deserved), but for his candour and penchant for plunder (it was reported that Napoleon once remarked that if he had had two Vandammes, he would have had to make one hang the other). Notably quarrelsome, he returned home from the 1812 campaign after a row, but when mentioned (entries for 24 and 30 August, and 1 September 1813), he was commanding I Corps. Defeated at Kulm, he was taken prisoner on 30 August – not killed as Napoleon feared – and failed to control his temper, even when introduced to the Tsar, whom he accused of murdering his own father.

Vaubois, General Charles-Henri, comte de Belgrand de (1748–1839). A general who served with some distinction in Italy, Vaubois is best known for his defence of Malta (1798–1800), but after the capture of the island, he served only in command of reserve formations.

Vedel, General Dominique-Honoré-Antoine-Marie (1771–1848). Sent to Spain with a division composed largely of recruits, Vedel was implicated in Dupont's surrender at Baylen, and was criticised for capitulating upon receiving an instruction to that effect from Dupont, whose orders could have been ignored, as they had been written from captivity. Vedel was court-martialled and convicted upon his return to France, but he was reinstated from December 1813.

Vence, Captain Clément Louis, marquis de (1783–1834). One of Napoleon's *officiers d'ordonnance*, Vence was appointed to the duty in November 1808 and served in that capacity until transferred to the 1st *Chasseurs à Cheval* in January 1813.

Verdier, General Jean-Antoine (1767–1839). Distinguished at Castiglione and promoted to general ten days later, Verdier saw service in Egypt, the Peninsula and the Russian campaign of 1812, during which he was seriously wounded at Polotsk.

Ver Huell, Admiral Charles-Henry (1764–1845). When Napoleon mentioned this Dutch naval officer, the Dutch forces were allied to those of France. Later, he served as Dutch minister of marine and as ambassador to Paris from the Kingdom of Holland. He entered French naval service when that kingdom was integrated with France.

Verne, General Pierre-François (1756–96). This officer served under Napoleon in Italy and was mortally wounded at Arcola.

Vicenza, Duke of: see Caulaincourt.

Viceroy (of Italy): see Beauharnais, Eugène de.

Victor, Marshal Claude (1764–1841). Claude Victor Perrin, who called himself Victor, came to prominence under Napoleon in Italy. Appointed a marshal in 1807 after serving with distinction at Friedland, he was ennobled in 1808 as Duke of Belluno. In the 1812 campaign, he commanded IX Corps, helping to cover the retreat of the *Grande Armée*, and in 1813 he led II Corps, but was relieved of command for being dilatory in the manoeuvres before Montereau (see entry for 19 February 1814). He refused to leave, saying that he would fight as an ordinary soldier if necessary, so Napoleon relented and gave him a command in the Imperial Guard. He is also mentioned especially (entry for 18 April 1815) as one of those who remained loyal to the king during the Hundred Days.

Vignolle, General Martin (1763–1824). Originally Napoleon's deputy chief of staff in Italy, Vignolle became a general in August 1796 and continued to hold staff appointments thereafter.

Villeneuve, Admiral Pierre-Charles-Jean-Baptiste-Silvestre (1763–1806). This French naval officer was given the task of luring away the British fleet so that Napoleon's invasion of England could proceed, but the plan miscarried. He was about to be relieved of command when he took the Franco-Spanish fleet out of Cadiz and was crushed at Trafalgar. Captured during the battle, he killed himself shortly after returning to France.

Visconti, Madame, Berthier's mistress.

Volney, Constantin-François-Chasseboeuf, comte de (1757–1820). When mentioned by Napoleon (entry for 20 September 1791), this French historian and man of letters was best known for his four years spent travelling in the Middle East and his *Voyage en Egypte et en Syrie* (1787). In 1792, he bought an estate in Corsica. A member of both the States-General and Constituent Assembly, he was appointed as a count and senator by Napoleon.

Voltaire, François-Marie Arouet (1694–1778). Napoleon's reference in the entry for 12 January 1803 concerns this great French philosopher and dramatist.

Voronzof, General Mikhail Semenovich (1782–1856). A member of a most distinguished Russian family (his father served as ambassador to Britain; his uncle was imperial chancellor), Voronzof served in the 1807 campaign, was wounded commanding a division at Borodino, fought in the campaigns of 1813–14, and led the Russian forces in the occupation of France in 1815.

Walewska, Countess Marie (1789–1817). Napoleon's liaison with his Polish mistress was encouraged by those seeking to influence him toward the granting of Polish independence, but it developed into a relationship of real affection. Although her aged husband acknowledged her child, Alexandre, as his own, the boy was actually Napoleon's son and accompanied Marie when she visited him on Elba. After the death of old Count Walewski, Marie married Napoleon's cousin, General Philippe d'Ornano (1816), who became the child's stepfather.

Walther, General Frédéric-Henri (1761–1813). When mentioned by Napoleon (entry for 9 October 1805), Walther was commanding the 2nd Dragoon Division of the *Grande Armée*; he was wounded at Austerlitz.

Washington, George (1732–99). The great American president had died at Mount Vernon on 14 December 1799; it is an indication of the time taken for news to be transmitted that Napoleon only mentioned the event in his order of 7 February 1800.

Weimar, Charles Augustus, Duke of Saxe-Weimar-Eisenach (1757–1828). One of the most influential princes of the smaller German states, Weimar served as a general officer with the Prussian Army in the Jena campaign. After the defeat, he was forced to join Napoleon's Confederation of the Rhine, but in 1813 reverted to his old alliance and commanded an Allied corps in 1814. It was Weimar who introduced Napoleon to Goethe. His wife, as mentioned by Napoleon in the entry for 28 April 1813, was Princess Louise of Hesse-Darmstadt.

Wellington, Field-Marshal Arthur Wellesley, Duke of (1769–1852), the leading British soldier of the era. Wellington was the victor of the Peninsular War and commanded the Anglo-Allied Army in the Waterloo campaign. Napoleon's comment (entry for 26 December 1810) refers to Wellington's defensive position of the Lines of Torres Vedras, which kept the Lisbon peninsula secure against Masséna's advance.

Werneck, *Feldmarschall-Leutnant* Franz, Baron, an Austrian divisional commander in the Ulm campaign, as mentioned by Napoleon (entries for 19 and 22 October 1805).

Whitworth, Charles, 1st Earl (1752–1825). British ambassador to Paris at the time of the Peace of Amiens, Whitworth also performed diplomatic duties in Poland, Russia and Denmark, and was Lord-Lieutenant of Ireland (1813–17).

William III, King of Great Britain (1650–1702). By referring to William III (entry for 3 March 1816), Napoleon was comparing his intended conquest of Britain to the 'Glorious Revolution' of 1688, by which William, then Prince of Orange, supplanted King James II. He must have been overlooking the fact that William was broadly popular, whereas his attempted conquest would have been opposed sternly.

William Frederick, Prince of Orange (1772–1840). Son of the Netherlands Stadtholder William V, William Frederick had close ties to Prussia by virtue of his mother and wife, and in the Jena campaign he commanded a Prussian division. In 1809, he joined Austria to continue his opposition to Napoleon, and in March 1815 became King William I of the Netherlands.

Willot, M. A member of the Clichy club and an agitator of insurrection against the Directory, Willot was transported to Guiana, but escaped with Pichegru to Britain, hence Napoleon's interest in his conduct (entry for 4 December 1802).

Wintzingerode, General Ferdinand (1770–1816). After initial service in the Austrian Army, Wintzingerode joined Russia, served in the 1805 campaign and commanded a corps in 1813–14. He was defeated at St Dizier (26 March 1814), the last of Napoleon's victories

Wittgenstein, General Ludwig Adolf Peter (1769–1843). Of Westphalian origin, Wittgenstein followed his father into the Russian Army and served at Austerlitz. In 1812, he led I Corps of the First West Army and, as the *Grande Armée* withdrew, was one of those who attempted to cut off Napoleon's retreat, marching from the north while Tchichagof moved up from the south. He replaced Kutuzov in overall command until after Bautzen, and served until wounded at Bar-sur-Aube in 1814.

Wrede, General Karl Philipp (1767–1838). The foremost Bavarian commander, Wrede served alongside the French from 1805, although probably was never happy with the alliance. In 1809, he commanded in the Tyrol and served at Wagram. He led a division of the *Grande Armée* in 1812, but in 1813–14 fought against Napoleon following Bavaria's change of allegiance, of which he approved.

Wurmser, Field Marshal Dagobert Sigismund (1724–97). A commander of the Austrian Army who opposed Napoleon in Italy in 1796–7, Wurmser was defeated at Castiglione and Bassano, and was forced to capitulate at Mantua.

Würtemberg, Elector, later King of: see Frederick I.

Wyndham (actually Windham), William (1750–1810). Pitt's secretary at war, Windham left office with Pitt and declined a position upon the latter's return in 1804, although he became secretary of state for war in Grenville's administration. As he was an influential member of the British political establishment, Napoleon was anxious to discredit him (see entry for 4 December 1802).

Xenophon (b. c. 430 BC). Napoleon's reference in the entry for 26 March 1798 concerns the Athenian historian, author and soldier, whose *Anabasis*, the account of the expedition of 401 BC in support of Cyrus against his brother, Artaxerxes II of Persia, is one of the most famous military texts from the classical period.

Xerxes. In the entry for 24 April 1809, Napoleon uses the example of the Persian king Xerxes I, whose forces were beaten at Salamis and Plataea, and who was murdered in 465 BC, to illustrate the difference between disciplined troops and more numerous, but less organised, 'hordes'.

Yarmouth, Francis Charles, Earl of (1777–1842). One of the British civilians interned in France following the collapse of the Peace of Amiens, Yarmouth was used by the French as a conduit for the tentative negotiations for peace in 1806. A friend of the Prince of Wales, he became the 3rd Marquess of Hertford, and was said to be the model for both 'Lord Steyne' in Thackeray's *Vanity Fair* and for 'Lord Monmouth' in Disraeli's *Coningsby*.

York (also Yorck), General Hans David Ludwig (1759–1830). Commander of the Prussian corps that formed part of Napoleon's *Grande Armée* during the invasion of Russia, York's 'treachery' (entry for 9 January 1813) was to negotiate the Treaty of Tauroggen with the Russians (30 December 1812), by which the Prussian forces became neutral, precipitating the change of sides by Prussia. He was one of the leaders of the Allied forces during the 'War of Liberation' (1813–14).

Zach, General Anton, Baron. This experienced Austrian officer was Melas's chief of staff in the Marengo campaign, and effectively led the army in the later stages of the battle after Melas was wounded. Later, he served as Archduke Charles's chief of staff at Caldiero.

Zayonchek, General Joseph (1762–1826). Having served under Koscziusko, this Polish officer entered French service in Italy in 1797. When mentioned by Napoleon (entry for 24 November 1812), he was commanding the 16th Division of Poniatowski's V Corps; on 28 November, he lost a leg at the Berezina and was captured by the Russians.

BIBLIOGRAPHY

Bertrand, H.G., *Napoleon at St. Helena: Memoirs of General Bertrand*, London, 1953; published originally as *Cahiers de Saint-Hélène*, ed. P.F. De Langle, Paris, 1949.

Bingham, D.A. (ed.), *A Selection from the Letters and Despatches from the First Napoleon*, London, 1884.

Bourrienne, L.A.F. de, *Mémoires de Monsieur de Bourrienne sur Napoléon, le Directoire, le Consulat, l'Empire, et la Restauration*, Paris, 1829; English translations from 1830, subsequently reprinted, including that by R.W. Phipps (ed.), London, 1893.

Brotonne, L. de (ed.), *Lettres Inédites de Napoléon Ier*, Paris, 1898, and supplement, *Dernières Lettres Inédites de Napoléon Ier*, Paris, 1903.

Cairnes, W.E. (ed.), *The Military Maxims of Napoleon*, London, 1901 (one of a number of editions; for the latest, see below).

Chair, S. de, *Napoleon on Napoleon*, London, 1992.

Chandler, D.G. (ed.), *The Military Maxims of Napoleon*, Greenhill, London, 1987 (the latest of a number of editions, this being a reprint of Cairnes [above] with new commentary).

Chuquet, A. (ed.), *Ordres et Apostilles de Napoléon 1799–1815*, Paris, 1911–12.

Chuquet, A. (ed.), *Inédits Napoléoniens*, Paris, 1913–19.

'Constant' (Louis Constant Wairy), *Memoirs of Constant, the Emperor Napoleon's Head Valet*, trans. P. Pinkerton, London, 1896; published originally as *Mémoires de Constant*, Paris, 1830–1.

Du Casse, Baron A. (ed.), *Supplément à la Correspondance de Napoléon Ier*, Paris, 1887.

Fain, A.J.F., *Mémoires de Baron Fain, Premier Secrétaire du Cabinet de l'Empereur*, Paris, 1884.

Fain, A.J.F., *Memoirs of the Invasion of France by the Allied Armies and of the Last Six Months of the Reign of Napoleon*, London, 1834; published originally as *Souvenirs de la Campagne de France*, Paris, 1824.

Gourgaud, G., *Sainte-Hélène: Journal Inédit de 1815 à 1818*, eds vicomte de Grouchy and A. Guillois, Paris, 1899.

Guedalla, P. (ed.), *The Letters of Napoleon to Marie-Louise*, London, 1935.

Hall, H.F. (ed.), *Napoleon's Letters to Josephine*, London, 1903.